TRENDS
IN SPEECH RECOGNITION

TRENDS
IN SPEECH RECOGNITION

Wayne A. Lea, Editor

Speech Communications Research Laboratory
and
University of Southern California

PRENTICE-HALL, INC., *Englewood Cliffs, New Jersey 07632*

Library of Congress Cataloging in Publication Data

    Main entry under title:
    Trends in speech recognition.

      Bibliography: p.
      Includes index.
        1. Automatic speech recognition.   I. Lea, Wayne A.
TK7882.S65T73   621.38'0412   79-23614
ISBN 0-13-930768-0

Editorial/production supervision: Nancy Moskowitz

Printed in the United States of America

10 9 8 7 6 5 4 3 2

PRENTICE-HALL INTERNATIONAL, INC., *London*
PRENTICE-HALL OF AUSTRALIA PTY. LIMITED, *Sydney*
PRENTICE-HALL OF CANADA, LTD., *Toronto*
PRENTICE-HALL OF INDIA PRIVATE LIMITED, *New Delhi*
PRENTICE-HALL OF JAPAN, INC., *Tokyo*
PRENTICE-HALL OF SOUTHEAST ASIA PTE. LTD., *Singapore*
WHITEHALL BOOKS LIMITED, *Wellington, New Zealand*

CONTENTS

v

vi

PREFACE

Speech recognition work now runs the gamut from practical 24-hour-a-day applications of isolated word recognizers in industrial or governmental operations, to research and development work on versatile recognizers of complex spoken sentences. The number of commercial devices being sold is apparently expanding exponentially, public awareness of the technology is up, and the prospects for future impact on human interaction with machines are very bright. Speech recognition is a part of a broader speech processing technology also involving computer identification or verification of speakers, computer synthesis of speech and production of stored spoken responses, computer analysis of the physical and psychological state of the speaker, efficient transmission of spoken conversations, detection of speech pathologies, and aids to the handicapped. Only the tasks of machine comprehension of the intended linguistic message are considered in this book. There is much yet to be done to make speech a practical and increasingly valuable modality for instructing machines, but ideas abound for achieving future successes in spoken control of machines.

This book is intended to serve both newcomers to the field of speech recognition, and various forms of experts. You do not have to be planning a career in speech recognition, or looking for detailed new ideas, to be served by the various chapters in this book. Some chapters are valuable for giving you a palatable dose of the technology and satisfying even a casual interest. If you are a business manager or government executive interested in the significance of this emerging technology, or if you are concerned about keeping up to date on computer input methods, you need to know what can and can not be done with voice control of machines. The science fiction forms of conversational computers may not be here yet, nor soon forthcoming, but there is little doubt that voice interactions will be a prominent part of future trends in computer technology.

If your interest in speech recognition goes far beyond casual curiosity, to the point where you are planning a new project in speech recognition, or considering the best way to make an entry into the field, this book is for you. Here you will find technically substantive but readable presentations of a variety of previous devices, proven successes and enlightening failures, promising techniques, and guidelines for further work. If you have specialized in one or a few aspects of this complex interdisciplinary technology, and wish to extend your intellectual horizons to encompass other aspects, you should find here several important topics to pursue. If you teach university courses on computers, signal processing, artificial intelligence, pattern recognition, speech science, linguistics, or related topics, you will find this book to be a valuable text or a comprehensive resource volume. I have taught two courses, in "Machines that Understand Speech" and "Seminar in Speech Recognition", to linguists, engineers, and computer scientists at the University of Southern California, using the preliminary versions of most of the chapters in this book as textbook materials. The students and I have been quite pleased by the comprehensiveness, readability, and stimuli for further work that the authors have provided.

Experts will hopefully find this book's various reviews of previous work to be excellent references that will hold their value over a long period of time. Regardless of the transient nature of present technology, the variety of techniques and issues that seem important today will have impact on most aspects of technology for years to come, if past experience is any indicator. All authors have been asked to not only report their own work, but to provide a representative assessment of the best of the available techniques in their areas of expertise, and to give guidelines for future work.

You will find in Part I several views about the reasons for interest in speech recognition systems. Chapter 1 provides arguments for why speech is a valuable modality for communication with computers, and outlines what types of systems and applications seem promising. In Chap. 2, Neuburg distinguishes between the actual <u>needs</u> for speech recognizers and the limited <u>competences</u> that current devices and ideas encompass. He advocates continued attention on limited systems and modest attempts at advancing the technology. A valuable part of the proof about the merits of limited systems comes from field successes of practical commercial recognizers, as discussed by Martin and Welch in Chap. 3. They also report on experiments that show conditions under which voice control of machines is or is not better than standard keyboard or graphical input facilities. An overview of the history of speech recognition, and a survey of current devices, current projects, gaps in current technology, and recommendations for future work is presented in Chap. 4. I attempt to provide therein a guide to all the other chapters, as well as a description of earlier work that is not otherwise discussed in this book. In addition, it seemed necessary to introduce in Chap. 4 some of the basic theoretical concepts of speech recognition, to guide newcomers and to help put history in a more systematic perspective. This comprehensive chapter suggests future needs and trends, which you may want to help turn into tomorrow's realities.

Thus, Part I of the book will not tell you the details about how to build the inner workings of tomorrow's recognizers, but it does put speech recognition work into an overall motivational framework that seems essential to the best future use of voice control of machines. Part II then will provide many ideas for how to accomplish some of the most important aspects of system design. This Part should be particularly useful to newcomers to the field, and yet it has much material worthy of the expert's perusal also. Zue and Schwartz provide in Chap. 5 an authoritative discussion of the best techniques and biggest challenges in converting acoustic data into sequences of vowels and consonants that compose the pronunciations of words and sentences. This topic of "acoustic phonetic processing", or the "acoustic phonetic front end" of a recognizer, is generally considered to be the top-priority aspect that needs further work and major advances. Shoup next discusses, in Chap. 6, another high-priority topic; namely, the phonological processing that handles speech variability and context effects on pronunciations. Critical, and fairly well advanced, aspects of recognition are the processes of hypothesizing and verifying words that match the pronunciations of incoming speech, which Smith and Sambur discuss in Chap. 7. That chapter includes good introductions to word matching algorithms, such as dynamic programming and the different techniques used in the HEARSAY II and HWIM systems (described later, in Chap. 16 and 14, respectively).

Almost no work has been done on the use of acoustic information for detecting linguistic units larger than the word. I argue in Chap. 8 that prosodic information (pitch and energy contours, and timing information) offer the opportunity of acoustically detecting large linguistic units and guiding several aspects of speech understanding systems. Prosodic features are a promising, but largely untried, aspect of sound structure that can help simplify phonetic analysis, select appropriate phonological rules, hypothesize and verify words, and, perhaps most importantly, guide parsing procedures. In Chap. 9, Hayes-Roth discusses the role of syntax, semantics, and pragmatics in speech understanding systems. For about twenty years, researchers have called for the use of such higher-level linguistic processing and task-dictated constaints in recognition, but only since 1973 have such processes been integrated into working systems. Finally, Part II of the book concludes with Chap. 10, in which Goodman and Reddy discuss alternative control structures for speech understanding systems. They show how, through a variety of models for component interactions, and some efficient search techniques and procedures for focusing attention on crucial information at each stage in the recognition process, one can hope to integrate all incomplete sources of knowledge into a cohesive system for understanding an utterance.

The discussion next advances from general tutorials to descriptions of specific systems and projects. Part III covers the largest project ever undertaken in speech recognition, the 5 year $15 million Speech Understanding Research project sponsored by the Advanced Research Projects Agency (ARPA) of the United States Department of Defense. Klatt provides a very helpful overview of the project, in Chap. 11. Barnett, Bernstein, Gillman, and Kameny describe the System Development Corporation system, which, despite its limited performance following an unfortunate loss of a computer system, offered some interesting advances in acoustic phonetic analysis, word hypothesizing, and component evaluations. Walker summarizes SRI research on speech understanding in Chap. 13, which work focused on the complement of SDC work, in the design of an integrated language description which incorporated syntactic productions, semantic constraints and relationships, and pragmatic information such as discourse and task constraints. These linguistic knowledge sources, and alternative control and search strategies, were experimentally tested using a simulation of performance of acoustic processing components. Chapter 14, by Wolf and Woods of Bolt Beranek and Newman, discusses the "Hear What I Mean" (HWIM) system, which incorporated excellent acoustic phonetic processing, an interesting idea of a "lexical decoding network", a very powerful syntax with prosodic analysis capabilities, and a systematic theory for scoring competing hypotheses throughout the system. Wolf and Woods also offer some provocative comparisons among various system philosophies, such as used in the HWIM, Harpy, HEARSAY II, and IBM systems. The Harpy system, developed at Carnegie-Mellon University (CMU) and described by Lowerre and Reddy in Chap. 15, was the most successful ARPA SUR system, and is worthy of careful study by all readers who are interested in currently successful techniques and "benchmark" performances for comparisons with future systems. The chapter on Harpy is the most readable and helpful description of that system that I have seen anywhere. Another high performance system developed at CMU was the HEARSAY II system of cooperative knowledge sources interacting through a common "blackboard", as described by Erman and Lesser in Chap. 16. This is one of the most flexible system structures for future research on speech understanding techniques.

I am convinced that the chapters summarizing the ARPA SUR projects are the best such sources available anywhere, presenting the most readable and comprehensive summaries of the interdisciplinary effort that went into that largest-ever project in speech recognition. To have such major technical contributions compiled in one volume is one of the highlights of the book. While that project is now history, it involved addressing almost all the major problems involved in computer understanding of spoken sentences, and it has substantially influenced the advancing technology and contributed to the growing interest in a broad spectrum of recognition capabilities. June Shoup and I were contracted by ARPA, and by the Office of Naval Research and the Air Force Office of Scientific Research, to review the scientific contributions of that ARPA SUR project, to survey the total current state of technology in speech recognition and understanding, and to recommend work that should be undertaken in future years. Our general review, which is summarized in Chap. 17, naturally led to an increased desire to provide the readers with a single sourcebook which could provoke and guide the needed advancements in this field.

Current projects exhibit a moderation to more limited goals than the ARPA SUR project addressed, and the successes reported in Part IV of this book show the merit of judicious use of constraints to reduce the recognition task to complexities that can currently be reliably handled. In Chap. 18, Flanagan, Levinson, Rabiner, and Rosenberg describe a series of successful development projects that have expanded the capabilities of practical speech recognizers, to include speaker-independent recognition of isolated words and limited forms of word-sequence recognition when spoken in continuous form. In Chap. 19, Medress describes a linguistically-based system that can handle connected word sequences and can spot key words in the context of naturally-flowing conversations (i.e., "word spotting"). My students and I have found this chapter to be an excellent readable description of the basic concepts and implementations of acoustic phonetic, prosodic, and phonological analyses.

Chapter 20 is unique, in that it is an attempt by a market consultant, Nye, to project the expanding market for speech recognizers into the next ten years. The conclusions include a bright future, especially for limited, low cost systems. This form of analysis is obviously useful in making present work pertinent to future technology.

Speech recognition work at ITT is described by White and Sambur in Chap. 21. They outline project plans in isolated word recognition, word spotting, and other areas, and describe work on dynamic programming algorithms, degraded speech, new feature extraction methods, and measures of the dissimilarity between input speech and stored templates.

Almost every group in the United States of America which is currently doing work on speech recognition is represented in the book, and work in other countries (in Europe and Asia) is summarized, in Chaps. 22 to 24. Wakita and Makino summarize, in Chap. 22, the recent work in Japan, including studies of phoneme recognition and segmentation, linguistic models, and talker differences, plus projects for developing isolated word recognizers and speech understanding systems. Work in Poland is described by Jassem in Chap. 23, while Haton discusses work in Western Europe in Chap. 24. These summaries show a variety of goals and techniques worthy of the reader's careful scrutiny.

While all authors were asked to write their chapters with a clear view to the future, and with a projection about future issues and trends, Part V of the book presents several specific assessments of future trends and promising approaches to the advancement of the technology. Chapter 25 contains two specific proposals for speech recognition techniques, by Klatt. His proposals seem to combine the best of the ideas and techniques of Harpy, HWIM, and other recent systems, plus some improved acoustic and phonetic analysis procedures. Doddington raises a provocative question of "Whither Speech Recognition?" in Chap. 26, and answers it in part by advocating work on well-constrained problems. In the final chapter (27), I try to summarize some issues raised during an open discussion on "Speech Recognition: What is Needed Now?", at the December, 1977, International Congress on Phonetic Sciences (IPS-77), Miami, Florida. That session, which I organized and chaired, was one stimulus for the development of this book. In Chap. 27, I also summarize a poll of expert opinions about the future of speech recognition, and offer a few of my own thoughts about future work.

This book thus contains 27 chapters by 35 leaders in the field of speech recognition. Coincidentally, that corresponds to the equivalent of one chapter for every year in the 27-year history since the first speech recognizer was described in 1952. Of course, every book has its limitations, and this book is no exception. No response was obtained to my requests for a chapter on work in the USSR. Another notable gap in the book concerns the large project on statistically-based continuous speech recognition, being conducted by Frederick Jelinek and his colleagues at the IBM Thomas J. Watson Research Center, Yorktown Heights, New York. At the time of this writing, the IBM project was the largest industrial development project in speech recognition in the United States of America. While Jelinek participated in the 1977 meeting that stimulated this book, an agreement could not be reached regarding the nature, timing, and part of the book in which a chapter on IBM work might appear. The reader is referred to journal articles and other reports by Jelinek and his IBM colleagues, as listed in Chap.4, for a comprehensive summary of the IBM project. Despite these limitations, I believe this to be the most comprehensive and timely single source of information about speech recognition theory, design, and application that is available anywhere.

I am grateful to each author for the valuable contributions each chapter adds to the book. Most authors were very responsive to publication deadlines, and I apologize to those authors and to all readers who have been waiting unusually long for the book to be completed. I trust that the quality of the final product will alleviate the frustrations of previous delays. I am especially grateful to those authors who provided crucial chapters on very short notice, including especially Rick Hayes-Roth and George Doddington. I also thank Harry Hollien for inviting me to chair the IPS-77 session that initially sparked this project, and thank Dennis Klatt, Raj Reddy, Jared Wolf, June Shoup, David Broad, and Hisashi Wakita for providing helpful ideas and criticisms about the contents of the book.

Most of all, I thank my wife and family for their patience in enduring my long occupation with this book. I am especially grateful to Gayle for her excellent and prompt typing and other help, which did much to spur me on and help me complete my aspects of this work. Thanks also go to Betty Muiderman for long hours of typing help. The patience and advice of Paul Becker, Bernard Goodwin, and Hank Kennedy of Prentice-Hall is also highly appreciated.

Wayne A. Lea
Santa Barbara, CA

PART I

MOTIVATIONS AND GENERAL REVIEWS

THE VALUE OF SPEECH RECOGNITION SYSTEMS

Wayne A. Lea
Speech Communications Research Laboratory

1-1. INTRODUCTION

Each reader of this book probably has some idea why it is valuable to have machines that can recognize spoken commands. Some of us could perhaps even offer explicit examples of how we would profitably use such systems if we could get access to them immediately. We all are aware of the growing importance of machines in business, school, government, and even in the home. One of our most frequent complaints about such machines is the difficulty of communicating with them in efficient and natural ways. Speech input seems to offer a truly natural mode for human-machine communication that, if attainable in a cost-effective way, would be unsurpassed in making computers and other mechanical devices truly cooperative servants of humankind, rather than increasing the demands on the human to adapt to the machine.

In this chapter, we shall first consider the many advantages of speech as an input modality for communication with machines (Sec. 1-2). Along with the advantages, we shall also consider the disadvantages, most of which can readily be alleviated, but which must not be neglected. We shall then compare speech with other input modalities, and discuss evidence that speech is the most effective single modality, and an integral part of the most effective multimodality communication links (Sec. 1-3).

Even if we acknowledge speech input to machines to be the best (or one of the best) machine-input modalities, we would find that knowledge to be of little use if speech recognition by machines were unattainable or if adequate systems were not practical. Consequently, we shall (in Sec. 1-4) define the dimensions of alternative system capabilities (isolated words versus connected speech, small versus large vocabulary of accepted words, number of speakers recognized, accuracy requirements, etc.) and consider how much recognition capability is needed to make a system useful for various applications. The ultimate practicality of speech recognition will depend upon the success of the various analysis techniques described throughout this book, and any others that are yet to be discovered, tested, and efficiently applied. While we can count on the scientists and engineers to come up with new ideas and algorithms for years to come, the ultimate utility of such advances will be determined by the commercial sources of devices, and the users in industry and government, who tailor those systems to real needs and test them in the crucible of field applications and repetitive conversations with machines. This book offers valuable tutorials about various important aspects of the inner workings of speech recognition systems (in Part II), and summaries of past, present, and future work in the field (in Chap. 4, and also in Parts III, IV, and V, respectively), but we need a solid foundation concerning why we want speech recognizers before we detail how they can be developed, tested, used, and improved.

Suppose you have a problem, and you intend to use your computer (or a command and control system, or the like) to help you solve it. Perhaps you are in industry, and would like to have the machine assist you in taking inventory of stock items whose stock numbers you could read and enter into the machine. Or perhaps while your hands and eyes are busy handling a large volume of items, you would like to dictate where objects go by commanding a computer that controls a conveyor system (such as some postal services have). Or perhaps you are involved with an airline reservation system and busy at other tasks. Or maybe you have a computer system that authorizes credit transactions, but you have a heavy turnover of employees who are unwilling to endure the tedium and pressure of receiving a large volume of telephone calls from merchants, all of whom have the same form of inquiry about the acceptability of a credit card and want the receiver of the call to check both the number and the amount to be charged to the account. Or maybe you're a manager who would like to communicate with that awesome machine down the hall without going through an expert programmer or some teletypewriting terminal--maybe you could go right through that telephone on your desk.

Alternatively, you might be an air traffic controller at a facility that uses a computer to assist in keeping information about the position, altitude, identity, fuel supply, and other critical conditions for a large number of aircraft in your vicinity. Or, you could be a forward observer in a military tactical situation where you would like to communicate with the gun control computer from your remote field site. Or you're in a crowded airplane cockpit with no room for another keyboard, display, or array of knobs, but you need another way of communicating to one more of the many aspects of the airborne system or a ground control facility. Or, perhaps you're "really far out", as an astronaut suited up for an extra-vehicular manuever in space.

You then are one of those to whom speech recognition advocates would try (or have tried) to sell their wares. Why? Does speech input offer special advantages in such cases as these? Indeed it does. We can see this more clearly by looking at the list of advantages of speech input given in Table 1-1. You will want to use speech wherever possible, because it is the human's most _natural_ communication modality. It is thus a familiar, convenient, spontaneous part of the capabilities the human brings to the situation of interacting with machines. One distinct aspect of that spontaneity and naturalness will be a propensity to use that natural modality when communicating under stress conditions. Like a native English speaker in a foreign country, who will revert to his native language when in danger, when angry, or otherwise under stress, you will be more inclined under duress to _speak_ (and speak _correctly_) in your native natural language than to type, punch buttons, or even speak an artificial code.

Untrained people speak but do not in all cases read, write, typewrite, or use buttons, knobs, or tactile devices with any efficiency. Speech thus _requires no training_, except for instructing you the user to confine your utterences to those which the machine can recognize or "understand". This latter aspect is one of the potential difficulties of using speech recognition facilities; namely, can you readily refrain from saying arbitrary sentences that the machine has not been programmed to understand, and rather constrain yourself to say only a restricted set of sentence structures and limited vocabulary (which may not necessarily be the most obvious way to say what was intended)? Once you speak, you are inclined to speak freely, forgetting any artificial constraints. "Habitability" (Watts, 1968; Klatt, 1977) is a common term for this desired ease of learning, and adhering to, constraints dictated by a restricted language. A habitable language is one for which you can be assured you won't keep getting system responses like "say again", "syntax error", "that doesn't compute", etc. The human's

TABLE 1-1.

ADVANTAGES AND DISADVANTAGES OF SPEECH INPUT TO MACHINES

EFFECTIVE USE OF HUMAN COMMUNICATIVE ABILITIES

- Human's Most Natural Modality Familiar, Convenient, Spontaneous, — but the user may say natural, yet unrecognizable utterances.

- Requires No Training of User, — except for how to constrain utterances to those recognizable by the machine.

- Human's Highest-Capacity Output Channel, — but slowed by pauses or unfamiliarity.

- Permits Multimodal Communication.

- Simultaneous Communication with Humans and Machines, — but the user may forget which is being addressed.

COMPATIBILITY WITH UNUSUAL CIRCUMSTANCES

- Possible in Darkness, Around Obstacles, and for the blind or handicapped.

- Unaffected by weightlessness, — though this feature is rarely important.

- Only Slightly Affected by High Acceleration and Mechanical Constraints.

- Permits Verifying Speaker's Identity, — but is sensitive to dialects and differences in pronunciation.

- Permits Monitoring Acoustical Environment, — but is susceptible to environmental noise and distortions.

- Requires no Panel Space, Displays, or Complex Apparatus, — but microphone must be worn or held.

MOBILITY AND FREEDOM FOR OTHER ACTIVITIES

- Possible at a Distance and at Various Orientations, — but at a loss of privacy.

- Permits Simultaneous Use of Hands and Eyes for Other Tasks.

- Permits Telephone to Serve as a Computer Terminal, — provided the potentially large speaker population, narrowband, noise, and distortions can be handled.

ability to adapt is, of course, quite impressive, and we might well expect that highly motivated users (e.g., trainees, subordinates under strict instructions, etc.) will accept and abide by even some of the most "unhabitable" forms of communication, but the more the machine adapts to the normal human speech mode (that is, the more versatile and structurally-unconstrained the interactive language), the more universally useful the speech input system will be. Such a trend will preserve the distinct "little or no training" feature of speech input to machines. In the meantime, as long as the machines are limited in what they can correctly understand, there will be _some_ amount of user training required, but it is usually far less than that required for other computer input devices.

A word of caution is appropriate related to training users to speak to a machine. Several informal studies (e.g., Bobrow and Klatt, 1968) suggest that speakers are more consistent from time to time, and thus _less_ prone to confuse the machine with unexpected differences in pronunciation, if they are instructed (or simply _allowed_) to speak "naturally", not to speak "carefully" or "clearly". The unusual articulations when users try to help the machine are so inconsistent from time to time that the conscientious user can do more harm than good if instructed to focus on the _manner_ of speaking.

Since speech is the natural communication mode between humans, and can be heard both by humans and machines, speech could offer _simultaneous communication_ with humans and machines. One distinct disadvantage that this might produce, however, is that the speaker might forget the machine's constraints on acceptable utterances as he or she turns from one utterance, directed at a human, to the next utterance, directed at the machine. Of course, the indiscriminate propagation of the speech signal in the vicinity of the speaker also jeopardizes the _privacy_ of the human-to-computer communication link.

Another important advantage of speech is that it is the human's _highest-capacity_ output communication channel. This has been quantitatively shown several times in the literature (Shannon and Weaver, 1949; Pierce and Korlin, 1957; Lea, 1968; Turn, 1974, p. 4). Spontaneous speech has a usual rate of around 2.0 to 3.6 words per second (Turn, 1974, p. 4). In contrast, only about 0.4 words per second are conveyed by handwriting or handprinting, while _skilled_ typists can type about 1.6 to 2.5 words per second, and _unskilled_ typists (that is, most computer users) can type only about 0.2 to 0.4 words per second. Newell et al. (1971) also reported that only about 1.2 to 1.5 words per second can be conveyed by using a touch-tone telephone. Chapanis, et al. (1977) found that even _experienced_ typists only achieved about _18_ words per minute in actual problem solving (thinking and typing), compared to about _176_ words per minute in speech (thinking and speaking). Speech clearly offers the highest potential capacity for human-to-computer communication.

We must, however, qualify these statements about the high rate of information transfer with speech. If you only can speak in sequences of _isolated words_, where each word is clearly delimited by preceding and following pauses (silences), then some of the gain in rate of information transfer is lost. Martin (1976) reported that _average_ speaking rates of about 0.5 to 1.1 isolated words per second (or, as he reported it, 30 to 70 words per minute) were achieved in factory environments by individuals using voice input systems, with peak rates (dictated by high workload) running close to 2.0 words per second. This overall performance is still somewhat better than the usual worker can accomplish by typewriting, keypunching, or button-pushing, but is less than the five-to-one (or larger) ratio obtained in comparing spontaneous connected speech with unskilled typewriting or handwriting, or the two-to-one ratio in comparing spontaneous speech with operating a touch-tone telephone.

Related to the issue of _rate_ of information transfer between human and machine is the advantage of _multimodal communication_, which speech permits. Speech input may be combined with other input modalities, so that, for example, you can point to a specific position on a graphical input device and speak at the same time, etc. Multimodal communication of course increases the possible rates of information transfer, and it also permits choosing the best input method for each new problem, and provides redundancy and increased reliability (since, if one input channel fails, another back-up channel is available).

Although I don't believe the advantages of speech listed in the second part of Table 1-1 usually represent the major reasons why speech recognizers are bought and used, they are worthy of some consideration. Speech communication is possible in darkness, and around obstacles, because it propagates omni-directionally, without light. For aerospace applications, it may be of some interest that speech is unaffected by weightlessness, and less affected by high levels of acceleration and mechanical constraint than are other conven-tional mechanical modes of machine input, such as typewriting, button pushing, twisting knobs and thumb-wheels, or handwriting (Lea, 1970; Turn, 1974).

For example, Turn (1974, pp. 9-10) reported on two studies that showed that it took 4.0 g. acceleration to cause 10% reduction in recognition accuracy, while only 0.8 g. vibration caused 10% reduction in input accuracy when using push buttons, rotary dials, or thumb wheels. On the other hand, speech can be significantly distorted by unusual atmospheric composition and pressure, such as occur for deep sea divers and astronauts.

The same speech that may be used to instruct the machine might also be used to monitor the physical and psychological state of the speaker. This might be of some value in monitoring astronaut capabilities (Lea, 1968), detecting fatigue and emotion, and observing variabilities in the speaker's pronuncia-tion, that need to be normalized for if successful recognition is to be main-tained. More important for some applications is the ability to use spoken commands to verify a speaker's identity before permitting access to a secure area or a computer facility, or before disclosing credit information or other secrets. Other aspects of the acoustic environment can also be monitored by the speech input channel.

A primary difficulty with speech recognition is this ability of the input system to pick up other sounds in the environment that act as interfering noise, making accurate recognition more difficult. Speech recognizers that work very well in quiet laboratory environments may fail miserably in fac-tories, computer rooms, or other field applications where acoustic noise is high. Part of the solution to such noise problems is to use close-talking (and noise-cancelling) microphones, that pick up the near-by speech better than the distant noises. Most commercial speech recognizers being used today are equipped with close-talking noise-cancelling microphones worn on light-weight headbands or mounted in telephone-like handsets. Another part of the solution to acoustic noise is to reduce the noise at its source, or to isolate the human from the noise by way of soundproofing and acoustic enclosures. This cannot always be done when the talker must be mobile or must simultane-ously work with the very machines that are making the noise. Besides keeping the microphone away from the noise, the effects of noise can be reduced if the acoustic features used in the recognition decisions are less susceptible to distortions or confusions from noise. Rather than giving equal attention to all arbitrary aspects of acoustic patterns, we may endeavor to focus on robust features that are closely associated with linguistic (phonetic) contrasts but that are not markedly affected by noise. This is one primary reason for attempting to use formant frequencies, pitch, general spectral shapes and other phonetic features, in the more sophisticated speech recog-nizers that will be discussed throughout this book.

Another complication introduced by the acoustic environment is any band-width limitations and spectral distortions that may be intrinsic in the trans-ducer and input communication system. Obviously, sibilants (e.g., s,z) and stop bursts, whose energy is distributed primarily at high frequencies, will be more difficult to reliably detect over telephones and narrowband radio

7

channels. Recognizers must not rely upon such phonetic units if the expected
input channel disallows their reliable detection.

One additional advantage of speech recognizers in certain specific applications (such as in crowded aircraft cockpits) is that there is no need for
displays, buttons, or more panel space on the interactive consoles being used.
The microphone that a pilot already wears or holds for other communications
then serves adequately as a computer input device.

I believe that the advantages listed in the last part of Table 1-1 include
the most important practical reasons for developing and using speech recognition facilities. Speech permits mobility and simultaneous performance of
other tasks, which are unusual in computer input facilities. In using
switches, typewriters, cathode ray tube displays, and even the more unusual
graphical input devices ("RAND tablets") and "joy sticks", the user must
either be in physical contact with the computer console or terminal or must
be oriented in fixed directions to produce input commands and monitor computer
outputs. With speech, you can walk around the room, read instruction manuals,
and turn your back on the console, while still inputting to the computer.
Your hands and eyes can be busy with other tasks, such as handling packages
in an inventory or postal distribution situation, or measuring critical
distances in a quality control or inspection task. You can perform other
primary tasks like hands-on experiments or adjustment of equipment while
speaking information into the computer. It is possible to be some distance
from the microphone, or to hold it or have it mounted on a headband, and you
may move your head, hands, and body without returning to a fixed position for
computer input. If you like, you may sit at your desk and talk over the
familiar telephone to the computer down the hall or across the country.

These are the most encouraging aspects of speech recognition technology,
that have opened up new vistas for a variety of practical applications. We
can talk all we want to about the academic virtues of speech or other modalities, but it truly strikes home, factory, and the pocketbook when work
efficiency is increased, input errors are reduced, and good workers are freed
from tedious unnatural tasks and constant movement of eyes and hands from
work pieces to computer input devices. Martin and Welch (Chap. 2; cf. also
Martin, 1976) and their colleagues and competitors (Herscher, 1977; Glenn,
1971) have found success in practical applications of speech recognizers for:
control and inspection of television faceplates, inspecting pull-ring can
lids, automobile assembly lines, inspecting incoming merchandise, automated
handling of materials (packages, etc., as in distribution systems within post
offices and nationwide chains of department stores), and "voice programming"
by supervisory personnel who are unskilled in computer programming. Most
satisfied customers who have bought and used speech recognizers have had
overloaded workers whose hands and eyes were thereby freed to simultaneously
handle other tasks.

1-3. EXPERIMENTAL EVALUATION OF VOICE INTERACTIONS

We have seen that speech has many advantages for human-to-computer communication, including being natural and fast, and also "liberating", so the user
can move around and be involved in other tasks. What clinches the case in
favor of speech recognition for me is the experimental evidence that voice
communication is critical to the best single- and multi-modality communication links. In 1974, Ochsman and Chapanis (cf. also Chapanis , 1975) reported
on experiments in which pairs of people communicated with each other via ten
alternative communication channels that might be used in human-computer
communications, and they determined which channels produced the most effective
problem solving. Included in the study were five basic channels: voice (via
microphones and speakers in adjoining rooms); typewriting (via slaved electric

typewriters); handwriting (via a telautograph); closed circuit video ("TV without voice"), and visual contact (through a sound-insulated glass panel). The teams of two communicators were given problem-solving tasks like scheduling classes for a college student, finding faults in an automobile ignition system, and identifying small parts that match requested parts (such as light sockets). Each member of the team had part of the necessary information, and they needed to communicate to successfully complete the task. (Chapanis, 1975, reported similar studies with other problem solving tasks, including: equipment-assembly; retrieval of newspaper articles about a specific topic; and a map-searching problem in which the team tried to find the office of a physician closest to a hypothetical home address.)

There were several major conclusions from these experiments, all of which strongly support the value of voice interaction (and hence support speech recognition capabilities). Their most important conclusion was that "there is a sharp dichotomy between modes of communication involving voice and those modes of communication that do not" (Ochsman and Chapanis, 1974, pp. 617-618). Their data showed that "regardless of extra embellishments, communication via typewriter or handwriting cannot even approach speech in terms of speed or task efficiency" (p. 618).

More specifically, Ochsman and Chapanis found that the average time it took for the communicating team to solve a problem was about 12 minutes for communication involving voice and handwriting, and about 16 minutes for voice alone. Other voice-assisted combinations of voice and typewriting, voice and video, and a communication-rich mode involving all five basic channels had mean solution times within those 12 and 16 minute limits. On the other hand, the fastest hard-copy mode (handwriting and video, without voice) took about 23 minutes, or 46% more time than the slowest mode involving voice alone. They could very reasonably conclude that, "The single most important decision in the design of a telecommunications link should center around the inclusion of a voice channel." (p. 618).

The inclusion or exclusion of the voice channel not only accounted for 90% of the statistical variance between problem solving times for the various modes, but also accounted for 72% of the variance in channel-switching actions that reflected the user preferences for various modes. They measured how often the communicators used activation buttons, seeking to use a channel, and found there were about four times as many activations, or messages sent, per unit time with speech modes as with the non-speech modes (p. 599). Speech thus seems to be the most "interactive" mode, allowing the users to work faster, and yet initiate more messages or interactions within that shorter problem solving time.

Finally, they found that the amount of time spent in non-communicative activities (like reading information, searching through the information folio given to each communicator, handling parts, making notes, waiting, etc.) was much greater in the non-speech modes than in the oral modes (12.1 versus 5.3 minutes, respectively; p. 608). With speech, they could do these other activities simultaneously with communicating, rather than at separate times. This is experimental evidence for one of the most important advantages of speech mentioned in Sec. 1-2; namely, that, more than any other communication modality, speech permits you to communicate while your hands and eyes are busy at other tasks. Other evidence comes from "field experience"; most commercial speech recognizers have been purchased and effectively used in industry because the user's hands and eyes were busy at other tasks and faster non-interruptive communication was desired (and attained, with definite customer satisfaction).

Later experiments (Chapanis et al., 1977; Kelly and Chapanis, 1977; Michaelis, et al., 1977) showed it is possible to find a small "basic" vocabulary (of around 200-300 words) that allows effective performing of realistic tasks, _provided_ the word list is carefully tailored to the application. Given no vocabulary limits, talkers used about 1200 different words. A few hundred carefully chosen words may thus be adequate in practical recognizers, but perhaps 1200 words are needed if the vocabulary is not tailored to the task and individual speakers.

1-4.   THE POTENTIAL FOR RECOGNIZERS OF VARIOUS CAPABILITIES

Even though we know that speech input to computers is valuable to have, we must, for each specific application, face the question of whether we can ever achieve the design, construction, and practical use of adequate speech recognizers. Exactly what is "adequate" needs to be clarified, and related to the specific uses of various speech input capabilities. A fully versatile, rapidly-responding speech input system capable of correctly recognizing all of the arbitrary natural-language sentences spoken by any arbitrary talker, over any communication link, would probably make best use of the advantages of the speech modality. But such a system is not available, and won't be forthcoming in any foreseeable future, so that spoken communication between human and computer will involve a _compromise_ between the human needs and desires and the computer's limited capabilities. A critical question for each potential application thus is, "How much recognition capability is really needed?"

Table 1-2 lists various dimensions of system capability that need to be considered in discussing system adequacy and specific task requirements. Many of the system design criteria associated with these dimensions will be discussed throughout this book, and need to be understood if we are to fully appreciate the value of speech recognizers and the difficulties involved in developing systems that are adequate for various applications.

The most basic dimension of relative capability of interest in speech recognizer design involves the _form of speech_ to be processed. The easiest task is the recognition of _isolated words_ taken from a small vocabulary of alternative words or short phrases. _Larger vocabularies_ of up to several hundred isolated words or commands make the problem more difficult and only a few prototype systems with such capabilities have been developed. Recently, initial systems have been developed to slightly extend the isolated-word capability by using _formatted sequences of isolated commands_, with strict (syntactic and task-dictated) constraints on the acceptable sequences of isolated words or commands.

If the form of speech is _continuous_ (uninterrupted), one of the next most simple recognition tasks is _word spotting_ (equivalently, "keyword spotting"), which is the detection of each (or, at least, many) of the occurrences of selected "keywords" in the context of flowing speech. Keyword spotting is fairly simple in one sense, in that not all of the speech need be analyzed and classified into words or phrases; only the occasional occurrences of the keywords need to be detected. Usually the interesting ("information-carrying") keywords are prominently stressed and clearly articulated, and many of the problems with continuous speech (e.g., coarticulation, missing segments, etc.) are minimized in finding such words. Yet, in another sense, word spotting is difficult, because the context of the word is not known and cannot be used to reinforce or verify decisions. In addition, the primary purpose of keyword spotting is to survey large amounts of information taken from narrow-bandwidth, noisy radio links, and to select conversations about topics of special interest. Consequently, word spotting is difficult on some _other_ dimensions listed in Table 1-2, since the speaker is unknown (and usually not

TABLE 1-2.

DIMENSIONS OF DIFFICULTY IN SPEECH RECOGNITION

INPUT CHARACTERISTICS	1. Form of Speech
	2. Speaker Population
	3. Transducer and Channel
LANGUAGE DESIGN	4. Vocabulary
	5. Syntactic Constraints
	6. Semantic Constraints
	7. Task Constraints
	8. Enhanceability
SYSTEM STRUCTURE	9. Control Strategy
	10. Knowledge Sources
	11. Scoring Procedures
PERFORMANCE CRITERIA	12. Recognition Accuracy
	13. Training the Machine
	14. Training the User; User Acceptance
	15. Speed
	16. Cost
	17. Time for delivery

cooperative), the channel distorts and adds noise, and the conversation is not limited by preselected vocabulary, syntax, or topic, and is naturally rather sloppily spoken (Beek, et al., 1977).

Another restricted recognizer of connected speech handles highly constrain-ed (but continuously spoken) sequences of words, like strings of digits (telephone numbers, stock numbers, measurements, etc.) or carefully formatted sequences of words (air traffic control commands, fixed-length commands with each word selected from a predetermined small vocabulary, etc.). This demands more complete analysis of the utterance than word spotting, so that all words must be determined. However, for some applications, the vocabulary of possible words used at each point in an utterance can be preselected so that the words are largely unaffected by their context (so that coarticulation effects are minimal). Also, the structural variety is kept to a minimum by the strict format demanded for all acceptable sequences, and the words spoken in such strict formats are generally spoken with unusual care. (See **Chap. 18 and 19 of this book for example word-sequence recognizers.)**

Farther along on the spectrum of increasing recognition difficulties are two distinct system types: <u>restricted sentence understanding</u> and what I shall call <u>autonomous continuous speech recognition</u>. Restricted sentence understanding was introduced by the Speech Understanding Research (ARPA SUR) project sponsored by the USA Advanced Research Projects Agency, which will be described more fully in Part III of this book (cf. also Newell, et al., 1971). A sentence understanding system could potentially use all the forms of knowledge available to a native listener of a language, including: acoustic processing, phonetic segmentation and labelling (that is, finding and categorizing all the vowels and consonants in the continuous speech); coarticulation and sound structure ("phonological") rules of the language; expected patterns or sound structures of words (to be matched with the sound patterns in the speech being analyzed); prosodic information; syntactic constraints on allowable word and phrase sequences; semantic knowledge ("intended meanings"); and pragmatic constraints such as the expected flow of discourse, user preferences for certain ways of saying things, and the task-dictated constraints on what needs to be communicated to have the machine truly aid the human in performing the specific task. The basic dogma of speech understanding is that for a machine to "understand" speech requires more than mere recognition of the sound structure and wording of the sentence; higher level linguistic information (associated with syntax, intended meanings, and task contexts) is also needed, and the acoustic speech signal alone is not adequate for understanding enough so that the machine can give the correct ultimate response. This dogma is not endorsed by all workers in the field of speech recognition.

Recent work in speech understanding (and future work for years to come) is clearly <u>restricted</u>, in that systems are tailored to specific problems and specific subsets of acceptable natural-language sentences. For example, the HEARSAY I speech understanding system developed at Carnegie-Mellon University (CMU) was initially developed using the specific task of playing chess with the computer, with the human's moves spoken as highly formatted utterances like "Pawn to king four." (Reddy, et al., 1973). In understanding the spoken move, the computer used explicit knowledge about allowable chess moves, the current state of the chess board, acceptable ways to express the moves, etc.

Autonomous continuous speech recognition (or, as it is usually called, simply "continuous speech recognition") is well represented by an old notion of automatically transcribing speech into word sequences. "Autonomous" here refers to the idea that these recognizers are to operate independent of syntactic, semantic, or pragmatic knowledge (cf. Postal, 1968). By endeavoring to do an excellent job in recognizing the sound structure of continuous speech and thus to locate all the words, the developers of such systems hope to avoid the heavy dependence upon syntactic, semantic, and pragmatic constraints that "speech understanding systems" must rely upon. The system theoretically can then be used on several new tasks without major adjustments or reprogramming (provided the vocabulary is still maintained). Obviously, without the verification help of total linguistic and pragmatic information, such systems must have a very reliable word recognition capability, and must be able to handle the effects of almost any word on its neighboring words.

In the extreme, the autonomous continuous speech recognizer might be directed towards recognizing any arbitrary English (or other-language) sentence, and might be visualized as a voice dictation machine or "phonetic typewriter" that would turn any spoken utterance into the appropriate word sequence. For the foreseeable future, some practical constraints have to be placed on such a system, primarily through limiting the vocabulary. Also, many researchers believe that adequate success in autonomous recognition is difficult or impossible to achieve. Most known applications for speech recognizers permit (in fact, encourage) use of task restrictions and linguistic constraints. Ultimately, if the recognizer is to be more than a phonetic typewriter, and is to use incoming messages to alter its future responses in aiding the human, speech "understanding" does seem to be necessary and in line with the "bionic" model of duplicating the successful human listener.

We have defined the primary dimension for distinguishing speech recognizers, on the basis of the form of speech. It appears that each type of recognizer in that spectrum of recognition capabilities has its own potential value and specific applications. However, in the past, most commercial interest, and even much of the _military_ field interest, in speech recognizers, has been dominated by the ready availability of isolated word recognizers. It seems to be a case of the available technology dictating to the application, rather than the application dictating what technology should be developed and used. Beek, et al. (1977, p. 315) noted that "There has never been a stated military requirement for CSR" (continuous speech recognition), but this may be due more to the military emphasis on using available technology than to the lack of real uses for such capabilities. A large number of military-sponsored projects in continuous speech recognition (cf. Beek, et al., 1977), of which the ARPA SUR project was the largest, suggest that significant military interest must exist in developing continuous speech recognizers. Recognition studies have been done for applications in aircraft cockpits, military tactical field-data entry, military training systems, voice input to cartographic processing systems, keyword spotting, and several other applications. A RAND report outlined a variety of military applications where various speech recognition capabilities may be useful (Turn, et al. 1974). Ultimately, the "burden of proof" is on the speech recognition advocate to show why speech recognition is useful in any specific application, and to determine what form of recognizer (handling isolated words, connected speech of specific formats, speech understanding, or whatever) is most appropriate to that application.

Another important dimension of difficulty is the _speaker population_ that must be handled. While a system can be tailored specifically to a single talker, most applications demand some ability (immediately, or after some training or retraining) to handle more than one talker, perhaps as many as 10, or 100, or 1000 talkers, or (for surveillance of communication systems, or for nationwide credit card authorizations) an unlimited number of talkers. The talker may be (a) "cooperative" (that is, willing to help the machine by saying exactly what the machine wants, or saying it in such a clear way as to help the machine), (b) "not cooperative" (perhaps unaware of, or not committed to, the need to help, and yet not endeavoring to confuse the machine), or (c) "uncooperative" (that is, unwilling to help, and working to prevent the machine from correctly understanding). Machines are also sensitive to the sex of the talker, and his or her dialect, and these are also critical aspects of the difficulty introduced by the speaker population.

The _transducer and communication channel_ used with a speech recognition system can also introduce several problems, including reduced bandwidth, low signal-to-noise ratio (that is, presence of considerable noise), and other distortions that are characteristic of microphones, telephones, and radio channels. Detection and classification of all the vowels and consonants can be handicapped by loss of high-and low-frequency energy, confusions introduced by noise, and spectral distortions that alter the apparent spectral content of the speech. It is easier to avoid all these problems by use of high quality broadband systems in quiet environments, but many systems (such as factory installations of word recognizers, word spotters, etc.) must deal with such complications. The ARPA SUR project made a _tradeoff_ in complexities, by dealing with ambitious sentence understanding tasks but a fairly small number of speakers and quite high quality speech.

The _vocabulary_ of recognizable words can vary in _size_ from a few words like the ten digits, up to 100; 1000; 10,000; or some larger number of entries. The ARPA SUR project, for example, greatly extended the target vocabulary size, by seeking to handle 1000 words. In addition to the number of words in the vocabulary, the _confusability_ of words in the vocabulary is also very important. It is more difficult to accurately recognize ten rhyming words that the ten digits zero (or "oh") to nine, and considerably easier to recognize ten other longer and more distinctive words, like the names of the ten largest cities in the USA, etc. In some applications, words can be carefully _selected_ to be clearly distinct from all other words in the vocabulary (such as using the phonetically-rich word "negative" instead of the shorter less distinctive word "no").

Other language constraints may be used to restrict the difficulty of recognizing continuous speech. _Syntactic constraints_ may range from simple constraints on what word can be next, based only on the identity of the previous word (so-called "Markov" models), to more complex constraints on phrase structure based on what are called context-free, context-sensitive, and "augmented transition network" (ATN) grammars which make more intricate use of the total structure of the sentence. _Semantic constraints_ specify which word sequences are meaningful in the human-machine communications. _Task constraints_ may exclude certain word sequences that cannot occur in the context of the previous human-computer discourse, the current state of the task environment (such as the current board positions in a chess game), and the expectations that certain speakers will use certain expressions. The more of these linguistic and situational constraints we use in a system, the more complex the system gets, but the better the chances of correct recognition can be (cf. Klatt, 1977).

Table 1-2 also includes the "_enhanceability_" of the language and system, meaning the ease with which new words or sentence structures could be incorporated into the system as time progresses and the changing usage demands some change in the vocabulary or other aspects of the language. We would hope that we need not start from scratch everytime the language or application is changed slightly. This aspect of recognizer design has been given little consideration in previous studies, but may be quite important to the long-term utility of a recognizer.

A speech recognizer may be structured in various ways, with various "_knowledge sources_", or components, communicating to each other in various ways, and an executive _control strategy_ that schedules and gives attention to various components at successive times in the analysis. In essence, this involves an implementation of alternative "divide and conquer" strategies, such as the alternative control structures discussed by Goodman and Reddy in Chap. 10 of this book. Alternatively, the recognition system can be based on an integrated network representation such as used in HARPY (see Chap. 15) and the DRAGON and IBM systems (Jelinek, 1976), which use statistical knowledge and generalized mathematical models (what Newell, 1976, called "generalized input-output systems"), rather than separate linguistically-defined components.

In any system, the available acoustic data can sometimes be compatible with more than one interpretation (such as when a word sounds a lot like the word "speech" but it is also somewhat like the word "beach", or "peach", or "spits", etc.), and some procedure is needed for selecting the best first guess. _Scoring procedures_ are then needed to define "nearest neighbors" or order of likelihood for alternative hypotheses. Such procedures also become particularly troublesome when several different types of information, or different knowledge sources, suggest different hypotheses, and the various "votes" for the competing alternatives need to be weighted so that a best choice can again be made. One of the more sophisticated scoring procedures was developed in the BBN HWIM system, to be described in Chapter 14.

Table 1-2 also lists six important PERFORMANCE CRITERIA that define system specifications that can dramatically affect the difficulty of attaining adequate recognizers. Recognition accuracy is the percentage of all utterances or units that are correctly identified, and the higher the demanded level of accuracy (such as 99%, rather that 95%, etc.) the more difficult the system development task will be. Most commercial isolated word recognizers achieve over 99% correct recognition when trained for the individual talker, but performance may drop significantly when speech of new talkers is processed, or the input channel picks up´ considerable noise or distortions. Occasionally a word will be rejected because it is not close enough to any one word to make a reliable decision. For word spotting systems, many more failures to locate keywords may be permitted, provided most of the important conversations are found from the correctly located words; however a false detection of a keyword when it wasn't really there is considered very undesirable in word spotting, since the intention is to weed out all conversations that aren't of interest. For continuous speech recognition or restricted speech understanding, one can speak of errors and accuracies at several levels, including identification of phonemes, words, sentence structures, and meanings. High accuracy requirements at each of these levels makes the recognition task very difficult. In judging the final performance for such complex systems and being guided toward future improvements, one needs to consider not only the overall final semantic accuracy or word sequence accuracy, but the accuracy of each of the components or knowledge sources, and the exact sources of error (or "weak spots") in system performance.

Another dimension of difficulty in the design of speech recognizers is the amount of training required by the machine. Can a new user come up to the machine and be accurately recognized without ever having trained the machine to his or her voice, or must the user initially say a small set of training words (one or more times) or say all the words in the vocabulary, or all the acceptable utterances, once, or more than once? For large vocabularies and a large range of alternative sentences or phrases that can be recognized, the need to say all alternative utterances becomes an unwieldy task. Recognizers that require little or no training are preferred, but are more difficult to develop.

Similarly, a system is to be preferred which requires little or no training of the user, so the user need not learn special ways of talking, unnatural constraints on acceptable sentence structures, highly limited vocabularies, or the need to speak formatted word sequences with pauses separating successive words. It is true that talking is pleasant and natural to the human, yet the user of a recognizer may be severely disturbed and possibly reduced in efficiency and reliability if he or she is radically restricted in "conversation" with the machine. To be forced to speak in only a highly restricted and "stilted" command language may be awkward and frustrating, and may thus reduce the acceptability of voice communication with computers. It would seem appropriate for advocates of speech recognition to determine what constraints on the vocabulary, syntax, semantics, and general "naturalness" and "expressive power" of an interactive language are most likely to be acceptable to the user of a recognition system. I know of only one study (Lea, 1968, 1969) of the operational acceptability to the user of practical constraints on vocabulary size, command or sentence structure, and verbal system response times, and that study has had virtually no effect on the design of useful speech recognizers. Behavioral studies of human operator performance could and should be performed to provide meaningful measures (such as error rates, times required to cooperatively solve problems, modality duty rates, etc.) of the effectiveness of restricted voice input systems. The final test of the value of the voice link between human and computer will be whether the users accept and use it with some low level of frustration and low error rate, and high efficiency.

Associated with efficiency is the speed of the machine; does it take

15

minutes to get a computer response to a three-second command, or does it respond immediately (in real time)? While initial laboratory models can be permitted to take 10, or 100, or even 1000 times real time to process an utterance through all their algorithms and make a final decision, such delays are usually unacceptable in operational recognizers. Commercial word recognizers usually provide almost instantaneous responses, and this has been a part of their growing acceptability. Recently, researchers have become increasingly concerned with speeding up their computer software for recognition, not only to demonstrate the ultimate feasibility of useful real-time recognition, but also to reduce time required to do experiments and analyze enough data to develop reliable algorithms. Of course, such demands for high-speed analysis do increase the difficulty of designing adequate recognizers, but in another sense the resultant ability to process lots of data and carefully tune algorithms to near optimum conditions increases the chance of providing reliable and useful recognizers.

The cost of a system is an important design criterion. Past experience and standard commercial procedures suggest that commercial customers will not pay the development cost of initial prototype systems, so the developers of recognizers must handle initial developments under contracts or grants, or internal funds. After such development projects, product lines can be introduced at fixed prices. The initial cost of available commercial speech recognition devices range from tens of thousands of dollars for the reliable self-contained word recognizers down to a few hundred dollars for a hobbyist's speech hardware interface to be used with an available small computer. Recent hardware advances suggest that most of the type of processing that has been done in speech recognizers (such as spectral analysis, autocorrelation, and decision logic) will be possible to obtain on a single "chip" costing at most a few hundred dollars (White, 1977), so that initial costs of such recognizers will probably drop dramatically. In addition, recognizers of connected speech, such as the LOCUST version of HARPY (cf. Lowerre and Reddy, Chap. 15 of this book), will probably be available in the price range of the earlier word recognizers. Another aspect of cost is the cost per second of speech processed, which may or may not be expressed to include an amortizing of the initial purchase price of the recognizer. In any case, cost of a system will obviously be one of the important performance criteria.

Another criterion of some interest is the time for delivery. Commercial word recognizers are now "off the shelf" items, available for use within days, whereas the interested user will wait longer for more sophisticated recognizers. Within the next few years (after the writing of this chapter in 1978), commercial recognizers will probably be available that can handle vocabularies of 200 or more isolated words, or restricted (HARPY-like) forms of connected speech, with near-real-time performance. It appears there will be prototype word spotting systems within that same time period. However, interested users will probably have to wait some years before versatile recognizers are available that can handle substantial subsets of spoken natural-language sentences that are not severely restricted by a small speaker population, stilted syntax, pre-selected task domains, and considerable training of the machine and user. Some informed researchers are not optimistic about having versatile speech understanding systems ("that will accept and understand unrestricted discourse from all speakers") in our lifetime (Flanagan, 1976, p. 411).

1-5. SUMMARY

In summary, we have seen that while speech offers many advantages for communication with machines, there are a variety of ways in which we can put demands on the machine that increase the difficulty of achieving success. The very advantage of naturalness of speech can promote versatile unrestricted recognizers that are to handle unrestricted forms of speech, but some compromise is needed between the human's desires for fully natural expression and the machine's limited capability for dealing with arbitrary sentence structures, extensive vocabularies, and casually slurred articulations. The larger the speaker population, the more difficult the system design will be. Also, while we have seen that primary advantages of speech input include the mobility it permits and the freeing of hands and eyes for other tasks, the recognizer's task is compounded by pickup of environmental noise and distortions in telephone systems and other communication links. The recognizer's chance of success can be increased by alleviating noise and distortions, tuning to the specific speakers, and restricting the vocabulary, syntactic structures, possible semantic interpretations, and task-related alternatives about what can be said. The system can be structured to use various forms of knowledge to develop and score alternative hypotheses that the system control strategy can select among. The final performance evaluation or utility of a system then hinges on its accuracy, the training effort it requires, the user acceptability, the speed and cost, and its availability.

Certain applications clearly demand certain choices in system design. For example, word spotters must handle nearly unlimited speaker populations, noisy and distorted speech data, and unrestricted forms of conversational speech. However, for most applications, the design choices are less rigid, so that while it might be nice to allow any speaker to use a telephone, and say nearly any arbitrary utterance, with almost no machine errors and with immediate and inexpensive response, less versatility may be acceptable. One of the crucial questions for each developer (or purchaser) of speech recognizers will be, "How much speech recognition ability is really adequate for the intended application?" By carefully answering this question in each such circumstance, using the dimensions shown in Table 1-2, the speech recognition advocate can successfully develop and evaluate speech input facilities, and give further evidence about the actual value of speech recognition systems.

1-6. REFERENCES

BEEK, B., E.P. NEUBERG, and D.C. HODGE (1977) "An Assessment of the Technology of Automatic Speech Recognition for Military Applications", IEEE Trans. Acoustics, Speech, and Signal Processing, ASSP-25, No. 4, 310-322.

BOBROW, D.G. and D.H. KLATT (1968) "A Limited Speech Recognition System", BBN Report 1667, Final Report, Contract NAS 12-138, Bolt Beranek and Newman, Cambridge, MA.

CHAPANIS, A. (1975), "Interactive Human Communication", Scientific American, 232, No. 3, 36-42.

CHAPANIS, A., R.N. PARRISH, R.B. OCHSMAN, and G.D. WEEKS (1977), Studies in Interactive Communication: II. The Effects of Four Communication Modes on the Linguistic Performance of Teams during Cooperative Problem Solving, Human Factors, 19, No. 2, 101-126.

FLANAGAN, J.L. (1976), "Computers that Talk and Listen: Man-Machine Communication by Voice", Proc. IEEE, 64, No. 4, 405-415.

GLENN, J. (1971), Voice Initiated Cockpit Control and Integrating (VICCI) System Test for Environmental Factors, Scope Electronics, Inc., Reston, Va.

HERSCHER, M.B. (1977), "Real-Time Interactive Speech Technology at Threshold Technology, Inc.", presented at Workshop on Voice Technology for Interactive Real-Time Command and Control System Application, NASA Ames Res. Center, December 6-8, 1977.

KELLY, M.J. and A. CHAPANIS (1977), Limited Vocabulary Natural Language Dialogue, Intern. J. Man-Machine Studies, 9, 479-501.

KLATT, D.H. (1977), "Review of the ARPA Speech Understanding Project", J. Acoust. Soc. America, 62, No. 6, December, 1977, 1345-1366.

LEA, W.A. (1968), "Establishing the Value of Voice Communication with Computers", IEEE Trans. Audio & Electroacoustics, vol. AU-16, 184-197.

_____(1969), The Impact of Speech Communication with Computers, Proc. Sixth Space Congress, Cocoa Beach, FL: Brevard Printers, pp. 15-19 to 15-31.

_____(1970a), "Evaluating Speech Recognition Work", J. Acoustic. Soc. America, 47, No. 6, 1612-1614.

_____(1970b), "Towards Versatile Speech Communication with Computers", Intern. J. Man-Machine Studies, 2, 107-155.

MARTIN, T.B. (1976), "Practical Applications of Voice Input to Machines", Proc. IEEE, 64, 487-500.

MICHAELIS, P.R., A. CHAPANIS, G.D. WEEKS, and M.J. KELLY (1977), Word Usage in Interactive Dialog with Restricted and Unrestricted Vocabularies, IEEE Trans. on Professional Communication, Vol. PC-20, No. 4, 214-221.

NEWELL, A., J. BARNETT, J. FORGIE, C. GREEN, D.H. KLATT, J.C.R. LICKLIDER, J. MUNSON, D.R. REDDY, and W.A. WOODS (1971), Speech Understanding Systems; Final Report of a Study Group, Carnegie-Mellon University, Pittsburgh, PA. (Reprinted by American Elsevier, Amsterdam, North-Holland, 1973).

OCHSMAN, R.B. and A. CHAPANIS (1974), "The Effects of 10 Communication Modes on the Behavior of Teams During Cooperative Problem Solving", Intern. J. Man-Machine Studies, 6, 579-619.

PIERCE, J.R. and J.E. KERLIN (1957), "Reading Rates and the Information Rate of a Human Channel, Bell System Techn. J., 36, 497-516.

POSTAL, P.M. (1968), Aspects of Phonological Theory. New York: Harper & Row.

REDDY, D.R., L.D. ERMAN, and R.B. NEELY (1973), "A Model and a System for Machine Recognition of Speech, IEEE Trans. Audio Electroacoustics, vol. AU-21, 229-238.

SHANNON, C.E. and W. WEAVER (1949), The Mathematical Theory of Communication, Urbana, IL: University of Illinois Press.

TURN, R. (1974), "The Use of Speech for Man-Computer Communication", RAND Report-1386-ARPA, RAND Corp., Santa Monica, CA.

_____, A. HOFFMAN, and T. LIPPIATT (1974), "Military Applications of Speech Understanding Systems, Defense Advanced Research Projects Agency, Arlington, VA, Report 14-34, AD 787394, June 1974.

WATT, W.C. (1968), "Habitability", American Documentation, 19, 338-351.

WHITE, G.M. (1977), "Implications of Low-Cost Signal-Processing Devices for Speech Science", J. Acoust. Soc. America, 62, Suppl. No. 1, 536-537 (A).

2.

NEEDS VS. COMPETENCE IN SPEECH RECOGNITION

Edward P. Neuburg
Department of Defense

2.1 INTRODUCTION

A celebrated letter from J.R. Pierce to the Editor of the Journal of the Acoustical Society of America [Pierce, 1969] took the then Speech Recognition world to task, holding that no real improvements in the art were taking place; that researchers were simply producing more of what already existed, namely isolated word recognition systems; and that because of our inability to use speech information other than the acoustic, the situation was not likely to change in the near future. Nine years and many dollars later there are numerous ambitious, complicated, sophisticated recognition systems, incorporating sources of knowledge such as syntax, semantics, pragmatics, but practical speech recognition has not moved far from where it was in 1969. Perhaps this is precisely because everyone wants to build a system that is ambitious, complicated, and sophisticated. How we got into this situation is a matter of history (a little of which is included below); in what follows a suggestion is made on how we might get out of it. Briefly, it is a suggestion (similar to Pierce's but probably not as well stated) that at least some segment of the speech research community should limit itself to a search for simple, sensible, achievable next steps beyond the practical speech recognition systems that now exist.

2-2 Problem vs. Solution

Fields of study generally flourish for one of two reasons: either there is a problem in need of solution, a problem of sufficient importance that considerable resources are brought to bear on it, or else there is a solution looking for a problem -- and finding it. Examples of major problems that attract money and effort are to be found in medicine and microbiology. Examples of ready-made solutions are a little harder to come by, but occur surprisingly often in the field of pure mathematics. Cayley is supposed to have remarked after developing his theory of matrices that he had at last succeeded in producing a mathematical structure that could never be put to any practical use.

2-2.1 Is There a Problem?

Continuous speech recognition does not fit too well into either of these categories. It certainly is <u>not</u> true that the world is clamoring for the ability to recognize words automatically. There is no speech recognition vacuum. For a while the Defense Department, through the Advanced Research Projects Agency (ARPA) Speech Understanding Research (SUR) project [Newell, 1971], did a certain amount of clamoring; but no one should think of this project as indicative of "Government need" for automatic speech understanding. Speech researchers -- any researchers -- naturally interpret support for a research project as an expression of consumer demand. Sometimes a research project is application-driven, and such a demand does exist; but often it does not. Research, whether industrial, academic, or governmental is directed by an R&D manager who must usually try to encourage both immediately applicable research and research that is considerably in advance of, or even tangential to, current operational needs. It is particularly confusing to try to guess at the needs of "Government" for a speech recognition technology, for "Government" is not a single will deciding what is needed and directing research accordingly. Even within the Defense Department there are many entities, each with its own ideas about what sort of speech-handling competence needs to be developed. Perhaps some central office, or at least a formal structure within the government for exchange of information, would make for more efficiency in meeting all speech research needs, pursuing the promising lines of research, and avoiding duplication. However at least at present, direction of "Government" speech research is marvelously fragmented.

2-2.1.1 The ARPA SUR Project

The foremost example of Government speech support was the ARPA SUR project, certainly the biggest event in speech research history. (When it began, the speech part of it alone cost as much as all other Government-supported speech research put together.) But it began not because of any pressure from DOD consumers, but from an internally-generated desire to see if so-called Artificial Intelligence (which ARPA had fostered, to a great extent) could recover the meaning of an utterance given the recognizedly inaccurate string of phonetic elements produced by current automatic extraction algorithms. (The answer, for practical application, appears to be "not yet" [Klatt, 1977].)

2-2.1.2 Other Government Work

There are, of course, speech areas in which Government and some industrial entities have immediate needs, areas such as speech bandwidth compression. Here there is enthusiastic and generous support of applied speech research and development. A lot of progress has been made, and much of what has been learned there about how to transmit speech information is helping us to understand how to automatically extract and use speech information. However if one again today adds up what is being spent by the Government on speech recognition and basic speech research (and excludes speech compression work) one finds that the amount is not substantially greater than it was in 1971; discounting inflation, speech recognition support is just about where it was at the start of the SUR project. The Government, it seems, is not jumping up and down in its eagerness for a successful speech recognition technology.

2-2.1.3 Industrial Work

It's true that there is a certain amount of internally-funded industrial work, (e.g. [Jelinek, 1976]) but again the motivation seems to come not from customer pressure but from internal R&D organizations that have convinced management that speech recognition is going to be feasible and someday even profitable. Furthermore, some of this work is riding on the coattails of other closely related speech work that has outside backing, such as speech compression, talker identification, and isolated word recognition.

2-2.2 Practical Recognition Systems; Isolated Words And Talker Verification

Well, if it's not a problem needing solution, how about a solution
looking for a problem? Do we have a technology that is ready to be applied
if only the right circumstances could be found? When we say "applied" we
are not talking about a laboratory system meeting certain specifications,
we are talking about a device that is comfortably usable by a customer in a
real-life situation. (It might even have to be cheap.) Application of a
technique thus implies that it is simple, robust, reliable, and
reproducible. In these terms speech research has so far produced just two
"applicable" automatic techniques; one is isolated word recognition
[Martin, 1975] and the other is talker verification [Doddington, 1974].
There is no longer any doubt that if a person is willing to train a word
recognition system with his own voice, with a fixed channel, with a vocabulary of a few hundred isolated words in fixed form, the system can be made
to recognize those words, spoken over that channel by that person, with
very high reliability. Also, a verification system can be produced such
that, given a talker who claims to be person X, and given that the talker is
willing to utter phrases when and as directed by the system, and given that
the system has on file examples of X uttering those phrases, the system can
be built to decide with high reliability whether or not the talker is
indeed person X. These two are the sum total of our pratical competence in
speech recognition.

What these successes tell us, of course, is that the particular algorithms
used are actually good enough; and lack of similar success on all the other
speech recognition problems means that the algorithms we are using, while
they may work sometimes and to some extent, are not good enough. Now
current implementations of talker and word recognition schemes have certain
features in common. First, they involve exactly one trained, cooperative
talker. (It can be argued that anyone can talk into a talker recognition
system, but in fact the task is only to judge whether one particular person
is talking.) In both cases, incoming speech is compared with prerecorded
template tokens recorded by the subject, templates formed from features
extracted mostly from the speech spectrum; the features used may be different in the two schemes, but in both they are supposed to have some phonetic
relevance. In both schemes there is a way of compensating for variations in
rate of talking; this time normalization, which is done on the string of
extracted features, is essentially the only normalization or distortion used
in the system. And finally each scheme uses a fairly unsophisticated
matching algorithm to compare the incoming feature string with the stored
templates.

2-2.3 Unsolved Problems of Continous Speech Recognition

Between these practical schemes and the kind of general continuous speech
recognition sought in, say, the SUR project, there is a difference not just
in degree but in kind. In order to pass from template matching of words
spoken in citation form to general sentence recognition we must first
overcome problems of channel difference (for example between template and
test utterance), such as additive noise, spectral amplitude distortion, and
phase distortion. Then we must cope with talker differences, such as in
spectral and temporal features of various speech sounds, in coarticulation,
rhythmic habits. Progress has of course been made: spectral channel
distortion is to some extent corrected by "blind deconvolution"
[Stockham, 1975] (but if an apparent channel effect was in reality a speaker
effect, blind deconvolution can be a disaster). At the spectral level,
feature patterns can be fairly successfully time-normalized to a standard
[Bridle, 1973; Neuburg, 1977]. Frequency normalization (of formants, say) is

21

still in its infancy [Gerstman, 1968; Wakita, 1977; Fant, 1976]. But even
if all channel and talker differences could be eliminated (perhaps by
sticking to one talker and one channel) the principal unsolved problems of
continuous speech recognition remain, the problems having to do with the
nature of continuous speech. We simply do not know enough, even for a
single speaker, about what happens to words when they occur in sentences
rather than in citation form, or even if words are the right units to be
looking for in continuous speech (but see [Cole, 1977]). We don't know how
to characterize supersegmental features quantitavely, or how much information
they convey above or about the phonemic features. We have only the crudest
notions of a local perceptual distance measure [Mermelstein, 1976], and
none for linguistic or semantic distance, so even when we do have a good
template for a word in running speech, we don't know what parts of the
template are important to match correctly. These and many other gaps in
our knowledge make continuous speech recognition a completely different
class of task from the two in which we have actually succeeded.

2-3 Simple Improvements to Existing Systems

The purpose of all this wailing and wringing of hands is not to cast
doubt on the eventual achievement of practical, useful continuous speech
recognition, or to put a damper on research in the field. Quite the
contrary; it is becoming clearer all the time that we can have working,
limited recognition systems, if limitations are realistic, and surely speech
research should get more support than it does. There is an argument,
however, for trying to solve one hard problem at a time, rather than trying
to solve them all at once. There is a great deal to be learned by trying to
build a speech system just one step more sophisticated than the one we have
already produced.

There _are_ applications now for the systems that are applicable. In all
likelihood there would be applications for such systems extended in just
one dimension or a small number of dimensions, if they really worked. For
example, there would surely be interest in a single-speaker system that
could reliably recognize alphanumeric strings of arbitrary length, or a
device that could interpret sentences made up of isolated words. In fact
people work on such systems e.g. [Haton, 1974; Sambur and Rabiner, 1975],
and they may be the ones who are on the best and most productive track.

2-4 Conclusion

And that brings us down to the point that all this was intended to
suggest; that those who have a need for a practical, high-reliability
speech-input device should limit their hopes and their support to a system
that is only one order of magnitude more sophisticated than what is already
practical; and those who are trying to further the science of speech
recognition without a particular application in mind would make more of a
contribution with a small solid advance in one direction than with another
complicated, comprehensive speech recognition system that is just a little
better than anybody else's.

2.5 REFERENCES

BRIDLE, JOHN S., "An efficient elastic-template method for detecting given words in running speech," Proc. British Acoust. Soc., Spring Meeting, April 1973.

COLE, R.A., "Model of word recognition from fluent speech" (Abstract), J. Acoust. Soc. Amer., vol. 62, Supplement no. 1 (Fall 1977), p. 49.

DODDINGTON, GEORGE R., "Speaker verification - Final report," Rome Air Development Center, Giffiss AFB, N.Y., Tech. Rep. RADC 74-179 (1974).

FANT, GUNNAR, "Vocal-tract determinants of resonance frequencies and bandwidths" (Abstract), J. Acoust. Soc. Amer., vol. 59, Supplement no. 1 (Spring 1976), p. 70.

GERSTMAN, L.J., "Classification of self-normalized vowels," IEEE Trans. Audio Electroucoust., vol. AU-16 (March 1968), pp. 78-80.

HATON, J.P., "A practical application of a real-time isolated word recognition system using syntactic constraints," IEEE Trans. ASSP-22, no. 6 (1974), pp. 416-419.

JELINEK, F., "Continuous speech recognition by statistical methods," Proc. IEEE, vol. 64, no. 4 (April 1976), pp. 535-556.

KLATT, DENNIS H., "Review of the ARPA Speech Understanding project," J. Acoust. Soc. Amer., vol. 62, no. 6 (Dec. 1977), pp. 1345-1366.

MARTIN, THOMAS B., "Applications of limited vocabulary systems," in Speech Recognition, D. Raj Reddy, Ed. Academic Press, N.Y. (1975).

MERMELSTEIN, PAUL, "Distance measures for speech recognition-psychological and instrumental," Haskins Laboratories Status Report on Speech Research SR-47 (1976), pp. 91-103.

NEUBURG, EDWARD P., "Dynamic methods in speech processing" (Abstract), J. Acoust. Soc. Amer., vol. 62, Supplement no. 1 (Fall 1977), p. 36.

NEWELL, A. et.al., Speech Understanding Systems, Final report of a study group. (1971), reprinted by North-Hollard/American Elsevier, 1973.

PIERCE, J.R., "Whither speech recognition?" (Letter), J. Acoust. Soc. Amer., vol. 46 (1969), p. 1049.

SAMBUR, M.R. and L.R. Rabiner, "A speaker independent digit recognition machine," Bell System Tech. Jour., vol. 59 (Jan. 1975).

STOCKHAM, T.G., T.M. Cannon and R.B. Ingbretsen, "Blind deconvolution through digital signal processing," Proc. IEEE, vol. 63, no. 4 (April 1975), pp. 678-692.

WAKITA, H., "Normalization of vowels by vocal-tract length and its application to vowel identification," IEEE Trans. Acoust. Speech Signal Process., ASSP-25 (1977), pp. 183-192.

3.

PRACTICAL SPEECH RECOGNIZERS

AND SOME PERFORMANCE EFFECTIVENESS PARAMETERS

Thomas B. Martin
John R. Welch
Threshold Technology Incorporated

3-1. INTRODUCTION

Automatic speech recognition (ASR) systems have indeed come of age in a practical sense, since there are hundreds of such systems in operation around the world in industrial and government applications, enabling workers to use their voices to control machines or to enter data into computers. The basic technical difficulties associated with machine recognition of speech are fairly well appreciated by most speech scientists. There are, in addition to these difficulties, however, a host of other problems which must be confronted when attempting to apply an ASR system in a practical situation. In this chapter, discussions of these problems will be based primarily on our experience with speaker-adaptive, isolated-word recognition systems, but references will be made to universal and continuous-speech systems for those problems which tend to be dependent upon the type of recognition that is performed. The chapter will include an outline of some of the economic justifications for using voice input systems. This will be followed by discussions of some of the system and human factor aspects of ASR applications. Results from a set of carefully controlled comparisons of an ASR system with two manual data entry systems will then be presented. Finally, a number of different practical applications of ASR systems will be described.

3-2. TYPES OF VOICE RECOGNITION SYSTEMS

3-2.1 Continuous Versus Isolated Speech

All ASR systems can be considered as belonging to one of two categories: continuous (connected) or isolated (discrete) speech systems. Continuous-speech systems are those which can extract information from strings of words even though the words are run together as in natural speech. Such systems range in complexity from those which simply recognize short strings of connected digits to those which attempt to perform speech understanding.

Isolated-speech systems, on the other hand, can be defined as those systems that require a short pause before and after utterances that are to be recognized as entities. The minimum-duration pause that can be reliably inserted by a human speaker is about 100 ms. Furthermore, anything shorter than 100 ms could be confused with the closure of stop consonants within words. Actually, a stop gap can exceed 100 ms duration. For example, the word "Victor" can be spoken with a relatively long silence interval after "Vic-". For a cooperative speaker entering data rapidly, however, a 100 ms separation between words is almost never confused with internal stop gaps. The maximum speaking rates that can be achieved with isolated speech are lower than with connected speech, but the differences are by no means overwhelming. The upper speed bound for an isolated word recognition system has been measured informally for trained speakers reading digits in random order.[1] Rates of 120 digits/min. have been achieved consistently by the best speakers, with error plus reject rates of two percent or less. In factory environments, average speaking rates between 30 and 70 isolated words (or phrases) per minute have been measured for individuals using isolated speech input systems during their entire 8-hour working day. These average rates included peak rates close to 120 words/min. and lower than average rates during periods of light workload (Martin, 1976). No comparable results are available for connected speech, since to date there is no real-time connected-speech recognition system of comparable performance. Informal tests of connected-speech reading rates indicate, however, that maximum machine recognizable entry rates with random digits will probably not exceed 180 digits/min.

Aside from increasing the speed of data entry it is generally assumed that continuous-speech recognizers will eliminate the artificiality associated with isolated speech. At high entry rates many speakers have trouble leaving enough separation between words to obtain satisfactory recognition results. If continuous-speech recognizers can provide a good solution to the word boundary problem for such speakers or in high noise environments they will have solved a major problem. It is possible, however, that the first continuous-speech recognizers will have even more problems with poor speakers and noisy environments than isolated-speech recognizers do, simply because they will be attempting to accomplish segmentation (or its equivalent) without any assistance from the speaker.

3-2.2 Universal Versus Speaker Dependent Recognition

One of the major obstacles to progress in the field of ASR is the variation in speech between individuals. Such differences have made the search for the "universal" speech recognizer a formidable task. A practical bypass of the problem can be achieved by adapting a recognition system to the characteristics of the user. Since interspeaker differences are far greater than intraspeaker differences, substantially higher recognition accuracy can be achieved for a given complexity of ASR system by using speaker adaptation. It is for this reason that the first ASR systems to be used in practical applications have almost all employed speaker adaptation.

3-3. ECONOMICS OF ASR

Economic factors are critical in determining whether ASR systems are employed in practice. In most applications, ASR systems will not be used unless their speeds and accuracies are high enough to provide cost savings over conventional data entry systems. Direct cost savings can result from either increased productivity or reduction in labor force. Indirect savings can result from elimination of training (since relatively unskilled personnel can use ASR systems).

It is interesting to note that to-date most ASR applications fall into the category of source data entry. There are essentially no applications in which ASR is being used simply to replace the functions of a skilled keypunch operator. There are several reasons for this. First, the performances of most ASR systems are such that they cannot compete directly with a skilled keypunch operator in terms of speed and accuracy of transcription.

---

[1] Independent tests conducted by both authors with Threshold Technology VIP-100 systems.

Second, it has been estimated that for every dollar spent in keying operations (keypunch, key-to-disc, key-to-tape) another three to four times this amount is spent in data capture (Dorn, 1973). Hence, a combination of technical limitations and economic payoffs strongly favors the application of ASR systems to source data entry.

With respect to source data entry it is apparent that anything performed by an ASR system can be achieved by a human listener with typing skills and a keyboard. In this regard the ASR system competes directly with the cost of a skilled human listener. When ASR systems cost less than the equivalent functions performed by humans, a strong cost justification results for ASR. Indeed, this is the classical justification for virtually all recent trends toward automation. It is not surprising, therefore, that the first practical applications of ASR in the early 1970's occurred in industries with 2 or 3 shift operations. The ASR system can perform quite adequately 24 hours a day, thereby increasing the cost justification in these applications.

There are several factors which affect the cost of ASR systems. First is the cost of the basic ASR hardware and software. At present a state-of-the art isolated word recognition system capable of achieving greater than 98 percent correct recognition for a thirty word vocabulary costs five to ten times as much as a good quality editing CRT terminal. In addition to this basic cost, however, the fact that the ASR system will probably be used for source data entry means that the system will in fact be an "intelligent" terminal, and that a substantial amount of custom software may have to be developed to provide that intelligence. The cost of developing the software can greatly exceed the cost of the ASR terminal itself, whereas failure to provide adequate software can weaken the performance of the system so that it will not provide the necessary increase in productivity to justify its cost. Clearly a library of applications software becomes quite an asset when attempting to market ASR systems.

Another way to minimize the high cost of software development is to provide an ASR system which is plug compatible with manual data entry terminals for which data entry software already exists. Once again the greatest payoffs will come from replacing the types of terminals that are presently used for source data collection. Application of ASR to these systems without modifying the software, may not result in an optimum voice data entry interface, but the lower cost of the total ASR system can compensate for that lack of optimality in many applications.

3-4. HOW THE APPLICATION AFFECTS THE ASR SYSTEM

The decision to use voice in data entry usually is made on an economic basis. Whether or not voice provides a productivity advantage with respect to other data entry devices depends moreover on the application. In this section we will discuss some of the system aspects of data entry applications which determine cost effectiveness of voice as an entry method.

3-4.1 Hand Occupation

ASR systems are unique in their ability to obtain data or commands from a user whose hands are already occupied with other functions. The alternatives to voice data entry when hands are occupied are to have the data recorded by tape or by a listener, or to require the user to interrupt his other activities for the purpose of data input. For situations which require simultaneous hand occupation and data entry on a continuous basis, voice data entry may enable one person to do nearly the work of two. Quality control, inspection and material sortation often fall in this category. In many other applications, however, either the hand occupation or the data

entry tasks are performed on a part-time or sporadic basis. In these cases
the productivity advantage of voice input depends upon the duty cycles of
hand occupation and data entry, and upon the specific nature of the task.
If the hand occupation duty cycle is low, then keyboard data entry may be
advantageous. If the data entry duty cycle is low then recording for later
transcription or interrupting the primary process may be feasible. On the
other hand, even though data entry performance is sporadic, a 100 percent
hand occupation requirement coupled with an occasional need for immediate
data input, may require the use of voice input.

3-4.2 Mind and Eye Occupation

Mind and eye occupation are often overlooked as justifications for
voice data entry because the advantages to be gained from freeing the mind
and eyes relate primarily to quality and only secondarily to quantity of
data entered. In a complex data entry task involving a substantial amount
of visual scanning it is a significant additional burden to have to locate
a keyboard or data menu and then to have to find the proper keys or menu
blanks to enter the data. A skilled touch typist can, of course, do this
without diverting his eyes or mind from the data source, but the amount of
training required to achieve that ability is substantial. With voice data
entry, operators with no typing skills can perform the data entry function
without having to remove their eyes from the data source. Recent experiments
(Welch, 1977) have indicated that voice data entry produces significantly
fewer reading and interpretation errors than keyboard or menu data entry in
this kind of situation. In practice, however, this reduction in the reading
error rate only has value if the voice data entry system has a low recognition error rate. An operational recognition error rate greater than three
percent (including rejects) will be high enough to cancel the advantages of
the lower reading error rate in many situations.

Since mind and eye occupation is a factor in most intelligent terminals
and interactive graphic systems, whether or not they involve extensive hand
occupation, application of voice data entry should find increasing usage
where it is possible to achieve limited vocabulary error rates consistently
below one percent for both skilled and unskilled talkers. In this situation
it is possible to demonstrate substantial increases in overall data entry
efficiency because of reductions in operator fatigue and in time and labor
required for verification and error correction.

3-4.3 Operator Mobility

Operator mobility is an advantage of voice input which ranks in importance with hand freedom in certain applications. Hand-held keyboards are
available which offer operator mobility but usually with reduced functions
because of size and weight limitations. Voice input suffers no loss in
functional capability when used by a non-stationary operator. Furthermore,
by the use of a wireless transmitter an operator can have complete freedom
of movement and still communicate with an ASR system. Small cigarette-pack
size transmitters are used with voice input to provide a considerable range
of operation. However, in such cases, feedback to the operator may require
the use of voice response or a portable display since he may be outside the
visual range of a fixed display.

3-4.4 Data Type

The advantages or disadvantages of voice data entry as compared to keyboard or other entry media depend to a great extent on the type of data to
be entered. Some factors which affect voice entry performance are size of
vocabulary, type of vocabulary, and length of data fields. Let us now consider how these factors can be expected to affect data entry performance differently for voice and for keyboard and for devices such as light pens, mark
sense forms and large pushbutton arrays, when used in a menu-selection mode.

A large vocabulary (greater than 100 items) generally includes items such as key words, function selectors, and control characters, in addition to alphanumerics. A keyboard can easily handle such a vocabulary but has the disadvantage that the words other than the alphanumerics and control characters must be spelled out either entirely or partially. Menu data entry has a disadvantage with this kind of vocabulary because of the excessive time required to scan a very large menu. Voice data entry, on the other hand, is ideal for large vocabularies of words (if speed and accuracy are suitably high) since an operator with no special skills can enter the equivalent of numerous keystrokes with a single utterance without resorting to abbreviations or having to remember special code words. Since voice recognition accuracy tends to decline with increasing vocabulary size, however, its advantages are best realized when the actual recognition vocabulary is reduced in size at each data entry node based on the syntax of the data entry problem. Such systems are sometimes referred to as "syntax driven", and most of the voice input terminals currently in operation for use with large vocabularies are of this type.

Medium-size vocabularies (greater than 30 but fewer than 100 items) generally fall into two categories, words or alphanumerics. Entry of a medium-sized vocabulary of words can often be accomplished very effectively by voice or menu systems. The vocabulary size does not exceed the practical limitations of commercial voice data entry, nor does it result in an impractical size of menu, except possibly near the upper limits of the size range. Keyboard also can do a good job in this size range, but it has the disadvantage of requiring multiple keystrokes. The use of abbreviations can reduce the number of keystrokes to no greater than two per entry, but memorization of abbreviations increases the training requirements.

If the medium-sized vocabulary is explicitly limited to alphanumerics either singly or as code strings, then keyboard no longer requires multiple keystrokes per entry. Menu data entry then has a disadvantage as compared to keyboard since, at best, it lets the operator proceed like a "one-fingered" typist. Voice entry may also have the disadvantage of requiring use of a phonetic alphabet. Some experience is required before an operator can rapidly spell words using a phonetic alphabet.

Small vocabularies (fewer than 30 words) can take the form of words, alphanumerics, or numerics. In this size range, vocabularies of words can be recognized very accurately by voice and the menu size is quite manageable for menu-oriented systems. Keyboard still has the disadvantage of requiring multiple keystrokes or memorization of abbreviations when words are to be entered. Small vocabularies of strictly alphanumeric data can be handled very well by keyboard. Menu input still has the disadvantage of being like one-fingered typing, but for very small vocabularies this is compensated by the fact that unlike a standard keyboard, the menu can be reduced in size and tailored exactly to match the vocabulary. Voice input again may have the disadvantage of requiring use of a phonetic alphabet.

Numeric-only vocabularies can be processed very rapidly by special numeric keypads or by the numeric row of keys on a standard teletypewriter. It is possible to learn to touch-type such numeric keyboards with relatively little training. Furthermore, such keyboards can be used one-handed in applications requiring use of the other hand. Menu data entry by contrast cannot compare to keyboard because of its "one-fingered" nature. Voice entry, likewise, cannot compete with a numeric keyboard solely on the basis of speed unless entire data strings can be entered by continuous speech. Even then, the continuous speech recognition system must have a very low error rate and must provide methods for circumventing the verification delay and string correction problems.

Length of data fields is a parameter which is applicable to alphanumerically coded fields or strictly numeric fields. If each field must be verified by a word such as "ENTER" or a carriage return, then short fields require more verification time per character than do long fields. On the other hand, time for entry of long fields is increased by the requirement that the operator mentally break the fields into smaller more easily memorized segments, which are then entered separately. Voice data entry has a greater advantage with long fields since the eyes can remain fixed on the data source during the entire entry process. This advantage can be lost, however, if the error rate is relatively high and it is not possible or convenient to make corrections to individual characters in the data strings.

3-4.5 Source Data Entry Versus Keypunching

Most data entry can be categorized as either source data entry or key-punching. Source data entry can be defined as the direct conversion of data to computer readable form as the data is being generated or extracted by a human. Keypunching can be (broadly) defined as bulk manual conversion of organized data from prepared format sheets to computer readable form.

Often source data entry is performed by a person who is not a skilled typist or keypunch operator but who is trained to perform functions other than enter data. Generally, the data extraction task requires at least a moderate degree of mental concentration and the data has some meaning to the operator. Speed may not always be important in source data entry, but accuracy is usually critical.

Voice is well suited to source data entry. The eye and hand occupation requirements generally favor the use of voice, and the speed of voice input can be competitive because of the user's lack of typing skill. The introduction of voice data entry to such keypunching functions as key-to-disk or key-to-tape conversion is harder to justify, however, since the dedicated full-time nature of these tasks makes it feasible to use highly trained data entry specialists. Voice input is not yet competitive in speed or accuracy with a skilled typist, and since a keypunch operator can generally keep his eyes on the data source while typing, there is no eye occupation advantage either.

The place where voice input may first become advantageous for keypunching is in the hands of skilled professionals such as scientists or computer programmers who typically do their own data entry but who are not skilled touch typists. Such individuals may find that voice input enables them to dispense with intermediate detailed data editing or coding since thinking and data entry can proceed simultaneously. The high labor costs for such individuals also means that smaller proportional time savings will be required to justify the higher cost of the voice entry system.

3-4.6 Flexibility of Application

It is not uncommon for a keyboard terminal to be available for use by a large number of people for a variety of applications such as in a time sharing environment. To-date, however, there are two factors which tend to discourage use of voice in this kind of flexible arrangement. The first factor is operator proficiency. Although it requires substantially less time to master voice input than to become a touch typist, it generally requires more time to obtain a low but useful level of proficiency with voice. With keyboard input the operator only has himself to worry about; the keyboard seldom makes mistakes and its requirements are relatively easy to comprehend. With voice, on the other hand, there is substantial interaction between the operator and the machine and it takes time to learn what the machine expects from the operator in terms of effective speaking style. As a result, most voice input systems tend to be used by individual operators continuously for sustained periods. In such a situation, the operator typically becomes a skilled talker, and voice input becomes an integral part of his job function.

The second factor which works against voice input as a flexible data entry medium is the time required for setting up different applications. Use of a voice terminal for various applications would require either that all entries be spelled one character at a time, which is not generally the most efficient way to use voice input, or that different vocabularies be made available for each different application. Vocabulary reference data can, of course, be stored for those applications which are used repeatedly, but new applications require respecification and retraining of the vocabulary, and may also require retraining by each individual operator. In other words, there is an overhead for defining and training a non-standard voice input vocabulary which can only be recovered if the data input task is a lengthy one, or if that task is expected to be repeated a number of times.

It is interesting to note that if universal recognition is employed, individual retraining will no longer be required, but the overhead involved in adding or changing vocabulary items may be substantially greater than with a speaker adaptive system.

3-5. HUMAN FACTORS

There are numerous human factors which affect the usefulness of automatic speech recognition systems in practical data entry and control applications. Since in many applications the justification for voice input is based upon fractional increases in productivity which depend upon the cooperation of the user, failure to attend to human factors can have catastrophic effects on system performance.

3-5.1 Microphone Mounting

A number of engineering considerations (Martin, 1976) lead to the requirement that the operator speak into a close-talking, head-mounted microphone, and that the microphone maintain the same position in front of the operator's mouth for long periods of time. Human considerations, on the other hand, require that the microphone assembly be light in weight, comfortably loose fitting, and that it not muss the operator's hair nor produce a strange or humorous appearance. Recent reductions in weight and size, and improvements in stability of microphone mounting systems have largely resolved the once substantial conflict between these engineering and human requirements and are proving to be of benefit to long term performance in many ASR systems.

3-5.2 Recognition Accuracy

Recognition accuracy in a practical ASR system must be high enough not to hinder the accomplishment of the intended task or result in loss of user confidence. Humans have a tendency to be oblivious to very low error rates in multitask operations; but if the error rate is high enough to interfere noticeably with the task, the operator will lose confidence and will not wish to use the voice input system. Interviews with users of operational voice input systems have shown that rarely is a voice input system accepted unless the error rate is very low (Martin, 1976). In a sense the operator makes a binary decision, i.e., the voice input system is either "good" or "bad". The actual error rate at which this happens is dependent upon the particular application and the data entry rate. Applications with voice data entry rates above 50 words per minute require lower error rates than those applications where the data rate is slow enough that the user has ample time to make corrections. This relationship to entry rate is unfortunate since, in isolated word systems, error rates tend to increase with increasing entry speed because of the increased difficulty of separating adjacent words when speaking rapidly.

It has also been observed that voice recognition accuracy tends to decrease when the operator loses confidence in the recognition system. That is, any factor which would normally increase the error rate, such as a damaged microphone, may have an additional adverse effect on performance when the operator senses that something is wrong and loses trust in the system. Conversely, a slight improvement in recognition equipment performance may result in a surprisingly large improvement in recognition accuracy, if the change raises the operator's confidence level above the acceptance threshold.

3-5.3 Error Correction

Since voice data entry systems are subject to several sources of error, it is necessary to provide convenient and reliable mechanisms for correcting errors. One approach to error correction is to provide a recognition output buffer which stores recognition results locally at the voice recognition terminal and transmits the results to the host or output device only upon receipt of a verification command. Two error-correction commands can be provided, one for erasing the last recognized word from the output data buffer and a second for erasing all entries recognized subsequent to the last verification command. For example, the word "OKAY" can be used for verification, "ERASE" for clearing the last recognition result and "CANCEL" for clearing the entire buffer.

In practice there is one difficulty with this procedure, which is easily overcome by experienced operators, but which can cause considerable confusion with new or infrequent users. The problem is that the verification and correction commands themselves can be misrecognized. Failure to recognize these words is frustrating and can add further errors to be corrected. False recognition of the commands can erase properly recognized data and always slows the data entry process. The fact that these words tend to be used more often when speakers are having some difficulty with recognition results, and hence are under stress, increases the likelihood of their being misrecognized. This problem must be minimized either by an inherently low error rate or by choosing the correction commands to be as phonetically different from the other words in the vocabulary as possible.

3-5.4 Response Time and Delay

In most applications the economic justification for voice data entry depends upon its ability to increase worker productivity. For this reason the speed of voice input is generally critical. In order for an isolated word recognition system to be competitive with other data entry media such as keyboards or light pens it is necessary to reduce recognition response time to the point where the system can repeatedly recognize words which are separated by as little as 100 ms and which have durations on the order of 200 ms. Consistency of response is also important since even an occasional delay above these limits will force the operator to increase his word spacing to accommodate the worst-case system response.

Provision of a ready indicator to signal that a new word can be accepted obviates the problem of premature entry only for very slow speaking rates. For entry at maximum rates, the operator cannot be expected to pay attention to a ready indicator, but must be able to rely on the system being ready if he has provided the required silence interval between words, and has kept word durations above the minimum value.

The time elapsed between speaking a word and display of the recognition result can also affect the throughput of the recognition system, since at the end of data strings the operator must wait for the display of the final word before he can finish verifying the string. By reducing the recognition processing delay nearly to zero, the verification overhead can be reduced to only the time required to speak the verification command.

Several proposed continuous word recognition systems (Sakoe and Chiba, 1971; Rabiner and Sambur, 1976; Porter, et.al., 1977) operate on a string of words at a time and produce an output after the last word of the string is spoken. Unless verification is deferred at least for several strings, as in a page-buffered system, the verification overhead in such a system can reduce considerably the overall throughput. Furthermore, if error correction is required in such a system, the entire string may have to be respoken. Because of these considerations, continuous speech recognizers will achieve higher overall data entry throughput than the best isolated word recognition systems, only if they employ extremely fast processing, have very low error rates and include sophisticated buffering and error correction capabilities.

3-5.5 Feedback and Prompting

Immediate feedback of recognition results must be given the user of a voice input system, either visually, aurally, or both. The feedback should either be a direct echo of the words entered or an unambiguous elaboration thereof. As mentioned in the section on response time and delay, efficient use of feedback for verification requires that the feedback delay be minimized.

In any data entry application which involves more than one or two data fields, conversational interactive prompting can be used to guide the operator through a data entry process. The design of an efficient prompting structure can be a very complicated process. Prompts must be clear and helpful without being too verbose. Gaines and Facey (1975) recommend that the user be given a simple method for selecting the degree of verbosity of the prompts, so that the prompts can be very helpful during learning but brief and efficient after the operator has memorized the data entry sequence. Such prompting can be applied in addition to direct echo feedback, but in some cases the prompts themselves provide sufficient verification of previous entries to enable direct feedback to be eliminated. For example, a response of "enter new address" serves both as verification feedback and as a prompt for the next input when it follows the input command "change address".

Interactive voice data entry systems can operate as intelligent terminals which provide syntax-driven error correction and prompting to the operator. Such systems can perform calculations, check formats and expected values of parameters, make data dependent modifications to entry procedures and request special functions from the operator. A very high percentage of the voice input terminals which have been installed to-date are intelligent. One reason for this is that voice input is often used in applications in which the operator must perform other functions. In those situations any assistance which can be provided by the terminal to simplify or clarify the data entry task, improves overall operator productivity. A second reason is that almost always voice data entry is "source data entry" so that any error checking and correction which can be performed locally reduces communication and processing costs, and eliminates the long delays, high costs and potential loss of data associated with after-the-fact error detection and correction.

3-5.6 Stability of Reference Data

An adaptive, limited vocabulary system recognizes by comparing an unknown utterance with a set of stored samples of the vocabulary words obtained from the user of the system. Once the reference data has been obtained, the operator should be able to use the voice input system for long periods of time with little or no "retraining". The ability to begin operations each day with no "warm up" or retraining will greatly enhance the operator's confidence. Similarly, he should not have to interrupt his normal operations frequently to retrain individual words.

3-5.7 Training Effects

In a speaker adaptive recognition system, it is necessary for the user to train the system by repeating each word in the vocabulary one or more times during a training phase. During the training mode many users tend to speak differently from the way they speak during the recognition mode. This is especially true for inexperienced users and in applications where voice data entry is performed simultaneously with other stressful tasks. The differences between the two modes of operation produce changes in many factors including: amplitude, timing, stress, vowel pronunciation, articulation of stops, abruptness of word terminations, breath noise, and co-articulation.

Good performance requires that recognition results be unaffected by variations in amplitude, timing and stress. But since elimination of all sensitivity to differences in vowel and stop pronunciation is not desirable and elimination of sensitivity to word boundary variations is very difficult, it is important to design the training procedure to be as realistic as possible. In practice this means that during training, several repetitions of each word should be required. Connolly (1977) has also indicated that there may be an advantage to randomizing the order of the repetitions to eliminate rhythmic patterning and to provide a variety of coarticulatory environments. Furthermore, the pace of the training routine should approximate the pace of the recognition process, and if possible the same external noise, stress and distraction factors should be present as will be present during normal operation.

Experienced voice data entry operators tend to differ from inexperienced operators both in how they speak during recognition and during training. They learn to speak effectively and consistently during recognition and to provide speech samples during training which are similar to the utterances which will be spoken during recognition. In other words, while the ultimate goal is to make a machine which can adapt to the speech variations of the user, good recognition performance can also be obtained by experienced users who adapt to the requirements of the machine.

3-6. A COMPARISON OF VOICE AND MANUAL DATA ENTRY

3-6.1 Background

In order to apply voice or any other data entry device effectively, it is necessary to obtain reliable experimental measures of the advantages, limitations, and the basic operating characteristics of the device in the specific data entry scenario to which it is to be applied. Voice, as an input mode, is so new that there have been few carefully controlled experiments to assess its capabilities.

Isolated word ASR systems have clear advantages in applications where the operator's hands are completely occupied or disabled, but it is harder to demonstrate the relative merits of ASR when hand occupation is not so complete as to eliminate manual data entry from consideration. Because of this, one of the authors (Welch, 1977)[1] recently performed a comparison of an isolated word ASR system, an ASCII keyboard and a Graf Pen[2] graphical menu data entry system as a function of several factors including presence or absence

---

[1] Work sponsored by Rome Air Development Center, Air Force Systems Command, Griffiss AFB, NY.

[2] The Graf Pen Sonic Digitizer is a product of Science Accesories Corp., Southport, Connecticut.

of hand occupation. These experiments were designed to answer the question, "Can an isolated word ASR system compete with other data entry methods when hand occupation is not so complete as to eliminate manual data entry from consideration?"

3-6.2 Description of Experiments

Two separate experiments were performed. The first experiment, which was called the High Speed Data Entry (HSDE) test, was a measure of entry performance in copying simple random strings of numeric and alphanumeric data. In this experiment, the three entry devices were tested with all possible combinations of the following factors:

    a. Data Type   - Numeric only, Alphanumeric.
    b. Data String Length - 3 Characters, 10 Characters.
    c. Hand Occupation   - Pushbutton required (single push per
                              string), not required.
    d. Feedback   - Visual and Voice response, visual only.

Forty-eight subjects were tested with three test trials per subject.

The second experiment, which was called the High Complexity Data Entry (HCDE) test was a measure of performance in entering simulated flight data control messages. In this task the subject's ability to interpret a complicated English language statement and convert it to a series of data entry fields had a large effect upon performance. This time the three entry devices were tested with all possible combinations of these factors:

    a. Hand Occupation   - With and without the requirement for a
                              pushbutton to be depressed at the end
                              of an entry sequence.
    b. Prompting   - Visual only and a combination of visual
                              and voice response.
    c. Subject Experience - No experience and some limited experience.

Twenty-four subjects were tested with three test trials per subject.

The subjects in the tests were not highly trained so that the absolute entry rates and error rates were not indicative of the rates that could be achieved by skilled data entry operators, but were more indicative of the problems that would be encountered by casual or infrequent users of a data entry system.

3-6.3 Discussion of Results

The most statistically significant results of the tests can be summarized as follows:

. Alphanumeric data entry was 25% slower and had twice the error rate of numeric data entry in the simple scenario of the HSDE test.

. Keyboard provided the fastest and most accurate entry of numeric data strings and the fastest entry of alphanumeric strings (by subjects most of whom had some keyboard experience) in the simple scenario.

. Voice entry provided the lowest error rate for entry of alphanumeric data strings in the simple scenario primarily because of its greater immunity to reading errors.

. In the complex scenario of the HCDE tests, voice was faster than keyboard for inexperienced subjects, and had a similar operational error rate, but had a substantially higher error rate before correction, primarily because of recognition and correction system errors.

. Graphical menu ranked between keyboard and voice in most of
  the simple scenario measures, except that it was least accurate
  with alphanumeric data, and had the lowest entry speed for long
  data strings.

. In the complex scenario, the performance of graphical menu
  differed significantly from that of voice only by virtue of its
  superior error rate before correction on the positive side and its
  greater loss in speed with hand occupation on the negative side.

. Overall, most of the errors with voice input involved misrecog-
  nition while those with keyboard and graphical menu involved
  misreading.

. The instantaneous pushbutton requirement in the HSDE test had
  no significant overall effect on entry speed or accuracy, but
  the more substantial (approximately 20 percent) hand occupation
  requirement in the HCDE test gave a significant speed advantage
  to voice input. It also increased the error rate for all three
  entry devices.

. Voice response feedback was too slow to be of value in the simple
  scenario, and actually increased the error rate for alphanumeric
  data entry and for keyboard data entry.

. Voice response prompting significantly reduced reading and interpretation errors in the complex scenario both before and after
  correction. This effect was the one clear demonstration that
  voice response, like voice input, can free the eyes from at least
  one of the burdens of the data entry task and can thereby improve
  data entry performance. The fact that voice response only showed
  this advantage in the prompting mode agreed with Hammerton's
  (1976) conclusion that instructions should be heard and data seen.

In addition, the following more general conclusions were also drawn
from these tests:

. When comparing voice with manual data entry it is necessary to
  use identical conditions and to perform realistic tasks. Maximum
  achievable accuracy levels or data entry speeds have little
  meaning in a difficult problem setting. ASR error rates go up,
  and manual data entry speeds come down. Reading errors, error
  correction problems and system difficulties all become apparent.

. It is more difficult to train an operator for casual data entry
  by voice than it is to do the same with keyboard or graphical
  menu input.

. Under pressure, data entry error rates are high for all devices
  so that error correction mechanisms must be easy to use, fast
  and reliable.

. Significant improvements in man-machine interaction may be
  obtainable by combining voice and manual data entry. For
  example, voice could be used for entry of words and keyboard
  for entry of numbers and for control of error correction, entry
  verification, tabulation, and editing.

Some of the areas to which voice input systems have been applied are:
1. Quality Control and Inspection
2. Automated Material Handling
3. Parts Programming for Numerically Controlled Machine Tools
4. Receiving Inspection
5. Cartography
6. Annotating Integrated Circuit Photo Masks

The first voice input systems to be used by industry in these various applications were installed in late 1972 and early 1973 (Martin, 1976). The results obtained from these initial operating systems indicated that a factory worker with minimal training can use a voice input system quite successfully. Recognition accuracies obtained were equal to or superior to keying accuracies obtained from the same personnel. Original training data for a speaker has been found to be stable over many months, thereby eliminating the need for frequent retraining and updating of the reference data.

3-7.1 Quality Control and Inspection

A normal procedure in industry for the inspection of products is for an inspector or an inspection team to prepare a handwritten report of defects or abnormal conditions. This record can then be keyed into a computer from an on-line or off-line terminal. Several people may be required to complete the procedure, the elapsed time may be substantial, and chances for error are abundant. If the inspection data is to be captured at the source, it is necessary for the inspector to key in the defects as they are observed. This keying requirement usually reduces the productivity of the operator and necessitates additional training. By using a voice data entry system it is possible to combine the inspector's normal work requirements with simultaneous entry of the data that he measures and observes. An inspector wearing a small microphone and having both hands free, follows a checklist appearing on an electronic display and simply describes each item's condition verbally. This information, can provide immediate status reports or can be transmitted to a central computer. In addition to providing cost savings, voice data entry improves production quality by providing more timely and more accurate inspection reports.

A typical quality control application involves the inspection of pull-ring beverage can lids. Both hands are necessary to handle production samples of such lids which are passed through a rigorous quality inspection. These lids must be handled and placed in and out of an assortment of gauges. In certain types of meters, the lids must be rocked back and forth to find minimum and maximum points. Capturing this data manually would require either two persons, one measuring and one writing or keying, or would require constant interruptions in the inspection process. With voice data entry it is now possible simultaneously to enter the measurements while the hand manipulations are being performed. A leading can manufacturer has reported throughput increases in several plants of up to 40%.

Another hands-busy quality control application involves the inspection by a leading glass manufacturer of color TV picture tube faceplates. As many as 54 separate measurements are made on each sample faceplate by a quality control inspector. This procedure required two people before voice data entry was installed. Now a single inspector handles (with both hands) the often large and heavy faceplates and the complicated measurement gauges while inputting measured parameters by voice.

3-7.2 Automated Material Handling

Automated sorting equipments of various types have been developed in recent years for the rapid movement of materials from one point to another.

Typically these materials consist of parcels, containers, baggage, sack mail, inventory, etc. Distribution and sorting centers use either belt or tray sorters and encoding at induction points to control the movements of the material. At each induction station a two-man team is usually employed; one who orients the label face-up and another, seated at a keyboard, who keys in the destination code. If one operator is used at the induction station, he must first handle each item, read the label, and then key the sorting code. A one-man operation is significantly slower than a two-man induction process.

Voice encoding for material handling applications can produce high sorting rates with a single operator at the induction station. Such systems have been in operation in a variety of applications since 1973. All of these systems have resulted in increased operator productivity and reduced errors from the operators who formerly key-entered the sorting destination codes. Examples of such systems are those at United Parcel Service, Baldwin Park, California and S.S. Kresge, Sparks, Nevada.

3-7.3 Parts Programming for NC Machine Tools

A traditional bottleneck in computer-based, numerical-control machining systems has been the interface between the machinist and the computer. An approach using voice programming (Plute and Cox, 1975) has made it possible for a machinist to do his own parts programming using normal English, with no requirement to convert the information into an artificial computer language. All the operator needs is a knowledge of blueprints and machine tool operation.

When using voice programming, the machinist calls out each operation into a microphone. Each command is displayed sequentially for positive verification, after which the next entry is requested. The display provides a means for immediate error detection and because the actual entry is by voice, the programmer's hands are free to handle prints or to perform measurements or calculations. At the end of the programming sequences, the cuts which have been specified are generally drawn on a graphics plotter so that any remaining programming errors can be detected without generating scrap. The combination of voice entry and a sophisticated interactive programming language eliminates the requirement for specialized computer training to perform NC parts programming.

3-7.4 Receiving Inspection

It is typically difficult to obtain timely and accurate information about the quantities arriving with each delivery at the receiving area of a large corporation. For example, Tecumseh Products Company manufactures over 50,000 different varieties of compressors and related products, ships 60,000 pieces per day and experiences a daily service return rate of 1 1/2 compressors per minute. These compressors have to be disassembled, analyzed for defects and credited to the returner. Prior to applying voice data entry, it was necessary to keypunch a form for each compressor. The form required such items as order no., item no., complete serial plate data, customer tag no., etc. The combination of handling compressors and writing down the information either required two operators or such a complicated mix of mechanical and clerical skills that error rates were on the order of 30 percent and delays ranged from six to eight weeks.

Now using direct voice entry the inspector speaks the data as he handles each compressor and is prompted through the entry sequence by the display. Illegal serial plate codes are checked and correction is possible immediately rather than after the compressor has been sent to a repair area. The system has increased operator productivity and has reduced response time for analysis and crediting of repairs to about three days.

3-7.5 Cartography

Voice data input is especially applicable where large digitizing tables are used in map making and related applications. At the Defense Mapping Agency Hydrographic Center, for example, voice data entry is used for entering ocean depth data while the operator's hands and eyes are busy positioning a cursor to provide X-Y coordinates. In this system, visual feedback is provided by a small LED display built into the cursor.

3-7.6 Annotating Integrated Circuit Photo Masks

A leading semiconductor manufacturer is using voice data entry in the generation of integrated circuit masks. A large light table with a free cursor occupies the eyes and hands of the operator in this application. The operator is able to input, by voice, data describing the circuit parameters or components as he or she positions the cursor over an enlarged photomaster of the circuitry.

3-8.   CONCLUSIONS

Limited vocabulary voice input systems have moved from the laboratory to successful applications in industry and government. A cost-effective voice input system requires careful attention to the variables affecting recognition accuracy, to the data entry scenario and to human factors. Generally, these variables and factors are interrelated so that successful application of voice data entry is a systems problem. Continued improvements in recognition accuracy, ease of use and simplicity of providing applications software are expected to result in ever increasing utilization of this powerful new technology.

3-9.   REFERENCES

Connolly, Donald W., "Voice Data Entry in Air Traffic Control," in 1977 Proc. of Conference on Voice Technology for Interactive Real-Time Command/Control Systems Applications, NASA Ames Research Center, Moffett Field, Calif., Dec. 1977.

Dorn, Phillip H., "Whither Data Entry?" Datamation, p. 41, March 1973.

Gaines, Brian R. and Peter V. Facey, "Some Experience in Interactive Systems Development and Application," Proc. IEEE, Vol. 63, No. 6, pp 894-911, June 1975.

Hammerton, M., "The Use of Same or Different Sensory Modalities in Information and Instructions," Royal Naval Personnel Research Committee Report, December 1974, AD-A026857.

Martin, Thomas B., "Practical Applications of Voice Input to Machines," Proc. IEEE, Vol. 64, No. 4, pp 487-501, April 1976.

Plute, Martin F. and Robert B. Cox, "Voice Programming - A New Dimension to NC," in NCS Proc. Tech. Conf. 1975 - NC/CAM EXPO '75 (Washington, DC), pp 89-97, May 1975.

Porter, J.E., M.W. Grady, M.B. Hicklin and L.F. Lowe, "Use of Computer Speech Understanding in Training: A Preliminary Investigation of a Limited Speech Recognition Capability," NAVTRAEQUIPCEN 74-C-0048-2, Final Report, June 1977.

Rabiner, Lawrence R. and Marvin R. Sambur, "Some Preliminary Experiments in the Recognition of Connected Digits," IEEE Trans. Acoust. Speech Signal Proc., Vol. ASSP-24, pp 170-182, April 1976.

Sakoe, Hiroaki and Seibi Chiba, "A Dynamic Programming Approach to Continuous Speech Recognition," in 1971 Proc. 7th ICA, Paper 20 C13, Aug. 1971.

Welch, John R. "Automatic Data Entry Analysis, "RADC TR-77-306, Final Technical Report., Sept. 1977.

4.

SPEECH RECOGNITION:

PAST, PRESENT, AND FUTURE

Wayne A. Lea
Speech Communications Research Laboratory

4-1. INTRODUCTION

The thirty year history of speech recognition is speckled with limited successes and repetitive rediscoveries of old ideas, and yet with a growing ability to successfully handle small vocabularies of words spoken in isolation. Recent trends have added successes in recognition of continuous speech such as strings of digits and spoken sentences related to a restricted task domain, and the technology is currently expanding rapidly. Some important gaps still remain, and future work will have to overcome some challenging problems.

In this chapter, I attempt to provide a brief but fairly comprehensive overview of all this past, present, and future work. One purpose is to guide the reader through the various projects that are described more fully elsewhere in the book, including the developments of sentence-understanding systems in the ARPA Speech Understanding Research (ARPA SUR) project as presented in Part III of the book, the recent or current USA industrial projects and work in other countries summarized in Part IV, and the suggestions for further work as outlined in Part V and at selected points in the various chapters. My primary purpose, however, is to describe the principles and historical context provided by other work not otherwise discussed in this book.

Some basic concepts involved in machine recognition of speech are introduced in Sec. 4-2, to provide a framework for characterizing various approaches to recognition. Then, historical developments of techniques and systems will be briefly summarized (Sec. 4-3), as will the variety of currently popular methods (Sec. 4-4), and the prospectus for future technology (Sec. 4-5).

For further reviews and historically significant summaries, the reader is referred to the following list of reviews, and references cited therein: (Lindgren, 1965; Hill, 1970; Lea, 1972; Reddy, 1975, 1976; Jelinek, 1976; Martin, 1976; Wolf, 1976; Breaux, et al., 1978; Lea and Shoup, 1979). Current work frequently appears in such journals as the IEEE Transactions on Acoustics, Speech, and, Signal Processing; other IEEE transactions, such as IEEE Transactions on Computers; the International Journal of Man-Machine Studies; the Journal of the Acoustical Society of America; the Journal of the Acoustical Society of Japan; the Bell System Technical Journal; and related journals from various countries. In addition, each of the groups cited throughout this book provides regular technical reports, available through their authors. Other information can be obtained from the proceedings of technical conferences such as the annual IEEE International Conferences on

4-2. GENERAL PRINCIPLES AND IDEAS

Speech signals convey information about <u>who</u> spoke <u>what message</u> in <u>what manner</u> and in <u>what environment</u>. The task of a speech recognizer is to automatically determine the message (i.e., what was said), regardless of (or perhaps with some help from knowledge of) the variabilities introduced by speaker identity, manner of speaking, and environmental conditions. In this section, we discuss some of the basic principles that have been (or might be) used in speech recognition processes.

4-2.1 <u>Ultimate Goals for Recognition</u>

Speech recognition can be generally defined as the process of transforming the continuous acoustic speech signal into discrete representations which may be assigned proper meanings and which, when comprehended, may be used to affect responsive behavior. The ultimate goal is to understand the input sufficiently to select and produce an appropriate response. This attention on ultimate responses was one motivation for the designers of the ARPA SUR project coining the phrase "speech understanding systems", since their systems were intended to "understand" sentences sufficiently to yield correct responses, not just to correctly "recognize" vowels and consonants, words, or other subunits. In actual fact, the effectiveness of <u>every</u> recognizer (even small devices for isolated word recognition) is determined by the appropriateness of its responses. Responses might be the mere lighting of one of ten display lights, the typing of words on a teletypewriter, the manipulation of a machine tool, the retrieval of stored data, the performing of a computation, or the production of a spoken response. Input utterances may be considered <u>equivalent</u> if they have the same intended response, or <u>different</u> if they should yield different responses. This produces "equivalence classes" of spoken inputs, regardless of any irrelevant signal changes due to changes in the talker, the speaking rate, the recording environment, or variabilities in details of pronunciation. A recognizer's decision is <u>correct</u> if the input is assigned to the right equivalence class, and <u>incorrect</u> if the wrong response would be produced (regardless of how many "phonemes", words, phrases, or other aspects of the signal are properly classified). The recognizer must recover the original intended message.

<u>Performance evaluation</u> of a recognizer is concerned in part with establishing what percentage of the spoken utterances produce a correct machine response. There is, of course, some <u>uncertainty</u> associated with the selection of the correct responses, so decisions are made with the hope of minimizing the number of errors, or equivalently, reducing the <u>probability</u> of an error. Also, one must determine which utterances produce incorrect responses, and why. Part of the establishment of <u>reasons</u> for errors is concerned with determining which aspect or component of the recognition process led to the error. This will help determine the "weak links" in the chain of processes within the recognizer. For example, if the recognizer identifies sentences by detecting certain phonetic sequences as occurrences of target words, and if one of the words was wrongly identified because a particular vowel or consonant was misidentified in an early stage of the recognizer, then specific improvement in vowel or consonant identification would be called for (<u>unless</u> an additional procedure can be defined for readily correcting for phonetic errors, based on their context or other information). However, the ultimate evaluation of the recognizer is concerned with the correctness of its final responses, not its intermediate results.

Another related aspect of system performance concerns how severely a system is affected by deficiencies of usual information, or deprivation such as the removal or malfunction of a system component. It is useful to know how much of the action of the recognizer is attributable to each knowledge source or system component, and to design systems so as to permit leeway or errors in one aspect, by permitting another component (such as syntactic analysis) to recover from errors in an earlier part of the system (such as the component that identifies small units). "Gradual degradation" is desired so that minor changes in either the input channel conditions or the system structure will not have catastrophic effects on system accuracy.

Other aspects of the evaluation of speech recognizers are concerned with what we might call the generality and enhanceability of the system. Each of the "dimensions of difficulty" listed in Chap. 1 of this book are important to determining the utility of the recognizer for various applications. Systems are obviously of more general utility if they permit a large number of speakers (of both sexes and various dialects) to speak in a natural manner (usually involving large vocabularies, continuous, uninterrupted speech and loosely constrained message structures), even in the environment of some noise and signal distortions such as a telephone channel might introduce. The speed with which machines make recognition decisions, the required memory size and processing power, and the cost are other factors that must be considered. Also of some importance is the ease with which an available limited recognition capability can be enhanced to handle somewhat more difficult tasks such as new vocabularies, new structures in the spoken commands, new talkers, etc. One of the primary reasons given for the use of more complex linguistically oriented recognition schemes instead of simpler mathematical techniques is the expected ease of enhancement and ultimate generality of linguistic approaches. However, for immediate success on limited problems, the more mathematically oriented approaches have repeatedly proven to give better results in shorter times. As one focuses more on a machine for a single task rather than a multi-purpose capability, mathematical techniques currently prevail in providing correct machine responses (Newell, 1975).

4-2.2 Alternative Viewpoints for How to Design Successful Recognizers

Let us look further at alternative approaches to recognition, such as mathematical schemes. Some designers of recognizers focus only (or primarily) on mathematical representations of the recognizer's input-output characteristics, asserting that each input must merely be compared with previously-stored representatives or templates of each equivalence class of inputs, and the nearest neighbor or minimally different representative must be selected as the identity (or equivalence class) of the current input signal (or, if no template is near enough, an error message might be given). This is the basis of generalized input-output functions (Newell, 1975), linear discriminant analyses, other statistical models, and general pattern recognition and signal processing schemes. Such recognition models could apply as well to signals other than speech, and indeed their technology is highly developed because of such other applications. They do not consider how the signal was produced by the speaker, nor how it is normally perceived by the human listener. They, of course, do not require that the recognizer operate internally in any way similar to the human's perception processes.

In essence, this generalized input-output or signal-processing approach represents the first of the following four basic viewpoints about how to be guided towards the design of successful speech recognizers:

1. The ACOUSTIC SIGNAL VIEWPOINT asserts that since the speech signal is just another waveform (or vector of numbers), we can simply apply general signal analysis techniques (e.g., Fourier frequency spectrum analysis, principal component analysis, statistical decision procedures, and other mathematical schemes), to establish the identity (or representative "nearest neighbor") of the input.

2. The SPEECH PRODUCTION VIEWPOINT suggests we understand the communicative "source" of the speech signal, and capture essential aspects of the way in which speech was produced by the human vocal system (e.g., look for vocal tract resonances, rate of vibration of the vocal cords, manner and place of articulation, coarticulatory movements, etc.).

3. The SENSORY RECEPTION VIEWPOINT suggests duplicating the human auditory reception process, by extracting parameters and classifying patterns as is done in the ear, auditory nerves, and sensory feature detectors.

4. The SPEECH PERCEPTION VIEWPOINT suggests we extract features and make categorical distinctions that are experimentally established as being important to human perception of speech (e.g., voice onset times and formant transitions as cues to state of consonant voicing, "single equivalent formants" as vowel distinguishers, perceptual "feature detectors", etc.).

Of course, mixtures or combinations of these viewpoints can also be devised, and have been evident in some of the previous work, as will be discussed in Sec. 4-3. The four viewpoints reflect different ways in which the linguistic message being communicated is encoded at various stages in the production and reception of speech. The sensory reception and speech perception viewpoints have had much less effect on actual recognition systems than the speech production and acoustic signal viewpoints, as will become evident from the review in Sec. 4-3.

The speech production, sensory reception, and speech perception viewpoints may be characterized as what Newell (1975, p. 15) called "knowledge-source-driven representations", which assume that recognition can be based on available knowledge of how speech is usually encoded or decoded. These three viewpoints assert that knowledge of the acoustic speech signal alone is not enough to fully determine the message (or intended machine response); other sources of knowledge must be brought to bear on the recognition problem. These viewpoints also acknowledge that, while a machine need not operate internally in the same manner as the human, the human speech processing abilities can serve as a successful "prototype system" for guiding the development of machine algorithms for speech recognition. The conversion from acoustic signal to machine response, without the intervention or help of the human, involves the machine functionally duplicating the overall (input-output) function of a human perceiver. It need not structurally duplicate the human ear-brain system, but the knowledge-source-driven viewpoints would suggest that recognizers may glean guidelines for effective recognition from study of human speech processing techniques.

Computers can currently do some analyses better than humans, and some others less adequately, and so a controversy continues between mathematical (statistical, information-theoretic, signal-processing, or pattern-classifying) methods and human-oriented (phonetic, linguistic, perceptual, or neurological) approaches. For example, statistical analyses such as IBM uses (Jelinek, 1976), or the dynamic programming methods such as Nippon Electric Company, ITT (cf. Chap. 21), and others use, can be contrasted with phonetic, phono-logical, and prosodic analysis schemes and sophisticated linguistic models, such as the ARPA speech understanding projects (cf. Part III of this book) and the current Sperry Univac systems (Chap. 19) have used. Of course, there is some use of probabilities, statistics, and other mathematical tools in even the most linguistically-oriented recognizers, and some use of linguistic units (especially "words") in the statistically defined recognizers or gener-alized input-output devices, so this is not a simple dichotomy. The Harpy system described in Chap. 15 is a good example of a recognizer that uses basic mathematical concepts like a Markov model and a mathematically-defined dis-tance measure for detecting "nearest neighbors" to specific spectra, coupled with linguistic analyses such as detection of sequences of subphonemic units, application of phonological rules, and use of syntactic constraints on likely utterances.

4-2.3 Matching Continuous Signals, and Extracting Important Features

There is an extensive amount of information in the speech signal, only some of which is related to selecting correct machine responses. A critical task is to extract from all that data all (and only) those parts that convey the message. No matter how many parts or time slices we divide the speech signal into, to permit minute study of all its data, an even finer analysis is always possible. Similarly, no matter how exactly we measure the pressure (or volt-age) of a speech wave at an instant, a finer grain analysis is conceivable. Thus, speech is a two-dimensional non-denumerable continuum. It is possible to analyze it as such, making no arbitrary or linguistically-motivated divisions into time segments and no quantizations into significant changes in signal levels. The incoming continuous wave can then be compared to other waves on the basis of point-by-point differences in signals, with no regard to the possibility that some signal differences are more important than others.

This continuous representation of speech signal comparisons is shown in Fig. 4-1 as the left-most branch of the "tree" of alternative decoding schemes. To determine the identity of the incoming speech and effect the correct machine response, a recognizer can determine the difference between the incoming sig-nal and the expected signal for each message. "Expected" signals, or tem-plates, can be actual stored training samples that were previously declared by the human to be associated with each appropriate machine response, or they can be averages or other composite signals obtained from many such training samples. For each equivalence class of utterances (associated with a specific correct response), a template (or perhaps several templates, representing allowable variations within the equivalence class) must be available for com-parison with the input waveform. A method for assessing the amount of diff-erence between the signal and the template must be specified, such as the calculation of a "Euclidean distance" formed from the squares of the point-by-point differences in signals. The selection of an appropriate "distance measure" is thus one of the important concerns in this signal-matching approach to recognition.

This (in it's simplest form) is basically an "ignorance model" of the significant aspects of the incoming signal. Each deviation from previously stored signals is assigned equal significance, and no particular features of the speech are considered more important than others. Besides ignoring what-ever we can learn about the important physiological and linguistic regularities of both the source of the speech and the intended intelligent receiver of

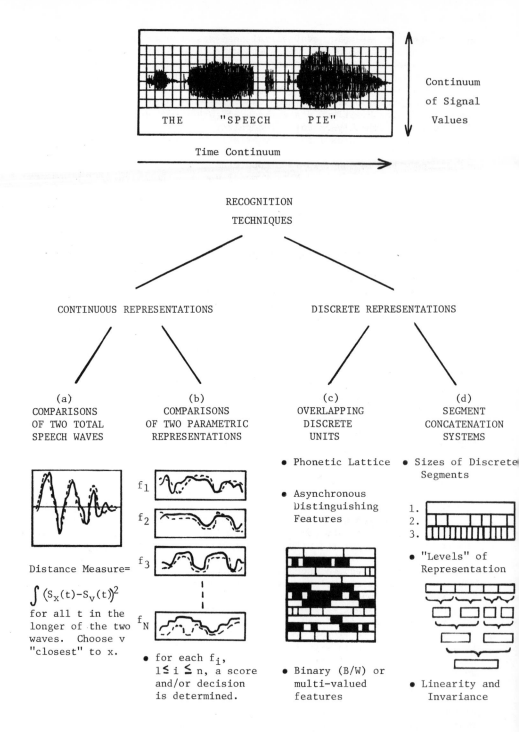

Figure 4-1   Alternative methods for dividing the two-dimensional speech continuum
("the speech pie") into parts. These methods may be used in matching
incoming speech with stored knowledge of possible pronunciations, so
that the identity of the utterance can be determined.

spoken messages, this approach has several other drawbacks. It requires
accumulation of representative training signals for each possible message.
For large message sets (large vocabularies of isolated words, or large numbers
of alternative sentences that might be continuously spoken), obtaining training templates is a time consuming and costly process, and results in extensive
storage requirements in the machine. In addition, it is difficult to obtain
truly "representative" training signals, that are quite distinct from message
to message and that are likely to be closely approximated by all speakers in
all environments. Speaker differences, variations from time to time, and
variations due to environmental noise, channel distortions, or even rate of
speaking all must be accounted for. This usually requires storing several
alternative templates for each message (e.g., one for each speaker in each
environment, etc.), thus further increasing storage requirements and making
recognition costly and unwieldly. However, with the rapidly advancing speeds
and storage capacities in low-cost computers, this is less of a problem than
it might have seemed in earlier years. Also, this approach to recognition
avoids the dangers of inadvertently "throwing away" important information.

One can attempt to assign higher weights (or levels of significance) to
certain aspects of the continuous waveforms, such as focusing on the higher
signal levels that are less susceptible to corruption by noise. One can also
warp the incoming signal to match certain features of the stored templates,
such as matching its duration to that of each alternative template before
they are compared. This time normalization process has proven useful in some
recognizers. Similar processes of speaker normalization or channel normalization can be attempted, so that certain features of the signal are detected
and used to adjust the signal to more closely match the correct stored templates. For example, by detecting the fundamental frequency or "pitch" of
the signal, or by complex processes that determine the speaker's vocal tract
length, one can adjust for speaker differences such as male versus female
speakers. Similarly, by monitoring the long-term average frequency spectrum
of the signal, and applying a mathematical process called "blind deconvolution"
(Stockham, et al., 1975), one can adjust for some differences in the spectral
characteristics of channels. Such feature extractions focus on relevant aspects of speech and remove or diminish the confusions introduced by irrelevant
differences from templates.

This is the beginning of the acknowledgement that no two utterances of the
same message are exactly alike, and the communicative ability of speech is due
to "resemblances" between successive utterances. The task of recognition is
thus said to be that of determining the "information-carrying features" common to all utterances of the "same" message, and using those features to classify utterances according to their intended meanings or expected responses.
Mathematical procedures exist for automatically "learning" features that are
common to all utterances which the human declares to be equivalent, while
assuring that the features are quite different for non-equivalent utterances.
Alternatively, features can be selected based on trial-and-error procedures
or heuristics which capture some of the regularities in previously processed
data.

4-2.4 Discrete Representations of Speech

We have observed that the acoustic speech signal has a non-denumerable
continuum of possible acoustic pressure values at any one time, and is continuously varying in time, so that for any two times you choose (or any two
pressure values, even within the finite limits of normal speech pressures),
you can find another value between them. It may be likened to a two dimensional "pie", as shown in Fig. 4-1(a). Selecting and comparing features of

the signal and stored templates, as outlined in Sec. 4-2.2, may be viewed as a process of slicing the speech "pie" into horizontal slices, with each slice still possibly being a <u>continuous</u> function of time (Fig. 4-1(b)). There is extensive justification for characterizing speech by <u>discrete units in time</u> and as a finite set of <u>simultaneous features</u>. Here we shall briefly explain those justifications, since they explain why much of speech recognition work has been done the way it has.

To begin with, some simple engineering and information-theoretic considerations suggest discrete representations. Since speech must be converted into <u>discrete voltages and switching states</u> in digital computers, a discrete representation will of necessity be required for speech recognition using practical digital computers. Also, the <u>sampling theorem</u> (cf., Pierce, 1961, pp. 66-6; Rabiner and Gold, 1975, pp. 26-28) asserts that any bandlimited signal (such as speech may be considered to be) can be completely represented by $2F_u$ samples per unit time, where F_u is the upper bound on the frequency content of the signal (which can certainly be taken to be at most 10KHz for speech). The <u>fidelity criterion</u> of communication theory (cf. Chomsky and Miller, 1963, p. 273) acknowledges that certain sound changes (e.g. those due to emotion, fatigue, speaker ideosyncrasies, etc.) are irrelevant to the receiver, while others are significant, so that the infinity of possible speech waves of a limited length can be partitioned into a finite set of discrete, mutually-exclusive "equivalence classes". Each such class, taken from the finite set of signal equivalence classes, may be represented by a discrete symbol taken from a finite "alphabet" of distinguishable signs.

Speech perception studies also suggest that certain acoustic changes are not perceivable until they reach a minimal change called a "just noticeable difference" or "limen" (Flanagan, 1972). Thus, there seem to be "quantum steps" in perceivable values of speech parameters. Thresholds of major acoustic distinction also exist in articulation of speech. For example, there are definite rates of respiratory airflow below which airflow is laminar and above which flow is turbulent, yielding sharp distinctions between what are called "sonorant" sounds and "fricatives". Also, there are rather abrupt changes in the acoustic features corresponding to opening the velic valve for nasalization. Not all articulatory changes produce significant acoustic changes, and many acoustic changes that do occur (e.g., whispering, speaking loudly, etc.) are not linguistically significant (i.e., do not usually signal a change in intended response at the receiver). Kenneth Stevens (1969) has indicated that there is a quantum nature in the acoustic changes that accompany articulatory motions, which natural languages tend to exploit, choosing sounds and articulation positions that are most stable, and not sensitive to slight misplacements of articulators. A discrete code results.

Linguist Morris Halle (1954, p. 198) has also noted that "if a discrete view be adopted, correction of errors can begin upon receipt of each discrete unit (quantum)", so we don't have to wait until the entire continuous signal is completed to correct errors in reception of such named segments. This may prove significant in the real-time recognition of spoken sentences. Finally, we may note that most messages for machine input would have identical intended responses if they had been written (or typewritten), rather than spoken, so the fact that the written code is discrete suggests the sufficiency of a discrete representation of speech.

Thus, there are a number of arguments favoring discrete representations of speech. Notice that no representation could be fully discrete unless it breaks up each of the two acoustic continua (continuum of time and continuum of pressure levels) into a countable (in practice, <u>finite</u>) number of discrete parts. A nondenumerable infinity of possible speech waveforms of a fixed length must be identified in the same discretely-representable class. Likewise, an infinity of possible lengths must be classified as "equivalent". Thus, a discrete representation of the time domain requires a segmentation of the continuous speech waveform into some sort of units or "segments". While the segments or units need not be separated with strict "boundaries" between them, and could actually overlap each other or be spaced apart from each other, the usual method is to segment speech into juxtaposed units of non-zero length, which classify as equivalent any of an infinity of "insignificantly different" wave shapes spanning about the same stretch of time. Sequences of such classified segments then determine the important information about the speech. Figure 4-1(c) illustrates discrete representations that do allow overlapping units ("lattices", or incomplete specifications of alternative units which may be in the incoming speech), and ones that involve strict concatenations, or sequences, of non-overlapping, juxtaposed segments. Both forms of representation have been used in speech recognizers, though the predominant approach is to use strict segmentations into non-overlapping units.

Given the many justifications for discrete representations, the primary question is: How should we quantize, or discretely represent speech, and how do we identify which of the finite set of categories each unit of speech belongs to? One of the simplest answers would be to segment speech at fixed time intervals. Commonly, such segments are selected to be short enough to be a small fraction of the length of normally-sustained vowels and consonants, but long enough to allow proper feature extractions, such as proper spectral averaging, or detections of periodicities in the waveform. This smallest unit of time (such as a short 10-millisecond unit) can be sensibly categorized into one of a finite number of sound categories, such as the most similar of a set of stored training templates obtained from previous processing of training data (cf. Baker, 1975). Alternatively, the segment may be assigned to a phonetic category based on the spectral content and other distinguishing features of the waveform within that unit.

At the other extreme, the total utterance (which may be a word, for isolated word recognizers, or a sentence, or discourse for continuous speech recognizers) can be interpreted as an undivided entity which determines the appropriate machine response. This maximal input unit also may be assigned to one of a countable (realistically, finite) set of discrete units (which are the labels of the equivalence classes of desired machine responses). Thus, we have the extremes in simple segmentation of speech as shown in Fig. 4-1 (d1 and d3). We shall see in section 3 that both the total-utterance-classification and the arbitrary classification of each short (10ms) segment into spectral categories have been used in previous speech recognition systems.

4-2.5 Phonological and Prosodic Structures, and Word Matching

The most controversial aspect of segmentation has concerned the relative values of intermediate size units, such as "phones"; phoneme-to-phoneme transitions or "diphones"; syllabic subunits like "syllabic onsets", "syllabic nuclei", and "coda"; "syllables"; "words"; and "phrases". There is a vast literature on the "psychological reality" and the linguistic utility of segments like phonemes and syllables (cf. Sapir, 1933; Bloomfield, 1933; Pike, 1945; Wells, 1947; Trager and Smith, 1951; Chomsky, 1957; Chomsky and Miller, 1963; Chomsky and Halle, 1968; Hockett, 1972). For example, it has long been observed that utterances can resemble or differ from other signals, based on similar or clearly distinctive portions of speech. For examples, pin begins like pig, pill, or pit, but ends differently; it ends about the same as fin, sin, tin; it contains something close to the sound of in but adds something

47

at the beginning. Also, <u>pin</u> begins like <u>pat</u>, <u>push</u>, or <u>peg</u>, but its resemb-
lance to them is less than that to <u>pig</u>, <u>pill</u>, or <u>pit</u>; it ends somewhat like
<u>man</u>, <u>sun</u>, or <u>when</u>, but its resemblence to them is smaller than to <u>fin</u>, <u>sin</u>,
<u>tin</u>, or <u>in</u>; its beginning and ending are both similar to those of <u>pen</u>, <u>pan</u>,
or <u>pun</u>, but the middle is different. Only the middle part of <u>pin</u> is like <u>dig</u>,
<u>fish</u>, or <u>will</u>.

Thus, <u>parts</u> of words are similar or different; further experiments with
such paired comparisons can (at least in the simplest cases) reveal how many
replaceable parts are in a word or utterance, and we can demonstrate that a
good representation of the word is that it is divisible into a certain number
(for the examples above, exactly three) linguistically-contrastive parts.
Such minimal units of distinctive contrast are called <u>phonemes</u>. Thus, <u>pin</u>
consists of three phonemes. Despite variations in the written form, the
following words also have only three phonemes: <u>thick</u>, <u>ping</u>, <u>phone</u>, <u>tough</u>,
etc. This motivates a message-distinguishing <u>segmentation</u> of the message
into phonemes.

Of course, segments are not simply interchangeable; if you remove a "p"
from <u>pan</u> and put it in place of the beginning of another word like "pin", or
vice versa, it may sound disjointed, "wrong" or confusing, or even, in some
extreme cases, may sound like another phoneme (Yilmaz, 1967). The reason, in
part, is that it is difficult to precisely define where one linguistic unit
ends and the next one begins; they tend to overlap, and affect each other, so
that some anticipation of the next sound may affect the pronunciation of its
predecessor, and there are lingering effects from previous sounds. To account
for the variations between versions of a particular phoneme that occur in
different contexts, linguists refer to each distinguishable subclass as an
<u>allophone</u> of the phoneme. Some recognizers have detected allophones as the
primary small units of recognition. Thus, for example, some versions (allophones) of unvoiced stops (/p,t,k/) will be "aspirated" (such as at the
beginnings of words) while others are "unaspirated" (after /s/ within a word,
etc.); some stops will be "released" while others will be manifested as
"unreleased" allophones. For further discussion, see Chap. 5.

Since transitions into and out of phonemes are affected by surrounding
sounds, some recognizers (e.g., Harpy, Ch. 15) use <u>sub-phonemic</u> units, such
as dividing a stop consonant into a silence, followed by a burst, then
aspiration, and then a transition into following vowels or other sounds.
Alternatively, one may segment speech at the steady-state <u>centers</u> of phonemes,
producing transitional sounds called <u>diphones</u>. With such segments, the coarticulatory influences of one sound on its predecessor and successor can be
directly incorporated into the nature of the two transitional units that meet
in the center of the phoneme. Some workers (e.g., c.f. Chap. 12 and 16) have
advocated the use of <u>syllable parts</u> (onsets, targets, and offsets) and whole
<u>syllables</u> as unanalyzed units, for which detection might be more reliable
since the coarticulatory transitions of speech are captured within the larger
syllabic unit. If such diphones, syllable parts, or total syllables are used,
the "alphabet" of the basic recognition units becomes much larger, but some
of the transitional phenomena of flowing speech are represented directly in
those minimal units. With smaller units like subphonemic units, allophones,
or phonemes, coarticulatory and "phonological" rules may be needed to account
for such transitional effects. In Chap. 6, June Shoup discusses these alternative ways of representing phonological units, and some rules for their
systematic combinations.

Regardless of which specific units are used, recognizers have usually been
implicitly based on two reasonable but seriously erroneous assumptions. These

assumptions were characterized by Chomsky and Miller (1963) as the LINEARITY and INVARIANCE conditions. The _linearity_ condition asserts that each segmental unit (phoneme or other-size unit) must have associated with it a particular stretch of soundwave, so that if unit A is before unit B in the segmental sequence, the stretch associated with A precedes the stretch associated with B in the acoustic wave. The _invariance_ condition asserts that to each segmental unit A (phoneme or other linguistic event) there is a specific defining set of physical (acoustic) features, such that each token or variant of A has all those features, and no segmental unit which is not a token or variant of A has all those features. Assuming that these two conditions were satisfied for phonemes A, B, ..., a machine could look for the invarient set of features for each phoneme, find all occurrences of each, string these together side by side, and have the basic message-distinguishing information needed to establish the wording of an utterance. This is the basis for segmentation and labeling schemes that seek to use "the information-carrying features" of each phoneme (or other unit) to decide what units occur in what sequence in an unknown utterance. Other popular linguistic notions such as "biuniqueness" and the "principle of complementary distribution" can be derived from these assumptions. Biuniqueness asserts a one-to-one relationship between abstract linguistic units like phonemes, and physically manifested ("surface") units like phones or allophones, so that each sequence of phones is represented by a unique sequence of phonemes, and each sequence of phonemes represents a sequence of physical phones that is "unique up to free variation" (i.e., the phonetic sequence is the same in each occurrence, except for irrelevant or non-linguistic variations).

On careful reflection, most phonemicists and most workers in speech recognition would reject the idea that phonemes or other units can always be identified from unique sets of physical features, independent of their context or other factors. Yet it seems that considerable (in fact, most) work in speech recognition has conformed to the linearity and invariance assumptions. They are taken to be at least a good approximation to reality, though admittedly it is difficult to find the beginning and ending points (boundaries) of phonemes in continuous speech, and it is acknowledged that phonetic context and other factors will prevent the same features from always occurring for any one unit like the phonemes /t/, /d/, /i/, etc.

What is involved in these usual efforts at labelling segments in speech is some assignment of _associations_ between "levels of representation", involving various size units in the utterance. Thus, sets of "features" are associated with occurrences of "phones", which are in turn assumed to be occurrences of minimal message-distinguishing units or "phonemes", which are in turn assumed to pattern into sequences that form "words", from which larger units like phrases and sentences are composed. Linearity and invariance assumptions make for simpler (usually, one-to-one) associations, but there are strong reasons to doubt that they are correct. Chomsky and Miller (1963, p. 311) offered examples of words _writer_ and _rider_ which phonemically differ in their fourth segment: /rayt ɝ/ versus /rayd ɝ/, but which are phonetically (i.e., physically) different not in their fourth segments, but rather their second segments: [rayDr] versus [ra·yDr], where the longer vowel [a·] versus the shorter [a] is the primary cue to the /d/ versus /t/ distinction. Thus, the linearity and invariance conditions are refuted by these and many other examples of actual distinctions between phonemic and phonetic structures. These results are by no means isolated exceptions; indeed, the primary reasons for recent interest in phonological rules for recognition procedures have to do with the context-dictated pronunciation variabilities of speech. Phonemes, syllables, and sometimes even whole words can be deleted in flowing speech; extra sounds can be inserted, as well. In addition to many violations of invariance and linearity that are dictated by the effects of phonetic contexts, other influences such as the grammatical structure of the sentence can alter phonetic manifestations of words (Chomsky and Miller, 1963; Chomsky and Halle, 1968; Lea, 1972).

Engineers and mathematically-inclined workers in speech recognition are inclined to interpret the actual variance and non-linearity associated with linguistic units like phonemes as evidence that those units "do not exist", "can't be reliably found", or "are of little or no use in practical recognizers" (cf. e.g., Grady, et al., 1978). More accurately, these difficulties show the inadequacy of the usual simplistic assumptions involved, and the need for properly characterizing the contextual interdependencies and phonological regularities of the language. Detection and identification of linguistic units need not depend on strictly segmenting into linear strings of separate units abutted at strict boundaries, or using features in those segments alone to identify them. Schemes have been devised for only _detecting_ (but not necessarily establishing the boundaries of) occurrences of various sound categories, using reliable information that is the least variable and most "robust", including use of contextual cues not coincident with the occurrence of the segment.

There are some situations where linearity and invariance are more closely approximated than usual. For example, as discussed in Chap. 8, _stressed syllables_ are more reliably decoded than unstressed or reduced syllables, and exhibit closer resemblances between surface phonetic form and the underlying phonemic sequence. Also, isolated words and _slowly spoken_ word sequences tend to be more carefully articulated, with less coarticulation and more likelihood of reaching target articulatory positions, so that phoneme-distinguishing features can be more reliably detected. Indeed, it appears (cf. Lea, 1975) that rhythm and rate of speech can be used to predict which phonological rules (for fast or slow speech, etc.) apply. Durations, intensities, and pitch of vowels can also provide secondary cues to vowel identity, and information about the nature of neighboring consonants. All this prosodic help to phonemic analysis is in addition to what help prosodics can provide in determining the large-unit (syntactic) structures of phrases and sentences.

Obviously, the fact that prosodic features like stress patterns, rhythm, and intonation (which extend over several syllables at once) carry some cues to the identities of phonemic units provides further proof of the non-linearity and variability of speech. What is more, it would be erroneous to assume that _prosodic_ contrasts themselves are invariably manifested in strict linear sequences. As shown in Chap. 8, stressed syllables are sometimes (particularly in phrase-initial positions) manifested by local increases in pitch or voice fundamental frequency, but in other positions other cues are used. Similarly, I outline in Chap. 8 how boundaries between major syntactic phrases can be detected (admittedly, not invariably) from fall-rise "valleys" in intonation, but those boundaries need not (and, indeed, often _do_ not) occur at the precise time of ending of the wording of one phrase and beginning of the next. The boundary cue may be displaced in time from its underlying abstract location at the phrase juncture, thus violating the linearity condition.

Linearity and invariance assumptions are also evident at the level of word matching. The template matching approach to word identification is based on an implicit invariance assumption, and a companion linearity assumption of being able to delimit a region of speech most closely corresponding to each word. The fact that word sequences like "did you" can be pronounced "dija", and the words can merge into each other, suggests the error of assuming invariant pronunciations of each word, which are to be strung in a linear row.

We have seen that stored templates and/or incoming acoustic patterns can be warped in duration (time normalized) or spectral form (e.g., for speaker normalization or channel normalization), to provide a closer match for words. The concept is to preserve, and indeed to _enhance_, invariances, by modifying either the input or the template in **systematic** ways. In similar fashion, expected pronunciations represented as phonemic strings can be altered by phonological rules, to allow for predictable variations (e.g., "did you" or "dija") in acceptable pronunciation in various contexts, and to overcome confusions introduced by errors (insertions, deletions, or substitutions). Generative phonological rules allow beginning from expected (dictionary) pronunciations of large linguistic units and deriving alternative pronunciations (sequences of small units) which can be directly compared with the acoustic phonetic input. _Analytic_ rules work the other way, converting incoming detailed acoustic data into possible abstract underlying forms that will match lexically stored pronunciations of large units like words or sentences. Most linguistic rules are represented in generative form, and the interest in recognition is to either convert to analytic rules for mapping from inputs to abstract units, or to incorporate a "hypothesize and test" routine which generates hypothesized messages and tries matching the input with generatively predicted physical forms for each hypothesized message, until a best match is attained.

4-2.6 <u>Grammatical Constraints and Parsing Procedures</u>

Given the uncertainty involved in converting acoustic data into hypothesized words, there is a high probability that many alternative words could be hypothesized within each local region of an utterance. Many of those hypothesized words will be erroneous, and additional information is needed to resolve remaining ambiguities and select correct word sequences. Syntactic constraints can be used to rule out certain ungrammatical word sequences. This after-the-fact screening of hypotheses has been effectively used with sequences of isolated words as well as with continuously-flowing word sequences (cf. Chap. 3, 9, 19). It may also be viewed as a subsetting of the vocabulary into small sets of acceptable words that could appear in the context of (usually following) previously-detected words.

Generative models of language define a grammar as a <u>vocabulary</u> of symbols for representing utterances and their parts, coupled with <u>rules</u> for combining the symbols to produce acceptable and interpretable utterances. A generative <u>derivation</u> of an acceptable sentence is then a series of steps by which a sentence is divided into phrases such as a noun-phrase "subject" followed by a verb-phrase "predicate", then the composition of those phrases is specified in a step-by-step fashion, until each word is specified and positioned in the final string of words. There are many <u>types</u> of grammars, of varying powers to generate complex languages (Lea, 1966 ; Chomsky and Miller, 1963) but perhaps the most important to speech recognition are "slot-and-frame", "finite state", "context-free", "context sensitive", and "augmented transition network" grammars.

A slot and frame grammar is a simple finite list of frames, or contexts, in which alternative words may be inserted at predetermined slots. Examples of such "menus" of alternative words that might be spoken in each context would be a small numeral ("one" or "three" etc.) in the first slot, and one of the azimuth numbers "one" to "twelve" in the second slot, for an aircraft advisory frame like "Traffic _____ miles from you, at _____ o'clock". Such simple grammars have been used in restricting alternative words in a sequence of isolated words, and are being explored in recognizers of continuously-spoken but strictly-formatted sequences of words (cf. Chap. 1, 3, 9, 18, 19).

51

Finite state grammars are at the forefront of current capabilities in highly reliable speech recognition. Harpy (cf. Chap. 15), the IBM systems (cf. Sec. 4-3.), and other recognizers (Chap. 18, 22-24) have endeavored to recognize with this restrictive form of a grammar, and systems like the BBN HWIM system that have tried to go beyond the limitations of finite state grammars have had comparatively limited successes. A finite state grammar is equivalent to a "finite state automaton" or "Markov model", in which generation (or recognition) of the next word in a sentence is determined by a fixed memory of the previous n words (where n is frequently only one, so the immediately previous word restricts the allowable next word). A common representation of the allowable word sequences is a state diagram composed of nodes representing states of machine memory, and transitions between the nodes which are labeled with words that are generated (or recognized) with that state change. Probabilities of taking transition can also be assigned to each transition. See Chap. 15 for further discussion of finite state grammar, working in the Harpy speech understanding system.

Linguists (e.g., Chomsky, 1957) have shown that finite state grammars cannot properly characterize major subsets of English sentences, if no fixed limit is placed on the complexity of sentences. Thus, finite state grammars cannot generate (or recognize) all such English sentences and only the acceptable sentences. Context free grammars have been devised to permit more generative power, in which sentences need not be generated a single word at a time, but large units can be divided into phrasal sub-units, which in turn get expanded until the smallest units are represented by words of the acceptable vocabulary. Yet, even such context free grammars can't capture some of the contextual constraints that seem to be involved in aspects of the English language, again assuming no fixed limit on sentence complexity. Transformational grammars (cf. Chomsky, 1957, 1965) were devised to systematically account for complex contextual effects, total derivational histories of sentences, and important grammatical relations between various sentences or sentence types (such as passive versus active sentences, etc.). However, transformational grammars have proven difficult to use in recognition procedures, so the "augmented transition network" (or ATN) grammar has been devised as a practical substitute, of equally general power. The ATN grammar operates like a finite state grammar with special transitions that are associated not with the generation of a single word, but rather with instructions to insert a whole phrasal unit at the next point in the structure, to "push" down into a subprocedure to fully expand those subunits, then to "pop" back to process the next node and transition in the network. Transitions are thus allowed to call for local subroutine-like expansions of phrases, and also to build total structural descriptions for the sentence and its phrases, and to assign relevant interpretations or "meanings". The HWIM system (Chap. 14) and the SRI work (Chap. 13) were based on the powerful ATN grammars.

Thus, there is a hierarchy of ever more powerful grammars, ranging from frame-and-slot formats and finite-state grammars up to ATN grammars. The more powerful the grammar, the more versatile the language that can be characterized. More importantly, however, for the current uses of syntax in recognition, the more restrictive the grammar, the better it is for strictly limiting the acceptable word sequences. Thus, frame-and-slot formatting is quite suitable for extremely restrictive recognizers of simple word sequences (with or without pauses between words; cf. Chap. 18 and 19). Finite state grammars such as Harpy used may be argued to be limited in utility to only small sentence understanding tasks, but they definitely constrain alternative word sequences, so that incorrect word hypotheses can be eliminated. Powerful grammars such as the ATN grammar in HWIM (Chap. 14) may offer more versatile, natural communications (i.e., closer to "habitable" languages; Watt, 1968), but their lack of constraints makes the recognition very difficult (perhaps to a degree just beyond the limits of current capabilities). Most current efforts in recognition involve limited languages that can be effectively handled with finite state grammars, despite the ultimate desirability of more versatile language structures. One good idea in the work at SRI (Chap. 13) was the use of a performance grammar, which described the syntax of English that was actually used in spontaneous dialogs relevant to a task, rather than developing a general grammar of typewritten English texts.

Grammars are usually intended to characterize at least four general human language-processing abilities: (1) to distinguish between well-formed, acceptable word sequences and ill-formed ones; (2) to determine the structure or phrasal divisions of sentences; (3) to label the phrases with syntactic categories that show similarites between parts in different positions (or in different sentences); and (4) to identify grammatical relations between parts of sentences (e.g., subject/verb relations, subordination, coordination, etc.) and between sentences or sentence types (passive vs. active forms, etc.). As noted previously, one problem with currently popular finite state grammars is that they cannot efficiently distinguish well-formed from ill-formed sequences, in a manner that agrees with the restricted English utterances that are likely to occur in various complex human-machine dialogs. What's more, finite state grammars assign highly restricted (typically, "right branching") structures that do not adequately characterize the phrasal groupings, syntactic categories, and grammatical relations in subsets of English sentences, which can be adequately characterized by more powerful grammars like ATN grammars (cf. Chap. 14).

Recognition of spoken utterances need not involve the usual generative processes used in grammar description, but rather involves parsing of sentences (ie., to determine well-formedness, to represent the structural phrases and categories, and, ultimately, to establish the intended meanings). Traditional parsing procedures with typewritten input will simply reject any inputs as soon as any error in spelling or format is detected, and they typically operate in strict "left-to-right" fashion, starting with the first (leftmost) word and checking successive acceptability conditions in the order in which the words come. However, parsing of spoken utterances involves several complications, including (1) uncertainty and conflicting alternatives about the identity (and beginning and ending points) of each word; (2) possible errors in word identifications (due to acoustic or phonetic errors, etc.); and (3) the need to consider starting the analysis from reliable words in the middle of the utterance, and working both directions from initially-reliable "islands". The structural analysis must be able to overcome occasional losses of whole words due to sloppy articulation or poor acoustic analysis. These concepts come up repeatedly throughout Chap. 9 and the structural descriptions found in the chapters of Part III and IV of this book.

The actual use of grammars and other higher-level linguistic processors in speech recognition procedures has been primarily confined to: (1) weeding out unacceptable word sequences after the words have been hypothesized; and (2) determining some minimal aspects of the structure and meaning of a sentence, and the relevance to the task being performed, so that words can be predicted for filling in gaps in the sentence where the wording has not yet been identified. These ideas are described more fully in Chaps. 9 and 13, and criticized briefly in Chap. 8.

An important issue in syntactic analysis for speech recognition concerns the assessment of the complexity of a language for speech interaction with machines. Goodman (1976) developed the idea of an average "branching factor", which indicates the average number of words that can appear next in a sentence of the voice-input language. The higher the branching factor, the more difficult the recognition task, though this is hardly a fully adequate measure. Other measures have been developed that also consider the confusability of words in the vocabulary and the statistical likelihoods of various word sequences occurring (Reddy, 1976, pp. 524-5; Sondhi and Levinson, 1977; Jelinek, et.al., 1977).

4-2.7 Semantics and Pragmatics

"Semantics" means different things to different people. While some work has been done on the use of "truth conditions" for testing the meaningfulness of word sequences in speech recognizers (cf. Wherry, 1976), most work on semantic constraints in speech recognition has been concerned with determining the meaningfulness or anomalous character of word sequences, based on either (a) semantic networks or (b) semantic conditions imbedded in the syntactic rules of the grammar. Semantic models for speech recognition do not try to capture all that is involved in a human's ability to attach meanings to utterances or to associate signs with referents; rather, they focus on relations between words or phrases, which can help verify the meaningfulness of sentences in which certain combinations of words are hypothesized. Theoretical linguistic models suggest semantic features that show commanality among meanings of words, such as "bull", "man", "uncle", "rooster" all being 'masculine'. Tests for common features ("semantic selectional restrictions", Woods, 1975) can be used to verify the semantic well-formedness or "meaningfulness" of two or more words occurring in specific places in utterances. Semantic networks can be used to show semantic relations between words, such as the inclusion of "uncle" as a special case of "males" and "humans", and the inclusion of all those in larger categories such as "animate" and "concrete object", etc. Objects that can be "contained in" other objects may be connected in a semantic network, like "calcium" being contained in "rock sample A", etc. Thus, a sentence with the phrase "calcium in rock sample A" is meaningful, while "rock sample A in calcium" may not be. In early works on speech understanding systems, semantic networks were expected to play an important independent role in determining the correct word sequences to hypothesize in a system, and which hypothesizable word sequences should be ruled out due to their semantic anomolies (Nash-Webber, 1975).

Later work on speech understanding systems has tended to more closely integrate semantics in with syntactic constraints. Thus, the BBN HWIM system (Chap. 14) used a "pragmatic grammar" with semantic knowledge built right into the ATN representation of expected phrase structures for acceptable sentences. Such pragmatic grammars tend to become very task-specific, and are expensive to alter for new or expanded tasks. The SRI 'performance grammar" and integrated linguistic descripion also tended to integrate syntax, semantics, and pragmatics together in the stored information about phrasal units, but it was done in a way (via attributes and factors, associated with transitions in the syntactic network) which permitted the overall linguistic description to be readily adjusted to each new or expanded task (cf. Chap. 13).

Pragmatic information may be used in speech recognizers to verify or rule out hypothesized word combinations by establishing their agreement with prior discourse or their applicability to the task being undertaken during the human-machine interaction. Knowledge of previous discourse can help and can permit the full expansion of elliptical (truncated) utterances that follow similar utterances (cf. Chap. 13).

There is a substantial gap between linguistic and semiotic theories of semantics and pragmatics, on the one hand, and the effective application of semantic and pragmatic information in speech recognizers, on the other hand. See Chaps. 9 and 13 for further discussion of these topics.

One excellent demonstration of the effectiveness of syntactic, semantic, and pragmatic constraints in easing the difficulty of recognition was given for the HEARSAY I system, which had very simple syntax, and heavy constraints dictated through the legal and reasonable moves in chess, plus information about the current state of the board. These constraints helped improve recognition accuracy substantially (cf. Chap. 16 and 17; Reddy, et al., 1973).

4-2.8 Statistical Information and System Structures

Two other topics that deserve mention in this summary of general principles involved in speech recognition are statistics and system structures. We shall touch only briefly on each of these.

Given the variability of speech signals due to conditions beyond the explicit control of the recognizer (e.g., speaker variability, emotion, rate of speech, noise, etc.), the process of determining the intended linguistic message is necessarily a non-deterministic one of decision making under uncertainty. The signal will not exactly match the stored templates for alternative messages, and we can use probabilities and statistics to predict which message was intended. This is true at each level of decision making in the machine, whether it be deciding whether a sound is voiced or unvoiced, or is an /s/ or an /f/, or if the word is "nine" or "five", or if the structure was declarative or a command. Statistics permit one to use summary characteristics of past experience to choose the hypothesis that is most likely to be correct, and to assign scores about our level of certainty based on likelihoods of errors. When one reflects that recognition is a process of functionally duplicating the usual receiver of a transmitted message, the techniques of statistical information theory come immediately to mind. This has been the basis of major efforts in speech recognition, such as that at IBM (Jelinek, 1976).

Even predominently linguistically-based recognizers use probabilities and statistics, as is evident in Chaps. 5, 7, 12 to 16, 18, 19, and 21-25. Maximum likelihood ratios are used in rating hypotheses, and Bayes' theorem is frequently used to predict the likely message intended, given the acoustic signal and the prior statistics of likely acoustic encoding of messages. Probably the most dangerous aspect of statistics to use in recognition is the relative frequency of occurrence of a message or part of a message. Unless extensive statistics are obtained, such as IBM does with hours of training speech (Jelinek, 1976; Bahl, et al., 1978), some messages (or words or phrases) may appear to have essentially no likelihood of occurring. Then, if hypotheses are selected in priority on the basis of their likelihood of occurrence, some unlikely but correct words will be ruled out (or delayed in being tested), forcing expensive analysis of more likely but wrong word sequences (cf. Woods, et al., 1976, Vol. I, p. 14). Since information content in a message increases with the unlikelihood of what was said, the most informative parts of messages might thus be least properly handled. For these reasons, HARPY (Chap. 15), HWIM (Chap. 14), and other recognizers have not considered the a priori probabilities of alternative hypotheses in their decisions about which hypotheses to pursue.

One link between statistics and system structures comes in scoring procedures. Typically, each component of a complex speech understanding system selects hypotheses on probabilistic grounds, and assigns a "score", or relative confidence to its selection, based on information gathered in that component of the system. Different components may give conflicting hypotheses about the wording of an utterance. How does the system as a whole then select what hypotheses to pursue, or which component(s) to 'listen to'? This depends in part on a general scoring philosophy and upon the system structure and control procedures.

In Chap. 14 and Woods, et al., 1976, Volume I, the BBN researchers outline systematic procedures for finding optimum or near-optimum selection processes, based on "uniform scoring procedures". Other systems make heuristic judgments about which components should direct the system to the "best" next hypothesis to pursue, and those judgments may vary from time to time or from one set of conditions to another. The goals are to reduce the likelihoods of going down very expensive futile "paths" (sequences of tentatively selected hypotheses), and to maximize the likelihood of selecting sequences of hypotheses that efficiently find the correct solutions. Some systems attempt to pursue the most promising ("best") path, by selecting the highest scoring hypothesis for a word (or other subunit), then extending that hypothesis with words that give the best score when combined with that word, and so forth. Such a best-first strategy gets the system ever more deeply committed to the consequences of the initially most promising hypothesis, giving a "depth first" search strategy. Other strategies acknowledge the possibility of promising alternatives, and conduct a "breadth first" search of alternatives, and only after all alternatives for one aspect of the analysis are exhausted and comparatively rated or ruled out do they go on to pursue extensions of those hypotheses to cover other parts of the utterance. In addition to such depth-first and breadth first strategies, there are also "optimal strategies" which exhaustively search all alternatives (e.g., the Dragon system; Baker, 1975) and hybrid or compromise strategies ("best few" or "beam" search strategies; cf. Chap. 15).

HARPY and Dragon (and a very few other systems) have integrated all their knowledge about acoustic properties, phonetic units, word pronunciations, phonological variations, and syntactic constraints into a large network of states or nodes labelled by small (sub-phonemic or smaller) segments, with allowable transitions from one node to another (i.e., allowable sound sequences) completely specified by a "finite state graph" or Markov model. Such systems form a single-level system, with a straightforward beam search through alternative node sequences being the way in which utterances are recognized. Other systems explicitly try to "divide and conquer", using a set of interacting components or knowledge sources, each contributing to the interpretation of an unknown input waveform. Components of a limited speech understanding system might perform functions such as:

- extracting acoustic parameters from the speech waveform ("acoustic analysis");

- identifying the vowels and consonants that are present ("phonetic analysis") ;

- using prosodic information (intonation, stress, rhythm) to detect large-unit linguistic structure like phrases, subordination, sentence type, etc. ("prosodic analysis");

- comparing this sequence of speech sounds with expected pronunciations of word ("words matching") ;

- testing whether a hypothesized word is syntactically consistent with words already recognized, and using syntactic constraints to predict likely upcoming words ("syntactic analysis");

- testing the meaningfulness of hypothesized word sequences ("semantic analysis") ; and

- predicting likely future words based on prior discourse and on the task being performed ("pragmatic analysis").

The problem is that none of these components currently can be made to perform reliably. A strategy must be found to combine incomplete information from all components in such a way that errors in intermediate stages of analysis do not result in errors of sentence understanding.

Systems with such components can be structured in many ways. Some systems, such as illustrated in Fig. 4-2, work in a "hierarchical" or "layered" way, with important acoustic parameters first being extracted from the speech signal, followed by phonetic and prosodic analysis, then phonological adjustments, then word matching with lexical entries, then syntactic, semantic and pragmatic analyses, in successive order. These are called "bottom-up" systems, since they begin with the basic small units and successively combine to larger ("higher level") linguistic units. "Top-down" systems reverse that process (i.e., reverse the arrows in Fig. 4-2) by predicting sentences and successively hypothesizing the phrases, words, prosodics, phonemes, phonetic features, and acoustic patterns that make up that sentence, and then comparing the predicted patterns with the input acoustics. Such systems have the danger that errors made early in the process will propagate through the other levels, and be difficult or expensive to recover from. Other systems let the various components work in some hybrid way, or permit them to independently and simultaneously develop hypotheses that may reinforce each other or contradict. For example, all the components in Fig. 4-2 could have their arrows feeding into a common database, or "blackboard" for recording hypotheses, rather than communicating directly with each other. Then an executive control strategy can select which information to consider next, and which component to activate next for further analysis.

Throughout this book, and throughout the speech recognition literature, systems of all these (and other) types are evident. For further discussion of system structures, see Chap. 10. Systems that focus on "understanding" speech give special attention to the higher level linguistic analyses shown in Fig. 4-2, while more traditional "recognition" systems focus on the task-independent transformation from acoustic signals to words and word sequences.

4-2.9 Primary "Types" of Recognizers

The literature on speech recognition characterizes a whole spectrum of types of recognizers, as illustrated in Fig. 4-3. The types of recognizers are defined by type of speech being processed, and the ultimate recognition goal. The easiest task is recognition of isolated words, surrounded by pauses. One can also use linguistic constraints on allowable sequences of such words, by still maintaining pauses, as in the sequence "...RIGHT...THIRTY...DEGREES...". When the speech flows freely in connected form, word boundaries are hard to find and words distort the pronunciation of the neighboring words, but the task can be limited by handling only strings of digits ("...ZERO THREE ZERO...") or strictly formatted word sequences ("...RIGHT 30 DEGREES..."), where only certain words can go in each slot in the structure. Key information-carrying words can be spotted in the context of conversations, so that one can decide that a conversation is worth listening to based on the occurrence of certain key words like "NIXON" and "WATERGATE". Restricted speech understanding is intended to handle total sentences relevant to a specific task, using all the knowledge that can be brought to bear about the grammatical and plausible sentences one can say when working in a specific task domain. Task-independent continuous speech recognition will allow a change in topic from one utterance to the next and still correctly identify the wording of the sentences, such as illustrated in Fig. 4-3 for the sentences "What is the big event in Anaheim?" and "How many aircraft carriers does Russia have?"

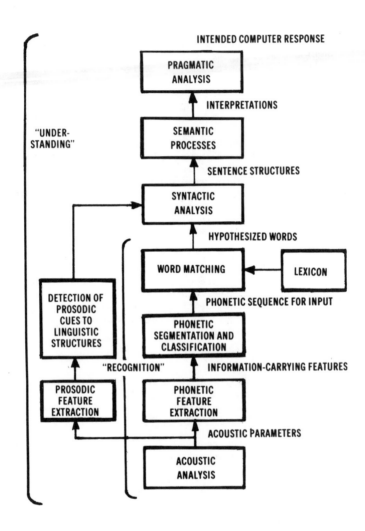

Figure 4-2. Processed involved in " recognition"and "understanding"

- **ISOLATED WORDS** ...(Pause)...**RIGHT**...(Pause)

- **SEQUENCES OF ISOLATED WORDS, USING LINGUISTIC CONSTRAINTS**
  ...**RIGHT**...**THIRTY**...**DEGREES**

- **CONNECTED SEQUENCES OF**
  —DIGITS, OR   ...**ZERO THREE ZERO**...
  —WORDS IN STRICT FORMATS   ...**RIGHT 30 DEGREES**...

- **SPOTTING KEY WORDS IN CONTEXT**   xxxxNIXONxxxxxxWATERGATExxxx

- **RESTRICTED SPEECH UNDERSTANDING**   "Tell me about Nixon and Watergate."

- **TASK-INDEPENDENT CONTINUOUS SPEECH**

  "What is the big event in Anaheim?"..."How many aircraft carriers does Russia have?

Figure 4-3. Forms of speech recognized by machines.

4-3. HISTORY OF SPEECH RECOGNITION

We have seen that speech recognition involves a variety of principles,
ranging from models of basic acoustics, articulation, sensory reception, and
perception, to a hierarchy of challenging sub-tasks like detecting vowels and
consonants, handling phonological variabilities, matching pronunciations of
words, using prosodics, syntax, semantics, statistics, and pragmatics, and
coordinating and controlling all these processes to search for correct hypotheses. We know the ultimate goal is to correctly respond to the message,
despite errors in sub-systems and variabilities in environmental conditions,
speakers, and tasks. In this section, we will try to quickly summarize (at
least some primary highlights of) the history of speech recognition, showing
how such principles repeatedly were selectively applied in developing systems
of various capabilities. Sec. 4-3.1 summarizes the long history of attempts
at building isolated word recognizers, which dominated the early history of
this field. Initial and recent attempts at connected speech recognition and
sentence understanding are outlined in Sec. 4-3.2, including the large ARPA SUR
project and some subsequent work. Unless otherwise indicated, studies discussed here were done with English speech.A summary appears in Sec. 4-3.3.

4-3.1 The Historical Development of Isolated Word Recognizers

4-3.1.1 Preliminary Advances in Acoustic Processing - Speech recognition is
an interdisciplinary problem that has its roots in centuries of historical
studies of language, sound, physiology, psychology, and automata. Yet, not
until this century were the knowledge and mechanisms sufficiently advanced to
seriously attempt machine recognition of speech. Since the beginning of the
·twentieth century, it had been increasingly evident that the speech signal (or
any other acoustic wave, or light, or radio waves) could be decomposed into
simple sinusoidal wave-forms by a "frequency spectrum analysis". Such ideal
·mathematical decompositions of signals could be approximated by electronic

59

"filters" which separated different frequencies from each other. Speech was acknowledged to be produced by the human vocal mechanism in such a way as to have many frequencies in it, with some frequencies highly accented by the mouth and throat acting like a specially-shaped acoustic tube. Such an acoustic tube has "resonances" that are related to the geometry of the tube; these natural resonances of the human vocal system are commonly called "formants" (cf. Chap. 5). Other important aspects of the speech that were expected to be important in speech recognition included the amplitude or loudness of the speech and the "pitch" of the voice (well represented by different musical notes on which a particular vowel like "ah" could be sung or said; cf. Chap. 8). Some speech sounds (for example, consonants "s", "k", and "p" in a word like "skip") are spoken without vibration of the talker's vocal cords, and are called "unvoiced" sounds, while others (like vowels, or some consonants like "m", "n", and "r") involve vocal cord vibration and are called "voiced". Other classes of speech sounds (called "phoneme classes") were distinguishable, like the hissing "fricatives" ("s", "f", etc.), the silent-or-near-silent-then-exploding "stop consonants" ("p", "t", "k", "b", "d", "g"), and "nasals" (which involve airflow out through the nose like in "n" or "m"). These concepts are discussed further in Chaps. 5, 6, and 7.

From the early stages of speech recognition, controversies arose about the utility of all these speech categories for the practical processes of machine recognition of speech. As we observed in Section 4-2, some argued that we need to understand how the human produces speech, and use distinctions or categories ("phonemes") that the human uses in producing or perceiving various vowels and consonants. Other more engineering-oriented or mathematically-inclined workers suggested that direct comparisons or "correlations" should be done between input signals and stored "templates" or exemplars of the expected words, obtained from training utterances of the words, as spoken earlier and stored away for comparison.

4-3.1.2 Limiting the Problem - Researchers have long recognized that a speech recognition (or "speech understanding") system of the most general kind would be a computer or other machine that could accept verbal commands and questions spoken into a microphone or telephone by any user, then figure out the intended meaning of the sentence, and generate an appropriate response. The technical difficulties associated with the design of a system this powerful were, from the beginning, acknowledged to be well beyond the growing, but still limited, capabilities of computer scientists, speech scientists, linguists, and engineers. Part of what makes the development of speech recognizers so hard is that different people speak in different ways. Also, a noisy acoustic environment may interfere with reliable interpretation of the acoustic speech signal. In addition, even the same single talker will vary from time to time in his pronunciations. The problem is complicated considerably by the complexities of naturally flowing connected speech, (cf. Sec. 4-2)

If the problem could be carefully limited, by restricting the population of speakers, working with good acoustic conditions, and avoiding the complexities of fluent speech, then perhaps some initial capabilities could be demonstrated. Thus, the early history of speech recognizers focused on isolated word recognizers, which could identify which word from a small vocabulary was spoken, when sufficient silence preceded and followed the word, to assure easy detection of word boundaries and avoid coarticulatory effects between neighboring words.

4-3.1.3 Early Work - It is interesting, in light of the recent interest of toy manufacturers in speech processing devices, that the earliest known speech recognizer was a little toy dog, "Radio Rex", which was designed to jump from its house when its internal mechanisms were triggered by its name being spoken.

It could, however, be activated by a variety of other spoken words or sounds only loosely resembling its name 'Rex'. It was affected by the quality of the voice, exemplifying the recurrent limitation of a recognizer's only responding to 'its master's voice'.

Probably the first serious attempt at automatic speech recognition was described by Dreyfus-Graf (in France) in 1950. In his 'stenosonograph', the speech signal was passed through six bandpass filters, whose signals were fed to deflection coils spaced around a circle, resulting in a dot (a deflected electron beam) which appeared on the screen of a cathode ray tube at a point depending on the relative energies in the six bands. Thus, low-frequency sounds like vowels were deflected to quite different spots from high frequency sounds like fricatives. Different sequences of sounds gave different tracks around the screen (effectively rediscovered by Yilmaz, 1967), but a subsequent automatic decision process would be needed to associate a particular pattern with the correct identity of the utterance.

Another speech-to-visual-pattern converter, which has played a major role in the history of speech recognition research, is the sound spectograph, developed in the 1930's and 1940's (cf. Potter, Kopp and Green, 1947). As illustrated in Fig. 4-4, the spectrogram provides a graphic display of the amount of energy (darkness) in various frequency bands (vertical axis) versus time (horizontal axis) during an utterance. Spectrographic analysis and the rise of electronic speech processing devices paved the way for a growing technology in speech recognition.

In 1952, Davis, Biddulph, and Balashek of Bell Telephone Laboratories developed the first complete speech recognizer, which divided the frequency spectrum into two bands, above and below 900 cycles per second (Hertz), and counted how often the two signal levels passed through zero volts ("axis crossings"). This indicated the equivalent frequency of energy concentration within each band. Feeding the two signals to the horizontal and vertical axes of a display yielded an approximation to what is now called a "formant 1 - formant 2" (F_1-F_2) plot. The pattern (two dimensional array of numbers) for an input signal was then cross correlated with ten spectral patterns already stored for each of the digits zero (oh) to nine, and the best-match (highest cross-correlation) or 'closest' of the ten stored patterns, was chosen as the identity of the sound. Over 97% of the time, the machine correctly identified which of the ten words was spoken, when patterns had been stored for that particular speaker. This was thus the first speaker-dependent digit recognizer, and it was based on the acoustic signal viewpoint and the unsegmented template matching procedures described in Sec. 4-2.2 and 4-2.3.

Several years later, Dudley and Balashek (1958) developed a recognizer called "Audrey' that used ten frequency bands and derived certain spectral features whose durations were compared with stored feature patterns for the words in the vocabulary. Another major aspect of the Dudley and Balashek recognizer (and other contemporary work; cf. Fry and Denes, 1958; Denes, 1960) was the segmentation of words into phonetic units, which were identified from their spectral patterns. Almost perfect recognition accuracy was reported, when the electronics were specifically optimized for the individual speaker. Performance dropped drastically for other speakers, although, by altering his voice, a new speaker could improve performance.

The first work using a digital computer came at around 1959-1960. Denes and Mathews (1960) introduced the important concept of time normalization, whereby (as shown in Fig. 4-4) short versions of an utterance that were spoken more rapidly than the training data were automatically stretched out or "normalized" to equal the normal duration of the training utterances, and slowly-

EARLY HISTORY OF MACHINE RECOGNITION OF SPEECH

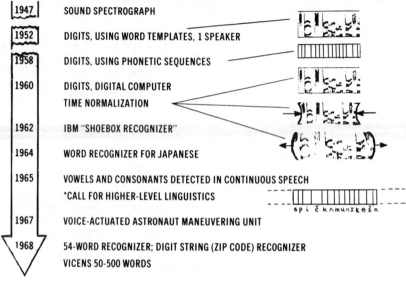

1947	SOUND SPECTROGRAPH
1952	DIGITS, USING WORD TEMPLATES, 1 SPEAKER
1958	DIGITS, USING PHONETIC SEQUENCES
1960	DIGITS, DIGITAL COMPUTER
	TIME NORMALIZATION
1962	IBM "SHOEBOX RECOGNIZER"
1964	WORD RECOGNIZER FOR JAPANESE
1965	VOWELS AND CONSONANTS DETECTED IN CONTINUOUS SPEECH
	*CALL FOR HIGHER-LEVEL LINGUISTICS
1967	VOICE-ACTUATED ASTRONAUT MANEUVERING UNIT
1968	54-WORD RECOGNIZER; DIGIT STRING (ZIP CODE) RECOGNIZER
	VICENS 50-500 WORDS

RECENT HISTORY

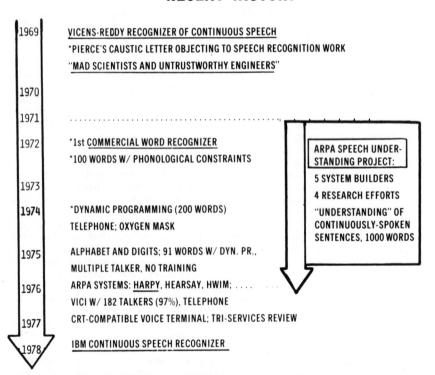

1969	VICENS-REDDY RECOGNIZER OF CONTINUOUS SPEECH
	*PIERCE'S CAUSTIC LETTER OBJECTING TO SPEECH RECOGNITION WORK
	"MAD SCIENTISTS AND UNTRUSTWORTHY ENGINEERS"
1970	
1971	
1972	*1st COMMERCIAL WORD RECOGNIZER
	*100 WORDS W/ PHONOLOGICAL CONSTRAINTS
1973	
1974	*DYNAMIC PROGRAMMING (200 WORDS)
	TELEPHONE; OXYGEN MASK
1975	ALPHABET AND DIGITS; 91 WORDS W/ DYN. PR.,
	MULTIPLE TALKER, NO TRAINING
1976	ARPA SYSTEMS: HARPY, HEARSAY, HWIM; ....
	VICI W/ 182 TALKERS (97%), TELEPHONE
1977	CRT-COMPATIBLE VOICE TERMINAL; TRI-SERVICES REVIEW
1978	IBM CONTINUOUS SPEECH RECOGNIZER

ARPA SPEECH UNDER-
STANDING PROJECT:

5 SYSTEM BUILDERS
4 RESEARCH EFFORTS
"UNDERSTANDING" OF
CONTINUOUSLY-SPOKEN
SENTENCES, 1000 WORDS

Figure 4-4.   Some highlights in the history of speech recognition.   (Work on isolated words is described in Sec. 4-3.1, while continuous speech recognition is outlined in Sec. 4-3.2.)

spoken long versions could get reduced to a normalized length before comparisons and matching were attempted to compensate for variable speaking rates. Experiments showed that considerably lower error rates could be achieved with time normalization than without it, even for multiple speakers.

Another early use of computers in recognition was the simple speech recognition programs of J. W. and C. D. Forgie of Lincoln Laboratory. The Forgies developed a vowel recognition program (1959), which depended almost solely on the position of the first two formants (F_1 and F_2). Using isolated words of the form /bVt/, where V is one of the English vowels, they achieved a reported accuracy of 93% correct recognition. They also designed a similar computer program for recognizing fricatives in initial and final positions of isolated words (words like fief, thief, thigh, thrill, frill, myth, etc.) (1962).

The 1960's also saw the advent of special-purpose hardware devices for recognition of isolated spoken words. In these cases, the hope has often been to develop a marketable product, usually of small physical size and minimal cost, that might recognize words spoken from a predetermined small vocabulary. One such shoe box or suitcase-size recognition device, demonstrated at the Seattle World's Fair in 1962, was commonly called the 'IBM shoebox recognizer' (Dersch, 1961). Government funders of speech research and development work were inundated by builders of such limited but transportable devices (cf. also the Philco-Ford 'single equivalent formant' recognizer; described by Teacher et al., 1967, or other special purpose recognizers described by Ross, 1967, Hill, 1969, Kelley, et al., 1968, Martin, et al, 1969, etc.) Kelley, Scott, Martin, and other RCA researchers illustrated the application of the sensory reception view described in Sec. 4-2.2 by working with "analog threshold logic" based on neuron models. Recognizers were also developed for other languages, such as Japanese (Nagata, et al., 1964) and German (Musman and Steiner, 1965).

4-3.1.4 Expanding Capabilities - The proposed applications for recognizers included voice control of machinery, voice dialing of telephones (Denes, 1959), zip code reading for the post office (Martin, et al., 1969), and a "far-out" idea of a voice-controlled astronaut manuevering unit (Kelly, et al., 1968). Expanded-vocabulary word recognizers endeavored to handle vocabularies of 50 to 500 words. Gold obtained 86% recognition accuracy with a 54 word vocabulary, spoken by 10 speakers; Bobrow and Klatt (1968) were able to improve the accuracy on the same task to 97%, for two speakers. An interesting aspect of the Bobrow-Klatt system was the use of independent asynchronous property vectors (voicing, stress, stridency, presence of nasals, "ah-like vowels", etc.) whose "on-off" transition patterns were used to independently select which words to hypothesize. A majority vote of such independent choices selected the word. This is an example of the unsegmented, feature-matching analysis illustrated in Fig. 4-1 (b). Another major stride in vocabulary size was attempted with the Vicens system, which was quite successful with a 500-word vocabulary. Medress (1969,1972) developed a recognizer for several vocabularies, including a 100-word vocabulary. This research system was based on the phonological constriants on acceptable English syllable onsets and offsets, so that if a word began with a fricative followed by a stop, the system knew the fricative must be an /s/ and the stop must be unvoiced and followed by a vowel or sonorant consonant.

A major event in the history of speech recognition occurred in 1972, when the first commercial products appeared, from Scope Electronics, Inc. and from Threshold Technology, Inc. Table 4-1 shows some rather impressive recognition scores reported in recent years for several commercially available recognizers,

TABLE 4-1. REPRESENTATIVE RECOGNITION SCORES FOR VARIOUS ISOLATED WORD RECOGNIZERS

REFERENCE	ENVIRONMENT	VOCABULARY	NUMBER OF SPEAKERS	NUMBER OF TEST UTTERANCES	PERCENTAGE OF WORDS CORRECTLY RECOGNIZED
Martin, Grunza, 1975 (also Martin, 1975)	High Quality Speech	10 Digits 12 Words	10 10	2400 1320	99.79% 99.32%
"	Pilot's mike and oxygen mask	12 Words	12	1440	97.15%
Martin, 1975	85-90dB background noise Actual baggage-handling application	34 Words	12	9149	98.5%
Itakura, 1975	Telephone Speech	200 Words (Japanese)	1 Male	2000	97.3%
"	Telephone Speech	36 Words (Alphabet & Digits)	1 Male	720	88.6%
Scott, 1975	No training required, "Speaker-independent"	10 Digits	30 Males	9300	98.0%
Scott, 1976	Speaker-independent, Taped and live tests	10 Digits and 4 control words	85 Males	16,200	98.0%
Scott, 1977	Speaker-independent, with error-correction dig its, Telephone Bandwidth	10 Digits and 4 control words	139 Males 54 Females	56,000	96.0%
Coler, et al., 1977	Scope VCS device	10 Digits	20 Males	20,000	87.6%
"	Best NASA/Ames Extension of Scope Algorithm	10 Digits	20 Males	20,000	99.9% correct 5% rejected
"	Best NASA/Ames Algorithm; High Quality Speech	100 Words	10 Males	100,000	93.2% or 95.7% with 5% rejections
"	Syntax tree dictates subvocabulary at each point in discourse	100 Words subsetted by syntax into subvocabularies	10 Males	100,00	98.6% or 99.6% with 5% rejections
Nippon Electric Co. Announcement 1978	Speaker-dependent	10 Digits	4 Males	2400	99.8%
"	Speaker-dependent	50 Japanese City Names	1 Male 1 Female	—	100%

operating under a variety of conditions. In general, scores of from 99% to as high as 99.9% correct recognition are possible in ideal laboratory conditions of no noise, adequate talker training, and consistent talking habits. However, actual field tests with ultimate users rarely come close to such high figures, and 97% is a high (and barely adequate) accuracy level for most field conditions. When noise is added (up to a high level of 90 dB, or an average signal to noise ratio of around 0 dB), even laboratory scores tend to drop to 98% or lower, as the noise signal gets confused with possible speech sounds, and the endpoints of the word become obscured. With some talkers, high recognition scores are hard to achieve under <u>any</u> conditions, partly because speakers will train the machine with carefully articulated speech, then speak more casually in actual working conditions (Martin, 1977, p. 37).

Other <u>research</u> efforts have achieved high recognition scores in recent years, using <u>laboratory</u> versions of isolated word recognizers. Itakura (1975) introduced the now-popular technique of dynamic programming for time normalization, and he defined a new metric for comparing frequency spectra. His system was quite successful (99%) with a vocabulary of 200 Japanese geographical names spoken by one talker over a telephone with 68 dB noise. On the difficult vocabulary of the alphabet and digits, Itakura obtained 88.6% recognition. White and Neely (1975) improved upon the Itakura ideas, and attained 98% correct recognition with the spoken alphabet and digits. Clearly, the digits "zero" to "nine" are more difficult to distinguish than other sets of ten words such as the names of the ten most populous cities in the United States. Even more difficult than the digits are groups of rhyming words such as "B,C,D,E,G,P,T,V,Z", or "A,J,K", in the spoken alphabet.

4-3.1.5 <u>Dimensions that Increase Recognition Difficulty</u> - It should be obvious that as a vocabulary gets larger it generally becomes more likely that similar words might get confused. This is evident in the results shown in Table 1. For example, Coler, et al. (1977) reported 99.9% correct recognition for the ten digits, and 95.7% for a 100-word vocabulary under otherwise similar conditions. In addition, they introduced a <u>syntax structure</u> that dictated a decision tree, or branching chain of commands, which allowed only certain words from the vocabulary to be spoken at various times in a discourse with the machine. This syntax structuring method reduced the number of possible commands that the recognizer had to distinguish at any given point in time, with fifteen subsets that ranged in size from three to ten words. As expected, recognition accuracy decreased as the size of the subvocabulary increased. The size of the vocabulary is clearly a major factor in determining the difficulty of a recognition task. Commercial recognizers have exploited this, and have been delivered with applications syntax software, to limit the acceptable vocabulary at each stage in a discourse with the machine.

Evidence thus verifies the obvious point that the <u>size</u>, and the <u>confusability</u>, of the vocabulary can substantially affect the possibility of recognition errors.

<u>Speaker variability</u> is another source of recognition errors. Most recognizers have worked only with a few male talkers, or have required extensive training for each new talker. However, in recent years, several <u>speaker-independent</u> recognizers have been successfully tested with large numbers of talkers (e.g., the "VICI" system handled 182 talkers in one study; Scott, 1977). At Bell Laboratories, a speaker-dependent word recognition system was tested with 13 talkers who dialed into the system from their own phones daily over a five-month period, and spoke words from an 84-word flight information

vocabulary, with a median rate of 91.6% correct recognition. (See Chap. 18.)
They were able to increase the recognition score to 98.5% by allowing
the talker up to three attempts to say the word before the system rejected
the speech as too dissimilar from any reference patterns. Another speaker-
independent recognizer developed at Bell Laboratories achieved 94.4% correct
recognition using 30 female and 25 male speakers, with recordings made in a
noisy computer room, using a low quality microphone. In 1978, Bell Laboratories researchers also reported on a system that is purported to be able to
handle 85% of all American speakers without training, and handle the other
speakers with minimal training. See Chap. 18 for Bell Laboratories studies.

Commercial recognizers also have been tested in the presence of noise and
over telephone lines, and those from Dialog Systems are specifically designed
to work over telephone lines. Recognizers have also been tested in airborne
conditions with an oxygen mask and simulated accelerations or vibrations.
(For a review of airborne applications of speech recognizers, see Lea, 1979.)

In 1978, the first commercial recognizer was announced that looks to a
computer just like a standard computer CRT terminal. The current status in
isolated word recognition will be summarized in Sec. 4-4.

4-3.2 History of Continuous Speech Recognition

4-3.2.1 Why Continuous Speech? - No one has adequately determined whether
smooth-flowing continuous speech is clearly desired or needed in computer input work, or how performance with continuous recognizers might differ from
that with recognizers which only handle separated words. One manufacturer
of isolated word recognizers told me that probably 80% of the currently known
applications for speech recognition can be adequately handled by isolated
word recognizers. Yet, there is widespread agreement that, if accurate continuous speech recognition were available, it would be the preferred mode of
human-to-machine communication. Usually when we speak, we don't pause between each two successive words, even in highly restricted communications
such as speaking telephone numbers, reading credit card numbers or manufacturing parts numbers, or saying highly formatted word sequences such as air
traffic control commands, mathematical formulas, weather reports, or programming language statements. Certainly, naturally spoken sentences involve
smoothly flowing speech. Continuous speech recognition would thus be more
natural and satisfying to the user. What is more, the rate of information
transfer is considerably higher with continuous speech. One can continuously
speak at a rate of about 150 to 300 words or more per minute, but when words
must be individually separated by pauses, the rate drops to less than 125
(usually to around 50 to 80) words per minute.

4-3.2.2 Steps Towards Continuous Speech Recognition - In the late 1960's and
early 1970's, several major projects were undertaken to develop appropriate
techniques for recognition of connected speech. Otten (1966) proposed the
application of syllabic units, prosodics, and a finite state language (Markov
model) to represent the structure of speech dialogue with a machine. Several
projects involved the phonetic segmentation of continuous speech (Sakai and
Doshita, 1963; Hemdal and Hughes, 1967; Reddy, 1967; Hughes, et al., 1969).
Reddy, for example, reportedly achieved over 80% correct identification of
phonemes in nonsense strings and meaningful phrases. Reddy and his student
Vicens demonstrated an initial capability in connected word sequence recognition, using a 16-word vocabulary (Vicens, 1969).

Throughout the 1950's and 1960's, several workers emphasized the need for
linguistic information in speech recognition (cf. eg. Fry and Denes, 1958;
Denes, 1959; Peterson, 1962). Fry and Denes (1953) incorporated a primitive

GOAL	RESULTS WITH 1976 ARPA SUR SYSTEMS			
	HARPY	HEARSAY II	HWIM	SDC
Accept continuous speech, ...	184 sentences	22 sentences	124 sentences	54 sentences
from many cooperative speakers, ...	3 male, 2 female	1 male	3 male	1 male
in a quiet room, ...	(computer terminal room)			quiet room
with a good microphone, ...	(inexpensive close-talking mike)			good mike
with slight adjustments for each speaker, ...	20 training sentences	60 training sentences	no training	no training
accepting 1000 words, ...	1011	1011	1097	1000
using an artificial syntax, ...	BF=33	BF=33 or 46	BF=196	BF=105
yielding less than 10% semantic error, ...	5%	9% or 26%	56%	76%
in a few times real time (=300 MIPSS)	28 MIPSS	85 MIPSS	500 MIPSS	92 MIPSS

Fig. 4-5. Goals and Final (1976) System Results for the ARPA SUR Project

The ambitious system specifications of the ARPA SUR project called for
machines that would accurately (i.e., for over 90% of the correctly spoken
sentences) accept continuous speech from many cooperative speakers, with near-
ideal conditions of quiet rooms and high-fidelity equipment. Sentences were
to be highly-stylized structures defined by a small grammar, using a 1000-
word vocabulary. Realizing both the complexity of the problem and the prospects for rapid advances in computer technology, they called for the recognition to be accomplished on very large fast computers that could handle
about 100 million internal instructions per second (which is about 100 or
more times as powerful as the actual computers the systems were finally built
on), and yet they allowed the computer processing to take several times as
much time as the duration of the spoken sentence.

In addition to five original system-building contractors, the project included four research contractors who were charged with developing advanced
ideas for improving the recognition techniques. In the fall of 1976, this
largest project came to an end with the demonstration of several systems that
could understand spoken sentences. Carnegie-Mellon University demonstrated
two alternative system designs (called "Harpy" and "Hearsay II"), Bolt Beranek and Newman, Inc. demonstrated the "Hear What I Mean" (HWIM) system, and
System Development Corporation demonstrated a system. One of the systems,
the Harpy system developed at Carnegie-Mellon University, basically met or
exceeded the system goals by correctly understanding 95% of the sentences
spoken by five talkers, using a 1011-word vocabulary and a highly-constrained
grammar of sentences relevant to a task concerning the retrieval of documents
from the computer memory. Five talkers is not "many", and the tests were
done on only a small set of 184 sentences, due to time and money limitations.
However, the system did work well even when the original specifications were
exceeded by having it handle somewhat noisy speech with inexpensive (lower-
fidelity) microphones. Harpy not only met the "letter of the law" by matching the ambitious goals for the project; it also fulfilled the "spirit" of
the project by demonstrating the feasibility of a limited (but potentially
useful) technology for computer understanding on continuously-spoken sentences. Also, in line with the spirit of the project, it made effective use
of strict constraints on allowable (grammatical, meaningful, and relevant)
word sequences, to bring the task within manageable limits. Other final
ARPA SUR demonstration systems had higher error rates primarily because they
dealt with more difficult tasks, used more general techniques that could have
been used for additional more ambitious tasks, and were not as carefully tested and adjusted as Harpy before the final demonstration tests. The Harpy
system also benefited from a new way to incorporate knowledge about the

acoustic properties of speech sounds and the phonetic composition of words into a special network. The network structure permitted very rapid examination of many alternative word sequences before selecting the best-scoring word sequence as the sentence spoken by the user.

4-3.2.4 <u>Other Recognizers of Continuous Speech</u> - Thus, the ARPA SUR project produced major strides in the necessary technology for commanding machines by naturally spoken sentences. However, there is a tendency for proponents of that project to forget that continuous speech recognition did <u>not</u> begin with ARPA SUR. Table 4-2 lists several studies which dealt with restricted (i.e., highly formatted) word sequences, such as sequences of digits or words from selected small vocabularies. Most of these admittedly dealt with far more restricted tasks than the ARPA SUR project. The Harpy, Bell Laboratories, and Sperry Univac studies are summarized in Chaps. 15, 18, and 19, respectively. The Lincoln Laboratory system and others of the twenty systems developed during the ARPA SUR project are briefly described in Chaps. 11 and 17; cf. also Medress, et al., 1977.

Years before the ARPA SUR project began, the largest single industrial project in speech recognition was begun at IBM (first at Raleigh, North Carolina, then transferred to the Thomas J. Watson Research Center in Yorktown Heights, New York; Tappert, et al., 1968; 1971; Dixon and Tappert, 1973; Jelinek, 1976; Bakis, 1977). IBM researchers developed a hierarchial "ARCS" system which segmented continuous speech into short transitional elements called <u>transemes</u>, which extended from the steady-state center of one phoneme to the center of the next phoneme. Such transemes capture some of the co-articulatory effects of flowing speech, and thus offer some hope of being more invariantly detectable than normal phonetic units. In their later work, IBM included both the transeme segmentation <u>and</u> a conventional phonetic ("steady-state") segmentation, working together in a dual segment classifier. They (Tappert, et al., 1971) reported 89% correct labeling of general phonetic categories, and 64% correct identification of specific phone labels. These researchers also advocated the use of stress and other prosodic features, "anchoring" of word hypothesization around robust segments, and feedback from a linguistic processor to refine segment classifications. The linguistic processor used a sequential decoding algorithm similar to a "best first" search procedure. A 250-word vocabulary was developed, and a highly-restricted finite-state graph specified 14 million allowable word sequences.

In 1973, the IBM ARCS system was the first system to perform automatic recognition of continuous speech based on a substantial command language. Performance was encouraging. The segmentation routines missed only 2% of the phonetic boundaries, and introduced 4% false boundaries. Phonetic-class identification on test data was 90% correct, with 81% correct identification of the specific phonetic units. Ninety-three percent of the words (of non-rejected sentences) were correctly identified, while 27% of the sentences were completely correct in identified wording.

In 1977, Bakis of IBM reported on another version of a finite state machine which used the power spectra of 10-millisecond ("centisecond") segments as the states. Trained to the speaker, it correctly recognized 96% of the 7-digit telephone numbers it was tested on, with a per-digit accuracy of better than 99%. He also tried a pilot study with the 250-word vocabulary and command language. The encouraging results with this centisecond-based system were prophetic of what was to come in 1978, when the IBM group reported that the centisecond-based system attained 95% sentence recognition and 99.4% word recognition on the 250-word command language. A striking fact was that this was substantially better accuracy than the 73% sentence recognition (96.4% word recognition) obtained with the usual IBM system with

70

TABLE 4-2. PERFORMANCE OF RECOGNIZERS OF CONNECTED WORD SEQUENCES

REFERENCE	CONDITIONS	WORD SEQUENCES	NUMBER OF TALKERS	NUMBER OF TEST UTTERANCES	PERCENTAGE OF STRINGS CORRECTLY RECOGNIZED
Vicens, 1969	High Quality Speech	From 16-word vocabulary	2 Male	192 strings	85%
IBM; Dixon and Tappert, 1973	High Quality Speech	New Raleigh language, 250-word vocabulary	3 Male	72 sentences	38%
IBM; Jelinek, 1976	High Quality Speech	7-Digit Strings New Raleigh Language, 250-word vocabulary	1 Male 1 Male	100 strings 363 strings	89% 81%
Bell Labs; Rabiner and Sambur, 1976	High Quality Speech Noisy Computer Room	7-Digit strings 3-Digit strings	5 Male, 5 Female 5 Male, 5 Female	200 strings 100 strings	91% 87%
Bell Labs; Sambur and Rabiner, 1976	Computer Room: Speaker-dependent Speaker independent	3-Digit strings	4 Male, 2 Female 10 Male	900 strings 200 strings	98.8% 95.3%
HARPY; Reddy, et al., 1976	Computer room Computer room Telephone lines Speaker independent	3-Digit strings 3-Digit strings 3-Digit strings 3-Digit strings	7 Male, 3 Female 1 Male 3 Male, 1 Female 14 Male, 6 Female	1000 strings 100 strings 400 strings 1200 strings	96% 96% 82% 83%
TI: Doddington, 1976	Good Quality Speech	6-Digit strings	NA*	NA*	99%
Kohda, et al., 1977	Good Quality Speech	Seat Reservations in Phrase Form (Japanese)	8 Male	320 reservations	86%
Saki and Nakayawa, 1977	Good Quality Speech	Commands for Computer (Japanese)	10 Male	200 sentences	64%
IBM; Bakis, 1977	High Quality Speech	7-Digit strings	1 Male	NA*	95%
Nippon Electric Co. Announcement, 1973	High Quality Speech	1 to 3 Digits (Japanese)	5 Male	1500 strings	99.8%
Medress, 1978	Quiet room Vocabulary = 36 words Quiet room Vocabulary = 64 words	2 to 4 alpha-numerics 2 to 7 words	3 Male 3 Male	24 strings 23 strings	79% 87%
IBM: Bahl, et al., 1978a	High Quality Speech – Phone Model – Centiscond Model – Centiscond Model	New Raleigh language 250 word vocabulary HARPY TASK, 1010 word vocabulary	1 Male 1 Male 1 Male	100 strings 100 strings 100 sentences	73% 95% 99%
IBM: Bahl, et al., 1978b	High Quality Speech	Laser patent texts 1000 word vocabulary	1 Male	20 sentences	67% word recognition

*NA = Information not available

71

phonetic-segmentation. Thus, the excellent phonetic segmentation methods developed at IBM, whose reported performance has been at the forefront of the field, were outperformed by the spectral matching at the centisecond level. The system was also tested with one speaker on the Harpy task of 1011-word recognition, attaining 99% correct sentence recognition for one speaker. On a corpus of 20 more-complex sentences from laser patent texts with a 1000 word vocabulary, 66.9% correct word recognition was attained. Success with the IBM systems has been promoted by confining the tests to high-quality recordings in sound-treated rooms, with extensive training to the statistical characteristics of an individual speaker. However, subsequent work has been directed at handling more than one speaker.

Texas Instruments (Doddington, 1976) has developed a highly successful system for recognizing strings of six spoken digits, followed by a speaker verification procedure. The ultimate goal of this system is to verify from the speaker's voice that he or she is qualified to have access to a secure computer room. However, the more advanced version of the system involves the system first recognizing a sequence of digits, to determine the individual's purported identification number. After the number is identified, then the speaker's specific voice characteristics are verified for granting access to the facility. Other work on restricted word-sequence recognition has been undertaken at Texas Instruments.

As shown in Table 4-2, considerable success has also been attained at Bell Laboratories in the recognition of connected sequences of digits and other words. In 1976, Rabiner and Sambur of Bell Laboratories developed a recognizer which detected boundaries between adjoining digits by finding unvoiced portions of the speech (i.e., portions during which the speaker's vocal cords were not vibrating), as well as observing significant dips in energy. These two cues were indicative of the stop consonants (in "two", "six", and "eight") and fricative consonants (in "zero", "three", "four", "five", "six", "seven") that occur at the boundaries between digits. Then, the known sound structure of each of the digits was built into the algorithms, so that their recognizer was carefully "tailored" to the digit vocabulary, and would not be directly applicable to other word sequences. Later, Sambur and Rabiner (1976) improved the accuracy of this digit-string recognizer by using an extra test (a special "distance measure") for handling some digit sequences with adjacent vowels or other hard-to-divide sound sequences (such as "one nine nine"). The high accuracy attained by their digit string recognizer is close to that commonly attained by isolated word recognizers, and suggests that accurate digit string recognition is currently just short of commercial practicality. Other digit string recognizers have also been fairly accurate, even when the recognizers were originally developed for other tasks, such as the HARPY system (Reddy, et al., 1976), which was developed for a sentence understanding task. With 3-digit strings spoken (after training) by 10 talkers, and 7-digit strings spoken by one talker, HARPY correctly recognized 96% of the strings. When telephone speech was used, or the system was not tuned to the talker's voice, performance dropped considerably. However, these results did demonstrate the ability of a speech understanding system like HARPY to be effectively applied to more restricted tasks than total sentence understanding.

Another system for handling connected word sequences has been developed at Nippon Electric Company of Japan, but the only available performance results are in commercial advertisements describing recognition efforts with strings of Japanese digits spoken by five men, for which the system is purported to have attained 99.8% correct word recognition (which usually is equivalent to a string-recognition score of over 99%). This system uses a two-level

72

pattern matching scheme in which short segments are first matched by a dynamic programming algorithm, then word sequences are matched by another level of dynamic programming (Tsuruta, 1978).

4-3.2.5 <u>Word Spotting Systems</u> - We have seen substantial progress toward limited versions of the challenging goal of recognizing continuous speech. Sometimes it is sufficient to detect key information-carrying words, without thoroughly analyzing the sound structure and wording of a sentence, so that a "keyword spotting system" is of interest. Fortunately, such "key" words are usually stressed and well articulated, and coarticulation with surrounding words is minimized, thus easing the problem. However, the conversations that are usually to be analyzed for word spotting are spoken over noisy communication channels by arbitrary talkers, so that other aspects of the task are usually difficult. A "word spotter" must detect words in the context of any other words, without being sensitive to talker differences and channel distortions. Consequently, most early work on word spotting was concerned with detecting linguistically-invariant units such as phonemes or phonetic classes (Hughes, et al., 1971; 1972) and matching phonetic strings of the lexicon with those analyzed in the incoming speech. It was also acknowledged that detection of stressed syllables and other prosodic structures should also help spot the prominent content words in smooth flowing speech (Lea, 1973; Medress, et al., 1978). Simple acoustic pattern-matching techniques were expected to be too sensitive to noise, distortions, and talker differences. Yet, as is true throughout the field of speech recognition, rapid progress has been made in the use of mathematical models and pattern matching techniques like dynamic programming, so that the current work includes both acoustic pattern-matching schemes and more linguistically-oriented analysis schemes that detect specific phoneme sequences.

Dialog Systems, Inc. (Moshier, et al., 1977, p. 1) developed a word spotter with the goal of "90% detection of key words and 5 or less false alarms per hour .... over telephone lines and radio links". False alarms must be kept to a minimum since the purpose of a word spotter is to focus attention on only those few conversations, out of thousands constantly going on over communication systems, that are of interest because of their topics of discussion. Dialog's technique was to extend an algorithm originally designed for recognizing words in isolation, and to detect half-syllable sized units whose sequence made up the single word "Kissinger". On initial tests with nine talkers <u>reading</u> a hypothetical news script, they achieved an "effectiveness of 90%-95% detection of a single key word, with 4-6 false alarms per hour against the limited number of test voices" (Moshier, et al., 1977, pp. 3-4). However, they found that the system "could not hold this accuracy against a wider population of test voices", yielding instead about "70% detection and 6 false alarms per hour" for tests with ten new voices.

The task Dialog Systems addressed was unusually easy, since there were a small number of talkers tested, the speech was <u>not</u> conversational such as occurs on communication links, and the single key word "Kissinger" is easier to spot than many other possible key words. Longer words like "Kissinger" have several syllables and fairly robust phonetic units like sibilants (/s/ or /z/, etc.) and some unvoiced stops (/k/) and nasals (/n/), which can combine with stressed vowels to provide considerable information for detecting target words, while ruling out other words that sound somewhat similar. In a study of the detection of <u>passwords</u> in free speech, as a part of a speaker verification procedure, Doddington and his colleagues at Texas Instruments (1978), found that the search for shorter words like "Congress", "Candidate", and "Pentagon" produced more false alarms (and more speaker verification errors) then using longer passwords like "Constitution" and "Secretary of State". Obviously, the more phonetic structure a word spotter can require to be present, and the more that structure is robustly evident regardless of context, noise, or speaker differences, the better will be the chance of detecting the keywords and rejecting all other words.

Medress, et al. (1978) have reported on a word spotter that undertakes the more ambitious task of spotting ten different keywords that have a good phonological diversity. They found a definite correlation between poor performance and the phonological structure of the keyword being spotted. When setting a strong demand of no more than 2 false keyword detections in 24 minutes of noise free speech, they correctly detected only 38% of the tokens of the ten keywords. However, they found that 60% of the missed tokens were occurrences of the four words ("Boonsboro", "interstate", "Middleton", and "mountain") which allowed the greatest phonological reduction in conversational speech. Indeed, these words had very few robust sounds in them, were subject to severe reductions in which whole syllables were all but lost, and involved voiced stops and voiced fricatives, which are among the more difficult sounds to detect acoustically. As is characteristic of almost all studies in speech recognition, system performance was much better on male speech than on female speech.

4-3.2.6 <u>Summary of Historical Progress</u> - The progress in over 27 years of work on speech recognition cannot simply be measured by increases in recognition accuracy, though there has been some progress on that performance factor. The primary gains have been made in the complexities of the tasks that have been accurately handled. In isolated word recognition, vocabulary sizes have increased from ten to several hundred words; highly confusable words have been distinguished; syntax trees have been incorporated to restrict acceptable next words to be within small sub-vocabularies; improved adaptation to the individual speaker and speaker-independent systems have both been developed; the telephone and noisy, distorting channels have been effectively used; effects of other environmental conditions like vibration, g-forces, and emotional stress have also been explored (cf. Lea, 1979); and commercial products have been produced and applied in practical interactions with machines. Expansions to limited forms of continuous speech have yielded a few modestly-successful systems for key word spotting, a number of fairly effective laboratory systems and one commercial product for recognizing digit strings and strictly formatted word sequences, and some limited but encouraging systems for total sentence understanding.

The pattern matching techniques, for establishing which of many stored templates is closest to the incoming speech data, have dominated the successes on limited problems. Simplified linguistic methods which have been based on strict linearity and invariance of identifying features, have produced more moderate successes, in part because they make errorful categorical decisions early in the recognition process and "throw away" most of the information before it can be used to reinforce or guide decisions at all levels of analysis. Initial encouraging strides have been made in handling coarticulation, context affects, phoneme sequence constraints, and phonological distortions such as deletion or insertion of segments. The most unused or ineffectively used information in the speech signal is the prosodic structure. The ARPA SUR project and other studies have clearly shown the merit of using syntactic, semantic, and pragmatic information to <u>constrain</u> the recognition task.

4-4. CURRENT CAPABILITIES IN SPEECH RECOGNITION

While the "present" is transitory, and a description of the "present state of technology" will be outdated somewhat by the time some readers examine this chapter, it does seem useful to take a "snapshot" of the state of the art and consider where all the past work has left us. We shall consider the current (i.e., early 1979) commercial recognizers (Sec. 4-4.1), the current research and development projects (Sec. 4-4.2), and the significant "gaps" that remain in the technology (Sec. 4-4.3). Such an assessment should help guide future work, as will be indicated in Sec. 4-5 and Chap. 27.

4-4.1 Commercial Speech Recognizers

After 27 years of increasingly more intensive work on machine recognition of speech, there is now a well-established technology for inputting highly-restricted spoken commands. Currently one can buy any of several isolated word recognition devices, as shown in Fig. 4-6. These current recognizers range over a broad spectrum from cheap hobbyist subsystems to expensive accurate systems ready for fully effective use in field applications. Heuristics, Incorporated makes a $200 hobbyist's "Speechlab", which provides only an acoustic front-end of a recognizer and requires a separate computer, although Heuristics offers software and ideas for small-vocabulary word recognition which are purported to provide over 95% correct word recognition (Enea and Reykjalin, 1978). Heuristics also offers manuals that introduce basic concepts of speech recognition and explain their recognition methods. Over 500 Heuristics Speechlabs are said to have been sold. Phonics, Incorporated offers their SR-8 "stand-alone" recognition system for $550, which is capable of speaker dependent recognition of 16-word vocabularies, or may be used with a separate computer for larger vocabularies. This system functions as an acoustic pattern classifier, processing the total spoken word as a single complex (unsegmented) pattern, and benefits considerably from use of a time normalization algorithm. It is purported to provide 98% recognition with a 2% reject rate for experienced users (Hitchcock, 1978). Centigram's "Mike" system is almost an order of magnitude more expensive at $3,000 to $5,000, and is intended to be used with the ADAM computer. I know of no public claims of performance figures for this recognizer, but it has been publicly demonstrated (e.g., at the 1978 National Computer Conference). Perception Technology, Incorporated is also reported to have offered speech recognizers, but I have no information on them.

More expensive (but generally more accurate and versatile) total recognition systems are available from Interstate Electronics, Dialog Systems, Threshold Technology, and Nippon Electric Company. Interstate Electronics now manufactures a version of an earlier "VDETS' recognizer developed by a

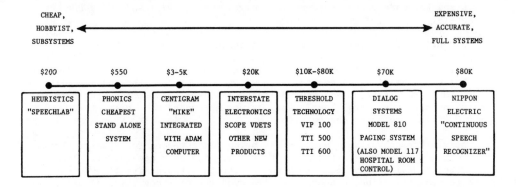

Figure 4-6. The spectrum of available commercial speech recognizers.

75

long-established speech recognition branch of Scope Electronics. Several VDETS (Voice Data Entry Terminal System) terminals and other Scope products have been used or tested by government agencies, and a Scope Electronics Voice Command System has been used and modified by NASA Ames Research Center (Coler, et al., 1978). The Interstate Model 1832 speaker-dependent VDETS is intended for moderate size vocabularies (up to 300 words) and costs $18,750. Another expanded model for 900-word speaker-dependent recognition (or 4-user, 250-word recognition) costs $22,500. Interstate also offers other optional devices and services to integrate voice data entry into a total applications system. For many practical applications, the effort and costs in developing a full application-oriented system far exceed the initial cost and trouble of obtaining a speech recognizer. Interstate, Dialog, and Threshold have offered total systems for voice input of data or commands, which represents a major step above initial recognizer capabilities alone.

Dialog Systems Incorporated has provided several recognizers for various applications, including the 99-word vocabulary Dialog 117 System for voice control of hospital room environmental conditions, for immobilized patients to control bed motors, lights, TV, nurse calls, etc. Dialog's standard Model 810 Voice Input Terminal is available for $70,000, for 12- or 31-word paging applications. This terminal, like many of Dialog's systems, works over telephone lines, and provides voice answer-back. Related Dialog Systems devices have been tested by government agencies with what was reported as considerable satisfaction.

Threshold Technology Incorporated has been the leading source of speech recognizers, selling well over 200 recognition systems since they offered their first project in 1972. The Threshold VIP 100 was tested and used in many commercial and governmental applications, and some are still in use or have been modified for advanced applications of isolated word recognition (Connolly, 1978). The VIP 100 was superceded by the Threshold 500, introduced in 1975, and the Threshold 600, introduced in 1977. The Threshold 600 is a CRT-compatible voice data entry terminal that looks to a computer just like a standard CRT terminal. Threshold Technology voice input systems cost from $10,000 up to $80,000 or more, depending greatly upon the customer's needs. Most of the successful applications of speech recognition in various commercial (and governmental) systems have been based on use of Threshold Technology devices, which provide speaker-adaptive, small vocabulary recognition with accuracies exceeding 99.5% in the best of cases. Threshold Technology's systems generally work with single speakers or a few speakers, using head-mounted close-talking microphones, but some tests have been done with speaker-independent recognition (e.g., Scott, 1976) and telephone channels.

Recently, Nippon Electric Company has announced a recognizer that reportedly can handle either 60 to 120 isolated words or else connected digits or word sequences, with over 99.5% correct recognition. The Nippon Electric DP Voice Recognition System uses a two-stage dynamic programming algorithm for time normalization, and uses distance measures between incoming spectral data and stored spectral templates. It was announced at a cost of around $80,000, for two input channels.

All of these available systems are primarily intended for speaker-adaptive use, requiring a moderate amount of training for each new talker. These commercial devices have done much to advance the credibility of voice input and to promote further concern with improved speech recognition capabilities. Current efforts are directed towards bringing the costs for such devices down to under $1,000, plus improving the ability to use telephone speech, and eliminating the need for each talker to train the system to the peculiarities

of his or her voice. Industry, government, and researchers are now concerned
with defining adequate standard tests to comparatively evaluate the available
systems, particularly since the number of commercial sources of such devices
has more than tripled in the last few years, and the systems being offered
vary greatly in accuracy and price.

Around 300 isolated word recognizers (besides over 500 hobbyist devices)
have been sold in the past six years, with roughly half of them now in daily
operational use, and others being tested in experimental government facilities and research laboratories. There have been many satisfied customers,
who report 50% to 90% reductions in manpower needs, time savings from 30%
to 95%, increased accuracy of data entry, and higher user morale. Figure
4-7 illustrates some of the commercial and military applications. Some applications have involved package sortation systems (such as at UPS, S.S.
Kresge, the U.S. Postal Service, and airline companies), where the operator's
hands are busy controlling packages on a conveyor belt system and orienting
the packages, while his spoken commands can simultaneously control on which
belt each package should go. Other applications involve inspecting TV faceplates at Owens Illinois, compressors at Tecumseh Projects, pull-top can
lids at Continental Can and Reynolds Metals, automobiles on assembly lines
at General Motors and Chrysler Motors, etc. Machine tools like lathes and
complex drilling machines can automatically be controlled by voice with
highly sophisticated Voice Numerical Control (VNC) systems such as have been
installed at Heat Controls, Inc., Calabrese and Sons, Joseph Moreng Iron
Works, Purcell Manufacturing Co., Diversified Manufacturing Co., and other
metal working facilities. Also, there is considerable interest in telephone
banking and voice authorization of credit card transactions. One of the most
successful recognizers ever developed was a system for securing personnel
access to a computer facility, at Texas Instruments (Doddington, 1976).
Other applications include voice actuated wheelchairs and hospital room environmental controls that are voice operated. The potential commerical applications of recognizers seem to be rapidly expanding.

The military has been the primary source of development funds in speech
recognition, and as shown in the bottom of Fig. 4-7, the current DOD applications include cartography or map making (Beek, et al., 1977; Goodman, et
al., 1977), computer-assisted training of skilled communicators like air
traffic controllers (Breaux, 1978; Grady, et al., 1978), recognition aids in
airplane and helicopter cockpit communications (Curran, 1978; Huff, et al.,
1978), monitoring of large communications systems to automatically detect
important conversations (Beek, et al., 1977), and natural forms of command
and control operations by high-ranking officers who would like to speak
natural commands to a machine without middlemen or complex input devices.

Other systems are being tested by the Federal Aviation Administration,
the Veterans' Administration, and the NASA Ames Research Center, for air
traffic control, voice-controlled wheelchairs, hands-off control of hospital
room environmental conditions, and simulations of pilot communications in
helicopters and aircraft.

One marketing consultant (cf. Chap. 20) predicts that in the next ten
years about 2.5 million speech processing units will be sold, for a total
market of about 4.8 billion dollars. At least one third of this market is
expected to be in isolated word recognizers. A recent survey of experts in
speech recognition work (Lea and Shoup, 1979) shows expected sales that can
be projected to similar figures. With the expectation that accurate isolated
word recognizers will come down in price within the next two years, from
their current several tens of thousands, to well under $1,000 each, we can

COMMERCIAL APPLICATIONS

PACKAGE SORTING

QUALITY CONTROL AND INSPECTION

PROGRAMMING OF NUMERIC
CONTROLLED MACHINES

VOICE-ACTUATED WHEELCHAIR

BANKING AND CREDIT CARD
TRANSACTIONS

SECURITY AND ACCESS CONT

MILITARY APPLICATIONS

CARTOGRAPHY IN DEFENSE MAPPING

TRAINING AIR TRAFFIC CONTROLLERS

COCKPIT COMMUNICATION

SPOTTING KEY WORDS IN
MONITORED CONVERSATIONS

COMMAND AND CONTROL BY HIGH-RANKING OFFICERS

Figure 4-7.   Commercial and military applications for speech recognition.

predict a rapidly expanding market, and a growing variety of applications.

4-4.2 Current Development Projects

Currently, a number of developmental projects are being conducted at Bell Laboratories, IBM, ITT, Logicon, Nippon Electric Company, Sperry Univac, and Texas Instruments. CMU is still continuing work on extensions of Harpy, while other advanced research projects, especially including speech understanding work, are being conducted in Japan, France, Germany, Italy, and other countries. Table 4-3 summarizes current projects. We will not describe all this work here, since Part IV of this book summarizes most of the current work. However, a few project highlights that have not been mentioned previously in this chapter should be noted.

Texas Instruments has a company-sponsored project in limited vocabulary continuous speech recognition, and has operational real-time demonstrations of isolated and continuous word recognition, for both enrolled (trained) and new speakers, using vocabularies up to 50 words. Their entry into the consumer product market with the "Speak and Spell" educational toy has substantially improved the marketability of speech processing devices. While their accurate voice verification system has other ultimate goals than message understanding, it has involved successful recognition of over 99% of the 6-digit identification numbers spoken to it. Two useful constraints in the Texas Instruments recognition algorithms include (1) the incorporation of two parity check digits, to automatically correct for recognition errors in the digit string, and (2) the forbidding of digit sequences that are particularly hard to segment and identify, such as "three eight", etc. An independent study by Mitre Corporation (Fejfar, 1977) concluded that the voice identification system was superior to other entry control systems such as handwriting or fingerprinting analysis, so that voice entry control systems should be a promising application of speech recognition technology in the future.

A new project in speech recognition was instituted at ITT's Defense Communications Division in 1977, and while no complete recognition system has yet been developed, the researchers led by White and Sambur (Chap. 21) are exploring speaker independent speech recognition, telephone bandwith and noisy speech, and low cost speech processing hardware. Isolated word recognition, word spotting, and talker identification are among the intended application areas, and prominent among the methods being investigated are dynamic programming and optimum distance (or "similarity") measures.

Several studies have been conducted at Logicon, Incorporated, concerning the feasibility and utility of speech recognition for such tasks as the Automated Adaptive Flight Training System, and training air traffic controllers for the ground controlled approach system. Another task attempted was recognition of voice commands of a conning officer aboard a ship, for which simulations showed 90% correct recognition of a small vocabulary of 63 navigation commands (isolated phrases) spoken by several talkers within a task-dictated syntax. From 1973 to 1977, Logicon used commercial (Threshold Technology VIP 100) isolated word recognizers coupled to their computer facility, and in 1977 they began developing a system (called "LISTEN") for real-time recognizing of connected speech with small vocabularies. This LISTEN system uses a Markov model like Harpy and the IBM systems use, but they replace Harpy-like linguistic processing with faster mathematical and statistical analyses. No performance results are yet available for this developing system. Its capabilities are clearly limited to small vocabulary, finite-state languages such as are appropriate in restricted tasks like navigation commands and training of air traffice controllers.

Table 4-3. Current Development Projects in Speech Recognition

BELL LABORATORIES	• High-accuracy isolated word recognition with linguistic and task-dictated constraints on sequences, and speaker-independence; • Telephone applications with digit strings and restricted word sequences (e.g., directory assisstance and travel reservations); • Research on entropy and task complexity neasures, speech science, and voice response.
CARNEGIE-MELLON UNIVERSITY	• Minicomputer version of HARPY; • Enhancements of HARPY for bigger tasks, incremental compilation of networks, and automatic knowledge acquisition.
IBM RESEARCH CENTER	• Statistically-based approach to general continuous speech recognition, without restrictive task constraints, but with use of extensive speaker-dependent statistics. Tested with a variety of tasks, including an ambitious 5000-word Lasar Patent Text task. Goal is automatic transcription of unrestricted spoken texts ("dictation machine").
ITT DEFENSE COMMUNICATIONS DIVISION	• Low-cost isolated word recognizers, and speaker independence; • Work spotting in connected speech; • Practical conditions of telephone bandwidth and noisy speech.
LOGICON	• Applications studies with available recognizers, for training air traffic controllers and for other military and training applications; • LISTEN system with Markov model for highly-restricted connected speech recognition.
NIPPON ELECTRIC COMPANY	• Digit string and restricted word sequence recognition; • Advanced dynamic programming methods; • (Other manufacturers are currently working on similar projects).
SPERRY UNIVAC	• Linguistically-based connected speech recognition system; • Word spotting in connected speech, with practical channel conditions.
TEXAS INSTRUMENTS	• All voice talker-verification system with initial recognition of six-digit strings; • Error-correcting methods in digit string recognition.
BRITAIN, FRANCE, GERMANY, ITALY, JAPAN, POLAND	• For various studies in isolated word recognition, digit string recognition, connected word sequence recognition, speech understanding systems, and airborne applications.

This review has primarily focused on work in the USA. Yet, several other speech recognition systems (for both isolated speech and continuous speech recognition or understanding) are being developed around the world. For example, limited continuous speech understanding work is actively going on in France, Germany, Italy, and Japan. In Orsay, France, at Laboratorie d'Informatique pour la Mechanique et les Sciences de l'Ingenieur, Mariani and Lienard and their colleagues are working on a speech understanding system (called "ESOPE") that uses phonological, lexical, syntactic, prosodic, and semantic constraints to correct errors in acoustic phonetic analysis, in a manner similar to the ARPA SUR systems. They are currently investigating performances with several very limited tasks such as phrases composed of subject-verb complement constructions (21-word vocabulary with a branching factor of 5), digit strings of unspecified length, numbers (like "thirty four"), arithmetic expressions (42-word vocabulary, branching factor of 12), and phrases used in standard telephony (for which they are testing how performance varies with size of the vocabulary and branching factor). At Centre de Recherche en Informatique, Universite de Nancy, France, Haton and his colleagues are working on speech understanding in the MYRTILLE project (cf. Chap. 24). In 1974-1976, a first version called MYRTILLE 1 was implemented using a top-down (syntax-driven) strategy. MYRTILLE 2 involves a new parser, prosodic segmentation schemes, new phonemic recognition procedures, and a versatile interactive system.

It appears that the European scholars are continuing where the ARPA SUR project left off, but proceding with some caution, initially dealing with fairly restricted problems. One of the interesting highlights of European work is the use of syntactic pattern recognition schemes, which model speech waves by structural features or units whose composition and combinations are determined by syntactic rules (e.g., cf. Baudry and Dupeyrat, 1978; DeMori, et al., 1975). This method has been well known in other (visual) forms of pattern recognition work in the USA (Fu, 1974), but has had little attention in American work in speech recognition.

In Japan, several recognition efforts are active (cf. Chap. 22 for a summary), but the primary work in speech understanding is at Kyoto University (however, work is also being done at Yamanachi University; Sekiguchi and Shigenaga, 1978). A multiple-knowledge-source system for recognition of a small vocabulary spoken version of the "BASIC" programming language was developed by Niimi and his colleagues (1975), with some success. It achieved 47% correct sentence recognition in 1975, and has since been improved considerably. A more ambitious project was the LITHAN (LIsten-THink-ANswer) speech understanding system (Nakagawa, 1976), which used a 20-channel filter bank in an Acoustic Processor, plus a Phoneme Recognizer, Word Identifier, Word Predictor, Parsing Director, and Responder, to achieve 64% correct recognition of sentences of 4 to 24 words, with a 100-word vocabulary.

4-4.3 Gaps in Current Technology

Machine recognition of speech has apparently "come of age", as evidenced for example by the title of an article in Science magazine, which asserted that "More people are talking to machines, as speech recognition enters the real world" (Robinson, 1979). Speech recognition devices have begun to impact the everyday commercial world, with considerable user satisfaction. The field shows some signs of rapid expansion, partly resulting from an expanded spectrum of available devices and an expectation of substantially lower costs in the next few years. Despite such maturing of the field, there are substantial "gaps" or inadequacies in current technology and extensive further work is needed. In this section, we shall briefly consider: expert opinions about the best current techniques (Sec. 4-4.3.1); a comprehensive framework for defining adequacies and gaps in current technology (Sec. 4-4.3.2); some current adequacies (Sec. 4-4.3.3); and a listing of important gaps (Sec. 4-4.3.4).

4-4.3.1 Best Current Techniques – In assessing the total technology in speech recognition and understanding, June Shoup and I conferred with over 100 workers in this field, and obtained detailed viewpoints from 34 experts (16 ARPA SUR participants, 18 non ARPA experts), via a 32-page question-naire. The experts (with an average of 10 years experience each) considered Harpy, HEARSAY II, the IBM system, and HWIM to be the most relevant systems for future work, in that order. Experts who were not participants in the ARPA SUR project ranked a "prosodically guided" speech understanding system (cf. Lea, et al., 1975) as a promising future approach.

When questioned about the best techniques for various aspects of speech recognition processes, the experts primarily favored the following methods:

Acoustic Parameters:	Use contours of the 3 formant frequencies (F_1, F_2, F_3), energy, and pitch (Fo), plus a spectral derivative, formant bandwidths, and other spectral parameters;
Phonetic Analysis:	Use a phonetic lattice (like HWIM did) on sub-phonemic templates (like Harpy);
Prosodic Information:	Use stressed syllables, number of syllables, syntactic pauses, and intonational phrase boundaries;
Word Matching:	Use phonologically-based word hypothesiza-tion (with a HWIM-like lexical decoding network), and word verification with acou-stic or phonetic patterns;
Search Strategy:	Use the beam ("best few first") search strategy, and island drive only if the islands are truly reliable;
System Structure:	The Harpy integrated network and the modu-lar HEARSAY II structure are two good structures, but the HWIM uniform scoring strategy looks promising.

4-4.3.2 A Framework for Defining Gaps – It is questionable whether one can define gaps in a technology without defining the complete needs and current adequacies. Figure 4-8 shows one organizational framework for defining adequacies, gaps, and issues in all aspects of speech recognition (cf. Lea, 1979). Included are not only technical dimensions of systems design and specific components, but also aspects of testing, evaluation, and project design that are important to defining good projects that will help fill gaps in the field. Supporting research and practical applications are also included as essential aspects of the process of developing a total technology in speech understanding.

Obviously, the task conditions determine the relative utility of speech input, and the applicability of recognizers to real tasks. The human needs and variabilities must be considered, and the language selected for inter-actions will significantly affect the complexity of the recognition task. Environmental conditions and transduction processes will interfere with

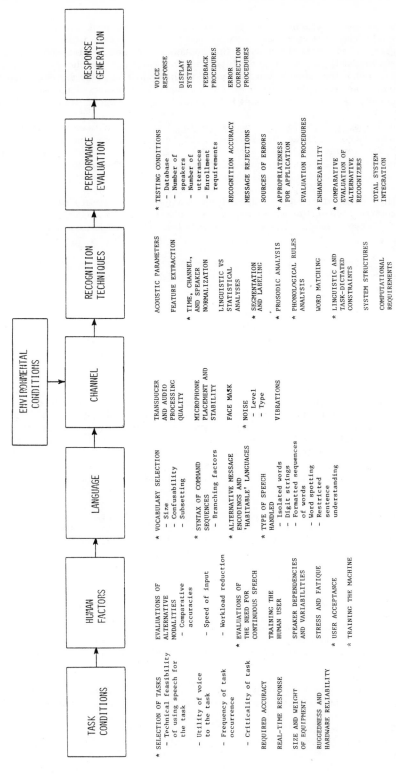

Figure 4-8 An organizational framework for summarizing the various issues involved in applications of speech recognizers.

83

acoustic regularities of the received signal. Recognition techniques must cover all the statistical, pattern-matching, and linguistic knowledge sources that may be effectively used. The system performance must obviously be carefully assessed, and an appropriate machine response produced. We shall briefly consider adequacies and gaps within this framework, but much could obviously be said about each of the associated topics. Unless otherwise indicated, further work is needed on each aspect listed in Fig. 4-8.

4-4.3.3 Adequacies in Current Technology - For each new recognition task, all the factors listed in Fig. 4-7 must be considered and either determined to be irrelevant, adequately handled by available systems, or in need of further work. Except for unusual circumstances, those factors not marked with a star under task conditions and human factors in Fig. 4-8 may need decisions to be made, but do not require extensive research and development or other work before these decisions can be informatively made. For example, the comparative value of speech as a machine input modality, and the high reliability of small-vocabulary isolated word recognizers, are well established.

Only limited work has been done on the channel and environmental conditions shown in Table 4-8, and the only conditions under which fully adequate recognition is attainable today are high-quality speech from a speaker for whom the system is trained. For isolated word recognizers, telephone speech, noise, and many speakers of both sexes and multiple dialects do appear to be within reach, with a few successes already shown in previous studies. Continuous speech recognizers are clearly limited in their abilities to handle the more challenging input conditions.

Isolated word recognizers are adequate for small (30 word) vocabularies, and several studies show nearly adequate performance in using syntactically constrained sequences of isolated words. Digit string recognizers appear close to becoming effective commercial products, and not far behind are recognizers of strictly formatted word sequences. The feasibility of limited speech understanding has been demonstrated, and the successful HARPY system and its integrated network structure are being adequately applied, extended, re-implemented on a smaller computer, and used in developing a system for a practical task of computer-assisted training (Breaux, et al., 1978).

Significant advancement has been made in system organizations, so that now there are several promising system structures that could be used in future work. Syntactic models have proved effective, so that systems performed best with highly constrained syntax that truly restricted word sequences, rather than just providing a good description of the language. The other areas that appear to be sufficiently adequate to allow some future system development include semantics, and lexicon and word matching procedures. Most experts polled in the Lea and Shoup (1979) survey believe that among the generally adequate aspects of recognition techniques are: the acoustic parameters like formants and LPC analysis results, syntactic analysis that sharply constrains word sequences, semantic models that work together with syntax, and phonetically or parametrically based word matching procedures.

4-4.3.4 Practical Limitations and Research Gaps - When queried by Lea and Shoup (1979) concerning the types of systems that are most needed now, the research-oriented ARPA SUR participants favored speech understanding systems and recognizers of connected word sequences, while the more practical non-ARPA participants favored more modest systems ranging from very low cost isolated word recognizers to recognizers of modestly-constrained connected word sequences. In summary, these opinions suggest interest in recognizers of several levels of capability, including, in decreasing order of importance:

- Connected word sequences and digit strings;
- Isolated word recognizers with syntax and low cost;
- Restricted speech understanding (Harpy-like) systems; and
- Research speech understanding systems (much more powerful than Harpy).

All the factors marked in Fig. 4-8 with an asterisk seem to need substantial further work. For each application, workers must explore the careful selection of tasks for which speech input is technically feasible, useful, likely to be frequently needed, and yet for which the consequences of recognition errors (which are a very real likelihood with today's limited technology) will not have critical impact on the mission or task being undertaken.

No systematic studies have been done to determine what accuracy (and other system features) it takes for user acceptance of a recognizer. However, informal studies with practical usage of isolated word recognizers indicate that 97% accuracy is usually needed, and at least that accuracy would probably be needed for the longer spoken sentences. For some situations, errors are so intolerable that feedback of recognition decisions is essential to correct occasional errors. Extensive testing and performance evaluating of total systems and their components is clearly needed for all systems, whether they be isolated word recognizers or speech understanding systems. Work with better use of linguistic constraints and habitable languages seems important, while speed, moderate-quality input channels, and multiple speakers don't appear to be limiting the utility of recognizers. There is no evidence that significantly larger vocabularies than about 300 words are needed. No absolute needs for continuous speech recognizers have been defined (Beek, et al., 1977), but this may in part be due to the available technology dictating to the application rather than allowing the applications to determine needed technology. The desirability of continuous speech (due to increased speed and naturalness, reduced training demands on the users, etc.) may be evident, but the necessity or comparative cost effectiveness of versatile continuous speech recognition is not yet established. Part of the problem is to determine how much recognition capability is really needed. How versatile does the language of possible utterances have to be, and can one define a hierarchy of tasks of increasing complexity that can and should be handled by speech recognizers? Can systems be defined that are useful but have capabilities somewhere between isolated words and speech understanding systems? If so, what are those intermediate systems? Also, how acceptable is it to have systems that require extensive training, such as Harpy and some other systems need, and can systems be developed that require little training?

Work still remains to be done (even with simple isolated word recognizers) on reducing the performance degradation that results from various levels of background noise, the effects of microphone characteristics and their physical mountings, and the difficulties introduced by physical stress (labor, heavy breathing, etc.) and mental stress (danger, critical operations, or being overloaded with things out of control).

With the advent of many commercial sources of word recognizers has come a growing demand for objective procedures for evaluating systems. Several manufacturers have mentioned the real need for industry standards, such as general speech databases of 100 or more talkers speaking many instances of the digits and other vocabularies such as the alphabet ("A, B, C, ..."), the phonetic alphabet ("alpha, bravo, charlie, ..."), the names of the 50 states, or vocabularies relevant to important applications. The Speech Recognition subcommittee of the IEEE Machine Intelligence and Pattern Analysis Technical Committee of the IEEE Computer Society is currently endeavoring to define several general purpose databases that can be used to comparatively evaluate recognizers. However, just having individual manufacturers run the same speech data through alternative recognizers does not provide totally adequate "bench-marks" for assessing recognizers. The total task of interactions between unsophisticated users and voice entry systems needs to be tested in accurate simulations of field usage, which could perhaps best be carried out by an independent evaluation facility.

From the linguistic analysis viewpoint of speech understanding, the problem of voice input is not solved. For example, human observers can do quite well (about 90 percent correct) in identifying vowels and consonants of nonsense words placed in spoken sentences. There is no theoretical reason why computers cannot approach this performance, but careful research is needed to reach such a goal. This is probably the research area with the highest potential payoff in terms of improving the performance of limited speech understanding systems. However, improvements are possible in all of the components of speech recognition and understanding systems. Recognizers also have not incorporated or adequately tested many of the published rules concerning English phonological structure. Prosodic structures show great promise of aiding word recognition and detection of several aspects of grammatical structure, but prosodic information has had virtually no impact on the performance of previous recognizers. While several promising techniques have previously been developed for identifying words by their resemblences to expected pronunciations, further work is still needed to increase the accuracy of word matching. At the higher levels of linguistic analysis (dealing with larger units like phrases and sentences), efficient constraints must be developed that will allow future expansions to more difficult tasks. We need precise methods for assessing the relative complexities of various recognition tasks and for adequately evaluating the total performance of a recognizer.

Thus, further work is needed in almost every aspect of recognition, despite the advances that the ARPA SUR project and other recent work have produced. Experts answering the Lea-Shoup survey considered that the following were among the top-priority aspects of recognition that need attention (listed in descending order of priority):

- Acoustic phonetic analysis;
- Prosodic cues to linguistic structures;
- Performance evaluation;
- Using linguistics to constrain ambiguities;
- System tuning on extensive data;
- Fast or near-real-time processing;
- Scoring procedures; and
- Phonological rules.

As is evident from these opinions (and the more detailed list of gaps in Fig. 17-9 of Chap. 17), the "front end" analysis routines which transform from acoustics to phonetics, phonology, words, and prosodics, are among the top priority components on which to focus. In addition, all systems need extensive testing and performance evaluation, which in turn requires fast processing techniques and research on comprehensive measures of task complexity. Total measures of recognition task complexity are needed, which more completely measure language complexity, sentence complexity, vocabulary confusability,

confusability of phrases and their possible extensions, and other dimensions of difficulty such as speaker population, environmental conditions, etc. It currently is difficult to comparatively evaluate two or more alternative systems if they are not applied to tasks of equivalent complexity and similar or identical speech data, and we do not know how to decide whether system A which yields 90% recognition on a simple task is better or worse than system B which yields 50% recognition on a difficult task.

It is also important to determine the <u>causes</u> of recognition errors, and the weak and strong links in system operation. Systems need to be adjusted, tested, and evaluated with extensive amounts of data. This is one reason why Harpy succeeded, since it was carefully adjusted with extensive speech data. Projects should be designed to allow time for such extensive tests, including over-all system accuracy scores and evaluations of the effectiveness and weakness of various system components.

Comparative evaluations of alternative speech recognizers must be undertaken, particularly for commercial isolated word recognizers, and the available practical recognizers need to be applied to various applications. Extensive thought must be given to systematically bridging the large gap between practical isolated word recognizers and long range work on ambitious speech understanding systems. Part of that task involves human factor studies of the accuracy and other system performance characteristics that are needed in various practical applications. Another part involves defining appropriate "next steps" in advancing speech recognition capabilities. Programs are needed, but already underway, in digit string recognition and recognition of formatted word sequences. Speech understanding systems are, however, not getting the attention they deserve. Also required is consideration of "technology transfer", to translate results of such advanced development projects into improvements in practical recognizers. Finally, there is a continuing need, intensified and clarified by the ARPA SUR advancements, to conduct needed experimental research on acoustic phonetic, phonological, and prosodic characteristics of spoken sentences, plus to determine what makes a limited interactive language "habitable" (easily learned and strictly adhered to by the regular user of the system).

All of these gaps in current technology are discussed by Lea and Shoup in Chap. 17 and a 1979 report. They suggest the future work outlined in the next section, and in Chap. 27.

4-5. FUTURE NEEDS AND TRENDS

4-5.1 Another ARPA SUR Project?

To "fill" the known gaps in current speech recognition technology would seem to be a primary goal for future work. Many of the specific topics listed in Fig. 4-8 are intertwined, with the methods taken in one aspect likely to affect the best way to accomplish other tasks. One possible way to foster the needed interactions and to ambitiously pursue advancements of the field, could be a large scale, ARPA-SUR-like multiple-contractor research program of cooperative and competitive developments of alternative systems. The expert respondents to the Lea and Shoup (1979) survey considered that, if another large scale coordinated program were attempted, they would favor development of several alternative systems, particularly if the systems address a <u>spectrum</u> of problem complexities, with one system directed at an easy problem, another at a moderately difficult task, and another at a quite difficult, challenging task. Other organizational features endorsed for a new project were the use of supporting research efforts conducted by specialist contractors, plus mid-term evaluations of the systems, extensive performance evaluation of the systems developed, and close interactions and frequent interchanges among contractors. The ARPA SUR project taught the value of mid-term milestones, back-up plans, and clearly demonstrated successes, rather than working on or modifying system features right up to the last minute.

The respondents were uncertain, or had mixed opinions, about completely defining fixed system specifications that must be achieved by fixed dates. As one colleague said, "You can't legislate or schedule scientific breakthroughs".

When asked what system design choices they would make if another large scale project were undertaken, the respondents recommended: a moderate vocabulary of several hundred words or more; 10 to 100 speakers; three levels of system or language complexity; practical input through close talking microphones, telephones, or other communication channels of various qualities; systems adjustable to the speaker with only a few utterances; more substantial use of semantic and pragmatic constraints; near-real-time operation; and accuracy of 95-99%, to be achieved within a project period of three to five years. The primary differences from the ARPA SUR project are: a series of progressively more difficult tasks; more attention to practical needs like realistic input channels, many speakers, and high accuracy in real time; and no programmed demand for success on a fixed deadline.

While such opinions may be of general interest, current needs do not necessarily demand the idea of another large-scale speech understanding project. For each of the problem areas listed in Fig. 4-7 separate programs could be undertaken. Another mechanism for stimulating interaction and cooperation among administratively independent projects would be a coordinating group which regularly meets and discusses issues and common problems. Funders of speech recognition work in the United States government have developed a voice interactions Technical Advisory Group (or "TAG"), to foster such cooperation. A similar cooperative group involves the NATO countries (through the RSG-10 speech recognition group).

Another idea for fostering cooperation would be the establishment of two or three "speech science centers", where powerful and flexible recognition systems can be combined with extensive expertise in speech science, linguistics, and computer science, to maintain a constantly advancing capability in machine recognition of speech. Visiting scholars can then use such facilities to try out their new ideas in aspects of recognition within the framework of a total working system, and practical applications-oriented tasks can be simulated to evaluate the effectiveness of voice input in various real-world situations. Such centers could compile valuable databases of spoken utterances for analysis, plus lists of publications on various related topics, and a variety of computer programs for various aspects of recognition. See Sec. 17-6 of Chap. 17.

4-5.2 Types of Needed Projects

Table 4-4 suggests four types of speech recognition programs that are needed now, including: 1. some applications studies with available commercial recognizers; 2. some comparative evaluations of alternative devices and specific improvements (without major re-design of systems) to handle noise, a large talker population, and limited forms of connected speech; 3. some advanced development projects to substantially expand recognition capabilities;

TABLE 4-4. RECOMMENDED TYPES OF SPEECH RECOGNITION PROJECTS

APPLYING AVAILABLE RECOGNIZERS	• Cockpit Communications (NASA Ames, NADC, NTEC, RADC) • Training Air Traffic Controllers (NTEC) • All-Voice Access Control to Secure Areas (RADC) • Voice Entry of Cartographic Data (RADC, DMA) • Key-Word Spotting (RADC, ONR) • Computer-Assisted Trouble Shooting

EVALUATING AND ADVANCING CURRENT TECHNOLOGY WITHOUT MAJOR RE-DESIGN OF SYSTEMS	• Comparative Evaluations of Alternative Input Modalities
	• Comparative Evaluations of Alternative Speech Recognizers
	    Selection of databases and benchmark tasks
	    Measuring complexities of tasks
	• Human Factors Studies
	    Effects of physical and mental stress
	    Design criteria for user acceptance
	• Realistic Channel Conditions
	    Microphone characteristics and placement; telephone input;
	    Noise; channel distortions
	• Larger Vocabularies
	• Application of Isolated Word Recognizers to Word Spotting
	• Speaker Independence without Extensive Training

DEVELOPING ADVANCED SYSTEMS	• Evaluating the Need for Continuous Speech • Digit String Recognizers • Word Sequence Recognizers • Moderately-Restricted Speech Understanding Systems • Autonomous Continuous Speech Recognizers • Methods for Fast Processing of Extensive Data
RESEARCH ON NECESSARY CONCEPTS AND KNOWLEDGE SOURCES	• Acoustic Phonetic Analysis • Prosodic Aids to Recognition • Performance Evaluation and Task Complexities • Phonological Rules • Linguistic Constraints on Ambiguities • Scoring Procedures for Selecting Hypotheses • Social Issues Concerning Uses of Recognizers

and 4. research on necessary knowledge sources and basic concepts relevant to future success in recognition.

Most of the project topics listed in Table 4-4 are self-explanatory and based directly on gaps listed in Sec. 4-4.(The projects are described in detail in available reports: Lea and Shoup, 1979; Lea, 1979.) However, a few projects need some explanation, and the list must also be supplemented by recommendations about the relative priorities of all these projects or topic areas.

Applications studies involve considering all the issues raised by the many factors listed in Fig. 4-8, especially those that are determined by the specific task involved, such as the value of speech in the specific intended application, the task requirements, the human factors, the language design, and the environmental conditions. For each Department of Defense (DOD) application shown in Table 4-4, studies can and should be done of the advantages and cost effectiveness of voice input facilities, the conditions and system specifications for the most appropriate form of recognizer, and the human factors of an effective system for interactions. An illustrative applications study has been done for cockpit applications of speech recognition (Lea, 1979). DOD agencies shown in parentheses in the top part of Table 4-4 have already funded or expressed interest in the applications as listed. A similar list of commercial applications could also be made, and each promising application carefully analyzed to determine how voice input fits into that context. Most applications studies will naturally grow out of interest in applying this new technology to human-to-machine interactions where the advantages of speech seem particularly relevant (cf. Chap. 1). However, in some complex applications, early attention must be given to defining those specific tasks that are most suitable for the restricted forms of voice dialog which can be accomplished with available devices (cf. Lea, 1979). Another top-priority issue concerns the determination of the best type of speech to use, and how versatile the language for interaction must be.

Very soon, government agencies and other independent groups need to comparatively evaluate alternative speech recognizers, and be able to select the best one(s) for use with specific vocabularies, the needed type of speech, appropriate channel conditions, and relevant speaker populations. It would also be desirable to predict (at least to some fairly good approximation) how well a system will do under new environmental conditions or new speakers, or new vocabularies and language structures, without having to conduct a complete new test of the system for each change of conditions, vocabulary, syntax, or speakers.

Some rather demanding applications, such as airborne uses of speech recognizers, will warrant considerable attention to environmental conditions like noise, physical and emotional (task-induced) stress and fatigue, g-forces and acceleration, small size and weight of equipment, etc. Since it seems unwise to use speech under the poorer and more-critical conditions of flight, the primary environmental issue to consider first would appear to be noise (Lea, 1979). For most applications in the next few years, such environmental complicating factors should be avoided, or dealt with as research enhancements to current technology.

Top priority improvements for manufacturers of speech recognizers would seem to be: (1) speaker independent recognition, so that extensive training procedures can be eliminated for most speakers; (2) low-cost ($1000) accurate isolated word recognizers; (3) accurate small-vocabulary connected-word-sequence recognizers; and (4) better handling of telephone, noise, and practical field conditions.

Undertaken separately, each of these looks possible (and likely) within a
few years. Expansions to telephone-accessed voice data entry systems would
open up a widespread market, such as for banking and credit card transactions,
but those applications require accurate analysis of telephone speech from
arbitrary speakers. Current indications are that manufacturers will be
spontaneously dealing with these enhancements, without any demand for special
stimulus from funding agencies.

The next market area, after digit-strings and formatted word sequences,
would probably be for Harpy-like forms of restricted sentence understanding
systems. These systems may not be spontaneously developed, and may need
stimulation from interested funding agencies. There are still some research
and development problems that need solution before such systems will become
practical. Harpy is currently very expensive to implement for each new task,
and minor changes (such as adding new words or structures) require extensive
processes for re-compiling the whole finite state network. Extensions to
Harpy that should really pay off (cf. Chap. 15) include incremental compilation, automatic knowledge acquisition, and introduction of additional knowledge sources (such as prosodics).

Research systems which permit the introduction and testing of new or improved components are also vitally needed, and should be permitted to test
system features like uniform scoring, admissible strategies, and reliable
island driving. Within those research systems, work is needed on phonetic,
phonological, prosodic, and other types of components, with the specific
tasks and priorities roughly as indicated in Fig. 4-7 and in Fig. 17-7 of
Chap. 17. Coupled with recognition studies should be necessary experimental
research on prosodic structures, human factors issues (especially concerning
what makes a language habitable), comparative evaluation of systems with
common tasks, and general acoustic phonetic characteristics of spoken sentences. One promising structure for a more ambitious speech understanding
system for such ambitious research would be a HEARSAY-like system of independent modules communicating through a blackboard. Such a system could
also incorporate the best components of HWIM and other systems, as well.

Future work on speech recognition should not only include widespread application of recognizers, enhancements to current devices and techniques,
and the development of advanced systems like extensions of Harpy and HEARSAY
models. Research on necessary concepts and knowledge sources must also be
vigorously pursued. Experts widely agree with the need for improved techniques in the acoustic phonetic and prosodic "front ends" of systems. Basic
studies should be done on the phonetic, prosodic, and phonological properties of sentences. Just as with the past, the future thus holds a challenge
for speech researchers, system developers, and those who effectively apply
speech recognizers to real needs and investigate the resulting performance
characteristics. Neuburg (Chap. 2) has suggested that at least some segment
of the speech research community concerned with speech recognition should be
addressing modest "next steps" in recognizer developments. This is in line
with the concept of "bootstrapping" oneself up to better and better recognition capabilities, by careful stages of progression. There is an ever-
present danger in such a cautious strategy that a dead-end may be reached,
analogous to when one tries to get to the moon by climbing a tree. Ambitious projects which reach far, with the best of the available tools, such as
the ARPA SUR project did with higher-level linguistic constraints, are also
needed to complement cautious efforts on modest advances.

In Part V of this book, the reader will find three views about what to do
in future speech recognition work. Klatt's proposal (Chap. 25) of the LAFS

91

and SCRIBER systems may be seen to be effectively applying the best of what Harpy, IBM work, and other spectral-template matching and acoustic phonetic detectors and mathematical ideas, have given as a legacy to future workers. Doddington (Chap. 26) advocates a cautious engineering approach similar to Neuburg's. He observes that current limitations of speech science knowledge require moderated and well-defined goals, and coordinated teams of researhers giving careful consideration to human perception processes as they design recognizers. Low cost devices are important in Doddington's view of the future. His title, "Whither Speech Recognition?", is identical to that of Pierce's powerful and provocative 1969 letter. My answer (in Chap. 27) to that question is, to me, strikingly different than it was in 1969 (cf. Lea, 1970), and I believe it shows how much progress has come in over a decade of interdisciplinary work. I remain inclined toward linguistic approaches to the largest problems in speech understanding, but acknowledge the rapid progress and accuracies available in mathematical techniques. There is room in the growing future of speech recognition technology for a variety of techniques, and a spectrum of tasks ranging from challenging to cautiously practical.

The next ten years or more would seem to offer a growing spectum of available devices, ranging from very low cost isolated word recognizers, through digit string recognizers, recognizers of strictly formatted word sequences, task-restricted speech understanding systems, and more powerful research systems for continuous speech recognition. All such systems will take advantage of low-cost microminiturized hardware that puts speech recognition within the reach of most potential users. A matured speech recognition technology will permit voice access to machines over the telephone and other communication channels. User acceptance of voice input will approach the "matter-of-fact" attitudes now prevalent with limited keyboard entry, even through full versatility and "habitabilty" of input languages will not have been attained to any major degree. I would expect substantial advances in the knowledge of acoustic phonetic characteristics of spoken sentences, prosodic correlates of linguistic structures, coarticulation and phonological rules, speaker variabilities and normalization procedures, and more-readily applicable models of syntax, semantics, discourse effects, and task constraints. Major strides will be made in comprehending what makes one recognition task more complex than another, and such knowledge will speed decisions about the best of competing techniques for each recognition task. An advanced performance evaluation technology will yield far better understanding of the strengths and weaknesses of each system. Advanced, readily modifiable system structures will offer some forms of ready adaptation to new tasks. Despite all these advances, we will be far from the science fiction image of fully versatile voice interaction with machines, and I doubt that unrestricted "phonetic typewriters" are a part of the next decade or more of practical work on speech recognition.

Funding of these advances, and of the many recommendations contained in all the chapters of this book, will not occur spontaneously. Careful program plans must be developed and coordinated to stimulate interdisciplinary progress on all the recommended topic areas for further work. Researchers and system developers would be ill-advised to depend solely on any government agency (or agencies) to provide complete and consistent support of the needed work. Other options, like industrial funding of development projects, and non-profit foundations supporting needed research, must be pursued.

Social issues will arise from machines that can automatically analyze our conversations. Experts have apprehensions about errorful attempts at voice control of gunfire in the military, and machine surveillance of conversations on large communication system, which might be used in intelligence activities to detect important conversations and invade privacy. Also, in banking by voice, or seeking authorization of credit card transactions, or in almost any other voice input of data, fraud and occasional errors will arise, and procedures will have to be developed to safeguard all those involved in such voice transactions. Issues like these are similar to others involving speech and machines, such as the adequacy of "voiceprint" analysis in criminal cases, the inaccuracies and personal infringements involved in use of "voice lie detectors", plus the standards for police tape recordings and wiretaps, etc. The Academy for Forensic Applications of Communication Sciences (AFACS) is concerned with such social, law-enforcement, and legal implications of speech communications devices (cf. Lea, TO APPEAR). With the growing interest in and use of speech recognizers, care will have to be taken to insure personal rights, reasonable industrial standards, and appropriate legal procedures in this new aspect of the impact of automation.

The long term goal of future work is to make speech input to computers a routine cost-effective channel that is reliable and truly helpful to the user. Speech recognition work does promise to be a fascinating and productive thrust in the future of computer technology.

6. REFERENCES

Bahl, L.R., J.K. Baker, P.S. Cohen, A.G. Cole, F. Jelinek, B.L. Lewis, and R.L. Mercer (1978), Automatic Recognition of Continuously Spoken Sentences from a Finite State Grammar, Proceedings of the 1978 IEEE International Conference on Acoustics, Speech, and Signal Processing, Tulsa, OK, April 1978, 418-421. Also, Recognition of a Continuously Read Natural Corpus, 422-424.

Baker, J. K. (1975), The Dragon System - An Overview, IEEE Transactions on Acoustics, Speech, and Signal Processing, vol. ASSP-23, 24-29.

Bakis, R. (1976), Continuous Speech Recognition via Centisecond Acoustic States, Journal of the Acoustical Society of America, Vol. 59, Supplement Number 1, 597(A).

Baudrey, M. and B. Dupeyrat (1978), Utilisation de Methodes Syntaxiques et de Filtrage Logique en Reconnaissance de la Parole, Congres AFCET/IRIA, Reconnaissance des Formes et Traitement des Images, Paris, February 21-23, 1978.

Beek, B., E.P. Neuberg, and D.C. Hodge (1977), An Assessment of the Technology of Automatic Speech Recognition for Military Applications, IEEE Transactions Acoustics, Speech and Signal Processing, ASSP-25, Number 4, 310-322.

Bloomfield, L. (1973), Language. New York; Holt.

Bobrow, D.G. and D.H. Klatt (1968), A Limited Speech Recognition System, in Proceedings of the AFIPS Fall Joint Computer Conference, Vol. 33, Washington D.C.: Thompson Book Co., 305-318.

Breaux, R. (1978), Laboratory Demonstration Computer Speech Recognition in Training, Proceedings of the Workshop on Voice Technology for Interactive Real-Time Command/Control System Application, (R. Breaux, M. Curran, and E.M. Huff, Editors), NASA Ames Research Center, Moffett Field, CA, December 6-8, 1977.

Breaux, R., P.M. Curran, and E.M. Huff (1978), Proceedings of the Workshop on Voice Technology for Interactive Real-Time Command/Control Systems Application, NASA Ames Research Center, Moffett Field, CA, December 4-6, 1977; revised for distribution, April, 1978.

Chomsky, N. (1957), Syntactic Structures. The Hague; Mouton.

Chomsky, N. and M. Halle (1968), The Sound Pattern of English. New York: Harper and Row.

Chomsky, N. and G.A. Miller (1963), Introduction to the Formal Analysis of Natural Languages, in Handbook of Mathematical Psychology, (Ed. R.D. Luce,

R.R. Bush, and E. Galanter). New York: John Wiley and Sons, Inc. 269-321.

Coler, C.R. E.M. Huff, R.P. Plummer, and M.H. Hitchcock (1978), Automatic Speech Recognition Research at NASA-Ames Research Center, Proceedings of the Workshop on Voice Technology for Interactive Real-Time Command/Control Systems Application (R. Breaux, M. Curran, and E. Huff, Editors), NASA Ames Research Center, Moffett Field, CA, 143-170.

Connolly, D.W. (1978), Voice Data Entry in Air Traffic Control, Proceedings of the Workshop on Voice Technology for Interactive Real-Time Command/ Control Systems Application (R. Breaux, M. Curran, and E. Huff, Editors). NASA Ames Research Center, Moffett Field, CA, 171-196.

Curran, M. (1978), Voice Integrated Systems, Proceedings of the Workshop on Voice Technology for Interactive Real-Time Command/Control Systems Application (R. Breaux, M. Curran, and E. Huff, Editors, NASA Ames Research Center, Moffett Field, CA, 123-137.

Davis, K.H., R. Biddulph, and J. Balashek (1952), Automatic Recognition of Spoken Digits, Journal of the Acoustical Society of America, Vol. 24, 637-645.

De Mori, R., S. Rivoira, and A. Serra (1975), A Speech Understanding System with Learning Capability, in Proceedings of the 4th International Joint Conference Artificial Intelligence, Tbilisi, USSR.

Denes, P.B. (1960), Automatic Speech Recognition: Experiments with a Recognizer Using Linguistic Statistics, U.S. Air Force Contract No. AF 61 (514)-1176, Technical Note No. 4.

Denes, P. and M.V. Mathews, Spoken Digit Recognition Using Time-Frequency Patterns Matching, Journal of the Acoustical Society of America, Vol. 32, 1450-1455.

Dersch, W.C. (1962), Shoebox -A Voice Responsive Machine, Datamation, Vol. 8, 47-50.

Dixon, N.R. and C.C. Tappert (1973), Intermediate Performance Evaluation of a Multi-Stage System for Automatic Recognition of Continuous Speech, Final IBM Report, RADC-TR-73-16 to Rome Air Development Center, Griffiss AFB, NY.

Doddington, G.R. (1976), Personal Identity Verification Using Voice, presented at ELECTRO 76, Boston, MA.

Doddington, G.R. (1978), Speech Systems Research at Texas Instruments, Proceedings of the Workshop on Voice Technology for Interactive Real-Time Command/Control Systems Application, NASA Ames Research Center, Moffet Field, CA, December 6-8, 1977.

Dreyfus-Graf, J. (1949), Sonograph and Sound Mechanics, Journal of the Acoustical Society of America, Vol. 22, 731-739.

Dudley, H., and S. Balashek (1958), Automatic Recognition of Phonetic Patterns in Speech, Journal of the Acoustical Society of America, Vol. 30, 721-739.

Enea, H., and J. Reykjalin (1978), Low Cost Speech Recognition for the Personal Computer Market, Proceedings of the Workshop on Voice Technology for Interactive Real-Time Command/Control Systems Application (R. Breaux, M. Curran, and E. Huff, Editors), NASA Ames Research Center, Moffett Field, CA, 285-288.

Fejfar, A. (1977), Test Results: Advanced Development Models of BISS Identity Verification Equipment (Vol. 1, Executive Summary), MITRE Technical Report MTR-3442, The MITRE Corporation, Bedford, MA.

Flanagan, J.L. (1972), Speech Analysis, Synthesis, and Perception. New York: Springer.

Forgie, J.W. and C.D. Forgie (1959), Results Obtained from a Vowel Recognition Computer Program, Journal of the Acoustical Society of America, Vol. 31, 1480-1489.

Forgie, J.W. and C.D. Forgie (1962), Automatic Method of Plosive Identification, Journal of the Acoustical Society of America, Vol. 34, 1979 (A).

Fry, D.B. and P.B. Denes (1953), Mechanical Speech Recognition, in Communication Theory (E.C. Cherry, Ed.), 426-432. London: Butterworths.

Fry, D.B. and P.B. Denes (1958), The Solution of Some Fundamental Problems in Mechanical Speech Recognition, Language and Speech, Vol. 1, 35-38.

Fu, K.S. (1974), Syntactic Methods in Pattern Recognition. New York: Academic Press.

Gold, B. (1966), Word-Recognition Computer Program, Technical Report 452, Research Laboratory of Electronics, M.I.T., Cambridge, MA.

Goodman, G. (1976), Analysis of Languages for Man-Machine Voice Communication, Technical Report CMUCSD, Ph.D. Dissertation (through Stanford University), Computer Science Department, Carnegie-Mellon University, Pittsburgh, PA.

Goodman, G., D. Scelza, and B. Beek (1977), An Application of Connected Speech to the Cartography Task, Proceedings of the 1977 IEEE International Conference on Acoustics, Speech, and Signal Processing, Hartford, CT, 811-814.

Grady, M.W., M.B. Hicklin, and J.E. Porter (1978), Practical Applications of Interactive Voice Technologies--Some Accomplishments and Prospects, Proceedings of the Workshop on Voice Technology for Interactive Real-Time Command/Control Systems Application (R. Breaux, M. Curran, and E. Huff, Editors), NASA Ames Research Center, Moffett Field, CA, 217-233.

Halle, M. (1954), The Strategy of Phonemics, Word, Vol. 10, 197-209.

Hemdal, J.F. and G.W. Hughes (1-67), A feature Based Computer Recognition Program for the Modeling of Vowel Perception, in Models for the Perception of Speech and Visual Form, W. Wathen-Dunn, Ed. Cambridge, MA: M.I.T. Press.

Hill, D.R. (1969), An ESOTerIc Approach to Some Problems in Automatic Speech Recognition, International Journal of Man-Machine Studies, Vol. 1, 101.

Hill, D.R. (1971), Man-Machine Interaction Using Speech, in Advances in Computers (F.L. Alt, M. Rubinoff, and M.C. Yovits, Editors). New York: Academic Press, Vol. 11, 165-230.

Hughes, G.W. (1961), The Recognition of Speech by Machine, Technical Report 395, Research Laboratory of Electronics, M.I.T., Cambridge, MA.

Hughes, G.W., A.S. House, and K.-P. Li (1969), Research on Word Spotting, Final Report AFCRL-69-0240, on contract F19628-67-C-0276 for AFCRL, Bedford, MA.

Hughes, G.W., K.-P. Li, and T.B Snow (1972), An Approach to Research on Word Spotting in Continuous Speech, Proceedings of the 1972 Conference on Speech Communication and Processing, IEEE Catolog No. 72 CHO 596-7AE, Newton, MA, 109-112, April, 1972.

Hughes, G.W., A.S. House, and K.-P. Li (1970), Research on Word Spotting, Final Report, Air Force Contract No. F 19628-69-C-0157, AFCRL-72-0014.

Itakura, F. (1975), Minimum Prediction Residual Principle Applied to Speech Recognition, IEEE Transactions on Acoustics Speech, and Signal Processing, Vol. ASSP-23, 67-72.

Jelinek, F. (1976), Continuous Speech Recognition by Statistical Methods, Proceedings of the IEEE, Vol. 64, No. 4, 532-556.

Jelinek, F., R.L. Mercer, L.R. Bahl, and J.K. Baker (1977), Perplexity - Measure of Difficulty of Speech Recognition Tasks, paper presented at 94th Meeting of Acoustical Society of America, Miami Beach, Florida, Dec. 15, 1977.

Kelley, T.P., J.T. Martin, and J.R. Barger (1968), Voice Controller for Astronaut Manuevering Unit, Technical Report AFAL-TR-68-308, Air Force Avionics Laboratory, Wright Patterson Air Force Base, OH.

Lea, W.A. (1966), The 'Spectrum' of Weak Generative Powers of Grammars, Mechanical Translation, Vol. 9, 10-14.

Lea, W.A. (1970), Evaluating Speech Recognition Work, Journal of the Acoustical Society of America, Vol. 47, 1612-1614.

Lea, W.A. (1972), Computer Recognition of Speech, Current Trends in Linguistics, (Vol. 12: Linguistics and Adjacent Arts and Sciences). The Hague: Mouton, 1561-1620.

Lea, W.A. (1973), An Approach to Syntactic Recognition Without Phonemics, IEEE Transactions on Audio and Electroacoustics, AU-21, 249-358.

Lea, W.A. (1975), Isochrony and Disjuncture as Aids to Phonological and Syntactic Analysis, presented at the 89th Meeting of the Acoustical Society of America, Austin, TX, Journal of the Acoustical Society of America, Vol. 57, Supplement 1.

Lea, W.A. (1979), Critical Issues in Airborne Applications of Speech Recognition, Final Task Report, Naval Air Development Center (Code 6041) Contract Number N 62269-78-M-3770, Warminster, PA.

Lea, W.A. (TO APPEAR), A Guide to Issues and Techniques in Forensic Communications, presented at the AFACS Voice Analysis on Trial Symposium, Salt Lake City, Utah. To appear in the book Voice Analysis on Trial (W.A. Lea, Editor).

Lea, W.A., M.F. Medress, and T.E. Skinner (1975), A Prosodically-Guided Speech Understanding Strategy, IEEE Transactions in Acoustics, Speech, and Signal Processing, ASSP-23, 30-38.

Lea, W.A. and J.E. Shoup (1979), Review of the ARPA SUR Project and Survey of Current Technology in Speech Understanding, Final Report on ONR Contract Number N00014-77-C-0570, Speech Communications Research Laboratory report to Office of Naval Research, January, 1979.

Lindgren, N. (1965), Machine Recognition of Human Language, IEEE Spectrum, Vol. 2, March, April, May issues.

Mariani, J.J. and J.S. Lienard (1978), ESOPE Ø: un programme de comprehension automatique de la parole procedant par prediction-verification aux niveaux phonetique, lexical et syntaxique, Congres AFCET/IRIA Reconnaissance des Formes et Traitment des Images, Paris, France.

Martin, T.B. (1976), Practical Applications of Voice Input to Machines, Proceedings of the IEEE, Vol. 64, No. 4, 487-501.

Martin, T.B. (1977), One Way to Talk to Computers, IEEE Spectrum, 35-39.

Martin, T.B., H. Zadell, E. Grunza, and M. Herscher (1969), Numeric Speech Translating Machine, in Automatic Pattern Recognition. Washington, D.C.: National Security Industrial Association, 113-141.

Medress, M. (1969), Computer Recognition of Single-Syllable English Words, Ph.D. dissertation, Department of Electrical Engineering, Massachusetts Institute of Technology, Cambridge, MA.

Medress, M.F. (1972), A Procedure for Machine Recognition of Speech, Conference Record of the 1972 Conference on Speech Communication and Processing. Newton, MA: IEEE Catalog Number AD-742236, 113-116.

Medress, M.F., T.C. Diller, D.R. Kloker, L.L. Lutton, H.N. Oredson, and T.E. Skinner (1978), An Automatic Word Spotting System for Conversational Speech, Proceedings of the 1978 IEEE International Conference on Acoustics, Speech, and Signal Processing, Tulsa, OK, IEEE Catalog No. 77CI1197-3 ASSP, 468-473.

Moshier, S.L., P.N. Leiby, and R.E. Smith (1977), Key Word Classification, Air Force Report Number RADC-TR-77-122, Final Report on Air Force Contract Number F30602-75-C-0171, Rome Air Development Center, Griffiss AFB, NY.

Musmann, H.G., and K.H. Steiner (1965), Phonetische Addiermaschine, Arch. Elek. Ubertragung, Vol. 19, 502-510.

Nagata, K., Y. Kato, and S. Chiba (1964), Spoken Digit Recognizer for the Japanese Language, in Preprints of the Audio Engineering Society Annual Meeting, Preprint 347.

Nakagawa, S.I. (1976), A Machine Understanding System for Spoken Japanese Sentences, Ph.D. Disseration, Department of Information Sciences, Kyoto University, Kyoto, Japan.

Nash-Webber, B. (1975), The Role of Semantics in Automatic Speech Understanding, Representation and Understanding (D.G. Bobrow and A. Collins, Editors).

Newell, A. (1975), A Tutorial on Speech Understanding Systems, Speech Recognition: Invited Papers Presented at the 1974 IEEE Symposium (D.R. Reddy, Editor), New York: Academic Press, 3-54.

Niimi, Y., Y. Kobayashi, T. Asami, and Y. Miki (1975), The Speech Recognition System of 'SPOKEN-BASIC', Proceedings of the 2nd USA-JAPAN Computer Conference, Tokyo, Japan, 375.

Otten, K.W. (1966), Automatic Recognition of Continuous Speech, Technical Report AFAL-TE-66-408, AF Avionics Laboratory, Wright-Patterson AFB, Ohio

Peterson, G.E. (1961), Automatic Speech Recognition Procedures, Language and Speech, Vol. 4, 200-219.

Pierce, J.R. (1961), Symbols, Signals, and Noise. New York: Harper Brothers.

Pike, K.L. (1947), Grammatical Prerequisites to Phonemic Analysis, Word, Vol. 3, 155-72.

Potter, R.K., G.A. Kopp, and H.C. Green (1947), Visible Speech, New York: D. van Nostrand Co.

Rabiner, L.R. and B. Gold (1975), Theory and Application of Digital Signal Processing. Englewood Cliffs, NJ: Prentice-Hall.

Rabiner, L.R. and M.R. Sambur (1976), Some Preliminary Experiments in the Recognition of Connected Digits, IEEE Transactions on Acoustics, Speech and Signal Processing, Vol. ASSP-24, No. 24, 170-182.

Reddy, D.R. (1973), The CMU Speech Understanding Project-Progress Report, October 15, 1973, Department of Computer Science, Carnegie-Mellon University, Pittsburgh, PA.

Reddy, D.R. (1975), Editor, Speech Recognition: Invited Papers of the IEEE Symposium, New York: Academic Press.

Reddy, D.R. (1976), Speech Recognition by Machine: A Review, Proceedings of the IEEE, Vol. 64, 501-531.

Reddy, D.R., et al. (1976), Speech Understanding Systems: Summary of Results of the Five Year Research Effort at Carnegie-Mellon University (2nd version, 1977), Department of Computer Science, Carnegie-Mellon University, Pittsburgh, PA.

Robinson, A.L. (1979), More People are Talking to Computers as Speech Recognition Enters the Real World, Science, Vol. 203, 16 February, 1979, 634-638.

Ross, P.W. (1967), A Limited-Vocabulary Adaptive Speech Recognition System, Journal of the Audio Engineering Society, Vol. 15, 414-418.

Sakai, T. and S. Doshita (1963), The Phonetic Typewriter, Information Processing 1962, Proceedings of IFIP Congress 62, 445-449.

Sambur, M.R. and L.R. Rabiner (1976), A Statistical Decision Approach to the Recognition of Connected Digits, IEEE Transactions on Acoustics, Speech, and Signal Processing, Vol. ASSP-24, No. 6, 550-558.

Sapir, E. (1933), La Réalité Psychologie des Phonèmes, J. Psycho., Vol. 30, 247-265.

Scott, P.B. (1976), Voice Input Code Identifier, Final Technology Report, Air Force Contract F30602-75-C-0111, Report Number RADC-TR-77-190, Rome Air Development Center, Air Force Systems Command, Griffiss AFB, NY.

Sekiguchi, Y. and M. Shigenaga (1978), Speech Recognition System for Japanese Sentences, Journal of the Acoustical Society of Japan, Vol. 34, No. 3, 204-213.

Sondhi, M.M. and S.E. Levinson (1977), Relative Difficulty and Robustness of Speech Recognition Tasks that Use Grammatical Constraints, Journal of the Acoustical Society of America, Vol. 63, Supplement 1, S64(A).

Stevens, K.N. (1969), Study of Acoustic Properties of Speech Sounds II, and Some Remarks on the Use of Acoustic Data in Schemes for Machine Recognition of Speech, Scientific Report No. 12, Contract No. F19628-68-C-0125, Report AFCR L-69-0339 prepared by Bolt Beranek and Newman, Cambridge, MA.

Tappert, C.C., N.R. Dixon, D.H. Bettle, and W.D. Chapman (1968), A Dynamic Segment Approach to the Recognition of Continuous Speech: An Exploratory Program, Technical Report No. RADC-TR-58-177 (prepared by IBM).

Tappert, C.C., N.R. Dixon, A.S. Rabinowitz, and W.D. Chapman (1971), Automatic Recognition of Continuous Speech Utilizing Dynamic Segmentation, Dual Classification, Sequential Decoding, and Error Recovery, Technical Report RADC-TR-71-146 (prepared by IBM).

Teacher, C.F., H.G. Kellett, and L.R. Focht (1967), Experimental Limited Vocabulary Speech Recognizer, IEEE Transactions on Audio and Electroacoustics, Vol. AU-15, 127-130.

Trager, G.L. and H.L. Smith, Jr. (1951) An Outline of English Structure, Studies in Linguistics: Occasional Papers 3, Norman, Oklahoma, Battenburg Press.

Tsuruta, S. (1978), DP-100 Voice Recognition System Achieves High Efficiency, JEE (Japanese Magazine), DEMPA Publications, Japan, July, 1978, 50-54.

Vicens, P.J. (1969), Aspects of Speech Recognition by Computer. Technical Report, Stanford University, AI Memo 85, Stanford, CA, (Ph.d. Dissertation).

Watt, W.C. (1968), Habitability, American Documentation, Vol 19, 338-351.

Wells, R.S. (1947), Immediate Constituents, Language, Vol 23, 81-117.

Wherry, C. (1976), VRAS: Voice Recognition and Synthesis, Naval Air Development Center, Warminster, PA.

White, G.M. and R.B. Neely (1975), Speech Recognition Experiments With Linear Prediction, Bandpass Filtering, and Dynamic Programming, IEEE Transactions Acoustics, Speech, and Signal Processing, Vol. ASSP-24, 183-188.

Wiren, J. and H.L. Stubbs (1956), Electronic Binary Selection System for Phoneme Classification, Journal of the Acoustical Society of America, Vol. 28, 1082-1091.

Wolf, J.J. (1976), Speech Recognition and Understanding, in Pattern Recognition, K.S. Fu, Ed., New York: Springer.

Woods, W.A. (1975), Motivation and Overview of SPEECHLIS: An Experimental Prototype for Speech Understanding Research, IEEE Transactions on Acoustics, Speech, and Signal Processing, ASSP-23, 2-10.

Woods, W.A. et al. (1976), Speech Understanding Systems, BBN Report No. 34-38 (5 Volumes), Final Report on ONR Contract No. N00014-75-C-0533, Bolt, Beranek and Newman, Cambridge, MA.

Yilmaz, H. (1967), A Theory of Speech Perception, Bulletin of Mathematical Biophysics, Vol. 29.

PART II

ASPECTS OF SYSTEM DESIGN
(TUTORIALS)

5

ACOUSTIC PROCESSING AND

PHONETIC ANALYSIS

Victor W. Zue*
Massachusetts Institute of Technology

Richard M. Schwartz
Bolt Beranek and Newman Inc.

5-1 INTRODUCTION

This chapter discusses the issues and approaches related to acoustic processing and phonetic analysis in a speech recognition system. The objective of an acoustic processing and phonetic analysis, or APPA, component is to accept the continuous speech signal (i.e., pressure variations as a function of time recorded from a microphone) as input and produce as output a string of discrete units that are often phonetic in size and nature. These strings are then accessed by other components of the system to perform lexical, syntactic, and semantic analysis in order to decode the utterance.

The performance of the APPA component is critical to the success of a speech recognition system for several reasons. First, APPA is usually the "lowest" component in the system. Results from such a component become the primary input to other parts of the system for additional analysis. The performance of the other components is therefore severely constrained by the performance of the APPA component. There is also the propagation of error effect, whereby mistakes made in earlier stages are more costly than those made later on. In addition, the APPA component is often the only place in the system that actually deals with the input speech at the continuous, acoustic level. With very few exceptions, all other system components treat the speech signal as a string of discrete units (either phonetic segments, syllables, words, or phrases). In performing the continuous-to-discrete transformation, the large scale data reduction is often accompanied by a loss of information. Whatever information the APPA component discards will no longer be available to the rest of the system.

The operation of an APPA component can be conceptualized, at least functionally, as a reversal of the speech production process. In the production of speech, discrete linguistic units are converted into motor commands that set the articulators into motion, eventually producing the acoustic output. Before proceeding further with our discussion of APPA, it

---

* Victor W. Zue is also a consultant at Bolt Beranek and Newman Inc.

is therefore appropriate to provide a brief account of the acoustic theory of speech production, and summarize the linguistic framework on which the following discussion will be based.

5-1.1 The Acoustic Theory of Speech Production

Speech is generated by closely coordinated movements of several groups of human anatomical structures. One such group of structures consists of those that enclose the air passage below the larynx. Through control of the muscles and through forces generated by the elastic recoil of the lungs, pressure can be built up below the larynx. This pressure provides the energy for the generation of sound.

Immediately above the trachea is the larynx, which constitutes the second group of structures essential to the production of speech. The vocal cords in the larynx can be positioned, and their tension adjusted in many ways so that air can flow through the glottis either with or without setting the vocal cords into vibration. When the vocal cords are set into vibration, the airflow through the glottis is interrupted quasi-periodically, thus creating the effect of modulation.

The third set of structures consists of the tongue, jaw, lips, velum, and other components that form the vocal and nasal cavities. By changing the configuration of the vocal tract, one can shape the detailed characteristics of the speech sounds being produced.

It is convenient to describe the acoustics of speech production in terms of three distinct stages. First, through interaction between airflow from the lungs and the laryngeal and supraglottal structures, a source of acoustic energy is created. This acoustic source may be one of several types, and may have several possible positions. The source acts as the excitation for the cavities above and below it. Each cavity has its own resonating characteristics. The filtering that is imposed on the source by the vocal tract cavities is the second stage in the generation of speech sounds. Finally, speech sound is radiated from the lips and/or the nostrils.

If the production of speech sounds can be modeled as a linear system, then the pressure variations recorded at some distance from the lips will have a spectrum that is the product of the source spectrum, the vocal tract transfer function, and the radiation characteristics (Fant, 1960).

Sources. There are two basic types of sound sources in speech production: periodic and turbulence noise. If the vocal cords are vibrating, then the signal generated at the glottis is basically periodic in nature, with a corresponding line spectrum that falls off in the high frequency region at 12 dB/octave. If a constriction is made somewhere in the vocal tract, turbulence noise may be generated at the constriction, with a continuous spectrum that is essentially flat. Depending upon the position of the constriction, the noise source is referred to as frication (supraglottal constrictions) or as aspiration (constriction at the glottis). It should also be noted that it is possible to have two different types of sources simultaneously in the production of speech sounds, such as the /z/ in "buzzer".

Transfer Function of the Vocal Tract. In the production of non-nasalized vowels, the transfer function of the vocal tract can be represented as a product of a number of complex pole-pairs. The frequencies

of the pole-pairs correspond to the resonant frequencies of the vocal tract, and are referred to as the formant frequencies, or simply formants. The spectrum of the transfer function usually shows sharp peaks at the frequency locations of the formants.

The formant frequencies are the resonant frequencies of the vocal tract and bear a direct relationship to the shape of the vocal tract. In the case where a side-branch exists, as in the production of nasals and fricatives, the vocal tract transfer function will have zeros, or anti-resonances, as well as poles. The presence of zeros will introduce minima in the spectrum of the transfer function. The interaction of poles and zeros can often change the frequency and amplitude of the formants.

Radiation Characteristics. The transfer characteristic relating the pressure variation at some distance from the lips to the volume velocity at the lips is a linear function of frequency. The radiation characteristics can thus be modeled as a single zero linear filter. The spectrum increases at 6 dB/octave.

5-1.2 Linguistic Framework and Related Issues

Studies of the way language is organized have produced overwhelming evidence that underlying the production and perception of speech there exists a sequence of basic discrete segments that are concatenated in time. These segments, called "phonemes," are assumed to have unique articulatory and acoustic characteristics. It has been proposed by Jakobson, Fant, and Halle (1963) that the phonemes can be characterized by a set of invariant attributes called distinctive features. The distinctive features bear a direct relationship to the articulatory gesture from which the speech sound is produced, and they have certain well-defined acoustic correlates. Therefore, at the phonemic level, the linguistic structure of an utterance can be represented by a two-dimensional matrix with columns representing the phonemes, rows listing the distinctive features, and the matrix entries indicating the presence or absence of a feature for a given phoneme.

It should be noted that at the phonemic level, the distinctive feature theory necessitates a discrete (or even binary) selection, whereas at the articulatory and acoustic levels, the feature correlates appear to take on a continuum of values.

During the production of speech, the linguistic contents of the feature matrix are transformed into neuromuscular commands that set the articulators (lips, jaw, tongue, etc.) into motion. Although the commands may be discrete, or stepwise, the actual motions of the articulators and the resulting acoustic signals are continuous, due to the interaction among various structures and their different degrees of sluggishness. The result is an overlap of phonemic information from one segment to another. In other words, although the features have well-defined acoustic correlates, there is no one-to-one correspondence between a given feature and its correlates. More precisely, the acoustic manifestation of a given feature appears to depend on the presence or absence of other features. Furthermore, when phonemes are concatenated to form an utterance, the acoustic correlates of the underlying features will undergo modification and distortion as a consequence of the phonetic environments.

As an illustrative example, consider the utterance, "Tom Burton tried to steal a butter plate," shown in Fig. 5-1. Every word, except "a", in this sentence contains a single occurrence of the phoneme /t/. However, depending upon the immediate phonetic environment and stress pattern, the underlying /t/'s are realized either an an aspirated /t/ ("Tom"), an unaspirated /t/ ("steal"), a /t/ with extended aspiration ("tried), an unreleased /t/ ("plate"), a flap ("butter"), or a glottal stop ("Burton"). The acoustic properties of the final realizations can be seen to be quite different.

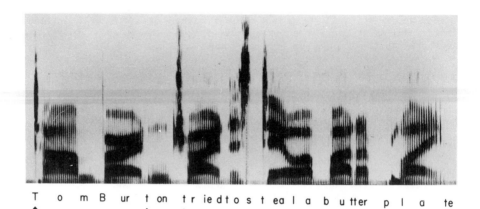

Fig. 5-1. Spectrogram of the utterance, "Tom Burton tried to steal a butter plate." All but one of the words contain an underlying /t/. However, the acoustic realizations of the /t/'s are quite different, depending upon the phonetic context.

The above example serves to illustrate the fact that the acoustic properties of phonetic segments vary considerably with phonetic context. In addition, a speaker can sometimes distort the acoustic properties of speech sounds so severely that even the environment will provide no acoustic cues to the identity of the phoneme. Figure 5-2 provides examples of such acoustic distortion. The schwa in the second syllable of the word "multiply" and the first syllable of the word "display" can be devoiced such that it exhibits no acoustic characteristics commonly associated with vowels. Such distortion is possible because a listener is capable of decoding an utterance not only from the acoustic signal, but also from his familiarity with the syntactic and semantic constraints, and with rules governing the allowable phoneme sequences of his language. In order to decode the intended phonetic sequences, it is, therefore, necessary to invoke various knowledge sources to compensate for the inherent distortions and modifications that will invariably be present in the acoustic signal.

Whereas it is true that the acoustic realizations of phonetic segments are highly context-sensitive, a great deal of the variations, such as the ones illustrated in Figs. 5-1 and 5-2, are, in fact, systematic and can be captured by rules. Although our present knowledge of the inventory of such rules is still incomplete, these rules must somehow be incorporated into the speech recognition system such that words can be recognized from the seemingly ambiguous acoustic signal.

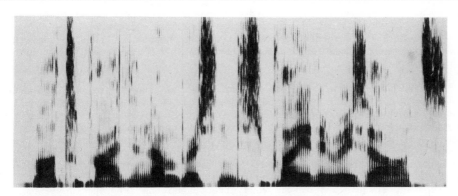

Fig. 5-2. Spectrogram of the utterance, "Multiply the numbers and display the results." The schwa in the second syllable of <u>multiply</u> and the first syllable of <u>display</u> is devoiced, leaving no acoustic characteristics commonly associated with a schwa.

5-1.3 <u>Overview of the Chapter</u>

In Section 5-2 we outline the signal processing techniques often employed in an APPA component. The parameters used for segmentation and labeling, and the algorithms to extract these parameters, will then be discussed. Various approaches to segmentation and labeling will be presented in Section 5-3.

Given the tutorial nature of this chapter and the vastness of the topic, most of the discussion in subsequent sections are necessarily brief and qualitative. We shall, wherever appropriate, indicate sources where detailed and more quantitative information regarding a specific topic may be obtained. The readers are also encouraged to take advantage of several comprehensive review articles that exist in the literature (Reddy, 1976; Klatt, 1978; Schafer and Rabiner,1975; Wolf,1976), as well as other chapters in this volume that deal with specific speech understanding systems.

5-2 SIGNAL PROCESSING AND PARAMETER EXTRACTION

Some of the first questions to be asked when designing an APPA component are: how the speech should be represented; what parameters should be used for phonetic processing; and how these parameters could be extracted reliably. An in-depth treatment of waveform and parametric representations of speech can be found in Schafer and Rabiner (1975).

5-2.1 <u>Time- and Frequency-Domain Representations of the Speech Signal</u>

Due to the increasing availability of digital computers and the advantages of computer environments, such as flexibility, large data storage capability, and accuracy, most researchers in speech recognition nowadays choose digital processing techniques over analog ones as a matter of course. The speech signal is usually sampled and digitized using an analog-to-digital converter, and stored in the computer. The sampling rate used varies from 6 to 20 kHz, and usually 9 to 16 bits are used to represent the speech samples.

Given a digital representation of the speech signal, various parametric representations can then be derived. Certain parameters, such as zero-crossing density and fundamental frequency of voicing (F0), can be derived in the time domain directly from the speech signal. On the other hand, experience has shown that frequency-domain representation of the speech signal often provides greater insights into the relationship between the articulatory and the acoustic realizations of speech. For example, spectral peaks in non-nasalized vowels can quite reliably be correlated with the resonant frequencies of the vocal tract, and the frequency location of the major energy concentration in a plosive release gives good indications about the location of the constriction in the vocal tract. It is, therefore, often desirable to obtain the short time spectrum of the speech signal.

The prevailing technique used in APPA systems to obtain the short-time spectrum of the signal is the linear prediction, or LPC, technique (Itakura and Saito, 1968; Atal and Hanauer, 1971; Markel, 1972; Makhoul and Wolf, 1972). A comprehensive treatment of the theory and application of linear prediction as applied to speech analysis and recognition can be found in Markel and Gray (1976) and Makhoul (1975a; 1975b).

Linear prediction analysis is based on a specific speech production model, namely that speech is produced by an all-pole digital filter that is excited by a periodic impulse train for voiced speech and random noise for unvoiced speech. To the extent that this production model is valid, estimation of the short-time spectrum of speech can be reduced to a problem of determining the coefficients of the all-pole filter, since the filter coefficients uniquely specify the transfer function.

Part of the appeal of linear prediction analysis lies in the fact that, by choosing a minimum mean-squared error criterion, estimation of the filter coefficients reduces to a solution of a set of p linear equations, where p is the order of the all-pole filter. The set of equations has certain mathematical properties that greatly reduce the computational complexity of the algorithm.

There are several advantages in choosing linear prediction over other spectrum analysis procedures. First, linear prediction separates the periodic excitation in voiced speech from the combined effect of the glottal characteristics, the vocal tract transfer function, and radiation characteristics. The harmonic structures in the original short-time spectrum are therefore removed. Secondly, by choosing the order of the predictor to adequately reflect the number of formants within the frequency range, the peaks in the filter transfer function often correspond well with the actual formants. This property greatly reduces the difficulties associated with the estimation of formant trajectories in continuous speech.

In addition, the residual error of linear prediction is valuable as an error metric that lends itself to applications where measured and stored values are to be compared (Itakura, 1975). As we shall see later, a number of parameters have been derived from the linear prediction formulation that are potentially useful in phonetic recognition. Last but not least, the predictor coefficients can be computed quite efficiently due to the mathematical properties of the set of equations. The additional computation required for linear prediction as compared to a straight forward discrete Fourier transform is thus justified in view of the potential pay-offs.

Figure 5-3 compares spectra of a synthetic vowel /a/ obtained by various spectral smoothing techniques: (a) and (b) by windowing (with different window widths) and Fourier transforming the waveform, (c) by cepstral smoothing (Oppenheim and Schafer, 1968), and (d) by linear prediction. In Fig. 5-3(a), the effect of glottal periodicities can be seen as the ripples superimposed on the spectral envelope. These ripples are greatly reduced in Fig. 5-3(b) because of the spectral smearing of the wide frequency window. In Fig. 5-3(c), the effect of the glottal excitation is removed by a homomorphic technique. This effect is also removed in Fig. 5-3(d). However, since the linear prediction analysis is based on a specific speech production model and thus limits the number of spectral peaks, there are no extraneous peaks in Fig. 5-3(d). If we compare the locations of the spectral peaks with the actual values of the five formants, it is clear that, for this example, the spectrum derived from linear prediction provides accurate formant information.

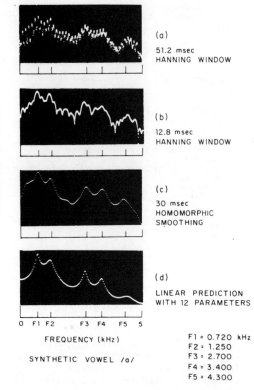

(a)
51.2 msec
HANNING WINDOW

(b)
12.8 msec
HANNING WINDOW

(c)
30 msec
HOMOMORPHIC
SMOOTHING

(d)
LINEAR PREDICTION
WITH 12 PARAMETERS

FREQUENCY (kHz)

SYNTHETIC VOWEL /a/

F1 = 0.720 kHz
F2 = 1.250
F3 = 2.700
F4 = 3.400
F5 = 4.300

Fig. 5-3 Spectra of a synthetic /a/ by various analysis techniques.

It should be noted that not all APPA systems employ linear prediction analysis to obtain the short-time spectrum. Silverman and Dixon (1974), for example, have found that a smoothed discrete Fourier transform spectrum is more desirable than the linear prediction spectrum, in the system that they have developed. In addition, Klatt (1976) has proposed a filter bank representation of the short-time spectrum, taking into account critical bands and psychophysical constraints of the human auditory system.

5-2.2 Parameters for Phonetic Analysis

Our discussion on the acoustic theory of speech production suggests a number of parameters that can be used to characterize different speech sounds. These parameters are in fact utilized by some APPA systems for phonetic processing. In this section, we shall present a representative, but by no means exhaustive, list of such parameters, and comment on their relative merit for phonetic analysis. Some of these parameters have been plotted in Fig. 5-4 to supplement our discussion. For a precise definition of the parameters, see Schwartz and Zue (1976).

107

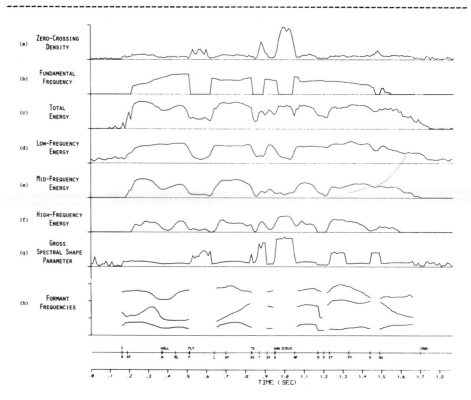

Fig. 5-4. A plot of several parameters for the utterance, "I will fly to San Diego." The parameters are (a) zero-crossing density; (b) fundamental frequency; (c) total energy; (d) low-frequency energy; (e) mid-frequency energy; (f) high-frequency energy; (g) a parameter characterizing the gross spectral shape; and (h) formant frequencies.

Zero-Crossing Density. Early work on speech recognition (Reddy, 1966; Vicens, 1969) relied heavily on the use of zero-crossing density, i.e., the count of zero crossing of the speech signal in a given interval, to perform segmentation. This is partly due to the fact that the algorithm can easily be realized in analog hardware. Although it is difficult to associate zero-crossing density directly with the underlying acoustic and articulatory correlates of speech sounds, this parameter continues to enjoy its popularity, mainly due to its relative ease in implementation. Several recent efforts in phonetic recognition have reported promising results using zero-crossing density, and modifications thereof, as the primary segmentation parameters (Goldberg and Reddy, 1976; Janet Baker, 1975).

Fundamental Frequency of Voicing. During the production of voiced sounds, the vocal cords are set into vibration. The fundamental frequency of voicing (F0), therefore, can be used as a voicing indicator. Although the above justification is theoretically sound, fundamental frequency has not been widely used in segmental analysis for several reasons. In the segmentation of vowels and sonorants, there exist acoustic parameters such as low-frequency energy that are just as robust and much simpler to derive. In the case of English consonants, the voicing distinction lies more in the durational difference than in the presence of F0. /s/ and /z/ differ primarily in the fact that /s/ is usually longer than /z/, and the difference between /t/ and /d/ appears mostly as a difference in voice onset time. In addition, voiced consonants tend to be devoiced in many environments, thus making the voicing decision of secondary importance. Most of the APPA systems tend to extract F0 as a matter of course, but rarely utilize this parameter significantly for segmentation or labeling.

It is well known that fundamental frequency contours also carry prosodic information, such as stress and intonation. Rise and fall in the fundamental frequency contour can also be used as a potential cue to mark major syntactic boundaries (Lea et al., 1975). However, most APPA systems developed thus far have not advanced to the stage that such ideas are fully implemented and tested.

There exist a number of pitch extraction algorithms in the literature. The paper by Rabiner et al. (1976) presents a comprehensive review and evaluation of both the time and frequency domain pitch extraction algorithms. In addition, several other pitch detectors (Gillman, 1975; Seneff, 1978) that are more robust in the presence of noise have since appeared in the literature.

Energy Related Parameters. One of the most important characteristics of the speech signal is the fact that the intensity varies as a function of time. Sharp intensity changes in different frequency regions often signify the boundaries between speech sounds. For example, low overall intensity usually signifies either a pause, a stop closure, or a weak fricative, whereas a drop in mid-frequency intensity in a vocalic segment usually indicates the presence of an intervocalic consonant.

Almost all APPA systems have several energy related parameters. These parameters are obtained either directly by digital or analog filtering of the waveform, or indirectly from the short-time spectrum.

Gross Spectral Shape Parameters. Some of the acoustic characteristics of speech events, such as the production of fricatives and the onset of plosive releases, are best characterized in terms of the gross spectral shape, as opposed to the frequency locations of the spectral peaks. Various parameters have been developed to capture the gross spectral shapes. Some have chosen to represent the spectrum with a low-order linear prediction analysis (Makhoul and Wolf, 1973; Molho, 1976), while others have attempted to characterize the spectrum by moment-related measures (Weinstein et al., 1975; Schwartz and Zue, 1976).

Formant Frequencies and Trajectories. It is well known that the first three formants for vowels and sonorants carry important information about the articulatory configuration in the production of speech sounds. Steady-state values of formant frequencies can be used to classify vowels and sonorants. In addition, formant trajectories can be used to classify diphthongs. Formant transitions in adjacent vowels can be used to determine the place of articulation of consonants.

Estimation of formant frequencies in the past has been a difficult and time-consuming problem. Since the introduction of linear prediction analysis, however, the problem of formant trajectory estimation has been greatly reduced. Various algorithms, from simple peak-picking (Markel, 1972) to complicated algorithms involving segmentation, anchor points, and spectral enhancement (McCandless, 1974), using linear prediction spectra, have been developed. A detailed comparison of various formant tracking algorithms can be found in Markel and Gray (1976).

<u>Other Novel Parameters</u>. A number of other parameters have been proposed for phonetic recognition. In the Harpy system (Lowerre, 1976), phonetic segments are characterized by the set of linear prediction coefficients with surprisingly good success. Other parameters derived from the linear prediction analysis (Kasuya and Wakita, 1976; Makhoul and Wolf, 1973) show promise, but require extensive testing before their validity can be assessed.

5-3 SEGMENTATION AND LABELING

The parameters for phonetic segmentation are usually computed at a fixed rate that ranges from 50 to 200 times per second. Once the parametric representation of the speech signal has been obtained, the next step in an APPA component is to segment the speech into larger units. These units are either linguistically motivated such that they correspond roughly to phonetic segments (Weinstein et al., 1975; Goldberg and Reddy, 1976; Schwartz and Zue, 1976; Medress, et al., 1977; Dixon, 1977), or they are defined strictly on the basis of acoustic homogeneity (Lowerre, 1976). It should be noted that not all APPA components perform segmentation and labeling (e.g. James Baker, 1975). The BBN word verifier (Cook, 1976), for example, compares templates that have been synthesized by rules directly with the speech spectra using dynamic programming techniques.

There are several advantages to segmenting the input. Since acoustically homogeneous regions are usually due to a single phoneme, they should logically be treated as a single unit, rather than as several unrelated frames of data that happen to be adjacent. Segmentation is also desirable from a computational point of view, since the speech signal undergoes yet another stage of data reduction. In addition, segmentation reduces the number of patterns to be compared, thus simplifying both the task of identifying these sounds and the lexical representation of the words.

Segmentation is often followed by a stage where the segments are identified and assigned a label that is consistent with the internal representation of the lexicon. The number of these units varies from system to system, but such units are usually phonetic in nature.

Although labeling usually follows segmentation, the distinction between these two stages is not always clear. In the process of segmentation, broad phonetic labels, such as silence, voiceless consonant, vowel, or sonorant are often assigned to the resulting unit. These labels are later modified and refined by the labeling program. Sometimes it is even possible to assign a rather specific label in the segmentation program. For example, a vowel that is less than 30 msec in duration can only be a schwa, and an intervocalic consonant with a duration of less than, say, 25 msec can only be an alveolar flap (as in "bu<u>tt</u>er"). On the other hand, sequences of labels that are not consistent with English phonology and phonotactics may lead to the insertion and/or deletion of segments. For example, it is not possible to start an English sentence with two stop consonants in a row. The detection of such a sequence will indicate that a segmentation error has been made.

Accurate segmentation and labeling of the speech signal is an extremely complicated and difficult task. It involves the proper representation of our knowledge of English phonology, acoustic-phonetics, and articulatory phonetics. Since our understanding in these areas is still incomplete, it is not surprising that a good phonetic recognizer has not yet been developed.

In the following subsections we shall first outline some of the issues concerning segmentation and labeling and then discuss some of the acoustic features that are potentially useful for segmentation and labeling in the present speech recognition systems.

5-3.1 Use of Context

We have stated earlier that the acoustic realizations of phonetic segments are highly dependent on the environment, and that this dependence should be incorporated in any speech recognition system. For most systems, the contextual knowledge is incorporated into the APPA component in a bottom-up fashion, in that measurements and decisions in earlier phases guide the program in subsequent phases. This, however, is not the only alternative. If contextual information can be represented directly in the lexicon, segmentation and labeling can be accomplished with very little attention to context.

5-3.1.1 Context-Independent Methods

In context-independent methods of segmentation, boundaries are hypothesized whenever the changes in parameter values exceed certain thresholds. Typical parameters used are: energy-related parameters, parameters measuring spectral change, such as the spectral derivative or accumulated spectral change (Lowerre, 1976), and zero crossing density. The main advantages of these context-independent methods is that they can be well defined, and are very simple to implement. The thresholds can be adjusted for the desired balance between missed and extra boundaries.

The most common form of context-independent labeling is "template matching". Template matching generally requires that a different pattern be stored for each possible dictionary entry (e.g., for each phoneme). A single phoneme might be represented as a sequence or even a network of required templates (See Chapter 25 in this volume). These templates may have been extracted from a single prototypical token from one speaker, or may be an average of several tokens from one or many speakers. They might even have been synthesized automatically from a set of rules describing how the phoneme should be realized (Klatt, 1975b; Cook, 1976). Then, for an unknown segment of speech, the same parametric model is extracted and compared with each of the stored templates. The choice of metric used to compare the unknown sample with the templates is critical and depends on the particular parametric representation used.

The template matching procedure is appealing because the templates can be determined automatically by examining a large amount of training data. Since the training is automated, as much detail as desired can be included as long as the measurements are well specified. However the inclusion of too much detail can also result in the templates being highly speaker dependent. Those systems that use templates derived from high order LPC spectra or DFT spectra experience severe degradation when used for a speaker other than the one from whom the templates were derived.

5-3.1.2 <u>Context-Dependent</u> <u>Methods</u> Rather than use the same features to detect all types of boundaries, context-dependent segmentation allows the set of features and the thresholds used to be dependent upon the apparent phonetic context. For example, if previous measurements indicate that a particular time region consists of sonorant sounds, boundaries within that region might best be detected by examining formant frequency trajectories and looking for small dips in wide-band energy parameters. If, on the other hand, the region contains all obstruent phonemes, a segmentation program would have to use more robust features of the high-frequency band and different thresholds. Instead of simply applying a threshold to a set of acoustic parameters, the segmentation is performed by a set of heuristic procedures or rules that operate on the results of previous rules.

Some acoustic parameters often go through peak-to-valley excursions, or dips. The detection of these dips can thus be used to signify potential acoustic segments. Several APPA systems have been developed (Weinstein, et al., 1975; Schwartz and Zue, 1976) in which dip detection routines were used extensively in the preliminary segmentation process. Dip detection routines are often desirable since they can concentrate on significant global changes in a parameter without relying on particular parameter values. Figure 5-5 shows the smoothed low-frequency energy parameter for the sentence, "I will fly to San Diego." The vertical lines indicate boundaries found by a dip detection algorithm. Although the parameter takes on a wide range of values, broad regions are easily distinguished. Comparison of these boundaries with the manual transcription shown below indicates that by applying a dip detector routine to the low-frequency energy parameter, we can separate sonorant phonemes from obstruent phonemes quite reliably. Experience has shown that dip detection on other parameters can supply additional segmentation information.

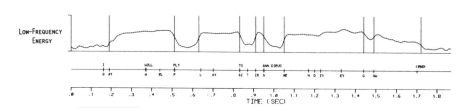

Fig. 5-5. Time plot of a smoothed low frequency energy parameter for the sentence, "I will fly to San Diego." Manually derived phoneme boundaries are shown on the bottom line. Boundaries derived by a dip detection algorithm are indicated by vertical lines superimposed on the parameter plot.

If the segmentation program uses the context and knowledge of the phonotactic constraints of the language, many segmentation errors can be eliminated. For example, a nasal can only occur adjacent to a vowel. An isolated nasal can thus be rejected based on this knowledge, despite robust acoustic evidence.

The hierarchical approach discussed above is often more esthetically pleasing to linguists and phoneticians because it is more likely to represent knowledge about the acoustic correlates of speech in a familiar way. Because it uses more detailed knowledge of the nature of the speech signal, it has the potential for performing better than context-independent methods.

112

Context-dependent labeling methods generally involve acoustic-phonetic feature extraction. Using explicit knowledge of the acoustic nature of different phonemes, the program extracts acoustic features, which are then used in heuristic algorithms or by statistical techniques to determine a phonetic or phonemic label.

There are several advantages in using feature extraction as an approach to labeling. It is well known that different speech sounds are characterized by different acoustic features. Fricatives, for example, are characterized by the presence of turbulence noise. The place of articulation of the fricatives can often be described by the gross shape of the short-time spectrum. Vowels, on the other hand, are usually characterized by the frequency values of the lowest three formants. If the proper set of features is selected and extracted, it is not unreasonable to argue that the APPA component will be able to distinguish the speech sounds better than if the speech is represented by some uniform and arbitrary measure, such as the LPC coefficients or the DFT spectra. In addition, by choosing features that characterize the phonemes, the influence of the recording environment and speaker-specific acoustic cues can often be minimized.

However, feature extraction is easier said than done. Our present understanding of the acoustic correlates of speech sounds is quite incomplete, and what little we know has been derived mostly from controlled studies in which the corpus usually consisted of a small number of tokens of nonsense utterances or words in citation form. While the general tendencies described in these studies hold true in continuous speech, the quantitative information is generally not applicable to the problem of continuous speech recognition. The variability of acoustic characteristics is considerably greater in continuous speech due to the wider range of context and the more relaxed pronunciations. For example, the vowels in continuous speech tend to be more centralized than the ones reported earlier by Peterson and Barney (1952). Determining vowel identity based on the Peterson and Barney data will invariably lead to error.

The problem is really two-fold. On one hand, we are faced with large gaps in our acoustic-phonetic knowledge which can only be filled by many man-years of basic research. The various acoustic realizations of the phoneme /t/ in Fig. 5-1, for example, must be examined and documented quantitatively. On the other hand, it is often necessary to repeat some of the earlier experiments just to get results that are applicable to the continuous speech environment. For instance, vowel formant data must be collected from continuous speech. A number of studies reported over the past few years (for example, Kameny, 1975; Zue, 1976) that deal with the acoustic properties of speech sounds have been motivated, at least in part, by research in speech recognition.

A related problem in using context-dependent strategies for segmentation and labeling is that a large body of data must be examined in order to include all possible phonetic contexts and to derive statistically meaningful decision strategies. For example, the duration of the phoneme /s/ varies considerably depending on context (Klatt, 1974). In continuous speech, however, it is also possible for two /s/'s to occur in sequence, as in "bus stop". Given an /s/-like segment of sufficient duration, it is difficult to decide whether the segment is a lengthened /s/ or a geminate /s/. Only through the examination of a large corpus of data can statistically significant thresholds be determined to distinguish the possibilities.

In order to alleviate this problem, facilities have been developed (e.g. Schwartz, 1976) that enable speech researchers to examine a large body of data, in order to derive thresholds and test algorithms. The availability of such a facility has been of great use in the development of segmentation and labeling algorithms (Woods, et al., 1976).

5-3.1.3 Hybrid Approaches The APPA components used by IBM (Dixon and Silverman, 1976) can be thought of as a hybrid in that the analysis frames are initially classified by speaker dependent templates, but are then grouped together and labeled using a multiple pass, context-dependent strategy. Excellent results have been reported for one speaker. The results for other speakers are not as good. Thus even though the system is tuned to each speaker, the methods used perform much better on one of the speakers than on others.

5-3.2 Dealing with Errors in Segmentation

A segmentation error is said to have occurred when more than one segment have been grouped into one, or a given segment is split by the program into more than one segment. It is difficult to define segmentation errors precisely because it depends on the choice of the correct segmentation to which the results are compared. If the results of the segmentation program are to be compared with the "ideal" transcription of a trained phonetician, any inconsistency between the two would be counted as an error. This criterion is troublesome for several reasons. A phonetician transcribing an utterance has, in addition to the acoustic signal, many other sources of knowledge that he routinely, and often subconsciously, applies to decide what was said. For example, he is likely to transcribe the /s/-like sound in "bus stop" as two segments because of his knowledge of the language. Therefore, an assessment of error based on a comparison with the "ideal" transcription will likely be questionable. In addition, one must not lose sight of the objective of a speech recognition system. The task at hand is to recognize or understand an utterance, and not to agree with the transcription of a phonetician. A more appropriate criterion might be to compare the results of segmentation with the way the lexicon is represented. If the lexical representation agrees with the segmentation results, the segmentation can be considered error-free, regardless of what the "ideal" representation might be.

Error-free segmentation is a difficult, if not impossible, goal to achieve for several reasons. First, the reliability of segmental boundaries in continuous speech is not at all uniform. While the boundary between /p/ and /yu/, as in the word "compute", is often clearly marked in several acoustic parameters, the boundary between the schwa and the /m/ in the same word will often be much less obvious. For this particular example, it is likely that one would not rely on the presence of precise boundaries to detect the /m/. The presence of nasalization in the schwa and the fact that the following consonant is a labial stop is probably sufficient to suggest an /m/. Secondly, we have not yet determined how to represent our acoustic-phonetic knowledge. While visual detection of nasalization from a spectrogram is often possible, no reliable automatic methods have yet been developed to duplicate such ability. Thirdly, the acoustic parameters of phonetic segments often have distributions that span a wide range. Going back to our earlier example of the /s/-like segment, the detection of a long fricative segment could indicate either a lengthened, single /s/, or a geminate of two /s/'s. Such ambiguities can only be resolved later on with the help of additional sources of knowledge.

One way to incorporate a confidence measure into the segmentation boundaries and to reduce segmentation errors is the "segment lattice" concept adopted in the BBN system (Woods, et al., 1976). Rather than forcing the lexical matching component to handle all missing or extra boundaries, the APPA component can supply as much supporting information as possible. For example, in those cases where the decision of whether to segment a region of speech into two cannot be made reliably, an APPA can hypothesize each decision, and supply the higher components with all the necessary information for each hypothesis. If possible, the APPA component should also supply a relative figure of merit (or score) for each option. However, care must be taken such that the problem of segmentation errors is not replaced by a problem of vagueness.

Segmentation errors are usually dealt with in the lexical matching component where the discrete units derived from the acoustic signal are matched against the entries of the lexicon to propose words and phrases. Segmentation errors that are systematic and predictable can often be dealt with by allowing lexical representations to have extra and/or missing segments. The missing nasal in the "compute" example given previously can fall into this category. For some other errors, the lexical matcher has to adjust the score of the particular match to account for the fact that a possible error has occurred. The algorithms for score adjustment depend on the phonetic nature of the segment and the type of error involved.

The balance between extra and missing segments is an adjustable variable in the design of an APPA component. A segmentation program can often be biased to favor one type of error over the other. The Harpy system, for example, set the threshold on the accumulated spectral change parameter so that extra boundaries are inserted liberally. The lexical matching component then severely penalizes word hypotheses that involve missing boundaries, while allowing several segments in the result to match a single lexical unit. In such a system, a missing boundary is often a fatal error in that the system will have little hope of recovery.

5-3.3 Scoring

There are several reasonable techniques for an APPA component to assign scores to the labels on the different segments. The simplest method is to adopt a binary score by setting a threshold on the value of the acoustic features. An example of such a technique might be to label the vowels by dividing the formant space into non-overlapping regions. Selecting the most likely phoneme based on a set of thresholds leads to errors since the distributions of features for different phonemes often overlap. Thus it is impossible to make a threshold lax enough to accept all of the occurrences of a phoneme, without falsely accepting a large number of occurrences of other phonemes.

A slightly more sophisticated approach is to use a weighted distance measure from an unknown segment to the expected targets of each of several likely phonemes. These distances can be used to determine the most likely candidates. However, even this alternative puts the burden onto the lexical matcher to decide the relative merit of the phonemes accepted. In fact, as long as distances are being computed, an APPA component might as well supply the distances measured for every possible phoneme, so that the lexical matcher has all the information it needs.

The lexical matcher must combine sequences of phoneme hypotheses to form words by deriving a total word score from the individual scores.

115

However, adding distances will not result in meaningful scores, since distance metrics vary from phoneme to phoneme. If, on the other hand, each of the scores were independent probabilities, they could be multiplied together to arrive at the joint probability density of all the acoustic measurements, given the presence of a word. In practice, the logarithms of the likelihood ratios are used in order that the scores can be added rather than multiplied. It should be noted that, while the assumption of statistical independence is only an approximation, it is generally adopted in order to make the computations and data gathering tractable. (See Chapter 14 in this volume.)

The only remaining issue is how to compute these probabilities. A simple method is to construct a long term confusion matrix indicating the labels chosen by the APPA component for each of the dictionary phonemes. A more accurate and difficult scheme is to compute the actual likelihood ratio based on the probability density of measured acoustic features. The BBN system used a mixture of the last two approaches. The IBM system (Bahl, et al., 1976) gathered a probabilistic network model of the output of the APPA component given a particular phoneme. This model was allowed to vary when embedded in different words. While this last approach requires large amounts of training data, the probabilistic network models can be derived automatically, resulting in good performance. Using automatic data gathering programs and large data bases, these methods are all relatively straightforward to implement.

Another important feature of probabilistic scoring methods is that they usually use information about expected variability of particular features for a particular phoneme. Other scoring schemes use the same unnormalized distance metric in all circumstances (see, for example, Lowerre, 1976). Such schemes can presumably be improved by the use of probabilistic scores.

It is often the case that errors in the hypothesis of the identity of the adjacent segment will lead to further errors. In those cases where hypotheses are likely to be incorrect it would be advantageous to consider all possible relevant contexts, and compute different results for each postulated context. For example, one way to distinguish between the unvoiced plosives /p,t,k/ is to examine the burst frequency when the plosive is followed by a vowel. However, if the unvoiced plosive is followed by a sonorant, the burst frequency is modified considerably. Since part of the sonorant is often devoiced, it is difficult to determine whether the plosive is followed by a vowel or by a sonorant-vowel sequence. We can, however, consider two allophones of each plosive; one followed by vowels, the other followed by sonorants. Then these can each be evaluated separately under their own assumptions of context. The lexical matcher will always look at the results for the allophone that is appropriate for the particular word.

In the template matching approach this problem is best dealt with by defining a network of templates where several different templates may be used for a single phoneme depending on the phonetic context. Since the measurements made are independent of context, many templates are needed for each phoneme. A single vowel may have a wide range of expected spectral sequences depending on the particular phonemes on either side. These different sequences have similarities and differences that are predictable from knowledge of the acoustic-phonetic effects of different contexts. However, such knowledge must be expressed as a different set of templates for each possible context. This results in a large number of templates, requiring a large amount of training for a new speaker.

5-3.4 <u>Normalization</u>

The acoustic parameters used for segmentation vary as a function of several extra-linguistic factors such as speaker-identity, speaking rate, and the recording environment. It is desirable to normalize the parameters such that the influences due to the above factors are minimized.

The speech signal recorded from a microphone depends on the placement of the microphone, the characteristics of the microphone, the room acoustics, and the characteristics of the ambient noise. For a discussion of some of the attempted normalization schemes, see Reddy (1976).

Further amplitude normalization of the speech signal is achieved either by analog automatic gain control circuits or by digital means in which the speech samples are normalized by a factor determined from the peak- or averaged-amplitude of the signal.

Any measurement of duration clearly depends heavily on the speaking rate. Although many measures of speaking rate have been proposed, the procedures for normalization of acoustic parameters have not been incorporated into most speech recognition systems. Instead, most systems require that the speaker speak at a moderate rate that is comparable to that of other speakers.

Of all the extra-linguistic factors being considered, speaker normalization has probably been attempted the most by speech researchers. Some systems (Silverman and Dixon, 1974) subtract the average long-term spectrum from the speech spectra to normalize for the effects of speaker and environment. Others choose to perform speaker normalization by scaling the speech spectrum by a linear factor that reflects the difference in vocal tract dimensions (Schwartz, 1971; Wakita and Kasuya, 1977). Although it has been shown that such a linear scaling will not fully account for the differences between males and females (Fant, 1966), such procedures are nevertheless used as a simple first order approximation.

Many systems avoid the issues of speaker normalization by retraining the entire acoustic front end for each new speaker. The IBM system redefines both the spectral templates, and the probabilistic lexical network for each speaker. The Harpy system keeps the lexicon the same, but adjusts the spectral templates according to those extracted from previously known or recognized and verified sentences of a new speaker. While these speaker normalization techniques can give very good performance, they require a separate, and often tedious training session. This may be quite reasonable for some systems, but other systems may need to do the best possible with normalization parameters extracted from the very sentences being recognized. Intermediate means include systems that extract a small number of normalization parameters from one or two standard sentences which were carefully designed for that purpose (Weinstein et al., 1975).

5-3.5 <u>Acoustic Features for Segmentation and Labeling</u>

Having discussed some of the issues, we shall now turn to the specific acoustic features that are useful for segmentation and labeling.

5-3.5.1 <u>Vowels</u> Vowels can be detected by the presence of substantial energy in the low- and mid-frequency regions. They are characterized mainly by the steady state values of the first three formant frequencies. Most vowel recognition methods measure the first three formants in the middle portion of the vowel and compare those values against stored targets. The modified Euclidean distance between an unknown vowel and a known vowel target has been used effectively to identify the vowels of a given speaker. However, vowel formants are not the same for all speakers. Vowel formants from an unknown speaker must be normalized before they can be compared with the formant targets. If the speaker is known, the models can be scaled according to the known vowel formant extrema of that speaker (Gerstman, 1968). When the speaker is unknown, other measurements must be derived to determine the scale factor. Some of the measures that have been used successfully are: average fundamental frequency (Schwartz, 1971), computed vocal tract length (Wakita and Kasuya, 1977), and formant log ratios (Skinner, 1977). It is well known that the characteristics of adjacent consonants tend to influence vowel articulation resulting in target undershoot or overshoot. In order to determine vowel identity, the influence of consonant coarticulation, such as lateralization and retroflexion, must be taken into consideration (e.g. Kameny, 1975).

There are other cues to the identity of vowels besides formant frequency targets and trajectories. For example, there are several short or "lax" vowels in English. These vowels have formant targets that are close to those of their long or "tense" counterparts, but they tend to have shorter durations. For instance, /i/ and /ɪ/ both have a low first formant and high second formant. /i/ is usually between 70 and 220 msec long when it occurs in non-final position, whereas /ɪ/ is usually between 40 and 100 msec. While these ranges in duration overlap somewhat, much of the overlap is due to vowel stress. If vowel stress is included with the phonetic spellings in the lexicon, vowel duration can be better utilized. For instance, if the formants of a vowel indicate that it is either an /i/ or an /ɪ/, and the duration is about 90 msec, then one can be fairly certain that it is either an unstressed /i/ or a stressed /ɪ/. Other tense/lax vowel pairs are /æ,ɛ/, /ɑ,ʌ/, /u,ʊ/.

Diphthongs are characterized by a transition from one steady state to another. Diphthongs are recognized not only by their steady states, but also by the rate of the transitions. In words such as "five" and "nine", the diphthong rarely reaches the second steady-state target due to coarticulation with the following consonant. In this case, one must rely on the rate of transition and the duration of the diphthong in order to recognize it. The recognition of diphthongs, therefore, requires that the formant trajectories of at least the lowest two formants be available.

5-3.5.2 <u>Consonants</u> The consonants can usually be divided into several groups depending on the manner in which they are articulated. There are five such groups in English, namely, plosives, fricatives, nasals, glides, and affricates. Consonants across "manner-of-articulation" groups often have widely different acoustic properties. For example, the acoustic properties of the first sound in the words "seed", "deed", and "need" differ substantially due to the degree of constriction in the vocal tract. In the case of /s/, a narrow constriction is formed, thus allowing the generation of turbulence noise. The vocal tract is completely closed off in the articulation of /d/ and /n/. In /n/, however, the velum is lowered to provide an air passage. For the stop consonant /d/, the complete closure enables pressure to build up behind the constriction.

Consonants within a "manner-of-articulation" group differ in their voicing characteristics and the position of the constriction. /t/ and /d/ differ in that /t/ is produced without setting the vocal cords into vibration, whereas the production of /d/ often involves vocal cord vibration. The difference between /p/ and /t/, on the other hand, lies in the positions of the constrictions. The constriction is formed at the lips for /p/ and at the alveolar ridge for /t/.

If a consonant is adjacent to a vowel, the transitions of the formants will often signify the place-of-articulation for the consonant, since formant transitions are a direct consequence of the articulatory gesture of consonantal closure or release. Consonants with the same place-of-articulation will have the same release gesture, and thus similar formant transitions. The first formant generally rises from a consonant to a vowel, and falls if the vowel is followed by another consonant. This property often enables the detection of weak consonants at the beginning of a sentence. If the first formant rises sharply at the beginning of a sentence, one can be fairly certain that the sentence must have started with a consonant.

Second- and third-formant transitions can be used as cues to the place of articulation of the consonants. Labial consonants, such as /b/, /v/, /m/, and /w/ cause rising formant transitions into the following vowel, whereas alveolar consonants tend to have falling transitions for the second and third formants. In the case of velar consonants, such as /k/ and /ŋ/, the formant transitions depend on the positions of the vowel formants. The second and third formants tend to "spread" into the following vowel.

To summarize, the acoustic properties of consonants differ both within the consonants themselves and in the adjacent vowels in the form of formant transitions. Both of these sources of information must be utilized to recognize the consonant.

Plosives. The plosives (/p,t,k,b,d,g/), are characterized acoustically by a period of prolonged silence, followed by an abrupt increase in amplitude at the consonantal release. The release is accompanied by a burst of frication noise. For the unvoiced stops in English (/p,t,k/), the frication noise is generated at the glottis. The voice-onset time (VOT), defined as the duration between the release and the onset of normal voicing for the following vowel, is quite different between voiced and voiceless stops (Lisker and Abramson, 1964; Klatt, 1975a; Zue, 1976).

Aside from a difference in VOT, English voiced and voiceless stops also differ in several respects. If the stop is followed by a vowel, the extent of the first-formant transition, and the fundamental frequency contours are different between voiced and voiceless stops (Lea, 1972). The voiced stops are often prevoiced, thus creating the voice-bar in the low-frequency region during the closure interval. In addition, voiced consonants tend to lengthen the duration of the preceding vowel (House and Fairbanks, 1953). It has also been found that the amplitude of the burst is significantly different between voiced and voiceless consonants (Zue, 1976).

The place of articulation of the stop consonants can be distinguished most reliably by the frequency characteristics of the burst as well as the formant transitions in adjacent vowels. In addition, it has also been found that the VOT varies systematically as a function of the place of articulation (Zue, 1976).

Stop consonants can often appear in clusters with /s/, and with sonorants /l,r,w/. In this case, the acoustic properties of the stop consonants will undergo substantial modification. For example, the aspiration of a /p/ can be increased (as in "preach") or decreased (as in "speech"), depending on the nature of the consonant forming the clusters. The influences of other consonants are also evident in the burst spectrum and the formant transitions. For instance, the /t/ in "tree" has a lower burst frequency, in addition to the longer VOT (Zue, 1976).

Fricatives. Fricatives (/f,v,s,z,š,ž,θ,ð/) are detectable by the presence of turbulence noise. Depending on the signal-to-noise ratio of the speech signal, however, it might be difficult to distinguish weak fricatives, such as /f,θ/, from silence based on energy alone.

Voicing contrast among fricatives can be determined from several acoustic cues. Voiced fricatives often have simultaneous noise and periodic excitations, and thus tend to have a greater amount of low-frequency energy. They also tend to be shorter and tend to lengthen the preceding vowel. However, duration as a voicing cue must be used with extreme caution, since factors governing segmental duration are numerous, and their interactions quite unclear (Klatt, 1974).

The place of articulation of the strident fricatives (/s,z,š,ž/) can often be determined by examining the gross spectral shape during the fricative (Weinstein, et al., 1975; Schwartz and Zue, 1976). The weak fricatives (/f,v,θ,ð/), on the other hand, are more difficult to distinguish. Formant transitions and higher-frequency spectral characteristics can, however, be used to distinguish among the weak fricatives.

Nasals. The nasals (/m,n,ŋ/) are invariably adjacent to a vowel, and are marked by a sharp change in intensity and spectrum, corresponding to the closing of the oral cavity and the opening of the velarpharyngeal port. In many cases, the presence of a nasal is indicated by the extensive nasalization of the adjacent vowels. As we have stated earlier, nasalization is often easy to detect by eye on a spectrogram. However, no algorithms have thus far been developed that will detect nasalization reliably in continuous speech. The nasals are distinguishable from other vowel-like sounds in that there are often discontinuities at the nasal boundaries. The first formant for the nasals is very low, typically below 300 Hz. In addition, the formants are usually stationary during a nasal murmur.

The nasals can be distinguished from one another in several ways. The formant transitions into and out of a nasal often provide reliable cues. The frequency locations of the zeros in the vocal tract transfer function also reflect the position of the constriction in the oral cavity. However, the detection of nasal zeros is a difficult task, and is rarely attempted. In English, it is not possible to have an /ŋ/ preceding a vowel in the same syllable.

Glides. Like nasals, glides (/w,r,l,y/) can occur only next to a vowel. The formant patterns of glides are at the extremes of the possible vowel formant positions: /w/ has the lowest F1 (first formant) and F2, /l/ has a low F1 and F2 with the highest F3, /r/ has the lowest F3, and /y/ has a very low F1 with the highest F2. For these phonemes, the formant transitions into a vowel are fairly smooth and are much slower than those of other consonants. While the formant patterns within a glide may be similar to some vowels, their distinguishing characteristics are in the dynamics of

120

the transitions to adjacent vowels. This is yet another case where it is important to be able to take account of the rate of change information in an APPA component.

Affricates. The affricates are often considered to be a plosive followed by a fricative. The two affricates of English are /č,ǰ/. While the affricates are often modeled as a sequence of two phonemes (/č/ as /t-š/ and /ǰ/ as /d-ž/), there are some subtle differences. The duration of the frication is typically half as long as in other occurrences of those fricatives. Also, the major energy concentration in the fricatives is typically much higher than those of the palatal fricatives. These differences can help to distinguish the consonants in "that ship" from those in "the chip".

Other Consonants. The alveolar consonants (/t,d,n/) are often realized as a flap when the surrounding stress pattern is falling (as in "writer", "rider"). The alveolar flaps are marked by an extremely short dip in energy (10-30 msec) in the higher frequencies. Since the acoustic characteristics are completely different from those of /t/, this phonological variation must be predicted and included in the lexicon as a possible pronunciation of those words.

Some reduced vowel-sonorant sequences can be realized as a single "syllabic" segment (as in "bottle", "button"). These segments have formant patterns similar to those of their consonantal counterparts, but have intensity more like that of reduced vowels. Since there may be no adjacent vowel and corresponding transition, these phonemes must be to be recognized from their steady state characteristics.

The phoneme /h/ is usually produced with the vocal tract in the configuration of the following vowel. However, the vocal cords are abducted, thus enabling aspiration noise to be generated at the glottis. The formant pattern is that of the following vowel. The total energy is about that of a weak fricative. When /h/ occurs at the beginning of a phrase, it can be detected by an increase in the mid-frequencies before the increase in low-frequency voicing energy.

Unreleased stops at the end of a sentence can be detected by an abrupt drop in energy, as opposed to the gradual decrease usually associated with a sentence final vowel.

5-4 SUMMARY

We have outlined in this chapter some of the techniques used for the processing of the speech signal. Time- and frequency-domain parameters that are potentially useful for phonetic recognition have been suggested. Issues related to segmentation and labeling of the speech signal were discussed. We ended with a brief outline of some of the specific acoustic features that are useful for segmentation and labeling.

Throughout the chapter we have stressed the fact that the acoustic realizations of speech sounds are highly context dependent, and that care must be taken to insure that our acoustic-phonetic knowledge is properly represented. The performance of current APPA components have been somewhat disappointing, especially in light of recent spectrogram reading experiments reported in the literature (Cole, et al., 1978). However, one must keep in mind that, with very few exceptions, large-scale efforts in speech recognition have only flourished over the past decade. These efforts have increased our awareness of the complexity of the problem and have produced significant advances in speech science in general, and automatic phonetic recognition in particular (See Chapter 17 in this volume). Continued interest and effort in speech recognition is likely to produce greater success in the years to come.

REFERENCES

Atal, B.S. and S.L. Hanauer, (1971). "Speech Analysis and Synthesis by Linear Prediction of the Speech Wave," J. Acoust. Soc. Amer., vol. 50, no. 2, pp. 637-655

Bahl, L., J. Baker, P. Cohen, N. Dixon, F. Jelinek, R. Mercer, and H. Silverman, (1976). "Preliminary Results on the Performance of a System for the Automatic Recognition of Continuous Speech," Conference Record, IEEE-ICASSP (Teacher, 1976), pp. 425-429.

Baker, James K. (1975). "The Dragon System--An Overview," IEEE Trans. Acoust. Speech Signal Process. ASSP-23 (Feb. 1975), pp. 24-29.

Baker, Janet M. (1975). "A New Time-Domain Analysis of Human Speech and other Complex Waveforms," Ph.D. dissertation, Carnegie-Mellon Univ., Pittsburgh, PA.

Cole, R.A., A. Rudnicky, R. Reddy, and V. Zue, (1978). "Speech as Patterns on Paper", in Perception and Production of Fluent Speech, R. Cole (Ed.), Erlbaum.

Cook, C.C. (1976). "Word Verification in a Speech Understanding System," Conference Record, IEEE-ICASSP (Teacher, 1976), pp. 553-556.

Dixon, N.R. (1977), "An Application Hierarchy for Heuristic Rules in Automatic Phonetic Segmentation of Continuous Speech", IEEE Int. Conf. ASSP, 671-674, IEEE Catalog No. 77CH1197-3 ASSP.

Dixon, N.R. and H.F. Silverman (1976). "A General Language-Operated Decision Implementation System (GLODIS): Its Application to Continuous speech Segmentation," IEEE Trans. Acoust. Speech, Signal Processing, vol. ASSP-24.

Fant, G.M. (1960). Acoustic Theory of Speech Production, 's-Gravehage: Mouton & Co. (1960).

Fant, G.M. (1966), "A Note on Vocal Tract Size Factors and Non-Uniform F-Pattern Scaling", Speech Transmission Labs. QPSR-4, 22-30.

Gerstman, L.J. (1968). "Classification of Self-Normalized Vowels," IEEE Trans. on Audio and Electroacoustics Vol. AU-16, No. 1 (March, 1968), pp. 78-80.

Gillman, R.A. (1975). "A Fast Frequency-Domain Pitch Algorithm," J. Acoust. Soc. Am. 58, S62(A).

Goldberg, H.G., and D.R. Reddy, (1976). "Feature Extraction, Segmentation and Labeling in the Harpy and Hearsay-II Systems," J. Acoust. Soc. Am. 60, S11(A).

House, A.S., and Fairbanks, G. (1953). "The Influence of Consonant Environment upon the Secondary Acoustical Characteristics of Vowels," J. Acoust. Soc. Am., vol. 25, pp. 105-113.

Itakura, F. (1975). "Minimum Prediction Residual Principle Applied to Speech Segmentation," IEEE Trans. Acoust. Speech, Signal Processing, 67-72.

Itakura, F. and S. Saito, (1968). "Analysis Synthesis Telephony Based on the Maximum Likelihood Method," in Proc. 6th Int. Congr. Acoustics, Paper C-5-5.

Jakobson, R., G.M. Fant, and M. Halle, (1963). Preliminaries to Speech Analysis, (MIT Press, Cambridge, MA.)

Kameny, I. (1975). "Comparison of Formant Spaces of Retroflexed and Nonretroflexed Vowels," IEEE Trans. Acoust. Speech Signal Process. ASSP-23 (Feb. 1975), pp. 38-49.

Kasuya, H., and H. Wakita (1976). "Speech Segmentation and Feature Normalization Based on Area Functions," Conference Record, IEEE-ICASSP (Teacher, 1976), pp. 29-32.

Klatt, D.H. (1974). "The Duration of /s/ in English Words," J. Speech and Hearing Research, vol. 17, pp. 51-63.

Klatt, D.H. (1975a). "Voice Onset Time, Frication, and Aspiration in Word-Initial Consonant Clusters," J. Speech Hear. Res., vol. 18, No. 4, (Dec. 1975), pp. 686-706.

Klatt, D.H. (1975b). "Word-Verification in a Speech Understanding System," in Reddy (1975), pp. 321-341.

Klatt, D.H. (1976). "A Digital Filter Bank for Spectral Matching," Conference Record, IEEE-ICASSP (Teacher, 1976), pp. 537-540.

Klatt, D.H. (1978). "Overview of the ARPA SUR Project," Chapter 11, this volume.

Lea, W.A. (1972). "Intonational Cues to the Constituent Structure and Phonemics of Spoken English," Ph.D. dissertation, Purdue Univ., Lafayette, IN.

Lea, W.A., M.F. Medress, and T.E. Skinner, (1975). "A Prosodically Guided Speech Understanding System," IEEE Trans. Acoust. Speech Signal Process, ASSP-23 (Feb. 1975), pp. 30-38.

Lisker, L., and A.S. Abramson, (1964). "A Cross-Language Study of Voicing in Initial Stops: Acoustic Measurements," Word, vol. 20, No. 3, (Dec. 1964), pp. 384-422.

Lowerre, B.T. (1976). "The Harpy Speech Recognition System," Ph.D. thesis Carnegie-Mellon University, Pittsburgh, PA.

Makhoul, J.I. and J.J. Wolf (1972). "Linear Prediction and the Spectral Analysis of Speech," Bolt Beranek and Newman Inc. Report No. 2304, Cambridge, MA.

Makhoul, J.I., and J.J. Wolf, (1973). "The Use of a Two-Pole Linear Prediction Model in Speech Recognition," Bolt Beranek and Newman Inc., Cambridge, MA, Report 2357.

Makhoul, J.I. (1975a). "Linear Prediction in Automatic Speech Recognition," in Reddy (1975), pp. 183-220.

Makhoul, J.I. (1975b). "Linear Prediction: A Tutorial Review," Proc. IEEE (Special Issue on Digital Signal Processing), vol. 63 (April, 1975), pp. 561-580.

Markel, J.D. (1972). "Digital Inverse Filtering - A New Tool for Formant Trajectory Estimation," IEEE Trans. Audio Electroacoust., vol. AU-20, pp. 129-137, June 1972.

Markel, J.D. and A.H. Gray, Jr. (1976). "Linear Prediction of Speech," (Springer, Berlin, Heidelberg, New York).

McCandless, S.S. (1974). "An Algorithm for Automatic Formant Extraction using Linear Prediction Spectra," IEEE Trans. Acoust., Speech, Signal Processing, vol. ASSP-22 (Apr. 1974), pp. 135-141.

Medress, M.F., T.E. Skinner, D.R. Kloker, T.C. Diller and W.A. Lea (1977). "A System for the Recognition of Spoken Connected Word Sequences," Conference Record, IEEE-ICASSP (Silverman, 1977), pp. 468-473.

Molho, L.M. (1976). "Automatic Acoustic-Phonetic Analysis of Fricatives and Plosives," Conference Record, IEEE-ICASSP (Teacher, 1976), pp. 182-185.

Oppenheim, A.V., and R.M. Schafer, (1968). "Homomorphic Analysis of Speech," IEEE Trans. Audio and Electroacoust., AU-16, No. 2, (June, 1968), pp. 27-31.

Peterson, G., and H. Barney (1952). "Control Methods used in a Study of Vowels," J. Acoust. Soc. Am., Vol. 24, pp. 175-184.

Rabiner, L.R., M.J. Cheng, A.E. Rosenberg, and C.A. McGonegal, (1976), "Comparative Performance Study of Several Pitch Detection Algorithms", IEEE Trans. ASSP-24, 399-417.

Reddy, D.R. (1966). "Segmentation of Speech Sounds," J. Acoust. Soc. Amer., vol. 40, pp. 307-312.

Reddy, D.R. (Editor) (1975). Speech Recognition: Invited Papers Presented at the 1974 IEEE Symposium (Academic Press, New York).

Reddy, D.R. (1976). "Speech Recognition by Machine: A Review," Proc. IEEE 64 (April, 1976), 501-531.

Schafer, R.N. and L.R. Rabiner (1975). "Parametric Representations of Speech," in Reddy (1975), pp. 99-150.

Schwartz, R.M. (1971). "Automatic Normalization for Recognition of Vowels of All Speakers," S.B. thesis, Mass. Inst. of Tech., Cambridge, MA, June.

Schwartz, R.M. (1976). "Acoustic-Phonetic Experiment Facility for the Study of Continuous Speech," Conference Record, IEEE-ICASSP (Teacher, 1976), pp. 1-4.

Schwartz, R.M., and V.W. Zue (1976). "Acoustic-Phonetic Recognition in BBN SPEECHLIS," Conference Record, IEEE-ICASSP (Teacher, 1976), pp. 21-24.

Seneff, S.S. (1978). "Real Time Harmonic Pitch Detector," IEEE Trans. Acoust. Speech Signal Process. in press.

Silverman, H.F. (Chairman) (1977). "Conference Record of the 1977 IEEE International Conference on Acoustics, Speech and Signal Processing," Hartford, 9-11 May (IEEE Catalog No. 77CH1197-3 ASSP).

Silverman, H.F. and N.R. Dixon (1974). "A Parametrically-Controlled Spectral Analysis System for Speech," IEEE Trans. Acoust., Speech, Signal Processing, vol. ASSP-22, pp. 362-381.

Skinner, T.E. (1977), "Speaker-Invariant Characteristics of Vowels, Liquids, and Glides Using Relative Formant Frequencies", J. Acoust. Soc. Am. 62, Supple. 1, 55 (A).

Teacher, C. (Chairman) (1976). Conference Record of the 1976 IEEE International Conference on Acoustics Speech and Signal Processing, Philadelphia, PA, 12-14 April (IEEE Catalog No. 76CH1067-8 ASSP).

Vicens, P.J. (1969). "Aspects of Speech Recognition by Computer," Ph.D. dissertation, Stanford Univ., Stanford, CA.

Wakita, H. and Kasuya, H. (1977). "A Study of Vowel Normalization and Identification in Connected Speech," Conference Record, IEEE-ICASSP (Silverman, 1977), pp. 648-651.

Weinstein, C.J., S.S. McCandless, L.F. Mondshein, and V.W. Zue, (1975). "A System for Acoustic-Phonetic Analysis of Continuous Speech," IEEE Trans. Acoust. Speech Signal Process. ASSP-23 (Feb. 1975), pp. 54-67.

Wolf, J.J. (1976). "Speech Recognition and Understanding," in Digital Pattern Recognition, edited by K.S. Fu (Springer-Verlag, Berlin), pp. 167-203.

Woods, W. A., M. Bates, G. Brown, B. Bruce, C. Cook, J. Klovstad, J. Makhoul, B. Nash-Webber, R. Schwartz, J. Wolf, and V. Zue, (1976). "Speech Understanding Systems - Final Technical Progress Report," Report No. 3438, Vols. I-V, Bolt Beranek and Newman Inc., Cambridge, Ma., 1976 (DDC ADA035165, ADA035166, ADA035167, ADA035277, ADA035278).

Zue, V.W. (1976). "Acoustic Characteristics of Stop Consonants: A Controlled Study," Sc.D. thesis, Mass. Inst. of Tech., Cambridge, MA.

6.

PHONOLOGICAL ASPECTS OF SPEECH RECOGNITION

June E. Shoup
Speech Communications Research Laboratory

6-1. INTRODUCTION

The acoustic speech signal, which is produced physiologically and interpreted linguistically, is recognized to be a complex phenomenon. The sounds
used by speakers in human communication are structured very differently in
various languages. The area of phonology within linguistics addresses the
many issues in the structure or function of speech sounds in a language.
Some of the questions that are to be answered in the investigation of any
given language include:
1. What are the phonological units used in this language?
2. How do these units relate to one another?
3. How do these units deviate in "defective" speech from the norm of the
    language?
4. How similar or dissimilar are the units and their relations of the
    given language to any and all other languages?
5. How stable or changeable are these units as a function of time from
    the earliest descriptions of the given language to the present spoken
    utterances under investigation?
It is generally agreed that the speech signal can be studied independent
of a given language by physiologically and acoustically identifying the
physical events that comprise the sequence of sounds. There is no general
agreement, however, as to the theoretical or methodological definition of
these sequences of sounds. The term "phone" is regularly used to denote a
minimal unit of speech sound, such as an [m] or an [o], but the rigors of
phonetic science are lacking in providing an adequate definition of this
term. Operationally most phoneticians and linguists have a gross understanding of these units of speech and they have developed ways of representing them symbolically, as illustrated above with [m] and [o]. From
these basic units of phonetics, which are actual physical events in the
speech stream, the linguist studies abstractions of the phones as they
function in given languages. These abstractions are variously referred to
as phonological segments and suprasegmentals, as segmental phonemes and
prosodemes, or as bundles of features. They are symbolized rather similarly to the phones of phonetics, but usually represented between slanted
lines, such as /m/ and /o/. The concatenation and superposition of phonological segments form larger phonological units, such as syllables and
words.
All of the abstract phonological units are studied as to their function
singly and in sequence within a language. One aspect of this study is the
formulation of phonological rules which operate on the phonological units
of the language in a predictable manner. Quite obviously, this type of
information is of great importance within automatic speech recognition (ASR),
for any known regularity of the language, if embedded appropriately within
the recognition system, should aid in the better performance of that device.
There remain many irregular phenomena of speech for which no general rules
of phonology will apply and which, consequently, add to the difficulties of
obtaining accurate speech recognition. Generally speaking, the more we can
understand of the phonological structure of the language and the more we

can make use of this knowledge in a recognition system, the more successful we should be in our work in ASR.

In the following discussion of the phonological aspects of speech recognition, two basic assumptions have been made: 1. that an appropriate set of acoustic-phonetic parameters can be extracted from the speech signal to provide a necessary and sufficient set of phonological features for further processing, and 2. that any desired lexicon can have its entries efficiently represented in the most useful phonological units. Although these basic assumptions are not yet fully realized, they can be met in large measure at this time. Consequently, four basic questions will be addressed:

1. What are the phonological units to be recognized in automatic speech recognition?
2. What are the issues to be considered for phonological rules?
3. What are the potential contributions to automatic speech recognition from prosodics?
4. What might be expected in the future within the phonological aspects of speech recognition?

These are questions to be addressed, not answered at this time! The obvious reason for not resolving them now is that no one as yet has found the final answers and, indeed, every alternative position taken on the fundamental issues has both advantages and disadvantages. Also, within any particular recognition system, there are often practical considerations that determine the decisions made on these issues.

6-2. UNITS FOR RECOGNITION

In considering the first question, "What are the phonological units to be recognized in automatic speech recognition?", the following possibilities are obvious: allophones, phonemes, diphones, syllables, words, or some combination of the above. It is asssumed that some type of features will be extracted from the speech signal, so the issue is really one of finding the best mapping of these features into one or more phonological units that are maximally useful in the recognition system. Each choice, as stated earlier, has its advantages and disadvantages.

6-2.1 Allophone
Some of the considerations for recognizing an allophonic unit will be discussed first. As used here, the term "allophone" is meant to represent a set of phones within a given language which have the same information-bearing parameters, or distinctive features, either physiologically or acoustically. Thus, all of the nasalized, rounded, back, high vowels of English might be represented as the allophone [ũ]. Figure 6-1 gives a listing of the ARPABET. This is the selection of symbols used within the Advanced Research Projects Agency Speech Understanding Research (ARPA SUR) project and it was found to be a convenient coding for the many participants in transcribing their spoken utterances. It is obvious that certain allophones, such as alveolar flap [ɾ] and glottal stop [ʔ], are included in the list, for these units are rather easily identified from the acoustic signal. In the spoken utterance of "better sentence" one might find phonetically the sequence [bɛɾəsɛ̃nʔəns] which might be phonemically symbolized as /bɛtəsɛntəns/. Although one phoneme /t/ occurs twice, the first allophone of alveolar flap, [ɾ], is acoustically distinct from the second allophone of glottal stop, [ʔ], and they both in turn are very different acoustically from the more common allophones of /t/; namely, [t] and [tʰ]. A speech recognizer can identify rather easily the distinctly different /t/ allophones, so there is some argument for using an allophone as a phonological unit of recognition.

126

Phoneme	Computer Representation		Example	Phoneme	Computer Representation		Example
	1-Character	2-Characters			1-Character	2-Characters	
i	i	IY	beat	p	p	P	pet
I	I	IH	bit	t	t	T	ten
e	e	EY	bait	k	k	K	kit
ε	E	EH	bet	b	b	B	bet
æ	@	AE	bat	d	d	D	debt
ɑ	a	AA	Bob	g	g	G	get
Λ	A	AH	but	h	h	HH	hat
ɔ	c	AO	bought	f	f	F	fat
o	o	OW	boat	θ	T	TH	thing
U	U	UH	book	s	s	S	sat
u	u	UW	boot	š or ʃ	S	SH	shut
ə	x	AX	about	v	v	V	vat
ɨ	X	IX	roses	ð	D	DH	that
ɝ	R	ER	bird	z	z	Z	zoo
ɑU or ɑw	W	AW	down	ž or ʒ	Z	ZH	azure
ɑI or ɑy	Y	AY	buy	č	C	CH	church
ɔI or ɔy	O	OY	boy	ǰ	J	JH	judge
y	y	Y	you	ʍ	H	WH	which
w	w	W	wit	syl l, l̩	L	EL	battle
r	ɾ	R	rent	syl m, m̩	M	EM	bottom
l	l	L	let	syl n, n̩	N	EN	button
m	m	M	met	flapped t, ɾ	F	DX	batter
n	n	N	net	glottal stop, ʔ	Q	Q	
ŋ	G	NX	sing	Silence	—	—	
				non-speech Segment	!	!	laugh, etc.

AUXILIARY SYMBOLS (1- AND 2-CHARACTER CODES ARE IDENTICAL)			
Symbol	Meaning	Symbol	Meaning
+	Morpheme boundary	: 3 or ,	Fall-rise or non-term juncture
/	Word boundary	* **	Comment (anything except * or **)
#	Utterance boundary	' '	Apos.-surround special symbol in comment
:	Tone group boundary	( )	Phoneme class information
: 1 or .	Falling or decl. juncture	( )	Phoneme class information
: 2 or ?	Rising or inter. juncture	< >	Phonetic or allophonic escape

STRESS REPRESENTATIONS (IF PRESENT, MUST IMMEDIATELY FOLLOW THE VOWEL)			
Value	Stress Assignment	Value	Stress Assignment
0	No stress	3	Tertiary stress
1	Primary stress	⋮	(Etc.)
2	Secondary Stress	⋮	

Figure 6-1. ARPABET symbols for representing within a computer the phoneme-like units of English.

It is also known that certain allophones provide syllable and/or word boundary information that can be useful in recognition. For example, in the two phonetic sequences of [hilɪtʰ] and [hiɫɪtʰ], which would have the same phonemic symbolization of /hilɪt/, the only distinctions lie at an allophonic level. The first utterance contains a "light [l]" and the second a "dark [ɫ]" allophone. The distribution of the allophones of the phoneme /l/ is such that a linguist knows that a syllable and/or word boundary lies before the "light [l]" and after the "dark [l]." Thus, if a recognizer operated on allophonic units, it would properly identify the first utterance as "he lit" and the second as "heal it."

A third advantage of identifying all of the allophones is that, if this were successfully accomplished, it would obviate the necessity of applying many acoustic-phonetic and coarticulation rules at a lower level. This will be discussed later in the section on rules. The disadvantages of selecting the allophone for recognition are: the instrumentation is not yet sophisticated enough for this task, the total number of allophones for any given language can be excessively large (in the thousands), and the identification of many allophones is very dependent on the environment in which they are located. This last objection will be more clearly seen in the discussion of the diphone given later.

6-2.2 Phoneme

The "phoneme" is a term that is used for the total collection of allophones that function similarly and do not make meaningful distinctions among themselves within a given language. Thus, in English the phoneme /u/ would include not only the previously mentioned nasalized allophone [ũ], but also the non-nasalized allophone [u] within the total group of its allophones. Likewise the English /t/ phoneme would have to include at least the four allophones referred to above; [ɾ], [ʔ], [t], and [tʰ]. Although it is a property of allophones within a phoneme to be "nonconstrastive," it is a required property of phonemes that they be "contrastive." Thus, /o/ and /u/ are separate phonemes in English, for they contrast in pairs of words, such as boat and boot, i.e., /bot/ and /but/. These contrastive word pairs are referred to as "minimal pairs" and are used to determine the phonemes of a language.

The advantages of selecting the phoneme as the phonological unit are well known. First, the set of phonemes for any language represents the smallest number of distinctive phonological classes to be recognized. This number is substantially less than the set of allophones, diphones, syllables, or words. To illustrate the small size advantage, ordinarily one would find the number of phonemes within any given language to be somewhere between 20 and 60, whereas the number of allophones, diphones, syllables, and words may be in the thousands. It would therefore appear to be a considerable saving to recognize such a small set of phonological units. The second advantage is that the phoneme maps the most directly to lexicon entries which are usually phonemic in nature. Quite obviously, dictionaries could be coded by using units other than phonemes, but it would require considerable storage space and possibly longer access time during the word matching procedure in ASR.

The disadvantages of using the phoneme as the phonological unit in recognition systems are not trivial. First and foremost, it is very difficult to identify acoustically the phonemes and their boundaries. Second, certain sounds, such as the final vowel in "party" or "city" may belong equally well to more than one phoneme, and if multiple choices of phonemes are allowed, this requires more work at the word matching level of recognition. Third, if phonemes are selected, it requires a substantial number of acoustic-phonetic and phonological rules at lower and higher levels within the recognition system, for none of the coarticulation and junctural phenomena of speech are represented in the phoneme.

6-2.3 Diphone

It is well known that a great deal of the acoustic information that is used to identify the consonants of a given language lies in the transitions between the consonants and vowels. It is not surprising, then, that for many years speech scientists have found it useful to work with a unit that includes such transitional information. This unit, which is referred to as a "diphone" or "transeme", is generally meant to represent, in a consonant-vowel sequence, the segment from the center of the consonant to the center of the vowel, and in a vowel-consonant sequence, the segment from the center of the vowel to the center of the consonant. Thus the diphones for a phonetic utterance representing the utterance "come here," which is symbolized phonemically, together with initial and final silence, as /#kəmhɪr#/ would include: #-k, k-ə, ə-m, m-h, h-ɪ, ɪ-r, and r-#. One of the most obvious advantages of selecting the diphone for recognition is the fact that it includes the transitional information which is necessary for many identifications. Another advantage is that the diphone includes some of the coarticulation rule information within itself, since this information lies in the transitions between sounds. The disadvantages of selecting the diphone are: the inventory may be relatively large (again in the thousands), and most phonological rules, as currently written, are not easily applied to diphones. It is an open question as to how difficult it would be to rewrite all the phonological rules with diphonic symbols and concepts.

6-2.4 Syllable

One of the more difficult-to-define phonological units is the "syllable." In very general terms, it is a vowel (or syllabic) nucleus and its functionally related neighboring consonants. The specification of the syllable can become a problem for utterances that have two or more nuclei with surrounding consonants, e.g., "common" is symbolized phonemically as /kɑmən/, but it is not clearly evident whether the syllables are /kɑm/+/ən/ or /kɑ/+/mən/. The theoretical basis for such decisions is not well agreed upon within linguistics. Recently more consideration has been given to the advantages of recognizing the syllable as the phonological unit. Perhaps the most important reason for selecting the syllable in ASR is that syllable nuclei are relatively easy to locate and identify. Indeed, the stressed vowels of speech are one of the first groups of sounds to be recognized. A second major advantage of the syllable is one previously mentioned for the diphone; that is, many coarticulation effects are included in the syllabic unit. A third, but relatively minor, advantage is that currently used phonological rules often include syllable boundary conditions. This last advantage loses some of its attractiveness upon citing one of the disadvantages, that is, the difficulty of determining all syllable boundaries. Ordinarily it is relatively easy to identify how many syllables are present and oftentimes it is also straightforward to know which syllables they are, but it is exceedingly hard to know the precise boundaries between syllables. There is some question, however, whether it is required in ASR to obtain anything more than gross boundary information. If not, then this lack of clearly defined boundaries would no longer be a disadvantage. Another possible disadvantage is that the syllable inventory can become very large with extensive vocabularies. The size does not approach that of allphones or words ordinarily, but it far exceeds that of phonemes.

6-2.5 Word

Although most all speakers and writers feel they know what a "word" is, the definition of this concept, in spoken form particularly, is not simple. One illustration of this problem is the rapid pronunciation of the sentence, "did you eat yet?" The clearly enunciated phoneme string may be /dɪdyuityɛt/, but in the fast, poorly-articulated versions the utterance may be /djiyɛt/. Currently, there is no rigorous algorithm for deciding how many phonological words this should be. So it is that the word, "word," is used as though it is fully understood, but the precise definition of "word" as a phonological unit is not yet clearly specified.

The obvious, overall advantages of proceeding directly from acoustically derived parameters or features to the word itself is that an entire level of recognition activity is eliminated. With any of the other units (allophones, phonemes, diphones, or syllables) there is a two-fold process involved: first, recognition of the sequence of units and second, matching the lexicon entries with these recognized strings to obtain a word match. If one can go directly from the acoustic processing to the template matching of the word, considerable time and effort are saved. One of the disadvantages of this approach, however, is that template matching becomes most difficult when vocabularies are extensive. Also, word boundary phenomena expressed in junctural phonological rules, i.e., the segmental changes on either side of the word boundaries, are difficult to characterize in the lexicon entries of the computer dictionaries.

6-2.6 Combination of Units

From the preceding discussion it can be seen that there is no phonological unit for recognition that is truly ideal, and for that reason it may be well to consider the use of a combination of units in ASR. Table 6-1 summarizes the advantages and disadvantages of each phonological unit which might be used in speech understanding systems. A study of this summary might be helpful in the selection of an appropriate combination of units. In view of the fact that all units have certain advantages and no unit is without disadvantages, it is not surprising that some system builders have indeed used a combination of phonological units in their recognition schemes. The strong position given by Fujimura of Bell Laboratories (1974) and researchers at Haskins Laboratories (Mermelstein and Kuhn, 1974) for the syllable as the basic phonological unit had a definite influence within the ARPA SUR project. Two of the system builders, Carnegie-Mellon University (CMU) and Systems Development Corporation (SDC), incorporated the syllable or syllable type as an intermediate level of recognition between the phone or phoneme and the word.

Experiments were conducted by Mermelstein (1975) in automatic segmentation techniques for continuous speech to derive syllable-size units. One segmentation algorithm was tested on approximately 400 syllables of continuous text with results of 6.9% syllables missed and 2.6% extra syllables. Mermelstein suggested that the inclusion of alternative fluent-form syllabifications for multi-syllabic words and the use of phonological rules for predicting syllabic contractions might further improve the results of the algorithm. Unfortunately, there have been no systematic experiments performed to see whether the syllable or some other unit is the most effective one in speech recognition or whether combinations of units are better than any one alone.

6-3. PHONOLOGICAL RULES

The second question to be answered is "What are the issues to be considered for phonological rules in automatic speech recognition?" Some of the questions that have been asked, and are still being asked, by those scholars concerned with phonological rules include:

1. What is the nature of the base form on which the rules operate?
2. Should there be one or multiple base forms for each lexicon entry?
3. Should the rules be analytic, generative, or both?
4. Should the rules be cyclic or noncyclic?
5. Should the rules be ordered, unordered, or partially ordered?
6. Should the rules be obligatory or optional?
7. Should the rules be at certain linguistic "levels"?

Phonological Unit	Possible Advantages	Possible Disadvantages
Allophone	1. Certain ones are easily identifiable acoustically.	1. Instrumentation is not yet sophisticated enough for the task.
	2. Some word boundaries are indicated by allophones.	2. The total number of allophones can be excessively large.
	3. They reduce the need for rules at a lower level.	3. Many allophones are very dependent on their environment.
Phoneme	1. The number of distinctive phonological classes is small.	1. Phonemes are not easily determined acoustically.
	2. Phonemes map the most directly to lexicon entries in present computer dictionaries.	2. Some sounds belong equally well to more than one phoneme.
		3. Many rules are needed at both lower and higher linguistic levels.
Diphone	1. Transitional information is included.	1. The total number of diphones can be relatively large.
	2. Some coarticulation rule information is included.	2. Most phonological rules are not easily applied to diphones.
Syllable	1. It is relatively easy to locate and identify.	1. Precise syllable boundaries are difficult to determine.
	2. It includes much coarticulation rule information.	2. The total number of syllables can be rather large.
	3. Certain phonological rules include syllable boundary conditions.	
Word	1. It eliminates an entire level of recognition activity.	1. Template matching is more difficult with large vocabularies.
		2. Junctural phonological rules are hard to characterize in lexicon entries.

Table 6-1 Summary of advantages and disadvantages of each phonological unit which might be used in automatic speech recognition.

8. Should the rules contain syllable, morpheme, or word boundary information?
9. Should certain (or all) rules be incorporated into the lexicon entries?
10. Should the rules be applied before or during dictionary look-up?
11. How many rules are needed?
12. How many rules are useful?
13. Do certain rules cause more problems than they solve?
14. What are the best forms for the rules?

These questions will be rather briefly discussed below and it will be seen that simple answers are not possible at this time for these complex issues.

6-3.1 Base Forms

The first question to be addressed regarding phonological rules is: "What is the nature of the base form on which the rules operate?" The base form is that listing of the lexicon entry in the dictionary on which a phonological rule operates to produce a derivative form. For example, if the base form for the word, the, were to be its unstressed form of pronunciation, /ðə/, then a phonological rule for the stressed condition would produce /ði/. Conversely, if the stressed form /ði/ were chosen as the base form of the lexical entry, the, then a rule of stress reduction would give the derived form /ðə/.

In most generative grammars the base forms of the lexicon tend to be of a more abstract nature than those used by the current builders of speech recognition systems. These abstract base forms are used to show relationships such as medical and medicine being derived from the same underlying root. Although it would be possible to use these abstract linguistic forms, it has not been found to be very practical in speech recognition. In fact, there are certain advantages for selecting a base form that actually occurs in speech production, as illustrated both by /ðə/ and /ði/, in the example discussed above. Ordinarily, however, the nature of the base form is determined by the robustness of the rule applicability on that form, i.e., by the largest number of derived forms that can be obtained from the base form through the application of the rules.

In addition to the decision as to the type of base form to be used, there is the consideration as to the advantages of limiting each lexicon entry to one base form, or of permitting more than one for each entry. Currently many dictionaries used in speech recognition allow multiple base form entries, such as [naiðɚ] and [niðɚ] for "neither", rather than limiting entries to single forms. It has not been found useful, however, to permit large numbers of base form entries, unless there is an intent to eliminate the need for most of the phonological rules by listing virtually all possible pronunciations of an entry.

6-3.2 Nature of Phonological Rules

Within current linguistic theory phonological rules are of a **phonological** nature. That is, the rules operate on one form to generate or derive another form. To illustrate, if the representation for sentence is $\underline{S}$ and that for noun phrase and verb phrase is $\underline{NP}$ and $\underline{VP}$, respectively, then $\underline{S \rightarrow NP+VP}$ means "Sentence is rewritten as Noun Phrase plus Verb Phrase." Quite naturally, both noun phrase and verb phrase can be rewritten to generate new forms, such as adjective plus noun, or verb plus noun phrase. By successive rules one can finally generate the actual phonetic string for the pronunciation of the sentence.

Since automatic speech recognition has the task of taking the speech signal and determining the spoken sentences, one might intuitively think that generative rules should be of an opposite direction, from the pronunciation which occurs in the speech signal to the base forms of the words spoken to their abstractions of linguistic units, such as nouns, verbs, phrases, etc., until one recovers the intended sentence. Such rules that take the actual event and analyze the structures are referred to as analytical rules.

The type of rule to use within speech recognition, i.e., generative or analytical, depends entirely on what its function is within a given ASR system. Bolt, Beranek, and Newman (BBN) is an example of a group that has incorporated both types of rules within its speech understanding system (Rovner, Makhoul, Wolf, and Colarusso, 1974). The analytic rules, describing acoustic-phonetic processes, are applied to sequences that may be errorful, such as the phonetic lattice, (described in Chapter 14), and generative rules, describing the phonological and coarticulation processes, are applied to idealized base forms in the dictionary.

A full description of the phonological rules and their use within the HWIM system developed by BBN can be found in their final report (W. Wood, et al., 1976). A Dictionary Expander is employed when the system is originally loaded. This expands the dictionary of baseform pronunciations by means of generative phonological rules to provide all pronunciation variants and the data structure necessary for the Lexical Retrieval component to apply across-word phonological rules during the matching process. The dictionary starts with 1138 base words which are expanded to 1363 words by means of regular inflections and these are expanded into 8642 pronunciations by the application of the phonological rules.

The acoustic-phonetic rules that were developed at BBN within their synthesis-by-rule program were used for word verification. The output of the phonological rule program included a sequence of phonetic segments, a stress assignment to each segment, a duration for each segment, and certain phonological aspects of fundamental frequency contour for vowel nuclei. The rules handled segmental insertions, deletions, and substitutions, as well as coarticulation phenomena. Improvements to the acoustic-phonetic rules are made in the following way. Broadband sound spectrograms of synthesized consonant-vowel nonsense syllables and sentences are made and compared with the speech of a single talker. The observed differences are used to evaluate and improve the rule program.

There are other considerations of the nature of phonological rules besides generative versus analytical. Decisions must be made whether the rules to be implemented should be cyclic or noncyclic. The concept of cyclic is that of repeating the application of the rules as many times as they will produce changes in the derived forms. For example, there are rules of vowel reduction from stressed pronunciation to weak or unstressed forms. In a word such as president the phonemic symbolization of the base form could be /prɛzɪdɛnt/, but the actual pronunciation could be [prɛzədənt]. The vowel reduction rule might be applied the first time to convert /ɪ/ to [ə] and again a second time to make the last /ɛ/ into [ə] also. Depending on how generalized the rule of vowel reduction was written in the system, one rule could be cycled through twice to obtain the desired pronunciation.

Another consideration for phonological rules is whether they should be ordered, unordered, or partially ordered. That is, if the system uses a set of phonological rules, will the generated forms from these rules differ depending upon the order in which the rules are applied. For example, three possible rules within a system are vowel reduction, consonant reduction, and syllabification of final nasals. In a word such as reading the last syllable ing may be pronounced in many ways, including [iŋ], [ɪn], [n̩]. The first pronunciation implies a certain degree of stressing and the last two require a reduction of emphasis or stress. If the base form were /ridiŋ/, then it might be useful to order the rules such that the syllabification rule would operate on the derived form [ɪn] which resulted from vowel and consonant reduction, rather than from the base form [iŋ]. If this were the case, then some type of ordering of the rules would be required so that vowel and consonant reduction rules preceded the syllabification of final nasal rule.

Still another consideration for the nature of phonological rules is that of whether they should be <u>obligatory</u> or <u>optional</u>. Within most languages speakers employ rules in different ways. In the illustration given above for <u>reading</u>, there are some speakers who might have trained themselves to use only the first option of [iɲ] whenever using a gerund or participle in English. Other speakers might use all three options upon different occasions. Thus, the rules of vowel reduction, consonant reduction, and syllabification of final nasals should be implemented as optional within a speech recognition system. The manner in which the base forms are selected and the list of rules required to generate all the possible variations of these base forms in actual speech determine which rules should be optional and which should be obligatory. It is possible to choose base forms and rules such that all rules are optional, but it might be efficient to select them in such a way that certain rules were indeed obligatory.

Although it is common linguistic practice to use cyclic, partially or fully ordered, and both obligatory and optional rules, some speech recognition groups, such as IBM (Cohen and Mercer, 1975), found it expedient in the past to use noncyclic, unordered, and totally optional rules. Other system builders chose to use some partially ordered rules and both obligatory and optional phonological rules. The decisions are an integral part of the total systems design and thus the "best" approach is not easily demonstrated.

6-3.3 Incorporation of Rules in Systems

It is informative to study in detail the rules selected by any given system builder to ascertain the rationale that influenced the decisions for selecting, formatting, and using particular phonological rules in the system. An IBM phonological-rule component is discussed in detail by Cohen and Mercer (1975). It is, therefore, suggested that any person seriously interested in the phonological aspects of speech recognition read this full description given by them. Only a brief statement of the phonological-rule component is given here.

The IBM lexicon had an inventory of entries called sub-utterances. These entries were basically equivalent to individual English words, and each of them had associated with it a small number of base forms. When the phonological rules were applied to this lexicon, an entire inventory of desired utterances and their associated pronunciations could be generated. For statistical decoding of the speech signal, there was associated with each utterance, u, and pronunciation, $\emptyset$, a number $P(\emptyset/u)$, which was the probability that $\emptyset$ would be produced as a pronunciation of u. There were likewise speaker-dependent probabilities associated with both the base forms and the phonological rules. Then it was possible to obtain an overall probability for a given pronunciation by combining the probabilities of all the base forms and rules involved in the creation of the particular pronunciation of an utterance. The base forms, phonological rules, and all associated probabilities were regarded as a speaker performance model.

The issue of having rules incorporated at linguistic "levels", that is, acoustic, phonetic, phonemic, or morphophonemic levels, <u>or across them</u> is likewise determined by system design. The more modular the system, the more appropriate to use rules at different levels, as mentioned above for the BBN HWIM system. The extreme case of non-modularity, such as demonstrated in the CMU HARPY system, virtually eliminates the possibility of rules being applied at linguistic levels in the usual sense.

Almost all sets of rules include certain boundary information for the syllable, the morpheme, or the word. There has been some preliminary study done at the Speech Communications Research Laboratory to see which rules can be rewritten without boundary considerations, but there are not conclusive results as yet on all boundary information.

The decision as to how many of the rules should be incorporated into the lexicon entries is somewhat determined now by the size of the vocabulary and the number of speakers with varying dialects who might use the system. As the vocabulary and speaker size increase, the difficulties of incorporating all the rules within the lexicon become greater likewise.

If many of the rules are not incorporated in the lexicon, then a decision must be made as to whether the rules should be applied before or during dictionary look-up. Within the ARPA SUR project, almost all the systems applied the rules before any entry was checked.

At this time it is not really known how many rules are absolutely needed within any recognition system, how many might be useful, and how many might actually cause more problems than they solve. The ARPA SUR group compiled a list of over 200 rules, but it is not known whether this is a necessary and sufficient set for recognition work. The number of rules compiled is not the important issue, but rather the generality of their application to account for all the data.

6-3.4 Forms of Phonological Rules

The forms of the rules are also diverse. Figure 6-2 illustrates various types of rules from the ARPA SUR project. The analytic rules from BBN at the acoustic-phonetic level are rather straightforward, as indicated: "for all inter-vocalic obstruent-fricative [IVOBS-FRIC] sequences, the two segments are replaced (non-optionally) with a single fricative [FRIC]." Inter-vocalic obstruent as used by BBN means a set of weak voiced obstruents, namely [v,ð,ʃ,h]. The format of the generative rules appears to be quite different at the three groups shown here: BBN, CMU, and SDC, but they all have a similar construction. That is, a given phoneme or set of features becomes a different phoneme under given stress conditions and/or in given environments. The BBN glottalization of T rule indicates that T becomes glottal stop following a stressed vowel before a syllabic "EN" or "EL". CMU's flap rule states that a given set of features become flap in the environment of a particular preceding and following set of features. SDC's vowel reduction rule indicates that a primary stressed [ɪ] becomes [ɪ̵] with reduced stress.

Of the 242 phonological rules compiled within the ARPA SUR project, certain categories appear to be absolutely essential in any speech recognition system, some of which include: vowel reduction, schwa deletion, syllabification, stop insertion, stop deletion, flapping, nasalization, nasal deletion, "Ruh" reduction, geminate reduction, palatalization, and devoicing. These general rules, plus spectographic displays that illustrate the phenomena, are presented in an article by Oshika, et al., (1975).

As previously illustrated, most stressed vowels becme reduced to a more central vowel position when unstressed or with reduced stress, for example, [ritɝn] for "retúrn" and [rɪtɝn] or [rətɝn] for "retúrn." Schwas can actually be eliminated when they occur in unstressed positions, such as "chocolate" becoming "choclate". Syllable-final schwa followd by [l] or a nasal can become syllabic [l̩] or nasal, such as in "bottle" [bɑtl̩] or "button" [bʌtn̩].

Stop consonants are both inserted and deleted in words. Homorganic formations are very common in this respect, such as "something" having a [p] inserted as in [sʌmpθiŋ], and "mostly" having the [t] deleted, as in [mosli]. Also, previously shown as an illustrative CMU rule is alveolar flapping that often occurs between vowels in place of a medial [t] or [d], as in "wedding" [wɛɾɪŋ].

The nasalization of vowels preceding or between nasal consonants is a common phenomenon, such as [ãn] for "on". Another nasal rule is that of nasal deletion which can occur with nasalization of the preceding vowel; for example, monosyllabic words such as "can't" are often realized as [kʰæ̃t] without an [n], but with a nasalized vowel.

"Ruh" reduction, as it is referred to, is the reducing of [r] plus a following vowel to a retroflexed [ɝ], such as [ɪ̃ntrədʌkʃən] becoming [ɪ̃ntɝdʌkʃən] in certain pronunciations of "introduction".

135

ANALYTIC:

BBN: FOR ALL IVOBS-FRIC SEQUENCES, THE TWO SEGMENTS ARE
REPLACED (NON-OPTIONALLY) WITH A SINGLE FRIC.

(RULE: IVOBSFRIC)

GENERATIVE:

BBN: GLOTTALIZATION OF T
E.G. "GOTTEN" G AA T EN $\Rightarrow$ G AA Q EN

(RULE (T Q / 12 * -- (EITHER EN OR EL)))

CMU: FLAP

$$\begin{bmatrix} \text{LOMXN} \\ \text{MINI} \\ \sim\text{NUNAS} \end{bmatrix} \longrightarrow \text{FLAP} \ / \ \begin{bmatrix} \text{HIMXN} \\ \text{HIVOC} \end{bmatrix}, \ \begin{bmatrix} \text{HIMXN} \\ \text{HIVOC} \end{bmatrix}$$

SDC: VOWEL REDUCTION

$ REDUCE2 IX=IH:1,

Figure 6-2. Types of rules from the ARPA Speech Understanding Research
Projects. (See the text for an explanation of the rules.)

Certain rules apply across word boundaries, such as the geminate reduction rule in formations, such as "some more" becoming [səmɔr]. Palatalization is also common across word boundaries; for example, [s] followed by [y]
is realized as [ʃ], as in [ðɪʃɪr] for "this year". Devoicing across word
boundaries, as well as at the end of sentences, is a well-known phenomenon;
"his foot" [hɪzfʊt] may be realized as [hɪsfʊt].

Only twelve rule categories that have proved to be important in speech
recognition have been illustrated and yet over 200 rules were compiled. A
natural question might be, "where are the others?" or "aren't the others
useful?" It should be pointed out that of the 242 rules within the ARPA SUR
project only 29 categories are represented. Within these groups there are
many rules of specificity. For example, within "vowel reduction" there are
11 individual rules listed that give different conditions of stress and environment which affect particular vowels that will be reduced. As mentioned
previously, the number of rules is not significant, but the results obtained
from their application are of prime consideration.

6-4. CONTRIBUTIONS FROM PROSODICS

The third question to be addressed is: "What are the potential contributions to automatic speech recognition from prosodics?" Most all of the present speech recognition system builders are using very limited amounts of prosodic information within their systems. The full use of this knowledge source has never been adequately tested. Extensive studies at Univac and other sites showed rather clearly that prosodic information can be used to help parse sentences into grammatical constituents and also it can locate syllabic nuclei of stressed syllables with a high degree of accuracy. Thus it is possible to find those areas which contain the most reliable phonetic information and also those places where the most complex computations of parameters must be done. It also seems possible to determine what phonological rules should apply at various regions of an utterance based on the prosodically-detectable rate of speech, since some rules apply for fast speech while others are applicable only to slow speech. It is generally recognized that prosodic information does offer much to the speech recognition work, but it needs to be fully implemented and tested within a working system.

6-5. FUTURE CONSIDERATIONS

The fourth, and last, question to be addressed is "What might be expected in the future within the phonological aspects of speech recognition?" From the earlier presentation of considerations for using the allophone, phoneme, diphone, syllable, word, or combination of these for recognition, it seems clear that many experimental tests are needed to obtain the most useful phonological unit for recognition, if indeed there is one preferred unit. And, simultaneously, investigators should ascertain whether a combination of units is more productive than any one alone.

A second major area of research is a systematic testing of all possible phonological rules to see their applicability to real speech data. Within the course of an extensive study on this subject, answers to all of the questions discussed previously under "What are the issues to be considered for phonological rules?" should be answered.

Both the testing of phonological units and of phonological rules should be done with human subjects and with recognition systems. If equivalent answers are obtained for both man and machine, the future directions will be clear. If, however, the answers obtained from experiments with humans differ from those with machines, a new set of questions should be asked: "Why the difference?", "What is their significance?", "Should machines try to simulate humans?", etc.

Another step in the future is to expand the capabilities of existing systems, improving the phonological aspects to their fullest extent, using all the knowledge available at this time. Only then will it be possible to define all the future needs in this area.

Another suggestion for the future is that systems be designed which use new approaches or new components. Univac proposed the development of a prosodically-guided speech recognition system (Lea, et al., 1975). Suggestions have been made for designing a perceptual-model recognition system (Klatt, 1977). From the current work in vocal tract modeling (Wakita, 1973), it is possible to think of adding physiologically-supportive components within a future speech recognition system.

The most important consideration for all of the above ideas is that much, much more speech data must be analyzed, processed, and tested before the necessary answers can be obtained for solving the speech recognition problems.

6-6. ACKNOWLEDGMENTS

This chapter was prepared with support from the Office of Naval Research, the Air Force Office of Scientific Research, and the Advanced Research Projects Agency under contract #N00014-77-C-0570 monitored by the Office of Naval Research.

6-7. REFERENCES

Cohen, P.S. and R.L. Mercer (1975), The Phonological Component of an Automatic Speech Recognition System, Speech Recognition, D. R. Reddy (editor), New York: Academic Press, 275-320.

Fujimura, O. (1974), Syllable as a Unit of Speech Recognition, IEEE Symposium on Speech Recognition, Carnegie-Mellon University, April 15-19, 148-153.

Klatt, D.H. (1977), Review of the ARPA Speech Understanding Project, Journal of the Acoustical Society of America, 62: 1345-1366.

Lea, W.A., M.F. Medress, and T.E. Skinner (1975), A Prosodically Guided Speech Understanding System, IEEE Transactions on Acoustics and Speech Signal Processing, ASSP-23: 30-38.

Mermelstein, P., Automatic Segmentation of Speech into Syllabic Units (1975), Journal of the Acoustical Society of America, 58: 880-883.

Mermelstein, P. and G.M. Kuhn (1974), Segmentation of Speech into Syllabic Units, Journal of the Acoustical Society of America, 55: Supplement, Spring, S22 (abstract).

Oshika, B.T., V. Zue, R. Weeks, H. Neu, and J. Aurbach (1975), The Role of Phonological Rules in Speech Understanding Research, IEEE Transactions on Acoustics, Speech, and Signal Processing, ASSP-23: 104-112.

Rovner, P., J. Makhoul, J. Wolf, and J. Colarusso (1974), Where the Words Are, Lexical Retrieval in a Speech Understanding System, IEEE Symposium on Speech Recognition, Carnegie-Mellon University, April 15-19, 160-164.

Wakita, H. (1973), Direct Estimation of the Vocal Tract Shape by Inverse Filtering of Acoustic Speech Waveforms, IEEE Transactions on Audio and Electroacoustics, AU-21: 417-427.

Woods, W., M. Bates, G. Brown, B. Bruce, C. Cook, J. Klovstad, J. Makhoul, B. Nash-Webber, R. Schwartz, J. Wolf, and V. Zue (1976), Speech Understanding Systems Final Technical Progress Report, Bolt, Beranek, and Newman, Inc., Report No. 3438, Cambridge, Massachusetts.

7.

HYPOTHESIZING AND VERIFYING WORDS

FOR SPEECH RECOGNITION

A. Richard Smith
Marvin R. Sambur
ITT - Defense Communicaton Division

7-1. INTRODUCTION

This chapter is a tutorial on the methods and problems of comparing stored representations of words with the acoustic information of unknown utterances for speech recognition. We will discuss word hypothesizing (also called lexical retrieval and lexical subsetting) and word verifying (also called word matching and word mapping). Word verifying is presented first (Sec. 7-2) and is defined to be the matching of an acoustic description of a word against the utterance to determine the likelihood that the word was spoken. We will concentrate on the tools used in word verifying rather than examples of word verifiers. The discussion of word hypothesizing (Sec. 7-3) deals primarily with word hypothesizing as a data-driven process in which the acoustic information of the unknown utterance proposes words which may have been spoken. Both methods and examples of word hypothesizing are given. We conclude the chapter (Sec. 7-4) with speculations on the trends in these areas of speech recognition.

The nature of speech is such that there is no direct mapping from acoustic information to a unique spoken word. Environmental noise, differences between speakers, differences for the same speaker at different times, and variations in pronunciations make it difficult to recognize what words were spoken in the utterance. For continuous speech, the acoustic pattern of a word is embedded within the total pattern of the utterance and modified by it. This gives rise to the coarticulation problem. Also a listener interprets an acoustic event not only by what actually occurs in the utterance but also by the surrounding context and even by what he expects to hear.

Solving the recognition problems arising from these characteristics of speech has required intensive work on all aspects of speech system design and has resulted in a varity of designs and techniques. Nevertheless, the basic structure of connected speech recognition systems can be summarized by the flow chart of Fig. 7-1. (Those parts of the structure shown enclosed in dotted lines are absent in some systems.) We use the figure to show the things that a speech system must do, not the particular parts a system must have. For example, the Harpy speech system [Lowerre, 1976] merges all but the lowest box of the figure into one state transition network. However, the network does the work represented by the higher boxes.

Typically, input speech is digitized and processed to obtain a set of parameters every 10 ms. Hopefully these parameters capture features that are

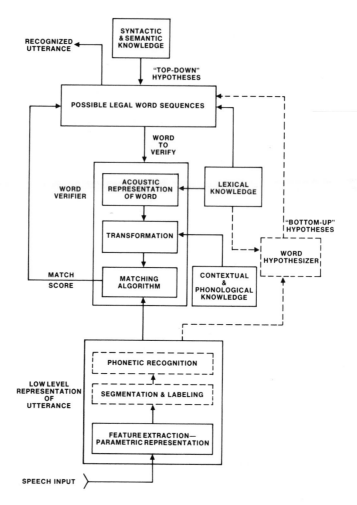

Figure 7-1: Flow Chart of Typical Connected-Speech
Recognition System

most useful for recognition, but tend to be independent of speaker, speech
context, background noise, etc. In some systems, feature extraction is
augmented by segmenting and labeling the speech into phonemic-like regions.

In order to solve the recognition problem, speech recognition systems
use the hypothesize-and-test paradigm in a variety of ways. That is, these
systems attempt to solve the problem by an iterative process of a) making
hypotheses, "educated guesses" about some part of the problem, and b) testing
the likelihood that each hypothesis is true. The form of the hypothesize-
and-test paradigm of interest to us is word hypothesizing and word verifying.

In approaching the problem of finding the acoustic pattern of a word
embedded within the total pattern of the utterance, researchers have
sometimes avoided hypothesizing words from the lower acoustic levels. Rather,
all hypothesizing is based on the semantic, syntactic, and lexical
constraints of the higher levels (shown as "top-down" word hypothesizing in
Fig. 7-1). (In isolated word recognition systems, this "top-down" word
hypothesizing appears as a simple iteration through the lexicon,

hypothesizing each word in turn.) Each word hypothesis is then verified by taking a stored acoustic description of the word, transforming that description to match the lower level representation and deriving a score for the match. It is the word verifier which must handle pronunciation variations, coarticulation effects, and time allignment of the word with the utterance. A word that matches well (i.e., is rated high by the word verifier) directs the system to other "top-down" hypotheses. The system repeats the process until it finds the best syntactically legal sequence of words matching the whole utterance.

Since word verifying is computationally expensive, the above strategy has its limits. If the recognition task is such that the vocabulary and grammer do not constrain the search sufficiently, the system soon becomes overwhelmed with the number of words needing verifying throughout the utterance; words which may be syntactically correct but have no acoustic support. The solution is to do "bottom-up" word hypothesizing (shown by the dotted line box on the right of Fig. 7-1). The method of "bottom-up" word hypothesizing attempts to infer from the lower acoustic information what subset of words from the vocabulary may have been spoken in each part of the utterance. In this chapter, we are primarily concerned with the methods and problems of "bottom-up" word hypothesizing.

Hypothesizing words based on the acoustic information does not compete in accuracy with word verifying. This is because the transformation and matching of words by the verifier takes place for each word with knowledge about the possible context about the word and with knowledge about how various acoustic events within the word might interact to produce the speech. Linguists have developed a fairly detailed generative model of speech describing these transformations from words to the speech signal. Unfortunately, these transformations are not easily or uniquely reversible. Before looking at these issues, we will first present the methods and problems of word verifying.

7-2. WORD VERIFYING

In the typical recognition system shown in Fig. 7-1, the task of the word verifier is to examine the list of hypothesized words at a particular point in the utterance and determine which word is most consistent with the observed acoustic signal. The hypothesized words are determined either "top-down" from a priori knowledge of the syntactical and semantical constraints of the language [Reddy, Erman, and Neely, 1973; Bates, 1975; Reddy, 1976] or "bottom- up" from the acoustic manifestation of the input (see Sec. 7-3).

Given the hypothesized word list, the word verifier retrieves a reference file containing the expected acoustic (or expected phonetic) realization of each candidate. Contextual and phonological rules then operate on each expected realization to form a set of multiple representations for each hypothesized word [Klatt, 1977]. These rules reflect knowledge of the possible perturbations in the expected representation due to coarticulation, to differences in pronunciations, and to optional deletions and insertions in pronunciations. The matching algorithm compares the acoustic (or phonetic) representation of the input speech with each of the possible representations of the hypothesized words to find that word that is most consistent with the observed speech.

The purpose of this section is to examine in more detail each component of the word verifier block of Fig. 7-1.

7-2.1 Word Representation

One of the critical issues in designing a speech recognition system is that of selecting an appropriate acoustic representation of the lexicon. Since, in continuous speech recognition, the representation of the word can vary dramatically in acoustic characteristics depending on the surrounding environment and context, it would be difficult to apply traditional methods of template matching across the entire utterance. This is true because of the problems in predicting how a template may be deformed in these situations. Instead, a word is represented by a sequence of finite acoustic states. An acoustic state can be defined as a relatively stationary segment of speech that can be associated with a set of broad phonetic classes [Woods et al., 1976] or to a set of spectral shapes [Lowerre, 1976]. The key advantage of this representation is that the effects of context and coarticulation can now be predicted by a set of rules that produce a finite state transition network descriptions of the possible modifications that may occur (see Sec. 7-2.3.2).

Given that a speech utterance is to be represented by a finite set of states, how can these states be represented and detected? This problem can be solved by the application of conventional methods of template matching. Thus, a particular state is represented by a set of acoustic features and then detected by determining which representation best matches the measured acoustic features. The success of this approach is associated with the choice of an acoustic feature set.

7-2.1.1 <u>Feature Selection</u> – The important information bearing elements of the speech signal are contained in the magnitude spectrum of the signal as evidenced by ones ability to synthesize speech from knowledge of only the magnitude spectrum, the pitch, and the power [Flanagan, 1972].

The most common features used by ASR systems are the linear prediction parameters [Markel & Gray, 1976]. These parameters are particularly appealing because they are uniquely determined from the speech waveform without any of the ambiguities associated with the measurement of pitch and formant frequencies. The linear prediction formulation models the speech signal as the output of an all pole filter (Fig. 7-2) with transfer function:

$$\text{Eq. (7-1)} \quad H(z) = \frac{1}{1 - a_1 z^{-1} - a_2 z^{-2} \cdots - a_n z^{-n}}$$

The model has proven to be a robust spectral representation of a wide variety of speech sounds. In the generation of speech as shown in Fig. 7-2b a sequence of pulses separated by the pitch period is used as an excitation signal of voice sounds and a pseudo random noise is used for the excitation of unvoiced sounds. This model implies that within a frame of speech the output speech sequence is given by:

$$\text{Eq. (7-2)} \quad s_n = \sum_{k=1}^{p} a_k s_{n-k} + G u_n$$

where p is the number of modeled poles, u_n is the appropriate input excitation, G is the gain of the filter, and the a_k's are the coefficients characterizing the filter. The linear prediction parameters not only specify the magnitude spectrum of the sound but they can also be used to derive the important formant frequencies and the vocal tract area parameters [Wakita, 1973; Markel, 1971]. Other transformations of the linear prediction parameter exist that are also important recognition features [Reddy, 1977].

Another popular speech recognition feature set is obtained as the outputs of a bank of carefully designed bandpass filters [Klatt, 1976b]. These parameters are computationaly less costly to compute than linear prediction parameters and provide a useful and robust spectral representation of the speech [White & Neely, 1976]. Like the linear prediction parameters,

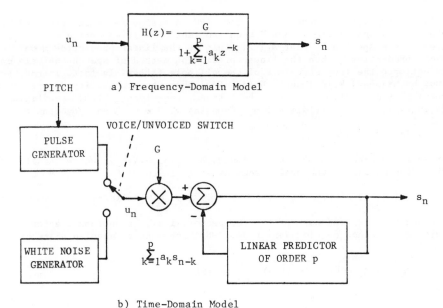

a) Frequency-Domain Model

b) Time-Domain Model

Figure 7-2: Linear Prediction Model of the Speech Signal

the filter bank outputs can be used to synthesize speech, to estimate formant frequencies and other useful parameters (see [Flanagan, 1972]).

Zero crossing measurements have also been successfully used as speech recognition features [Niederjohn, 1975]. These measurements are easy to calculate and can be related to the important first formant and the second formant [Peterson, 1951].

Prosodic cues (fundamental frequency, duration and intensity) are other popular features that have been tried in ASR systems [Lea et al., 1975].

The problem of selecting an optimum feature set for speech recognition purposes is still an open area of research. The selection process is complicated by the fact that the speech utterance contains much more information than the mere identity of the spoken words. The speech conveys information about the identity of the speaker, his educational background, his emotional state and even his physical makeup. The speech is also modified by such factors as the characteristics of the transmission channel and the background noise conditions. The most useful recognition features should be insensitive to characteristics of the talker, the transmission channel and the background noise conditions. Although some preliminary results have been obtained in normalization of these factors [Sambur & Rabiner, 1975; Sambur & Rabiner, 1976; Wakita, 1977], much work needs to be done.

7-2.1.2 <u>State Detection</u> - If the states used to represent the words are associated with a set of spectral templates (as in the Carnegie-Mellon Harpy system [Lowerre, 1976]), the task of detecting a state is an easier task than that of detecting a phonemic state [Klatt, 1977]. If, for example, the linear prediction parameters are used as features, than a convenient distance measure exists that can be used to compare a measured set of LPC coefficients with the set of reference templates [Itakura, 1975]. Because of the importance of the LPC distance measure to state detection for both spectrally defined and phonetically defined states, it is important to understand this measure.

143

7-2.1.2.1 <u>LPC Distance Measure</u> -- The LPC distance measure proposed by Itakura [Itakura, 1975] is based upon the fact that if we excite an all pole filter with a spectrally flat signal (this is the linear prediction model of speech production), then the linear prediction method of speech analysis can only <u>estimate</u> the true structure of the all pole filter. In fact, it has been shown by Mann and Wald [Mann & Wald, 1943] that the probability distribution governing the estimate of the true underlying LPC coefficients $A=(a_1,a_2,...,a_p)$ is multidimensional Gaussian with mean A and covariance:

$$Eq. (7-3) \quad S = \frac{R^{-1}(BRB^t)}{N}$$

where B is the measured LPC coefficients, $B=(b_1,b_2,...,b_p)$, where R is the correlation matrix of the speech segment with elements:

$$Eq. (7-4) \quad r_{ij} = r(|i-j|) = r(k) = \frac{1}{N}\sum_{n=1}^{N-k}s(n)s(n+k)$$

and t denotes the transpose of the row vector, i.e., a column vector. The resulting distance metric [Van Trees, 1968] for such a Gaussian distribution is:

$$Eq. (7-5) \quad d(A,B) = (A-B)[\frac{NR}{BRB^t}](A-B)^t$$

It should be noted that for computational considerations Itakura proposed the closely related distance measure (not metric):

$$Eq. (7-6) \quad d(A,B) = log(ARA^t/BRB^t)$$

Other distance measures for the LPC parameters can also be derived [Gray & Markel, 1976]. These measures are related to the mean square distance between the observed LPC computed spectra and the template LPC computed spectra. Some additional refinements in the distance measure need to be developed so as to reflect the varying degrees of perceptual significance in each region of the spectrum.

When LPC coefficients are not used as recognition features, standard Gaussian type distance metrics have been frequently used [Sebestyen, 1962].

7-2.1.2.2 <u>Spectrally Defined states</u> - The process involved in determining a spectrally defined state consists of first locating approximately stationary acoustic regions. This can be done by sequentially comparing (using an appropriate distance measure) adjacent 10 msec frames to determine if they are sufficiently similar. If the distances between adjacent frames exceeds a suitable threshold [Makhoul, et al., 1974], the quasi stationary segment is then classified as belonging to one of the possible spectral states. In the Harpy system, a label is assigned to each segment based on the LPC distance between the middle 10 msec frame of the segment and a set of 98 templates. A rank order of other template candidates is also computed and used in the final matching algorithm.

7-2.1.2.3 <u>Phonetically Defined states</u> - The phonetically defined states are categorized in terms of a set of broad phonetic class such as voiced or unvoiced, nasal-like or nonnasal- like, front vowel or back vowel, etc. Many excellent papers have been written on methods for characterizing these classes in terms of a set of acoustic features [Martin & Reddy, 1975; Becker & Poza, 1975; Broad & Shoup, 1975] (see also Chap. 5).

Classically the distinction between various vowel sounds have been done on the bases of formant frequences [Peterson & Barney, 1952]. Fig. 7-3 shows the separability of vowel sounds when classified according to the first and second formants.

The distinction between unvoiced and voiced sounds is based upon the

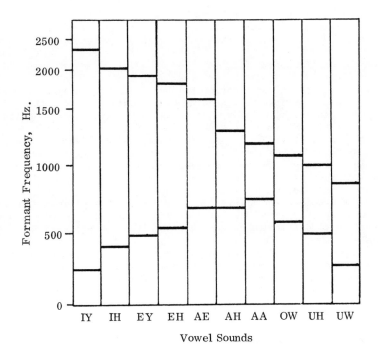

Figure 7-3: First and Second Formants of Vowel Sounds
for a Male Speaker

fact that the unvoiced sounds have a higher concentration of energy in the
high frequency band than the low frequency band, and that the unvoiced sounds
have a lower overall energy than voiced sounds. Such parameters as zero
crossing rate, energy, first LPC coefficient, first autocorrelation
coefficient are linked to these characteristics and can be used to
distinguish between the sounds [Atal & Rabiner, 1976]. The exact shape of the
spectrum can also be used to decide whether a sound is voiced or unvoiced
[Rabiner & Sambur, 1977].

The distinction between nasal and nonnasal sounds is quite difficult
and more research is needed in this area. Similarly, the distinction between
types of fricative sound also needs more research effort.

7-2.2 Transformation

The task of the Transformation box in the verifier is to take the
expected state sequence for the hypothesized words and expand each
representation to account for the possible acoustic forms that could result.
The Matching box then searches through the possible sequence to determine
which sequence is most consistent with the input.

The output of the Transformation box is a state transition network that
represents the possible perturbations of the expected (reference) state
sequence. To derive this network, a set of phonological rules or spectral
transition rules operate on the expected sequence (see Sec 7-2.3.2). Word
boundary rules then operate on the structure to account for the possible
effects of coarticulation. For example, in the digit sequence "4-8-1", the
word "eight" is pronounced as the word "rate" because of the effects of
coarticulation. This fact is captured in the network structure for an

utterance containing the hypothesized word "eight".

The Transformation box relies heavily on detailed phonological rules that are beyond the scope of this chapter (see Chapter 6).

7-2.3 Matching Algorithm

The real job of verification is done in the matching box. The key tool that the most successful matching algorithms use is that of dynamic programming [Bellman, 1957]. The dynamic programming algorithm is a computationally efficient procedure for determining an optimal path through a set of finite states. When used in this manner dynamic programming is sometimes referred to the Viterbi algorithm. The term "Stochastic Matching" can be applied to systems (e.g., Dragon [Baker, 1975]) that employ such a matching procedure.

Alternatively, the dynamic programming algorithm can be used to find the best possible time alignment between an unknown utterance template and a reference template. Most isolated word recognition systems use dynamic programming algorithms to solve the time alignment process. The "analysis by synthesis" method of verification used in the BBN system also employs dynamic programmming for this purpose. Their verifier sends the various representations formed by the transformation box to a synthesis by rule program [Klatt, 1976a] to form a sequence of spectra. Verification scores are obtained by comparing 10ms frames of synthesized spectra with selected spectral frames of the unknown utternace, using dynamic programming algorithm to find the best possible alignment [Woods et al., 1976, Vol. 2].

7-2.3.1 <u>Dynamic Programming</u> -- The method of dynamic programming used for time alignment can best be understood by a concrete example. Suppose that we have hypothesized that the spoken word was the word "four" and that the expected state sequence was five frames in length and was represented as "FFOOR". Now assume that we wish to compare this expected state sequence with some unknown input sequence with a length of four time frames. (We have assumed in this example that we were able to determine the endpoints of the unknown by some technique [Rabiner & Sambur, 1975]). Figure 7-4 shows some of the ways in which the reference sequence can be contracted to fit the unknown input sequence. The ensemble of possible alignments of the reference and the

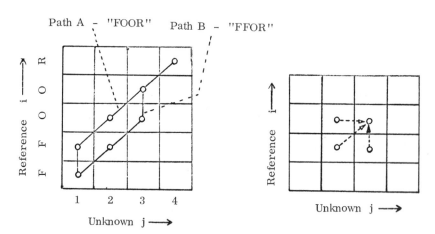

Figure 7-4: Two Alignments of the   Figure 7-5: Possible Path Steps
Reference and Unknown

146

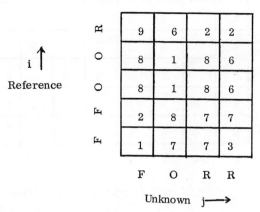

a) Matrix of speech sound similarity between reference and unknown

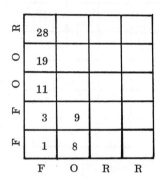

b) Column by column computation of minimum accumulated distance to each point

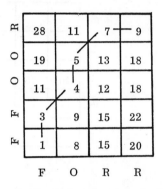

c) Final Matrix with total accumulated distance = 9

Figure 7-6:   Illustration of Dynamic Programming

unknown is represented by all paths originating at the lower left hand point (box) and ending at the upper right hand point (box). The length of the path in going from one point to the next is measured by the acoustic similarity between the reference and the unknown input at the point. Dynamic programming is a recursive procedure for determining the shortest path leading to the upper right hand point. This path results in a time alignment in which the reference word has the maximum acoustic similarity with the input.

The dynamic programming algorithm is based upon the observation that the optimal path to point (i,j) in the two dimensional matrix illustrated in Fig. 7-4 must pass through either the point (i-1,j), or (i-1,j-1), or (i,j-1) as shown in Fig. 7-5.   The minimum accumulated distance to point (i,j) is then given by

Eq. (7-7) $D(i,j) = DIST(i,j) + \min \{D(i-1,j), D(i-1,j-1), D(i,j-1)\}$

where $DIST(i,j)$ is the distance (as determined by a suitable measure) between the reference utterance at time i and the unknown utterance at time j. The algorithm recursively computes this distance column by column to determine the minimum accumulated distance to the point (M,N) where M is the number of

147

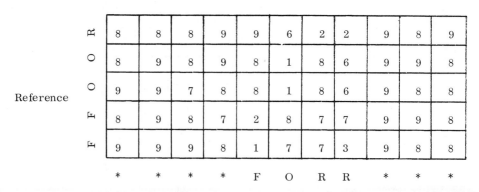

R	8	8	8	9	9	6	2	2	9	8	9
O	8	9	8	9	8	1	8	6	9	9	8
O	9	9	7	8	8	1	8	6	9	8	8
F	8	9	8	7	2	8	7	7	9	9	8
F	9	9	9	8	1	7	7	3	9	8	8
	*	*	*	*	F	O	R	R	*	*	*

Reference

a) Unknown Dissimilarity Matrix

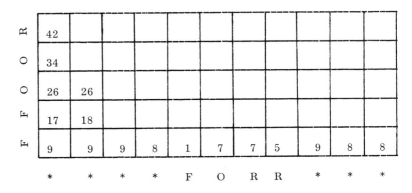

R	42										
O	34										
O	26	26									
F	17	18									
F	9	9	9	8	1	7	7	5	9	8	8
	*	*	*	*	F	O	R	R	*	*	*

b) Column by column computation of minimum accumulated distance

Minimum Distance

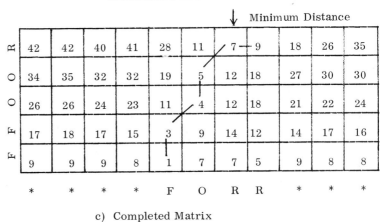

R	42	42	40	41	28	11	7	9	18	26	35
O	34	35	32	32	19	5	12	18	27	30	30
O	26	26	24	23	11	4	12	18	21	22	24
F	17	18	17	15	3	9	14	12	14	17	16
F	9	9	9	8	1	7	7	5	9	8	8
	*	*	*	*	F	O	R	R	*	*	*

c) Completed Matrix

Figure (7-7): Illustration of Dynamic Programming when the end points are not known

frames in the reference and N is the number of frames in the unknown.

Figure 7-6 illustrates how the dynamic programming algorithm would operate if the unknown utterance was the utterance "four" with state sequence "FORR" and the acoustic distances between the input and the references are as indicated in part a) of the figure.

White has suggested a method for performing time alignment without the need for endpoint detection [White, 1978b]. The method is similar to the dynamic programming algorithm described above except that:

Eq. (7-8) $D(1,j) = DIST(1,j)$ for all j

Figure 7-7 shows how this dynamic programming algorithm would be applied if the unknown was "****FORR***" where "*" represents a frame of silence. The surrounding silence indicates that we were unable to accurately determine the endpoints of the unknown. The minimum score in the top row corresponds to the similarity between the utterances.

7-2.3.2 <u>Viterbi Algorithm</u> -- The Viterbi Algorithm (VA) [Forney, 1973] is a form of dynamic programming in which a recursive search is used to determine the optimal path through a network. To illustrate the VA method, assume that the transformation box has produced the state diagram shown in Fig. 7-8a for the word "four". In this figure, nodes represent states, branches represent transitions, and over the course of time the process traces some path from state to state through the state diagram.

In Fig. 7-8b, a more redundant description of the same process is illustrated. This description is called a trellis and each node corresponds to a distinct state at a given time (frame) and each branch represents a transition to some new state at the next frame. The most important property of the trellis is that to every possible state sequence, there corresponds a unique path through the trellis and vice versa.

The underlying assumption in the VA method is that the transition from a state at time j to a state at time j+1 is only dependent on the value of the state at time j (first order Markov). In addition, the state sequence is observed in memoryless noise. What this statement means is that we are not actually observing a particular state at any given time, but some acoustic realization for the state that has been corrupted in some unknown manner. The corruption (which may be due to noise, coarticulation, variability in the particular way a state is pronounced, etc.) is only dependent on the value of the state at the time of observation.

These assumptions mean that we can associate a distance for each branch

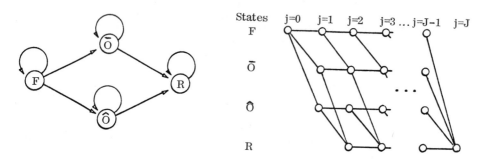

a) State Diagram
   for the Word "FOUR"

b) Trellis

Figure 7-8: State Representation for the Viterbi Algorithm

149

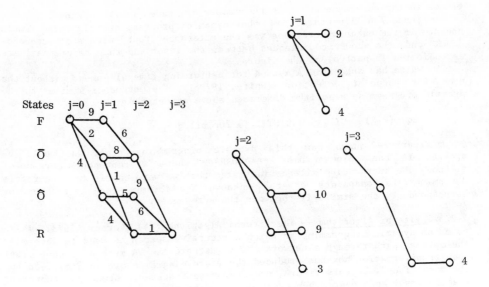

a) Trellis Labeled
   with Branch Lengths

b) Recursive Determination
   of the Shortest Path

Figure 7-9: Operation of the Viterbi Algorithm

in the state diagram given by:

Eq. (7-9) $D(S(i,j),S(k,j-1)) = -\ln P(S(i,j)|S(k,j-1)) - \ln P(X|S(i,j))$

where $S(i,j)$ indicates that at time j we are in the ith state, $P(X|S(i,j))$ is
the probability of observing the acoustic feature set X given that at time j
the ith state was present, and $P(S(i,j)|S(k,j-1))$ denotes the probability of
going from the kth state at time j-1 to the ith state at time j. Given this
definition of distance, dynamic programming is utilized to find the shortest
route through the state diagram. This route corresponds to a state sequence
that is most consistent (in a maximum likelihood sense) with the observed
acoustic features.

Figure 7-9 illustrates how the VA would operate when the length of the
unknown was four units and the unknown was "FORR". The distances are given in
Fig. 7-9a. At each node, the shortest path is determined. This procedure is
recursively continued until the shortest path to the final state is computed
as shown in Fig. 7-9b.

7-3. WORD HYPOTHESIZING

Before looking at particular methods of ("bottom-up") word
hypothesizing, we will discuss word hypothesizing in general and present some
of the problems it must handle.

7-3.1 General Issues

7-3.1.1 <u>Need and Purpose</u> -- As was mentioned in the introduction, a word can
be hypothesized "top-down" from the syntactic and semantic information or

"bottom-up" from acoustic information. The "top-down" method is relatively straight forward. If part of the utterance has been recognized, the grammar and vocabulary of the system and the topic of the utterance will permit only certain sets of words for the remaining parts of the utterance. It is these words which are hypothesized. "Bottom-up" word hypothesizing is more difficult and becomes more important as the vocabularies and grammars of speech systems get larger. As these constraints weaken (i.e. towards the characteristics of general English), a speech system with only a "top-down" word hypothesizer is overwhelmed with the number of words needing verifying; more constraint must come from the acoustics. We discuss only "bottom-up" word hypothesizing below. (Thus, the term "bottom-up" will be assumed).

The primary purpose of word hypothesizing is to make recognition faster not more accurate. A speech system's accuracy is determined by the performance of its word verifier and the characteristics of the bottom-end acoustic processing. However, to achieve that accuracy in an acceptable amount of time for a large vocabulary and grammer, the system will need to do word hypothesizing. The performance of the hypothesizer itself, is a factor in determining how much recognition time is reduced. As was mentioned above, coarticulation, pronunciation variations, and noisy input make it impossible to uniquely determine a word from its acoustic pattern in the utterance. Thus, many of the hypotheses of the word hypothesizer will be in error. One measure of performance is the ratio of the number of correct hypotheses (i.e. words matching the spoken words in name and position) to the number of incorrect hypotheses. Another measure is the relative ratings of the correct and incorrect hypotheses. When the word hypothesizer gives the speech system highly rated correct hypotheses and few incorrect hypotheses, the system does not waste time trying to match incorrect word sequences to the unknown utterance.

7-3.1.2 <u>Large Vocabulary Problems</u> -- Large vocabularies not only require a system to do word hypothesizing but also cause problems for the word hypothesizer, which must be handled by its design. (These same problems must be handled by the word verifier). As the vocabulary increases, storage requirements and computation costs increase. Another problem is performance degradation. As more words are added to a vocabulary, the more likely it is that words will be confused with one another. Sometimes this is because one word is a subpart of another, such as "Plea" being confused with "Please". Other times the confusion comes because words have similar acoustic descriptions and the word hypothesizer (and/or the acoustic processors) cannot distinguish between the acoustic patterns. An example of this is the words "What" and "Watt".

A potentially crippling problem is knowledge acquisition. This is a common and important problem for Artificial Intelligence knowledge-based systems [Feigenbaum, 1977]. For each word to be recognized by the word hypothesizer, a description of how it will appear in speech is needed. This acoustic description must somehow include the variations which the word will undergo due to the speech problems mentioned above (coarticulation, pronunciation variations, etc.). A necessary goal for the word hypothesizer is the ability to add words to its vocabulary easily.

7-3.1.2 <u>Human Performance</u> -- It is interesting to see how well humans perform as "bottom-up" word hypothesizers. Although it is hard to constrain humans to such a role, some measure of human performance is found in the work of Miller and Isard [Miller & Isard, 1963]. Part of their work involved testing the ability of subjects to recognize (i.e. repeat back) the words of ungrammatical utterances spoken to them (e.g., "The built a was tamer fortune blaze by lazy"). Thus, the syntactic and semantic constraints were removed, forcing the subjects to recognize the words from the acoustic information alone. In a test of 50 utterances (5 to 9 words each), 56.1% of the

utterances were repeated back exactly (i.e. all words recognized) and 88.3%
of the principal words (i.e., not function words like "the" and "by") were
recognized. The accuracy for function words was found to be lower (however,
those numbers are not available). Despite a preliminary training period for
the task, the subjects improved significantly during the experiment. The
utterance accuracy for the first 10 utterances was 35.7%; the accuracy for
the last 10 utterances was 62.1%. (Word accuracy was not given.)

Often these results are quoted to show that syntactic and semantic
information is needed to recognize speech. However, the results can also be
used to show the great ability of humans (relative to current speech systems)
to use the acoustic information alone to recognize words in an utterance.
Better than 85% of the utterance words were given correctly as the best
choice hypothesis. In addition, if the tendency of subjects to force a
syntactic and semantic pattern on the utterances could be inhibited, the word
accuracy might be higher yet. (This tendency may explain the improvement with
practice; the subjects may have learned to turn off their semantic and
syntactic "processors".) At any rate, this accuracy is much better than the
best performance obtained by a machine word hypothesizer. Only 34% of the
utterance words are given correctly as the best choice hypotheses, and this
is using a vocabulary of only 1000-words (see Sec 7-3.2.2.1).

7-3.2 Methods and Examples

A word hypothesizer takes an acoustic description of a vocabulary, an
acoustic description of part of an utterance, and outputs word hypotheses
having an acoustic similarity with that part of the utterance. It will help
to look at this task more abstractly. One can imagine a multidimensional
space in which the sound of a word is represented by a point in the space (or
perhaps by a set of points to account for the many ways the word might occur
in speech) and the similarity between the sound of two words is represented
by the distance between their corresponding points as measured by some
metric. We call this the word sound similarity space. This space is defined
by the acoustic descriptions of the words, the acoustic information taken
from the speech, and the methods that the word hypothesizer uses to combine
these to rate its hypotheses. The goal of the hypothesizer is to output for
each part of the unknown utterance the smallest region of the space which
consistently includes the correct word.

There are at least three methods for finding this small region. We will
call them hypothesizing by iterative matching, hypothesizing by directed
matching, and hypothesizing by data-driven matching. In the first,
hypothesizing by iterative matching, the word space is scanned quickly and
not toocarefully to find the words which seem to match the acoustic data. The
resulting subregion of the space is scanned again, not as quickly but more
carefully, to find a smaller region containing better matching words. This
process iterates until the smallest region which is likely to contain the
correct word is found. The method has been suggested by White [White-1978a]
as a means of handling large vocabularies in an isolated word recognition
system. In such an application, the process continues until the final
subregion contains only one word. (In this case, the final scan should
probably be called word verifying.)

The idea behind the second method, hypothesizing by directed matching,
comes from the techniques used in nearest neighbor algorithms. If we think of
the acoustic information for a particular word of the utterance as defining a
point in the word sound similarity space, then hypothsizing can viewed as the
task of finding the nearest neighboring points (i.e., vocabulary words) to
the unknown point. One technique is to do a directed search of the space. The
distance from a known point (or a set of known points) to the unknown point
is used to determine what point (or set of points) should be compared next to
the unknown point. In the same way, the result of matching a word (or a set

of words) directs the hypothesizer to another word (or a set of words) to match. Thus, the hypothesizer focuses in on the best word hypotheses.

The last method is hypothesizing by <u>data-driven matching</u>. Though the other two methods are certainly data driven (i.e. acoustic driven), this method uses the acoustic information to control a step by step search through a data structure combining the descriptions of all the vocabulary words. During the search, subparts (or perhaps characteristics) of words are matched, but not complete words as in the previous methods. The acoustic information can be veiwed as an "index" into the structure. As an index, the information is most easily used in the form of segment-labels or phones.

The first method has been used slightly, the second not at all (to our knowledge), and the last most frequently. Examples of the first and last methods will be described in the next sections. We must emphasize that the "word sound similarity space" has only been used as a way of describing the problems and methods of hypothesizing. Word hypothesizers do not explicitly define the dimensions of the space or a distance metric for it.

7-3.2.1 <u>Hypothesizing by Iterative Matching</u> -- This method of iteratively matching smaller and smaller subsets of the vocabulary with greater and greater precision depends on a hierarchy of acoustic descriptions of the vocabulary and the unknown utterance. At the lowest level the words are represented incompetely, permitting a very fast matching of the whole vocabulary against the unknown. At each higher level, words are described in more detail, until at the highest level a complete representation is given, requiring a costly match for each word (but, of course, the set of words matched at this level is small).

There are several ways to define the levels. If a parametric representation is used (e.g., LPC coefficients for each 10 msec frame of speech), the lower levels can use greater time compression [White, 1978a], use a fewer number of coefficients (this is especially useful if the coefficients can be ordered by the amount of information they carry), or a faster metric for comparing frames of speech. If the representation is based on a sequence of states (e.g., segment-labels or phones) than the lower levels might merge adjacent states, use only the more distinctive states (i.e., gross features), or use equivalence classes of states. An example of the last possibility is found in an isolated word recognition system [Rivorra & Torasso, 1977]. The system uses a two level finite state automaton to describe each word. In the first level the states are broad classes of phonemes such as vowel, stop, silence, etc; the second level uses phonemes.

Hypothesizing by iterative matching may be limited to moderate sized vocabularies (<5000-words). Even with fast matching of words, the method will become too expensive for a large vocabulary. The method also requires the storage of several representations of each word. (However the different levels may be given implicitly in the way a word description is accessed.) For large vocabularies the acoustic information must be used to subset the vocabulary directly. This is done in the next method.

7-3.2.2 <u>Hypothesizing by Data-Driven Matching</u> -- In this method the acoustic information of the utterance controls a search through a data structure combining the descriptions of all the vocabulary words. The amount of acoustic information used by hypothesizers varies. One rarely used version of the Carnegie-Mellon Hearsay-I speech system [Reddy, Erman, and Neely, 1972] tried to use gross acoustic events, such as the "SH" in "Bishop", to suggest words. (The vocabulary was divided into sets of words having the same acoustic event.) We know of only three examples of word hypothesizers using extensive acoustic information. They are the word hypothesizer [Smith, 1976] in Carnegie-Mellon Hearsay-II [Reddy, et al., 1977; Erman, 1977], the "Probabilistic Lexical Retrieval Component" [Klovstad, 1978] for the BBN (Bolt, Beranek, and Newman, Inc.) HWIM system [Woods, 1976] and the Noah word

hypothesizer developed to study the effect of large vocabularies on word hypothesizing [Smith, 1977]. We will describe each of these showing how they acquire and represent acoustic descriptions of words, how they handle coarticulation problems and proununciation variations, and how they use the acoustic information of the utterance to search for word hypotheses.

7-3.2.2.1 <u>The Hearsay-II Word Hypothesizer</u> -- Design -- The Hearsay-II word hypothesizer [Smith, 1976] is shown in Fig. 7-10. It uses a Markov probability model to convert sequences of segment-labels to classes of syllables called "syltypes". Then, for each syltype hypothesized, all words containing a stressed syllable which is a member of that syltype class are suggested for hypothesizing. Multisyllabic words which match poorly against adjacent syltypes are rejected.

The definition of syltypes is based on grouping the phonemes into seven classes: A-like vowels, I-like vowels, U-like vowels, liquids, nasals, stops and fricatives. Fig. 7-11 gives the class membership for the phonemes. The pronunciation of each vocabulary word found in a pronunciation dictionary is converted to a sequence of syltypes by mapping each phoneme to its phoneme class. (The dictionary contains alternate pronunciations to handle a few coarticulation problems). For example, let the above phoneme classes be represented by the symbols A, I, U, L, N, P, and F respectively (as in the first column of Fig. 7-11). The word "Airplanes", with the pronunciation EH R - P L EY N Z" is mapped to the syltypes "IL" and "PLINF". Whenever the syltype "PLINF" is hypothesized, it is used to index an inverted lexicon and retrieve the set of words containing it (like "Airplanes", "Trains", and "Grins"). If the syltype hypothesis "IL" is found, to the left of "PLINF", then the word "Airplanes" would be hypothesized.

A network is used to describe the legal syltypes for a vocabulary, by associating with each state a phoneme class. A Markov probability model gives a way of calculating the probability of each path through the network (i.e., each syltype) for a segment-label sequence. The probabilities for the state transitions are estimated from phonetically hand-labeled training utterances. The phones in these utterances are converted to phoneme classes and then to state sequences. Segment-labels from the Hearsay-II sementer-labeler for the utterances are aligned with these states so that frequency counts of <current state, next state, next segment-label> triples can be made. These are normalized to give the probability of going from a current state to a new state given the next segment-label. The state transition probabilities and the segment-label sequences of an unknown utterance determine syltype hypotheses which are used to hypothesize words.

Results and Discussion -- In Hearsay-II all hypotheses from the word hypothesizer are passed immediately to the word verifier for rating. Thus, the word hypothesizer acts as a word filter for the word verifier. The performance measure relevant to this task is the number of words hypothesized correctly and the average number of hypothesized per utterance word. (The ratings of hypotheses are only used to determine what words are passed to the verifier). Testing on 48 utterances (none of which where included in the 60 training utterances) and using a 1011-word vocabulary resulted in hypothesizing 65% of the utterance words, along with about 90 hypotheses per utterance word. The word verifier rejects 51% of the incorrect hypotheses and about 6% of the correct hypotheses (for a particular rejection threshold setting).*

The Hearsay-II word hypothesizer attempts to handle the problems of coarticulation and pronunciation variations by a) using broad phoneme classes which tend to be not affected by these problems and b) including alternate

---

*Hearsay-II raises the resulting 61% word accuracy to above 70% by using the verifier to match all words that can syntactically begin (end) an utterance against the beginning (ending) of the utterance.

154

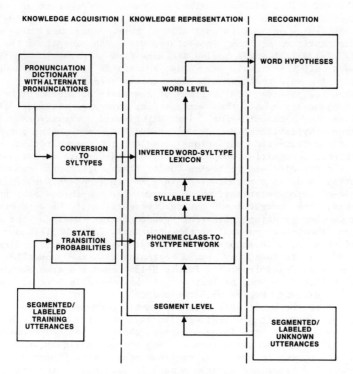

Figure 7-10: Word Hypothesizing in Hearsay-II

CODE	CLASS	PHONEME
A	A-LIKE	AE,AA,AH,AO,AX
I	I-LIKE	IY,IH,EY,EH,IX,AY
U	U-LIKE	OW,UH,U,UW,ER,AW,OY,EL,EM,EN
L	LIQUID	Y,W,R,L
N	NASAL	M,N,NX
P	STOP	P,T,K,B,D,G,DX
F	FRIC	HH,F,TH,S,SH,V,DH,Z,ZH,CH,ZH,WH

Figure 7-11: Phoneme Equivalence Classes

pronunciations in the dictionary (put in by hand) for any of the speech problems not handled by (a). Though the phoneme classes may make some of the speech problems disappear, increasing the accuracy, a high price is paid in the number of hypotheses per utterance word. The phoneme classes make each syllable a member of one and only one syltype class. However, it is impossible to separate syllables or phonemes into strict classes. Those phonemes which tend to lie "between" classes cause a loss in discrimination between the classes, which results in a loss in discrimination between syltypes and words. One solution is to use more phoneme classes and more syltypes, and in the limit to use phonemes and syllables. Another solution is to go directly from recognized phones in the utterance to pronunciations of the words explicitly giving coarticulation variations. This is what the next hypothesizer does.

155

7-3.2.2.2 The BBN HWIM Word Hypothesizer -- Design -- The heart of the HWIM word hypothesizer, shown in Fig. 7-12, is a lexical decoding network [Klovstad, 1978]. The network is basically a tree containing all expected phonetic realizations of the vocabulary words. An example of the tree is given in Fig. 7-13a. All words having the same first N phones share the same initial nodes of the tree. Any node containing the last node of the pronunciation of a word contains a pointer to the word.

The expected phonetic realizations of a word is obtained by expanding the base pronunciation of the word to an average of more than six pronunciations to account for 1) within-word variations due to palatalization, syllabification, vowel reduction, and other phonological phenomena, 2) within-word variations due to the pecularities of the acoustic-phonetic recognition component, and 3) end-of-word variations due to the effect of preceeding and following words. This dictionary expansion is done automatically using a phonological rule system [Woods & Zue, 1976].

The end-of-word variations, which account for two-thirds of the extra pronunciations, are constrained during recognition if the word context is known. This is done by using different pronunciation endings for a word depending on the next phones of the utterance. For example, consider the phonological rule: OPT {ND # L} → {N # L}, that is, when a word ending in the phones "N D" is followed by a word beginning with the phone "L", the "D" may disappear (e.g. "hand labels"). Figure 8-13b shows the tree augmented by this rule. The final "D" may be left off of the pronunciations of "Hand" and "And" when the next word begins with the phone "L".

The input to the hypothesizer is a phonetic segment lattice generated by the Acoustic-Phonetic Recognizer [Woods, et al., 1976]. The lattice structure gives a way of specifying alternate phonetic descriptions of the utterance. While scanning the utterance each segment position in the lattice can begin a path search in the tree, continue other paths (which began at an earlier segment), or complete a path. A path is extended in the tree to a new node if the phone of the node matches any of the phones in the next segment. Errors in segmentation are handled by permitting a merge or split of segments. That is, instead of matching one node in the tree per segment, one node is matched to two segments (a merge of the segments) or two nodes are matched to one segment (a split of the segment). Penalties are added for

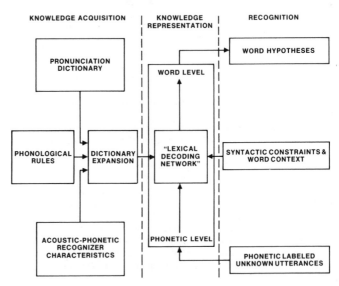

Figure 7-12: Word Hypothesizing in HWIM

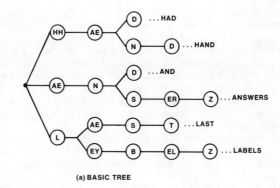

(a) BASIC TREE

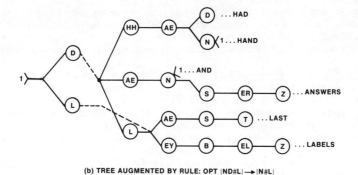

(b) TREE AUGMENTED BY RULE: OPT |ND#L| → |N#L|

Figure 7-13: An Example of the "Lexical Decoding Network"
in the HWIM Word Hypothesizer

splitting and merging. Only the best paths in the tree are searched, so that
only the best N hypotheses are found for the utterance. Typically N is
restricted to about 12 in the initial scan of the utterance (explained
below).

The hypothesizer includes features for using non-acoustic information
about the utterance. If the hypothesizer is given the syntactic class of the
words for a particular part of the utterance, it can constrain its search to
find only words in that class. This is done by storing at each node in the
tree the syntactic classes of all words in the subtree of the node (i.e., all
words pointed to by the terminal nodes of the subtree). Similarly,
information is stored at each node about the length of the words in the
subtree. This permits constraining the hypothesizer to look for words of a
particular length.

Results and Discussion -- The recognition strategy of the HWIM speech system
is different then that used by Hearsay-II. HWIM uses its hypothesizer to do
an initial scan of the utterance to find a few good hypotheses. The
hypotheses are used as "seeds" to start "top-down" recognition. Beginning
with the best seed the syntactic component of the system uses the
hypothesizer to find words adjacent to the seed using the (now known)
constraints of word context and syntax. The best rated hypothesis is joined
with the seed and the hypothesizer is called again to find words adjacent to
the pair of words. This process continues until a complete sequence of words
is found matching the acoustic information of the unknown utterance. Usually

157

the process involves backtracking to abandon a poorly matching partial sequence of words to pickup a better sequence or perhaps another seed.

In the inital scan of the utterance the hypothesizer typically returns 12 hypotheses, 2 of which are correct, from a 1097-word vocabulary with sentences averaging 6 words in length. A correct word hypothesis is rated best 58% of the time and as one of the top five 85% of the time. The hypothesizer fails to find any correct seed for 8% of the utterances. This ranking of the correct hypotheses compared to the incorrect hypotheses is important because it determines how frequently the speech system wastes time with incorrect seeds.

The hypothesizer has many good features: 1) It attempts to distinguish every word in the vocabulary, 2) It explicitly handles many coarticulation problems including word-to-word phonomena (when the word context is known), 3) The phonological rules for this are added to the dictionary automatically, 4) The final phonetic word descriptions are stored in a tree structure for relatively efficient matching to the utterance, and 5) Syntactic constraints can be used when available.

There is some question about the size of vocabulary the hypothesizer could handle. Since the phonological rules expand the number of word pronunciations six times, the tree may soon get too large to store and search. This size would increase if more phonological rules were added.

7-3.2.2.3 <u>The Noah Word Hypothesizer</u> -- The Noah Word Hypothesizer was designed, implemented and tested as part of a dissertation which investigated the problems of large vocabularies (greater than 10,000-words) and their effect on word hypothesizing [Smith, 1977] The hypothesizer uses the same segment-label input as the Hearsay-II word hypothesizer and was built with the idea of replacing it. Noah sets out to solve the following problems which are sensitive to vocabulary size: 1) Knowledge representation: storing the acoustic descriptions of words efficiently for fast retrieval, 2) Knowledge acquistion: obtaining the acoustic descriptions for a large number of words easily, 3) Flexibility: permitting improvements to be made to the segmenter-labeler without requiring an expensive reacquisition of knowledge, and 4) Performance: hypothesizing many of the correct words of an utterance with few incorrect ones, within "reasonable" computation constraints.

Design -- The solutions to these problems center around the knowledge representation of the hypothesizer. As shown in Fig. 7-14, Noah uses three trees and four levels of representation at the point where the HWIM word hypothesizer uses one tree between two levels. Speech is represented in a hierarchy of levels containing (from bottom to top): segment labels, "sylparts", syllables, and words. The sylpart level consists of parts of syllables: onsets, vowels and codas. (Onsets and codas are the initial and final non- nucleus part of syllables, respectively.) For example, the second syllable of "Abstraction" (AE B - S T R AE K - SH AX N), "S T R AE K" has an onset of "S T R" a vowel of "AE" and a coda of "K". (The first syllable of the word has a null onset.) The syllable level contains complete syllables and not syltypes as found in Hearsay-II word hypothesizer.

Between each pair of adjacent levels (segment-sylpart, sylpart-syllable, and syllable-word pairs) is a tree structure storing sequences of the lower level units to define a higher level unit. (In the same way phone sequences defined words in the HWIM hypothesizer.) Fig. 7-15 gives an example of a syllable-word tree, the top tree of the structure. The middle tree defines syllables in terms of sylparts and the lowest tree defines sylparts in terms of segment-label patterns. (The lowest tree is really three separate trees corresponding to onset, vowel, and coda sylparts.)

The knowledge stored in the two higher level trees is obtained by processing a pronunciation dictionary containing only base pronunciations. While converting the dictionary to the structure of the trees some of the

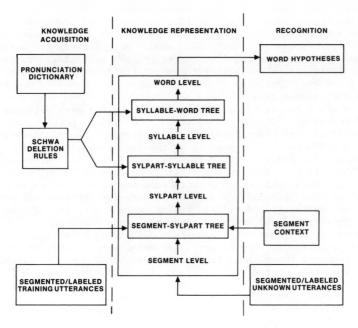

Figure 7-14: The NOAH Word Hypothesizer

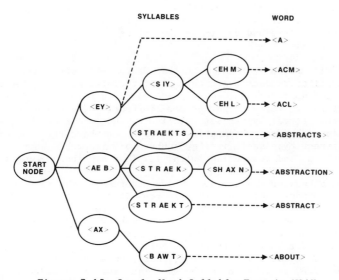

Figure 7-15: Sample Word-Syllable Tree in NOAH

words receive alternate pronunciations based on schwa deletion rules. (Schwas are reduced vowels that are sometimes deleted in normal speech.) For example, the second syllable in "Summary": S AX M - AX - R IY is often deleted giving: S AX M - R IY. Since the hypothesizer is syllable based, it is important to handle word variations which change the syllable count of words. Schwa deletion rules is one method. Another is "vowel sequence" learning, discussed below.

The knowledge stored in the segment-sylpart trees is acquired by training the hypothesizer on speech that has been hand-segmented into onset, vowels, and coda segment patterns. By aligning this training data with the segment-labels (produced by the same segmenter-labler used during recognition), segment patterns are learned for the sylparts. It is between the segment and sylpart levels that the pecularities of the segmenter-labeler and many of the coarticulation problems of speech are handled. One method is to learn "vowel-sequences".

Vowels often run together in speech, sharing the same syllable nucleus (as in "the abstract"). At other times, the segment pattern of a vowel is greatly modified by the preceding or following phone. Sometimes this modification of the vowel pattern is the only clue to the identity of the adjacent phone (as when the "IH L" in Nilsson": N IH L – S AX N appears as one vowel). It is for these reasons that the method of "vowel sequences" was developed. Basically, the method permits merging together adjacent phones with a vowel and learning the segment pattern for the complete sequence of phones. If the pattern is identified during recognition, the same sequence of phones is hypothesized and broken into onsets, vowels and codas.

Segment context learning is a second method. When learning the segment pattern of a sylpart, the adjacent segment-labels of the pattern are also learned as context. Though many factors influence the segment pattern of a particular sylpart, the greatest influence is given by the speech immediately before and after the pattern. During recognition, this context is used to limit the possible interpretations of the segment pattern.

Word hypothesizing in Noah is a bottom-up recognition process through four levels: 1) Syllables nuclei are recognized at the segment level, 2) For each syllable nuclei the segment-vowel tree is searched to hypothesize vowels; then onsets and codas are hypothesized, 3) Syllables are hypothesized using the sylpart-syllable tree, and finally 4) Words are hypothesized using the syllable-word tree. At each level the ratings of the hypotheses direct the search of the tree and determine the ratings of the hypotheses at the next higher level.

Results and Discussion -- Noah, like the Hearsay-II word hypothesizer, is used to hypothesize many words throughout the utterance. Its performance is measured by the number of words hypothesized per utterance word, the percent of the utterance words hypothesized correctly (word accuracy), and the ratings of the correct hypotheses relative to the incorrect hypotheses. The last measure is given by computing the ranks of the correct hypotheses. The rank of a correct hypothesis is the number of incorrect hypotheses rated better than it and competing with it. (Two hypotheses compete when they overlap in time significantly.)

The hypothesizer was trained on 174 utterances (about 1600 syllables) that had been hand-segmented into sylparts. It was tested on a different set of 105 utterances (about 700 words; one speaker) for 7 different vocabulary sizes ranging from 500 words to 19,000 words. In each test the number of hypotheses was limited to about 20 per utterance word. Fig. 7-16 shows the word accuracy for all 20 ranks and for each of the first 5 ranks over the range of vocabulary sizes. The average rank of the correct word hypotheses climbs from 2.6 to 5.8 over the same increase in vocabulary size. By one measure of performance (word accuracy weighted by the rank of the correct hypotheses), the performance degraded approximately logrithmically with vocabulary size. The computation costs also increased logrithmically with vocabulary size increasing from 2.4 MIPSS (million instructions per second of speech) to 6.6 MIPSS. For a 1000 word vocabulary the computation cost is almost an order of magnitude less than the cost of word hypothesizing in Hearsay-II.

For the task of finding the best "seeds" for an utterance, Noah finds about the same ratio of correct hypotheses to incorrect hypotheses (for a

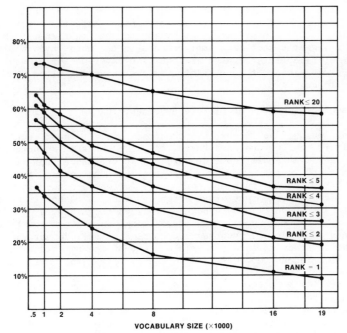

Figure 7-16: Word Accuracy for NOAH in the Best M Ranks
for Different Vocabulary Sizes

1000-word vocabulary) as the HWIM word hypothesizer. However, the correct hypotheses are more likely to be rated better. A correct hypothesis was rated best 69% of the time (compared to 58%) and within the top five 92% of the time (compared to 85%). The hypothesizer fails to find any correct seed for 2% of the utterances (compared to 8%) .

The advantages of this hierarchy of trees are two fold. First, the structure increases the speed of recognition for the following reasons: a) Because of the multiple levels a sylpart is recognized only once in each part of the utterance for all syllables using it; the same is true for syllables and words; b) The trees between each level permit a semi-parallel search for the hypotheses represented by the lower level hypotheses; c) Searching in the structure begins only at syllable nuclei, rather than at each segment; and d) The multiple levels permit controlling the number of hypotheses at each level preventing a possible combinatoric explosion of word hypotheses for large vocabularies.

Second, the structure permits separating the knowledge acquistion into the relatively easy task of acquiring base pronunciations of words and difficult task of acquiring segment-label patterns describing the pecularities of speech and coarticulation phonemena as interpreted by a particular segmenter-labeler. Once "enough" segment-patterns are learned for the sylparts, the word hypothesizer is ready to recognize any word from the base pronunciation of the word.

However, these advantages rest on what may be a weak assumption. The assumption is that the coarticulation problems of speech can be handled at the sylpart level. There is no provision for handling word-to-word (or syllable-to-syllable) coarticulation other than the same methods used between any two sylparts. It may prove that for better performance and multiple speakers, more of the coarticulation problems will have to be handled at higher levels (as schwa deletion has been).

The main conclusion of the research with Noah is that "bottom-up" word

161

hypothesizing is not greatly affected by the size of the vocabulary. It is a pleasant surprise that the vocabulary size affected performance and computation costs approximately according to the logarithm of the vocabulary size. This suggests that with improvements in the word hypothesizer and in the segmenter-labeler, speech recognition systems for general English can obtain a great amount of constraint from the acoustics alone, just as humans seem able to do.

7-3.3 Speech System Control of Word Hypothesizing

What words should be hypothesized? Is it best to permit the hypothesizer to try to recognize all the words of an unknown utterance? Generally not. The small function words of an utterance such as "the", "and", "a", and "of" should not be hypothesized "bottom-up" for the following reasons: First, small-function words are often hypothesized incorrectly, since their acoustic patterns often appear as subparts of other words. Second, they are usually not hypothesized when they should be, since they appear with reduced vowels and are "hidden" in the speech. Finally, if the small function words are hypothesized correctly, they do not give much clue about the syntactic and semantic content of the utterance. In brief, they have little "acoustic constraint" and little syntactic and semantic "content-value".

In testing Noah it was observed that 1% of the 1000-word vocabulary (the ten words: "an", "at", "in", "it", "the", "of", "a", "to", "done", and "Ann") accounted for almost 30% of the incorrect hypotheses, but less than 10% of the utterance words. The first eight words of the list which have little acoustic constraint and content-value should not be hypothesized "bottom-up". Rather, they should be hypothesized "top-down" when most of the utterance words have been recognized. It is more difficult to correctly handle words like "done" and "Ann", which have more syntactic and semantic content.

Vocabulary words can be divided into four (fuzzy) groups shown in Fig. 7-17. An example of each group is given in parentheses. A word hypothesizer has little trouble in hypothesizing words from Groups II and IV; the strong acoustic constraints reduce the number of misses for these words. The problem is with the words of Groups I and III. The speech system should control the hypothesizer so a word is hypothesized based on its acoustic match with the utterance, its a priori likelihood of being correct (based on its acoustic constraint), and its value for recognizing the rest of the utterance. The acceptance threshold for each word could be based on the product of a measure of the content-value of the word and the acoustic constraint of the word; Group I having the strictest acceptance threshold and Group IV having the most lenient acceptance threshold.

A speech system which searches word hypotheses to find syntacticlly legal sequences of words should assume the existence of a Group I word any time it needs one to extend a sequence. Later, these words can be verified for what seem to be the best sequences. The important thing to note is that the word hypothesizer should be controlled by preset thresholds or dynamically by the system to hypothesize those words most useful to the task of understanding speech.

		Acoustic-Constraints	
		Weak	Strong
Syntactic/Semantic	Weak	I. "the"	II. "also"
Content-Value	Strong	III. "Ann"	IV. "abstracts"

Figure 7-17: Four Types of Vocabulary Words

7-4. TRENDS AND FUTURE RESEARCH NEEDS

Since it is difficult to identify trends in an area of research as young as word hypothesizing and verifying, we can only speculate on the future. There are two obvious goals driving developments in word hypothesizing and verifying; these are the same goals which drive speech recognition in general. They are: a) the goal to increase the complexity of the recognition task towards that of general English and b) the goal to increase recognition accuracy for any size task.

The closer a speech system approaches the goal of real time recognition of general English, the more it must depend on the acoustic constraints of the unknown utterance, just as humans seem capable of doing (see Sec. 7-3.1.2). This means a greater emphasis on "bottom-up" word hypothesizing.

In addition, more complex tasks will require greater system control of hypothesizing and verifying. The "bottom-up" hypothesizer must be directed to hypothesize those words which are syntactically and semantically valuable for recognizing the complete utterance, thus, avoiding words such as "the", "an" and "of" (see Sec 7-3.3). For general English recognition, it will be important to direct the word hypothesizer to a subset of the total vocabulary (5000 out of 100,000-words?) when the topic of the utterance is known. The verifier should be controlled to do word matching with different levels of precision, restricting the most costly and precise matching for words which are syntactically and acoustically similar (e.g., "split" and "slit").

The second goal of increased recognition accuracy will require more research to find features which are more speaker independent and distance metrics which are more preceptually related. Along with Klatt [Klatt, 1977], we speculate that there will be a trend away from the phonetically defined states towards spectrally defined states for word representation (see Sec. 7-2.1.2.).

We think that there will appear several modifications of the popular dynamic programming algorithm. The modifications will be aimed at better beginning and ending detection of words, and more perceptually related weighting of the parts of words for better scoring.

Finally, we speculate that as systems face more ambitious recognition tasks and strive for greater accuracy, there will be a trend away from hand acquired knowledge for word hypothesizing and verifying towards automatic knowledge acquisition and adaptive learning systems.

7-5. BIBLIOGRAPHY

Atal B., and L. Rabiner "A Pattern Recognition Approach to Voiced-Unvoiced-Silence Classification with Applications to Speech Recognition," IEEE Transactions on Acoustics, Speech, and Signal Processing, ASSP-24, no. 3, 1976, 201-211.

Baker, J. K., "The DRAGON System - An Overview," IEEE Transactions on Acoustics, Speech, and Signal Processing, ASSP-23, no. 1, 1975, 24-29.

Bates, M., "The Use of Syntax in a Speech Understanding System," IEEE Transactions on Acoustics, Speech, and Signal Processing, ASSP-23, 1975, 112-117.

Becker R., and F. Poza, "Acoustic Phonetic Research in Speech Understanding," IEEE Transactions on Acoustics, Speech, and Signal Processing, ASSP-23, no. 5, 1975, 416-426.

Bellman, R., Dynamic Programming, Princeton, NJ: Princeton University Press, 1957.

Broad, D. J., and J. E. Shoup, "Concepts for Acoustic Phonetic Recognition," in Speech Recognition, ed. D. R. Reddy, New York: Academic Press, 1975, 275-320.

Erman, L. D., "A Functional Description of the Hearsay-II System," Proceedings IEEE International Conference on Acoustics, Speech, and Signal Processing, Hartford, Conn., 1977, 799-802.

Feigenbaum, E., "The Art of Artificial Intelligence: I. Themes and Case Studies of Knowledge Engineering," Proceedings of the 5th International Joint Conference on Artificial Intelligence, Mass., 1977, Vol II, 1014-1029.

Flanagan, J., Speech Analysis, Synthesis, and Perception, Springer Verlag, 1972.

Forney, G. Jr., "The Viterbi Algorithm," Proceedings of the IEEE, 61, no. 3, 1973, 268-278.

Gray, A., Jr., and Markel J., "Distance Measures for Speech Processing," IEEE Transactions on Acoustics, Speech, and Signal Processing, ASSP-24, no. 5, 1976, 380-390.

Itakura, F., "Minimum Prediction Residual Principle Applied to Speech Recognition," IEEE Transactions on Acoustics, Speech, and Signal Processing, ASSP-23, 1975, 67-72.

Klatt D. H., "Review of the ARPA Speech Understanding Project," Journal of the Acoustical Society of America, 62, no. 4, 1977, 1345-1366.

Klatt D. H., "Structure of a Phonological Rule Component for a Synthesis-by-Rule Program," IEEE Transactions on Acoustics, Speech, and Signal Processing, ASSP-24, 1976(a), 391-398.

Klatt, D. H., "A Digital Filter Bank for Spectral Matching," IEEE International Conference on Acoustics, Speech, and Signal Processing, Philadelphia, Pa., 1976(b), 537-540.

Klovstad, J. W., "Computer-Automated Speech Perception System," Ph. D. thesis in progress, Massachussets Institute of Technology, 1978. The research refered to in this chapter was sponsored by the Advanced Research Projects Agency, ARPA order No. 2904 at Bolt, Beranek, and Newman, Inc.

Lea, W. A., M. F. Medress, and T. E. Skinner, "A Prosodically Guided Speech Understanding System," IEEE Transactions on Acoustics, Speech, and Signal Processing, ASSP-23, 1975, 30-38.

Lowerre, B. T., "The Harpy Speech Recognition System," Ph. D. thesis (Department of Computer Science, Carnegie-Mellon University, Pittsburgh, Pa.), 1976.

Makhoul, J., R. Viswanathan, L. Cosel, and W. Russel, "Natural Communications with Computers: Speech Compression Research at BBN," Bolt Beranek and Newman, Inc., Cambridge, Mass., BBN Rep. 2976, vol. II, 1974.

Mann, H., and A. Wald, "On the Statistical Treatment of Linear Stochastic Difference Equations," Econometrica, 2, no. 3 and 4., 1943.

Markel, J. "Formant Trajectory Estimation from a Linear Least Squares Inverse Filter Formulation," Speech Communication Research Laboratory, Santa Barbara, Ca., Monogram 7, 1971.

Markel, J. and A. Gray Jr., Linear Predictions of Speech, Springer Verlag, 1977.

Martin, M. B. and D. R. Reddy, ed., Special Issue on IEEE Symposium on Speech Recognition, pp. 79-111, IEEE Transactions on Acoustics, Speech, and Signal Processing, ASSP-23, no. 1, 1975.

Miller, G., and S. Isard, "Some Perceptual Consequences of Linquistic Rules," Journal of Verbal Learning and Verbal Behavior, 2, 1963, 217-228.

Niederjohn, R., "A Mathematical Formulation and Comparison of Zero Crossing, Analysis Techniques which have been Applied to Automatic Speech Recognition," IEEE Transactions on Acoustics, Speech, and Signal Processing, ASSP-23, no. 4, 1975, 373-379.

Peterson, E., "Frequency Detection and Speech Formants," Journal of the Acoustic Society of America, 23, 1951, 668-674.

164

Peterson, G. E., and H. L. Barney, "Control Methods Used in a Study of the Vowels," Journal of the Acoustic Society of America, 24, 1952, 175-185.

Rabiner, L. R., and M. R. Sambur, "An Algorithm for Determining the Endpoints of Isolated Utterances," Bell System Technical Journal, 54, 1975, 297-315.

Rabiner, L. R., and M. R. Sambur, "Voice-Unvoiced Silence Detection using the Itakura LPC Distance Measure," IEEE International Conference on Acoustics, Speech, and Signal Processing., Hartford, Conn., 1977, 323-327.

Reddy, D. R., "Speech Recognition by Machine: A Review," Proceedings of the IEEE, 64, 1976, 501-531.

Reddy, D. R., L. D. Erman and R. B. Neely, "A Mechanistic Model of Speech Perception," Proceedings IEEE Conference on Speech Communication and Processing, Newton, Mass., 1972, 334-337.

Reddy, D. R., L. D. Erman, and R. B. Neely, "A Model and a System for Machine Recognition of Speech," IEEE Transactions, AU-21, 1973, 229-238.

Reddy, D. R., et al. "Speech Understanding Systems Final Report," Computer Science Department, Carnegie-Mellon University, 1977.

Ritea, B., "Automatic Speech Understanding Systems," Proceedings of the 11th IEEE Computer Society Conference, Washington, DC, 1975.

Rivoira, S. and P. Torasso, "Syntax-Directed Recognition of Spoken Words in Real-Time," Proceedings of IEEE International Conference on Acoustics, Speech, and Signal Processing, Hartford, Conn., 1977, 475-478.

Sambur, M. R. and L. R. Rabiner, "Speaker Independent Digit Recognition," Bell System Technical Journal, 54, 1975, 81-102.

Sambur, M. R. and L. R. Rabiner, "A Statistical Decision Approach to the Recognition of Connected Digits," IEEE Transactions on Acoustics,, Speech, and Signal Processing, ASSP-24, no. 6, 1976, 550-558.

Sebestyen, G., Decision Making Processes in Pattern Recognition, New York: Macmillan, 1962.

Smith, A. R., "Word Hypothesization for Large-Vocabulary Speech Understanding Systems,", Ph. D. thesis, Carnegie-Mellon University, 1977.

Smith, A. R., "Word Hypothesization in the Hearsay-II Speech Understanding System," IEEE International Conference on Acoustics, Speech, and Signal Processing, Philadelphia, Pa., 1976, 549-552.

Van Trees, H., Detection, Estimation and Modulation Theory, New York: Wiley, 1968.

Wakita, H., "Normalization of Vowels by Vocal Tract Length and its Application to Vowel Identification," IEEE Transactions on Acoustics, Speech and Signal Processing, ASSP-25, no. 2, 1977, 183-192.

Wakita, H., "Direct Estimation of the Vocal Tract Shape by Inverse Filtering of Acoustic Speech Waveform," IEEE Transactions on Audio Electroacoustics, AU-21, 1973, 417-427.

White G. W. and R. B. Neely, "Speech Recognition Experiments with Linear Predication, Bandpass Filtering, and Dynamic Programming," IEEE Transactions on Acoustics, Speech and Signal Processing, ASSP-24, no. 2, 1976a, 183-187.

White G. W., "Automatic Speech Recognition of Large Vocabularies," in Natural Language Communication with Compute s, L. Bloc, ed., Springer Verlag, to be published 1978b.

White, G. W., "Dynamic Programing, Viterbi Algorithm, and Low Cost Speech Recognition," IEEE International Conference on Acoustics, Speech and Signal Processing, Tulsa, Oklahoma, 1978.

Woods, W., M. Bates, G. Brown, B. Bruce, C. Cook, J. Klovstad, J. Makhoul, B. Nash-Webber, R. Schwartz, J. Wolf, and V. Zue, "Speech Understanding Systems: Final Technical Progress Report," Bolt Beranek and Newman, Inc., Report No. 3438, Cambridge, Mass., (in 5 volumes), 1976.

Woods, W. A., and V. Zue, "Dictionary Expansion via Phonological Rules for a Speech Understanding System," IEEE International Conference on Acoustics, Speech, and Signal Processing, Philadelphia, Pa., 1976, 561-564.

8.

PROSODIC AIDS TO SPEECH RECOGNITION

Wayne A. Lea
Speech Communications Research Laboratory*

8-1. INTRODUCTION TO PROSODICS

If there is one aspect of the information in the speech signal that seems promising and yet "untapped", it is the "suprasegmental" information such as stress patterns, intonation, pauses, and timing structures in the speech. Here a newcomer to speech recognition studies can readily make an original contribution, and experienced speech recognition workers can find additional tools for substantially improving the performance of speech understanding systems. Prosodic analysis is one of the "gaps" in speech recognition technology that has been repeatedly (and increasingly) noted since work on sentence understanding systems began (cf. Peterson, 1963; Denes, 1975, pp. 77-78; Fant, 1975, p. XI; Lea, 1972; 1973b; Neuburg, 1975, p. 90; Reddy, 1976, pp. 521-522; Wolf, 1976; Woods, et al., 1974).

8-1.1 A Preview of this Chapter
Since work on prosodic aids to speech understanding is admittedly in its infancy, much of what can be said in this chapter is motivational and experimental. That is, we can discuss (in Sec. 8-1.2) why prosodics do seem important to recognition, and consider some general examples (in Sec. 8-1.3) of how such features are closely associated with structural contrasts that are hard to extract from any other aspects of the acoustic signal. We can then consider a variety of arguments and experiments that demonstrate how prosodic information can be useful in speech understanding systems. The most basic prosodic feature of stress (or "syllabic prominence") will be shown in Sec. 8-2 to be important to phonetic, phonological, lexical, and syntactic analysis. Other explicit linguistic cues are found in the timing of speech, as described in Sec. 8-3. Next, in Sec. 8-4, we will consider how intonation (i.e., the pitch contour of the utterance) also provides vital cues to the linguistic structures of sentences. We shall then (in Sec. 8-5) describe basic algorithms for extracting prosodic information from the speech signal and discuss how to use that information to aid in phonetic analysis, selection of appropriate phonological rules, hypothesization and verification of words, and, perhaps most importantly, parsing of sentences.

To date, there is little to report in the way of contributions that prosodics have already made to the success of previous speech recognizers. That is a subject we would hope to hear good news about in years to come (and I believe we will, since, as is outlined in Sec. 8-6, we can expect prosodic analysis to be a valuable part of the future trends in speech recognition).

----

*Research reported in this chapter was conducted at Sperry Univac, under ARPA Contract Nos. DAHC 15-73-C-0310 and DAHC 15-72-0138. Preparation of the chapter was supported by the U.S. Air Force Office of Scientific Research/ AFSC, under Contract No. F44620-74-C-0034 to SCRL.

8-1.2 Acoustic Cues that are Independent of Hypothesized Words

A look at much of the past three decades of speech recognition work might lead you to conclude that the only incoming acoustic data usable in recognition are the acoustic correlates of the sequence of vowels and consonants in the speech, or (equivalently) the total acoustic pattern associated with spoken words (plus some acoustic distortions due to coarticulation and word boundary effects). Words thus have constituted the central reference level, at which (or "below" which) all acoustic data has ceased to be relevant, and the stored linguistic information takes over the job of characterizing the incoming message above the word level.

This is an important point. While syntactic, semantic, and pragmatic information has been very crucial to the success of recent speech understanding systems (cf. Klatt, 1977), it has served an "after the fact" role of weeding out the unlikely (i.e., unallowed, meaningless, or irrelevant) word sequences, based on pre-compiled information about acceptable, meaningful, and task-related sentences. Words are hypothesized throughout an utterance, to account for the phonetic data in all regions of the signal, and thus many of the hypothesized words overlap in position or directly compete as alternative hypotheses about the wording in each specific portion of the utterance. Then, because the recognizer has to allow for potential errors in the phonetic analysis, there may be a "combinatorial explosion" of thousands of alternative word sequences for any one simple sentence, and the higher level linguistic analysis has to select the most likely sequences of non-overlapping, closely abutted words which form grammatical, meaningful and relevant strings.

Unfortunately, the syntactic parser and semantic and pragmatic analyzers must then use as their only "input data" the collection of errorfully hypothesized words, from which to select good sequences. If there is errorful "garbage" fed into such linguistic processing, it is a big challenge to make sure that we don't get "garbage" out.

In contrast, prosodic analysis offers an independent way of acoustically detecting some aspects of syntactic structure, without depending upon the potentially-errorful sequences of hypothesized words derived from the incoming acoustic phonetic information.

8-1.3 Examples of Prosodic Markings of Linguistic Structures

A few examples may illustrate the many ways in which prosodic structures provide crucial information about the intended interpretations of utterances. For example, the type of sentence spoken is marked by the overall falling or rising intonation. A humorous but representative example of such intonational marking of sentence type is given by comparing an uninterrupted interrogative with falling pitch:

(1a) What is that in the road ahead?

versus an interrupted structure with a short yes/no "tag question" (with rising intonation) tacked on the end:

(1b) What is that in the road? A head?

What distinguishes such sentences is not the sequences of vowels and consonants (or words); rather, it is the way they are intoned and timed. There are also many sentences where the structural bracketing of the word sequence is ambiguous, and only the way the utterance is spoken, with properly placed pauses, "comma intonation," and stress patterns, can establish which interpretation is intended:

(2a) We fed (her) (dog biscuits).

(2b) We fed (her dog) (biscuits).

There are also "garden path" sentences, whose early words can mislead you (or a machine), and whose correct interpretation must await the reading of the complete written sentence:

(3) Cotton clothing is made of grows in Georgia.

However, when such sentences are spoken with the right pauses, stresses, and timing, the human listener can quickly rule out the more likely (but wrong) initial interpretation. Other contrasts are distinguishable from minor spelling changes plus punctuation in written form, and from stress patterns, intonation, and timing when spoken:

(4) (Convicts) (record) (permit violations).
(5) (Convicts' records) (permit) (violations).
(6) (Little good) will come from that.
(7) (Little (good will)) comes from that.

From these various examples, we can see that suprasegmental aspects of speech provide cues as to which type of sentence was spoken, how it can be divided into clauses and phrases, how to avoid misleading ("garden path") parses, and how to recover from minor phonetic mistakes like missing the /s/'s in sentences 5 and 7.

   In case such sentences seem to be contrived instances of rarely occurring phenomena, I offer the following sentences taken from actual experiments with the SPEECHLIS speech understanding system developed by Bolt Beranek and Newman to handle lunar rock analysis (Woods, et al, 1974; Lea, 1974, pp. 46-52). In an actual demonstration of SPEECHLIS, the yes/no question (8) was erroneously recognized as beginning with the word "Give" rather than "Have", making it appear to be a command. Sentences (9a) and (9b) show that the wording of this command is ambiguous in structure:

(8) Have any people done chemical analyses on this rock?
(9a) Give (any people)(done chemical analyses) on this rock.
(9b) Give any ((people-done) (chemical analyses)) on this rock.

The speech understanding system found both the structures of (9a) and (9b) in agreement with the grammar and semantics of the task, and could not recover from the error in hypothesized words.

   However, a study (Lea, 1974, pp. 46-52) of the prosodic patterns in sample pronunciations of these sentences gave encouraging indications that prosodics can provide important cues to help disambiguate such structures and help recover from the erroneous hypothesization of the word "Give". As many linguists might have predicted, the auxiliary verb "have" in the yes/no question was classified (on the basis of its acoustic prosodic correlates) as unstressed, while the command verb "give" was stressed. This alone may be enough to rule out the erroneous command structures. Other structural distinctions were also evident, however. The word "done" was stressed except when it was in the compound construction "people-done" of sentence (9b). There was a phrase boundary (marked by a large local dip in pitch) between "people" and "done" in command (9a) but not in the "people-done" interpretation of (9b). There were also distinctive timings of speech events in the contrasting structures. These sentences thus gave explicit evidence of the prosodic cues to contrasting sentence types and contrastive syntactic bracketings. Later in this chapter, we shall show that stress patterns and other prosodic information can also help improve phonetic and phonemic analyses and the accuracy of word identifications. We confine all discussion to English prosody, unless otherwise indicated.

8-2. THE IMPORTANCE OF STRESS PATTERNS

Perhaps the most basic abstract prosodic feature is what is commonly called "stress", or "accent". Much of what we will have to say about intonation, rhythm, phonological phrases, and the timing of pauses depends upon stress patterns. Stress is usually considered to be associated either with increased vocal effort on the part of the talker, or with a listener's perception of increased prominence on a syllable.

8-2.1 General Significance of Stressed Syllables

Stressed syllables occur in the important ("content") words of speech. Those words which are most informative and unpredictable (verbs, adjectives, adverbs, and especially nouns) contain stressed syllables while vowels in grammatically predictable words like articles, prepositions, and other "function words" are often reduced. When we want to emphasize a word, we give it particularly strong stress, by making it particularly loud, long, or prominent in pitch. Contrastive stress (such as in "I said productive, not seductive" or in coordinate constructions like "I saw an old house and a new house") particularly exemplifies how important words or syllables get stressed. Some words such as noun/verb pairs (permit/permit, convict/convict) are distinguished from each other almost entirely on the basis of stress. (cf. Lea, 1976c, p. 37).

Many published phonological rules, including those implemented in speech understanding systems (Friedman, 1974; Oshika, et al, 1974), require information about whether a syllable (vowel) is stressed, unstressed, or reduced. Stress is also acknowledged to be a crucial factor in the accomplishment of correct meter (rhythm) and rhyme in poetry and prose. Stress patterns (and other prosodies) are important in the early stages of language acquisition, and must be properly mastered in second-language learning if one is to speak without a "foreign accent". Also, inadvertent phonetic errors in speech production (spoonerisms or "slips of the tongue"; Fromkin, 1971; 1973) usually exhibit the correct stress patterns, suggesting that stress plays a significant role in the organization of speech productions and perceptions.

We may summarize these general arguments by noting that stress is important to:

- distinctions between words (permit/permit);
- conditions for application of phonological rules;
- listeners' perceptions of phonological structures;
- organization of articulatory units; and
- location of important words, emphasis, and special contrasts.

To complete this listing of important features of stress, we may add the following points, which will be demonstrated at the appropriate points later in this chapter:

- stressed syllables provide islands of phonetic reliability;
- detected phonetic structure is more nearly identical to underlying phonemic structure in stressed syllables;
- stress patterns are closely associated with specific syntactic structures;
- stress is a primary ingredient determining the intonation contour of an utterance;
- rhythm, pause intervals, and the rate of speech are all based on time intervals between stressed syllables; and
- phonological distortions (and errors in automatic phonetic analysis) are more frequent when time intervals between stresses are shortened (i.e., the speech gets faster and sloppier).

169

8-2.2 Islands of Phonetic Reliability

In languages like English and Russian (but not all languages), stress clearly has the effect of lengthening a vowel and enhancing its characteristic coloration, so that stressed vowels are expected to be clearer and more likely to reach target articulatory positions. Indeed, in experiments with trained subjects reading spectrograms, Klatt and Stevens (1972) have shown that partial transcriptions of vowels were correct 50 per cent of the time for stressed vowels, 44 per cent for unstressed vowels, and 30 per cent for reduced vowels. Prestressed consonants were also shown to be more accurately recognized from visual study of spectrograms than were consonants in other positions (74 per cent correct identification in the prestressed consonants compared to a maximum of 29 per cent in any other positions; Klatt and Stevens, 1972).

To more precisely investigate the effects of stress on phonetic recognition procedures, I studied the results of five groups who had participated in automatic segmentation and labelling of 31 test sentences, at the 1973 Carnegie-Mellon University Speech Segmentation Workshop (Lea, 1973e, 1974a). I investigated whether these available techniques for categorizing phonetic segments from acoustic features corresponded more closely with a linguist's phonetic transcription in the stressed syllables than in unstressed or reduced syllables. (A panel of listeners provided the information about which syllables were stressed, unstressed, or reduced; Lea, 1973d,e).

Figure 8-1 illustrates some typical results, for the automatic segment labelling by one research group. Plotted are the percentages of all segment labels that were found to be unacceptable (that is, the "error rate") for each phone class in syllables of each stress level. Vowels, stops, and fricatives clearly are most likely to be adequately categorized in stressed syllables (i.e., stressed syllables had the lowest error rates). Reduced vowels show particularly poor correspondence with the transcriptions. Many reduced vowels were automatically categorized by such grossly inadequate labels as "voiced stop".

Sonorant consonants exhibit an interesting exception to this trend of vowels and obstruents being more adequately categorized in stressed syllables. As shown in Figure 8-1 (and similar results were obtained for the other groups), sonorants in reduced syllables were most adequately categorized (that is, had the lowest error rates of all sonorants). This appears to be because those sonorants in reduced syllables are actually syllabic sonorants, forming the high-energy nuclei of the syllables, which are much easier to locate and analyze than the stressed or unstressed sonorants which adjoin higher-energy vowels (and appear as transitions into those vowels).

We may conclude that stressed syllables provide islands of phonetic reliability in vowel, fricative, and stop recognition; and reduced syllables appear to offer islands of reliability in sonorant consonant categorization.

We may also expect that phonetic structure (whether it is automatically determined or determined by humans listening to speech or reading spectrograms) will correspond more closely with underlying lexical representations (or phonemic structure) in stressed syllables than in unstressed or reduced syllables. It is well known that as the rate of speech changes, or the speech style changes, it is the unstressed or reduced syllables that experience the largest variations (Peterson and Lehiste, 1960; Friedman, 1974; Oshika, et al., 1974). For example, the (usually unstressed) word "and" may be realized variously as [ænd], [æn], [ən], or merely [n̩], while the stressed word "band" is less subject to such phonological perversions.

8-2.3 Stress Cues to Word Matching

Because stressed syllables are islands of phonetic and phonemic reliability, it is reasonable to use them as "anchor points" around which a word matching component of a speech understanding system may seek to find occur-

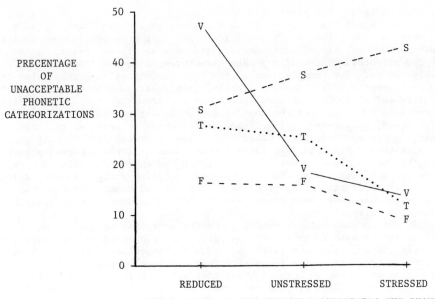

50

PRECENTAGE
OF
UNACCEPTABLE
PHONETIC
CATEGORIZATIONS

40

30

20

10

0

REDUCED   UNSTRESSED   STRESSED

STRESS LEVEL OF THE SYLLABLE CONTAINING THE PHONES

Figure 8-1. Error rates in automatic phonetic categorization
are a function of stress level. The percentages of phonetic
categorizations that were unacceptably different from the
available phonetic transcription are shown separately for
vowels (V), stops (T), fricatives (F) and sonorants (S) in
reduced, unstressed or stressed syllables.

rences of words in the flow of speech. In long phonetic sequences, it is
difficult to tell where a candidate word might begin and where it might end.
By locating stressed syllables, and doing a thorough phonetic analysis within
the reliably-encoded stressed syllable, a speech analysis system can give
particular weight or attention to the most reliable information in the wording of the speech.

Several speech recognition systems have used vowels (especially stressed or
"strong" vowels (Weinstein, 1975; Medress, et al., 1977) as "highly reliable
segments" around which to anchor a word matching procedure. In addition, I
understand (Medress, 1977) that Sperry Univac is exploring the comparison of
expected and acoustically detected stress patterns, to confirm the presence
of certain words in connected speech. Thus, for example, if a word looks
like "abridge" or "average", but the first syllable appears stressed in the
acoustic data, a higher likelihood would be assigned to the word "average"
than to "abridge". In essence, the stress pattern can be used as just another
distinguishing feature, not unlike the presence or absence of an initial
fricative or some other segmental highlight.

8-2.4 Stress Cues to Syntactic Structure

A variety of rules have been published that generate or predict expected
stressed patterns, given that the syntactic structure and wording of an
utterance are known (cf. Chomsky and Halle, 1968; Halle and Keyser, 1971;
Bresnan, 1971, 1972). For example, phonologists say that monosyllabic function words such as articles, prepositions, pronouns, and conjunctions are
unstressed or reduced (or "weakly stressed", Halle and Keyser, 1971, p. 9).
"Substantives" like nouns, and most verbs and adjectives, are often stressed.

Thus, when reversing the process in speech _analysis_, if you find a word (or a syllable in a word) that appears to be stressed, it is more likely to be a noun, verb, or adjective than a "function word" like a preposition or article.

Not only do specific word categories have regular stress levels, but _sequences_ of words, or specific phrase structures, also have distinctive stress patterns. For example, one of the best known English stress rules (the "Compound Stress Rule"; Chomsky and Halle, 1968) asserts that the first lexically stressed syllable in a constituent has the primary stress if the constituent is a compound construction forming an adjective, verb, or noun, such as _light_house, _house_keeper, _light_house keeper, com_pu_ter science, _rail_road crossing, _mea_ly mouthed, etc. Other (so-called "non-lexical" or "full phrasal") constituents have the _last_ lexically stressed syllable assigned primary stress, by the "Nuclear Stress Rule". This is the expected (rising-stress) pattern for all simple non-compound phrases, including whole sentences and noun phrases consisting of descriptive adjectives and nouns. We thus can see that knowing something about stress patterns can guide one to what syntactic structures a talker intended.

Beside the compound constituents, one other exception to the rising (nuclear) stress pattern is the stress pattern in conjoined noun phrases with contrasting parts. When one talks about "an old house and a new house", he wishes to contrast (and thus focus attention on) "old" versus "new", so extra stress is placed on both of those contrasting parts (Gleitman, 1965). Otherwise, he might say "old and new houses", with no contrasting intended. The shortest, least redundant expression is used in conjoined structures unless such contrast is intended. This is also true for conjoining of sentences or clauses. The following will usually have contrastive stress placed on the underlined words:

10. Ron knew _Lynn_ and Ron knew _Ann_.
11. _Ron_ knew Lynn and _Lou_ knew Lynn.
12. Ron may _love_ Lynn and _marry_ Lynn.
13. I saw an old _house_ and an old _barn_.

It is also of interest that the repeated parts in sentences 10 to 13 ("Ron" in 10, "Lynn" in 11 and 12, "old" in 13, and "knew" in 10 and 11, etc.) are substantially reduced in stress from what they would be if they were not repeated (Lea, 1976c). The repetitive syntactic structure dictates this stress pattern.

We could devote many pages to various linguist's claims or theoretical predictions about expected stress patterns, and how they relate to syntactic structures. However, much more to the point are the stress patterns that are actually _perceived_ by listeners who hear the speech and mark down what stress levels they hear for all the syllables. I have shown by a series of experiments that listeners can consistently perceive which syllables are stressed and which are not, with only about 5% of the syllables being confused between stressed and unstressed levels from time to time or from listener to listener (Lea, 1973d; 1976a,c). Here we shall consider some results from those studies that clearly show that specific stress patterns are closely associated with specific syntactic structures. Then, when we consider in Sec. 8-5 algorithms for detecting stresses from acoustic prosodic data, we will be able to relate those stress patterns to syntactic structures, and thus be able to determine aspects of sentence structure from the acoustic signal.

Five listeners who were quite consistent in their stress perceptions were asked to mark, for each syllable in a set of 255 carefully designed sentences, whether they heard the syllable as stressed, unstressed, or reduced (Lea, 1976 b,c). The majority decisions from the panel thus provide a three-way classification of stress levels. However we can also assign a finer-grained stress score which is equivalent to adding the number of listeners that judge a syllable as stressed, and subtracting the number who hear it as reduced.

For five listeners, then, a score of +5 is the most stressed a syllable can seem to be, and -5 means it is the most reduced possible. Thus, counting the number of listeners that agree that a syllable is stressed roughly indicates the relative stress level in a spectrum of possible values. Such a stress score is akin to the stress "levels" assigned to syllables by various stress assignment theories (Pike, 1945; Trager and Smith, 1951) and linguist's rules (Chomsky and Halle, 1968; Halle and Keyser, 1971; Halle, 1973; Bresnan, 1971, 1972).

Average stress scores for all such occurrences of words in each syntactic category have been plotted in increasing order in Fig. 8-2 (along with a tabulation of mean values and standard deviations). Those categories with the highest average stress scores (as shown on the right in Fig. 8-2) thus are, on the average, the most stressed. The figure shows that, on the average, command verbs, quantifiers, nouns, adverbs, and adjectives are more stressed than main verbs or negatives. Of considerable interest in automatic analysis of speech is that command verbs are highly stressed, while auxiliary verbs are unstressed, so that by determining whether a sentence begins with a stress or not, a speech recognizer can often determine whether the sentence is a command or a yes/no question, as was discussed earlier for sentences (8) and (9a,b).

Perhaps it will be a long time before speech recognizers can effectively use all the fine structure of relative stress levels shown in Figure 8-2. However, two general features worthy of early attention in prosodic aids to speech recognition are the effects of subordination and coordination on expected stress levels. For example, the cases where main verbs were not perceived as stressed illustrate how various syntactic structures interact with overall average stress scores. About three-fifths of the unstressed main verbs were in coordinate structures like sentences (10) and (11), where repetition of the same verbs occurred and contrast was placed elsewhere in the sentence, resulting in reduced stress levels on the verbs. Almost all of the other cases where a main verb was not stressed were in sentences with relative clauses. Clearly subordination, and repetition of the verb in the context of contrastive stress, account for the cases where main verbs are not stressed.

Figure 8-2 graphically shows that subordination causes reduced stress levels on not only main verbs, but also conjunctions, prepositions, copulatives, and auxiliary verbs. Interestingly, nouns in subordinate positions (such as the word "Maine" in "many young men from Maine" or the word "syntax" in the phrase "violations of syntax") do not have lower stress than in superordinate (matrix) positions. Both "men" and "Maine" in "men from Maine" are highly stressed. Nouns seem to maintain their high stress values except when de-emphasized in coordinate constructions (like sentences (10) to (12)) which have contrasting stress elsewhere in the sentence. In the future, we need to study further the relationships between perceived stress levels and syntactic structures, and to develop "reverse" stress rules that can predict some aspects of syntactic structure given the stress pattern. Then stress patterns will provide not only islands of phonetic and phonemic reliability, and additional features for verifying the presence of specific words, but also direct cues to syntactic structures. Of course, we also need procedures for determining stress patterns from the acoustic data and I will describe some successful procedures in Sec. 8-5. However, first we need to discuss intonational and timing regularities that interact closely with the acoustic correlates of stress, and that must be accounted for in any procedures for detecting stress patterns from acoustic data.

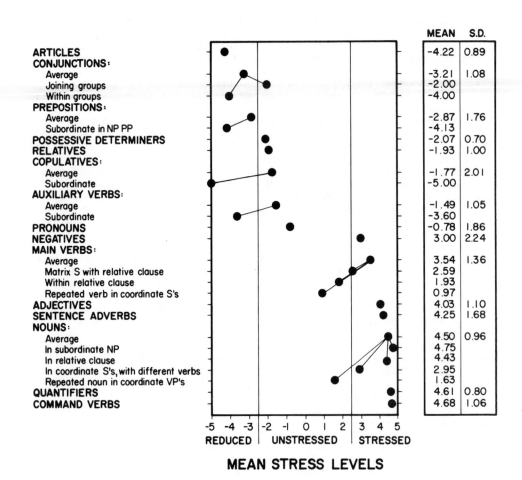

	MEAN	S.D.
ARTICLES	-4.22	0.89
CONJUNCTIONS:		
Average	-3.21	1.08
Joining groups	-2.00	
Within groups	-4.00	
PREPOSITIONS:		
Average	-2.87	1.76
Subordinate in NP PP	-4.13	
POSSESSIVE DETERMINERS	-2.07	0.70
RELATIVES	-1.93	1.00
COPULATIVES:		
Average	-1.77	2.01
Subordinate	-5.00	
AUXILIARY VERBS:		
Average	-1.49	1.05
Subordinate	-3.60	
PRONOUNS	-0.78	1.86
NEGATIVES	3.00	2.24
MAIN VERBS:		
Average	3.54	1.36
Matrix S with relative clause	2.59	
Within relative clause	1.93	
Repeated verb in coordinate S's	0.97	
ADJECTIVES	4.03	1.10
SENTENCE ADVERBS	4.25	1.68
NOUNS:		
Average	4.50	0.96
In subordinate NP	4.75	
In relative clause	4.43	
In coordinate S's, with different verbs	2.95	
Repeated noun in coordinate VP's	1.63	
QUANTIFIERS	4.61	0.80
COMMAND VERBS	4.68	1.06

-5 -4 -3 -2 -1 0 1 2 3 4 5
REDUCED   UNSTRESSED   STRESSED

MEAN STRESS LEVELS

Figure 8-2. Average perceived stress scores for various word categories, shown in order of increasing stress.

8-3. TIMING CUES TO LINGUISTIC STRUCTURE

It is usually expected that a recognizer's classification of an English phoneme or word should be substantially independent of prosodic features such as how long the unit is, or how far away in time it is from other units. In fact, time normalization procedures (e.g., dynamic programming) are used in many recognizers to eliminate (or drastically reduce) the irrelevant variations between the timings of two spoken versions of the same word or sentence. A sentence or word is assumed to be the same whether said slowly or rapidly, animately or monitonically, etc.

An important question then is: What role is left for underline{timing information} in speech, other than for providing the order in which discrete units occur? Several answers will be offered here, including:

- Comparing the durations of detected phonetic segments with expected durations for various phones or combinations of phones (Sec. 8-3.2);
- Detecting phrase boundaries from phrase-final lengthening of phonetic segments (Sec. 8-3.2);
- Detecting phrase boundaries from long intervals between stressed syllables (Sec. 8-3.3);
- Using the interstress interval as a measure of speech rate, for selecting appropriate (fast-speech or slow-speech) phonological rules (Sec. 8-3.4); and
- Detecting clause and sentence boundaries from durations of pauses (Sec. 8-3.5).

8-3.1 Phonetic Durations

One answer regarding the utility of timing information in speech is that there are extreme values of duration beyond which a segment's identity _is_ in question. For example, an appropriate fricative-like spectrum has to last for a minimum length (say 50 milliseconds or so) before it is clearly distinguishable from a stop burst with aspiration, and thus before it is accepted as an occurence of an /f/ or other fricative segment. · This concept was used as a condition on occurrences of phonetic segments in the HARPY speech understanding system, for example (Lowerre and Reddy, Chap. 15 of this book). This is one primitive sense in which a prosodic feature (namely, phonetic _duration_) has already been used in speech recognition. A related application is to say that when a sibilant (or other sound) is _longer_ than a certain duration, it may be a candidate for division (by phonological rule) into two successive sibilants.

To use phonetic durations in speech recognition procedures, you need to know something about normal durations for the various vowels and consonants, as summarized in Figure 8-3. (For further details on these durational results, refer to the articles cited with each graph.) Figure 8-3(a) shows characteristic durations for vowels, with low vowels (æ,ɑ) longer than high vowels (i, ɪ, ɔ, ʊ, u), and tense vowels (i,u) longer than corresponding lax vowels (ɪ, ʊ). This length characteristic can actually be used as one cue for distinguishing tense and lax vowels in a speech recognizer. Similarly, Fig. 8-3(b) shows that the consonant following a vowel also influences the vowel duration, with voiced consonants in particular causing a lengthening of their preceding vowels. Also shown are the different measured lengths for either total syllabic nuclei (Peterson and Lehiste, 1961), vowels in isolated words (House and Fairbanks, 1953), or stressed vowels in prepausal syllables of connected speech (Umeda, 1975). This brings up the crucial point of how to measure durations and where to set segment boundaries. All durational measures will be significantly influenced by segmentation procedures, and some of these previous duration studies may have to be repeated with a researcher's own segmentation method (or any new machine segmentation procedure). The previously published

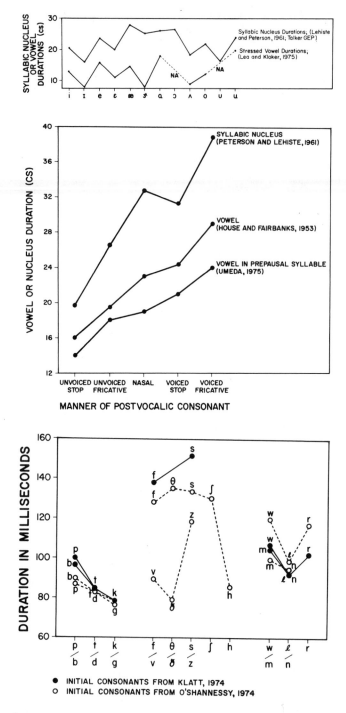

Figure 8-3. Characteristic phonetic durations, and factors that influence them.

results provide useful _trends_, however, and thus are worth reviewing here.

Consonants also have intrinsic durations, as shown in Fig. 8-3(c). As is evident in each of these plots, mean values may vary from study to study. Also, the context and position of the unit is important; word-final consonants have different durations from those shown in Fig. 8-3(c) for initial consonants. In general, the speech recognizer must consider not only mean values, but also total _distributions_ of values, and how to characterize the various contextual and situational effects on durations. Durational rules for speech synthesis (e.g., Klatt, 1974; O'Shannesy, 1974; Umeda, 1976) capture some of the regularities, but they of course only require that _some_ specific duration is provided that is reasonable (for full intelligibility and acceptable naturalness) for all the conditions involved, and they do not necessarily provide full guidelines about how much the durations can _vary_ without affecting lexical decisions in a speech recognizer.

Another factor which must be taken into account when predicting phonetic durations is the stress on the syllable. A stressed /i/ is longer than an unstressed /i/, and also may even be longer than an unstressed /ɑ/ or /æ/. Similarly, at fast speaking rates, stressed syllables will be somewhat shorter, and unstressed syllables will be _substantially_ shortened (Lehiste, 1970).

Thus, in using phonetic durations in speech recognition, one must be cautious about several issues:

- The method of segmentation and duration measurement;
- The phonetic context of the unit;
- The stress level of the syllable;
- The rate of speaking; and
- The position of the unit in the syllable, phrase, and sentence.

These interacting factors make it difficult to rely on any more than the most robust, largest distinctions in phonetic durations, unless elaborate procedures are taken, to account for all the contextual and situational factors.

A word of caution is also in order regarding the use of time normalization procedures, which effectively squeeze long versions of words or other units down to a standard length, and stretch short versions to that standard. Timing information, including durations of units and their subunits, may be lost by such distortions, and some aspects of recognition may suffer.

8-3.2 _Phrase-Final Lengthening_

Another answer to the question of what the time dimensions of speech can provide to recognition procedures is the _detection of phrase boundaries_ from a phenomenon known as "phrase-final lengthening" of vowels and consonants. Phrase-final and pre-pausal syllables have vowels (and sonorant consonants) whose durations are lengthened by 20 to 50% over their values in other positions (Lehiste, 1970; Klatt, 1973, 1975; Kloker, 1975; Lea and Kloker, 1975). Indeed, Kloker (1975; cf. Lea and Kloker, 1975) showed that 91% of all the phrase boundaries that listeners heard in spoken sentences could be detected by finding vowels and sonorant consonants that were at least 20% above the median lengths of the same vowel or sonorant in all its occurrances in the speech. The sentences used in Kloker's study were distorted by spectral inversion so as to remove the wording and semantic content and leave only the prosodic cues intact, then five listeners were asked to mark where they heard phrase boundaries and stressed and unstressed syllables (obviously based on the prosodic information only). Vowel and sonorant durations were measured from spectrograms, and median values were calculated separately for stressed and unstressed versions of each vowel or sonorant.

Of course, the detection of phrase boundaries from lengthened phones requires identification of all the phonetic segments in the speech, and measurements of _all_ vowel and sonorant durations, with all the difficulties and consequent issues mentioned in Sec. 8-3.1. Also, stress levels must be determined, median durations calculated, and occurrences of excessive lengths detected. Unfortunately, 31% of all the detected groups of lengthened syllables were not at perceived phrase boundaries, and were thus "false alarms" in phrase boundary detection. Another problem Kloker found was that the ends of groups of lengthened syllables didn't line up with the ends of syntactic phrases, so that the phrase boundaries were detected, but not accurately located. Thus, while monitoring lengthened phonetic durations may be a possible way of detecting phrase boundaries, it involves quite a complex process, and currently appears to have some definite limitations in effectiveness.

8-3.3 Long Interstress Intervals as Phrase Boundary Markers

Fortunately, there is other timing information that can be used to detect phrase boundaries. From the data of Kloker's five listeners marking stresses and boundaries in spectrally inverted speech, I measured the time intervals between onsets of vowels in syllables they heard as stressed. Figure 8-4 shows a plot of the results for a typical sentence. Here the time interval between two stresses (the "interstress interval") is plotted along the ordinate, and the time succession of stress-to-stress intervals is shown along the abscissa. Thus, the first interstress interval for sentence C5-1 was 0.38 seconds in duration and did not span a perceived boundary, as shown by the leftmost black dot. The second interval was 0.90 seconds, and did span a perceived boundary, as shown by the leftmost open circle. The tendency for most intervals to be about 0.3 to 0.4 seconds in duration is vividly shown as one progresses through the series of intervals shown by the black dots. This is a measure of the rate of speech. However, wherever there is a major phonological boundary, such that the listeners perceived a boundary in the spectrally distorted (inverted) speech, there usually is a very long interstress interval, as shown by the open circles in Figure 8-4.

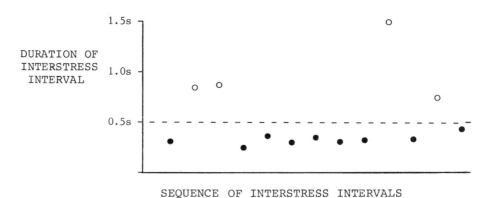

Fig. 8-4. Long interstress intervals are cues to perceived phonological boundaries. KEY: ● = Intervals NOT spanning perceived boundaries
o = Intervals spanning perceived boundaries

These results suggested a simple hypothesis: a phonological boundary is perceived wherever the interstress interval is greater than 5 tenths of a second. This hypothesis correctly detected over 95% of the boundaries perceived (by a majority of the listeners). While it is true that 64% of these perceived boundaries were accompanied by silent pauses of at least 200 ms (so that a pause detector alone would find 64% of these boundaries; see Sec. 8-3.5), still it is encouraging that such a large percentage as 95% of the perceived boundaries can be detected from a simple threshold on the interstress duration.

178

Twenty-three percent of all interstress intervals that were over 5 tenths of a second were <u>not</u> accompanied by perceptions of a boundary. However, these 'false alarms' in boundary detection did, in fact, span a major <u>syntactic</u> boundary in almost all cases. (Specifically, 25 of the 29 'false alarms' did involve major syntactic boundaries, even though the boundary was not perceived by listeners hearing the distorted speech).

In another experiment, I measured the interstress intervals in the Rainbow Script (Fairbanks, 1940), spoken by six talkers. As illustrated in Fig. 8-5 for one talker, the durations of interstress intervals tend to be small when only a word boundary intervenes but durations are increasingly longer for syntactically-predicted boundaries between phrases, clauses, and sentences (Lea, 1975; Lea and Kloker, 1975).

We may conclude that major phonological boundaries (which often correlate with underlying syntactic boundaries) can be reliably detected from long inter-stress intervals in the speech. A recognizer can then verify hypothesized wording of a sentence, or select among alternative parses for the sentence, based on which hypothesized structures would have phrase boundaries between the stresses where they are actually detected in the acoustic input. All that is required is a syllabification and stress location procedure, so onsets of stressed vowels can be determined. No phonetic analysis is required. However, as with phrase-final lengthening (and, as we shall see, with intonationally-detected phrase boundaries), the boundary is not strictly <u>located</u>, only <u>detected</u> and bracketed to lie between the stresses. Very few boundaries between speech units (phones, syllables, words, or phrases) are precisely and unambiguously located.

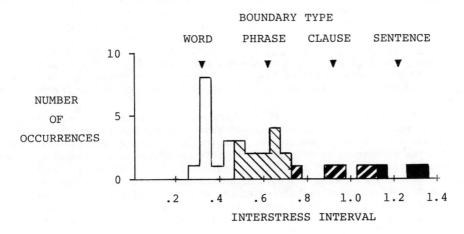

Fig. 8-5. Longer interstress intervals span boundaries between larger syntactic units. (Text was the 6-sentence Rainbow Script, spoken by Talker ASH.)

8-3.4 <u>Rhythm, Rate, and Phonological Distortions</u>

One other major factor that influences time intervals in speech is the tempo, or rate of speech. Studies have shown that it is difficult for talkers to alter their rate of speech to match a desired rate very exactly, and when asked to double the rate or halve it, they usually only change the rate by 30 to 50% in the syllables or words per unit time. An increase in tempo is accomplished primarily by reducing the durations of <u>unstressed</u> syllables. The stressed syllables are much less affected (Lehiste and Peterson, 1961;

Lehiste, 1970).

Little research has been done on tempo and its various effects. Perhaps one reason is that there is no single generally accepted definition of tempo or speech rate. How does one decide, for each new speech text, whether the talker is talking fast, medium, or slow, and how does one quantify such notions? The following have all been referred to in various discussions of speech rate:

- The total duration of a specific spoken text (as compared to the duration for another talker or for another repetition by the same talker);
- The average (or local, and thus, variable) measure of the number of words per unit time;
- The average number of stresses per unit time, or, locally, the reciprocal of the interstress time interval;
- The average or local number of syllables per unit time (the reciprocal of the intersyllabic time interval); and
- The average or local number of phones per unit time (reciprocal of phone durations).

It seems likely that for most purposes one overall figure, such as the time it takes to speak a whole text or the average number of words per minute, would not adequately represent "tempo," since the rate may vary from one area of a sentence or paragraph or discourse to another, and the words may vary dramatically in length. On the other hand, phones also vary dramatically in length and only some phones are significantly affected by changes in tempo. Also, as speaking rate increases, certain phones are deleted and sound sequences become simplified, tending to leave the phone rate more constant. What successive speech units or time intervals do seem to be fairly consistent in length at a fixed tempo, yet do vary considerably as the tempo varies from slow, to normal, to fast? The answer seems clear from Fig. 8-4; namely, the time intervals between stresses (after subtracting out phrase or sentence boundary marking) are fairly consistent throughout an utterance (as illustrated for the black dots in Fig. 8-4), and yet they vary as perceived tempo does. It would seem that stresses per unit time would be appropriate for measurement of tempo.

My studies (Lea, 1975, 1977) show that interstress intervals can be one of the most useful measures of speech rate. In one experiment, I explored the question: "Just what measure (or measures) of speech rate correlates well with the changes in phonological structure that have to be handled by phonological rules in speech recognition systems?" It is, of course, well known that speech rate can have a significant effect on the phonological and acoustic phonetic structure of spoken sentences, so that non-ideal pronunciations occur and adjustments in expected structure need to be made by "fast-speech rules", such as rules for vowel reduction and alveolar flapping (cf. Shoup's review in Chap. 6 of this book).

The best correlation between alternative measures of speech rate and the variation in phonetic structures was established as follows. Participants at the 1973 Speech Segmentation Workshop at Carnegie-Mellon University presented automatic segmentations of 31 selected sentences for man-computer interaction into phonetically-labelled units. Their automatic labelling of segments was compared with phonetic transcription provided by a linguist. Major discrepancies between the phonetic categories assigned by machine and linguist were considered to be errors. An investigation showed that most of these errors occurred where the interstress interval was short; for each group's method of machine labelling, the error rate was inversely related to the duration of the interstress interval.

180

This correlation between phonetic error rates and measures of speech rate was not as evident for the average (or, mean) interstress interval, or for other measures of speech rate, as shown by the correlation coefficients given in Table 8-1. The local measure of speech rate provided by the individual interstress interval usually yielded the highest-magnitude correlation coefficient, indicating that the phonetic error rate is more readily predictable from the interstress interval than from other measures. One other measure investigated was the average time per syllable (obtained by measuring the time between the onset of the first stressed vowel in a sentence and the onset of the last stressed vowel in the sentence, and dividing by the number of syllables included in that time). This time per syllable is a direct inverse of the number of syllables per second, which might have been expected to be a reasonable measure of speech rate. Table 8-1 shows a lack of substantial correlation between such a syllable-timing measure and the phonetic error rate. Another conceivable measure of speech rate, the average time per phone (obtained by dividing the time interval between the onsets of the first and last stressed vowels by the number of phones spanned), showed even poorer correlation with the phonetic error rates.

Table 8-1. Correlation Coefficients of Phonetic Error

Rates and Measures of Speech Rate

MEASURE OF SPEECH RATE	PHONETIC SEGMENTATION METHOD		
	A	B	C
Interstress Interval	$-.60$	$-.76$	$-.65$
Mean Interstress Interval	$-.55$	$-.74$	$-.70$
Time Per Syllable	$-.10$	$-.18$	$-.56$
Time Per Phone	$+.01$	$+.24$	$-.26$

It may actually prove to be very advantageous that a local measure of speech rate such as the interstress interval should prove to be more informative about phonetic errors than any average rate is. The local measure is easier to obtain, requires no additional averaging computations, and most important of all, can be determined on-line in a real-time manner, without requiring a delay until the whole utterance is completed.

In summary, it appears that the duration of the individual interstress interval is the best measure (or one of the best measures) for relating speech rate to applicable phonetic or phonological rules. Knowing the interstress interval, one can then predict how likely it is that phonetic categorization errors may occur. Since it is the purpose of acoustic phonetic and phonological rules to account for such changes in phonological structure, we may expect that the interstress interval as a measure of speech rate may be used to predict what phonological rules may be suitable at various points in spoken utterances.

In this total discussion of timing, rhythm, and rate of speech, we have shown several ways in which the interstress interval is important: as a good measure of speech rate (and, hence, an indicator of applicable phonological rules), as a cue to syntactic boundaries, and as the major unit in the rhythm of English speech. Next, we will show another way in which the interstress interval enters into speech; namely, in the timing of structurally-dictated pauses.

8-3.5 Pause Cues to Structural Divisions

The primary distinguishing feature of silent pauses is that the speech stops momentarily and starts again, with alternative <u>durations</u> of pause offering the only symbolic distinctions. There are extreme limits beyond which it is unreasonable to speak of a silent period as a pause; if it extends too long, it is the semiotic ("pregnant") but non-linguistic silence; if it is too short, it cannot be distinguished from brief interruptions in vocal output due to vocal tract or laryngeal closure during stop consonants. Pause consequently is and must be suprasegmental, or prosodic, if it serves any linguistic function.

We noted in Sec. 8-3.3 that successive interstress intervals were of similar duration, except that longer interstress intervals occur at phonological phrase boundaries. All interstress intervals spanning <u>pauses</u> in the speech were excluded from the data illustrated in Fig. 8-4, so the length of pause would not interfere with investigations of regularities in interstress intervals in uninterrupted speech. In Fig. 8-5, we saw an indication that interstress intervals spanning <u>clause</u> boundaries were clearly longer than those spanning phrase boundaries, and that intervals spanning <u>sentence</u> boundaries were even longer. Fig. 8-6 illustrates the obvious reason; namely, that pauses occur at clause and sentence boundaries. In essence, these pauses are the spoken equivalents of written punctuation marks (commas and periods).

Figure 8-6 includes only those interstress intervals that did span a pause in speech. (The spoken texts were six talkers' readings of the Rainbow Scripts; Lea, 1975a.) As shown in the top left histogram of Fig. 8-6, interstress intervals spanning pauses at <u>clause</u> boundaries tend to cluster at values near <u>two</u> times the average interstress interval found within uninterrupted speech. The dotted vertical lines show integral multiples of the 0.47 second <u>mean interstress interval</u> that was found for the uninterrupted intervals in the Rainbow Script (cf. Lea, 1974a, p. 35). The mean for intervals spanning clause boundaries is 0.99 seconds, which is quite close to twice the uninterrupted mean. Also, as shown at the top right in Fig. 8-6, the duration of unvoicing at the clausal pause itself clusters around a mean of 0.46 second, which is almost equal to the 0.47 second mean for uninterrupted interstress intervals. The 'pause' at a clause boundary is thus a one-unit interruption of the speech.

Similarly, the interstress interval between <u>sentences</u> is shown at the bottom left of Fig. 8-6. The mean interval is 1.43 seconds, which is very close to <u>three</u> times the interval of uninterrupted speech. This is due to a <u>two-unit pause at sentence boundaries</u>, as shown by the bottom right histogram in Fig. 8-6. Again, the mean value is very close to an integral multiple of the rhythmic interval in speech which is not interrupted by pauses.

Thus, syntactically-dictated pauses appear to be one- or two-unit interruptions of rhythm.

Syntactic pauses are usually substantially shorter than most multiple-second hesitation pauses that occur before high-information-content words in spontaneous speech (Goldman-Eisler, 1958, 1961; Boomer, 1965), and so they can usually be distinguished from hesitations. Obviously, since speech recognizers usually receive only one sentence at a time in a dialogue, only the <u>clause-marking pause</u> is expected to be of any structural importance in speech recognition. It can readily be detected from 200 millisecond or longer periods of silence (Kloker, 1975), or from 350 millisecond or longer periods of unvoicing (Lea, 1973b, 1974a).

An interesting study by O'Malley, et al. (1973), showed that when talkers spoke algebraic expressions, parantheses that mark major groupings of mathematical terms could be detected from silent pauses. Rules were developed that successfully inserted parantheses in expressions, based on the locations and

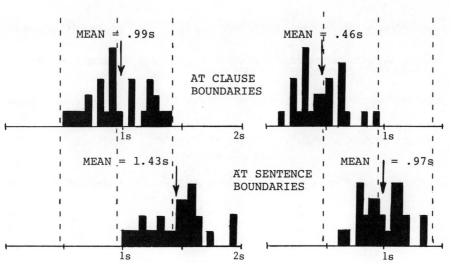

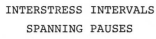

Fig. 8-6. Syntactic Pauses Are Integral-Unit Interruptions of Rhythm

measured durations of silent pauses, and the rule-predicted junctures agreed
over 90% of the time with listeners' perceptions of junctures.

Another aspect of pausing in speech is the occurence of non-silent pauses;
namely, <u>filled pauses</u> ("aaa...", "uh...", "er...", "mmm..."), <u>repeats</u> ("He...
He said that".), and <u>false starts</u> ("He...she said that.") These will be difficult but frequent aspects of natural creative "conversations" with machines,
and must ultimately be dealt with in speech recognition procedures. Some work
has already been undertaken to handle false starts, repeats, filled pauses, and
incomplete expressions in the HARPY speech understanding system (Reddy, personal communication).

8-3.6 A Composite Model of Timing Information

We have seen that the timing of events in speech is determined by the number of clauses, the pauses, the phrase boundaries, the stress pattern, and the
phonetic sequence. Fig. 8-7 illustrates how these timing regularities might
be combined in generative rules for verifying hypotheses about the identity of
a sentence. The selection of what words are hypothesized dictates the number
of syllables in each part of the utterance. We can initially assume that each
syllable has the same duration, such as the mean duration of a syllable for
the particular talker at the particular rate of speech. The energy contour
of Fig. 8-7 thus indicates the syllabic sequence in the utterance. Then, when
stress levels are taken into account by some form of generative rules of stress
assignment, the stressed syllables should become quite long (say about one and
one half times the initial mean value), and reduced syllables become shorter
(as illustrated, at about three quarters of the mean length). The relative
durations of stressed, unstressed, and reduced syllables will be functions of
speech rate, with reduced syllables shortened drastically at high speeds, but
stressed syllables only slightly shortened by the fast rate. In some cases,
such as for the third underlying syllable in the word "temperature", the syllable might be reduced to not being spoken at all. Next, phrase-final lengthen-

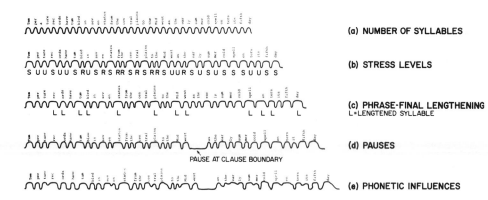

Fig. 8-7. The combination of various factors that determine the timing of
syllabic events in energy contours.

ing causes each final stress (and any following unstresses) within each major
phrase to be lengthened about 20 to 40% (assuming a crude approximation to
Kloker's groups of lengthened syllables). This is one cue to the phrase structure of the utterance. Pauses of about one rhythm unit (equal to one mean
interstress interval) get inserted between clauses. Finally, we must consider
the relative lengths of syllables and phones that are determined by intrinsic
vowel durations, intrinsic consonant durations, longer vowels being before
voiced consonants, etc. Thus, low vowels and diphthongs (such as in "states",
"plains", "cold", "dog") are intrinsically long, while higher vowels such as
in "mid" are shorter. Other refinements might take into account finer-grained
stress levels (reduced, unstressed, levels 5,4,3,2,1,etc.) and relative sizes
and significances of various phrase categories.

While no recognizer has yet used such generative combining of timing factors to compare predicted with acoustically detected energy contours, or to
verify that hypothesized word sequences agree with the timing of the actual
detected speech events, there does seem to be some promise in such composing
(or decomposing) of timing patterns.

8-4. INTONATIONAL CUES TO LINGUISTIC STRUCTURES

Intonation is the systematic variation of perceived pitch throughout a
spoken sentence. It is a vital aspect of speech which conveys information
about the type of sentence spoken, the divisions and categories in phrase
structures, the stress patterns, paragraphing and topic change, semantics, and
emotion. Children learn intonational cues to phrase structure and sentence
type even before acquiring any competence with the specific phonemics of their
language community. We are all aware that the basic meaning and connotations
of a sentence can be altered, without changing its wording, by just changing
the intonation. The examples given at the beginning of this chapter illustrate such intonational distinctions.

184

In this section, we will briefly consider the importance of intonational cues to sentence type (Sec. 8-4.1), pitch "valleys" as cues to the occurrence of syntactic boundaries (Sec. 8-4.2), specific ways in which pitch contours indicate subordination and coordination (Sec. 8-4.3), effects of phonetic sequences on pitch contours (Sec. 8-4.4), and the general way in which intonation seems to be decomposed into linguistic features (Sec. 8-4.5).

8-4.1 Intonation and Sentence Types

Intonation varies somewhat from language to language, but what will be said here for English is applicable to many other languages, and each language will show some intonational system. Intonation is a language universal.

The overall intonation of English sentences has been characterized (Armstrong and Ward, 1929) in terms of two alternative "tunes" or contours, as shown in Fig. 8-8. Tune I has a characteristic rising of pitch (or its acoustic correlate, voice fundamental frequency, abbreviated F_0) until the first stressed syllable in the sentence is reached, and a falling of the pitch from the first stressed syllable to the last. Sentence-final intonation was said to fall dramatically (for declarative sentences, exclamations, and questions with interrogative words). Tune II is like Tune I, but is terminated by a brief rise (or leveling) in pitch (within the last stressed syllable, if it is sentence-final; otherwise in the final unstressed syllables). Tune II was said to mark yes/no questions, uncertainty or indifference in expression, and various forms of incompleteness (cf. Lehiste, 1970, p. 99).

F_0 or

Pitch

Time

(a) TUNE I CONTOUR:
   For declaratives,
   WH Questions, or
   Completed Clauses

F_0 or

Pitch

Time

(b) TUNE II CONTOUR:
   For yes/no questions,
   Incompletion or
   Uncertainty

Fig. 8-8. Tune I and Tune II Intonation Contours.

I tested the general claim that F_0 follows the Tune I or II contours, using a set of 255 sentences that were especially designed to isolate intonational effects due to sentence type, phrase structure, stress patterns, and phonetic sequences (Lea, 1976e, pp. 33-38). The sentences were spoken by only one talker, but other studies show similar results with other talkers (Lea, 1974b; Olive, 1974). Here are some major features of English intonation that were

185

verified by these studies, along with the percentages of the occurrences for
which the effect was verified in the 255 sentences:

- F_0 rises steadily in the initial part of a sentence, until the
  first stress, where it peaks (99%);
- F_0 falls, after its highest F_0 value in the last stress, to a
  low value at the end of each declarative, command, and WH
  question (99.5%);
- F_0 dips, then rises, within the last stress of yes/no questions,
  and rises throughout subsequent unstresses (95%);
- F_0 falls from one stress to the next in a sentence (or clause).
  (This was verified for 91% of the cases in a subset of 58
  sentences, with the exceptions spanning major syntactic
  boundaries that were followed by highly stressed syllables.
  See Sec. 8-3.2).
- F_0 on each unstressed syllable is lower than on all preceding
  stresses, and is usually at or below a value along the line
  between the values of the immediately preceding and following
  stresses (91%).

These regularities were unusually well verified because the sentences had
been carefully designed to isolate basic "Tune" contours from other intonational effects such as phrase structures, stress patterns, and phonetic sequences. In undesigned sentences intended to simulate man-machine interactions
(Lea, 1976a), less consistency was shown. In particular, the expected terminal
rise in F_0 in yes/no questions was often <u>not</u> found, although the yes/no questions had less decrease in F_0 from the first stressed syllable to the last, so
the overall F_0 <u>slope</u> was more like a rise (or less of a fall) for a yes/no
question than for other sentence types (cf. Ohala, 1972; Lea, 1974a, p. 51).
Results to date thus suggest that a speech recognizer cannot count on a terminal rise to detect yes/no questions, but further studies might verify that
the overall slope of the contour can provide some reliable indication of sentence type.

8-4.2 <u>Pitch 'Valleys' as Phrase Boundary Markers</u>

For decades, linguists have claimed that intonation indicates the phrase
structure of English sentences (Jones 1909, 1932; Pike 1945; Wells 1947).
Trager and Smith, whose pitch and stress "levels" are widely used, claimed that
monitoring F_0 makes it possible to have "solidly established objective procedures" for "the recognition of immediate constituents and parts of speech
syntax" (1951, p. 77). Gleason (1961, p. 169) considered intonation and
stress as "the dominant elements in the syntax-signalling system". For example,
consider the following two sentences which have only one difference in vowel,
and thus might be confused in a speech recognition system:

     (14)   After they met, John and Bill put the money on the
            table by the door.
     (15)   After they meet John and Bill, put the money on the
            table by the door.

Sentence (14) will usually be spoken with a terminal rise in the vicinity of
the word <u>met</u>, followed by a possible pause, a large rise in F_0 at the clause-
initial word <u>John</u>, and the word <u>put</u> unstressed or at least not highly stressed.

Sentence (15), in contrast, will likely be spoken with a clause-marking terminal rise on the word <u>Bill</u>, a possible pause after <u>Bill</u>, a large rise in F_o at the clause-initial word <u>put</u>, and with the command verb strongly stressed.

A series of experiments on F_o in several forms of connected texts have confirmed the ability to detect syntactic divisions from F_o contours. My thesis research at Purdue University (Lea, 1972a, Chap. 2 and 3) involved four male and two female talkers reading several texts, including a five-sentence paragraph composed of only monosyllabic words, plus portions of three weather reports, and a portion of a news report. Also, I processed some excerpts from conversational interviews, bringing the total amount of speech processed to 500 seconds of speech, from nine talkers. More recently, I (1973a; 1975) extended such studies to include six talkers reading a paragraph of the "Rainbow Passage" (Fairbanks, 1940), ten talkers spontaneously speaking instructions (mostly questions or commands) for simulated or actual interaction with computers, and three talkers reading the database of 255 sentences with isolation of minimal linguistic contrasts. This made a total of over 1500 seconds of speech analyzed.

My results showed that a decrease (of about 7% or more) in F_o usually (i.e., about 90% of the time) occurred at the end of each major syntactic constituent, and an increase (of about 7% or more) in F_o occurred near (but not necessarily coinciding with) the beginning of the following constituent.

Fig. 8-9 illustrates the F_o contour (that is F_o values, in Hertz, versus time in seconds throughout the utterance) of a typical sentence taken from a weather report. Fall-rise "valleys" (marked by vertical dotted lines) accompany the syntactically predicted boundaries (marked by arrows labelled with the categories of surrounding constituents). Later, we will discuss a computer program that uses such F_o valleys to detect phrase boundaries. In my earliest studies (Lea, 1972, Chap. 3), I investigated the effects of specific constituent <u>categories</u> (noun phrase, verb, prepositional phrase, etc.) on boundary detection. The lack of regular boundary marking between noun phrases and following verbals was one of the most striking results. That is, even though the subject-predicate division is considered one of the major breaks in a sentence, that division was not clearly evident in F_o contours. On the other hand, around 95% of all boundaries before prepositional phrases were detected by F_o fall-rise valleys. Also, coordinate noun phrases or coordinate adjectives were always accompanied by F_o valleys between the conjuncts.

<u>Sentence</u> boundaries were always accompanied by fall-rise F_o contours. In fact, the rise in F_o (around 90% change) after a sentence boundary was substantially larger than the usual rises (about 40% or less) after non-sentential constituent boundaries. Pauses (periods of unvoicing for at least 350 milliseconds) were also detected at 95% of the clause and sentence boundaries.

Boundaries were occasionally <u>falsely</u> detected at F_o valleys that were apparently not in any way syntactically related. These resulted primarily from F_o variations between vowels and consonants. As we will discuss more fully in Sec. 8-4.4, sudden increases or "jumps" in F_o occur following unvoiced consonants, and are followed by rapid fall of F_o within a few centiseconds (hundredths of a second, equivalent to tens of milliseconds). Fundamental frequency will also decrease suddenly, or "dip", within voiced obstruents, then increase suddenly again at opening of the vocal tract, then increase gradually in the first few centiseconds of vowels (or sonorants) following such voiced obstruents.

Recently (Lea, 1976, 1977), my studies of F_o detected phrase boundaries in the 255 carefully designed sentences firmly established that <u>the F_o valley occurs just before the first stress in each major syntactic constituent</u>. The set of F_o-demarcated "major syntactic constituents" that are preceded by F_o valleys includes noun phrases, sentence adverbs, conjuncts, relative clauses, and parentheticals, as well as stressed main verbs (and auxiliary verb phrases, if and only if they contain a stress such as a negative).

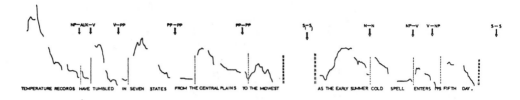

Fig. 8-9.   An F_o contour (vertical axis frequency; horizontal axis, time) of a sentence, with predicted constituent boundaries shown by arrows (labelled with category symbols for surrounding constituents), and detected boundaries shown by vertical lines.

The two parts of a compound noun are also separated by an F_o boundary. Since some words, like main verbs, lose their stress in some constructions (e.g., in coordinate constructions and subordinate phrases), those words will not be preceded by F_o boundaries in such positions.

We may summarize these major boundary-marking cues (or "deliminative" and "culminative elements"; Trubetskoy, 1939) of F_o contours as follows:

- Boundaries between clauses are detectable from very large (e.g., more than 90%) increases in F_o at the beginning of the new clause;
- Boundaries between major syntactic phrases are detectable from substantial (7% or more) increases in F_o, where the F_o increase begins at the first stress of the later phrase. 'Major syntactic phrases' before which such F_o fall-rise "valleys" occur include: noun phrases, sentence adverbs, relative clauses, paranthetical phrases, stressed main verbs, and auxiliary verbs with a stress. Boundaries are also marked between conjoined noun phrases and between the parts of a compound noun.

Further studies are needed to more precisely define exactly which phrase boundaries are marked in F_o contours, but we will demonstrate in Sec. 8-5 that F_o-detected phrase boundaries already have shown promise for aiding the syntactic parser in a speech understanding machine.

8-4.3   Intonational Cues to Subordination and Coordination

Some authors (e.g. Armstrong and Ward, 1929) claim that subordination of one phrase under another is detectable from F_o contours, in that F_o values will be lower and F_o variations will be smaller in subordinate phrases. We showed in Sec. 8-2.4 that subordination does decrease the perceived stress levels, and thus one might expect reduced F_o values to result in the subordinate positions. Sentences (14) and (15) introduced at the beginning of Sec. 8-4.2 include sequences of words that may be interpreted as structurally ambiguous, as indicated by the structural diagrams (simplified "trees") and alternative syntactic bracketings shown in Fig. 8-10, (a) and (b). The claim is that when "on the table" is a subordinate modifier under "the money", (as in Fig. 8-10b) showing that the money already is located on the table, then the subordinate phrase "on the table" will have lower F_o values and more monotonic intonation (reduced variations in F_o), compared to "the money" or "by the door". If, on the other hand, "by the door" is subordinate under "the table", then "by the door" will have the reduced F_o values and monotonic variations, as in Fig. 8-10(a). Hence, relative F_o values in the three phrases could be used to determine which structure was intended, and where the subordination occurs.

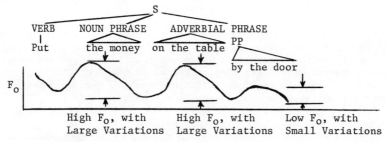

(a) Put (the money) (on the table (by the door)).

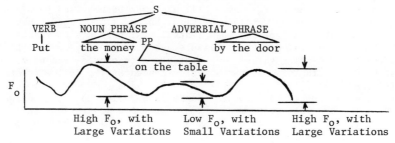

(b) Put (the money (on the table)) (by the door).

Fig. 8-10 Contrasts in Subordination and Purported Consequences in F_0 Contours

  This claim has not been well documented, however, and such F_0 cues to subordination were <u>not</u> apparent in one small study I conducted (Lea, 1976d).
Further study is warrented on this issue, since such structural distinctions
may be useful in speech recognition procedures. However, even if F_0 values
are not systematically correlated with subordination, other prosodic cues, such
as different local rates of speech and longer pauses after "money" in Fig. 8-
10(a) and after "table" in Fig. 8-11(b), may give some indication of subordination and grouping of phrases.
  Another subordinate structure that appears to be marked in prosodic patterns is the paranthetical or appositive (non-restrictive) relative clause in
sentence (16), which is to be contrasted with the restrictive relative clause
of (17):

   (16) Lynn, who knew the man in Rome, ran Maine.
   (17) Men who knew the man in Rome ran Maine.
Pauses, distinct "comma intonation" contours, and rhythmic effects are expected
to accompany the structural breaks of the paranthetical, but such interuptive
markers will be absent for the regular restrictive relative clause.
  A pilot study of prosodic features in five pairs of such contrasting sentences (Lea, 1976d, pp. 36-37) showed that in comparison with the non-restrictive relative clauses, parantheticals are demarcated by: larger F_0 variations
(F_0 falls about 20% more before the parenthetical and rises about 20% more
after the parenthetical); longer intersyllabic time intervals (equivalent to
"short pauses") at their boundaries (an average of 25 centiseconds longer than
for the restrictive relative clauses); and Tune II F_0 contours either before
or at the end of the paranthetical (but not so for the restrictive relative).
  <u>Coordination</u> is another syntactic construction which might be detectable
from F_0 contours. Since coordinate elements (such as noun phrases) usually
have equal stress levels, and there is an F_0 fall-rise valley between conjuncts,

each such conjunct is at least well marked as a phrase in the F_0 contour. To actually detect that a particular sequence of words is specifically a coordinate construction is another matter, however. Lea (1972) found that some coordinate structures seemed to have near-equal F_0 values on the conjuncts, with a peak F_0 on the conjunction between them. Linguists have also suggested that coordinate units have a pitch "concord" (Cantrell, 1969), but such claims about F_0 correlates of coordination have not been well tested and are not currently suitable for use in speech recognizers.

8-4.4 <u>Intonational Cues to Phonetic Structures</u>

As a primary correlate of stress, F_0 provides some cues about the positions of phonetic and phonemic reliability in an utterance. Also, the absence of F_0 values in a region of speech is an intuitively obvious sign of unvoicing of the consonant. However, F_0 values will also not be provided by a fundamental frequency tracker during portions of some phonemically <u>voiced</u> consonants, due to actual cessation of voicing when transglottal pressure decreases during some voice obstruents, or due to failures to track during low energies or rapid transitions in F_0 values. F_0 <u>contours</u> then provide secondary cues to the state of voicing of consonants, as evidenced by the following experimental results (Lea, 1972; 1973b):

- After F_0 contours are blanked out during unvoiced consonants, F_0 will start again at a high value and rapidly fall (about 10 to 20% in the first 5 centiseconds) in the subsequent vowel or sonorant sound; and
- F_0 dips about 10% during voiced obstruents (due to reduced transglottal pressure during closure or occlusion of the vocal tract), rises suddenly again at vocal tract opening, and continues to gradually rise (another 10% or so) in the first 5 or 10 centiseconds of the following vowel or sonorant sound.

These F_0 variations due to voiced and unvoiced obstruents interfere with the reliable detection of intonational phrase boundaries and stressed syllables. As shown in Fig. 8-9, sudden jumps of F_0 occur after unvoiced consonants such as within the words "temperature" and "records", and local dips of F_0 occur in the voiced obstruents of words like "tumbled", "seven", etc. The threshold for "substantial" sizes of F_0 valleys must be set high enough to avoid false boundaries being detected at such places. Similarly, since (as was noted in Sec. 8-2, and as will be discussed further in Sec. 8-5) rising F_0 is a primary cue to stress, some F_0 increases after <u>voiced</u> obstruents will produce false detections of stressed syllables, and some stressed syllables following <u>unvoiced</u> consonants will have falling F_0 and thus may miss being called stressed.

Another phonetic influence on F_0 that must be considered in detecting phrase boundaries, locating stresses, and assessing overall F_0 contours is shown in Fig. 8-11. High vowels have higher F_0 than low vowels, so some differences in F_0 from syllable to syllable may be due to vowel heights, not due to intended stress distinctions or structural contrasts. I observed that some errors in automatic stress location were due to such phonetic differences, whereby an unstressed high vowel can be selected over its neighboring low vowel as the stressed syllable. It appears that this effect could be reduced by adjusting F_0 values slightly down or up, according to whether the first formant is low (i.e., for high vowels) or high (for low vowels), respectively. On the other hand, relative F_0 values <u>could</u> be used to confirm or call into question a vowel's hypothesized identity, as a further prosodic aid to phonemic analysis.

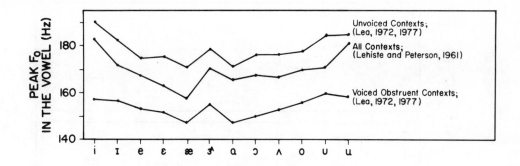

Fig. 8-11. Peak values of F_O for English vowels in various consorantal contexts, averaged for many utterances by male talkers, as reported in the publications indicated.

The glottal stop is still another source of phonetic influences on F_O contours. Glottal stops may be preceded by either rapid decreases in F_O, or rapid increases, and followed by opposite or similar trends, as illustrated in Fig. 8-12. Depending upon how the F_O analysis window lines up with timings of silences and glottal pulses at the short stoppages of airflow during glottal stops, a pitch tracker can get either higher-than-usual, or lower-than-usual, F_O values near the glottal stop. These F_O variations can be mistaken for phrase boundaries (Lea, 1975d; 1977). It is also worth noting that the glottal stop is an interesting secondary cue to stress in English, with glottal stops 12 times more likely to precede stressed vowels than unstressed ones (Lea, 1975d, p. 28).

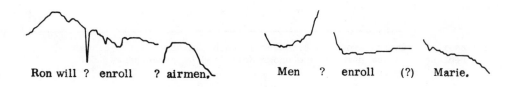

Ron will ? enroll ? airmen.   Men ? enroll (?) Marie.

Fig. 8-12. Examples of F_O Contours Near Glottal Stops

8-4.5 A Composite Model of F_O Contours

We have seen that several factors influence F_O contours, so a recognizer must be able to isolate each factor or generatively characterize how they combine to produce actual F_O contours (cf. Lea, 1977). Fig. 8-13 illustrates how some of the major factors can generate an F_O contour, which could be compared (by a recognizer) with an actual incoming contour to verify whether hypothesized wording and structures are correct. F_O is highest on the first stress, and staircases down on successive stresses. F_O jumps high again after the clausal pause, but, as illustrated in Fig. 8-13(a), it does not get quite as high in the second clause as it was in the beginning of the sentence (Lea,1972).

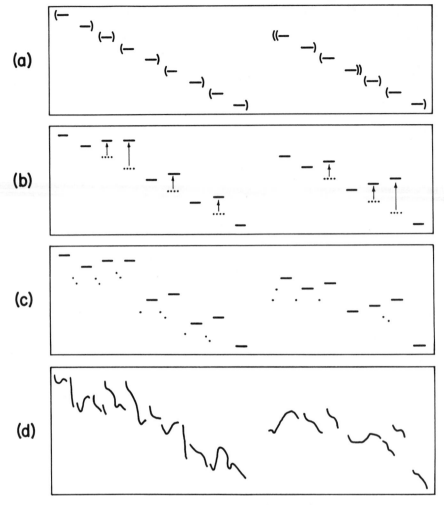

(a) Basic F_0 staircase on the stresses in each clause of a two-clause sentence. Major phrases are shown delimited by parantheses, for use in later rules.

(b) F_0 on each phrase-initial stress is raised to above the F_0 value of the previous stress. The F_0 rises now serve as acoustic substitutes for the parantheses in figure (a).

(c) F_0 on each unstressed syllable is predicted as below the F_0 value on its neighboring stresses.

(d) F_0 variations due to phonetic sequences cause lacal perturbations and slopes in the smoothed F_0 contours.

Figure 8-13. Progressive composition of a complex intonation contour from the staircasing of stresses, the F_0 rises at phrase-initial stresses, the values on intervening unstressed syllables, and the effects of intrinsic phonetic features and contour smoothing. The timing of all events, as determined in Fig. 8-7, has been replaced by discrete increments here, for simplicity. The final contour with timing is shown in Figure 8-9.

Note that stress assignment is a prerequisite to assigning F_0 contours, and subsequent rules which characterize initial and terminal contours, F_0 in unstressed syllables, and phonetic variations all require prior consideration of stress effects on F_0 values.

F_0 rises substantially at the first stress in a major phrase, as illustrated in Fig. 8-13(b). A modest absolute rise in F_0 is enough to mark the boundary, since F_0 would otherwise fall steadily from stress to stress, and any substantial non-fall cues the boundary.

Fig. 8-13(c) illustrates how unstressed syllables are assigned F_0 values that are below their immediately surrounding stresses. As with stresses, we also assume that F_0 drops from one unstress to the next following unstress. However, F_0 rises on successive clause-initial unstresses before the peak F_0 at the first stress in the second clause, and F_0 should fall rapidly after the final stress, though no example of final unstresses is shown in Fig. 8-13. If a Tune II terminal rise in F_0 were to be introduced due to the sentence being a question, or due to some connotative nuance such as uncertainty or incompletion, then F_0 would rise from unstress to unstress after the last stress in the clause. Sometimes such a terminal rise will begin within the final stressed syllable.

Some phonetic effects on F_0 are illustrated in Fig. 8-13(d). Obviously, during unvoiced consonants, F_0 contours are blanked out. Immediately following the unvoiced consonants, F_0 starts higher than the contour from Fig. 8-13(c), and rapidly falls. During voiced obstruents, F_0 dips slightly below the contour of Fig. 8-13(c). Also, F_0 is slightly higher in high vowels like /i, ɪ, ʊ, u/ than in the lower vowels like /æ, ɑ/. Fig. 8-13(d) then illustrates most major aspects of realistic F_0 contours except the proper timing of events, which, at each step in such composition, could be obtained as illustrated in Fig. 8-7.

Hopefully, it is clear that the superimposing of influences due to timing, sentence intonation, constituent structure, stress placements, and phonetic influences has yielded an F_0 contour quite similar to the actual one in Fig. 8-9. Finer-grain adjustments in the timing and specific F_0 values in the contours could be made, based on such additional aspects as relative levels of stress, syntactic subordination, vowel heights, consonantal place of articulation, glottal stops, etc. (Lea, 1972, 1977).

8-5. ALGORITHMS FOR PROSODIC ANALYSIS

In this section, we shall discuss actual computer programs or devices that have been developed to permit the various prosodic analyses outlined previously in this Chapter. The basic extraction of acoustic prosodic parameters (energy and fundamental frequency contours) is discussed in Sec. 8-5.1. An algorithm for detecting phrase boundaries from F_0 contours is described in Sec. 8-5.2. Detection of syllables (or syllabic nuclei), and the subsequent determination of which of those syllables are stressed, are presented in Sec. 8-5.3 and 8-5.4, respectively. General strategies for using prosodic information in recognition, and an example of some success in an application within the BBN HWIM system, are presented in Sec. 8-5.6.

8-5.1 Extracting Acoustic Prosodic Features

It is a small task to obtain the total energy contour of a speech signal, either by a digital sum of the squares of time samples or frequency components in a time window of the wave, or by an analog filter, rectifier, and smoothing filter. However, a frequency band limited "sonorant energy function" that measures the energy from 60 to 3000 Hz has been shown to be far better for prosodic analysis than the broadband total energy, since total energy remains high during obstruents while the sonorant energy dips at obstruents (which occur at syllable boundaries). Other bandwidth-limited energy functions, such as a weighted "loudness function" (Mermelstein, 1975), have also been shown effective for syllabification, and an energy function limited to the band 650 to 3000 Hz is useful for separating vowel nuclei from surrounding nasals, liquids, and glides (Lea, 1973b). A "very low frequency energy function" in the bandwidth 60 to 400 Hz can provide an independent decision about the voicing state of the speech. Each of the energy calculations is usually done about every 10 milliseconds (ms), with a 25.6 ms Hanning window, then converted to a relative decibel (dB) scale.

There are many algorithms or devices for determining the fundamental-frequency or "pitch" of the speech wave, but among the best is an auto-correlation pitch tracker developed by Sondhi (1968) and repeatedly implemented, simplified, modified, and converted to hardware versions by other authors (Skinner, 1973; Rabiner et al., 1975; Gillman, 1975; Dubnowski, et al., 1976). The basic algorithm involves center clipping the speech waveform (to preserve only the large peaks at the beginnings of pitch periods), then autocorrelating the signal to determine what time offset produces maximum autocorrelation, and hence detecting that the signal is again repeating its basic pitch cycle. Refinements to the basic algorithm have involved replacing multiplications involved in the autocorrelation by simple additions or subtractions, down-sampling and infinite peak clipping the signal to reduce the data that must be processed, and using energy thresholds and voicing decisions to decide when the pitch value will be reliable.

For prosodic analysis, we are interested only in the general trends and shapes throughout syllables and longer units, so longer sampling windows (on the order of 50ms; Lea, 1974a) are used. Also, since severe jitter, or wide variations of pitch values, will occur at the onsets and offsets of voicing (where part of the window is in the unvoiced region), it is good to use separate energy thresholds in the beginning and ending halves of the window and to set the energy thresholds for acceptable F_0 values quite high. Such a conservative pitch tracker may not provide F_0 values for some segments of speech which would be considered voiced, but, it is better to have no F_0 value in prosodic analysis than an unreliable value and jittery contour. Also, waiting until energy has built up substantially after an unvoiced region reduces the magnitude of the F_0 jump associated with unvoiced obstruents, and thus reduces the likelihood of false phrase boundary detections or erroneous stress decisions.

Previous pitch trackers have successfully reduced the number of octave errors in pitch tracking, by limiting the range of expected F_0 values to a normal 70 to 250 Hz for males, or 140 to 400 Hz for females, and by "smoothing" (or "error-correcting") the F_0 contour by disallowing large F_0 jumps that last for only one or two 10ms segments. Another useful refinement is to convert F_0 from Hertz to a relative scale, such as eighth tones (one fourth of a musical semi-tone, produced by a frequency ratio of $\sqrt[48]{2.0}$ = 1.014545335, which is about twice the just-noticeable-difference in perceived pitches. This yields 48 eighth tones per octave, and makes the 7% phrase-boundary-marking change in a female voice equivalent to a 7% change in a male voice (both being about 5 eighth tones difference).

8-5.2 F_0 Phrase Boundary Detector

A FORTRAN computer program for detecting boundaries between major syntactic constituents has been implemented (Lea, 1972; 1973b; 1976d). It looks for substantial (5 eighth tone, or 7%) decreases in F_0 followed by substantial F_0 increases (5 eighth tones), and marks a boundary at the last of the lowest F_0 values in the valley. Each local F_0 minimum or maximum must be beyond the 5-eighth tone threshold for at least two 10 ms segments, to eliminate false detections from single F_0 values that are out of line with neighboring values. A subroutine in the program also detects periods of unvoicing (no F_0 values) of duration 35 cs or longer, and declares those to be clausal or sentential pauses. A confidence measure is assigned to each detected boundary based on the magnitude and duration of the F_0 rise, whether the F_0 maximum occurred just after a period of unvoicing (and thus whether the F_0 variation may be phonetically-produced, not syntactically dictated), and how long any accompanying pause may be. More complete descriptions are available for the original program (Lea, 1972) and later refinements (Lea and Kloker, 1975).

The program has been tested on a total of over 1500 seconds of speech, involving 20 talkers, with texts that include readings of weather reports, newscasts, paragraphs with only monosyllabic words, the Rainbow Passage, and a database of 255 sentences (all 255 read by one talker, plus 37 sentences each by two other talkers), plus a variety of sentences intended for man-machine dialog, and short excerpts from conversations. In general, the program detects (but does not precisely locate) over 90% of the syntactically predicted boundaries, with about 5 to 10% of all detections being false (phonetically-dictated) and another 10 to 15% appearing to be syntactically related, but not predicted by prior expectations as to which boundaries should be intonationally marked.

The primary need in intonational phrase boundary detection is to determine which phrases are demarcated by such F_0 valleys and which are not. Over 99% of all clause and sentence boundaries in previous studies have been marked by substantial F_0 variations, and over 90% were accompanied by pauses of 35 cs or longer. Some phrase boundaries (e.g., at V-ADV and N-N Compound boundaries, between conjuncts, and between preposed ADV's and NP's) were detected 100% of the time in controlled studies, and many others were detected over 90% of the time. Yet, other expected boundaries were much less reliably detected, and many boundaries occurred where they were not expected. Controlled studies are needed that isolate phrase boundary effects from various other intonational effects, for a variety of structures. Except for this needed work on accurately predicting what boundaries should be marked, the intonation boundary detection process seems to work quite adequately for speech recognition purposes. (Of course, one could always hope to refine the algorithm to eliminate more phonetically-dictated false boundaries and to better handle both monotonically and animatedly spoken intonation contours from a greater variety of talkers.)

8-5.3 Syllabification

Syllabic nuclei have been successfully detected at Sperry Univac (Lea and Kloker, 1975) by a subroutine that finds high-sonorant-energy regions ("chunks") bounded by substantial (4 or 5 dB) dips in energy associated with pre- and post-vocalic consonants. The best definitions of the beginning and ending points of the nuclei were found to be at the halfway points in the dips, where energy drops half of the way down to its bottom value in the dip. Another test for a high-energy chunk to be considered a syllabic nucleus is whether it is voiced for at least 30 ms. Even in the "worst case" of detecting syllables in all-sonorant sequences (wherein most syllabic boundaries don't have large dips in energy), the program successfully found over 91% of the syllables, with only about 1% false detections of nuclei. A more sophisticated program developed at Haskins Laboratories uses a spectrally weighted "loudness" function to compensate for different intrinsic energies in various vowels, and uses an interative application of a "hull function" to first detect large energy dips, then later subdivide long chunks between those big dips, by locating smaller dips within the chunks (Mermelstein, 1975). The Haskins algorithm obtained over 92% of the syllabic nuclei.

Further refinements in syllabification procedures could make adjustments due to phonetically-detected vowel identity, and could use formant transitions as additional cues to syllabic boundaries.

8-5.4 Stressed Syllable Location

The primary acoustic correlates of stress are: high intensity (i.e., sonorant energy); long syllabic (or vowel) duration; and high and rising F_0 (Fry, 1955; 1958; Lea, 1976c). Combinations of these basic cues are even more effective. For example, Medress, et al. (1971) showed that while 72% of the stressed syllables in isolated words could be detected from the higher peak energy levels, and 70% and 68% could be detected from syllabic durations and peak F_0 values, respectively, over 85% could be located from the energy integral (sum of dB throughout the duration of the nucleus) and 90% could be located from rising F_0 contours. In sentence contexts, the energy integral worked best. In later studies with various spoken sentences (Lea, 1974a), I showed that 89% of the stresses could be detected by a procedure for locating stressed syllables from an "archetype algorithm" that used F_0 increases and energy integrals (with 21% false stress assignments), compared to 84% for durations of nuclei alone (with 32% false stresses) and 77% for regions of 100 ms of rising F_0 (with 24% false stresses).

Fig. 8-14 illustrates the basic steps involved in the archetype algorithm for stress location. The speech is first (Fig. 8-14a) segmented into sentences and major grammatical constituents by the algorithm for detecting phrase boundaries at the bottoms of substantial fall-rise "valleys" in fundamental frequency contours. The increasing fundamental frequency near the beginning of each constituent is assumed to be attributable to the first stressed syllable or "HEAD" of the constituent, as shown in Fig. 8-14a. A portion of the speech which is high in energy with increasing fundamental frequency values, and which is bounded by points where the energy dips 5 dB or more, is asserted to be the stressed nucleus of this HEAD syllable. This is shown by the cross-hatched portions in Fig. 8-14b. Previous studies have shown that this stress-induced initial rise in fundamental frequency in a constituent is usually followed by a gradual fall in fundamental frequency, which may be approximated by a straight line on the eighth tone scale. As shown in Fig. 8-14c, the "archetype line" steadily drops in eighth tone values from the maximum fundamental frequency in the constituent down to the low value at the end of the constituent. Other stressed syllables in the constituent are expected to be accompanied by local increases in fundamental frequency-increases which make the fundamental frequency contour locally rise above the archetype line. Thus, even though fundamental frequency may not be rising absolutely at such stressed syllables, the fact that it is not falling at its usual rate can be a cue to the presence of a stressed syllable. The stressed syllable is again located within a high-energy region bounded by 5 dB dips in energy, as shown by the new cross-hatched portions in Fig. 8-14c.

Further refinements have been incorporated into the algorithm to locate stresses: at long (12 cs) nuclei in pre-pausal positions; at long nuclei within unusually long constituents, in which F_0 never rises above the archetype line; and within unusually long rising-F_0 regions (i.e., before the maximum-F_0 points and HEAD stresses). Other refinements could permit more alternative levels of assigned stress (cf. Sargent, 1975; Cheung, 1975) and adjustments of intensity, duration, and F_0 cues based on the identity and consonental context of the vowel. Confidence measures or "scores" should also be attached to stress decisions.

Overall results suggest that only about 15% of all syllables are confused between stressed and unstressed levels in comparing machine decisions with listeners' perceptions, but more work is needed to reduce such confusions down to near the 5% confusions found in listeners' perceptions of stress.

196

(a) The first step in stressed
syllable location with the
archetype algorithm is to
divide the speech into
syntactic constituents with
the F_0 phrase boundary
detector.

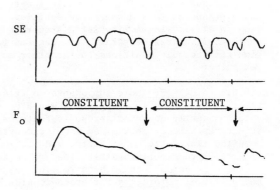

(b) Substantial increases in
F_0 are cues to nearby
stressed "HEADS" in the
beginnings of the syntactic
constituents. The stressed
HEAD syllables are then
associated with nearby
high-energy "chunks".

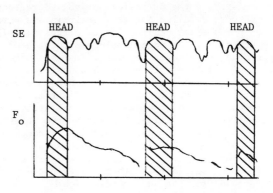

(c) Local increases above the
straight archetype lines
indicate other stressed
syllables in the constit-
ents. These are then
located within nearby high-
energy "chunks".

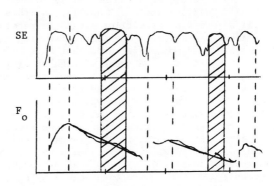

Fig. 8-14.   Basic Steps in the Location of Stressed Syllables with the
Archetype Algorithm. (SE = sonorant energy, in dB; F_0 =
fundamental frequency, in eighth tones)

197

8-5.5 Strategies for Using Prosodics in Recognition

You have your choice of a whole spectrum of alternative strategies for using prosodics to aid speech recognition, since we have seen that it offers aids in all levels of linguistic structure. Here we shall consider aspects of three illustrative strategies, ranging from a very cautious "conservative" plan for prosodic additions to the other extreme of a "bold" prosodics-only recognizer.

8-5.5.1 Adding Prosodic Components to Existing Systems

8-5.5.1 Adding Prosodic Components to Existing Systems – A cautious approach to using prosodics in recognition would be to use only the most robust (reli-able and easily detected) prosodic features to verify, or modify the scores of, structures already determined from segmental phonetic information and pre-compiled linguistic constraints, and not to weigh the prosodic information too highly. More experimental studies are needed before most prosodic information can be considered to have been reliably associated with linguistic structures, and a list of priorities for prosodic aids is needed. I would guess that the number and positions of F_0-detected phrase boundaries, the number of syllabic nuclei, and the detections of voiced regions (within which formant tracking and more detailed spectral analysis are warranted) are among the best aspects of prosody to consider first. Stressed syllable locations would also be useful to try, for additional cues to word matching and for assigning reliability scores to phonetic segments. Stress cues may also help detect sentence type. A problem with both phrase boundaries and stress decisions is that they are still not detected reliably enough to depend upon them too much. Interstress intervals might then be tested as rate measures, indicating which phonological rules apply to an utterance. Moderately interesting procedures might then be: verifying the timing of hypothesized phrases; using F_0 contours (e.g., terminal rises) to detect yes/no questions; anchoring phonetic analysis on stressed islands of reliability; and using pauses to detect structural boundaries. Must less reliability, simplicity, and attention should be initially associated with phrase final lengthening, expected phonetic durations, and prosodic cues to subordination and coordination.

A reasonable initial step in using prosodics in a speech recognition system would be to incorporate an expandable prosodic analysis component as an independently-operating knowledge source in a HEARSAY I-like structure, or to add supplemental tests to phonetic, lexical, or syntactic analysis procedures in a HEARSAY II, HWIM, or HARPY-like structure. For example, an attempt has been made to use F_0-detected phrase boundaries to aid the syntactic parser in the BBN HWIM system (cf. Chap. 14), so that correct words and phrase hypotheses will be proposed at earlier stages in parsing, and erroneous hypotheses can be avoided. As shown in the simplified diagram of Fig. 8-15, HWIM does a phonetic analysis to hypothesize words that have high scores of correspondence with the acoustic data. A queue of high scoring words, and their hypothesized positions, is given by way of the system control to the parser. These one-word islands can then be evaluated by the parser, and an adjusted list of likely words transferred back to system control. Prosodics may be introduced into the process, by adjusting the priority order of promising words that the parser transfers to system control. The procedure actually used involved first marking all the words in the grammar that were expected to be immediately preceded by F_0 valleys (i.e., main verbs, the first stressed words in noun phrases, adverbs, etc.). Only about one sixth of the wording generated by the grammar was expected to be preceded by F_0-detected boundaries, so once the system knows that a boundary occurred, the possible wording is highly constrained. Since at least one boundary occurs in almost every sentence, the prosodic information should be helpful in almost every sentence. If a word is expected to be preceded by a boundary, and a boundary is acoustically detected, then the priority or "score" for that word is increased substantially; if the expected boundary was not detected, the word's score is decreased.

198

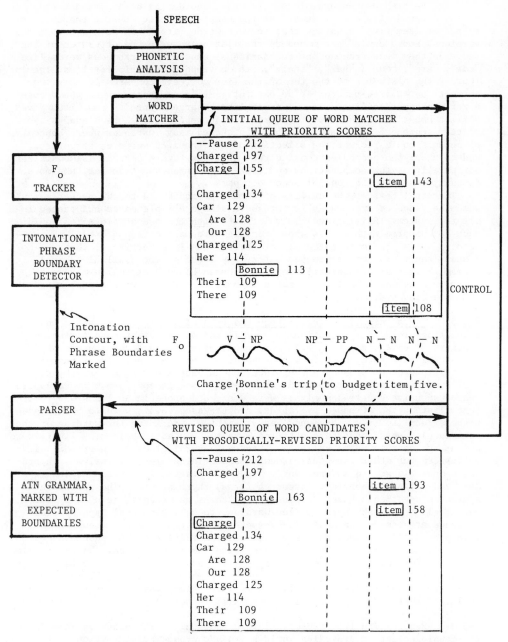

SPEECH

PHONETIC
ANALYSIS

WORD
MATCHER

F_O
TRACKER

INTONATIONAL
PHRASE
BOUNDARY
DETECTOR

Intonation
Contour, with
Phrase Boundaries
Marked

PARSER

ATN GRAMMAR,
MARKED WITH
EXPECTED
BOUNDARIES

CONTROL

INITIAL QUEUE OF WORD MATCHER
WITH PRIORITY SCORES

--Pause 212
Charged 197
Charge 155
                                    item 143
Charged 134
Car 129
  Are 128
  Our 128
Charged 125
Her 114
         Bonnie 113
Their 109
There 109
                              item 108

F_O V — NP   NP — PP   N — N   N — N

Charge Bonnie's trip to budget item five.

REVISED QUEUE OF WORD CANDIDATES
WITH PROSODICALLY-REVISED PRIORITY SCORES

--Pause 212
Charged 197
                              item 193
         Bonnie 163
                              item 158
Charge
Charged 134
Car 129
  Are 128
  Our 128
Charged 125
Her 114
Their 109
There 109

8-15   Simplified diagram of the BBN HWIM System, showing how prosodic
       analysis can be inserted to guide the parser. The initial queue
       of word candidates shows an ordered list of words and their scores.
       Using the four detected phrase boundaries in the intonation contour,
       the system can increase the scores on words "Bonnie" and "item",
       that are predicted, and found, to be preceded by phrase boundaries.

Fig. 8-15 shows one example of the major reordering of hypotheses that prosodic boundaries can produce, for the sample sentence "Charge Bonnie's trip to budget item five". Notice that correct words "item" (in both hypothesized versions) and "Bonnie" get moved up the list because in the utterance of the sentence they were preceded by boundaries as expected. Erroneous words like "car", "are", "our", "her", "their", etc. move <u>down</u> the priority list, leaving four of the six words at the top of the list correct, compared to only two correct top choices before the adjustment. At later stages, when the recognizer was hypothesizing word sequences like "Charge Bonnie's" and "item five", similar boosting of correct structures was accomplished. A hand analysis of sixteen sentences using these techniques showed many instances where boundary placements could reorder the selection of hypothesized words or structures, and thereby, the prosodics could direct analysis toward correct islands first, potentially saving computations on lower-score erroneous theories, and more directly reaching the goal of a correct parse.

The final test of the utility of such a prosodic aid to the parser comes when the proposed procedures for prosodic aids are implemented and tested in a total system. Parsing and control traces <u>with</u> the use of prosodics could then be compared with traces when prosodic information is <u>not</u> used. Unfortunately, while BBN implemented all of these ideas in a version of their HWIM System, their project terminated before any results were available. Still it seems likely that prosodically-detected phrase boundaries could improve the order in which alternative syntactic theories are tested within such a speech understanding system.

8-5.5.2 <u>A Prosodically-Guided Speech Understanding Strategy</u> - Rather than relegating prosodic information to a small add-on aspect of recognition, we can give it equal weighting with segmental analysis and other aspects of overall system structure, such as was proposed by Lea, Medress, and Skinner (1975). In their proposed "prosodically-guided speech understanding strategy", prosodics were to be used throughout the system. Energy contours were to control where expensive spectral analyses were done, and phonetic analysis was to be done first in the stressed syllables, and stressed vowels were to be assigned high reliability (i.e., assigned heavy weights in deciding the wording of the utterance). Detected stress patterns were to be used in selecting likely words which have corresponding syllables stressed. Parallel with the prosodically-influenced but otherwise usual acoustic phonetic and lexical analysis, a prosodic analysis was to independently predict syntactic structures, using F_0-detected phrase boundaries, stress patterns, rhythms, etc. The preliminary syntactic hypothesis based on prosodic patterns was then to be used by the parser along with the hypothesized wording, to select a total hypothesized sentence structure. An analysis-by-synthesis procedure could then generate (via prosodically-guided phonological rules) a total acoustic phonetic <u>and</u> prosodic pattern that could be compared with the input speech. Ways were also suggested for using prosodics to aid semantic analysis. Some aspects of this general prosodically-guided strategy were implemented in recognizers developed at Sperry Univac (Medress, et al., 1977; 1978; also, Chap. 19 of this book). Full implementation of such a strategy still is needed.

8-5.5.3 <u>Recognition from Prosodic Information Only</u> - The other extreme from the usual neglect of prosodics would be to use prosodic information as the <u>only</u> acoustically derived input, neglecting instead the usual segmental phonetic information. In 1972, Willems attempted recognition of numerical expressions ("zero", "one" ... "twenty two",..."one hundred sixty seven"...) using only prosodic information, with considerable success. It would be possible to learn much about an utterance from pauses, F_0 valleys, stress decisions, rhythm measures, rate measures, numbers of syllabic nuclei, other F_0 features such as Tune II terminal rises, and prosodic cues to segmental occurrences (such as F_0

slopes to detect voicing states of obstruents, F_O variations to detect glottal stops, energy dips as obstruent detectors, etc.). Of particular interest would be attempts to successfully recognize databases that have been handled by previous recognizers, such as the 100 sentences used to test HARPY and IBM recognizers (Reddy, et al., 1976; Bahl, et al., 1978). From such studies, we could get a clearer picture of just how much can be accomplished with prosodic recognition procedures. Phonemic information could be added later.

We thus see that while there currently are some algorithms for prosodic analysis, much is still to be done before prosodics will have been fully tested in speech recognition systems.

8-6. SUMMARY

This chapter has necessarily been more of a tutorial about prosodic correlates of linguistic structures than the presentation of successful procedures for guiding decisions in specific speech recognizers. Our initial introduction of prosodic features emphasized their potential for acoustically detecting aspects of the large-unit (multiple-word) structures of sentences, in contrast to conventional recognition schemes which lose association with acoustic data above the word level. We saw how sentence types might be detectable from terminal F_O contours or general slopes, or from placements of stress (on command verbs but not on auxiliaries that begin yes/no questions, etc.). From pauses and very large F_O variations, we can divide discourses into sentences, and sentences into clauses, and perhaps detect some structures like parentheticals or breaks in mathematical expressions. Perhaps one of the most useful and hopeful applications of prosodics would be the division of sentences into phrases by F_O valleys, with some help possible from phrase-final lengthening of vowels and sonorants or, more realistically, from long interstress intervals. We may be able to determine phrase categories from aspects of stress patterns, special F_O contours, or other prosodics. Grammatical relations like subordination may be detectable from lowered and more monotone intonation, or from stress patterns and rhythm and rate changes. Stress patterns can be used to select likely words, and to provide "islands of reliability" or anchors for reliable phonetic analysis. Rate measures such as interstress intervals may be used to select applicable phonological rules, and stress patterns may be crucial parts of the environment for applying phonological rules. Prosodics can provide a variety of secondary aids to phonetic analysis, such as cues to voicing, locations of syllabic nuclei (vowels), cues to occurrences of glottal stops, guidelines for efficient acoustic analysis, etc.

Fairly good computer programs have been developed for obtaining energy and F_O contours, making voicing decisions, detecting phrase boundaries at F_O valleys, locating syllabic nuclei, and locating stresses, but much more is to be done for improved prosodic analysis and application of prosodic information to speech recognizers. An initial attempt at using F_O-detected phrase boundaries in the HWIM system showed some real promise of helping a syntactic parser to select the correct hypotheses about the wording and structure of a sentence. A total prosodically-guided speech recognition strategy has been outlined but still awaits full implementation, and there is even some merit in testing prosodics with a prosodics-only recognizer.

It seems the stage has been set and the act has begun, and we await the evidence that prosodics will play a valuable and effective role in future speech recognition systems. From all indications, prosodic aids to speech recognition should be a star performer in many aspects of the scenes of human-to-computer communications.

8-7. REFERENCES

Abe, I. (1967), English Sentence Rhythm and Synchronism, _Bulletin Phonetic Society of Japan_, Number 125, 9-11.

Allen, G.D. (1967), Two Behavioral Experiments on the Location of the Syllable Beat in Spoken American English, _Studies in Language and Language Behavior_, 2-179.

Allen, G.D. (1968), On Testing for Certain Stress-timing Effects, _Working Papers in Phonetics Number 10_, UCLA, 1968a, 47-59. Also, The Place of Rhythm in a Theory of Language, 60-84.

Armstrong, L.E. (1929) and I.C. Ward, _Handbook of English Intonation_, Cambridge: Heffer (2nd Edition).

Bahl, L.R., J.K. Baker, P.S. Cohen, A.G. Cole, F. Jelinek, B.L. Lewis, and R.L. Mercer (1978), "Automatic Recognition of Continuously Spoken Sentences from a Finite State Grammar," _Proceeding of the 1978 IEEE International Conference on Acoustics, Speech, and Signal Processing_, Tulsa, OK., 418-421.

Bolinger, D.L. (1972), Accent Is Predictable (If You're a Mind Reader), _Language_, 48: 633-644.

Boomer, D.S. (1965), Hesitation and Grammatical Encoding, _Language and Speech_, 8: 148-158.

Bresnan, J. (1971), Sentence Stress and Syntactic Transformations, _Language_, 47: 157-181.

Bresnan, J. (1972), Stress and Syntax: A Reply, _Language_, 48: 326-342.

Cantrell, W.R. (1969), Pitch, Stress, and Grammatical Relations, Papers from the Fifth Regional Meeting of the Chicago Linguistic Society, Chicago: University of Chicago Press, 12-24.

Cheung, J.Y. (1975), Computer Estimates and Modelling of Linguistic Stress Patterns in Speech, Ph.D. Dissertation (EE Technical Report Number 188), Department of Electrical Engineering, University of Washington, Seattle.

Chomsky, N. and M. Halle (1968), _The Sound Pattern of English_, New York: Harper and Row.

Denes, P. (1975), Speech Recognition: Old and New Ideas, in _Speech Recognition_: Invited Papers Presented at the 1974 IEEE Symposium (D.R. Reddy, Editor). New York: Academic Press, 73-82.

Dubnowski, J.J., R.W. Shafer, and L.R. Rabiner, (1976), Real-Time Digital Hardware Pitch Detector, _IEEE Transactions on Acoustics, Speech, and Signal Processing_, ASSP-24, No. 1, 2-8.

Fairbanks, G. (1940), _Voice and Articulation Drillbook_, New York: Harper and Row.

Fant, G. (1975), Key-Note Address, in _Speech Recognition_: Invited Papers Presented at the 1974 IEEE Symposium (D.R. Reddy, Editor). New York: Academic Press, ix-xiii.

Friedman, J. (1974), Computer Exploration of Fast Speech Rules, _Proceedings IEEE Symposium on Speech Recognition_, Carnegie-Mellon University, 197-203.

Fromkin, V.A. (1971), The Non-anamolous Nature of Anamolous Utterances, _Language_, 47: 27-52.

Fromkin, V.A. (1973), Slips of the Tongue, _Scientific American_, Vol. 229, 110-117.

Fry, D.B. (1955), Duration and Intensity as Physical Correlates of Linguistic Stress, _Journal of the Acoustical Society of America_, 35: 765-769.

Fry, D.B. (1958), Experiments in the Perception of Stress, _Language and Speech_, 1: 120-152.

Gillman, R.A. (1975), A Fast Frequency Domain Pitch Algorithm, _Journal of the Acoustical Society of America_, Vol. 58, Supplement, p. S62 (A).

Gleason, H.A. Jr. (1961), _An Introduction to Descriptive Linguistics_, New York: Holt, Rinehart and Winston.

Gleitman, L.R. (1965), Coordinating Conjunctions In English. _Language_ 41: 260-293.

Goldman-Eisler, H. (1958), The Predictability of Words in Context and the Length of Pause in Speech, Language and Speech, 1: 220-231.

Goldman-Eisler, H. (1961), A comparative Study of Two Hesitation Phonemena, Language and Speech, 4: 451-454.

Halle, M. (1973), Stress Rules in English: a New Version, Linguistic Inquiry, Vol. IV, No. 4, 451-464.

Halle, M. and S.J. Keyser (1971), English Stress, New York: Harper and Row.

Jones, D. (1909) Intonation Curves, Leipzig and Berlin: B.G. Teubner.

Jones, D. (1932), An Outline of English Phonetics, New York: Dulton.

Khozhevnikov, V.A., and L.A. Chistovich (1965), Speech: Articulation and Perception, Translated by JPRS, Washington, D.C., Number JPRS30, p. 543.

Klatt, D.H. (1973), Interaction between Two Factors that Influence Vowel Duration, Journal of the Acoustical Society of America, 54: 1102-1104.

Klatt, D.H. (1974), The Duration of (s) in English Words, Journal of Speech and Hearing Research, 17: 51-63.

Klatt, D.H. (1975), Vowel Lengthening Is Syntactically Determined in a Connected Discourse, Journal of Phonetics, 3: 161-172.

Klatt, D.H. (1976), Linguistic Uses of Segmental Duration in English: Acoustic and Perceptual Evidence, Journal of the Acoustical Society of America, 59: 1208-1221.

Klatt, D.H. (1977), "Review of the ARPA Speech Understanding Project," Journal of the Acoustical Society of America, 62: 1345-1366.

Klatt, D.H. and K.N. Stevens (1972), Sentence Recognition from Visual Examination of Spectrograms and Machine-aided Lexical Searching, Proceedings 1972 Conference on Speech Communication and Processing, IEEE and AFCRL: Bedford, Massachusetts, 315-318.

Kloker, D.R. (1975), Vowel and Sonorant Lengthening as Cues to Phonological Phrase Boundaries, Journal of the Acoustical Society of America, 57: Supplement, pp. S33-S34.

Lea, W.A. (1972), Intonational Cues to the Constituent Structure and Phonemics of Spoken English, Ph.D. Dissertation, School of Electrical Engineering, Purdue University.

Lea, W.A. (1973a), Syntactic Boundaries and Stress Patterns in Spoken English Texts, Univac Report Number PX 10146, Sperry Univac DSD, St. Paul, Mn.

Lea, W.A. (1973b), An Approach to Syntactic Recognition Without Phonemics, IEEE Transactions on Audio and Electroacoustics, Vol. AU-21: 249-358.

Lea, W.A. (1973c), Segmental and Suprasegmental Influences on Fundamental Frequency Contours, Consonant Types and Tone (Proceedings of the First Annual Southern California Round Table in Linguistics, L. Hyman, Editor). Los Angeles: University of Southern California Press.

Lea, W.A. (1973d), Evidence that Stressed Syllables Are the Most Readily Decoded Portions of Continuous Speech, Journal of the Acoustical Society of America, 55: 410(A).

Lea, W.A. (1973e), Perceived Stress as the "Standard" for Judging Acoustical Correlates of Stress, Journal of the Acoustical Society of America, 55: 436(A).

Lea, W.A. (1973f), An Algorithm for Locating Stressed Syllables in Continuous Speech, Journal of the Acoustical Society of America, 55: 411(A).

Lea, W.A. (1974), Prosodic Aids to Speech Recognition: IV. A General Strategy for Prosodically-guided Speech Understanding, Univac Report Number PX10791, Sperry Univac, DSD, St. Paul, MN.

Lea, W.A. (1975a), Isochrony and Disjuncture as Aids to Syntactic and Phonological Analysis, Journal of the Acoustical Society of America, 57: Supplement, p. 533.

Lea, W.A. (1975), Prosodic Aids to Speech Recognition: VII. Experiments on Detecting and Locating Phrase Boundaries, Univac Report Number PX11534, Sperry Univac DSD, St. Paul, MN.

Lea, W.A. (1976a), Acoustic Correlates of Stress and Juncture, Univac Report

Number PX11693, June, 1976. Published in Studies in Stress and Accent, (L. Hyman, Editor), University of Southern California Press, Los Angeles, pp. 83-119, 1977.

Lea, W.A. (1976b), The Importance of Prosodic Analysis in Speech Understanding Systems, Univac Report Number PX11694, Sperry Univac DAD, St. Paul, MN.

Lea, W.A. (1976c), Prosodic Aids to Speech Recognition: VIII. Listeners' Perceptions of Selected English Stress Patterns, Univac Report Number PX11711, Sperry Univac DSD, St. Paul, MN.

Lea, W.A. (1976d), Perceived Stress Patterns in Selected English Phrase Structures, presented to the American Association of Phonetic Sciences, San Diego, California, Nov. 1976.

Lea, W.A. (1976e), Prosodic Aids to Speech Recognition: IX. Acoustic-prosodic Patterns in Selected English Phrase Structures, Univac Report Number PX 11963, Sperry Univac DSD, St. Paul, MN.

Lea, W.A. (1977), Prosodic Correlates of Linguistic Structures, in Topics in Speech Science (D.J. Broad, Editor), Speech Communications Research Laboratory, Santa Barbara, CA., 394-564.

Lea, W.A. and D.R. Kloker (1975), Prosodic Aids to Speech Recognition: VI. Timing Cues to Linguistic Structures, Univac Report Number PX11534, Sperry Univac DSD, St. Paul, MN.

Lea, W.A., M.F. Medress, and T.E. Skinner (1975), A Prosodically-guided Speech Understanding Strategy, IEEE Transactions in Acoustics, Speech, and Signal Processing, Vol. ASSP-23, 30-38.

Lehiste, I. (1970), Suprasegmentals, Cambridge: MIT Press, 1970.

Lieberman, P. (1967), Intonation, Perception and Language, Cambridge: MIT Press.

Medress, M.F. (1977), Personal communication.

Medress, M.F., T.E. Skinner and D.E. Anderson (1971), Acoustic Correlates of Word Stress, presented to the 82nd Meeting of the Acoustical Society of America, Denver, CO., Paper K3.

Medress, M.F., T.E. Skinner, D.R. Kloker, T.C. Diller, and W.A. Lea (1977), "A System for the Recognition of Spoken Connected Word Sequences," Proceedings of the 1977 IEEE International Conference on Acoustics, Speech, and Signal Processing, Hartford, CT, IEEE Catalog Number 77CH1197-3ASSP, 468-473.

Medress, M.F., T.C. Diller, D.R. Kloker, L.L. Lutton, H.N. Oredson, and T.E. Skinner (1978), "An Automatic Word Spotting System for Conversational Speech," Proceedings of the 1978 IEEE International Conference on Acoustics, Speech, and Signal Processing, Tulsa, OK., IEEE Catalog Number 77CI1197-3 ASSP, 712-717.

Mermelstein, P. (1975), Automatic Segmentation of Speech into Syllabic Units, The Journal of the Acoustical Society of America, 58: 880-883.

Neuburg, E.P. (1975), Philosophies of Speech Recognition, in Speech Recognition: Invited Papers of the 1975 Symposium. New York: Academic Press, 83-95.

Ohala, J.J. (1970), Aspects of the Control and Production of Speech, Working Papers in Phonetics Number 15, UCLA.

Olive, J. (1974), Pitch Rules for the Synthesis of Simple Declarative English Sentences, Journal of the Acoustical Society of America, 55: 117 (A).

O'Malley, M., D.R. Kloker and D. Dara-Abrams (1973), Recovering Parentheses from Spoken Algebraic Expressions, IEEE Transactions Audio and Electroacoustics Vol. AU-21, 219-220.

O'Shaunessy, D. (1976), Modelling Fundamental Frequency, and Its Relationship to Syntax, Semantics, and Phonetics, Ph.D. Dissertation, School of Electrical Engineering, MIT, Cambridge, Mass.

Oshika, B.T., et al. (1974), The Role of Phonological Rules in Speech Understanding Research, Proceedings IEEE Symposium on Speech Recognition, Carnegie-Mellon University, Pittsburgh, PA. 204-207.

Peterson, G.E. (1961), "Automatic Speech Recognition Procedures," in <u>Automatic</u> <u>Speech</u> <u>Recognition</u>, Vol. II. Ann Arbor: University of Michigan, 1963. (Reprinted from <u>Language</u> <u>and</u> <u>Speech</u>, 4: 200-219.)

Peterson, G.E. and I. Lehiste (1960), Duration of Syllabic Nuclei in English, <u>Journal</u> <u>of</u> <u>the</u> <u>Acoustical</u> <u>Society</u> <u>of</u> <u>America</u>, 32: 693-703.

Pike, K.L. (1945), <u>The</u> <u>Intonation</u> <u>of</u> <u>American</u> <u>English</u>, Ann Arbor: University of Michigan.

Rabiner, L. et al. (1976), Comparative Performance Evaluation of Pitch Trackers, <u>IEEE</u> <u>Transactions</u> <u>Acoustics</u>, <u>Speech</u>, <u>Signal</u> <u>Processing</u>, Vol. ASSP-24.

Reddy, D.R. (1976), "Computer Recognition of Connected Speech," <u>Proceedings</u> <u>of</u> <u>the</u> <u>IEEE</u>, 42: 329-347.

Reddy, D.R., et al. (1977), "Speech Understanding Systems: Summary of Results of the Five-Year Research Effort at Carnegie-Mellon University, Department of Computer Science, Carnegie-Mellon University, (reprinted 1977).

Sargent, D.C. (1975), Computer Algorithms for the Extractions and Applications of Stress Contours from Continuous Speech Sentences, Report Number <u>TR-EE75-44</u>, School of Electrical Engineering, Purdue University, West Lafayette, IN.

Shen, Y., and G.G. Peterson (1962), Isochronism in English, <u>Studies</u> <u>in</u> <u>Linguistics</u> <u>Occasional</u> <u>Papers</u> <u>9</u>.

Skinner, T.E. (1973), Speech Parameter Extraction: Fundamental Frequency, Spectral and Formant Frequency Processing, <u>Univac</u> <u>Report</u> <u>Number</u> <u>PX10376</u>, Univac Park, St. Paul, MN.

Sondhi, M.M. (1968), New Methods of Pitch Extraction, <u>IEEE</u> <u>Transactions</u> <u>on</u> <u>Audio</u> <u>and</u> <u>Electroacoustics</u>, Vol. AU-16: 262-266.

Trager, G.L. and H.L. Smith, Jr. (1951), <u>An</u> <u>Outline</u> <u>of</u> <u>English</u> <u>Structure</u>, Studies in Linguistics: Occasional Papers, Norman, OK: Battenburg Press.

Trubetskoy, N.S. (1930), Principles of Phonology. Translated from the French, 1969. Berkeley: U. California Press.

Umeda, N. (1975), Vowel Duration in American English, <u>Journal</u> <u>of</u> <u>the</u> <u>Acoustical</u> <u>Society</u> <u>of</u> <u>America</u>, 58: 434-445.

Umeda, N. (1976), Linguistic Rules for Text-to-speech Synthesis, <u>Proceedings</u> <u>IEEE</u>, 64: 443-351.

Wells, R.S. (1947), Immediate Constituents, <u>Language</u>, 23: 81-117.

Weinstein, C.J., S.S. McCandless, L.F. Mondshein, and V.W. Zue (1975), "A System for Acoustic-Phonetic Analysis of Continuous Speech," <u>IEEE</u> <u>Transactions</u> <u>on</u> <u>Acoustics</u>, <u>Speech</u>, <u>and</u> <u>Signal</u> <u>Processing</u>, Vol. ASSP-23: 54-67.

Willems, Y. (1972), The Use of Prosodics in the Automatic Recognition of Spoken English Numbers, Ph.D. Dissertation, Massachusetts Institute of Technology, Department of Electrical Engineering.

Wolf, J.J. (1975), "Speech Recognition and Understanding," in <u>Pattern</u> <u>Recognition</u>, K.S. Fu, Editor, New York: Springer.

Woods, W.A. (1975), "Motivation and Overview of SPEECHLIS: An Experimental Prototype for Speech Understanding Research," <u>IEEE</u> <u>Transactions</u> <u>on</u> <u>Acoustics</u>, <u>Speech</u>, <u>and</u> <u>Signal</u> <u>Processing</u>, Vol. ASSP-23: 2-10.

9.

SYNTAX, SEMANTICS, AND PRAGMATICS
IN SPEECH UNDERSTANDING SYSTEMS

Frederick Hayes-Roth
The Rand Corporation
Santa Monica, California

9-1. INTRODUCTION

Several kinds of higher-level knowledge can assist us in solving the speech understanding problem. Uncertainties arising from acoustic-phonetic errors and ambiguities can often be resolved by subjecting the conflicting word hypotheses to syntactic, semantic, or pragmatic analyses. Syntactic knowledge enables us to determine whether a particular sequence of hypothesized words can occur within a grammatical sentence. In addition, syntax provides a basis for predicting additional but unhypothesized fragments of the sentence. Semantic knowledge provides a capability to determine if a syntactically correct sentence is actually meaningful. It may also predict sentence constituents that could relate to current fragments in meaningful ways. Finally, pragmatic knowledge enables us to determine if a meaningful sentence is plausible and appropriate in the context of an ongoing dialogue. Or, conversely, such knowledge can predictively constrain the types of sentences that might meaningfully prolong an ongoing dialogue. Each type of higher-level knowledge defines additional constraints that sentence interpretations must satisfy. If properly exploited, these constraints can suggest promising hypotheses to pursue or can eliminate unlikely interpretations from consideration. As a consequence, these actions can reduce the number of incorrect hypotheses generated, extended, or accepted.

Psychological experiments have shown that humans use all of these types of knowledge in recognizing speech (cf. Miller & Isard, 1963). Human performance in transcribing utterances decreases significantly when the spoken sentences violate one or more types of higher-level knowledge or when transcribers do not possess appropriate knowledge. For example, error rates increase when sentences are heard out of context (i.e., are pragmatically inconsistent), are nonsensical (semantically inconsistent), or are in a language unknown to the subject (syntactically inconsistent). Furthermore, state-of-the-art automatic word recognizers (i.e., recognizers for connected speech that operate without the use of higher-level knowledge) perform substantially worse than humans. As a result, artificial speech understanding systems must utilize these types of knowledge effectively.

Because these three types of knowledge play related roles, we can examine them comparatively to analyze the efficiency of alternative constraints derivable from speech knowledge. While lower-level types of knowledge (e.g., acoustics, phonetics, or lexical verifiers) seem intrinsically identified with speech recognition per se, the higher-level knowledge sources appear more abstract and analyzable. We can discern in them numerous sources of constraint, and a decision to implement some or all of these constraints requires some justification. As a consequence, it seems easier to delineate abstract questions concerning knowledge utility and alternatives for implementation and control in their domains. From such

analysis we should gain a better appreciation of the design alternatives
for knowledge-based speech understanding systems.

The major questions encountered in developing these sources of
knowledge for a speech system include:

- o How should we gain the appropriate knowledge?
- o How should we represent this knowledge?
- o How should we implement (compile, interpret) it?
- o How can we selectively control its application?
- o How much knowledge is enough?
- o How can knowledge improve speech <u>understanding</u>
  as opposed to <u>recognition</u>?

This chapter will suggest a variety of answers to these questions
culled from previous research. It will provide both a general survey of
useful techniques and a set of principles to guide further theoretical and
engineering developments. At the outset, however, let me explicitly disavow
any claims of completeness or scholarly thoroughness. The volumes of
literature on each of these three areas would exceed the scope of any single
tutorial. On the other hand, most previous reports would not satisfy the
student or researcher who wishes to grasp quickly the state of the art in
computer speech understanding. This Chapter aims to serve the needs of such
readers.

The remainder of the chapter covers seven topics. The next three
sections discuss each of the types of higher-level knowledge in turn. For
each type (syntax, semantics, and pragmatics), the section addresses the
problems of acquiring knowledge and implementing the corresponding
knowledge-based constraints. Section 9-5 discusses the costs and benefits
of alternative schemes for integrating and applying diverse sorts of
knowledge. First, we consider what makes various constraints more or less
effective for speech understanding problems. Our analysis highlights
numerous types of potential uses for knowledge. This suggests that speech
analysis properly belongs to a class of problems admitting heuristic, rather
than formally rigorous, solutions. Some particularly effective methods for
exploiting grammatical knowledge are proposed. Section 9-6 describes what
speech understanding systems must do to accept and reply to a sentence
interpretation. The best current techniques are collated in Section 9-7.
Finally, Section 9-8 discusses five distinct problem areas for future
research. These include alternative problem solving paradigms; knowledge
acquisition; knowledge evaluation and validation; knowledge compilation; and
performance assessment and improvement.

9-2. SYNTACTIC KNOWLEDGE

Syntactic knowledge provides the simplest form of constraint on word
sequences. We consider a sequence of words "syntactically acceptable" if it
satisfies the <u>syntactic constraints</u>. This circular definition reflects the
empirical or pragmatic nature of syntax. Those structural properties of
sentences that seem to determine their superficial grammaticality constitute
the rules of syntax.

The notion of a <u>grammar</u> comprising a set of rules that specify
legitimate linguistic expressions arises often in such fields as linguistics
(cf. Chomsky, 1957; Fillmore, 1966; Langendoen, 1969), automata theory (cf.
Hopcroft & Ullman, 1969; Minsky, 1967), and programming languages (cf. Aho &

Ullman, 1972; Foster, 1970). In those domains, a grammar conventionally defines a vocabulary of possible words (called terminal symbols), a set of possible phrase types (called nonterminal symbols), one particular phrase type designating complete sentences (called the starting symbol), and a set of grammar rules. Typically, each rule expresses a possible way of transforming a phrase symbol into a sequence of one or more symbols (terminals, nonterminals, or both). Since such rules define acceptable methods of rewriting a higher-level phrase symbol in terms of lower-level symbol sequences, they are often called phrase structure or rewrite rules.

Grammar rules support two different functions. Used generatively, the rules enable us to investigate the language of grammatical sentences. The language includes all word sequences derivable from the start symbol as a result of arbitrarily selecting and applying rewrite rules. Used analytically, the rules enable us to test the grammaticality of any sentence. A sentence is grammatical if it belongs to the language derivable from the starting symbol. The process of testing a sentence's grammaticality is called parsing. If a sentence parses, we say the grammar accepts it; otherwise, we say it rejects it. Sentence parsing usually produces, as a by-product, a phrase structure tree that links the starting symbol with its constituent phrase symbols, which link recursively with lower-order phrases until, ultimately, all lowest-order nonterminal symbols connect in sequence with the words of the sentence.

Many formal languages, such as those used for programming computers, derive directly from detailed specifications of their grammars. Most speech understanding projects, however, follow another tack. They begin by collecting representative sentence samples and then attempt to model the more general language with a corresponding grammar. This approach reflects a desire to adapt the language design to the demands of communication in naturalistic man-machine interactions. However, the approach entails some difficulties. First, we cannot be certain that we have generalized from the sample sentences to the complete language correctly. Second, we cannot verify that the derived grammar rules parse just those sentences we would want. In short, because we compile syntax rules empirically, we cannot prove the sufficiency or necessity of any individual rule or of a complete rule set.

The primary desiderata for a suggested syntax include simplicity, generality, and specificity. We assess the simplicity of a syntax in terms of the number and complexity of its constituent rules. The generality of the syntax measures its capacity to accept all of the intelligible sentences of the language. The specificity of the syntax, conversely, measures the capacity of the syntax rules to diagnose and reject unintelligible sentences.

9-2.1 Acquiring Syntactic Knowledge

Because they recognize its empirical, informal character, most researchers develop syntactic knowledge by attempting to characterize samples of acceptable and unacceptable sentences in the chosen problem domain. Several fairly general syntactic grammars have been developed in recent years for computerized natural language understanding (cf. Woods, 1972; Winograd, 1975). However, since speech understanding projects typically undertake more limited tasks, they usually construct special-purpose syntaxes.

In a task domain such as document retrieval, the knowledge acquisition process typically begins with the collection of samples of sentences from simulated man-machine interactions. These simulations produce a corpus of exemplary sentences. To illustrate, the corpus might include the following:

Syntactic Type 1:

>   Are there some new articles by Smith?
>   Do you have any 1975 reports by Jones and Thomas?
>   Is there a recent paper by Johnson?

Syntactic Type 2:

>   Did Smith write some new articles?
>   Have Jones and Thomas written any 1975 reports?
>   Has Johnson published a recent paper?

Syntactic Type 3:

>   Give me some new articles by Smith.
>   Get me any 1975 reports by Jones and Thomas.
>   I want a recent paper by Johnson.

Of course, any reasonably extensive corpus would include many more "types" of syntactic constructions than the three shown here. But these suffice to illustrate the principal features of knowledge acquisition. By noting the similarities among sentences of the same type, we can discover their basic syntactic pattern. We can represent these regularities in terms of the following kinds of pattern templates:

Syntactic Template 1:

> $EXIST $NUMBER $DATE $ARTICLES by $AUTHORS?

Syntactic Template 2:

> $AUXILIARY-VERB $AUTHORS $WRITE $NUMBER $DATE $ARTICLES?

Syntactic Template 3:

> $FETCH $NUMBER $DATE $ARTICLES by $AUTHORS.

In these pattern templates, the nonterminals (uppercase terms prefixed by $) represent generalized word categories or phrase structures that can be inferred from the examples. For example, the category $EXIST includes phrases of the form "are there," "do you have," and "is there." We can define the allowable substitutions in terms of lower-level phrase structure rules. The first rule below expresses the substitutions allowed for the category $EXIST, and the other rules define additional categories similarly.

Syntactic Rule 1:

> $EXIST => are there ¦ do you have ¦ is there

Syntactic Rule 2:

> $NUMBER => some ¦ any ¦ a

Syntactic Rule 3:

$DATE => new ¦ 1975 ¦ recent

Syntactic Rule 4:

$ARTICLES => articles ¦ reports ¦ paper

Syntactic Rule 5:

$AUTHORS => $AUTHOR ¦ $AUTHOR and $AUTHOR

Syntactic Rule 6:

$AUTHOR => Smith ¦ Jones ¦ Thomas ¦ Johnson

Syntactic Rule 7:

$WRITE => write ¦ written ¦ published

In a similar way, the general category comprising sentences of all three types--i.e., requests for articles by author and date--might be represented in the following rule:

Syntactic Rule 8:

$REQUEST-BY-AUTHOR-DATE =>
    $EXIST $NUMBER $DATE $ARTICLES by $AUTHORS? ¦
    $AUXILIARY-VERB $AUTHORS $WRITE $NUMBER $DATE $ARTICLES? ¦
    $FETCH $NUMBER $DATE $ARTICLES by $AUTHORS.

The second template form in Rule 8 is overly general, because it does not specify the requirement for agreement between the $AUXILIARY-VERB ("did," "has," "have") and the various forms of the concept $WRITE ("write," "written," "published"). Because we have described the corpus in terms of context-free rules, we could not embed such a restriction easily into this rule. To express the additional constraints required, we would define corresponding requirements or restrictions on these general rules. For example, as part of this specification we might require:

Syntactic Restriction 8.1:

If $AUXILIARY-VERB = "did" and $WRITE = x, require that tense(x) = present.

Syntactic Restriction 8.2:

If $AUXILIARY-VERB = x is a form of $HAVE (e.g., "has," "have"), require agreement in number between x (singular or plural) and the number of authors.

The first of these restriction rules insures that we would accept "Did Jones write ..." but would accept neither "Did Jones written ..." nor "Did Jones wrote ...." The second restriction expresses the constraint that "Has Jones written ..." is acceptable, but neither "Have Jones written ..." nor "Has Jones and Smith published ..." is.

Although this very small rule set would not suffice for most practical tasks, it illustrates the basic aspects of the empirical knowledge acquisition paradigm. This endeavor typically produces a set of general templates or phrase structure forms, with accompanying restrictional rules that further constrain acceptability of potential word sequences. Despite the obvious weaknesses of this empirical approach, no preferable strategy has yet emerged. On the other hand, several computer-based aids have been developed to assist in rule formation. These techniques include programs to cluster sample sentences into comparable types and to abstract general categories from specific sentences (Goodman, 1976; Hirschman, 1975; Tretiakoff, 1974). Of course, once we have generalized templates to incorporate generalized categories, we can repeat the process to develop more general ones. To do this, we replace the specific initial sentences in the corpus by their generalized templates and subsequently consider these as exemplary "sentences." To my knowledge, no automatic aids currently exist that can assist in the generation of restriction rules. These rules are handcrafted, as needed, to make overly general rules sufficiently specific. Typically, the need for a restriction is discovered when the current system accepts an incorrect sentence. The problem is diagnosed and a new rule is created.

For some applications, we may prefer to design a language rather than infer one from exemplary sentences. This alternative is the conventional approach toward developing programming languages and other man-machine interfaces. However, even when we attempt to design a language by specifying its grammar, we often find that it overly restricts or inadequately delimits the language of acceptable sentences. In such cases, the empirically discovered limitations motivate appropriate design changes to the grammar.

9-2.2 Potential Uses of Syntactic Knowledge

It seems that knowledge of any constraining relationship can serve four possible functions (Hayes-Roth, et al., 1978): (1) It can enable us to recognize a familiar pattern in the current situation and then interpret this situation as an instance of the more general pattern (of course, this interpretation may be speculative or hypothetical). (2) It can enable us to predict a likely concomitant event. (3) It can allow us to enumerate the various realizations of a prediction. (4) It can enable us to confirm an hypothesis which is consistent with the constraint. We refer to these four functions as <u>recognition</u>, <u>prediction</u>, <u>enumeration</u>, <u>and postdiction</u>. The following paragraphs discuss how syntactic knowledge can accomplish these types of behavior.

Given a body of syntax rules such as those previously illustrated, the recognition function requires checking a sequence of words to see if it matches the templates and satisfies the corresponding restrictions of the syntax. Specifically, we rule out hypothesized word sequences that the grammar rules cannot parse. Conversely, we can interpret a sequence of words as a hypothetical instance of any general category whose constituency and restriction rules it satisfies. In any case, we may consider any word sequence credible that does not violate the syntax rules.

The second function, prediction, is made possible by first inferring from some hypothesized word sequence its syntactic category and then conjecturing that syntactically adjacent categories also occur. For example, if we recognized the words "Did Jones write" as an instance of the phrase $AUXILIARY-VERB $AUTHORS $WRITE, we might predict that the category $NUMBER would follow in the utterance (see Rule 8).

The third function, enumeration, employs knowlege of the phrase structure rules to translate a general prediction into a set of alternative, specific predictions. Thus, in the preceding example, the prediction for the category $NUMBER might be translated into the set of alternative predictions comprising "some," "any," or "a."

The fourth function, postdiction, temporally reverses the action of prediction. Rather than predicting that $NUMBER could follow "Did Jones write" and subsequently expanding this prediction into a set of specific word predictions, postdiction employs the same knowledge in a post hoc way. To illustrate, assume that $AUXILIARY-VERB $AUTHORS $WRITE had already been recognized and then, at some later time, a word-spotter detected the word "some." In this case, postdiction could confirm the new hypothesis, because it satisfies a potential prediction (even though the prediction might have been deferred). The important difference between prediction and postdiction, as in any empirical science, derives from the higher probability of an inference error in postdiction. In brief, we confirm an hypothesis more when we first predict, then gather data. When we construct or identify hypotheses consistent with existing data, we increase the probability of judging some accidental event as significant.

These are the four kinds of uses we can contemplate for our syntactic knowledge. Exactly which we choose depends on how well we can implement this knowledge and how we must integrate it with other sources of knowledge in a speech system. These topics are considered below.

9-2.3 Implementing Syntactic Knowledge

Syntactic knowledge, as already suggested, usually comprises a body of rules. Typically, these are phrase-structure rules like those of formal grammars (cf. Chapters 13 and 16 in this volume). Alternatively, most syntactic constraints can be embodied in finite-state or Markov networks, where each word or word class is linked to the word classes that can follow it in grammatical sentences (cf. Chapter 15 in this volume). More generally, syntactic constraints can be represented in augmented transition networks (ATNs) that allow phrase embeddings (as in push-down automata) and can incorporate additional arbitrarily complex test and store operations on intermediate results (cf. Chapter 14 in this volume). Following a different approach, the knowledge could be embodied in condition-action (production) rules that would monitor the changing hypotheses for suitable situations and would then respond with corresponding actions of any of the four types (recognition, prediction, enumeration, or postdiction) (cf. Mostow & Hayes-Roth, 1978). As a final alternative, syntax rules could be embedded in a computational procedure that first parses the structure and then tests the restrictions.

Harpy (see Chapter 15 in this volume) is an example of a system that embeds syntactic rules in a finite-state network which, in effect, tests transitions only at the acoustic segmental level. Dragon (Baker, 1975) and the proposed IBM system (Bahl, et al., 1978) employ more general Markov network models. The HWIM system (see Chapter 14 in this volume) uses the ATN framework for representing syntax. One configuration of Hearsay-II employed production rules (Mostow & Hayes-Roth, 1978). Efficient formal parsing procedures, operating directly on the grammar rules, were adopted in the final configurations of Hearsay-II and the SRI system (see Chapters 13 and 16 in this volume). Later, we shall discuss some of the costs and benefits of these alternative types of implementation.

Perhaps syntactic knowledge seems ad hoc and empirical because we have limited experience at formalizing grammatical relations. In the case of semantic knowledge, this problem is even more severe. Our understanding of semantics continues to increase daily. Few if any domains have yielded to complete descriptions of their meaningful intrinsic relationships or the alternative modes of speaking about them. One of the most thorough semantic analyses in the literature concerns a domain of toy blocks on a table (Winograd, 1975).

Issues of semantics arise in many areas of scientific research. One general approach to defining meaning attempts to relate logical expressions to world models that would insure their validity (cf. Tarski, 1965). A world model constitutes a description of objects, events, and relationships known to exist at some time and place. A logical expression consists of propositional assertions, joined by Boolean connectives, which may optionally be quantified. For example, the logical expression "For all x, Man(x) implies Mortal(x)" asserts that all men are mortal. This expression, presumably, is true in our world but could conceivably be false in others. In most computer systems, world models consist of data base relations that represent just atomic assertions that are assumed valid. Atomic assertions, such as Man(Jeffrey K. Smith) and Mortal(Jeffrey K. Smith), provide the elementary data against which more complex expressions are evaluated using logical inference rules.

Sentence _meanings_ include at least three components. The first component of meaning would be a logical expression corresponding to the assertion or query the speaker intended. The second component characterizes the relationship between the logical expression and the world model. For example, within some model, the expression could be true or false, or might designate a list of objects or values satisfying its parameters. Finally, a sentence can perform or characterize desired actions on the part of the listener or speaker. Each of these types of effects belongs to the meaning of a sentence. The field of semantics attempts to formulate these relationships in terms of semantic rules or semantic models.

Semantic knowledge in a speech understanding system can eliminate syntactically valid word sequence hypotheses that are not actually meaningful. As suggested in the previous section, where restriction rules were added to eliminate incorrect sentence forms from overly general templates, similarly we can develop semantic rules to incorporate meaningfulness restrictions. Moreover, if the computer system must perform some function (such as document retrieval), it will ultimately extract the specifications needed for its actions from the semantic interpretation of the sentence.

9-3.1 Acquiring Semantic Knowledge

Typically, researchers abstract semantic relationships from a corpus of exemplary sentences and general knowledge of the task domain. Meaningful relations are identified by examining specific examples, and general methods for extracting meaning expressions from sentences are represented in terms of interpretation rules. Usually, distinctive semantic functions of different types of syntactic constituents are discovered. For example, the semantic rules might select the primary or "head" noun in the main noun phrase as the "agent" of the verb. Additional nouns and adjectives preceding it would be interpreted as modifiers. Elements of the verb phrase, such as the verb and the direct and indirect objects, are extracted and interpreted as corresponding elements of the intended meaning. Thus, the verb could be viewed as designating a particular kind of semantic relation, such as "telling," "listing," or "writing." Similarly, the verb objects could be interpreted as specifying particular constants for specific "slots" in the verb's relational concept. Such relations typically map directly into logical expressions representing the semantic meaning of the sentence. This meaning, in turn, could be compared with the stored assertions in the world model by some uniform matching procedure (like those in relational data base systems).

A notable counterexample to this empirical, engineering approach is the formalized semantic system of Montague (Hobbs & Rosenschein, 1978; Montague, 1974). This system attempts to formulate semantic meanings as functions that can be applied directly to assertional world models. To do this, Montague's system associates meanings with each word in the language and defines rules for combining meanings whenever words or phrases combine syntactically. Generally, the meaning of a noun in this system is a function that tests for the defining characteristics of the corresponding entity. Thus, "horse" and "car," for example, are represented as computable predicates that evaluate to "True" only if a horse or car is present in the world model. The meanings of modifiers constitute functionals (functions whose domains are functions) which, when applied to the meanings of head nouns, produce appropriately modified meaning functions for the noun phrase. Thus, to interpret the phrase, "a fast brown horse," we apply the meaning of "brown" to that of "horse," then the meaning of "fast" to that of "brown horse," and finally the meaning of "a" to the previous result. The final product is a function that evaluates to "True" only if its argument (some context) exhibits a horse that is fast and brown. Two things are unique in this approach to natural language semantics. First, Montague's system associates very general semantic interpretation rules directly with syntactic phrase structure rules. Similar strategies often work well for programming language semantics. Second, rather than translating syntactic analyses into logical expressions, Montague's system generates meaning structures that are executable programs. These programs manifest meaning in their potential for performing appropriate actions.

Regardless of the approach, the validation of semantic rules to date remains an entirely empirical problem. Proposed rules are tested on sample sentences, and when overly general or overly specific rules are detected, they are modified appropriately.

One simple approach toward acquiring the semantic rules follows the syntactic acquisition method discussed previously. In fact, the rules suggested in Section 9-2 already manifest rudimentary semantic notions. For example, the nonterminals $AUTHORS and $DATE represent types of meaningful categories in the retrieval domain. Because the proposed syntax refers throughout to meaningful categories, the corresponding phrase structure rules are called <u>semantic</u> <u>templates</u>. The resultant grammar is known variously as a semantic template grammar, a semantic grammar, or a pragmatic grammar. The following semantic rules might appropriately accompany the corresponding syntactic rules:

Semantic Rule 1:

> If $AUTHORS = word(1) ... word(n), then form a set of Requested Authors including each word(j) which is itself recognized as an instance of $AUTHOR.

Semantic Rule 2:

> If $DATE = x where x is a year (e.g., 1975), then verify that the year is reasonable (e.g., in the range 1900-1979), and specify the date-of-interest for the retrieval as x.

Semantic Rule 3:

> If $NUMBER = x and x is "any," "some," or "a," then specify one attribute of the speaker's intention as "wanting to know first if the number is non-zero and, if so, 'How many?' as well as 'Which ones?'"

9-3.2 Uses of Semantic Knowledge

The first of these semantic rules illustrates two points. First, the type of syntax rule adopted in our examples implicitly embeds some semantic tests. By permitting only proper names in the category $AUTHOR, the grammar obviates testing whether or not the recognized words instantiating $AUTHORS actually name people. A more general syntax rule would require more complex semantic restriction rules. The second point concerns what information needs to be extracted to perform the requested action correctly. In this case, the names of the authors of interest must be extracted from the sentence to specify the document retrieval.

The second semantic rule similarly serves two functions. First, it encodes a semantic restriction that could rule out implausible dates for document requests (i.e., those too old or those which have not yet arrived). Second, it extracts another piece of specification for the eventual request. Of course, if the current hypothesis were subsequently invalidated, extracting that information immediately would prove wasteful. If the current hypothesis is later rejected, the corresponding retrieval would be canceled.

Both of these examples suggest a natural way to associate meaningfulness with syntactic units. That is, we should associate meaning components directly with the syntactic units. In this case, semantic information could be extracted from corresponding syntactic structures. The third semantic rule, however, illustrates a more general meaning extraction problem. This example illustrates how different nuances of expression can indicate substantially different intentions. For example, asking for "any articles" might connote something different from the intention behind a request for "the article" or "one article." Thus, part of the semantic analysis of a sentence requires discriminations between similar syntactic structures that imply substantially different interpretations. In this particular example, a request for "any articles" by an author indicates that the questioner does not know the answer to an implicit question ("Did the author write at least one article?") but also desires an answer to a second, more specific, implied question ("Which ones?"). If the system has good evidence that the questioner already knows the answer to the first implicit question, it should probably reject the current hypothesized sentence interpretation. (This type of inference requires pragmatic knowledge, as discussed in the next section.)

In short, a task domain may be characterized by a variety of different types of semantic relationships. In general, these specify the requirements for membership in meaningful conceptual categories and for participation in meaningful domain relationships. These categories and relationships may be defined best by a combination of phrase structure rules and semantic restriction rules. With only the hypothesized sentence available, only a fraction of these restrictions can be evaluated. Often, however, an evaluation of semantic plausibility requires checking the validity of the implicit assertions against a data base, a world model, or a discourse model. Although the possibility exists during speech recognition for interactively evaluating partial sentence fragments against such data bases or models, no successful speech system has exploited this opportunity.

9-3.3 Implementing Semantic Knowledge

As already suggested, we can implement a set of semantic restriction rules in various ways. By embedding semantic relations directly in the syntactic categories, the mechanisms that determine syntactic acceptability automatically check a large portion of the semantic restrictions. On the other hand, we need not adopt this type of semantic embedding. In work using augmented transition networks, some systems have fully separated syntax and semantics. The systems incorporate arbitrarily complex semantic rules to construct, store, and test intermediate data structures representing the useful information extracted from the syntactic structure (cf. Burton, 1976; Woods et al., 1972). The formation and evaluation of semantic structures could also be performed by production rules or by specific procedures invoked before, during, or after syntactic processing (cf. Chapters 13, 14, and 16 in this volume).

All of the current speech systems embed most of their semantic restrictions directly in their syntax. On the other hand, they perform additional semantic extractions and analyses on complete sentences that appear plausible. Specifically, they develop representations of the implicit command or query by extracting appropriate arguments from the parsed sentence and then attempt to execute the implied action. Only when the action is nonsensical or the result implausible would this final semantic function cause rejection of the sentence hypothesis.

In short, of the four generic types of knowledge-based functions, semantic knowledge seems to support primarily recognition. To the extent that semantic categories are embedded in syntax, semantic knowledge also constrains prediction, enumeration, and postdiction. However, no current systems exploit semantic knowledge for constraints that extend beyond the current sentence. Knowing what a human would be likely to say at some point in a dialogue, speech systems could predict the general meaning of an entire sentence or some of its constituents. For example, if the computer had just asked the person a yes-no question, the system should expect an utterance whose meaning would be an appropriate answer (e.g., "Yes," "No," or "I don't know"). More sophisticated mechanisms could generate and then exploit expectations for likely fillers for certain meaningful slots in a sentence. For example, if the user previously had established an apparent interest in documents about problem solving systems, we should expect his subsequent sentences to relate specifically to this topic. To exploit this expectation would require dynamically modifiable semantic rules. These capabilities are simply beyond the scope of today's systems.

9-4.   PRAGMATIC KNOWLEDGE

Pragmatic knowledge provides the capability for understanding a sentence in the context of an ongoing discourse. The same sentence can have different interpretations depending upon who the speaker and listeners are, what both are presumed to know, and what both have previously said. The purpose of a pragmatic knowledge source in a speech understanding system is to model these effects.

9-4.1 Acquiring Pragmatic Knowledge

The way most speech and language understanding projects have acquired their pragmatic knowledge sources has been through empirical methods, as previously discussed for both syntactic and semantic knowledge. In a task such as document retrieval, a model is constructed that represents the possible states of knowledge of the speaker at any point in time through various types of dialogs. For example, if the user explicitly says, "I am only interested in articles since 1965," we need to preserve this information to restrict the interpretations of subsequent requests accordingly. This type of inference might be represented by the following rule:

Pragmatics Rule 1:

> If the hypothesized utterance matches the template $USER $BE-MAINLY-INTERESTED $ABOUT $ARTICLES $DATE, the $DATE term should be stored for subsequent, implicit restrictions of $DATE interpretations.

Other types of pragmatic knowledge influence the plausibility of hypothesized interpretations. Most people have experienced situations where a listener misinterpreted them in ways that violate the listener's own knowledge of the speaker's intentions. Besides being frustrating to the speaker, this kind of error seems unnecessary. At least, we could envisage another rule to limit such errors:

Pragmatics Rule 2:

> If the understood utterance implies that the speaker believes some proposition P which you know the speaker disbelieves, reject the hypothesized interpretation.

The third type of pragmatics rule concerns the speaker's assertions and expectations that may be implicit in a sentence. One such example was discussed in Section 9-3.1. In that case, a question such as "Did Jones write any articles ..." was interpreted to mean that the system should first answer "How many?" and then answer "Which ones?" (see Semantic Rule 3). In current language understanding research, knowledge of this type is accumulating rapidly (cf. Kaplan, 1978). Some additional rules that illustrate this type of knowledge follow:

Pragmatics Rule 3:

> If all possible answers to a speaker's question imply some assertion P, assume the speaker presumes P to be true. Add "Speaker believes P" to the dynamic model of the user.

Pragmatics Rule 4:

> If all possible answers to a question Q are already presumed known
> by the user, Q is inappropriate unless the speaker intends to test
> the system. If you can reject that assumption, reject the
> hypothesized interpretation Q of the utterance.

9-4.2 Uses of Pragmatics Knowledge

As with previous types of knowledge, pragmatic knowledge enables us to
perform several functions.   Rules like Rule 1 help define and maintain
proper context descriptions so that appropriate responses can be generated.
A rule of the second type actually enables the system to reject (or reduce
its credence in) some specific hypothesized interpretation.   This is the
same type of constraint other lower-level sources of knowledge in speech
provide. A rule like Rule 3 operationalizes our understanding of how a
dynamic model of the speaker's knowledge might be inferred and updated. The
inferred beliefs of the speaker provide a basis upon which subsequent
disconfirmations of sentence interpretations can rest. Finally, Rule 4
illustrates a class of rules that attempt to relate the interpreted meaning
of an utterance to the overall pragmatic function of the cooperative man-
machine discourse. Because we typically believe a speaker would not ask for
information he already possesses, we ought to doubt any interpretation that
constitutes a question whose answer he already possesses.

Obviously, these rules are heuristics or "rules-of-thumb." Their
proposed actions, such as "reject the interpretation," require
qualifications such as "weakly" or "absolutely." They are neither provable
nor always correct.   Rather, each of these rules captures a bit of human
knowledge about speech perception and the functional purposes of speech. An
intelligent listener must find the most likely interpretation within this
set of fuzzy and perhaps inconsistent constraints.

9-4.3 Implementing Pragmatic Knowledge

The same types of implementation options we have considered previously
arise in pragmatics.   Specifically, the various rules of knowledge can be
appended as restrictions to syntactic or semantic templates. Or these rules
can operate as postprocessors to the speech "recognition" phase.

Two basic strategies have been used most often in pragmatics.   One
represents the stages of a dialogue in terms of a finite-state (or
augmented) network (Hayes-Roth, Gill, & Mostow, 1976).   This approach
employs the same type of formalisms that have proved useful for representing
allowable sequences of speech elements for similarly representing and
monitoring hypothesized sequences of man-machine communications. The second
approach attempts to maintain an up-to-date data base on the knowledge state
of the speaker and to check presumptions implied by interpretations against
that data base (cf. Chapters 13 and 14 in this volume). In this approach,
relational data bases or semantic network formalisms store assertions about
the system's knowledge, the state of the speaker's knowledge, and the
speaker's knowledge of the system's knowledge.

Currently, speech systems derive little useful constraint from
pragmatics because of the open-ended nature of the knowledge.   Each
pragmatic rule may be quite specific, and as a consequence, although each
applicable rule can potentially eliminate several specious interpretations
or misperceptions, no single rule will apply frequently to randomly selected
sentences.   Thus, the high cost-benefit ratio for including pragmatic

knowledge has inhibited most researchers from developing comprehensive knowledge sources.

9-5. THE COMPARATIVE EFFICIENCIES OF KNOWLEDGE-BASED CONSTRAINTS

The value of knowledge in a speech understanding system, regardless of its representation, derives from its capacity to constrain or restrict the set of plausible interpretations. We have suggested that most inferences warranted by higher-level knowledge could be simply described in terms of If-Then heuristic rules. Many of these rules provide absolute bases for rejecting hypothesized interpretations. Most, however, provide some ad hoc basis for supporting or rejecting an hypothesis. The qualitative and quantitative differences in knowledge-based constraints motivate us to seek some general principles for comparatively evaluating alternative computational forms for the rules, alternative rules themselves, and the alternative hypotheses they engender.

9-5.1 Analyzing Constraint Effectiveness

Given a wide variety of knowledge-based constraints to choose from, we must decide which to include in our speech systems. The first problem we face is to understand how each constraint can improve speech perception. The second problem is to analyze the relative efficiencies of alternative constraints. In this section, we attempt to describe the state of the art in such analysis. Section 9-5.3 discusses how to implement efficiently a chosen set of effective constraints.

In speech recognition, the basic problem is to identify a credible sequence of word hypotheses. The credibility of a word-sequence hypothesis should increase as consistent evidence accumulates (and should decrease as inconsistent data are discovered). In this view, knowledge-based constraints determine the evidentiary value of data.

Consider, as an example, the sentence "Give me the articles." The rules of syntax specify restrictions that this sentence presumably would satisfy. Each restriction satisfied by an arbitrary sequence of words is, to some extent, an improbable event. The credibility of an hypothesis derives directly from the capability of the hypothesis to satisfy such constraints. Of course, in judging credibility, we must also consider the probability that those constraints could be satisfied by chance. If the chance probability of satisfying a constraint is great, the constraint provides little information. These intuitions constitute the foundations of both Bayesian analysis and confirmation theory.

We can apply constraints to hypothesized sentence fragments as well as to complete sentence interpretations. Similar confirmation principles would apply to other cases as well. As an example, consider the sequence "me the." If these two words had been hypothesized bottom-up, what higher-level constraints would they satisfy? We note first that since the sentence "Give me the articles" is presumably valid, the sequence "me the" must also be valid. Of course, that statement must be qualified in several ways. No sentence can begin "me the," so we could test the proximity of the word "me" to the closest previous period of silence. Similarly, no sentence can end in "me the." In designing a particular task grammar, the number of words that grammatically could follow "me" could vary widely from 1% to 99% of the vocabulary. Any hypothesis of the form "the word me followed by word x" satisfies a very restrictive constraint if very few words grammatically could follow "me." Thus, we should place more credibility in the hypothesis "me the" when only "the" can follow "me" than when hundreds of possible words can follow "me."

Every possible restriction acts as a constraint with some chance probability of being satisfied by randomly selected hypotheses. Three principal characteristics of these constraints determine their utility in a speech understanding system: their diagnosticity, their satisfiability, and their computational cost. A constraint's diagnosticity measures the amount of information it adduces. Equivalently, a diagnostic test rules out a maximum number of competing hypotheses and thereby eliminates a maximum amount of uncertainty. A highly diagnostic syntax rule would be a specific one that disallowed nearly all possible combinations of words. The satisfiability of a constraint, on the other hand, measures the expected frequency for a test to yield positive results. Thus, a very general syntax rule would have high satisfiability, but low diagnosticity. Apparently, constraints can trade satisfiability for diagnosticity. This motivates us to develop efficient constraints, those maximizing both diagnosticity and satisfiability while minimizing computational cost.

All of the successful speech systems reflect design choices influenced by these considerations. Moreover, many of the ARPA projects have exhibited evolutionary developments responsive to just such tradeoffs. We shall discuss some of the current strategies after addressing the question of whether speech analysis can be rigorous.

9-5.2 Can Speech Analysis Be Formally Rigorous?

Any hypothesis in a speech system is an ad hoc interpretation based on some arbitrarily justified data. The significance we attribute to particular types of data and conceptual frameworks in speech analysis is shaped by our empirical successes and failures. We select sampling strategies, pattern matching algorithms, and rating functions by combining various intuitions, empiricism, and mathematical analysis. For example, a bottom-up word hypothesis derived from matching a lexical template to successive temporal segments of parameterized waveform data will necessarily carry an ad hoc evaluation of its credibility. This evaluation should estimate the Bayesian probability of the word, given the data. Such an estimate requires estimating the likelihood of observing those data if the word were valid, the a priori probability that the word would occur, and the overall a priori probability of observing such data. Certainly, we can implement some functions that we believe reasonably well approximate the likelihood estimate. Almost by definition, however, it seems unlikely that we can construct formally justifiable estimates of the a priori probabilities of interest. The fact that most current speech systems employ likelihoods and ignore a priori probabilities reflects these difficulties. Of course, it is well known in psychology and statistics that poorer judgments result when decisions employ likelihoods alone and neglect the a priori probabilities that differentiate between likely and unlikely events (cf. Kahneman & Tversky, 1973).

A basic question thus arises about the types of credibility measures that can be used to contrast alternative hypothetical interpretations: Can they be made analytically rigorous without sacrificing empirical usefulness and efficiency? Obviously, rigorous analyses can be formulated. The only interesting credibility functions, however, are those that help discover desirable answers within allowable resource limitations.

220

Several systems have formalized their credibility functions and used these to develop search strategies that seek to find maximally credible interpretations. Harpy, for example, accumulates log likelihoods as it searches all possible sentence interpretations left-to-right. It heuristically prunes the search space whenever fringe interpretations become significantly less credible than the best ones in the "beam" (see Chapter 15 in this volume). In a similar way, the HWIM system employs log probabilities to combine words into word sequences. It then employs a search strategy that assuredly finds the highest-rated word sequence first (see Chapter 14 in this volume).

Since the inferences demanded in speech analysis are as complex as those of other empirical, inductive enterprises, we should doubt that analytical or optimal solutions to its problems exist. Some proposed rating and scheduling methods may work well in some contexts and poorly in others, but no proposal yet developed "solves" the credibility or search control problems. In fact, philosophers, scientists, and statisticians have been unable to reach agreement on acceptable methods for most inductive problems, many of which are far simpler (cf. Salmon, 1973; Shortliffe, 1975).

What are the strengths and weaknesses of the rigorous formulations proposed for these systems? Their primary benefits include computational simplicity and uniformity. Any hypothesis, regardless of how it was generated or what constraints it satisfies, can be characterized by a single number generated by a simple rating algorithm. These algorithms presume that each high-level constraint is all-or-none; discovering that some hypothesis cannot satisfy the constraints eliminates it from further consideration. The weaknesses of this approach are corollaries of these benefits. The simple rating algorithms neglect statistical sampling principles, such as ones that would differentiate the credibilities of improbable joint events from those of more probable joint events. They also ignore the number and type of constraints applied and predictions confirmed. Thus, as knowledge sources evolve to include more valid and specific restrictions, the credibilities assigned do not reflect increased certainties of corresponding hypotheses. Conversely, the adoption of such simple rating functions may actually inhibit the development of more extensive and heuristic knowledge by dampening its practical effects.

Other problems with proposed rigorous schemes may be even more important. Because they do not consider computational costs of alternative methods, they provide a very limited basis for scheduling decisions (Hayes-Roth & Lesser, 1977). In slower, knowledge-intensive systems (e.g., Hearsay-II or HWIM, as compared to Harpy) that can explore only a small number of hypotheses in the time available, simple rating and control regimes likes those proposed produce undesirable effects. Specifically, they promote breadth-first searches of the tree of possible interpretations. These searches often exhaust the available time pursuing many incorrect hypotheses.

Thus an "admissible" control algorithm like HWIM's may sacrifice empirical feasibility to the goal of analytical simplicity. (An admissible algorithm guarantees finding an optimal solution faster than random searches and inadmissible algorithms.) To guarantee that the first solution found will necessarily be the highest rated one, the system must explore a very large, probably infeasible, search space. More practical control regimes will probably evolve that attempt to balance and integrate our naive intuitions about confirmation theory, diverse types of knowledge-based constraints, and improved knowledge of resource allocation strategies for heuristic problem solving. In fact, even in the HWIM system, several alternative control strategies were experimentally evaluated, and the best overall performance resulted from an "inadmissible" heuristic algorithm (see Chapter 14 in this volume).

9-5.3 Efficiency in Grammatical Analysis

One major insight into the efficiency of grammatical analysis has been foreshadowed by our previous discussions of semantic template grammars. These grammars integrate semantic and syntactic constraints in computationally efficient representations.

The concept of semantic template grammars was most fully explored in the PARRY system, which simulates a paranoid patient being interviewed (Parkinson, Colby, & Faught, 1977). PARRY's linguistic knowledge consists of 1700 templates representing standard types of questions abstracted from transcripts of psychiatric interviews. The template-based parsing scheme developed for PARRY can interpret most typed (as opposed to spoken) utterances in unconstrained English in less than one second.

Some doubts remain concerning the flexibility and extensibility of semantic grammars. Whenever category definitions change or new syntactic variants arise, the grammars require modification. Because semantic grammars are more specific than general syntactic grammars, they may necessitate more frequent or complicated changes. These questions merit continued investigation. On the other hand, semantic grammars provide many opportunities for efficiencies, as the following paragraphs illustrate.

From the outset, the designers of Hearsay-II opted for a semantic grammar approach similar to that in PARRY (Hayes-Roth & Mostow, 1976). In their original implementation of syntactic and semantic constraints, they converted semantic templates directly into production rules that could recognize valid fragments, predict adjacent constituents, enumerate specific variants of general predictions, and confirm compatible hypotheses by postdiction. The condition components of these production rules tested for the presence of specific word or category hypotheses. Their corresponding actions generated new hypotheses or confirmed prior ones. These conditions could be associatively matched, by searching the blackboard for hypotheses of the exact type desired. Since the cost of finding a member of a category like $ARTICLES was no more than the cost of finding a member of a more general category like $NOUN, but the corresponding constraints were considerably more diagnostic, the semantic templates seemed obviously preferable.

The Hearsay-II designers ultimately abandoned the production rule approach to implementing grammatical constraints, because it proved too weak to control combinatorics (Mostow & Hayes-Roth, 1978). However, the underlying qualities of the semantic template grammars continued to be recognized. Semantic template grammars reduced the cost and improved the satisfiability of tests by enabling the selection of all appropriate tests through associative look-up. Simultaneously, the semantic categories improved the diagnosticity of constraints. By the end of the ARPA project, all of the major contractors had either adopted such syntactic and semantic blends or recognized their practicality (e.g., in the SRI system, this was accomplished by immediate tests of semantic features; in the HWIM system, comparable "pragmatic grammars" were developed). As a result, the idea of grammatical knowledge emerged that integrated originally disparate ideas of syntactic and semantic knowledge. For computational efficiency, such integrated knowledge representations proved most advantageous. (The Harpy system carries knowledge integration even further; see Chapter 15 in this volume.)

A second important idea emerged from studies of efficiency in grammatical constraint satisfaction. The Hearsay-II designers discovered a method of identifying preliminary word-sequence hypotheses that satisfied some but not all of the grammatical constraints (Lesser, Hayes-Roth, Birnbaum, & Cronk, 1977). That method exploited the most efficiently computable constraints and enabled the system to focus initially on multiword hypotheses that were more credible than individual-word hypotheses. As a consequence, Hearsay-II pursued many fewer incorrect hypotheses and often found the correct interpretation immediately.

The word-sequence knowledge source (WOSEQ) in Hearsay-II searched among previously generated bottom-up word hypotheses to hypothesize credible word sequences. It did this by finding sequences of words that included at least one highly rated hypothesis (a "seed") and additional word hypotheses that were both time-adjacent and language-adjacent. The time-adjacency constraint tested the feasibility of the assumed junctures between words. The language-adjacency constraint tested the grammaticality of each contiguous pair of words in the hypothesized sequence. This test was expedited by using a sparse bit matrix of word-word adjacency relations precomputed from the grammar. Furthermore, WOSEQ's credibility ratings and internal search strategy exploited both individual word validity ratings and statistical sampling corrections. WOSEQ terminated its search for good word sequences whenever extensions of the ones it had already found seemed to reduce net credibility either through incorporating poorer data or by attaching an additional word from an excessively high branching-factor choice point in the language.

WOSEQ worked well because it could adduce confirmation to word hypotheses very quickly and cheaply. Although it could not guarantee that the sequences it found would satisfy all of the grammatical constraints (i.e., would parse), its hypotheses empirically proved to be excellent. Its success is attributed to the fact that its multiword hypotheses satisfied many more constraints than any single word did. Thus, pursuing WOSEQ's best hypotheses was a better overall strategy than pursuing many of the best bottom-up word hypotheses simultaneously. The top N (e.g., 10 to 20) words hypothesized at the start of the utterance have approximately a 10% to 20% chance of excluding the correct word. Thus, search strategies that begin by trying to extend the top N words have at least a 10% chance of eventually requiring backup. (This backup would probably never occur in practice, because the systems would run out of time first.) On the other hand, WOSEQ chose its top N "seed" words from the utterance at large. We can be nearly certain that one of these words, at least, is valid. In nearly all cases where several valid adjacent words had been hypothesized, WOSEQ discovered their sequence. Conversely, WOSEQ's failures usually resulted because too few contiguous hypotheses of correct words had been generated by the word-spotter.

Two potential complaints might be voiced against WOSEQ as a source of knowledge for less restricted speech understanding tasks. First, WOSEQ's word adjacency matrix grows quadratically with the size of the vocabulary, and storing increasingly large matrices is infeasible. Second, WOSEQ's performance depends upon the matrix being relatively sparse, and as grammatical complexity increases, the matrix may become too dense to provide effective constraint. Both of these questions warrant further analysis. However, it is apparent that the effective notion of <u>grammatical</u> <u>adjacency</u> could be generalized readily from <u>word</u> adjacency to <u>semantic</u> <u>category</u> adjacency. This would insure that both small and sparse adjacency matrices would suffice. Moreover, until better performance can be obtained from lower-level sources of knowledge, few effective alternatives exist. For the current state of technology, WOSEQ represents an efficient and effective mechanism for improving the system's ability to identify valid initial hypotheses.

The importance of valid initial hypotheses derives from several factors. First, speech systems may not have enough time to recover from pursuing several invalid initial hypotheses. Second, grammatically testing (parsing) an arbitrary sequence of words requires significant amounts of computation. Although fast algorithms exist for parsing initial sequences of words left-to-right from the start of an utterance, only computationally expensive algorithms have been developed to parse internal sentence fragments. For example, in Hearsay-II's efficiently coded algorithm for parsing partial sentence hypotheses (PPARSE), each hypothesized sequence requires 0.1 sec of PDP-10 KA-10 cpu time (Hayes-Roth, Erman, Fox, & Mostow, 1977). Other system implementations of this commonly discovered problem have required comparably long times. No system can afford to compute this type of function many times. In addition to identifying more credible initial hypotheses, WOSEQ also significantly reduced the number of sequences requiring this expensive type of partial parsing.

Aside from systems like HARPY that employ uniform, left-to-right searches, other designs now reflect several common principles. Although only Hearsay-II exploited the cheap and effective types of constraints in WOSEQ, all of the other systems employed similar techniques for processing multiword sequence hypotheses. Specifically, those sequences that proved to be grammatical were used to predict adjacent word hypotheses. Sometimes these predictions could be confirmed directly by prior hypotheses. At other times, they demanded new actions by word-verifiers. Subsequently, any words found to confirm these predictions were concatenated to their predictor sequences to compose compound hypotheses. When predicted words already supported adjacent multiword sequences, the two sequences were concatenated if they could satisfy the partial-parsing test. This predict-confirm-concatenate process was iterated until it produced word sequences interpretable as complete sentences that spanned the entire utterance.

9-5.4 Effective Higher-Order Constraints

In an isolated sentence recognition task, the types of constraints apparent in semantic templates constitute the most useful and most cost-effective tests available. In fact, most speech systems operate in such task contexts.

However, significant additional constraints could be realized through improved task and discourse design. Just as we can engineer the vocabulary and syntax to reduce uncertainty and computational complexity, so we could design man-machine dialogues to exploit comparable constraints. For example, we might structure a document retrieval task so that the user would need to descend through a hierarchy of increasingly precise topic menus before formulating a specific document request. The developers of several man-machine interfaces have adopted this approach independent of speech input considerations. If we imposed such a hierarchy of concepts and

224

situations in a speech task, the momentary dialogue context would provide valuable higher-order constraints. Specifically, we could generate strong predictions for the types of sentences and words expected at each point. These types of capabilities have been developed in experimental systems (Hayes-Roth, Gill, & Mostow, 1977) but were largely unexploited in the systems tested only on isolated sentences.

Conversely, we can reverse this general idea and suggest that one indicator that speech input would be feasible for a complex task would be a strong sequential discourse model. If the user naturally moved from one limited concept set to another in solving his problem, we could convert this task structure into effective constraints on the dynamic grammatical and lexical complexity. Thus, without adversely impacting the speaker, the system designer could simplify the performance requirements for the speech understanding system. Candidate domains of this sort would include automated form completion (e.g., income tax forms or medical histories), automated instrument readout (e.g., for aircraft pilots), and document retrieval.

9-6. ACCEPTING A SENTENCE INTERPRETATION

At some point, every speech system must decide whether or not to accept a hypothetical sentence interpretation. The problems that arise in this context include deciding whether the interpretation is credible, whether it's meaningful and reasonable, whether some undiscovered sentence interpretation could be preferable, and what to do in response. This section discusses each of these problems.

9-6.1 Deciding that the Sentence Hypothesis is Credible

Two basic strategies have surfaced for deciding whether or not some sentence hypothesis is credible. Both treat the question of credibility within the larger problem of control. The first method attempts to resolve the credibility question by systematically searching and pruning the entire space of alternatives to guarantee that the first interpretation found would necessarily be the most credible one. This sort of strategy is used in Dragon, the IBM system, Harpy, and HWIM. By adopting a verification approach to holistic sentence hypotheses, these systems assess credibility simply in terms of the goodness of fit of their constituent word hypotheses to the acoustic data. They accept an hypothesis as credible just because it fits the acoustic data more closely than any other hypothesis. If systems had to cope with somewhat ungrammatical sentences, these verification methods would require modification. For example, they might be augmented by establishing acceptability thresholds, in which case a credible sentence would need to possess several parts whose ratings exceeded that threshold. (Such thresholds would require normalization for sentence length, in some arbitrary unit system.)

The second strategy, used in Hearsay-II, attempts to find the best interpretation first, without systematically ordering the search of the hypothesis spaces. Hearsay-II attempts to explore a few of the most promising hypotheses simultaneously in disparate regions of the utterance. As a consequence of its opportunistic exploration of hypotheses, this strategy may hold several promising alternatives in abeyance while developing one credible sentence interpretation. Hearsay-II assesses the credibility of an hypothesis based on an ad hoc rating function that increases the credibility of phrasal hypotheses for each syllable and each word they subtend. These units are considered more reliable and informative than acoustic segments. Additional support for hypotheses is adduced when they satisfy semantic expectations (e.g., when a query includes a word in an expected category). As soon as the system generates a sentence hypothesis that exceeds the acceptance threshold, it invokes a knowledge source that can prune pending hypotheses below some comparative threshold. Since it may then succeed in finding additional, superior interpretations, Hearsay-II iterates this evaluation and pruning process as required.

9-6.2 Semantic and Pragmatic Acceptability

Those advanced speech systems that incorporate task components (e.g., Hearsay-II, HWIM, and the SRI system) extract the semantic representation of the sentence hypothesis and pass it to a task performance module. These external programs can decide if the sentence is nonsensical, in which case the system would continue searching for additional sentence interpretations. Alternatively, the task components may accept the semantic interpretation and respond appropriately. In the future, we can anticipate more sophisticated interactions between the higher-level sources of knowledge. For example, knowledge sources might extract sensible sentence fragments from overall meaningless sentences. These, in turn, could suggest alternative interpretations of the misunderstood fragments.

9-6.3 Pruning Remaining Hypotheses

A variety of techniques have been developed for pruning word and word-sequence hypotheses while searching for a sentence interpretation or for pruning those remaining after the first credible sentence hypothesis emerges. These include the beam search pruning of Harpy, the shortfall density pruning of HWIM, and the competitive pruning of Hearsay-II (see Chapters 14, 15, and 16 in this volume). All of these methods exploit the common notion that the credibility of each hypothesis establishes a threshold for comparing alternatives. Specifically, once a credible sentence hypothesis emerges, systems may prune any remaining hypotheses that could not conceivably contribute to a more credible sentence hypothesis (Mostow, 1977).

9-6.4 Responding to Incompletely Understood Utterances

Very little work has been reported on methods for responding intelligently to incompletely understood utterances. Some experimental methods have been explored by the Hearsay-II group (Fox & Mostow, 1977), which attempted to extract semantically meaningful fragments from the most plausible incomplete sentence hypotheses. These meaningful fragments can be easily identified, since they instantiate semantic categories of the grammar. For example, a fragment such as "... 1975 papers by Jones ..." would provide both $DATE and $AUTHORS information. In such a case, the system could generate a graceful response, although it might conceivably err.

This suggests another possibility as well. Since the ultimate measure of a speech system is its ability to respond appropriately, some partial-sentence interpretations could obviate full-sentence recognition. No system yet has exploited the opportunity to realize when it had enough semantic information to discontinue processing additional words.

9-6.5 Updating the Discourse Model

Once the system has interpreted the sentence and has responded appropriately, it must update its discourse model. Hearsay-II accomplishes this by advancing the finite-state discourse model to the next state and storing specific semantic category information (e.g., $AUTHORS) in dynamic registers (Hayes-Roth, Gill, & Mostow, 1977). In HWIM and the SRI system, relevant information is stored in semantic network representations (see Chapters 13 and 14 in this volume). By saving state information, the systems insure their ability to resolve subsequent pronominal references (e.g., "Are there other papers by him?") or anaphora (e.g., "Any more?").

The need to save various types of information and access it later depends heavily on the specific task. No general discourse models for speech currently exist.

9-7. CURRENT BEST TECHNIQUES

Scattered throughout this tutorial are many ideas about developing higher-level sources of knowledge. In this section, they have been collated in the following set of heuristic rules.

Rule 1, Task Design.

> If possible, attack tasks that have favorable domain characteristics, including hierarchically structured conceptual domains that are explored by several successively lower-level speech acts.

Rule 2, Language Design.

> Find or develop language environments that minimize the number of alternatives in semantic equivalence classes and the number of allowable transitions between semantic categories.

Rule 3, Knowledge Acquisition:

> Understand the task domain. Collect representative samples of man-machine interactions. Compare them and abstract their similarities. Represent the similarities in semantic templates. Take advantage of computational aids for managing this process. Represent additional constraints of semantics and pragmatics as heuristic rules.

Rule 4, Knowledge Compilation:

> The collected semantic templates and rules may be compiled into different forms to expedite calculations. Networks promote efficient left-to-right processing. Production rules promote direct (associative) indexing of knowledge based on current attributes of hypotheses. Templates themselves can suitably support algorithms for partial-parsing sentence fragments. Adjacency matrices support rapid testing of word-word hypotheses.

Rule 5, Grammatical Processing:

If (a) the language has a small branching factor, (b) utterances are guaranteed to be grammatical, and (c) sufficient computation cycles are available, evaluate word hypotheses left-to-right. This evaluation must be complete in the sense that the search samples every word sequence whose potential credibility could exceed the first sentence hypothesized. In particular, arbitrarily cutting off the initial hypothesis set at the top N initial-word hypotheses will lead to many errors (unless N is sufficiently large to guarantee including the correct first word).

Rule 6, Grammatical Processing:

If the conditions of Rule 5 are not met, a preferable strategy would first generate the best bottom-up word hypotheses, then look for mutually predicting words, and finally choose these as initial word-sequence hypotheses. This method enables a system to capitalize on its most efficient methods and its best acoustic data, even in the presence of noise and ungrammaticality.

Rule 7, Efficiency:

Test satisfiable and easily computed constraints first, reserving specific and costly methods until necessary.

Rule 8, Credibility:

Credibility ratings of hypotheses should increase with the number and strength of the constraints they satisfy.

Rule 9, Desirability:

Diverse theoretical, economic, and empirical factors affect the desirability of any potential action. Neither rigorously analytical approaches nor heuristic schemes for integrating these diverse factors have demonstrated empirical superiority. Moreover, the empirical effects of alternative scheduling strategies will vary as the performance characteristics of various knowledge sources change.

9-8. OUTSTANDING PROBLEMS AND FUTURE TRENDS

Throughout this chapter, we have referred to problems defying formal solutions and to many empirical questions for which few data exist to guide us. This section compiles a small set of such issues worthy of additional attention.

9-8.1 Systematic vs. Heuristic Searches

One of the foremost questions in speech understanding (as in other areas of artificial intelligence) concerns the relative benefits of systematic tree searches as opposed to more heuristic, generate-and-test approaches to problem solving. Both Harpy and the Northwestern Chess 4.5 program (Michie, 1977) have achieved outstanding performance levels within traditional AI tree-searching paradigms. Their capacities will increase directly with faster computers, and at the same time their costs will decrease.   On the other hand, in many areas of human endeavor, expertise at a task often consists of very selective and opportunistic use of knowledge. As the complexity of problem domains increases, cooperative, flexible problem solving frameworks (such as Hearsay-II, discussed in Chapter 16 in this volume) become increasingly attractive.

Architectures like Hearsay-II seem appropriate for future experimental systems for still another reason. Because speech system R&D is itself an empirical, trial-and-error endeavor, some flexible framework must exist for "plugging in" new sources of knowledge and exploring new ideas for focus and control.   The need for this flexibility suggests architectures like that of Hearsay-II as the testbed for much future research. Of course, specific applications should yield to specialized architectures that provide significant efficiencies over more general research systems.

9-8.2 Knowledge Acquisition

The tasks of formulating knowledge about speech and its task domain are currently quite empirical.   Only rudimentary computational aids have been developed to assist in this process. As we expand the domains of speech applications, the value of developing improved machine-aided knowledge acquisition capabilities will increase accordingly.

Specific areas where machine-aided knowledge acquisition would seem appropriate include:

o Gathering sample (simulated) man-machine interactions.
o Clustering syntactically similar sentences.
o Forming semantic categories and templates.
o Estimating a priori probabilities and improving empirical
      likelihood ratios.
o Assisting in the collection and representation   of
      semantic and pragmatic knowledge.

9-8.3 Testing and Correcting Knowledge

Enormous difficulties impede the evaluation of empirically gathered knowledge.   The problem of verifying knowledge subsumes a more general problem of verifying computer procedures. Both of these problems should see major advances in the coming decade, because they are the major bottlenecks in the development of reliable systems. Machine aids for generating and evaluating test data should be the first objective. A more difficult problem worthy of attention is that of inferring appropriate semantic models directly from explicit pragmatic models. From these semantic models, in turn, we would like to deduce suitably habitable syntaxes.

9-8.4   Compiling and Accessing Knowledge

Any piece of knowledge, such as a semantic template, can support several different types of inferences (see Section 9-5.3). We have little experience at compiling knowledge into different forms to support different types of functions.   To date, grammatical knowledge has been converted automatically both into production rules and Markov networks.   Higher-level restriction rules have been compiled only into test procedures invoked when corresponding phrase structures are recognized. In the next decade, the problem of compiling and accessing large bodies of knowledge for varied purposes will become one of the foremost problems in AI. This will also be true for speech systems aimed at increasingly complex tasks.

9-8.5 Credit Assignment and System Tuning

The last problem area concerns the empirical nature of system tuning. To improve a complex speech system, we must identify which aspects of its performance help and which hinder proper performance. For many aspects of the speech problem, this process seems mechanizable. In the Hearsay-II research project, for example, programs were written to compare desired knowledge source behavior with observed actual behavior. Actions that led to incorrect or irrelevant hypothesization became candidates for examination by the knowledge source programmers. This type of automated aid to credit assignment could significantly increase our abilities to detect and rectify errors and anomalies.

REFERENCES

Aho, A. F., & Ullman, J. D. (1972) The Theory of Parsing, Translation, and Compiling. Vols. I & II, Prentice-Hall, Englewood Cliffs NJ.

Bahl, L. R., Baker, J. K., Cohen, P. S., Cole, A. G., Jelinek, F., Lewis, B. L., & Mercer, R. L. (1978) Automatic recognition of continuously spoken sentences from a finite state grammar. Proc. 1978 IEEE Int. Conf. on ASSP, Tulsa, OK, 418-421.

Baker, J. K. (1975) The DRAGON system--an overview. IEEE Transactions on Acoustics, Speech, and Signal Processing, 23, 24-29.

Barnet, J. A., et al. (in press) The SDC speech understanding system. In this volume.

Burton, R. R. (1976) Semantic grammar: an engineering technique for constructing natural language understanding systems. BBN Report No. 3453. Cambridge, MA: Bolt, Beranek, Newman.

Chomsky, Noam (1957) Syntactic Structures. The Hague: Mouton and Company.

Computer Science Speech Group. (1976) Working papers in speech recognition - IV - The HEARSAY-II System. Carnegie-Mellon University, Pittsburgh, PA.

Deutsch, B. G. (1975) Establishing context in task-oriented dialogs. Tech Note 114, Artificial Intelligence Center, Stanford Research Institute, Menlo Park, CA.

Erman, L. D., & Lesser, V. R. (in press) The HEARSAY-II speech understanding system: a tutorial. In this volume.

Fox, M. S., & Mostow, D. J. (1977) Maximal consistent interpretations of errorful data in hierarchically modelled domains. Proceedings of the 5th International Joint Conference on Artificial Intelligence, Boston, MA, 165-171.

Fillmore, Charles J. (1966) A proposal concerning English prepositions. In Dinneen (Ed.), Monograph Series on Languages and Linguistics. No. 19, Washington: Georgetown University Press.

Goodman, G. (1976) Analysis of languages for man-machine voice communication. Tech report, Computer Science Department, Carnegie-Mellon University, Pittsburgh, PA.

Grosz, B. J. (1977) The representation and use of focus in dialogue understanding. Tech Note 151, Artificial Intelligence Center, Stanford Research Institute, Menlo Park, CA.

Hayes-Roth, F. (1976) Patterns of induction and associated knowledge acquisition algorithms. Computer Science Department, Carnegie-Mellon University, Pittsburgh, PA.

Hayes-Roth, F., Erman, L. D., Fox, M. S., & Mostow, D. J. (1977) Syntactic processing in Hearsay-II. Speech Understanding Systems, Summary of Five-Year Report. Carnegie-Mellon University, Pittsburgh, PA.

Hayes-Roth, F., Gill, G., & Mostow, D. J. (1976) Discourse analysis and task performance in Hearsay-II. Speech Understanding Systems, Summary of Five-Year Report. Department of Computer Science, Carnegie-Mellon University, Pittsburgh, PA.

Hayes-Roth, F., & Lesser, V. R. (1977) Focus of attention in the Hearsay-II speech understanding system. Proceedings of the 5th International Joint Conference on Artificial Intelligence, Boston, MA, 27-35.

Hayes-Roth, F., & Mostow, D. J. (1976) Syntax and semantics in a distributed logic speech understanding system. Proceedings of the 1976 IEEE International Conference on Acoustics, Speech, and Signal Processing. Philadelphia, PA, 421-424.

Hayes-Roth, F., Mostow, D. J., & Fox, M. S. (1978) Understanding speech in the Hearsay-II system. In L. Bolc (Ed.), Natural Communication with Computers. Berlin: Springer-Verlag.

Hendrix, G. G. (1977) The LIFER manual. A guide to building practical natural language interfaces. Tech Note 138, Stanford Research Institute, Artificial Intelligence Center, Menlo Park, CA.

Hendrix, G. G. (1978) Encoding knowledge in partitioned networks. Tech Note 164, Artificial Intelligence Center, SRI International, Menlo Park, CA.

Hendrix, G. G., Sacerdoti, E. D., Sagalowicz, D., & Slocum, J. (1978) Developing a natural language interface to complex data. ACM Transactions on Database Systems, 3, 105-147.

Hirschman, L., Grishman, R., & Sager, N. (1975) Grammatically-based automatic word class formation. Information Processing Management 11. 39-57.

Hobbs, J. R., & Rosenschein, S. J. (1977) Making computational sense of Montague's intensional logic. Artificial Intelligence, 9, 287-306.

Kahneman, D., & Tversky, A. (1973) On the psychology of prediction. Psychological Review, 80, 237-251.

Kaplan, S. J. (1978) Indirect responses to loaded questions. Proc. Second Workshop on Theoretical Issues in Natural Language Processing, Champaign-Urbana, IL.

Lesser, V. R., Hayes-Roth, F., Birnbaum, M., & Cronk, R. (1977) Selection of word islands in the Hearsay-II speech system. *Proceedings of the 1977 IEEE International Conference on Acoustics, Speech, and Signal Processing*, Hartford, CT, 791-795

Lowerre, B. T. (1976) The HARPY speech recognition system. Department of Computer Science, Carnegie-Mellon University, Pittsburgh, PA.

Lowerre, B. T., & Reddy R. (in press) The HARPY speech understanding system. In this volume.

Michie, D. (1977) David Levy challenges game, 1 April 1977. *SIGART Newsletter*, No. 62, 10-11.

Miller, G. A., & Isard, S. (1963) Some perceptual consequences of linguistic rules. *Journal of Verbal Learning and Verbal Behavior*, 2 217-218.

Minsky, M. L. (1967) In *Computation: Finite and Infinite Machines*. Prentice-Hall, Englewood Clifs, NJ.

Montague, R. (1974) *Formal Philosophy*. Yale University Press, New Haven and London.

Mostow, D. J., & Hayes-Roth, F. (1978) A production system for speech understanding. In D. A. Waterman & F. Hayes-Roth (Eds.), *Pattern-DIrected Inference Systems*. Academic Press, New York, NY, 471-481.

Mostow, D. J. (1977) A halting condition and related pruning heuristics for combinatorial search. In *Speech Understanding Systems, Five-Year Report*. Carnegie-Mellon University, Pittsburgh, PA.

Nash-Webber, B. L. (1976) Semantic interpretation revisited. Report No. 3335, Bolt Beranek and Newman Inc., Cambridge, MA.

Neely, R. B. (1973) On the use of syntax and semantics in a speech understanding system. Department of Computer Science, Carnegie-Mellon University, Pittsburgh, PA.

Parkison, R. C., Colby, K. M., & Faught, W. S. (1977) Conversational language comprehension using integrated pattern-matching and parsing. *Artificial Intelligence*, 9, 111-134.

Reddy, D. R., et al. (1977) Speech Understanding Systems. *Summary of Results of the Five-Year Research Effort at Carnegie-Mellon University*. Department of Computer Science, Carnegie-Mellon University, Pittsburgh, PA.

Robinson, J. J. (1975) A tuneable performance grammar. Tech Note 112, Artificial Intelligence Center, Stanford Research Institute, Menlo Park, CA.

Shortliffe, E. H., & Buchanan, B. G. (1975) A model of inexact reasoning in medicine. *Math. Bioscience*, 23 351-379.

Salmon, W. C. (1973) Confirmation. *Scientific American*, 228, 75-83.

Slocum, J. (1975) Speech generation from semantic nets. Tech Note 115, Artificial Intelligence Center, Stanford Research Institute, Menlo Park, CA.

Tretiakoff, A. (1974) Computer-generated word classes and sentence structures. Information Processing 1974, Proc. IFIPS Congress, 74,

Walker, D. E. (in press) SRI Research on speech understanding. In this volume.

Walker, D. E., et al. (1976) Speech understanding research. Final technical report, Stanford Research Institute, Menlo Park, CA.

Winograd, T. (1975) Frame representations and the declarative/procedural controversy. In D. G. Bobrow & A. Collins (Eds.), Representation and Understanding: Studies in Cognitive Science. Academic Press, New York, NY.

Wolf, J. J., & Woods, W. A. (in press) The HWIM speech understanding system. In this volume.

Woods, W. A. (1975) What's in a link: foundations for semantic networks. Report No. 3072, Bolt Beranek and Newman Inc., Cambridge, MA.

Woods, W. A. (1977) Shortfall and density scoring strategies for speech understanding control. Proceedings of the 5th International Joint Conference on Artificial Inteligence, Boston, MA, 18-26.

Woods, W. A., Kaplan, R. M., & Nash-Webber, B. (1972) The lunar sciences natural language information system: final report. BBN Report No. 2378, Bolt Beranek and Newman Inc., Cambridge, MA.

Woods, W. A., et al. (1976) Speech understanding systems. Final Report, Vols. I, IV, V. Report No. 3438, Bolt Beranek and Newman Inc., Cambridge, MA.

10.

ALTERNATIVE CONTROL STRUCTURES FOR SPEECH UNDERSTANDING SYSTEMS

Gary Goodman
Raj Reddy
Carnegie-Mellon University
Pittsburgh, PA 15213

10-1. ABSTRACT

Control Structures are an essential part of any speech recognition system. They are the devices by which passive knowledge about the task and language is transformed into active and effective processes. In this chapter we define and discuss three areas of control structures: knowledge source interaction, knowledge source activation, and knowledge source focusing. Discussion relates the concepts presented to systems developed during the five-year ARPA speech understanding project.

10-2. INTRODUCTION

Speech understanding systems are characterized by high data rates, diverse sources of knowledge representing large numbers of rules and facts, incomplete and inaccurate knowledge, and error and uncertainty in individual decisions. We know that all the available sources of knowledge must communicate and cooperate in the presence of error and uncertainty. We do not know how to do it effectively or efficiently. The problem of control in a speech understanding system refers to how knowledge is organized, activated, and focused to constrain the search. In this chapter we show how error leads to search, how knowledge constrains search, and how decisions about activation and focusing of knowledge affect the **computational complexity** of the recognition process. The control strategy, i.e. activation and focusing of knowledge, used by a speech understanding system thus seriously affects the speed and accuracy of the recognition process.

In Section 10-3 we discuss the problem and paradigms of knowledge source interaction, i.e., how knowledge sources communicate with each other. In Section 10-4 we show how the problem of error can be viewed as a search problem and discuss various search techniques useful to speech understanding systems. In Section 10-5 we show how various systems cope with the problem of focusing, that is, how they decide which of the many competing requests for knowledge source activation should be satisfied.

10-3. KNOWLEDGE SOURCE INTERACTION

Various forms of knowledge must be applied if a speech understanding system is to be effective in deducing the intended message from the speech signal. Further, these sources of knowledge must be able to cooperate with one another. The kinds of knowledge employed and the ways in which they interact are part of the many design decisions affecting the structure and control of speech understanding systems.

10-3.1 Knowledge Sources

The distinctive characteristic of speech understanding systems is the active use of knowledge of the language, the environment and the context in understanding an utterance. These sources of knowledge (KSs) include the characteristics of speech sounds (phonetics), variability in pronunciations (phonology), the stress and intonation patterns of speech (prosodics), the sound patterns of words (lexicon), the grammatical structure of language (syntax), the meaning of words and sentences (semantics), and the context of the conversation (pragmatics). Part II of this volume covers the definition and use of these types of knowledge. The following discussion refers to the levels of representation shown in Figure 10-1. These correspond, roughly, to a hierarchical structure of the forms of knowledge.

10-3.2 Models for Knowledge Source Interaction

A model of knowledge source interaction presumes some information on which the knowledge is to act. Knowledge sources speak "different languages" in the sense that they deal with diverse areas of knowledge. However, some common representation is necessary if knowledge sources are to interact cooperatively. The application of knowledge may affect this representation in essentially two different ways. Knowledge may be used to alter the representation within a level. This may happen at the lexical level when the occurrence of a word (e.g., author's first name) is used to predict an adjacent word (e.g., author's last name). This use of intra-level knowledge usually occurs at the phonetic level because of coarticulation. Another form of application occurs when the knowledge, as it relates to some level, functions to alter or infer the representation at another level. An example of this is when syntactic knowledge is used to infer <author> at the phrasal level after identifying the sequence of first-name and last-name at the lexical level. The direction of knowledge flow is not necessarily from a lower level to a higher level. The opposite case arises when syntactic knowledge is able to "strongly" predict a missing word from an otherwise complete sentence.

The types of knowledge employed, the communication paths, and their directions form the primitives for models of knowledge source interaction. The remainder of this section describes several general models in this framework. Interaction models specific to the ARPA recognition systems may be found in the excellent review by Klatt (1977).

Hierarchical model: The model, shown in Fig. 10-2, is the most straightforward model of interaction. It is completely data-driven with all communication paths going from level to level, bottom to top. Interpretations of the data at any level are available only to the next higher level. The direct, one-way KS interconnections greatly simplify control for this model. The model is limited, however, because an error in interpretation at some level propagates to the next level resulting in compounding of errors and an error of omission is difficult, if not impossible, to correct. Consider, for instance, one word of an otherwise complete sentence missing at the lexical level. Syntactic or other

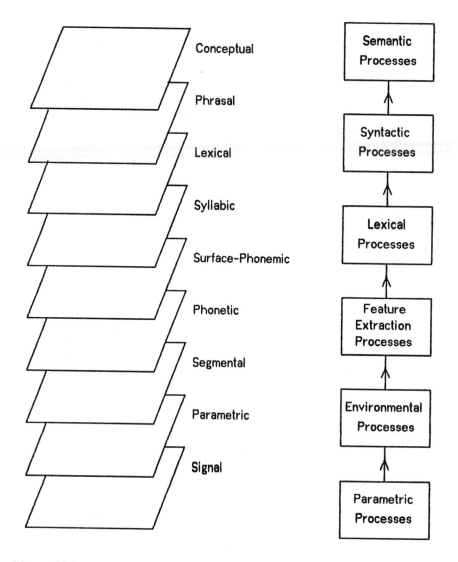

Figure 10-1.

Levels of representation for speech understanding systems.

Figure 10-2.

The hierarchical model.

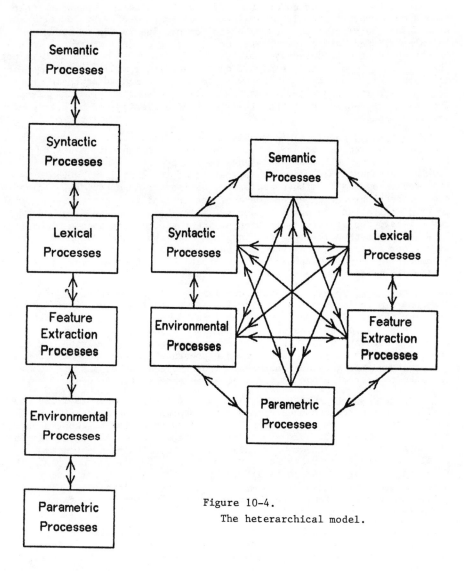

Figure 10-4.
   The heterarchical model.

Figure 10-3.
   The goal-directed model.

237

knowledge at the phrasal level must blindly assume the missing word was spoken in order for the sentence to have an interpretation at the sentential level. A KS has no opportunity, in this model, to request other knowledge sources to verify the existence of that word. This model, because of its simplicity, would be the correct one to use if no uncertainties existed in the interpretation (i.e., no errors) or if all uncertainty could be eliminated by application of knowledge. Since this is not the case in current speech recognition systems, this model is not used in its pure form. Some systems, however, do use this model for their front-end, transforming the signal, hierarchically, to some intermediate level. Uncertainties remaining at that level must be disambiguated by higher-level knowledge.

Goal-directed model: This model, shown in Fig. 10-3, is also known as the top-down, generative, or predictive model. Communication begins at the highest level with each knowledge source predicting at the next lower level. This continues until the signal level is reached, at which time the prediction may be either confirmed, denied, or more typically, given some score representing an estimate of the credibility that the prediction is true. Although the primary mode of interaction is higher level to lower level, the decisions, or scores, are reported back to the higher level. This method suffers from the fact that the search space starting at the top level is quite large for any reasonably sized, habitable grammar. The simple nature of the interaction, in the presence of error, limits the effectiveness of these first two models.

Heterarchical model: The heterarchical model, shown in Fig. 10-4, abandons simple interaction by allowing any knowledge source to interact with any other. One pays a price for this in the increased complexity of the representation and search. If there are k knowledge sources, then $k*(k-1)/2$ separate data paths exist where $k-1$ previously existed. Each new data path requires another common representation and increases the complexity of the knowledge source. Also, the search becomes more complicated to control since it may proceed in many different ways.

Blackboard model: Control of the search process may be simplified by having each knowledge source communicate through a central data base having one form of representation. This is known as the blackboard model, Fig. 10-5. Each knowledge source is an independent entity which examines the data base and after doing so may evaluate hypotheses created by other knowledge sources or create its own hypotheses. Even with this simplification, control of search is difficult for this model. This model was used successfully in the Hearsay-II (HS-II) system developed at Carnegie-Mellon University. More detail concerning this system may be found in Erman & Lesser (this volume).

Locus model: In the locus model (Fig. 10-6), all syntactic, lexical, and word juncture knowledge has been precompiled into an integrated network representing a complete description of every pronunciation of every possible sentence. The input signal is hierarchically transformed into a segmented and phonetically labeled form which is matched against the network to yield an optimal network path. The locus model of search uses a graph-searching technique in which all except a "beam" of near-miss alternatives around the best path are pruned from the search tree at each segmental decision point, thus containing the exponential growth without requiring backtracking. Control is greatly simplified because of a single uniform representation of all the different sources of knowledge.

The Harpy speech understanding system (Lowerre, 1976) is an example of the locus model. It was the first connected speech system to satisfy the original specifications given in the Newell report (Newell, et al., 1971)

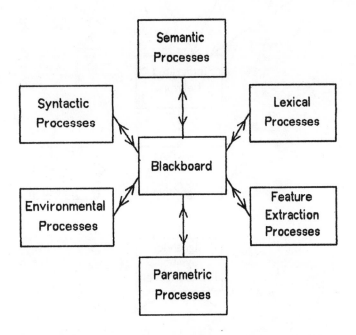

Figure 10-5.
The blackboard model.

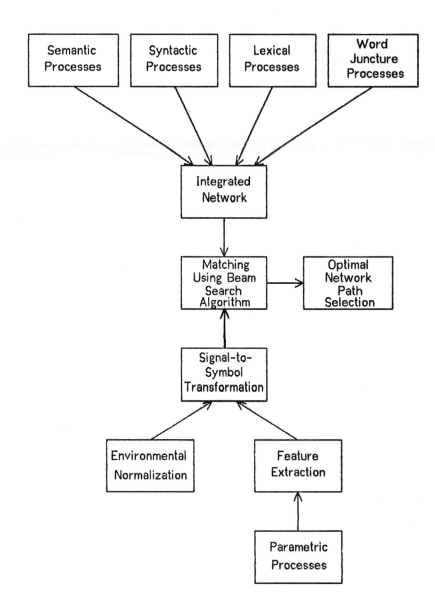

Figure 10-6. The locus model.

and was first demonstrated in September of 1976. A complete description and discussion of this system may be found in Lowerre & Reddy (this volume).

10-4. KNOWLEDGE SOURCE ACTIVATION

The goal of a speech understanding system is to find the most plausible interpretation consistent with knowledge at every level, including the input utterance (signal level). The role of acoustic-phonetic knowledge is to propose plausible interpretations of the signal using pattern classification techniques (Part II, this volume; Itakura, 1975; Makhoul, 1975; and Schafer & Rabiner, 1975). Because these techniques are not capable of making unique choices with perfect accuracy, several interpretations must be considered plausible. Figure 10-7 shows a speech waveform with multiple interpretations at the phone level. If acoustic-phonetic knowledge were perfect, only one alternative would exist for each segment, there would be only one interpretation of the utterance at the phone level, and recognition could proceed in a straightforward manner.

Pattern matching techniques utilize distance functions to decide on the plausibility of a particular choice. The result is a value which represents relative plausibility and can be used to order the alternatives. In the absence of other knowledge the most plausible interpretation would be formed by selecting the best of each set of alternatives. Since the techniques are less than perfect this generally leads to nonsense such as /ah r m aw t/. Higher level knowledge must be utilized to resolve the ambiguity. The goal is to find the most plausible sequence of candidates which is also consistent with the higher level knowledge. It would be possible to evaluate the path likelihood of every possible sequence, as in the Dragon recognition system (Baker, 1975). Since this can be very time consuming, some form of pruning strategy is usually desirable. The knowledge applicable at each level serves to constrain the search by considering only those sequences which are consistent with the knowledge. In the example of Fig. 10-7, lexical knowledge has constrained the last word to be "but", "out", or "about". The word "mutt" does not appear because it is not in the language and therefore inconsistent with lexical knowledge.

Here, we will briefly describe search mechanisms for activating knowledge. For clarification and more detail see Nilsson (1971) and Winston (1977).

10-4.1 Basic Search Mechanisms

During a recognition, partial interpretations are built in an attempt to find the most plausible one. The ways in which knowledge sources are activated are governed by the search strategies employed. As alternative interpretations are generated, the choice of the next alternative to attend to must be made. In a depth-first search, the most recent alternative is the one chosen. In a speech understanding system this means examining the implications of some hypothesis at every level before attending to other hypotheses. In the example of Fig. 10-7, suppose segmental alternatives were ordered (/o/, /ah/, /aw/). Segment /aw/ would be chosen to be explored next. This would lead to the generation of /aw/ at the phone level. Then lexical knowledge would be activated. If, in this instance, there are no words starting with /aw/ which also start a sentence of the language, the lexical search would generate no new

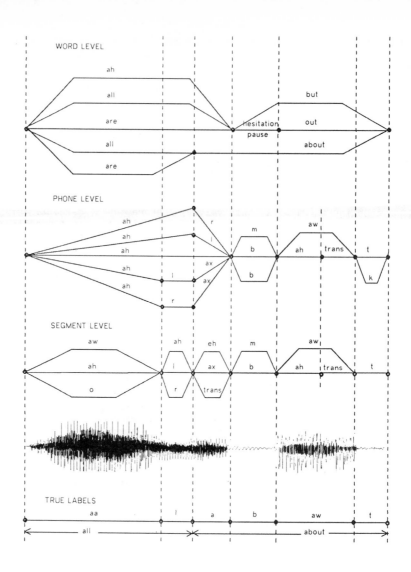

Figure 10-7.
Example of alternative interpretations at various levels
(from Reddy and Erman, 1975).

hypotheses. The depth-first premise would then select /ah/ at the segment
level as the most recent, unattended alternative. This hypothesis would
generate /ah/ at the phone level and "all" and "are" at the word level.
Depth-first search is risky in the sense that the search may waste much
time following a partial interpretation which is eventually found to be
inconsistent with some knowledge.

Breadth-_first_ is another form of basic search. This method of search examines all options at any level before proceeding to another level. Alternatives are explored uniformly so that the true path receives as much attention as any other path. In order not to overlook the correct path, many alternative labelings must be kept at every level, leading to combinatorial explosion.

10-4.2 Probabilistic Search

Search efficiency can be greatly improved if pattern matching knowledge is used to order the alternatives so that the most promising are explored first. If the selected alternatives are pursued in a depth-first manner, this is called best-_first_ search. Suppose, in the example of Fig. 10-7, that the scores resulting from a signal-to-symbol transformation for (/aw/, /ah/, and /o/) are (.7, .9, .05). Implications of /ah/ at the word level would be explored before those for /aw/ or /o/ were considered. The words generated would be likewise ordered so that the most promising would be pursued. The best-_few_ method expands breadth-first, evaluates the new hypotheses, and continues to explore only the most promising ones in a breadth-first fashion. In the example above /o/ would be discarded as unlikely with /aw/ and /ah/ being explored further.

The effectiveness of these methods depends highly on the accuracy with which the matching procedure orders the alternatives. Current signal-to-symbol matching yields 50-70% first choice accuracy (Klatt, 1977). Given this, the method works well only when moderate lexical and syntactic constraint is available.

10-5. KNOWLEDGE SOURCE FOCUSING

The search methods discussed in the previous section were concerned with examining alternatives at various levels. However, the search space may be regarded as having 3 dimensions: level, alternative, and time. In a global sense, each partial interpretation is a tree structure made up of alternatives at various levels and covering some portion of the utterance. Focus of attention mechanisms are control structures for deciding which of the competitive partial interpretations should be extended. A simple focusing strategy, used by Harpy, is to perform a best-few search moving left-to-right in time. Of the many ways in which search may proceed, there are two popular viewpoints: left-to-right and island driving (Erman & Lesser, this volume; Woods, 1977). This latter form of search begins by establishing anchor points which are portions of the utterance where the credibility of a word or sequence of segments is very high. These small partial interpretations are then extended in a best-first manner. The idea is to build interpretations covering larger time periods until an interpretation is found which covers the entire utterance.

Proponents of island driving argue that extending the globally best interpretation is more efficient since it approaches the recognition goal in the obvious, direct manner. Further, accuracy is better because the method does not consider portions of the utterance with low credibility until they become possible extensions of the current best interpretation, whereas a left-to-right strategy is forced to deal with unpromising portions as they occur in the utterance. If this happens at the beginning of an utterance, a left-to-right strategy may consume a great amount of time examining interpretations which look good initially, but cannot be completed.

Proponents of left-to-right strategy argue that it is much simplier, requiring far less bookkeeping, and thus leads to greater efficiency. Also, this method can achieve the same accuracy by using a best-few search which explores more alternatives during portions of the utterances where credibility is low.

Speech systems developed during the ARPA project used some form of probabilistically guided search. Hearsay-I (Reddy, Erman, & Neely, 1973), and the speech systems developed at Lincoln Labs (Forgie, et al., 1974) and SDC (Ritea, 1975) used a best-first left-to-right search with back-tracking. Hearsay-II and HWIM (Woods, et al., 1976) also employed best-first search but with an island driving strategy. Harpy (Lowerre, this volume) moves left to right with a best-few search, called "beam search", which requires no backtracking.

Control strategies for speech systems which use island driving may be classified as <u>explicit</u> or <u>distributed</u>. Explicit strategies, after deciding which interpretation to extend, call a predefined sequence of knowledge sources to extend and rate the new interpretation. Distributed strategies are necessary when knowledge sources are independently activated.

An example of an explicit focusing strategy is the Shortfall Scoring Method used in the HWIM system (Woods, 1977). This method assigns priorities to partial interpretations, called islands, by comparing the actual score obtained for an island with the maximum attainable score for the time period covered by the island. An island is a sequence of words which is part of a legal sentence. The maximum attainable score is computed by summing the best scores for all the sub-units (words) in the associated time period. Each island is assigned a priority equal to the actual score for the island plus the maximum attainable score(s) for the region(s) not covered by the island. Refering to the diagram of Fig. 10-8, Priority(Island) = Actual Score(Island) + Max-attainable(Region1) + Max-attainable(Region3). This represents an optimistic estimate of an island's final score. The algorithm extends the island having the highest priority. This priority scheme is interesting because it guarantees "admissibility"; i.e., it guarantees the discovery of the best matching interpretation of the utterance. Note also, that the method will work not only for island-driven strategies, but for left-to-right and right-to-left strategies as well.

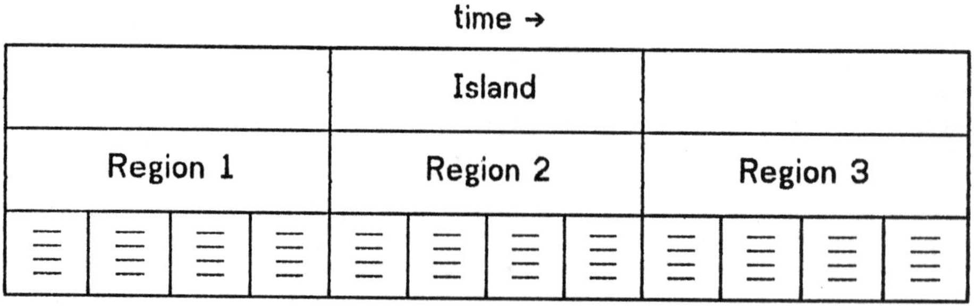

time →

	Island	
Region 1	Region 2	Region 3
▤ ▤ ▤ ▤	▤ ▤ ▤ ▤	▤ ▤ ▤ ▤

Figure 10-8.

Example of regions used in shortfall scoring.

A distributed focus mechanism was used in the Hearsay-II system (Hayes-Roth & Lesser, 1976). In this system, knowledge sources are data-directed and invoked whenever certain preconditions are observed in the data base. The control problem is to execute first those knowledge sources which are more likely to lead to a successful recognition. The approach was to lay down several principles for control: (1) The Competition Principle: the best of several alternatives should be explored first; (2) The Validity Principle: more processing should be given to knowledge sources operating on more valid data; (3) The Significance Principle: more processing should be given to knowledge sources whose expected results are more significant; (4) The Efficiency Principle: more processing should be given to knowledge sources that perform more reliably and inexpensively; (5) The Goal Satisfaction Principle: more processing should be given to knowledge sources whose responses are more likely to satisfy processing goals. Knowledge source priorities were based upon the degree to which they satisfied these principles. By tuning various weighting factors, a desirable balance between breadth- and depth-first search was achieved.

10-6. DISCUSSION

The complexity of speech understanding requires the use of many diverse sources of knowledge cooperating to achieve a solution. Ambiguity inherent in the speech signal necessitates search and the computational complexity of the search demands that it be carefully controlled. The designer of a speech understanding system has to make many decisions which affect the nature of control. He would like to know which kinds of knowledge should be used, how knowledge sources should interact, and how they should be activated and focused. In this chapter we have discussed different solutions to these problems. Obviously, we have not specified the best combination of design choices. In fact, there may be no single best set of choices. Each task probably requires a different combination of control decisions; i.e., if the task is simple, such as the recognition of digit sequences, a left-to-right best-first strategy may be adequate. If it is as complex as the "unrestricted English" task, some form of blackboard model with island driving and best-few strategy might be necessary.

One might suggest that the appropriate action is to build the best system possible using the most advanced forms of knowledge application. This is a worthy goal, but a flexible general system capable of handling unrestricted English will, in general, require too much space, too much time, and is not likely to be cost effective for simple tasks. Thus, the choice of optimal control strategies is affected by various aspects of the task; such as, connected speech versus isolated words or phrases, the degree of semantic and syntactic constraint, vocabulary size, and the degree of phonetic similarity of lexical items.

10-7. ACKNOWLEDGEMENTS

We would like to thank Jack Mostow and B. Yegnanarayana for their helpful comments on this manuscript and John Zsarnay for his help in generating the illustrations.

10-8. REFERENCES

Baker, J.K., "The DRAGON System - An overview", IEEE Trans. ASSP, vol 23, no 1, 1975.

Erman, L.D., & V.R. Lesser, "The Hearsay-II speech understanding system", chapter 18 this volume.

Forgie, J.W., et al., Speech Understanding Systems - Semiannual Technical Summary Report, MIT Lincoln Laboratories, Lexington, MA, 1974.

Hayes-Roth, F., & V.R. Lesser, "Focus of attention in a distributed-logic speech understanding system", Proc. IEEE Int. Conf. on ASSP, 1976, Philadelphia, PA.

Itakura, F., "Minimum prediction residual principle applied to speech recognition", IEEE Trans. ASSP, vol 23, 1975.

Klatt, D.H., "Review of the ARPA Speech Understanding Project" J. Acoust. Soc. Amer. vol 62, no 6, 1977.

Lowerre, B., "The Harpy speech recognition system", Tech. Rep., Computer Science Dept., Carnegie-Mellon Univ., 1976.

Lowerre, B., & D.R. Reddy, "The Harpy speech understanding system", chapter 15 this volume.

Makhoul, J., "Linear Prediction: A Tutorial Review", IEEE Proc., vol 63, no 4, 1975.

Newell, A., et al., Speech Understanding Systems: Final Report of a Study Group, 1971 (Reprinted by North-Holland/American Elsevier, Amsterdam, Netherlands, 1973).

Nilsson, N.J., Problem-Solving Methods in Artificial Intelligence, McGraw-Hill, 1971.

Reddy, D.R., L.D. Erman, & R.B. Neely, "A Model and a System for Machine Recognition of Speech", IEEE Trans, AU-21, 1973.

Ritea, B., "Automatic Speech Understanding Systems", Proceedings of the IEEE Computer Society Conference, Washington, DC, 1975.

Schafer, R.W., & L.R. Rabiner, "Digital Representations of Speech Signals", Proc. IEEE, vol 63, no 4, 1975.

Winston, P.H., Artificial Intelligence, Addison-Wesley, 1977.

Woods, W.A., "Shortfall and Density Scoring Strategies for Speech Understanding Control", Proc. IJCAI-77, Cambridge, MA, 1977.

Woods, W.A., et al., "Speech Understanding Systems: Final Technical Progress Report", Bolt Beranek and Newman, Inc., Report No. 3438, Cambridge, MA, 1976.

PART III

IMPACT OF THE ARPA SUR PROJECT

11.

OVERVIEW OF THE ARPA SPEECH UNDERSTANDING PROJECT(1)

Dennis H. Klatt
Massachusetts Institute of Technology

11-1 INTRODUCTION

In November of 1971, the Information Processing Technology Office of the Advanced Research Projects Agency of the Department of Defense (ARPA) initiated a five-year research and development program with the objective of obtaining a breakthrough in speech understanding capability that could then be used toward the development of practical man-machine communication systems (Newell et al., 1973). The specific goals set forth by an ARPA study group are outlined in Table 11-1.

The objectives were to develop several speech understanding systems that accept continuous speech from many cooperative speakers of a General American dialect. Recordings were to be made in a quiet room using a good-quality microphone. Slight tuning of the system would be allowed to handle new speakers, but the users could be required to make only natural adaptations to the system. The language definition would include a slightly selected vocabulary of at least 1000 words and an artificial syntax appropriate to the limited task situation (e.g. a data management task). Less than 10 percent semantic error would be tolerated and the system would have to run in a few times real time using the next generation of computers (i.e. machines capable of executing 100 million machine instructions per second (MIPS)). These goals were to be achieved by November, 1976.

Significantly (and deliberately) absent from the specifications were requirements that the demonstration tasks be relevant to real-world problems, that the languages be habitable, and that the systems be cost effective. These omissions helped to get the project focused on scientific and computational issues, but they have resulted in questions concerning the work remaining to develop future practical systems.

The study group emphasized the concept of speech understanding as opposed to speech recognition. They believed that the hope for the program lay in analyzing speech within the context of specific tasks that employed strong grammatical constraints, as well as strong semantic and dialogue constraints, so that many sources of knowledge could be brought to bear to attain successful understanding of what was said or intended by the speaker.

---

(1)
This chapter is an abbreviated version of a paper "Review of the ARPA Speech Understanding Project" which first appeared in J.Acoust. Soc. Am. 62, 1345-1366 (1977) (copyright 1977 by the Acoustical Society of America).

Table 11-1. The ARPA five-year goals are compared with the performance of Harpy.

GOAL (Nov., 1971)	Harpy (Nov., 1976)
ACCEPT CONNECTED SPEECH	YES
FROM MANY	5 (3 MALE, 2 FEMALE)
COOPERATIVE SPEAKERS	YES
IN A QUIET ROOM	COMPUTER TERMINAL ROOM
USING A GOOD MICROPHONE	CLOSE-TALKING MICROPHONE
WITH SLIGHT TUNING/SPEAKER	20 TRAINING SENTENCES/TALKER
ACCEPTING 1000 WORDS	1011
USING AN ARTIFICIAL SYNTAX	AVG. BRANCHING FACTOR = 33
IN A CONSTRAINING TASK	DOCUMENT RETRIEVAL
YIELDING < 10% SEMANTIC ERROR	5%
IN A FEW TIMES REAL TIME	80 TIMES REAL TIME
ON A 100 MIPS MACHINE	ON A .4 MIPS PDP-KA10,
	USING 256K OF 36-BIT WORDS, AND
	COSTING $5 PER SENTENCE PROCESSED

Accuracy was to be measured by the correctness of the response and not by whether all of the words were correctly recognized.

There were two possible ways to meet the ARPA goals: (1) simplify the general speech recognition problem by finding ways to apply syntactic and semantic constraints and (2) improve upon previous speech recognition capabilities. As noted above, the steering committee emphasized the first alternative and recommended that funding be given to research groups that were composed mainly of computer scientists, not speech scientists. It turned out that the various research groups tried different combinations of the two strategies, but the only clearly successful speech understanding system, Harpy, relied heavily on the first technique. In fact, if the ARPA project were to be judged on its contributions to speech recognition and the speech sciences, rather than judging it against its stated goals, a more negative appraisal might have to be given.

The second column of Table 11-1 characterizes the performance of the Harpy speech understanding system, which was developed at Carnegie-Mellon University (Lowerre, 1976). Harpy essentially meets or exceeds each of the specifications. Given this set of criteria, Harpy performed the best of all the systems that were demonstrated at the end of the project.

The primary concern of this overview is to introduce and compare the structures and components of the four speech understanding systems that were developed (1). The remainder of the chapter is divided into a section that sets forth the scientific problems to be solved, a section describing the main

---

(1)
    The original 5 system builders were a group at Bolt Beranek and Newman Inc. (BBN) headed by W.A. Woods, a group at Carnegie-Mellon University (CMU) headed by D.R. Reddy, a group at Lincoln Laboratories (LL) headed by J. Forgie, a group at Stanford Research Institute (SRI) headed by D. Walker, and a group at System Development Corporation (SDC) headed by B. Ritea. After two years, funding was concentrated on three main system builders. Smaller supporting research efforts were funded at Haskins Laboratories (F.S. Cooper), at Speech Communications Research Laboratory (J.E. Shoup), at Univac (M.F. Medress), and at Univ. California at Berkeley (M.H. O'Malley).

features of the four systems, and a section concerned with an overall scientific evaluation of the systems.

The ARPA project, while large in funding terms, is only one of many past and present efforts to recognize spoken utterances. The reader is referred to Chapters 18-24 and other sources for a more complete picture. For example, there are reviews such as have been published by Lindgren (1965), Pierce (1969), Fant (1970), Hyde (1972), Wolf (1976), and especially Reddy (1976); conference proceedings such as have been edited by Erman (1974), Reddy (1975), Fant (1975), Teacher (1976), and Silverman (1977); and descriptions of other recent speech understanding systems such as have been published by Bahl et al. (1976), Jelinek (1976), De Mori et al. (1975), Sakai and Nakagawa (1975), Haton and Pierrel (1976), and Medress et al. (1977).

11-2 THE SPEECH UNDERSTANDING PROBLEM

At the beginning of the ARPA project, isolated word recognition by pattern matching techniques was enjoying some initial success. However, it was realized that many words appearing in sentence contexts varied dramatically in acoustic characteristics depending on the surrounding phonetic environment and depending on certain phonological processes of English (Klatt and Stevens, 1973; Oshika et al., 1975), so a simple-minded pattern-matching word identification strategy could not be applied to the sentence understanding problem. Therefore it seemed necessary to follow a more traditional approach, the first step of which was to process the acoustic input to recover a phonetic transcription of what had been said. A phonetic transcription is a discrete representation of articulatory activity in terms of a sequence of configurational goals or states called phonetic segments.

The second step in the hypothetical understanding strategy would be to take the (probably errorful) phonetic transcription of an unknown utterance and try to find candidate words and word sequences that might be present. Consider the phonetic transcription:

$$[d I \widecheck{j} \vartheta h I \Lap I t \vartheta t a m] \tag{1}$$

No word boundaries are indicated in (1) because acoustic cues to word boundary locations are rarely present. The lexical search problem (to find the sequence of words corresponding to (1)) is extremely difficult because of the combinatorics of possible word boundary locations, because the phonetic transcription may contain substitution errors, omissions, and extra segments, and because the talker uses a system of phonological rules to modify and simplify the pronunciation of individual words in some sentence environments. For example, the normal way to say "Did you" is [d I ǰ ə], i.e. "Dija" but "you" is pronounced differently in "are you". The "t" in "hit" usually is realized as a very brief tongue flap [ɾ] in "hit it", but not in "hit some". The two adjacent "t"s of "it to" reduce to a single [t], resulting in (1) as the normal way to pronounce "Did you hit it to Tom?"

Each of the simplifications in (1) can be described by general phonological rules that presuppose an underlying basic representation for the word (called the phonemic representation). The phonemic string that would be stored in the lexicon for "you" might be /y u/. A phonological rule [d # y] --> [ǰ] transforms the /y/ into [ǰ] if the previous word ends in a [d]. The application of inverse phonological rules for sentence decoding is complicated by the fact that there is no unique inverse rule in most cases. A [ǰ] that is observed could be the first or last sound of a word like "judge", or it could be the surface manifestation of /d/-/y/ in a word pair like "did you". Similarly an observed flap [ɾ] may indicate a word containing a /t/, a /d/, or possibly even an /n/. Almost any segment could be simultaneously the manifestation of the last phoneme of one word and the first phoneme of the next word.

All of these phonological phenomena result in lexical ambiguity so that even the best lexical hypothesis routines will propose many words that are not in the original sentence, simply due to fortuitous matches. The third step in the sentence-decoding process would therefore be to use syntactic-semantic modules to weed out the false lexical hypotheses and put together a word string that represents what was spoken.

The block diagram shown in Fig. 11-1 summarizes what we have just said. Speech understanding systems may be thought to consist of two main components, a "bottom end" that converts acoustic data into lexical hypotheses and a "top end" that accepts lexical hypotheses and tries to find the most likely sentence that could have been spoken.

An important point to make concerning Fig. 11-1 is that the top end can provide the bottom end processor with constraints concerning what might be expected next. The relative success of the four speech understanding systems to be described is more highly correlated with the type of constraint provided by the top end than with any other variable. The most successful system, Harpy, exhaustively lists those and only those <u>acoustic segment sequences</u> that form acceptable input sentences, and the Harpy grammar severely constrains the acoustic alternatives much of the time. The advantage of applying strong constraints at the acoustic level is that one can avoid having to perform generalized phonetic recognition or generalized lexical hypothesization that would otherwise generate a large number of spurious hypotheses that have to be rejected later by the top end (a computationally costly and often difficult undertaking).

The scientific problems associated with top end design were concerned with how to combine lexical hypotheses into larger and larger sentence fragments that are (1) syntactically acceptable, (2) semantically acceptable, (3) and plausible given what the user has said previously and some notion of what he/she wants to do. Syntactic analyzers used earlier in text processing applications would have to be modified to function in the face of errorful input, to consider and score multiple alternatives, and to include semantic knowledge before sufficient constraints could be applied effectively in the speech understanding context. The algorithms would have to be fast enough to permit evaluation of many word combinations and they would have to include sophisticated scoring algorithms to select among those alternatives that are grammatically acceptable. Progress in each of these areas is summarized in Sec. 11-4.

The scientific problems associated with bottom end design included (1) selecting an acoustic representation, (2) improving segmentation and phonetic labeling strategies that had been developed previously, and (3) recognizing words that have undergone phonetic modifications at word boundaries and/or phonological recoding. Unanswered questions were: What kinds of improvements could be made to existing phonetic recognition strategies? How good does phonetic recognition have to be? Does one have to normalize for speaking rate? Can routines be made to work for any talker? How can one take advantage of prosodic cues (the pattern of voicing fundamental frequency, segmental durations, and intensity fluctuations), which indicate syllable stress and the syntactic structure of a spoken sentence? Progress in these areas and an interesting alternative to phonetic recognition are discussed in Sec. 11-4 and Chapter 25.

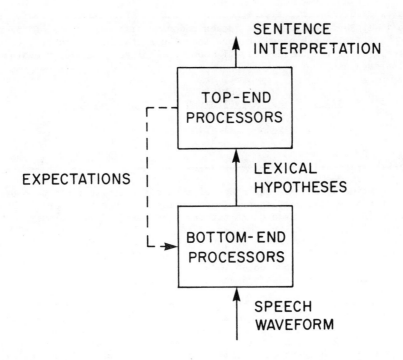

Fig. 11-1. Simplified overview of the speech understanding problem.

The block diagram of Fig. 11-1 describes a system. Some issues of speech understanding system design are obscured if one simply discusses component performance requirements. The system design problems extant at the onset of the ARPA program included (1) how to coordinate the effort to bring up and debug effectively a very large system, (2) how to define communication links between system components, (3) how to schedule activity among components, and (4) how to combine conflicting scores from different knowledge sources.

11-3 THE SPEECH UNDERSTANDING SYSTEMS

The performance of the final four speech understanding systems, when processing sentences composed from a 1000 word lexicon, is summarized in Table 11-2. Also presented is one measure of the constraint provided by the syntactic and semantic knowledge. The average branching factor is defined here to be the average number of words that would have to be considered at each point along the correct left-to-right path through the syntactic production rules during the processing of a typical utterance. Branching factor has been shown to be a better measure of task difficulty than vocabulary size per se, although other aspects of the grammar and inherent confusability of lexical items contribute to task complexity (Jelinek et al., 1977). Some systems do not process an utterance in a strictly left-to-right manner, but the estimated branching factors are roughly comparable.

Table 11-2. Performance of the speech understanding systems as of November 1, 1976. Statistics are based on more than 100 sentences spoken by several talkers, except for CMU Hearsay-II whose preliminary evaluation employed a smaller data set.

SYSTEM	SENTENCES UNDERSTOOD	AVERAGE BRANCHING FACTOR
CMU Harpy	95%	33
CMU Hearsay-2	91, 74	33, 46
BBN Hwim	44	195
SDC	24	105

Taking account of the range of task difficulties implied in part by the different branching factors, it is unclear whether there are large differences in ability among the top three systems. However, only Carnegie-Mellon University (CMU) was able to meet the ARPA goals. In judging the performance figures given in Table 11-2, it should also be noted that System Development Corporation (SDC) was handicapped by the loss of one of their computers, which prevented them from making use of components being developed jointly with Stanford Research Institute.

The tasks employed by the three system builders are summarized in Table 11-3. Also included is an example of a sentence accepted by the grammar. Each task involves data management of one sort or another. While only questions are given as examples in Table 11-3, each of the systems was also capable of understanding commands and statements of various types.

Table 11-3. Task domains of the four systems and an example of an acceptable input sentence.

Group	Task/Sample sentence
SDC	FACTS ABOUT SHIPS "How fast is the Theodore Roosevelt?"
BBN Hwim	TRAVEL BUDGET MANAGEMENT "What is the plane fare to Ottawa?"
CMU Hearsay II and Harpy	DOCUMENT RETRIEVAL "How many articles on psychology are there?"

11-3.1 Systems Development Corporation

The structure of the final SDC speech understanding system is shown in Fig. 11-2 (Ritea, 1975; Weeks, 1974); Bernstein, 1976). Formant frequencies and other parameters are first extracted from the input waveform. A phonetic transcription is obtained, including several alternative labels for each 10-ms waveform segment, and all of this information is placed in a data array called the A-matrix for later examination by top-end routines.

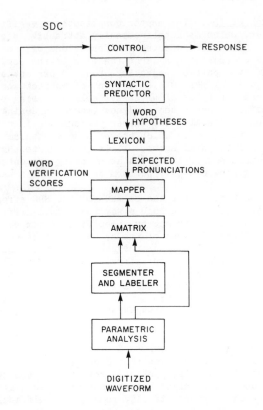

SDC

Fig. 11-2. Block diagram of the SDC system organization.

The utterance is processed from left to right by first generating a list of all possible sentence-initial words. The control box then retrieves an abstract phonemic representation from the lexicon for each lexical hypothesis and computes expected phonetic variants, resulting in a graph of phonetic alternatives. The phonetic graphs are sent, one at a time, to the mapper to see how good an acoustic match is obtained with the current position in the unknown utterance. The mapper is organized according to the syllable structure of a word and it examines the A-matrix in order to determine if the expected vowels and proper allophones of adjacent consonants are present. Since an exact match is unlikely, the mapper includes techniques for estimating the probability that the expected word is present given the phonetic and acoustic data. Performance of the mapper is indicated in Table 11-4.

On the basis of mapper scores, the control box decides which word or partial sentence hypothesis to pursue next, and generates a list of all words that can follow this sentence fragment. A similar "best-first" control strategy was used earlier in the Hearsay I speech understanding system (Reddy,

Erman, and Neely, 1973) and in a system developed at Lincoln Laboratories (Klovstad and Mondshein, 1975). A more detailed description of the SDC system is presented in Chapter 12 and in Klatt (1977).

   Discussion of SDC. The mapper constitutes a verification strategy based on syllables, which is a theoretically attractive design for embedding context-dependent rules for expected manifestations of phonetic segments. The mapper is capable of rejecting a large fraction of the word hypotheses not in the sentence, but at a cost of rejecting about 10 percent of the words actually present. Fatal absolute rejections of correct words occurred either because the mapper lost track of which syllable was being processed or because a phonetic confusion occurred that had not been seen during a prior statistics gathering run. Unfortunately, the mapper performance is not good enough for a top-end system organization in which there is no mechanism for recovering from a single bad lexical matching score. It is unfortunate that SDC had so little time to design a more powerful top end after being prevented from using an SRI module, because a system can only perform as well as its weakest link.

   The main criticism that can be made of the SDC effort is that their system failed its objectives in such a way that it is difficult to say what more restricted goals could be met by a modified system design. Is it simply a matter of shaking the bugs out of the system, or must one place further restrictions on the vocabulary and/or syntax? Or is it that the simple control strategy employed is essentially incapable of performing at an acceptable understanding rate in any moderate sized task because of the nature of speech and the inherent inaccuracies to be expected in any kind of mapper? Answers to these and other questions might have come from a year of system performance evaluation that was planned by the steering committee, but not funded by ARPA.

   An interesting aspect of the SDC system emerged in comparing its performance with an earlier version that did better on an easier task. The earlier system understood 65 percent of a set of test sentences formed from a 200-word lexicon and a more rigid syntax that was devoid of function words. Function words are usually acoustically reduced and difficult to identify. One might speculate that one reason for the poor performance of the more ambitious system was the dependence on function word recognition. Creation of a syntax that perhaps allowed some function words, but in no way depended on their identification to choose a path in the grammar, might be a better strategy for the realization of limited systems. (It is interesting to note that the Harpy grammar is essentially of this form.)

11-3.2 Bolt Beranek and Newman Inc. Hwim

   The general organization of the BBN Hwim (Hear what I mean) system is shown in Fig. 11-3 (Woods et al., 1976). As a first step in the processing of an unknown utterance, formant frequencies and other parameters are extracted from the digitized waveform. This information is used to derive a set of phonetic transcription alternatives that are arranged in a "segment lattice". The advantage claimed for the lattice structure is that it can represent segmentation ambiguity in those cases where decisions are most difficult.

   The identification process begins by searching through the segmental representation of the utterance for good matching words (anywhere in the utterance) that can be used as "seeds" for building up longer partial sentence hypotheses. The best-scoring initial word match is sent to a word verification component which returns to the parametric data to get a quasi-independent measure of the quality of the match. The method of

```
--------------------------------------------------------------------------------
```
Table 11-4. Performance statistics for three word verification components --
the SDC mapper, the BBN verifier, and the CMU Hearsay-II verifier. The last
row indicates that the SDC verifier is presented with lexical hypotheses from
a syntactic module, whereas the BBN and CMU verifiers are preceded by lexical
hypothesizers that screen out all but the best acoustic candidates.

	VERIFICATION DECISION					
LEXICAL PROPOSAL	SDC		BBN		CMU	
	ACCEPT	REJECT	ACCEPT	REJECT	ACCEPT	REJECT
CORRECT WORD	65	6	101	19	312	20
PERCENT	92%	8%	84%	16%	94%	6%
INCORRECT WORD	372	11,253	367	713	6462	6591
PERCENT	3%	97%	34%	66%	49%	51%
WORDS HYPOTH./ CORRECT WORD	165		10		40	
ACOUST. SIMILARITY	RANDOM		BEST 5%		BEST 14%	

```
--------------------------------------------------------------------------------
```

verification is analysis by synthesis (Klatt, 1975). The verification score
is combined with the lexical matching score, and if the combined score is
high, the word hypothesis is then sent to a syntactic predictor component
which proposes words that can appear to the left and to the right of the seed
word, given the grammatical constraints. An augmented transition network
grammar (Woods, 1970) is used to characterize syntactic and semantic
constraints.

Matching scores are obtained for all of these word proposals, using a
lexical decoding network (Klovstad, 1977). The lexical decoding network
contains a representation of the expected phonetic realizations of each word
in all possible phonetic contexts. To derive this network, a set of
phonological rules (Woods and Zue, 1976) first transforms a phonemic lexicon
into phonetic alternatives arranged in a tree structure such that common
initial portions of lexical items are grouped together. Then a second set of
word-boundary phonological rules attaches ends of words back to selected
initial nodes of the tree, creating a network of permissible phonetic strings
for all possible word sequences from the 1000-word lexicon. Similar concepts
were developed earlier at IBM (Tappert, et al., 1973; Tappert, 1975).

For example, the word "list" may be pronounced as [l I s], i.e.
without the [t], in "list some" due to an optional word boundary phonological
rule OPT{s t # s} --> {s}. This fact is captured in the network by creating a
path from the [s] of "list" to all words starting with [s]. In this way, the
network requires that, if "list" is to be recognized without the [t], a word
beginning with [s] must follow. The advantage of such a network
representation of word boundary phonology is that search is rapid and
phonological rule application is restricted only to those word sequences where
it applies; not every [s] in the input need be expanded into [s t # s] to see
if the inverse phonological rule had been applied.

Each word receiving a good score from the lexical decoding network is
combined with the seed word to produce a two-word hypothesis, a verification
score is derived for the new two-word hypothesis and the hypothesis is then

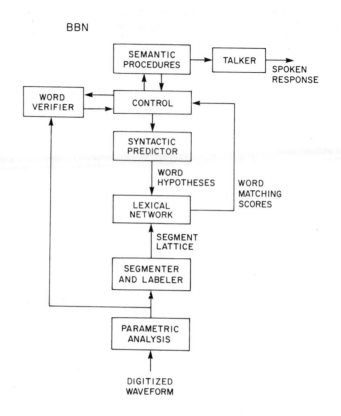

Fig. 11-3. Block diagram of the BBN Hwim system organization.

placed in an "event queue". The best scoring partial sentence hypothesis is always extended next. When a complete sentence is found, a deep structure representation of the word string can be sent to the semantic procedures component in order to compute an appropriate response. The response is spoken over a loudspeaker, using a speech synthesis by rule program. A more detailed description of the system is given in   Chapter 14 and in Klatt (1977).

   Discussion of BBN. The BBN speech understanding system has a task domain with a more general syntax than the other systems, so it is difficult to judge how much better or worse the system design and individual components are. The same criticism applies to BBN that was leveled at SDC: the way in which the demonstration system failed to meet the ARPA goals makes it impossible to determine what more limited task domain might have resulted in acceptable performance. It would be interesting to know, for example, how much of an improvement in certain critical components is needed to achieve acceptable performance, or how much improvement would be gained by restricting the language definition in various ways.

The most interesting ideas to come out of the BBN project were a lexical decoding network incorporating sophisticated phonological rules, the technique of representing segmentation ambiguity by a lattice of alternatives, and the concept of word verification at the parametric level. However the performance of these components individually and as a total system did not seem to live up to their theoretical potential. Because of the slowness of the system, there was apparently not enough effort devoted to debugging and optimizing individual components in a system context. Specific problems that were never resolved were (1) how to ensure that the segment lattice was in fact providing more information than a linear string of best guesses, (2) how to normalize for talker differences, (3) whether sufficient data were analyzed to rely on the probability estimates of various phonetic confusions, extra segments, and missing segments, and (4) whether the system would perform significantly better if it were fast enough to evaluate many more partial sentence fragments.

11-3.3 Carnegie-Mellon University Hearsay-II

The CMU Hearsay-II system organization is shown in Fig. 11-4 (Lesser, et al., 1975; Hayes-Roth and Lesser, 1976, Lesser and Erman, 1977). The recognition process is similar in some respects to that employed in BBN Hwim, although the block diagrams and organizational philosophies are disparate. The CMU system configuration consists of a set of parallel asynchronous processes that simulate each of the component knowledge sources of a speech understanding system. Knowledge sources communicate via a global "blackboard" data base. When activated by the appearance of certain types of new information on the blackboard, a knowledge source tries to extend the analysis.

The information on the blackboard is divided into several major categories: sequences of segment labels, syllables, lexical items proposed, accepted words, and partial phrase theories. A knowledge source accepts information at one level and attempts to provide new information at a higher level (bottom-up analysis) or lower level (top-down prediction and verification).

Initially, amplitude and zero-crossing parameters are used to divide an utterance into segments that are categorized by manner-of-articulation features (Goldberg and Reddy, 1976). Good performance is obtained by avoiding the more difficult place-of-articulation decisions in the preliminary analysis.

A word hypothesizer lists all words having a syllable structure compatible with the partial phonetic representation. For example, there might be ten lexical items that are consistent with a fricative-stop-vowel-stop pattern, three items consistent with a fricative-stop-vowel sub-pattern, and five more items consistent with a stop-vowel sub-pattern. The performance of the lexical hypothesizer is such that only about 70 percent of the correct words are detected (Smith, 1976), but others are found by top-down prediction at a later stage.

A word verification component scores each lexical hypothesis by comparing an expected sequence of spectra with observed linear-prediction spectra. The lexicon used for verification is adapted from Harpy and thus is defined in terms of expected spectral patterns instead of expected phonetic patterns. Coarticulation across word boundaries is a problem using this approach, but some word-boundary acoustic rules are included. Performance of the verification component is indicated in Table 11-4.

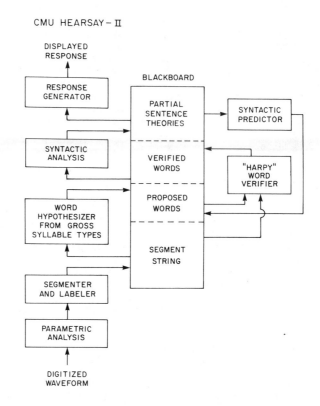

Fig. 11-4. A block diagram of the CMU Hearsay-II system organization.

High-scoring words activate a syntactic component which tries to put words together into partial sentence theories. Grammatically acceptable adjacent words are also predicted since the word hypothesizer is not expected to get all of the words of the sentence. The control strategy is similar to that used by BBN in that best-scoring words or sentence-fragment pieces are sought anywhere in the utterance and extended to the left and/or to the right. CMU obtained significantly better performance with an island-driven strategy than BBN, but it is argued below that the Harpy left-to-right control strategy has advantages over any middle-out strategy. Once a complete sentence has been found, a response could be computed by accessing a data base. A more detailed description of the system is presented in Chapter 16 and in Klatt (1977).

Discussion of CMU Hearsay-II. Hearsay-II exhibited the best performance of the systems other than Harpy. Since it is not at all clear that Hearsay-II used components having better absolute performance, it is of interest to speculate on those aspects of the overall system design that account for its superior behavior. There are three essential reasons in my view: (1) as in the BBN system, absolute decisions (e.g. to reject a word hypothesis) were avoided by assigning graded scores so that component errors were not necessarily fatal, (2) computational efficiency issues were always of primary concern so that more alternatives could be considered, and (3) syntactic complexity (i.e. the average number of words to be considered to the right of any correct word) was directly controlled and reduced to a point where the system performance was acceptable. The use of strong syntactic and semantic constraints was encouraged by the ARPA goal structure, and should be utilized in future practical systems to improve performance.

11-3.4 Carnegie-Mellon University Harpy

The Harpy system, as implemented by Lowerre (1976), is shown in Fig. 11-5. The system includes a network of 15,000 states. Embedded in the state transition network are (1) all possible paths through the finite state grammar (i.e. a graph representation of all possible sentences), (2) alternate representations of all lexical items in terms of acoustic segments, and (3) a set of rules describing expected changes to acoustic segment sequences across word boundaries. The set of word-boundary rules, lexical representations, and grammar equations are automatically compiled into the efficient network representation shown in the figure.

The input utterance is divided into brief roughly stationary acoustic segments. Each segment is compared with 98 talker-specific linear-prediction spectral templates to obtain a set of 98 spectral distances, using the minimum residual error metric (Itakura, 1975). Template selection for a new talker is automatic, but requires that the user read about 20 selected sentences. More recently, the system has been run in a mode where it begins with an average speaker-independent set of templates and adapts dynamically to the characteristics of the current talker (Lowerre, 1977). Initial performance is down about 10 percent, but recovery seems rapid, making this technique a powerful new method of talker normalization.

Each state in the network has an associated spectral template. The decoding strategy is to try to find the best scoring path through the state transition network by comparing the distance between the observed spectra and template sequences given in the network. Generally a state can accept a sequence of several sufficiently similar input segments, although some states are constrained so as to grab a specified minimum or maximum duration of the input. Thus the time dimension is only loosely constrained in the matching process, and the best possible time alignment is usually obtained.

Harpy is an extension of a Markov model of sentence decoding originally employed by Baker (1974) in a sentence recognition system called Dragon. In Dragon, a "breadth-first" dynamic programming strategy was used to find the optimal path through a network, but in the Harpy implementation a "beam-search" technique is used in which a restricted beam of near-miss alternatives around the best-scoring path are considered, thus reducing the search time significantly. Dragon also used a priori probabilities in choosing the most likely path through the network, while Harpy considers only spectral distance. A more detailed description of the CMU Harpy system is presented in Chapter 15 and in Klatt (1977).

Discussion of CMU Harpy. Harpy and its predecessor Dragon represent a significant breakthrough in the application of simple structured models to speech recognition. It might seem to someone versed in the intricacies of phonology and the acoustic-phonetic characteristics of speech that a search of a graph of expected acoustic segments is a naive and foolish technique to use to decode a sentence. In fact such a graph and search strategy (and probably

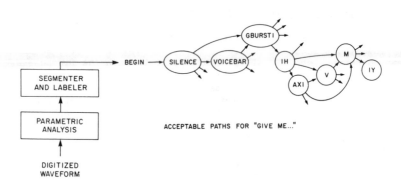

HARPY NETWORK FROM
 — LEXICAL REPRESENTATIONS
 —SYNTACTIC PRODUCTION RULES
 —WORD BOUNDARY RULES

ACCEPTABLE PATHS FOR "GIVE ME..."

SEGMENTER AND LABELER

PARAMETRIC ANALYSIS

DIGITIZED WAVEFORM

Fig. 11-5. A block diagram of the CMU Harpy system organization. Shown is a small (hypothetical) fragment of the Harpy state transition network, including paths accepted for sentences beginning with "Give me". Each node is named by the expected linear-prediction spectrum pattern. In general, many paths leave each node, corresponding to other possible sentence-initial words. A finite set of about 10**8 sentences (of length up to 8 words drawn from a 1011 word lexicon) can be recognized by the 15,000 state Harpy network.

a number of other simple models) can be constructed and made to work very well indeed if the proper acoustic-phonetic details are embodied in the structure. The keys to success seem to me to be (1) the way that important structural aspects of language and speech can be folded into an initial network structure, (2) the possibility of optimizing the network and the spectral templates using a very large body of training utterances, and (3) imposition of strong syntactic constraints.

Harpy is essentially a verification strategy. All alternative sentences are specified by the network, and the task is to verify which sequence of spectral states (path through the network) corresponds to the input sequence of spectra. It has been argued elsewhere (Klatt and Stevens, 1973) that verification of expected acoustic patterns for words is an easier task than phonetic analysis due to the inherent ambiguity of acoustic-phonetic decoding rules. To the extent that phonologists are better able to write generative than analytic rules to describe speech, the advantages of verification strategies will remain.

Due to syntactic constraints, the Harpy network is not particularly dense, so that minimal acoustic-phonetic distinctions are rarely required to distinguish between utterances. The present spectral sequence network may be capable of distinguishing minimal pairs of words quite well, but there is no direct evidence that it can, and some reason to doubt its detailed phonetic abilities given only 98 templates and limited word-boundary acoustic-phonetic rules. Even when syntactic constraints have been applied and the correct sentence has been identified, only 40% of the time does the top-scoring template match the expected template for each state in the best-scoring path through the network. If the templates were analogous to phonetic segments (which is roughly true for consonants in the current implementation, but not as true for vowels) this statistic would imply a less than 40% phonetic transcription performance in the absence of syntactic constraints, which is worse than in any of the other systems. However, there seems to be no fundamental limit to the ultimate transcription performance ability of Harpy-like networks if the lexical representations and word-boundary rules are sufficiently detailed.

The grammar on which Harpy and Hearsay-II were demonstrated was actually a member of a set of related grammars manifesting different branching factors and thus a range of task difficulties. One of the reasons for CMU's success was the ability to manipulate branching factor and observe changes to performance. This was a significant achievement given the ARPA objectives. Unfortunately, within the set of branching factors investigated, excellent performance was achieved only by using a rather low branching factor grammar, i.e. one that constrained acceptable sentences so that just two large syntactic classes were allowed: topics, and authors. Test sentences were always constrained so that at least one of these two classes appeared in each test sentence.

There clearly exist tasks for which a Harpy-like network would appear to be applicable (e.g. connected digit recognition or even perhaps air traffic control, but the languages for such applications will have to be fairly artificial and not a so-called "habitable subset of English" (Watt, 1968). Still the job of creating a Harpy system for a new task domain is not simple; it took careful analysis of 747 sentences to achieve the present level of Harpy performance on this particular 1000-word lexicon.

11-3.5 Other ARPA-Funded Speech Understanding Research

The ARPA project included a number of supporting efforts that were important to the task of creating the four large speech understanding systems just described. In this overview, we have emphasized the systems, but a brief mention of the activities of the other contractors is provided in the paragraphs below.

Lincoln Laboratory. Researchers at M.I.T. Lincoln Laboratory spent considerable effort on the development of phonetic recognition strategies (Weinstein et al., 1975). Techniques included formant tracking and the use of formant transition information for stop place-of-articulation categorization. The performance and documentation of these strategies was probably the best of the initial system builders at the time when funds were re-allocated from 5 to the 3 research groups showing promise of putting together the best total systems. Lincoln staff also developed a lexical network representation (Klovstad and Mondshein, 1975) that later evolved into the BBN lexical decoding network.

Stanford Research Institute. When a planned joint SDC/SRI system development program was no longer possible, Stanford Research Institute staff were forced to carry out their development and testing of system components and strategies using a simple simulation of the behavior of a SDC mapper for word verification. Simulation proved to be a valuable technique for optimizing several system design choices concerning speed/accuracy trade-offs, without the added run-time cost of using the actual mapper (Paxton, 1976; 1977). The results of the simulations were used, for example, to specify the performance required from the mapper for a given vocabulary size in order to obtain 90 percent sentence understanding, using a language definition that allows fairly general syntactic constructions, an independent semantic component, and capabilities for anaphoric references and ellipsis in processing sequential items in a dialogue (Walker, 1976).

Special Contractors. As part of the overall research and development plan, funds were allocated to several research groups to provide support in the area of acoustic-phonetic analysis. The research contributions of the special smaller contractors have not been discussed in this review. However, significant work was performed toward the development of phonological/phonetic rules for the description of spoken English sentences (Oshika et al., 1975), prosodic decoding rules (Lea et al., 1975), acoustic-phonetic recognition strategies (Mermelstein, 1975a; 1975b), and evaluation of the complexity of the grammars employed in the four systems (O'Malley, unpublished).

11-4 DISCUSSION AND CONCLUSIONS

System Organization. The structures of Harpy and Dragon represent a significant improvement in the realization of sentence verification procedures. System organization is immensely simplified by precompiling disparate knowledge into a uniform network representation at the spectrum level. A second new organizational concept comes from Hearsay-II and involves creation of a set of parallel asynchronous processes that communicate via a blackboard. As a conceptual model, the approach may be applicable in other problem solving domains.

Grammar Design. The ability to manipulate grammatical complexity and observe changes to system performance as the task is simplified was an important factor in the success of CMU. The shift of attention from size of the lexicon to effective grammatical branching factor is an important advance in the quantification of task difficulty from the original ARPA goal of a 1000-word lexicon. It means that a difficult problem can be made easier by reducing the apparent size of the lexicon. What is needed now are techniques to reduce grammatical complexity while maintaining task objectives and retaining language habitability.

Better measures of task difficulty are also needed. One promising proposal is to apply entropy concepts to the grammar (Jelinek et al., 1977). Using this kind of measure, the "perplexity" (akin to the effective average branching factor) of the Harpy grammar is estimated to be less than 10 words.

Control Strategy. Control strategies that work from the middle out, starting with a good-matching content word utilize less syntactic constraint and have been found to cost a great deal more in complexity and computation time than strategies based on strict left-to-right processing through an utterance. If phonological rules handle function word variability well, then a strict left-to-right strategy with a breadth-of-search capability, as in Harpy, seems to be the best choice.

Semantics and Context. Most semantic constraints employed by these systems are realized within the syntactic production rules. BBN Hwim contained a separate semantics module, but it was not used very much during sentence recognition. None of the four systems were able to use prior discourse information to reject a sentence such as "What is their registration fee?" because there was no assignable referent for "their". However, earlier, Hearsay-I (Reddy et al., 1973) contained a chess-playing program that checked requested moves for plausibility.

Syntax. It is likely that almost any parser structure will do for simple speech understanding tasks in which all that is required is an enumeration of the possible lexical items following a given sentence fragment. In fact, the best solution for a finite grammar is very likely to precompile a list of the permissible word sequences into a network, as is done in Harpy.

The speech understanding project has benefited from prior work on the automatic parsing (syntactic analysis) of written sentences. Powerful mechanisms such as an augmented transition network grammar and parser (Woods, 1970) have already been developed for processing word strings from left to right. While many grammar formulations could be considered, the augmented transition network grammar has the advantages of permitting semantic constraints to be written into the grammar and allowing many alternative parses to be computed efficiently in parallel (Woods, 1970). The grammar also includes simple methods for searching most-likely structures first and can produce structural representations that are ideal input for semantic processing routines involved in response generation.

Prosody. Prosodic cues (fundamental frequency, segmental duration, and the intensity contour) suggest a stress pattern for the incoming syllable string, and thus could assist in lexical hypothesization. Prosodic cues also indicate clause boundaries, phrase boundaries, and, to a minor extent, word boundaries. While relatively little use was made of prosodic information in the four speech understanding systems, some ideas for prosodic analysis were proposed (Lea, Medress, and Skinner, 1975).

Word Identification/Verification. Each word or morpheme of the lexicon has been specified at a fairly abstract phonemic level in several of the systems. This makes lexical development and augmentation much easier than if all possible detailed phonetic or acoustic forms must be listed. Phonological rules that operate within words and/or across word boundaries are used to expand the lexicon into multiple representations. Phonology seems to have come of age over the past few years in that formal rules of considerable predictive power have been developed. As a starting point the morphological expansions and phonological rules of Zue (Woods et al., Vol. 3, 57-72, 1976) might be used. Additional more general rules are to be found in the work of Cohen and Mercer (1975) and Oshika et al. (1975).

The potential role of the syllable in lexical verification was elaborated by SDC, who suggested that allophonic variations can be predicted in a relatively straight-forward way if one begins verification at a syllable peak and then looks for acoustic evidence of adjacent consonants that are expected. The advantages of the syllable as a recognition unit are less clear. It might be argued that the dyad (Peterson, Wang and Sivertson, 1958), an interval from the middle of one phonetic segment to the middle of the next segment, is a unit having about the same theoretical advantages. There are far fewer dyad types than syllable types in English. Silverman and Dixon (1976) have employed the dyad as a recognition unit with good success for a single talker. The diad has been termed a "diphone" when used as a building block for speech synthesis (Dixon and Maxey, 1968).

Word identification in sentence contexts is possible only if the effects of phonetic/phonological recoding at word boundaries can be decoded. This requires that the phonological encoding rules be known, and that computational procedures be available for applying the inverse rules rapidly

and selectively. To take the example of the rule [s t # s] --> [s] as in
"list some , it would be costly to test every [s] in an utterance for a
possible underlying [s t # s], especially considering the number of
word-boundary rules that would have to be treated in this way. The solution
that comes from the BBN system is to incorporate word boundary phonology into
the stored lexical representations by first constructing a lexical tree of
expected phonetic sequences, and then transforming the tree into a network of
permitted phonetic sequences for all possible word sequences.

    Acoustic-Phonetic Processing. An advance in the area of
acoustic-phonetic processing has been the realization that phonetic
segmentation and labeling is not necessary to word identification in connected
speech. The Harpy philosophy of representing words by sequences of spectral
templates in a network that takes into account word boundary phonology shows
great promise.

    The actual spectral representation (linear prediction spectral
analysis) used in Harpy and the spectral distance measure (the minimum
residual error) used are computationally very efficient, but probably not
optimal and not related very closely to perceptual distance. For example, the
metric does not incorporate overall spectral intensity and may therefore
confuse a silence spectrum with some speech sound having a similar spectral
shape. Also Harpy used only 98 templates to represent the entire inventory of
spectral variations in speech. The excellent performance of Harpy may mean
that the details of spectral representations and distance measures are not
critical. On the other hand, perhaps even better performance in harder task
domains is possible within the Harpy framework by using improved metrics.

    Comparison of the general performance of the phonetic analysis
components of the SDC, BBN, and CMU Hearsay-II systems in phonetic labeling
with for example, Silverman and Dixon (1976), (Weinstein et al., 1975), and
earlier work suggests that the contribution of the ARPA project to improved
phonetic recognition strategies is not in proportion to the level of effort
expended. Schwartz and Cook (1977) have recently attained 67% correct
phonetic transcription capabilities using 71 phonetic categories in a phonetic
vocoder application, but their system is not well documented. There is a
clear need for continued work in this area.

    Shockey and Reddy (1975) discovered that linguists are actually not
very consistent at phonetic transcription if the language is unfamiliar. From
their data, they speculate that machines should not be expected to be better
than 60 to 70 percent accurate in producing a phonetic transcription. We
believe that their results may be a reasonable test of the current status of a
universal phonetic theory, but they do not measure transcription abilities of
listeners who are permitted to make use of the phonetic and phonological
constraints of English. Recent experiments by Mark Liberman and Lloyd
Nakatani (personal communication) suggest that listeners can transcribe
English nonsense names embedded in sentences (and obeying the phonological
constraints of English) with about 90 percent phonemic accuracy. It is likely
that machine performance must approach this figure before very powerful speech
understanding systems are realized. Alternatively, perhaps the best bet is
not to do phonetic labeling at all, as in Harpy.

    Use of Statistics. Jelinek (1976) argues for the use of decision
strategies that are based on the collection of an appropriate set of
probabilities determined experimentally. Several of the speech understanding
systems used estimates of the probability of a phonetic or lexical decision
given the acoustic data in scoring the goodness of a theory, and each seems to
have gotten into trouble by so doing. The intelligent deployment of

266

statistical procedures is highly desirable, but the problem is to analyze enough data to be sure of the probability of infrequent confusions. This is nearly impossible if one wants to take into consideration factors such as phonetic environment.

Acoustic Analysis. It is now known that the important information-bearing elements of the speech code are contained in the magnitude spectrum of speech, i.e. in a sequence of well-chosen short-term spectra. Linear prediction spectra have proven to be a robust spectral representation having the additional advantages of being a pleasing visual idealization of speech, of having an existing simple metric for spectral comparisons, and of permitting the estimation of formant frequencies. On the other hand, it appears that filter banks designed carefully to take into account critical bands and other psychophysical constraints are equally useful as spectral representations (Klatt, 1976b).

Talker Normalization. A surprisingly powerful method of talker normalization is incorporated in the Harpy system. About twenty known sentences are processed to derive talker-specific spectral templates automatically. These templates are capable of capturing a wide range of talker characteristics including important differences between men and women. Other "dynamic" talker-specific characteristics such as differences in dialect are best overcome for the present by restricting system usage to talkers of a single fairly uniform dialect.

Response Generation. The BBN Hwim system and CMU Hearsay-II included a data base and response generator (although these components were not usually connected during a recognition demonstration). In this sense, a distinction between speech understanding (is the response correct?) and speech recognition (are all of the words correct?) was realized. Cases where a correct response would be generated in spite of lexical identification errors were fairly frequent in Hearsay-II. To that extent, the systems described here represent the beginnings of true machine understanding of spoken language.

To generate a proper response, one must solve an information retrieval problem, choose an appropriate frame sentence for a response, and synthesize an audio output. Some progress in general solutions to these problems was achieved at BBN (Woods, et al., 1976; Klatt, 1976a).

Future Research. The key to improved bottom-end performance (lexical hypothesization) in future speech understanding systems, it seems to me, is the transformation of a phonetic identification problem into a spectral state verification problem, as was done in Harpy. Phonetic representations for words of the lexicon are replaced by sequences of expected spectra and some durational constraints. This translation problem is non-trivial and required many trial-and-error iterations during Harpy development. The availability of a list of expected template sequences for all possible phonetic strings of English would considerably aid in bringing up new lexicons. The main objective of future research in this area should therefore be the accumulation of more detailed linguistic and acoustic-phonetic facts about English.

Future research on top-end design might focus on the imposition of realistic semantic and task constraints and on computational efficiencies that will ultimately permit the use of more general grammars. Another worthwhile pursuit might be to interface a Harpy-like lexical recognition network (Klatt, 1978) to a top end with a non-finite grammar.

Additional research will be required to build a practical speech understanding system that has a complete human-engineered interactive capability. Problem areas in need of further work include the design of habitable languages, how to monitor the input to know when a signal is present (Rabiner and Sambur, 1975), including rejecting "umm's" and breath noise (Martin, 1975), how to know when an utterance is complete, whether it will be necessary for a user to see a display of the request and give a "yes"-"no" response, etc.

The steering committee prepared a follow-on research plan (Newell et al., 1975) that took up a number of these issues and also proposed that the four speech understanding systems not be allowed to die. They argued that the systems required substantial additional debugging and tuning before reaching their full potential and that experiments were needed to better understand their capabilities and limitations. The committee proposed that the systems ought to be preserved as a resource for use by a wider community because considerable scientific insight might be gained from widespread experimentation with these systems. Based on the current funding picture, it appears that none of these recommendations will come to pass.

As a final note, we may ask "How hard is the sentence understanding problem in the limited contexts investigated during the ARPA project?". In 1970, when compared with isolated word recognition, the problems seemed immense. After the limited success of Harpy, one becomes more optimistic about the abilities of future systems. Still, the nature of the problem is elusive. Even the dimensions of task difficulty have yet to be adequately defined. Limited experience suggests that significant increases in difficulty are associated with increased grammar branching factor (caused by increased lexical size or increased syntactic freedom), the inherent acoustic ambiguity of words that must be distinguished, and the importance of unstressed function word recognition to sentence decoding. If these factors can be controlled in a particular task domain, speech understanding by machines is now a practical goal.

References

Bahl, L., J. Baker, P. Cohen, N. Dixon, F. Jelinek, R. Mercer and H. Silverman (1976), "Preliminary results on the Performance of a System for the Automatic Recognition of Continuous Speech", 425-429 in Teacher (1976).

Baker, J. (1975), "The Dragon System -- An Overview", IEEE Trans. Acoustics, Speech, and Signal Processing ASSP-23, 24-29.

Bates, M. (1975), "The Use of Syntax in a Speech Understanding System", IEEE Trans. Acoust., Speech, and Signal Proc. ASSP-23, 112-117.

Bernstein, M.I. (1976), "Interactive Systems Research: Final Report to the Director, Advanced Research Projects Agency", System Development Corporation, Santa Monica, CA, Report No. TM-5243/006/00.

Cohen, P.S. and R.L. Mercer (1975), "The Phonological Component of an Automatic Speech Recognition System", 275-320 in Reddy (1975).

De Mori, R., S. Rivoira, and A. Serra (1975), "A Speech Understanding System with Learning Capability", Proc. 4th Int. Joint Conf. Artificial Intelligence, Tbilisi, USSR.

Dixon, N.R. and H.D. Maxey (1968), "Terminal Analog Speech Synthesis of Continuous Speech Using the Diphone Method of Segment Assembly", IEEE Trans. Audio and Electroacoust. AU-16, 40-50.

Erman, L.D., (Ed.) (1974), Contributed Papers of the IEEE Symposium on Speech Recognition, (IEEE Catalog No. 74CHO878-9 AE).

Fant, G. (1970), "Automatic Recognition and Speech Research", Quart. Prog. and Status Rep. QPSR-1, Speech Transmission Labs., KTH, Stockholm, Sweden, 16-31.

Fant, G., (Ed.) (1975), Proc. Stockholm Speech Communications Seminar, Almqvist and Wiksell (Stockholm) and Wiley (New York).

Goldberg, H.G. and Reddy (1976), "Feature Extraction, Segmentation and Labeling in the Harpy and Hearsay-II Systems", J. Acoust. Soc. Am. 60, S11 (A).

Haton, J.-P., and J.-M. Pierrel (1976), "Organization and Operation of a Connected Speech Understanding System at Lexical, Syntactic and Semantic Levels", 430-433 in Teacher (1976).

Hayes-Roth, F. and V.R. Lesser (1976), "Focus of Attention in a Distributed-Logic Speech Understanding System", 416-420 in Teacher (1976).

Hyde, S.R. (1972), "Automatic Speech Recognition: A Critical Survey and Discussion of the Literature", in E.E. David and P.B. Denes, (Eds.), Human Communication: A Unified View, McGraw-Hill.

Itakura, F. (1975), "Minimum Prediction Residual Principle Applied to Speech Recognition", IEEE Trans. Acoustics, Speech, and Signal Processing ASSP-23, 67-72.

Jelinek, F. (1976), "Continuous Speech Recognition by Statistical Methods", Proc. IEEE 64, 532-556.

Jelinek, F. Mercer, R.L., Bahl, L.R., and Baker, J.K. (1977), "Perplexity -- A Measure of the Difficulty of Speech Recognition Tasks", J. Acoust. Soc. Am. 62, Supplement 1, p. 63 (A).

Klatt, D.H. (1975), "Word Verification in a Speech Understanding System", 321-341 in Reddy (1975).

Klatt, D.H. (1976a), "Structure of a Phonological Rule Component for a Synthesis-by-Rule Program", IEEE Trans. Acoustics, Speech, and Signal Processing ASSP-24, 391-398.

Klatt, D.H. (1976b), "A Digital Filter Bank for Spectral Matching", 537-540 in Teacher (1976).

Klatt, D.H. (1977), "Review of the ARPA Speech Understanding Project", J. Acoust. Soc. Am. 62, 1345-1366.

Klatt, D.H. (1978), "Speech Perception: A New Look at the Problem of Lexical Access", in The Carnegie Symposium on Speech Perception, R. Cole (Ed.), Erlbaum.

Klatt, D.H. and K.N. Stevens (1973), "On the Automatic Recognition of Continuous Speech: Implications of a Spectrogram-Reading Experiment", IEEE Trans. Audio and Electroacoust. AU-21, 210-217.

Klovstad, J.W. (1977), "Computer-Automated Speech Perception System", Ph.D. thesis, MIT.

Klovstad, J. W. and L.F. Mondshein (1975), "The CASPERS Linguistic Analysis System", IEEE Trans. Acoustics, Speech, and Signal Processing ASSP-23, 18-123.

Lea, W.A., M.F. Medress, and T.E. Skinner (1975), "A Prosodically Guided Speech Understanding System", IEEE Trans. Acoustics, Speech, and Signal Processing ASSP-23, 30-38.

Lesser, V.R., R.D. Fennell, L.D. Erman, and D.R. Reddy (1975), "Organization of the Hearsay-II Speech Understanding System", IEEE Trans. Acoustics, Speech, and Signal Processing ASSP-23, 11-23.

Lesser, V.R. and L.D. Erman (in press), "A Retrospective View of the Hearsay-II Architecture", IJCAI-77.

Liberman, A.M., F.S. Cooper, D.S. Shankweiler, and M. Studdert-Kennedy (1967), "Perception of the Speech Code", Psych. Review 74, 431-461.

Lindgren, N. (1965), "Machine Recognition of Human Language", IEEE Spectrum 2, Mar., Apr., May,.

Lowerre, B.T. (1976), The Harpy Speech Recognition System, Ph.D. Thesis, Dept. of Computer Science, Carnegie-Mellon Univ., Pittsburgh, PA 15213.

Lowerre, B.T. (1977), "Dynamic Speaker Adaptation in the Harpy Speech Recognition System", 788-790 in Silverman (1977).

Martin, T.B. (1975), Applications of Limited Vocabulary Recognition Systems", 55-71 in Reddy (1975).

Medress, M.F., T.E. Skinner, D.R. Kloker, T.C. Diller, and W.A. Lea (1977), "A System for Recognition of Spoken Connected Word Sequences", 468-473 in Silverman (1977).

Mermelstein, P. (1975a), "A Phonetic-Context Controlled Strategy for Segmentation and Phonetic Labeling of Speech", IEEE Trans. Acoustics, Speech, and Signal Processing ASSP-23, 79-82.

Mermelstein, P. (1975b), "Automatic Segmentation of Speech into Syllable Units", J. Acoust. Soc. Am. 58, 880-883.

Newell, A., J. Barnett, J.W. Forgie, C.C. Green, D.H. Klatt, J.C.R. Licklider, J. Munson, D.R. Reddy, W.A. Woods (1973), Speech Understanding Systems: Final Report of a Study Group, North-Holland/American Elsevier.

Newell, A., F.S. Cooper, J.W. Forgie, C.C. Green, D.H. Klatt, M.F. Medress, E.P. Neuburg, M.H. O'Malley, D.R. Reddy, B. Ritea, J.E. Shoup-Hummel, D.E. Walker, and W.A. Woods (1975), Considerations for a Follow-on ARPA Research Program for Speech Understanding Systems, August, 1975, available from Computer Science Department, Carnegie-Mellon University, Pittsburgh, PA. 15213.

O'Malley, M.H. (1975), "The Children of Lunar: An Exercise in Comparative Grammar", unpublished.

Oshika, B., V.W. Zue, R.V. Weeks, H. Nue, and J. Aurbach (1975), "The Role of Phonological Rules in Speech Understanding Research", IEEE Trans. Acoustics, Speech, and Signal Processing ASSP-23, 104-112.

Paxton, W.H. (1977), A Framework for Speech Understanding, Stanford University Ph.D. dissertation.

Paxton, W.H. (1976), "Experiments in Speech Understanding System Control", Artificial Intelligence Center Technical Note 134, Stanford Research Institute Project 4762, Menlo Park, CA.

Peterson, G., W. Wang, and E. Sivertsen (1958), "Segmentation Techniques in Speech Synthesis", J. Acoust. Soc. Am. 30, 739-742.

Pierce, J.R. (1969), "Whither Speech Recognition", J. Acoust. Soc. Am. 46, 1049-1051.

Rabiner, L.R. and M.R. Sambur (1975), "An Algorithm for Determining the Endpoints of Isolated Utterances", Bell Syst. Tech. J. 54 297-315.

Reddy, D.R. (1975), Speech Recognition: Invited Papers Presented at the 1974 IEEE Symposium, Academic Press.

Reddy, D.R. (1976), "Speech Recognition by Machine: A Review", Proc. IEEE 64, 501-531.

Reddy,D.R., L.D. Erman, and R.B. Neely (1973), "A Model and a System for Machine Recognition of Speech", IEEE Trans. AU-21, 229-238.

Ritea B. (1975), "Automatic Speech Understanding Systems", Proc. 11th IEEE Computer Society Conf., 319-322, Washington, D.C., (1975).

Sakai, T. and S. Nakagawa (1975), "Continuous Speech Understanding System LITHAN", Tech. Report, Dept. Information Science, Kyoto Univ., Kyoto Japan.

Schwartz, R.M. and Cook, C.C. (1977), "Advanced Acoustic Techniques in Automatic Speech Understanding", in Silverman (1977), 663-666.

Shockey, L. and D.R. Reddy (1975), "Quantitative Analysis of Speech Perception", paper presented at the Stockholm Speech Communications Seminar.

Silverman, H.F. (Chairman) (1977), "Conference Record of the 1977 IEEE International Conference on Acoustics, Speech and Signal Processing", Hartford, May 9-11, 1977, IEEE Catalog No. 77CH1197-3 ASSP.

Silverman, H.F. and N.R. Dixon (1976), "The 1976 Modular Acoustic Processor (MAP): Diadic Segment Classification and Final Phoneme String Estimation", 15-20 in Teacher (1976).

Smith, A.R. (1976), "Word Hypothesization in the Hearsay-II Speech Understanding System", 549-552 in Teacher.

Tappert, C.C. (1975), "Experiments with a Tree-Search Method for Converting Noisy Phonetic Representations into Standard Orthography", IEEE Trans. Acoustics Speech and Signal Processing ASSP-23, 129-135.

Tappert, C.C., N.R. Dixon, and A.S. Rabinowitz (1973), "Application of
Sequential Decoding for Converting Phonetic to Graphic Representation in
Automatic Speech Recognition of Continuous Speech (ARCS)", IEEE
Trans. Audio Electroacoust. AU-21, 225-228.

Teacher, C., (Chairman) (1976), Conference Record of the 1976 IEEE
International Conference on Acoustics Speech and Signal Processing,
Philadelphia, PA., April 12-14, 1976, (IEEE Catalog No. 76CH1067-8 ASSP).

Walker, D.E. (Ed.) (1976), "Speech Understanding Research: Final Technical
Report", Stanford Research Institute, Menlo Park, CA.

Watt, W.C. (1968), "Habitability", American Documentation 19, 338-351.

Weeks, R.V. (1974), "Predictive Syllable Mapping in a Continuous Speech
Understanding System", 154-158 in Erman (1974).

Weinstein, C.J., S.S. McCandless, L.F. Mondshein, and V.W. Zue (1975), "A
System for Acoustic-Phonetic Analysis of Continuous Speech", IEEE
Trans. Acoustics Speech and Signal Processing ASSP-23, 54-67.

Wolf, J.J. (1976), "Speech Recognition and Understanding", in Digital Pattern
Recognition, K.S. Fu, (Ed.), Springer-Verlag.

Woods, W.A. (1970), "Transition Network Grammars for Natural Language
Analysis", Commun. Ass. Comput. Mach. 13, 591-602.

Woods, W.A. and V. Zue (1976), "Dictionary Expansion via Phonological Rules
for a Speech Understanding System", 561-564 in Teacher (1976).

Woods, W., M. Bates, G. Brown, B. Bruce, C. Cook, J. Klovstad, J. Makhoul,
B. Nash-Webber, R. Schwartz, J. Wolf, and V. Zue (1976), "Speech
Understanding Systems: Final Technical Progress Report", Bolt Beranek and
Newman, Inc. Report No. 3438, Cambridge, Mass. (in 5 volumes).

THE SDC SPEECH UNDERSTANDING SYSTEM

Jeffrey A. Barnett
Morton I. Bernstein
Richard A. Gillmann
Iris M. Kameny
System Development Corporation

12-1. INTRODUCTION

SDC's involvement with the ARPA Speech Understanding Research (SUR) Program began in 1969 with our participation in the ARPA Speech Understanding Systems Study Group. In 1971, SDC became one of the five original Speech Understanding System contractors. During the ensuing years, SDC developed a variety of components, techniques and experimental speech understanding systems. Only the final system is presented in summary here. Those interested in greater detail about the systems structure, its components, testing and results are referred to Bernstein, 1976, which also contains references to much of the prior work.

SDC's approach, along with all of the other ARPA SUR system contractors, was primarily guided by the goals and objectives set forth by the Study Group in 1971 (Newell, 1973). In addition to attempting to meet this set of specifications, SDC was guided by other considerations. Among these were that the system should operate as efficiently (and rapidly) as possible on present-day computers, be able to handle a complex grammar with few constraints, accommodate a 1,000 word vocabulary (not counting regular declensions and pluralizations) in a symbolically constructed lexicon (that is, a lexicon constructed from regular phonetic spelling by phonological rules as opposed to construction by user training), and last but not least, that each component and the total system be thoroughly tested (within the limitations of the available resources).

We believe that the ARPA SUR Program collectively, and the SDC SUR project in particular have significantly advanced the state of the art and the body of scientific and technological knowledge in several areas: (1) signal processing of acoustic data, in terms of both parameter extraction and pattern recognition and classification, (2) phonology, in terms of identifying and applying phonological rules, (3) new techniques for symbolic pattern matching, as exemplified in the lexical matching procedure, and (4) new concepts and techniques in the design, construction, and control of very large and complex computer systems.

12-2. SYSTEM CONFIGURATION--AN OVERVIEW

The system comprises the three major components shown in Figure 12-1. The acoustic-phonetic processor extracts parameters and features from the incoming speech signal and produces an array of acoustic-phonetic data, called the A-matrix, which is the only representation of the input used by the rest of the system. The mapper receives hypotheses in the form of questions from the

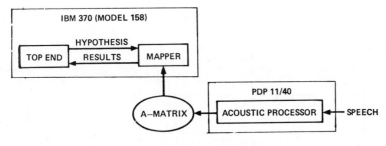

Figure 12-1. System Configuration

top end, such as "Is the word 'submarine' present at approximately five
hundred milliseconds into the utterance?" The mapper compares the request
with the contents of the A-matrix and returns a merit score reflecting the
possibility that the question should be answered affirmatively. The top end
uses the mapper's responses to guide its search in parsing the utterance.

12-2.1 The Acoustic-Phonetic Processor
   The acoustic-phonetic processor (AP) accepts, digitizes, and records the
speech input in real time. Subsequent processing in non-real time generates
parametric information in the A-matrix, which contains information for each
centisecond of input speech. Figure 12-2 shows the various AP components.

   After being passed through a low-pass filter, input speech is digitized
at the rate of 20,000 samples per second by a 12-bit analog-to-digital converter. The system presently operates consistently only on recordings made
in a quiet room by a high-quality microphone. (Some limited experiments
have been performed using telephone speech, but no accurate estimate is available of performance degradation.) Below is a brief overview of the AP; a
more detailed account is available in Bernstein, 1975. Many of the techniques used are described in more detail in papers published elsewhere.

   The first task performed by the AP after recording is to compute a pitch
track (F0) (Gillmann, 1975). The pitch tracker operates in three phases:
(1) a digital filter is used to down-sample the recorded speech from 20,000
to 2,000 samples per second, (2) the peaks are picked from an autocorrelation
spectrum (using a 50-msec. window) and an attempt is made to correct octave
errors, and (3) the pitch track is edited to deal with anomalous values and
discontinuities using a median smoothing technique. The AP then calculates
a smoothed RMS value for each centisecond and marks silence areas.

   On its next pass, the AP performs an LPC analysis (see, e.g., Markel,
1971) on 25.6-msec. speech frames that have been passed through a Hamming
window and attempts to pick out as many as five energy peaks per frame for
later use by the formant tracker. If isolated, large-bandwidth peaks are
detected, an "off-axis" spectrum is run in an attempt to better detect the
actual spectral peaks. Using this spectral-peak information, a formant
tracker next attempts to produce the digital equivalent of a voiceprint
(Kameny, 1974a).

   Following the formant-tracking pass, the number of slope changes (in the
digitized speech) per centisecond is calculated, and dip areas are marked
using an algorithm similar to that described in Weinstein, 1975. Dip
information is used to enhance detection of plosives, nasals, and flap
gestures as well as boundaries.

   On its next pass the AP attempts to segment and label those vowel-sonorant
areas that can be reliably handled (Kameny, 1976). To meet this goal, it is
necessary to use three levels of labels: (1) phoneme symbols in ARPABET,
(2) feature bits (retroflexion, nasalization, etc.), and (3) rough labels.
Labels in all three categories are emitted in reliable areas. In more

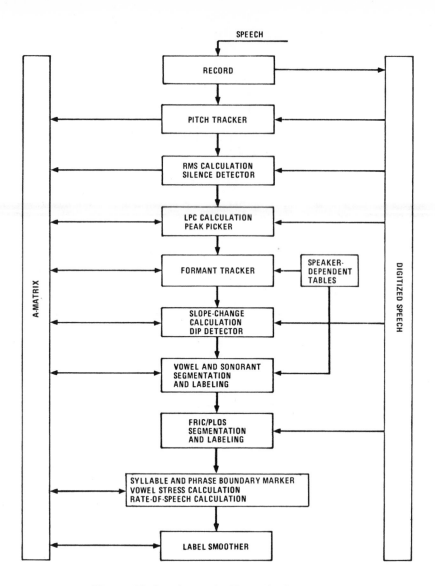

Figure 12-2. Acoustic-Phonetic Processor

ambiguous areas, only labels in category 2 and 3 or just in 3 are output.
The major technique used by the AP on this pass is the computation of a
distance measure from known points in a speaker-dependent vowel table.
(Idealized formant positions for the sonorants are derived from the vowel
information.) Reasonably steady-state areas are located, and the distance
measure is used to generate label choices and scores. The remaining task
is to determine approximate phone boundaries using rate-of-change,
continuity, and duration data.

Following the segmentation and labeling of vowel and sonorant areas, an
attempt is made to segment and label fricatives and plosives. To do this,
specialized LPCs are calculated having a narrow window and very few poles
(Molho, 1976). The spectra generated by the specialized LPCs are then

matched to templates to determine place and manner of articulation. This information is combined with rate-of-change and duration information to make label, score, and segmentation decisions. As above, a hierarchy of labeling is available comprising ARPABET, feature bits, and rough segment labels.

On its next pass the AP calculates prosodic information. A "convex hull" (Mermelstein, 1974) is used to identify syllable and phrase boundaries. Intensity, duration, and pitch information is used to determine level of vowel stress. Rate of speech is then calculated using a 1-sec. window. All of these processes have special provisions for handling end-of-utterance speech because of the effects of special FO trajectories and lengthening. Phrase boundaries are labeled as falling, rise-fall, etc.

On its final pass the AP makes a "best" label choice for each centisecond and enters it in an A-matrix column. This column is then corrected by a symbolic smoothing algorithm that removes label "jitters" and applies some linguistic constraints. The A-matrix now contains all information needed by the mapper and is ready for use by the rest of the system.

12-2.2 The Mapper and the Lexicon

The mapper is made up of three components: WORDMAP, PHRASEMAP, and SUBSETTER. WORDMAP verifies whether the A-matrix may contain a word hypothesized by the top end. PHRASEMAP calculates the likelihood of two adjacent words verified by WORDMAP existing side by side, and SUBSETTER uses "quick" clues to reject members of a list of hypothesized words. In addition to the A-matrix, the mapper uses a lexicon that contains alternative pronunciations of each vocabulary word.

12-2.2.1 Phonological Rules and the Lexicon

The lexicon is a data structure that maintains, for each vocabulary item, a pronunciation template called a "spelling graph." Figure 12-3 shows the spelling graph for the word "Baltimore." Each node is a phoneme in ARPABET and each path through the graph is an alternative pronunciation.

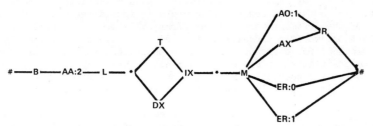

```
: 0, 1, 2  = STRESS LEVEL
     *     = SYLLABLE BOUNDARY
     #     = WORD BOUNDARY
```

BASE FORM: #BAA:2L*TIX*MAO:1 R#
GENERATED FORMS: #BAA:2L*DXIX*MAO:1R#
                 #BAA:2L*TIX*MAXR#
                 #BAA:2L*DXIX*MAXR#
                 #BAA:2L*TIX*MER:1#
                 #BAA:2L*DXIX*MER:1#
                 #BAA:2L*TIX*MER:0#
                 #BAA:2L*DXIX*MER:0#

Figure 12-3. Spelling Graph of the Word "Baltimore"

275

Generation of the lexicon is a part of system compilation. First, one or more ARPABET base-form pronunciations are entered for each vocabulary item. Next a set of phonological rules is applied to the base forms to produce additional alternative pronunciations. All of the base forms and derived pronunciations for the same vocabulary item are then merged into a spelling graph. There are two major advantages to the use of spelling graphs: (1) Since the graph is a compact representation of information, it provides memory savings; in the example of the word "Baltimore" (Figure 12-3), only 17% of the nodes and 23% of the links needed to store the eight pronunciations separately are necessary; and (2) Because most graphs are generated at compile time rather than on an as-needed basis, there are also time savings.

12-2.2.2 The Word Mapper (WORDMAP) - WORDMAP receives four arguments: an hypothesized word, whether the word is pluralized or not, an approximate starting time for the word (relative to the beginning of the utterance), and whether or not the word should complete the utterance. The major job of the word mapper is to determine whether the predicted word is a reasonable hypothesis. If it is, a numeric score is returned that represents the goodness of the match. The word mapper also returns, in addition to the score, four time boundaries for matched words: actual beginning time, end time, end of the first syllable in the word, and beginning of the last syllable in the word. The syllable boundary information is used later by the phrase mapper.

WORDMAP proceeds by tracing through the spelling graph of the predicted word and matching the phonemes on the nodes to information in the A-matrix; if the predicted word is pluralized, the graph is temporarily modified to contain the appropriate additional phonemes. Not only must WORDMAP determine whether any path through the graph is a reasonable match to the A-matrix, but if more than one path works the best path must be selected. This task is complicated by the fact that the A-matrix often contains mislabeled phoneme units, as well as additions and deletions. A modified dynamic program control structure is used, so that the time to map a word is approximately a linear function of the number of nodes and arcs in the spelling graph.

12-2.2.3 The Phrase Mapper (PHRASEMAP) - The arguments given to PHRASEMAP are two words that have previously been verified by WORDMAP. PHRASEMAP must determine whether or not it is compatible to assume that those words are adjacent. To do this, a new spelling graph is formed that contains the last syllable of the leftmost word and the first syllable of the rightmost word; if the leftmost word is pluralized, the additional phones are also included. The phonological rules are used as the graph is constructed to allow possible inter-word coarticulation effects to surface. The newly constructed graph is then mapped and scored against the A-matrix by the word mapper between the syllable time boundaries found for the individual words.

12-2.2.4 The Subsetter - The subsetter receives a set of words and an approximate beginning time boundary. For each of the words in the set, a few quick checks are made to determine whether it is conceivable that the word could be mapped by the word mapper. The value returned by the subsetter is the subset that passes the quick checks. No score or order ranking is associated with the members of the value set. The current version of the subsetter makes two attempts to reject a word. First, by comparing the number of syllables, it determines whether the shortest path through the spelling graph is longer than the remaining amount of A-matrix. Second, the word mapper is used to map the first half-syllable of the word (with loose tolerance). This process ensures that the subsetter will never reject a word that would be verified by the word mapper.

12-2.3 The Top End

The top end of a speech-understanding system provides two major services to the total system. The first is the representation and application of all non-acoustic knowledge sources. Among these are syntax, semantics, pragmatics, discourse analysis, user models, and task characteristics. The second service is the provision of the system's global control mechanism. The global control mechanism is responsible for determining what amount of resources to expend on each of the many possible tasks that may be necessary to complete the recognition and understanding of an input utterance. The job of the control mechanism is complicated because the set of possible tasks is derived from inconsistent and ambiguous theories about the results of already completed processing.

In our system, the only available knowledge source is a set of grammar rules. These rules and the parser (described in Sections 12-3 and 12-4) encode both syntactic knowledge and a modicum of semantic and pragmatic knowledge. Other knowledge sources are not employed because the system is not interactive--i.e., there is no task-performance component. The control program is described in Section 12-5.

12-3. THE GRAMMAR

The current grammar is a set of context-free production rules that describe a language for interacting with a data-management system whose data base contains facts about ship fleets of England, Russia, and the United States. Some typical legal utterances are:

Give me the speed of the Constellation.

Who is captain of the Whale?

Is the length of the sub more than 200 feet?

What American destroyer is in the port of San Francisco?

Where is each nuke?

Is N. Victorov on a carrier?

Does the Todd Pacific Shipyards build all Foxtrots?

List the number of torpedo tubes for each sub.

Though the language is context free, several constraints that may be thought of as semantic are incorporated. This is accomplished by making each verb appear explicitly in the grammar rules. Thus, number agreement is enforced by using different rules for singulars and plurals. Also, some case restrictions appear when the general categories of noun and adjective are subdivided into overlapping subsets by usage. For example, "Lafayette" belongs to both the set of ship names and the set of ship classes. So constructed, the grammar provides a reasonable amount of constraints without undue complexity. Obviously, many phenomena of natural language cannot be dealt with by this technique. However, given the current state of the art in acoustic processing and speech understanding, these limitations are not the pacing items.

The basic grammar has 400 non-syntactic terminals--i.e., vocabulary words. In addition, the word classes were augmented to achieve total lexicon sizes of 600, 800, and 1,000 terminals. All input utterances were selected from the grammar using only the 400-word vocabulary; this allowed the system's performance to be also tested with each of the larger vocabularies.

12-4. THE PARSER

The parser is an interpreter of the set of context-free grammar rules. Though the grammar could have been compiled into procedural form, the loss of flexibility and ease of change incurred would not have been compensated for by the slight efficiency introduced. After the A-matrix is completed, the system generally spends less than 4% of its total processing time within the parser and control program combined.

The parser is a simple program that is structured to take advantage of the multiprocessing capabilities of CRISP (Barnett, 1974). The strategy used is to create an independent process for each parsing path that is to be followed as a result of interpreting the grammar. A new process may be created when either of two conditions is encountered: (1) When the parser encounters an alternative in the grammar, a copy of the process is created to pursue each alternative independently; and (2) if the grammar hypothesizes a word class (i.e., ship names) and the mapper verifies the potential existence of more than one member of the hypothesized class, a copy of the requesting process is made for each verified word and resumed with that word as the only result. With this process-copying mechanism, a process is never resumed with a negative result and need not have provisions for backing up.

Essentially, the parser uses the control program as its lexical analyzer. Whenever a non-syntactic terminal (e.g., vocabulary word or class name) is encountered, it is hypothesized by passing it to the control program, where all priority rankings of request are determined. The parser is thus simplified because the control program contains all the decision-making logic.

12-5. THE CONTROL PROGRAM

The control program contains three groups of modules. The first group, called queueing functions, receives requests for activities and enters these requests in a priority queue (Section 12-5.1 describes the queueing functions). The second group, called the mapper interfaces, calls the various mapper components and enters the results into queues for further processing (Section 12-5.2 describes these). The third group consists of a single module, the dispatcher. The dispatcher selects a request from the queue and carries it out (Section 12-5.3 describes the dispatcher).

12-5.1 The Queueing Functions

The control program routes data among the parser and the mapper components and establishes priorities that determine who will operate on what data. The control program maintains a queue that contains five kinds of requests, each of which corresponds to a data path shown in Figure 12-4: (1) a word hypothesized by a parsing process that is to be mapped, (2) a word class hypothesized by a parsing process that is to be subsetted and mapped, (3) a subset of a word class (that has survived the subsetter) that is to be mapped, (4) mapped words that are to be phrase-mapped, and (5) found words that are to be returned to a parsing process. Queue entries of types (1) through (4) are maintained in request groups; for example, if several parsing processes hypothesize the existence of members of the same word class at the same spot in the utterance, they are all joined together in a single request group. (The priority of a group is that of its highest-priority member.) When the subset of the word group is found, the results are available to all group members. In addition to the above five kinds of requests, two others are also maintained in the queue: (6) a restart request by a process that is about to relinquish control but must complete some priority activities, and (7) a request to kill a parser process.

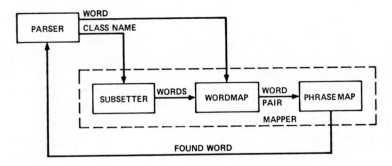

Figure 12-4. Parser-Mapper Interaction

12-5.1.1 <u>Queue Priorities</u> - A priority is assigned to each request (or request group) as it is entered into the queue. Priorities are the major factor used by the dispatcher in determining the next request to be honored. Restart requests are given the highest priority and are therefore satisfied ahead of any other kind of request. There is no distinction in priority among these requests, so they may operate in arbitrary order. Kill requests are of the next highest priority level; as with restart requests, no priority distinction is made between kill requests.

The remaining request kinds are for mapping and for resuming a parsing request with mapping results. These requests compete for attention on the basis of the priority of the request group to which they belong. The request group's priority is the highest priority assigned to any member of the group. The priorities of individual requests are computed by the queueing functions so that the queue can be maintained in sorted order. The common component used in computing the priority of these requests is based solely on the parsing path to date, and is called the <u>pathprio</u>:

$$pathprio(path)=depth(path) \cdot scores(path)$$

<u>Scores</u> computes a composite score based upon the word-map and phrase-map scores for each word in the path. <u>Depth</u> is used to effect either depth-first or breadth-first control.

$$depth(path)=d \cdot p+(1-d) \cdot (1-p)$$

where o<d<1 and p=path length/utterance length; i.e., p is the fraction of the utterance spanned by path.

12-5.2 <u>The Mapper Interface</u>

The mapper-interface functions receive request groups from the dispatcher and perform the requested activities by calling the mapper or finding a previous result for a similar request in a lookaside memory. The interface also normalizes the merit scores that the mapper returns by converting them into probabilistic measures. Based upon these probabilistic scores, the requests in the group are appropriately requeued. Figure 12-5 graphically represents the interconnections of the mapper interface and the mapper.

12-5.2.1 <u>The Lookaside Memory</u> - The top end has two mechanisms that operate to minimize the number of redundant mapper calls. The first is the formation of request groups by the queueing functions. The second is the lookaside memory. The lookaside contains a copy of each set of arguments passed to a mapper function (subsetter, word map, phrase map) paired with the results produced. Before the mapper interface actually calls the mapper,

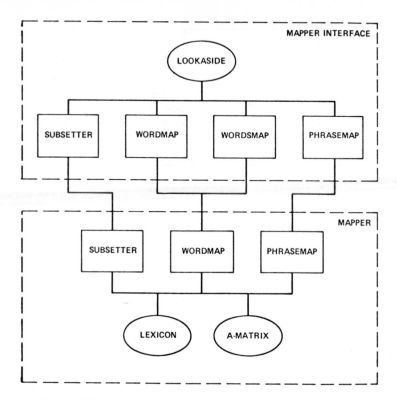

Figure 12-5. Mapper-Interface Connections to the Mapper

the lookaside is interrogated to see whether the same request has already been processed. If so, the previous result is used.

In some instances, a negative result for a predicted word can be inferred from a similar but different request that produced a negative result. There are four cases in which such a negative result can be inferred for a predicted word; in each case, the predicted word and approximate beginning time must agree with the information in the lookaside. The cases are: (1) an utterance-final plural word is predicted and the utterance-nonfinal plural fails, (2) an utterance-final plural word is predicted and the utterance-nonfinal singular fails, (3) an utterance-nonfinal plural is predicted and the utterance-nonfinal singular fails, and (4) an utterance-final singular is predicted and the utterance-nonfinal singular fails. These techniques are used only for regular plurals.

The fraction of requests satisfied by the lookaside varies with the settings of the control program's parameters. The observed range of this variation is .1 to .95. In any event, it has been determined that the fraction is greater when the system is processing utterances that are not properly understood. The reason for this is that utterances that are properly understood are processed in a straightforward manner with little wandering in the search. For other utterances, paths become blocked, and control continually returns to parse paths with bad initial scores. As this happens, the mapper requests tend to hit things already done--and hence the answers in the lookaside. Another reason for this is that parse paths with good scores tend to form into request groups in the early going. Therefore, the request-group mechanism, and not the lookaside, captures the redundancy.

12-5.2.2 <u>Score Conversion</u> - One of the major problems facing any builder of a speech-understanding system is finding adequate techniques for generating and interpreting scores produced by the mapping components. The most primitive (and most widely used) technique is to generate scores at one level of representation from a mean or weighted mean of the scores at the next lower level of representation. For example, a word would be the arithmetic mean of the scores of the syllables that make up the word. The favorite method of deriving word and syllable scores has become the geometric mean (with fudge factors) of the scores assigned to the generated phones. (See Neuistein, 1976 for a rationale of this technique.) Another approach is the use of conditional probabilities (Jelinek, 1976) in IBM's system. In our approach to this problem, the issues of score generation by the mapper and score utilization by the top end have been separated. The mapper attempts, on the basis of experimental evidence, to use a collection of scoring techniques that have the following characteristics: (1) they reject as many inappropriate predictions as possible by making binary-valued decisions, (2) they reject as few predictions as possible of things that actually exist, and (3) then for predictions not rejected, they generate scores that are monotonically related (statistically) to the probability that the prediction should be verified. We believe that a mapper component can be tuned to these three criteria by employing sets of scoring algorithms and heuristics that are natural to its pragmatic organization.

What we have done is to develop a statistical technique that allows us to sample the mapper's performance and derive an interpretation of its scoring. Figure 12-6 illustrates the results of such a sampling. The curves are probability-distribution curves normalized so that the area under each curve is the same. The T1 curve is derived by word mapping the words from several utterances at the places where they actually exist. (Part of the area under the T1 curve is at zero and is not shown; in this case, a score of zero is a Type 1 error, an error of omission, i.e., a false no.)

The T2 curve in Figure 12-6 is derived by word-mapping words at spots where they have not been spoken. The nonzero scores, which represent Type 2 errors, are collected and the distribution plotted. As can be seen in the figure, the T1 and T2 modes are separated, and the common area under both curves is approximately one-third of the total area. This means that the mapper provides reasonable discrimination via scores on words that are not rejected by binary decisions. From the T1 and T2 curves the transformed scoring function is derived, as shown in Figure 12-7. The transformed score, p, is defined by

$$p(s) = \frac{T1(s)}{T1(s)+c \cdot T2(s)}$$

(The curve in Figure 12-6 was derived by smoothing p and assuming c=1.) The variable, c, is the ratio of the number of questions asked by the mapper interface that ought to be answered "no", but are not, to the number of questions asked that ought to be answered "yes". Thus, p(s) is the likelihood, given a particular control mechanism, that a mapper score of s is a real "yes". An interesting problem arises here. When a p function is used to transform raw mapper scores, the system's performance, and hence the value of c, change. Therefore, a new p function needs to be computed. It is not known what conditions are necessary to guarantee that the sequence of c's so generated converges. Assuming that the sequence converges, the limiting value of c would provide a measure of the effectiveness of the combined mapper and top end, in that lower values of c imply either better discrimination by the mapper, or more accurate predictions from the top end, or both.

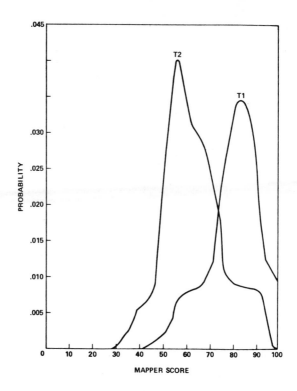

Figure 12-6. Distribution Curves of Mapper Scores

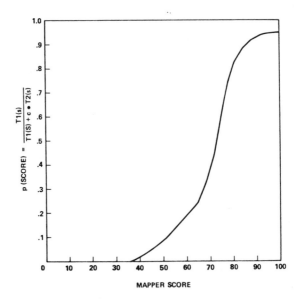

Figure 12-7. Transformed Mapper Scores

12-5.2.3 <u>Mapper Interface Functions</u> - There are four mapper interface func-
tions--one corresponding to each kind of queue request group that needs
mapper services. The argument given to an interface function by the dispatcher is a request group. The action of the function is to find the answer
to the request from either the lookaside or the mapper and to requeue the
request using the information so found. If the mapper is called, the results
are entered into the lookaside.

12-5.3 <u>The Dispatcher</u>

The dispatcher is a coroutine that is called by each parsing process when
its mapper requests have been queued and control can be relinquished. The
dispatcher examines the queue and selects, by priority, an activity to perform. The dispatcher continues working through the queue until the highest-
priority request results in resuming a parsing process. If the queue is
empty, then the attempt to understand the utterance terminates with the message "I don't understand you."

All restart requests are operated first, followed by all kill requests.
After the queue has been cleared of these two request types, resume requests
compete with mapping requests, by priority, for attention; after work is
finished on a mapper request, any new kill requests are obeyed and the rest
of the queue is operated in priority order.

12-6. MEASUREMENT AND EVALUATION

Testing of the SDC Speech Understanding System was conducted at three
levels: (1) acoustic-phonetic processor (AP), (2) mapper, and (3) total
system performance. Both time and resource limitations precluded testing
the system components as thoroughly as desired, and limited the use of the
test results in improving the overall system performance.

12-6.1 <u>Acoustic-Phonetic Processor Testing</u>

The accuracy of the acoustic-phonetic processor (AP) in generating labels
for the A-matrix has been documented elsewhere (Gillmann, 1974a, 1974b;
Kameny, 1976, 1975, 1974b; Molho, 1976, 1974a, 1974b) and will not be
presented here. The performance of the AP in terms of processing time could
only be estimated from external observation. The elapsed time that was
needed to process a large number of utterances through the AP on a PDP-11/40
was collected. The average value was 150 seconds per second of input speech.
Since this time included a substantial amount of I/O overhead for overlaying
program segments and data segments of the A-matrix, and the necessary
instrumentation was lacking, no accurate value for system overhead was
obtainable. It is our best estimate that the effective computation rate
for the AP was 20 MIPSS (million instructions per second of speech).

12-6.2 <u>Mapper Testing</u>

The mapper components have been tested in two environments, in isolation
and in the context of the total system. The following subsections describe
the methods and results of tests run in these two environments. Both kinds
of information are necessary to evaluate the mapper as a component in our
system and to extrapolate its use into other systems.

12-6.2.1 <u>Testing the Mapper in Isolation</u> - This body of tests was run to
generate the score transformations (P curves) described in Section 12-5.2.2.
As a byproduct, that information can also be viewed as describing mapper performance. The data were collected by three separate procedures. The first
was calling the word mapper, where the words were actually spoken. The
second procedure was to call the word mapper with all (singular) words in
the 1,000-word vocabulary at random spots in several utterances. The final

procedure was the gathering of data about performance of the phrase mapper. This was more difficult, since the phrase mapper should be called only when both of its argument words have been verified by the word mapper. These procedures are described below.

For the first procedure, a set of approximately 100 utterances was recorded. The orthographic word string for each utterance was then passed to the word mapper. Each word in the string was assumed to start where its predecessor stopped; this is reasonable, since the top end uses the same alignment scheme. If the mapper rejects a word, or successfully completes operation on the final word of the string, then processing of that test utterance is complete. For each word that is successfully mapped, two data are remembered--its score and whether the mapped pronunciation was mono- or polysyllabic. For words rejected by the mapper, the only datum noted is whether its base-form pronunciation is mono- or polysyllabic. Also, phrase-map scores (including rejections) were kept for phrase maps between each adjacent word pair accepted by the word mapper.

For the second test procedure, several of the original utterances were selected, and the entire 1,000-word vocabulary was passed to the word mapper at a single spot in each utterance. For one utterance, the selected spot was the beginning; for the others, it was an interior syllable boundary. In no case was the mapper called "very close" to the utterance end; so there were few, if any, rejects because of length of the predicted word. For each incorrect map (false "yes"), two data were noted; its score and whether the mapped pronunciation was mono- or polysyllabic.

The third procedure was to gather information about the phrase mapper in situations in which it ought to reject the proposed word pairs. It is difficult to find legitimate data for this test because the phrase mapper is "guaranteed" that both members of the word pair were individually accepted by the word mapper and that the predicted beginning time of the second word was the same as the actual ending time of the first word. In order to get enough data to accurately describe the phrase mappers, we therefore selected 17 utterances and ran them through the total system. From this exercise we derived the false "yes" and true "no" statistics. Table 12-1 summarizes the data gathered by the above three procedures.

Table 12-1. Performance Measures for Mapper in Isolation Test

	True Yes		False No		True No		False Yes	
All Word Maps	472	92.7%	37	7.3%	8349	92.8%	651	7.2%
Monosyllable Word Maps	294	96.1%	12	3.9%	761	76.2%	238	23.8%
Polysyllable Word Maps	178	87.7%	25	12.3%	7588	94.8%	413	5.2%
Phrase Maps	337	97.1%	10	2.9%	211	27.8%	547	72.2%

Figure 12-8 summarizes the data from mapper testing for polysyllabic words by showing probability density functions. The T1 curve shows the fraction of true "yeses" that occur with a score less than or equal to the abscissa value. The value of the T1 density curve at zero is the fraction of false "noes". The values on the T2 density curve gives the fraction of false "yeses" whose scores are less than or equal to the abscissa value. The MU density curve shows the fraction of tested utterances whose lowest score is less than or equal to the abscissa value and would therefore not be understood if a threshold were set at or above the abscissa value. The value of an MU curve at zero is the fraction of utterances that contain a Type 1 error (false "no").

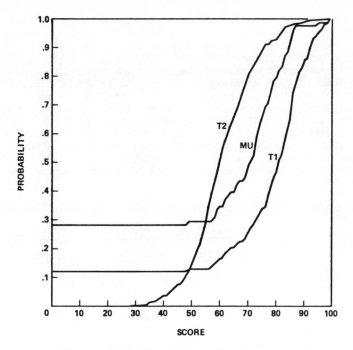

Figure 12-8. Polysyllabic Word-Map Density Functions

Figure 12-9 shows the corresponding probability distribution functions for the data shown in Figure 12-8. Also shown is the P function used for

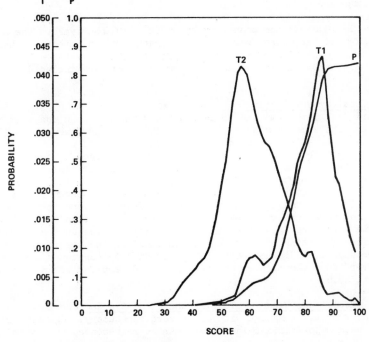

Figure 12-9. Polysyllabic Word-Map Distribution Curves and Score Transform Function

285

conversion of mapper scores by the top end. The theoretical definition of the
the distribution function is the derivative of the density function, assuming
continuity, etc. The curves shown were derived by smoothing (not clumping),
using a nine-point weighted window with weights 1, 2, 3, 4, 5, 4, 3, 2, and
1. Near the extrema, the size of the window was reduced to the number of
available points in the usual way. The area under the T2 curve is unity,
but the area under the T1 curve is not; the Type 1 errors cause a large
spike at a score of zero and are not shown. The P curves were then derived
as described in Section 12-5.2.2 and hand-smoothed to eliminate some minor
non-monotonicities. The C factor used in calculating the P function was
estimated from the grammar's branching factor (assuming a 600-word vocabulary), number of mapper and lookaside calls, and the data in Table 12-2.
Testing results for monosyllabic words and for phrase mapping are given in
Bernstein, 1976.

Table 12-2. Performance Measures for Word Mapper in System Test

	CLASS I				CLASS II			
	True	Yes	False	No	True	No	False	Yes
All Word Predictions by Class	65	91.5%	6	8.5%	11253	96.8%	372	3.2%
All Word Predictions	65	0.55%	6	.05%	11253	96.2%	372	3.2%

12-6.2.2 <u>Testing the Mapper as a System Component</u> - The experiments
described in this section were performed by running eleven utterances
through the system with the 1,000-word vocabulary and observing all calls
on the word mapper and phrase mapper. Questions answered by the lookaside
were not counted in the statistics. Table 12-2 summarizes the results from
the word mapper.

Figure 12-10 shows the mean time spent in the mapper versus the numbers
of syllables in the mapped words. It is gratifying to note that there is no
combinatorial explosion of mapping time for the longer words. Data from
other tests run on the mapper as a system component are included in Bernstein,
1976.

12-6.3 <u>Total System Testing</u>
Our original intention was to record 200 utterances and run them through
the system with vocabularies of 400, 600, 800, and 1,000 words and simply
record the results in each of the four cases. However, resource constraints
made that impossible. All 200 utterances were processed through the system
with the 400-word vocabulary; but progressively smaller subsets were selected
for processing through each of the larger vocabularies. The selected subsets
consisted of disproportionately large collections of utterances that had
worked in the next smaller vocabulary size. This was done for two reasons.
First, utterances that work take less processing time than those that do not.
Second, we were more interested in accurate information on the degradation in
performance on working utterances than in possible changes in failure modes
for utterances that did not work. The statistical techniques that were used
to "recover" from the problem created by skewed sampling are documented in
Bernstein, 1976.

12-6.3.1 <u>Techniques Used for Testing the Total System</u> - We hand-selected 200
utterances from the language with a 400-word vocabulary. One criterion used
was that each major variant in the grammar be represented by several

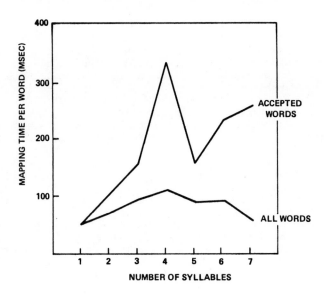

Figure 12-10. Mapper Timing

utterances. The other criterion was that a large subset of the 400-word vocabulary be used. Given the hand-selection process, there can be no guarantee that the chosen utterances represent a typical population as to length, phonetic confusion, or grammatical complexity. However, without collection of many protocols of human/system interaction, no confidence could be assigned to their typicality in any event.

The 200 utterances were recorded by a single speaker, and an A-matrix was produced for each. Next, all the utterances were run through the system using the 400-word vocabulary. Then, almost all the utterances that worked or were "close," plus a random sample of the others, were run through the system with the 600-word vocabulary. For the systems with 800-word and 1,000-word vocabularies, a subset of the utterances run in the system with the next smaller vocabulary size were selected for testing. The selection was a random sample of the utterances grouped by result class (described below). A larger fraction of the utterances were selected from those in result classes that worked or were close. For each run of an utterance, several quantities were collected for later analysis; a summary is presented below.

The results of running an utterance through the system fall into one of five categories, called result classes. The result classes are *, EQ, T2S, T2L, and T1. The result of running an utterance is in the class * if and only if the system understands the utterance exactly, i.e., each word in the utterance is identical to the recognized word. Results fall into the class EQ if the meaning of the understood and original utterance are identical. For instance, the speaker said, "Where are all of the Midways?" and the system understood "Where are all the Midways?" Results fall into T2S (Type 2 error, small) when the system understanding is different in meaning from the spoken utterance but the word strings are very similar. For example, the speaker said, "Who is captain of the Whale?" and the system understood "Who was captain of the Whale?" (This result class is sometimes referred to as "connoisseur's" errors.) Results fall into the T2L (Type 2 error, large) when the system understanding and the recognized word string are both dissimilar to the spoken utterance. For example, the speaker said, "How many cruisers are there?" and the system understood "What November has a boiler?"

Necessarily, judgment must be used in assigning results among the classes EQ, T2S, and T2L. Sometimes the distinction between EQ and T2S can be made with reference to the data base being queried. For example, an "a" vs. "the" distinction is usually significant in meaning if the following noun phrase describes a class of objects. The final result class is T1 (Type 1 error). A result falls into this class if the system outputs the message, "I don't understand you." Since the top end of the system did not use thresholds to prune paths, only a few results fall into this class.

For the results presented herein, the result classes * and EQ have been lumped together (as *) because utterances in both classes count as correctly understood.

12-6.3.2 <u>Results of Total System Testing</u> - All accuracy and performance results for other than the 400-word vocabulary reported in this section have been de-skewed by the statistical techniques described in Bernstein, 1976.

Table 12-3 gives the fraction of utterances that fall into each result class as a function of vocabulary size. As would be expected, the fraction of currently understood utterances (result class *) decreases as the vocabulary becomes larger. Also, the system commits more Type 2 errors (result classes T2S and T2L) as the vocabulary size increases, because there is more opportunity for a false path to outscore the current path.

Table 12-3. Projected Results for Total System vs. Vocabulary Size

		Vocabulary Size			
		400	600	800	1000
	*	.305	.270	.255	.235
Result	T2S	.155	.170	.173	.183
Class	T2L	.370	.450	.462	.472
	T1	.170	.110	.110	.110

System performance was found to depend upon utterance length as well as vocabulary size. Table 12-4 shows the fraction and number (in parentheses) of utterances that fall into each result class as a function of utterance length. (Derived from the 400-word vocabulary.) The results in Table 12-4 were derived by clumping. The fraction of correctly understood utterances falls off sharply with increasing utterance length. Also, the number of Type 1 errors rises sharply with increasing length because of the reduced likelihood that a false parse will be able to span the entire utterance. The last column of the table shows the number and percentage of utterances in each length category.

Table 12-5 summarizes performance statistics for the total system as a function of result class and vocabulary size. Results are stated as both per utterance and per second of speech measures. Processing time is given in seconds and is exclusive of time spent in the acoustic processor. The system ran on an IBM 370/158-3, which executes approximately one million instructions per second, thus the processing time/second data can be interpreted as a MIPSS measure. Using the estimate of 20 MIPSS for the AP, the total system processing rate for the 1,000-word vocabulary can be estimated at 92 MIPSS.

Table 12-4. Results by Utterance Length for 400-Word Vocabulary

		Result Class				
		*	T2S	T2L	T1	Total
	$1 \leq t < 2$	.70(14)	.10(2)	.15(3)	.05(1)	20(10%)
Utterance Length in Sec.	$2 \leq t < 3$	.36(31)	.19(16)	.38(33)	.07(6)	86(43%)
	$3 \leq t < 4$	.22(13)	.15(9)	.41(24)	.22(13)	59(29.5%)
	$t \leq 4$	.09(3)	.11(4)	.40(14)	.40(14)	35(17.5%)
	Total	.305(61)	.155(31)	.37(74)	.17(34)	200

Table 12-5. Results of Total System Testing

Measures		Vocabulary Size			
		400	600	800	1000
Processing time/utterance		90.17	144.52	185.18	233.86
	*	42.56	65.54	94.38	109.48
	T2S	56.23	85.58	118.35	147.83
	T2L	103.68	168.20	195.92	246.65
	T1	176.91	332.59	455.65	587.79
Processing time/second		28.54	45.63	57.92	71.75
	*	16.95	26.27	37.04	42.60
	T2S	18.88	28.16	39.21	48.80
	T2L	33.22	53.77	62.13	77.22
	T1	47.98	86.84	118.10	148.82
Mapper calls/utterance		964.27	1573.66	1939.93	2444.10
	*	471.10	739.63	998.50	1208.18
	T2S	561.68	894.25	1172.60	1539.82
	T2L	1135.09	1880.66	2167.28	2726.67
	T1	1826.15	3414.90	4371.93	5376.42
Mapper calls/second		314.14	514.83	634.29	793.26
	*	198.78	314.07	414.58	501.64
	T2S	196.84	299.34	397.07	517.02
	T2L	373.53	624.31	725.44	908.05
	T1	498.77	892.80	1135.85	1383.30
Lookaside hits/utterance		2227.12	5542.68	9304.66	12945.80
	*	306.85	751.78	2120.03	2607.63
	T2S	446.52	732.40	1168.81	1297.51
	T2L	2039.26	6975.09	8914.16	11316.60
	T1	7740.65	18876.39	40395.48	61401.13
Lookaside hits/second		646.18	1648.65	2586.58	3470.30
	*	136.46	330.23	733.12	894.40
	T2S	151.67	252.41	410.93	459.54
	T2L	628.77	2207.92	2843.91	3611.80
	T1	2049.45	4754.72	9224.16	13375.04

The SDC Speech Understanding Research project produced three things of significance:

- A working prototype speech understanding system that achieved a meaningful set of ARPA's original objectives,

- A clear enough understanding of the particular shortcomings in the system to be confident that a greatly superior version that would meet or exceed the original objectives is attainable, and

- Insight into the issues and problems of producing systems as complex as those for understanding speech.

We have learned a great deal about solving the particular problems of constructing and testing speech understanding systems at all levels, from processing the acoustic signal to understanding language. For instance, the lower levels' processes and knowledge sources must provide negative information when positive results are not obtained, rather than no information. A uniform and mathematically consistent scoring system must be used at all levels of the system. Effort must be expended, even during the research phase, to make every process as efficient of its use of computer resources as possible if sufficient tests are to be run from which to arrive at useful conclusions. Our major regret is that there was not sufficient time or resources to enable us to thoroughly test the system in ways that would permit a more accurate characterization of it from the component level and that would allow us to thoroughly understand the contribution of each element of the system to the observed successes and failures. In order to do the testing that was accomplished, we froze the system with some known existing minor flaws; others were discovered in the testing process. None but the most grievous were fixed. Therefore, it is difficult to say with certainty what the performance of a flaw-free version of the present system would actually be. We conjecture that the remaining flaws were not a primary cause of the observed errors, and that at best, the performance would have been improved only slightly.

Of potentially even greater value than what we have learned about speech processing systems per se is what we have learned about the general class of systems they represent: very large, very complex processing systems with many levels of interaction, such as those for extracting usable information from imaging and other complex sensor inputs, and command and control systems that incorporate many "intelligent" components.

Were the SDC Speech Understanding Research project to continue, it would concentrate on several crucial elements of the system process and take somewhat different approaches to implementing some of the components and subsystems. Various changes would be made in the Acoustic-Phonetic processor to improve its accuracy, its efficiency, and the way it communicates with the higher-level processes. With respect to the kind of information it provides, the scoring algorithm needs to be more coherent and more consistent with the rest of the system. Its output must contain data about what it reliably does not know as well as what it does know. In other words, it must degrade gracefully in the face of low-quality input. Much more effort must be expended in more accurately and reliably identifying and classifying fricatives, plosives, and nasalized sounds. Both labeling and scoring of phones can be improved by application of additional linguistic constraints. It should be observed that the more reliance the rest of the system can put on the output of the Acoustic-Phonetic processor, the more efficient and accurate the total system will be. In other words, there is more leverage to be gained at the bottom end for a given effort than almost anywhere else in the total system. Thus, the goal of a bottom-driven system is the proper one.

The creation and application of practical phonological rules to produce the various alternative pronunciations from the base forms of the lexicon was a significant achievement of the SUR project. It had been conjectured as being possible, but the realization of usable phonological rules was actually accomplished as part of this research. The rule set that is used is, however, not perfect; additional research is needed to discover more precise rules that produce more consistent and usable pronunciation variants. Even with better rules, the resultant pronunciation lexicon would contain inappropriate variants. Therefore, it would be highly desirable to find a method for post-editing the output of the rules pass to delete undesirable or unneeded entries. This would not only reduce the opportunities for Type 2 errors, but would also improve the efficiency of the Lexical Mapper (the component in which the majority of the time and effort is spent) by reducing the number of possible mappings.

Since the Lexical Mapper is one of the most critical components in the system for both efficiency and accuracy considerations, improvements here would have a salutary effect on overall performance. Three possible ways of improving the mapper became apparent during the system tests. Many of the errors that were observed were caused by improper alignment between the proposed word from the lexicon and the content of the A-matrix. This led to missing words that should have been found as well as finding words that were not actually there. Many utterances were not properly understood because of difficulties that occur when the mapper is attempting to identify the last word in an utterance, in which the energy tends to drop off. Much more work remains to be done to fully understand how to cope with this particularly unique portion of an utterance. Last, but not least, the mapper must be constructed to more adequately use the coarticulation environment of the interior words in utterances. The method presently used is ad hoc and barely adequate, and leads to more errors than are acceptable.

Even with the existing competence of the various system components, performance would have been significantly higher had we chosen a more constrained grammar. The grammar we did select was a quite rich and habitable subset of natural language for the domain of discourse. It is difficult to say what form these constraints should take, because the simple measures of fanout or branching factor do not adequately describe the complexity of a grammar. We do believe that the large number of potential choices that had to be made in the grammar we used, and the length-weighted average used in scoring, were inappropriate and led to errors that should have been avoided. In some instances, length-weighted scoring would favor a word with a lower score than another word when both were used to extend the same parse path. This anomaly can occur when the score of both words is less than the score of the parse path without either word's being appended, and the word with the lower score is shorter, because it penalizes the new parse path score less.

The system that was demonstrated was completely lacking in higher-level knowledge sources such as an independent semantic component, a discourse model, and a thematic memory. Each of these could have made a contribution in limiting the search and minimizing the large Type 2 errors, and in some cases the small Type 2 errors. Whether the system would function more efficiently is moot; that its performance could be improved is evident.

12-8. BIBLIOGRAPHY

Barnett, J. A., and D. L. Pintar. (1974) CRISP: A Programming Language and System, System Development Corporation TM-5455/000/00 (Draft).

Bernstein, M. I. (1976) Interactive Systems Research: Final Report to the Director, Advanced Research Projects Agency, for the Period 16 September 1975 to 15 September 1976, System Development Corporation TM-5243/006/00.

291

_____. (1975) <u>Interactive Systems Research: Final Report to the Director,</u> <u>Advanced Research Projects Agency, for the Period 16 September 1974 to</u> <u>15 September 1975</u>, System Development Corporation TM-5243/004/00. NTIS AD-A020-314

Gillmann, R. (1975) "A Fast Frequency Domain Pitch Algorithm," <u>J. Acoust.</u> <u>Soc. Am.</u> 58 (Supplement No. 1):S62 (Abstract).

————. (1974a) "Automatic Recognition of Nasal Phonemes," <u>Proceedings of</u> <u>the IEEE Symposium on Speech Recognition</u>, Pittsburgh, Pa., pp. 74-79.

————, and H. B. Ritea. (1974b) "Automatic Isolation and Analysis of Nasals and Nasalized Vowels in Continuous Speech," <u>J. Acoust. Soc. Am.</u> 55 (Supplement):S21 (Abstract).

Jelinek, F. (1976) "Continuous Speech Recognition by Statistical Methods," <u>Proceedings of the IEEE</u>, 64:4, pp. 532-556.

Kameny, I. (1976) "Automatic Acoustic-Phonetic Analysis of Vowels and Sonorants," <u>Conference Record, 1976 IEEE International Conference on</u> <u>Acoustics, Speech, and Signal Processing</u>, pp. 166-169.

————. (1975) "Comparison of Formant Spaces of Retroflexed and Non-retroflexed Vowels," <u>IEEE Transactions on Acoustics, Speech, and Signal</u> <u>Processing</u>, ASSP-23(1), pp. 38-49.

————, W. A. Brackenridge, and R. Gillmann. (1974a) "Automatic Formant Tracking," <u>J. Acoust. Soc. Am.</u> 56 (Supplement):S28 (Abstract).

————, and R. Weeks. (1974b) "An Experiment in Automatic Isolation and Identification of Vowels in Continuous Speech," <u>J. Acoust. Soc. Am.</u> 55:411 (Abstract).

Markel, J. D. (1971) <u>Formant Trajectory Estimation from a Linear Least-</u> <u>Squares Inverse Filter Formulation</u>, Monograph No. 7, Speech Communications Research Laboratory, Inc., Santa Barbara.

Mermelstein, P., and G. M. Kuhn. (1974) "Segmentation of Speech into Syllabic Units," <u>J. Acoust. Soc. Am.</u> 55 (Supplement):S22 (Abstract).

Molho, L. M. (1976) "Automatic Acoustic-Phonetic Analysis of Fricatives and Plosives," <u>Conference Record, 1976 IEEE International Conference on</u> <u>Acoustics, Speech, and Signal Processing</u>, pp. 182-185.

————. (1974a) "Automatic Recognition of Fricatives and Plosives in Continuous Speech," <u>Proceedings of the IEEE Symposium on Speech</u> <u>Recognition</u>, Pittsburgh, Pa., pp. 68-73.

————. (1974b) "Automatic Recognition of Fricatives and Plosives in Continuous Speech Using a Linear Prediction Method," <u>J. Acoust. Soc. Am.</u> 5(2):411 (Abstract).

Neuistein, C. J., and D. H. Johnson. (1976) <u>Initial Version of the Phrase</u> <u>Recognition Component for the Network User Interface</u>, MIT Lincoln Laboratory, NSC Note #91.

Newell, A., et al. (1973) <u>Speech-Understanding Systems</u>, North Holland Publishing Co., Amsterdam.

Weinstein, C. J., S. S. McCandless, L. F. Mondshein, and V. W. Zue. (1975) "A System for Acoustic-Phonetic Analysis of Continuous Speech," IEEE Transactions on Acoustics, Speech, and Signal Processing, ASSP-23(1), pp. 54-67.

13.

SRI RESEARCH ON SPEECH UNDERSTANDING[1]

Donald E. Walker
SRI International

13-1. INTRODUCTION

For a period of five years, SRI International participated in a major
program of research on the analysis of continuous speech by computer,
sponsored by the Advanced Research Projects Agency of the Department of
Defense.[2] The goal of the   program was the development of a speech
understanding system capable of engaging a human operator in a natural
conversation about the performance of a particular task (see Newell et al.,
1973).   A rather complex set of specifications defined the parameters more
precisely. The program culminated in the demonstration of a system that did
meet the target specifications (see the chapter by Lowerre and Reddy in this
volume), but more important   for the future of this technology were
developments in the various constituents or knowledge resources--particularly
syntax, semantics, and discourse--and in the system architecture necessary
for coordinating them efficiently and effectively (see Medress et al., 1977).
   Our work at SRI on speech understanding builds directly on the results of
research in computational linguistics and artificial intelligence.   It
emphasizes the importance both of the structure of natural language and of
the processes entailed   in understanding human communication.   We are
interested in speech that occurs spontaneously in a natural context, the
kinds of conversations that take place when one person interacts with another
or with a computer system to carry out a meaningful task.   Conventional
grammars do not always characterize the language used in such situations.
For example, an utterance may consist of a single noun phrase, like "The
United States."   As a reply to the question, "What country owns the
Lafayette?", that utterance should be interpreted as meaning "The United
States owns the Lafayette." In addition, depending on the speaker and the
context, certain constructions are more or less likely to be used.   To
capture these kinds of information, we have embodied the syntactic knowledge

----
[1] This chapter provides an introduction to and summary of research reported
more fully in a monograph, Understanding Spoken Language, edited by Walker
(1978). Material from that publication and from a paper by Walker and Paxton
et al. (1977) is included here by permission of Elsevier North-Holland and of
the International Joint Conferences on Artificial Intelligence. The research
was performed by Barbara Grosz, Gary Hendrix, Ann Robinson, and Jane
Robinson, all of SRI, and by William Paxton and Richard Fikes, who are now at
the Xerox Palo Alto Research Center.   Their contributions are reflected
directly in the content of the chapter.

[2] This research was funded under the following ARPA contracts, all
administered through the Army Research Office: DAHC04-72-C-0009, DAHC04-75-C-
0006, and DAAG29-76-C-0011.

of the system in the form of a linguistically motivated _performance grammar_ (Robinson, 1975). Semantic knowledge about the task itself is encoded in networks, which are partitioned to allow selective access (Hendrix, 1975). Discourse procedures make it possible to select relevant material from both the task structure and the preceding dialog (Grosz, 1977).

Deciding when and how to use the different kinds of knowledge during the interpretation of an utterance is a complex issue. The various sources of acoustic uncertainty combine with the large number of linguistic choices to create an extremely large number of alternative hypotheses. Relevant knowledge must be applied as early as possible to reduce the size of the search space by eliminating unpromising hypotheses and to allow the more likely of the remaining alternatives to be tested first. We have designed our system so that the constraints provided by acoustics, syntax, semantics, and discourse can influence the evaluation of each phrase. The rules for phrase formation, which are embodied in a language definition system, are applied by the system executive, which organizes the different interpretations and intermediate results, and assigns priorities for the system tasks.

In our system design, we stress _integration_--the establishment of a framework for unifying a collection of components--and _control_--the dynamic direction of the overall activity of the system during the processing of an input utterance. Our approach to integration allows specifying the interactions of information from various knowledge resources in a procedural representation; it makes it possible to adjust the language definition to particular domains without loss of generality; and it avoids commitment to a particular system control strategy, thus ensuring flexibility in combining words and phrases. Our approach to control allows an input to be processed left-to-right, right-to-left, or from the middle out; it enables combining top-down, predictive procedures, with bottom-up, data-directed procedures; and it permits evaluating partial results (phrases) within the larger linguistic contexts (sentences) in which they could be embedded.

Separating the language definition from the executive has made it possible to conduct experiments that evaluate alternative control strategies. The ability to experiment is a critical requirement for research on speech understanding and, more generally, on language understanding. It is not sufficient to demonstrate that a system works, unless one's goals are stated solely in practical terms. A concern with the scientific implications of the results requires a detailed inquiry into how and why the system works. In such a complex area, it is particularly important to be able to discover the actual effects and interactions of the system design features. The results of our experiments have provided a better understanding of the features that contribute to system performance and have suggested new lines of development to pursue.

The rest of this chapter contains an overview of the SRI Speech Understanding System, followed by a consideration of relevant experimental results. More detailed discussions on all points can be found in corresponding chapters of Walker (1978).

13-2. AN OVERVIEW OF THE SRI SPEECH UNDERSTANDING SYSTEM

In this section, the major features of our speech understanding system are reviewed. A discussion of the task domains and of the operation of the system provides context. Descriptions are given of the language definition system that establishes a framework for coordinating the various knowledge resources and of the executive routines that control their interactions. Then, in sequence, each of the system constituents are considered: the acoustic components, syntactic knowledge, semantic knowledge, discourse knowledge, deduction capabilities, and response generation.

13-2.1 The Task Domains

Two major task domains or discourse contexts have been considered during our research:

* Providing responses to queries from a file containing information about ships from the fleets of the United States, the Soviet Union, and the United Kingdom.
* Maintenance of an air compressor in a work station environment with the system as an advisor or "computer consultant."

We expected to implement systems that could process utterances relevant to each domain, but a reduction in funding made it necessary to concentrate our efforts on the first task. However, much of our work on discourse reflects analyses of the task-oriented dialogs of equipment maintenance, so it is appropriate to describe that domain as well.

The data base for the ship-information domain contains such characteristics as owner, builder, size, and speed for several hundred ships. Utterances can be formulated that refer to attributes of a particular ship or of ships meeting a certain description; to part-subpart relations between a ship and, for example, its crew; to set membership and kind relationships between various individuals and classes (such as "all ships" and "Are all ships diesels?"). It is possible to specify an object on the basis of its properties ("What country owns the Skate?"; "What American destroyer has a speed of 33 knots?") or of the number of individuals meeting a given description ("How many diesel submarines are owned by the U.S.?"). Queries may be quantified to seek information over classes of individuals ("What is the speed of each American sub?"). Dialog sequences can be processed with previous utterances serving as context; as a result, pronouns can be used, the referents of determined noun phrases can be identified, and it is not necessary to use complete utterances if the reference is clear ("What is the speed of the Lafayette?"; "The Ethan Allen?"; "Do both ships belong to the U.S.?").

The air compressor domain provided for assembling that device, which consists principally of a pump, a motor, a tank, a pressure gauge, the pieces that connect these items, and a platform on which things are mounted. The steps required to put together various parts of the compressor were analyzed and described formally. We considered various kinds of dialog interactions, with the person asking questions, responding to requests for information, or describing aspects of the immediate situation. Of particular interest were sequences of utterances in which the referents of certain objects could be identified only by knowing the structure of the subtask ("Attach the pump to the platform." "What size bolts should I use?") or where the structure of the previous utterance is necessary to analyze an elliptical utterance ("What tool should I use to fasten the bolts?" "The box end wrench.")

13-2.2 The Operation of the System[3]

When a speaker records an utterance, it is analyzed acoustically and phonetically, and the results are stored in a file. When these data are available, the executive begins to predict words and phrases, guided by the rules in the language definition, and to build up phrases from words that have been identified acoustically in the utterance. When a word is predicted

----

[3] The programs developed at SRI for the speech understanding system were written in INTERLISP-10 (Teitelman, 1975) on a Digital Equipment Corporation PDP/KA-10 running under a TENEX operating system. Subsequently, because our work was being conducted cooperatively with the System Development Corporation, the programs were transferred to the IBM 370/145 at SDC, using INTERLISP/370 (Uppsala University, 1975). We are grateful to Jaak Urmi and the Uppsala University Computer Center for their help in installing INTERLISP/370 on the IBM computer.

at a specified place in the utterance, alternative phonological forms of that word are mapped onto the acoustic data for that place, and a score indicating the degree of correspondence is returned. As each phrase is constructed, syntactic, semantic, and discourse information are checked, and, if appropriate, a semantic network representation of the phrase is developed. When an interpretation for the entire utterance is complete, relevant structures from the semantic model of the domain and from an associated relational data base are processed to identify in semantic network form the content of an appropriate response. This response is then generated either in text form or through the use of a speech synthesizer.

A rough flowchart of the internal organization of the system is shown in Figure 13-1. The direction of the arrows in the figure indicates the general flow of information (rather than control) as an utterance is interpreted and an appropriate response returned to the speaker. Descriptions of the components in the following sections will help clarify this diagram.

13-2.3 The Language Definition System

The input language is a subset of natural, colloquial English that is suitable for carrying on a dialog between a user and the system regarding information relevant to the given task. The form of the language is specified in a language definition system that consists of a lexicon containing the vocabulary and a set of composition rules for combining words and phrases into larger phrases. A rule consists of a phrase-structure declaration, which specifies the possible constituents of a phrase, augmented by a procedure that is executed whenever the rule constructs a phrase. Information provided by the procedure includes both <u>attributes</u> of the phrase based on the attributes of its constituents and <u>factors</u> for use in judging the acceptability of the phrase.

Attribute statements determine the properties of particular phrases constructed by the rule. They may compute values that specify acoustic properties related to the input signal, syntactic properties such as mood (declarative or interrogative) and number (singular or plural), semantic properties such as the semantic network representation of the meaning of the phrase, and discourse properties such as the entity to which a pronoun refers.

Factor statements compute acceptability ratings for a particular instance of the phrase. Scores for factors are <u>nonboolean</u>; that is, they may assume a range of values. As a result, a proposed phrase is not simply accepted or rejected; it may be rated as more or less acceptable, depending on a combination of factor values. Like attributes, factors may be acoustic, syntactic, semantic, or discourse related. Acoustic factors reflect how well the words match the actual input; syntactic factors perform tests like number agreement between various constituents; semantic factors assure that the phrase has a meaning in the task domain; and discourse factors indicate whether a definite noun phrase is appropriate in the given dialog context.

The attribute and factor statements in the procedural parts of the rules contain specifications for most of the potential interactions among system components. Attributes and factors either have constant values or have values that depend on attributes of constituents and global information (such as a model of the discourse or the results of preliminary, low-level acoustic processing). By design, the attributes and factors of a phrase are not allowed to depend on the context formed by other phrases that can combine with it to produce larger structures. By giving up explicit context dependency, it becomes easier to share phrases among different contexts, which allows the executive to reduce duplication of effort. However, contextual restrictions provide heuristic information that in practice is too valuable to ignore, so the executive algorithms for priority setting take them into account by special techniques described below. Essentially, we

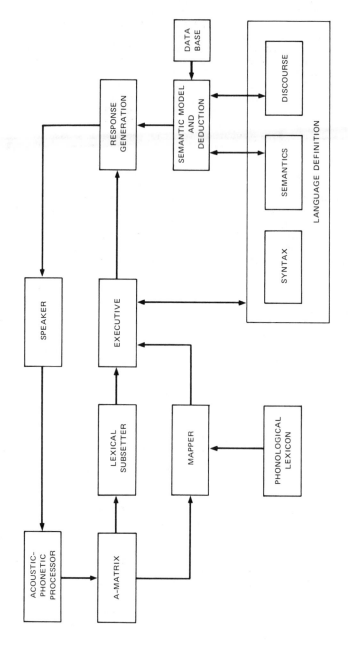

FIGURE 13-1 SYSTEM ORGANIZATION

have taken the explicit context dependencies out of the rules so that phrases can be shared by different contexts, and have developed methods in the executive so that contextual restrictions can still be used in controlling the operation of the system.

The form of the rules is designed to avoid commitments to particular system control strategies. For example, the rule procedures can be executed with any subset of constituents, so incomplete phrases can be constructed to provide intermediate results, and it is not necessary to acquire constituents in a strictly left-to-right order.

13-2.4 The Executive

Control of processing in the system is performed by the executive; it applies the rules of the language definition, organizes hypotheses and results, and assigns priorities. The principal data structure used by the executive is called the parse net.[4] It is a network with two types of nodes: phrases and predictions. Phrases correspond to words or composition rules from the language definition; phrases can be complete, containing all their constituents, or incomplete, with some or all of their constituents missing. A prediction is for a particular category of phrase associated with a particular location in the utterance. As the interpretation of an utterance progresses, new phrases that have been constructed from existing phrases or from words found in the utterance are added to the parse net. At the same time, new predictions are made as more information is obtained. Thus, as the interpretation process advances, the parse net, which holds intermediate hypotheses and results, grows. A complete root category phrase (typically, a sentence) with its attributes and factors constitutes an interpretation of the utterance.

Two types of tasks interact to build the parse net. The predict task leads to predictions for a word or phrase in the utterance that can help complete an incomplete phrase. The word task calls the acoustic mapper to look for a particular word in a particular location; if the word is found, it is used to build new phrases. Whenever a new constituent is inserted into an incomplete phrase, any adjacent constituents that had been missing can be predicted. New predictions can include predictions for particular words, leading to new instances of calls on the word task. Thus, each task ends by scheduling the other. When a successful interpretation for the utterance has been found, the executive invokes the response functions, which produce a reply.

A prediction serves as an intermediary between two sets of incomplete phrases: consumer phrases that all are missing a constituent of the predicted category at the predicted location in the input, and producer phrases that all might supply the missing constituents. Note that a phrase can be a consumer for one prediction and a producer for another. The full set of producer-consumer connections in the parse net makes explicit the different sentential contexts for each phrase. This contextual information is used by the executive in setting priorities and in lookahead.

Establishing the priority of a task begins with determining the score of the phrase involved. The score is computed from the results of the acoustic mapping of any of the words contained in the phrase, from the factor statements for the phrase, and from the scores of the constituents. The score is thus a local, context-free piece of information that does not depend on higher-level phrases that might use that phrase as a constituent. After the score is determined, the phrase is assigned a rating, which is an estimate of the best score for an interpretation of the entire utterance that could be constructed using the given phrase. The rating for a phrase does

----

[4] The design of the parse net was inspired by Kaplan's (1973) multi-processing consumer-producer approach.

depend on the other phrases in which it may be embedded to form a sentence. It takes into account the procedural information in the rules by exploring paths in the parse net and executing the corresponding procedures to gather attribute and factor information. Each producer-consumer path from a phrase P to a root category phrase reflects a way of constructing an interpretation using P. Various paths from P are formed, and the rating for P is its best rating with respect to any of the constructed paths.

To reduce the cost of rating alternatives, a heuristic search is made in the parse net for a near optimal path rather than exhaustively trying all possibilities. The heuristic exploits the fact that, typically, when a phrase is being rated, the higher level phrases that form its context have already been rated. (The parse net is initialized so that a context of previously rated phrases exists even when the system is doing bottom-up processing.) These prior ratings provide important heuristic information. The object is to find the path giving the best score, so the paths with the highest prior rating are explored first. When a complete path is found, one that leads to a root-category phrase, the score for that path is used as a threshold to prune other paths that have lower expected ratings.

Both the word and the predict task can work either left-to-right through an input or in either direction beginning from words selected at arbitrary positions within an utterance. This ability to add constituents to phrases in any order has made it possible to experiment with a variety of control strategies. Also important for experimental studies is the fact that each task does a limited amount of processing and then stops after scheduling further operations for later. The scheduling does not specify a particular time, but instead gives each operation a certain priority. The operation is performed when its priority is highest. Since the executive sets the task priorities, changing the way these priorities are set alters the overall system strategy.

13-2.5 Acoustic Components[5]

The acoustic-phonetic processor digitizes the input, extracts various amplitude and frequency parameters, assigns feature bits, segments the speech into phoneme-like units, and generates phonemic labels with associated merit scores for each segment. All of the acoustic-phonetic information is stored as an A-matrix for the utterance. Given a word predicted by the executive together with a location in the speech input, the mapper compares the acoustic data at that point in the A-matrix with alternative possible pronunciations of the word, as determined by the phonological lexicon. The mapper assigns a score between 0 and 100 that indicates how well the word matches the input. If the value exceeds a given threshold, the mapper reports the beginning and ending times of the word together with the score. To reduce the number of words that otherwise would have to be checked by the mapper, the lexical subsetter can be used to provide a list of words that could begin (or end) at a specified location.

13-2.6 Syntactic Knowledge

The syntactic knowledge in the system is encoded both in the phrase structure part of the language definition rules and in the attribute and factor statements in the procedure part of the rules. Syntax provides

----
[5] The acoustic components were designed and implemented by the System Development Corporation, with whom we worked during the last part of our participation in the ARPA program. The preliminary acoustic processing was performed on a PDP-11 computer, and the resulting data were transferred to the IBM 370/145. The mapper ran on the IBM 370/145 under control of the system executive. More detailed descriptions of these parts of the system can be found in Bernstein (1975).

computationally inexpensive information about which words or phrases may combine and how well they go together. In testing word or phrase combinations, syntactic information alone often can reject an incorrect phrase without requiring costly semantic and discourse analysis. Factors are used for traditional syntactic tests, such as agreement for person or number, but factors also are used to reduce the scores of unlikely phrases. For example, WH questions that are negative (e.g., "What submarine doesn't the U.S. own?") are not likely to occur. A factor statement lowers the value for this interpretation but does not eliminate it completely, so that if no better hypothesis can be formed to account for the input utterance, this interpretation will be accepted. Since the language definition system provides the capability for evaluating phrases in context by means of nonboolean factors, the grammar can be _tuned_ to particular discourse situations and language users simply by adjusting factors that enhance or diminish the acceptability of particular interpretations. It is not necessary to rewrite the language definition for each new domain.

The constituent structures allowed by the composition rules in the system allow WH questions, How Many questions, How+Adjective questions, imperatives, and statements; BE and DO verb forms are included. Noun phrases can be a variety of types. We have concentrated on those relevant for the ship-information domain having WH determiners (what, which, whose), quantifiers (all, any, both, each, either, every, neither, no, none, some), partitive expressions (containing "of"), expressions with numbers (from one through the millions) and units (tons, feet, knots), and comparisons involving numbers. There are more than 100 different kinds of basic noun phrases, to which may be added recursively "of NP" expressions and some classes of prepositional phrases. The current lexicon contains over 600 entries; regular plurals, past and past participle forms, and other suffixes are handled by rules.

13-2.7 _Semantic_ _Knowledge_

The system's knowledge about the task domain is embodied in a partitioned semantic network. A semantic network consists of a collection of nodes and arcs, where each node represents an object (a physical object, situation, event, set, or the like) and each arc establishes a binary relation. This representation of the task domain serves as the basis for building and testing semantic structures corresponding to successively more inclusive phrases. The network also is a source of information for answering queries.

The structure of our semantic networks differs from that of conventional networks in that nodes and arcs are _partitioned_ into spaces. These spaces, playing in networks a role roughly analogous to that played by parentheses in logical notation, group information into bundles that help to condense and organize the network's knowledge. Network partitioning serves a variety of purposes in the speech understanding system: encoding logical connectives and higher-order predicates, especially quantifiers; associating syntactic units with their network images; relating new inputs to previous network knowledge, while maintaining a definite boundary between the new and the old; simultaneously encoding in one network structure multiple hypotheses concerning alternative incorporations of a given constituent into larger phrases; sharing network representations among competing hypotheses; maintaining intermediate results during the question-answering process; defining hierarchies of local contexts for discourse analysis.

Concepts in the domain that can be referenced by individual words are so listed in the lexicon. As lexical items are combined into phrases, these network references are passed to the semantic composition routines. These routines construct new network structures that represent the meanings of the composite phrase, encoding new instances or new combinations of concepts. As phrases are combined into larger phrase units, the composition routines are applied until an interpretation for the entire utterance has been constructed. In this process, case relations provide a basis for using syntactic information in constructing semantic interpretations; they also allow rejecting unallowable semantic structures and blocking syntactic predictions for words that cannot fit in the current context. The interpretation for the entire utterance takes the form of a network fragment anchored to concepts in the original domain model, but maintained in a separate partition, the scratch net.

The scoping of quantifiers, contained implicitly or explicitly in the utterance, is performed in a separate step after an interpretation has been assigned to the total input. Scoping is accomplished by adding new partitioning to the network fragment without changing the topology of the existing structure.

Once a network structure encoding a fully quantified interpretation of an input is formulated, it is passed to the response component. For questions and commands requesting information, calls to the deduction component are generated to retrieve or derive the requested information from the network encoding of the domain model.

13-2.8 Discourse Knowledge

The discourse knowledge in the speech understanding system is used to relate a given utterance (or a portion of it) to the overall dialog context and to entities and structures in the domain. The procedures we have developed are based on systematic studies of dialogs between two people performing some activity together. Contextual influences were found to operate on two different levels in a discourse. The global context--the total discourse and situational setting--provides one set of constraints on the interpretation of an utterance. These constraints are used in the system to identify the referents of definite noun phrases. The second set of constraints is provided by the immediate context of closely preceding utterances. These constraints are used to expand utterance fragments into complete utterances. For the ship-information task domain of the system, the discourse context is limited to a linear history of preceding interactions. For more complex task-oriented dialogs, like those in equipment maintenance, the linear discourse history is replaced by a more structured history related to the organization of the task being performed.

To determine the referents of definite noun phrases, it is necessary to be able to group together those parts of the global knowledge base (that is, the knowledge about the domain of discourse) that are in the focus of attention of the dialog participants. To encode this focus, we have introduced a special partitioning that is independent of the logical partitioning used to represent semantic information. Spaces in this focus partitioning are used to group together and highlight those items in the knowledge base that are relevant at a given point in a dialog. The focus partitioning also is used to highlight a particular way of looking at some concept. For example, if different aspects of an object are focused on in two separate parts of a dialog, different relations in which the object participates will be in the two focus spaces.

The central process necessary for resolving definite noun phrases is finding a network structure that matches the structure of the noun phrase. The matching is performed by the deduction component, which associates nodes and arcs in the network fragment corresponding to the noun phrase with nodes and arcs in the knowledge base. Actual deductions may be required, using theorems--information stored in the network as general rules applicable to whole sets of concepts. The focus representation is used to constrain the search required by this matching process on the basis of the discourse context.

The constituents missing from an elliptical utterance are found in the immediately preceding utterance. The process of building an interpretation for an elliptical phrase entails two steps. First, the items missing from the current utterance must be found in the preceding utterance (or, equivalently, the slot the elliptical phrase fills in the preceding utterance must be determined). Syntactic information plays a major role in this identification, because the corresponding elements usually are structural units of the same type. Semantic closeness, determined from the element and superset hierarchy of the network, also may need to be considered. Second, a complete phrase must be built using the elliptical phrase and the missing constituents found in the previous utterance. This step requires maintaining syntactic, semantic, and discourse information about each of the noun phrases and verb phrases in the preceding utterances.

13-2.9 Deduction Capabilities

Along with the ability to represent entities and their interrelationships in a task domain, it is necessary to reason about them. Thus, the system also contains an inference mechanism that operates directly on semantic network structures. This mechanism serves a dual purpose: during the interpretation of an utterance, it supplies information needed to produce the appropriate semantic structure corresponding to each phrase and to relate it to the dialog context; after an interpretation has been found for a question, it is used to find an answer. It is possible to retrieve information explicitly stored in the networks, to derive information using general statements or theorems in the network, and to invoke user-supplied functions that can obtain information from knowledge sources other than the network, such as data files.

The processing entails matching a network fragment with some portion of the knowledge network. Each element in the fragment is bound to a corresponding one in the knowledge space. The list of bindings contains answers corresponding to the specific links identified. Information from the knowledge network is retrieved directly using the indexing properties of the nets. The derivational mechanism is equivalent to a logically complete first-order predicate calculus theorem prover.

13-2.10 Response Generation

We also have developed the capability of generating, as a response from the system, an English phrase or sentence that corresponds to a semantic network substructure. This substructure usually is the answer to a question asked by the user. Words and phrases are chosen to express the semantic content; a syntactic frame for their organization is selected; and the response is expressed in text form, although we have sometimes used a commercial speech synthesizer to produce a spoken output.

Verbs and grammar rules (in the form of templates) are associated with specific word senses (prototypical nodes) in the network structure. Separate algorithms are then called to generate a response, which may be a sentence, a clause, a noun phrase, and the like. The noun templates order the constituents in a noun phrase by specifying a function to be called with the corresponding network constituent. Using a distributed generation grammar, the generator expresses the content of the input nodes and arcs by employing the closest applicable templates (rules) in the superset hierarchy of those nodes. The answer to a WH question, for example, can be either a noun phrase or a complete sentence, depending on the exact content of the input. The generator can produce a variety of paraphrases of a constituent (e.g., "General Dynamics built the Whale."; "The Whale was manufactured by General Dynamics."). At present, the particular paraphrase is chosen at random.

The experiments to determine the effects of variations in control strategy for our speech understanding system were conducted using a simulated version of the acoustic processing component that performs the mapping operation (see 13-2.5 above).[6] There are compelling reasons for doing simulation experiments in speech understanding research. Extensive testing with the actual mapper would have been impossible both because of the time required and because of increased demands on memory with the large delays for page swapping by the time sharing system. In addition, we were able to study control strategies that would have been too slow for the mapper to perform.

The mapper simulation reproduces the observed mapper performance statistics for the hit scores (correct identifications), the false-alarm rate (incorrect identifications), and the particular false-alarm words and their scores.[7] Because of insufficient data, we were not able to include more complex statistics such as the cooccurrence of hits and false alarms or the dependence of scores on position within the utterance. Consequently, the experimental results provide comparisons between performance levels for the different design alternatives and should not be taken as estimates of the absolute value of the system's performance with a real mapper. For this reason, we do not try to assess the effectiveness of the system as a whole, although there are observations that are relevant for an evaluation of the overall results of the ARPA Speech Understanding Research Program.

13-3.1 Control Strategy Design Choices

In the main experiment of the series, the performance of the speech understanding system, with a lexicon of 305 words, was measured on a set of 60 test utterances,[8] while varying four major control-strategy design choices:

* To check context or not: take into account the restrictions of the possible sentence contexts as part of setting priorities versus ignoring the contextual restrictions except for use in eliminating already formed structures. Context checking should give more information for setting priorities and should lead to better predictions, but the checks may take more time and require more information to be stored.

* To map all or one: test all the words at once at a given location versus trying them one at a time and delaying further testing when a good match is found. Mapping all at once identifies the best acoustic

----

[6] The experiments were carried out on the DEC PDP/KA-10 TENEX system at SRI. We lost access to the IBM 370/145 computer facility, on which the system was being implemented at the System Development Corporation, shortly after the system became operational and before there was an opportunity to exercise it extensively or to refine the interface between the acoustic components and those providing higher level language processing. However, before the computer was removed, we were able to collect sufficient data on the performance of the acoustic components to permit extensive testing of our components and of the system framework.

[7] There were no "misses", cases in which the mapper failed to accept a correct word; however, as a result, the false alarm rate was high: there was an average of almost 40 false alarms for each hit.

[8] The utterances covered a wide range of vocabulary and included questions, commands, and elliptical sentences. The 60 utterances ranged in length from 0.8 to 2.3 seconds. There were 10 utterances at each 0.3 second interval. The utterances averaged 5.9 words in length, with a maximum of 9 words.

candidates and reduces the chances of following false paths, but if there are too many false alarms, it may take substantially more time.

* To <u>island drive</u> <u>or</u> <u>not</u>: go in both directions from arbitrary starting points in the input versus proceeding strictly left-to-right from the beginning. Island driving allows interpretations to be built up around words that match well anywhere in the input, but the added complexity may be less efficient.

* To <u>focus</u> <u>or</u> <u>not</u>: assign priorities for tasks focusing on selected alternatives by inhibiting competion versus proceeding each time with the task with the highest score. Focusing would allow continuing along successful directions and prevent thrashing, but if the focus is wrong too often, the effects would be detrimental.

The experimental design allows us to compare the 16 combinations of control choices and to evaluate, by analysis of variance, the effects of the control strategy variables, that is, the change in performance each produces, averaged over all the possibilities for the other variables. In the discussion that follows, the probabilities associated with an effect are expressed as p<.01, p<.05, and p<.10, corresponding to the different likelihoods that the effect is the result of random variation.

The most important performance measures for the system are <u>accuracy</u> (the percentage of utterances for which the correct sequence of words is found) and <u>runtime</u> (the computation required by the system, including simulated acoustic processing time). For these measures, the control strategy variables had large, significant effects. There was a wide range of values for both measures, from 46.7% to 73.3% for accuracy, and from 221 to 559 seconds processing per utterance for runtime. These wide ranges confirm the importance of control strategy in determining system performance. With respect to the individual control variables, context checking resulted in better accuracy and faster runtimes; mapping all at once improves accuracy but increases runtime; both island driving and focusing by inhibition reduce accuracy and increase runtime.

13-3.2 <u>Effects</u> <u>of</u> <u>Control</u> <u>Strategy</u> <u>Variables</u> <u>on</u> <u>Accuracy</u>

Figure 13-2 shows the effect of the control strategy variables on accuracy. As mentioned above, both context checking and mapping all at once improve accuracy, while island driving and focus by inhibition reduce it. The island driving effect was not significant statistically because of a large interaction with utterance length. For the long utterances, island driving decreased accuracy by 15.8%, but for the short ones it increased accuracy by 7.5%. There was a significant interaction between island driving and focus by inhibition. The bad effect of island driving is less with focus, and the bad effect of focus is less with island driving. To explain this collection of results, we must first consider how accuracy is influenced by control strategy.

	WITH	WITHOUT	DIFFERENCE
CONTEXT CHECKING	66.0	54.4	11.6 *
MAPPING ALL	64.6	55.8	8.8 *
ISLAND DRIVING	58.1	62.3	-4.2
FOCUSING	57.5	62.9	-5.4 *

(percent correct)

* $p<0.05$

Figure 13-2. MAIN EFFECTS OF CONTROL STRATEGY VARIABLES ON ACCURACY

Control strategy affects accuracy only indirectly: all the strategies are <u>complete</u> in the sense that they only reorder, and never eliminate, alternatives. If there were no false alarms, all the systems would get 100%

of the test utterances correct. Even with false alarms, the strategies would get an equal percent correct, if all the possible alternatives could be tried before the system picked an interpretation. Errors would only occur when false alarms had high enough scores to displace hits in the highest rated interpretations. However, in the actual system, the large number of alternatives makes it impossible to consider all of them in the space and time available. As a result, the order in which the alternatives are considered can affect the accuracy, and so can the demands on space and time. Control strategy thus affects accuracy indirectly by reordering alternatives and by modifying space and time requirements. To explain the accuracy effects, we must look at these other factors.

In this experiment, the storage limit had an important influence on accuracy. In the 960 tests (60 utterances times 16 systems), 578 (60.2%) were correct and 382 (39.8%) were wrong. Of the errors, 175 (46%) had an incorrect interpretation, while 207 (54%) had no interpretation at all. Since each system could potentially get the correct answer, and no time limit was imposed until at least one interpretation had been found, all of the 207 utterances with no interpretation were a result of running out of storage.

The storage limit used in the tests was based on the number of phrases constructed. When the total reached 500, the system would stop trying new alternatives and, if any interpretation had been found, pick the highest rated interpretation as its answer. The average number of phrases constructed over all systems was 204 nonterminal and 63 terminal. The system with the best accuracy (with context checking and mapping all at once, but without island driving and focus by inhibition) had the lowest average (113 nonterminals and 45 terminals), while the system with the worst accuracy (with focus by inhibition, but without context checking, mapping all at once, and island driving) had one of the highest averages (260 nonterminals and 68 terminals). Overall, there was a strong negative correlation (-.93) between system accuracy and average number of phrases constructed.

Figure 13-3 shows the effects of the control strategy variables on the number of phrases. The pattern is the same as for accuracy; context checking and mapping all at once have good effects, while island driving and focus by inhibition have bad effects. Again, because of a large interaction with length, the island driving effect is not significant statistically. There are significant interactions, $p < .05$, between island driving and focus by inhibition for storage, and between context checking and mapping all at once.

	WITH	WITHOUT	DIFFERENCE
CONTEXT CHECKING	240	294	-54 **
MAPPING ALL	244	290	-46 **
ISLAND DRIVING	287	247	40
FOCUSING	281	253	28 *

(number of phrases)

** $p < 0.01$ * $p < 0.05$

Figure 13-3. MAIN EFFECTS OF CONTROL STRATEGY VARIABLES ON STORAGE

The beneficial effects of mapping all at once are caused by a reduction in the proportion of false alarm terminal phrases. Mapping all at once significantly reduces the proportion of terminal phrases that are false alarms--from 88.0% to 85.7%, $p < .01$. The false terminal proportion is in turn significantly correlated with the number of phrases (.72) and with accuracy (-.75). When the words are all mapped at once at a given location, the system is able to take advantage of the differences in false alarm and hit score distributions to reduce the likelihood of constructing false terminal phrases. Notice that a relatively small change in false terminal percentage has a large effect on system performance.

Surprisingly, context checking also results in a significant reduction in the false terminal percentages--from 87.5% to 86.2%, p<.01. This reduction may be evidence that context checking is giving lower priority to looking for words adjacent to false alarms than it gives to looking for words next to hits. This change could affect the false alarm terminal likelihood, since a hit is always adjacent to a hit, while false alarms often have nothing but other false alarms next to them. In addition to its effect on false terminals, context checking may be improving the storage requirements and accuracy by generally improving the priority setting, thereby reducing the likelihood of following false paths.

Focus by inhibition slightly increases the proportion of false alarm terminal phrases (from 86.3% to 87.3%), but this increase is not statistically significant. The explanation of the ill effects of focus is essentially the converse of the explanation of the effects of context checking. Context checking makes performance better by improving priorities, while focus by inhibition makes it worse by distorting priorities. Focus too often changes priorities to bias the system in favor of a false alarm instead of a hit. In the focus-systems, there was an average of 3.5 hits put in focus per utterance compared to 12.9 false alarms. Focus conflicts changed priorities in favor of a false alarm 112 times per utterance and in favor of a hit only 15 times per utterance. Thus the priorities, and the system performance, were better with the unbiased best-first strategy than with focus by inhibition.

Island driving did not affect the false terminal proportion, but it did have bad effects on storage and accuracy for the longer utterances. To get an utterance correct, island driving must start at least one island with a hit. If all the seeds--words selected to start islands--are false alarms, the utterance will not be interpreted correctly. The overall average was 3.7 false alarm seeds per utterance and 0.9 hit seeds. There were one or more hit seeds in 82% of the tests using island driving. The bad effects of island driving on long utterances were not caused by an increase in the number of false alarm seeds. The average rank of the first hit in the sequence of words for use in forming islands was 4.8, and the rank did not increase with utterance length. (The correlation between rank and length was .04.) For utterances 1.7 seconds or longer, instead of an increase in the number of seeds necessary to get a hit, there was an increase in the amount of storage consumed per island. Perhaps the greater length allowed islands to grow in both directions, whereas in shorter utterances the utterance boundaries blocked one direction or the other.

The interaction of island driving and focus by inhibition can be explained as the result of the storage limit. The limit put a ceiling on the size of the possible combined effect. The limit was reached frequently, and, thus, the combined effect was less than the sum of the individual effects. Similarly, the interaction between context checking and mapping all at once is a result of overlapping good effects, which consequently fail to add. The same interaction pattern for context checking and mapping all at once appears in false terminal proportion, p<.05, and in accuracy, p<.10.

It is appropriate to present a brief analysis of the utterances that got one or more interpretations but were incorrect because their highest rated interpretation was wrong. As mentioned previously, this happened in 175 tests. In 109 of these (62%), the chosen interpretation was reasonable linguistically but contained incorrect words. In 10 cases (6%), the chosen interpretation could have been eliminated by a better (i.e., more restrictive) language definition. Finally, 56 of the errors (32%) were harmless, in that the system would probably produce the same answer as if it had found the correct sequence of words (e.g., substitutions of "the" for "a", or plural for singular). If the harmless errors are counted as correct in calculating accuracy, the most accurate system increases in percent correct from 73.3% to 81.7%, and the average accuracy for all systems increases about 5.8%.

The accuracy effects have been explained in terms of storage requirements, proportions of false terminal phrases, and priorities. The important role of the storage limit raises the question of whether the accuracy effects would have disappeared if more storage had been available. We believe that the effects would have been smaller but still important. The effects on the proportion of false terminal phrases would remain, as would the effects on priorities. A smaller percentage of false terminals and better priorities will cause the system to find the correct interpretation sooner, and, even if the storage limit were relaxed, the limit on runtime would remain to penalize systems that were slow to find the right answer. The effects of control strategy choices on accuracy would only vanish if space and runtime considerations were both removed.

13-3.3 Effects of Control Variables on Runtime

The system runtime is another important performance measure. Here, we will use the phrase total runtime to refer to the simulated acoustic processing, plus the actual processing time (on a DEC PDP/KA-10) for the executive and the semantic components. The executive time is mainly spent setting priorities and parsing. The semantics time is used in constructing semantic translations and in dealing with anaphoric references and ellipsis. The reported total runtime does not include acoustic preprocessing or question answering, since neither is affected by the experimental variables. We report results only for total, executive, and acoustic times; semantic times are not reported, both because they are redundant given the other three measures, and because they are relatively small in comparison to the others.

The main effects of the control variables on total runtime are given in Figure 13-4. All the variables except context checking increase the runtime. Dividing the utterances into a short group (0.8 to 1.4 seconds) and a long group (1.7 to 2.3 seconds) shows that island driving has a much worse effect on runtime for long than for short utterances. For short utterances, island driving increased the mean runtime from 262 to 290 seconds, a difference of 28. For long utterances, the increase was from 457 to 598 seconds, a difference of 141. Recall that for long utterances, island driving also had worse effects on storage and accuracy.

	WITH	WITHOUT	DIFFERENCE
CONTEXT CHECKING	383	421	-38 **
MAPPING ALL	498	305	193 **
ISLAND DRIVING	444	359	85 #
FOCUSING	417	386	31 *

(seconds per utterance)

** $p < 0.01$ * $p < 0.05$ # $p < .10$

Figure 13-4. MAIN EFFECTS OF CONTROL STRATEGY VARIABLES ON TOTAL RUNTIME

Figures 13-5 and 13-6 show the main effects on executive runtime and acoustic runtime respectively. In both cases, context checking decreases the runtime, while island driving and focus by inhibition increase it. Mapping all at once improves the executive runtime, but leads to a huge increase in acoustic processing time. As usual, the examination of the results according to utterance length shows that island driving is worse for longer utterances. The average executive and acoustic times together account for 95% of the average total, so, as mentioned previously, separate effects for semantics are not reported.

Analysis of variance for total, executive, and acoustic runtimes reveals a significant interaction between context checking and mapping all at once

(p<.01 for total and acoustics; p<.05 for executive). For total and acoustic
runtime, the good effect of context checking was reduced when words were
mapped all at once at each location, and the increase in runtime caused by
mapping all at once was greater when also context checking. For executive
runtime, both context checking and mapping all at once had good effects, and
there was actually a synergistic relation; context checking helped more when
mapping all at once, and vice versa.

	WITH	WITHOUT	DIFFERENCE
CONTEXT CHECKING	109	117	-8 #
MAPPING ALL	90	135	-45 **
ISLAND DRIVING	127	98	29 #
FOCUSING	120	106	14 **

(seconds per utterance)
** p<0.01 # p<.10

Figure 13-5. MAIN EFFECTS OF CONTROL STRATEGY VARIABLES ON EXECUTIVE RUNTIME

	WITH	WITHOUT	DIFFERENCE
CONTEXT CHECKING	254	282	-28 **
MAPPING ALL	389	147	242 **
ISLAND DRIVING	295	241	54 #
FOCUSING	276	260	16 #

(seconds per utterance)
** p<0.01 # p<.10

Figure 13-6. MAIN EFFECTS OF CONTROL STRATEGY VARIABLES ON ACOUSTIC RUNTIME

The runtime results follow basically the same pattern as the accuracy and
storage results. Island driving and focus by inhibition have bad effects,
with worse results from island driving for longer utterances, while context
checking has consistently good effects. Mapping all at once has a good
effect on executive runtime, but, unfortunately, it causes large increases in
acoustic and total runtimes. The only inconsistency with the previous
pattern of effects for accuracy and storage is the bad effect of mapping all
at once on the acoustic runtime. This fact is explained by pointing out that
the mapper was designed for checking words one at a time, and, in the
simulation, does not accumulate or share information to make subsequent tests
more efficient. Finally, it is worth noting that the extra effort for
context checking resulted in a net decrease in processing time. The best
context checking system spent an average of 6.1 seconds more per utterance
doing the extra processing, but it was still 41 seconds faster per utterance
than the corresponding system without context checking.

13-3.4 Implications of the Results of the Control Strategy Design Experiment
The experimental results suggest a number of modifications that could be
expected to improve the accuracy and speed of the system. Mapping all at
once improves accuracy and executive runtime, but at a large cost in acoustic
and total runtime. Redesign of the mapper, for example, by just cutting the
acoustic processing in half would make mapping all at once as efficient. The
choice, whether to map all or not, is explored further in Experiment 3.
The overall effects of island driving were bad, and they were particularly
bad for longer utterances. Island driving was hurt by false alarm seeds,
especially when the utterance was long enough for the islands to grow in both
directions. Perhaps island driving can be modified to overcome this problem.
For example, a multiword seed technique might reduce the number of false
alarm seeds, and a restriction to keep seeds near the start of the utterance

might reduce the storage needed per island. Another alternative would be to pick seeds anywhere in the utterance but to restrict them to growing in one direction to an utterance boundary before allowing them to grow in the other direction.

The effects of focus by inhibition were bad on all measures. The cause of the bad effects was too much focusing on false alarms, so we have tried a modified version that is much more conservative about which words to put in focus. It uses the false-alarm likelihood estimates as a primary criterion in selecting words for focus. The modified focus method was tested on the 60 utterances using the best of the original focus systems. The modification greatly reduced the number of false alarms in focus and improved the performance of all measures. In fact, this modified system proved to be the most accurate of all the systems tested. However, it is still slightly more costly in storage and runtime. The effect of the modification are small (because so few words are put in focus by the modified technique), but they suggest that focus by inhibition might have significant good effects if further effort was devoted to tuning the algorithm for selecting focus words.

Context checking had uniformly good effects. For both accuracy and runtime, it was worth the extra effort to get better priority setting. This result clearly depends on the fact that we put a large amount of the system's knowledge into the rule procedures of the language definition rather than into the structural declarations. It would be interesting to repeat these tests with different language definitions that had the same linguistic scope but put more information into the structure and less in the procedures.

13-3.5 The Effects of Gaps and Overlaps on System Performance

The mapper performance data do not aid us in simulating the mapper when it is called on to test whether two words accepted individually are also acceptable as a contiguous pair. Such tests, referred to as "phrase mapping", are necessary whenever words and phrases are combined to form larger units. In the simulation of the mapper, we replaced phrase mapping by a simple threshold test; we allowed gaps and overlaps of up to 0.05 second of speech, but rejected those that were larger. The second experiment we conducted tests the effect of different values of the gap-overlap parameter on the performance of the best system from the control strategy design experiment. It gives the results for a variety of measures with gap-overlap sizes of 0.00, 0.05, and 0.10 second.

The performance is much better for 0.00 and much worse for 0.10 second of gap or overlap. Notice that a technique using a simple threshold on the size of gaps and overlaps would not be acceptable in practice; further studies show that the threshold would have to be at least 15 centiseconds to guarantee 100% accuracy, and the data reported in Figure 13-7 suggest that the resulting performance would be terrible. These results provide strong evidence for the importance of special acoustic tests to verify word-pair junctions. Such tests can lead to a large reduction in the average hit rank and, consequently, to significant improvements in both accuracy and runtime.

	GAP-OVERLAP SIZE		
	0.00	0.05	0.10
RAW ACCURACY (percent)	96.7	73.3	48.3
FORGIVING ACCURACY (percent)	98.3	81.7	58.3
FALSE TERMINAL (percent)	58.2	83.2	89.1
NUMBER OF NONTERMINALS	31	113	217
TOTAL RUNTIME (sec/sec-speech)	140	247	333
EXECUTIVE RUNTIME (sec/sec-speech)	10	34	69
ACOUSTIC RUNTIME (sec/sec-speech)	128	205	243

Figure 13-7. EFFECTS OF GAPS AND OVERLAPS IN MAPPING

13-3.6 The Effects of Bigger Vocabulary and Better Acoustics on System Performance

The third experiment studies the effects of increased vocabulary size and improved acoustic-processing accuracy. As test systems, we use the two best systems from the control strategy design experiment: those with context checking, without island driving or focus by inhibition, and with and without mapping all at once. These are the best systems for accuracy and speed, respectively, and they also give us more information about the mapping all at once control strategy choice. Thus, there are three experimental variables: vocabulary size, acoustic accuracy, and mapping all at once or not. Data for two of the eight combinations, mapping all at once or not for smaller vocabulary and regular acoustic accuracy, come from the first experiment. For the third experiment the other six combinations were tested to provide a complete set of data for analysis of the effects of the variables.

The large vocabulary is a 451-word superset of the 305-word vocabulary used in the other experiments. The mapper performance data showed that, with the 451-word vocabulary, the mapper made 2026 false alarms and had a false alarm rate of 142 false alarms per second of speech (compared with 114 for the 305-word vocabulary). Using this information, the mapper performance was simulated for the large vocabulary on the same set of 60 test utterances.

Improved acoustic-processing accuracy was simulated by a 7% downward stretch of the false alarm score distribution, while leaving the hit scores unchanged. In other words, a false alarm score X, in the range 45 to 100, was replaced by 1.07X-7. If the result was below the threshold of 45, the false alarm was eliminated. This process reduced the number of false alarms for the 305-word vocabulary from 1564 to 1204, and for the 451-word vocabulary, from 2026 to 1541. Because the subthreshold scores were eliminated, the simulated improvement left the average false alarm score almost unchanged: for the 305-word vocabulary, it went from 59.4 to 60.2, and for the 451-word vocabulary, it went from 58.2 to 58.8. We feel that an improvement in acoustic accuracy of the magnitude simulated here could have been achieved by careful tuning of the mapper.

Figure 13-8 records the accuracy results, using the notation "M" for tests with mapping all at once, "m" for those without, "A" for systems with improved acoustic accuracy, "a" for those without, "V" for systems with increased vocabulary, and "v" for those without. Improved acoustics raises the accuracy of the system with mapping all at once from 73.3% to 85.0%, or from 81.7% to 95.0% if harmless errors are forgiven. However, if vocabulary size is also increased, accuracy drops slightly from 73.3% to 71.6%. Thus, in this experiment, a 7% improvement in acoustic accuracy almost compensates for a 48% increase in vocabulary. Comparison of the M-results to the m-results shows that mapping all at once consistently helps accuracy.

	AMv	Amv	aMv	AMV	amv	AmV	aMV	amV
RAW (percent)	85.0	78.3	73.3	71.6	70.0	68.3	68.3	53.3
FORGIVING (percent)	95.0	85.0	81.7	78.3	76.7	76.7	75.0	58.3

Figure 13-8. EFFECTS OF VOCABULARY AND IMPROVED ACOUSTICS ON ACCURACY

The main effects on accuracy and several other measures are given in Figure 13-9. Improved acoustics leads to big gains in accuracy, storage, and runtime. Increased vocabulary makes performance worse, but at least the system does not collapse. As in the first experiment, mapping all at once improves everything except acoustic and total runtimes. Vocabulary size and mapping all at once interacted significantly for acoustic runtime (p<.05). The increase in runtime caused by mapping all at once is greater for the bigger vocabulary, and, surprisingly, the increase in vocabulary size leads to a reduction in processing, if the system is not mapping all at once. The latter effect is presumably the result of an increased number of false alarms making it easier to form complete (but wrong) interpretations. Mapping all at once also interacted significantly with acoustics for acoustic runtime (p<.01), total runtime (p<.01), and false terminal percentage (p<.05). There was a synergistic interaction causing mapping all at once to be more effective with better acoustics, and vice versa. This result is readily explained since mapping all at once is designed to take advantage of the difference between false-alarm and hit-score distributions, and improving the acoustics enhances that difference by reducing the number of high scoring false alarms.

		WITH	WITHOUT	DIFFERENCE	
RAW ACCURACY (percent)					
	A	75.8	66.3	9.5	**
	V	65.4	76.7	-11.3	#
	M	74.6	67.5	7.1	*
PHRASES (total number terminal and nonterminal)					
	A	155	208	-53	**
	V	204	159	45	**
	M	156	206	-51	**
FALSE TERMINALS (percent)					
	A	80.6	85.9	-5.3	**
	V	84.3	82.1	2.2	
	M	81.7	84.8	-3.1	**
TOTAL RUNTIME (seconds/utterance)					
	A	266	320	-54	**
	V	312	275	37	*
	M	383	204	179	**
ACOUSTIC RUNTIME (seconds/utterance)					
	A	187	213	-26	**
	V	205	195	10	
	M	315	84	231	**
EXECUTIVE RUNTIME (seconds/utterance)					
	A	66	89	-23	**
	V	88	67	21	**
	M	55	101	-46	**

** p<.01   * p<.05   # p<.10

Figure 13-9. MAIN EFFECTS OF ACOUSTICS, VOCABULARY, AND MAPPING ALL AT ONCE

In addition to the main tests for this experiment, we also ran another test to study the effect of improved acoustics on a system using island driving. When the best island driving system from the control strategy design experiment was tested on the 305-word vocabulary with 7% simulated improvement in acoustics, it gained in accuracy from 68.3% to 78.3%. It was still below the non-island driving system, and the gap between them remained large. Thus, improvements in acoustics of the size considered here appear to be inadequate to solve the problems with island driving.

In summary, this experiment has given us information about how badly the system is hurt by increased vocabulary, and how much it is helped by improved acoustics. With respect to the control-strategy design choices, further evidence appeared in favor of mapping all at once, and against the current version of island driving.

13-3.7 Discussion of the Most Accurate System

The final measurements to be discussed deal with the system with the highest accuracy: with context checking and mapping all at once, but without island driving and focus by inhibition. Figure 13-10 shows the accuracy breakdown in terms of the existence and relative scores of correct and incorrect interpretations. Overall, this system got 44 utterances correct and missed 16. Of the 16 errors, five were harmless; three consisted of leaving out a plural morpheme. These accounted for all of the cases in which an interpretation was found but had a worse score than an incorrect interpretation that was also found. The other two harmless errors were among the cases in which only incorrect interpretations were found. In one, the system picked an interpretation containing "has" instead of a plural morpheme followed by "have". In the other, a singular verb suffix was accepted instead of a past tense suffix. In both cases, the incorrect interpretation had a higher score than would have been given to the correct interpretation (if it had been found). Thus, because of high scoring false alarms, the optimal solution (the interpretation with the highest score possible) was not the correct solution.

```
32 times only got correct interpretation
 8 times only got incorrect interpretation
 3 times got no interpretation
12 times correct score better than bad score
 2 times correct score same as bad score
 3 times correct score worse than bad score
---------
60 total--44 correct and 16 errors.
```

Figure 13-10. ACCURACY BREAKDOWN FOR THE MOST ACCURATE SYSTEM

The two cases having correct and incorrect interpretations with equal scores were caused by the presence of false alarms that could not be rejected by linguistic considerations alone. The three cases getting no interpretation all had a low scoring word in either the first or second position (mapper scores of 59 or less), and in two of the cases, island driving succeeded in finding the correct answer.

The eight cases in which only an incorrect interpretation was found can be divided into three categories: forgiven errors, optimal but not correct, and suboptimal. As mentioned previously, two of the eight with no correct interpretation were forgiven errors. Three were the result of finding an optimal interpretation that was not correct. (Surprisingly, island driving got one of these correct by stopping with a suboptimal, correct interpretation.) The final three were the result of stopping with a suboptimal, incorrect interpretation. In these last three, the correct interpretation started with either a bad score (56) or a small word ("how" or "the"). In each case, island driving got the correct answer.

Of the 16 utterances that the system missed, five were forgivable acoustic errors, six were correctly interpreted by an island driving system, four were the result of finding optimal but incorrect interpretations, and one had so many attractive false paths that it could not be handled within the storage limits by any of the systems. These results indicate that a different control strategy might have correctly answered at least five utterances more than this system did: three for which it picked a suboptimal interpretation and two for which it found no interpretation although a system with island driving found the correct one. Such an improved strategy would have an 81.7% accuracy (90.0% forgiving), with nonforgiven errors traceable to either acoustics (five cases) or storage limits (one case). This result gives a rough upper bound for improvements by modifying the control strategy versus modifying the acoustics. Of the 16 errors by fCMi, five were the result of the control-strategy failing to find the optimal interpretation, and 11 were the result of acoustic errors--but five of the 11 acoustic errors could be forgiven.

313

Understanding spoken language requires a variety of different kinds of knowledge about language and about how language information should be used during the interpretation of an utterance. In our speech understanding system development we have incorporated resources for acoustics, syntax, semantics, and discourse that provide:

* A characterization of the basic elements that can be found in a speech signal, how these elements combine into larger units, how words are formed from these units, and how each of these aggregations can be detected computationally.
* A specification of the words that are used and how they are combined into phrases.
* A representation of the set of concepts (including objects, relationships, and situations) that can be talked about.
* A statement of the relationships between the words and phrases used and the concepts they reference, together with procedures for deriving these relationships.
* A representation of the context determined by a dialog and how the context influences, and is influenced by, the interpretation of an utterance.
* A specification of the procedures which relate all or part of an utterance to particular domain entities in a specific context.

To ensure that the process functions as a whole, we have provided a framework within which these knowledge resources are combined and coordinated effectively. This framework includes:

* An ability to indicate close interactions among the various sources of knowledge in a manner that allows the distinctions between the individual sources to be maintained.
* A flexible means of stating and changing the kinds of knowledge available and the ways in which they interact.
* A flexible control structure, allowing alternative processing strategies to be tested and evaluated without affecting the statement of the knowledge and its interactions.
* An effective way to use all possible knowledge in choosing among and limiting alternatives.

Integrating the knowledge resources around phrases provides an easy means of stating the relations among the different kinds of knowledge, thus providing clarity of organization. The choice of the phrase as a unit also contributes to processing efficiency by balancing the tradeoffs between the cost of managing many small processes and that of performing larger processes which may pursue the wrong alternative longer than desired.

Separating the specification of the language to be understood from the decision about the control procedures to be applied allows the rules defining the language to be stated independently of any specification of the order in which they are to be used. In addition, alternative control procedures can be modified, tested, and evaluated without modifying the language definition.

Being able to use information from each knowledge resource during the evaluation of each phrase whether complete or only partially interpreted has three important benefits. First, erroneous interpretations can be rejected as early as possible in the processing. Second, evaluations from whatever knowledge resources are appropriate can be combined and used in choosing among the alternatives to be considered during processing. Finally, if more than one interpretation of an utterance is produced, evaluations from all the resources can be used in ordering them to determine the most likely one.

The research on speech understanding at SRI has produced system control concepts and a set of system components that are well suited for further work on speech understanding and also for research on natural language systems with text input. Under ARPA support,[9] we are applying the products of the speech understanding project in a Navy command and control context to provide natural language text access to a distributed data base stored on a number of different computers. Under National Science Foundation support,[10] we are exploring the significance of these products for understanding natural language dialog betwen humans and computers for the accomplishment of a structured task in a dynamic situation. We believe that the elaboration of complex knowledge sources and sophisticated mechanisms for integrating and controlling them will prove to have major implications for future work in both artificial intelligence and linguistics, as well as in speech understanding itself.

13-5. REFERENCES

Bernstein, Morton I., Interactive Systems Research: Final Report. TM-5243/004, System Development Corporation, Santa Monica, California, November, 1975.

Grosz, Barbara J., "The Representation and Use of Focus in a System for Understanding Dialogs," <Proceedings of the Fifth International Joint Conference on Artificial Intelligence>. Pittsburgh, Pennsylvania: Carnegie-Mellon University, 1977, pp. 67-76.

Hendrix, Gary G. Expanding the Utility of Semantic Networks Through Partitioning. Advance Papers, International Joint Conference on Artificial Intelligence, Cambridge, Massachusetts: Massachusetts Institute of Technology, 1975, pp. 115-121.

Kaplan, Ronald M., "A Multi-processing Approach to Natural Language," Proceedings, National Computer Conference, Volume 42. Montvale, New Jersey: AFIPS Press, 1973, pp. 435-440.

Medress, Mark F., et al., "Speech Understanding Systems: Report of a Steering Committee," Artificial Intelligence, 1977, 9, 307-316, and SIGART Newsletter, April 1977, 62, 4-8.

Newell, Allen, et al., Speech Understanding Systems. Amsterdam: North-Holland Publishing Company, 1973.

Robinson, Jane J., "Performance Grammars." In: Speech Recognition: Invited Papers of the 1974 IEEE Symposium, edited by D. Raj Reddy. Academic Press, New York, 1975, pp. 401-427.

Walker, Donald E. (ed.), Understanding Spoken Language. New York: Elsevier North-Holland, 1978.

Walker, Donald E., and William H. Paxton, et al., "Procedures for Integrating Knowledge in a Speech Understanding System," Proceedings of the Fifth International Joint Conference on Artificial Intelligence. Pittsburgh, Pennsylvania: Carnegie-Mellon University, 1977, pp. 36-42.

----

[9] Contract No. DAAG29-76-C-0012.

[10] Grant No. MCS76-22004.

14.

THE HWIM SPEECH UNDERSTANDING SYSTEM

Jared J. Wolf
William A. Woods
Bolt Beranek and Newman Inc.

14-1. INTRODUCTION

This chapter describes the research and development in speech understanding systems carried out at Bolt Beranek and Newman Inc. (BBN) during the ARPA Speech Understanding Project. This work included the development of bottom-up and top-down acoustic-phonetic recognizers, a lexical matching scheme that accounts for within-word and across-word phonological effects, the use of ATN grammars for combining syntactic, semantic, pragmatic, and prosodic information, an efficient bidirectional parsing algorithm for ATN grammars, a uniform scoring philosophy for combining the evaluations of different knowledge sources, and the exploration of approximate and admissible control strategies. These developments were implemented in a speech understanding system called HWIM (for "Hear What I Mean").

In this chapter, we shall discuss the philosophy underlying the design of HWIM (Sec. 14-2), the system, its knowledge components, and its control strategy (Sec. 14-3), the system performance at the end of the project (Sec. 14-4), and some conclusions about what we've learned (Sec. 14-5). We can describe this research only briefly here. For more complete descriptions of all parts of the HWIM system, see (Woods et al., 1976).

14-2. DESIGN PHILOSOPHY OF HWIM

14-2.1 Knowledge Components for Speech Understanding

When the ARPA speech understanding program first began in 1971, our state of knowledge about how a speech understanding system should be organized was quite limited. The only existing example, the Vicens-Reddy system at Stanford University (Vicens, 1969), was so specialized that its understanding strategy relied on such system-specific facts as that most words began and ended with stop consonants and that all sentences contained the word "block". The techniques used were clearly not general enough to provide a model of how a speech understanding system should be organized. Looking instead to initial experience with human spectrogram readers (Klatt and Stevens, 1973) for our model, we became convinced that a potentially viable speech understanding system would involve some organization of the following conceptually distinct sources of knowledge:

a) Phonetic Segmentation and Labeling - a process of detecting acoustic - phonetic events in the speech signal and characterizing the nature of the individual segments of the signal.

b) Lexical Retrieval - a process of retrieving candidate words from the lexicon that are acoustically similar to the labeled segments.

c) Word Matching - a process of determining a measure of the degree of similarity between a word hypothesis at a given point in the speech signal and the acoustic evidence there.

d) <u>Syntax</u> - the ability to determine whether a given sequence of words is a possible subpart of a grammatical sentence and to predict possible continuations for such sentence fragments.

e) <u>Semantics</u> - the ability to determine if, in addition to being grammatical, a given hypothesized sentence is meaningful or nonsensical.

f) <u>Pragmatics</u> - the ability to determine if a sentence is appropriate to the context in which it is uttered, given knowledge of the particular speaker, the task he is trying to accomplish, and what has been said previously in the discourse.

In addition to these sources of knowledge, it was obvious that the spectrogram readers were making use of an additional ability that was considerably less overt. By some criteria, they were making decisions about which fragmentary hypotheses to rule out, which ones to pursue further by trying to find compatible interpretations of adjacent portions of the utterance, and when to return to a previously rejected hypothesis in light of new information. These decisions imply the existence of a <u>control strategy</u> <u>for speech understanding</u>, and from the beginning, our speech understanding system has been designed to facilitate the discovery and exploration of such strategies.

14-2.2 Incremental Simulation

The method that we adopted to begin our research was one of <u>incremental</u> <u>simulation</u> (Woods and Makhoul, 1973), in which an overall system is "implemented" with some combination of computer programs and human simulators filling the roles of the different components. Initially, we implemented lexical retrieval and word matching components with computer programs, and then used one human to simulate a segmenting and labeling component, and another one, in another room, to simulate the syntax, semantics, pragmatics, and control components. Since this organization tended to break up the Gestalt recognition available to a single person both forming and matching word hypotheses against a spectrogram, it allowed us to explore the control strategy issue by making visible the intermediate steps that would otherwise be subconscious. Our original experiences with this mode of exploration have long since been widely supplemented by running a fully programmed system, with detailed tracings of intermediate results. These tracings, an example of which is given in (Woods et al., 1976, Vol. I), were subjected to detailed "failure analyses". As a result, our understanding of speech understanding problems and control strategy issues increased steadily during the project.

14-2.3 Task Domain

The difficulty of constructing a speech understanding system depends on (among other things) an inherent level of difficulty imposed by the task. Tasks differ in difficulty due to factors such as the amount of noise in the speaker's environment, the quality of the transmission channel through which the signal is acquired, the amount of individualized training of the speaker permitted, the number of different speakers and the differences of their dialects, the size of the vocabulary, and the inherent difficulty of the language spoken. All of these factors except the last one were effectively controlled by the target goals of the ARPA speech understanding program. The difficulty of the language that the speaker is permitted to use (i.e., the scope of the syntax that is permitted and the range of semantic concepts to which the system can refer) was specifically left open, although permitted to be artificial and constraining. The selection of a task determines this language, including the basic vocabulary that will be recognized and the basic knowledge that will be used by the syntactic, semantic, and pragmatic components to judge the acceptability of hypothesized interpretations of the utterance.

In the first speech understanding system developed at BBN, called SPEECHLIS (for "SPEECH Language Information System"), we worked in the context of an existing natural language question-answering system, LUNAR (Woods et al., 1972), which had a well-defined vocabulary, syntax, and semantics. This system answered English questions of the kind that would be asked by a lunar geologist about the chemical analyses of the Apollo 11 moon rocks. Its vocabulary and syntax were extensive, but its range of semantic concepts was extremely narrow. In this respect, the SPEECHLIS task was comparable to that of the CMU Harpy and Hearsay-II systems, which deal with authors and topics and the relationship between them (although SPEECHLIS' grammar was much more extensive). SPEECHLIS was characterized by a semantics-first understanding strategy that used a semantic network to identify the underlying semantic relationships possible among matches of content words found in the utterance and then used syntactic information to predict and fill in small function words and check the overall syntactic consistency of the utterance. The SPEECHLIS system dealt with a vocabulary of 250 words (drawn from the 3500 word vocabulary of the LUNAR system) and was demonstrated in 1973 (Bates, 1975; Nash-Webber, 1975a, 1975b; Rovner et al., 1974, 1975; Schwartz and Makhoul, 1975; Woods, 1975). The kinds of sentences that it understood are illustrated by the following:

Have any people done chemical analyses on this rock?
Give me all lunar samples with magnetite.
Do we have samples which contain silicon?
List all the samples which contain silicon.

BBN's second system, called HWIM (for "Hear What I Mean"), attempted to deal with a more diverse range of semantic concepts. HWIM dealt with a domain of trip planning and travel budget management. The system was intended to be an assistant to a travel budget manager, handling information about planned and taken trips, travel budgets and their status, plane fares and per diems, and other information important to trip planning. Whereas the vast majority of sentences in SPEECHLIS were variants on a few basic concepts -- "printout", "samples", and the containment of a mineral, element, or isotope in a sample -- HWIM covered a range of semantic concepts including people, places, budgets, budget items, times, dates, amounts of money, modes of travel, types of fare, trips, legs of trips, per diems, etc.

The travel budget task was chosen as a small and easily comprehensible version of a generalized management problem. Although it is a much more difficult task than the SPEECHLIS and Harpy tasks because of its increased semantic range (e.g., it is less easy to guess what the speaker is saying on the basis of a priori expectations or a few key words), the HWIM domain has a potential advantage of being able to develop a more realistic pragmatic model of the user. Consequently, it is easier to characterize the pragmatic constraints on the meaningfulness and possible interpretations of sentences in the context of a preceding dialogue. (Unfortunately the effect of using these contextual constraints has yet to be measured, since the final test runs of the HWIM system were made on sentences in isolation.)

A very brief sample dialogue with the system is shown below, with the travel budget manager's spoken input preceded by ">".

>Where is the next ASA meeting?
THE NEXT ASA MEETING WILL BE IN SAN DIEGO, CALIFORNIA.
>What is the round trip fare to San Diego?
THE ROUND-TRIP BOSTON TO SAN DIEGO AIR FARE IS $446.
>How much is left in the speech budget?
THE SPEECH BUDGET HAS $872.93 REMAINING.
>How many trips has Rich taken?
RICH SCHWARTZ HAS TAKEN ONE TRIP TO PHILADELPHIA FOR THE IEEE CONFERENCE.
>Enter a trip for Rich Schwartz to San Diego.
WHEN IS THE TRAVELER LEAVING BOSTON?
>November 14.

14-2.4 A Computational Framework for Perception

The BBN speech understanding system has evolved within a general framework for viewing perceptual processes. Central to this framework is an entity called a theory. A theory represents a particular hypothesis about some or all of the sensory stimuli that are present. Perception is viewed as the process of forming a believable, coherent theory that can account for all the stimuli. In our framework, this is achieved by successive refinement and extension of partial theories until a best complete theory is found.

In general, the perception process requires the ability to recognize any member of a potentially infinite class of perceptible objects that are constructed out of elementary constituents according to known rules. That is, the object perceived is generally a compound object, constructed from members of a finite set of elementary constituents according to some kind of well-formedness rules. These elementary constituents, as well as the relationships among them that are tested in the well-formedness rules, must be directly perceptible. Thus, a perceptual system must incorporate some basic epistemological assumptions about the things that it can perceive and the rules governing their assembly. The well-formedness rules can be used to reject impossible interpretations of the input stimuli and may also be usable to predict other constituents that could be present if a given partial theory were correct.

This perception framework assumes mechanisms for using subsets of the input stimuli to form initial "seed" hypotheses for certain elementary constituents (stimulus-driven hypothesization) and mechanisms for deriving hypotheses for additional elementary constituents that could be compatible with a given partial theory (theory-driven, or predicted, hypothesization). It also assumes mechanisms for verifying hypotheses against the input stimuli and evaluating the well-formedness of a compound hypothesis to assign it some measure of quality and/or likelihood. A theory may therefore be thought of as a hypothesis that has been evaluated in this way and assigned a measure of confidence.

In the case of speech understanding, a theory can range from an elementary hypothesis that a particular word is present at a particular point in the input (a word match) to a complete hypothesis of a covering word sequence with a syntactic and semantic interpretation. (In general, a theory is a set of compatible word hypotheses with possible gaps between them and with partial syntactic and semantic interpretations.) A partial theory may be able to generate predictions for appropriate words or word classes either adjacent to the words already hypothesized or elsewhere in the utterance.

Predictions are dealt with in our computational framework by two kinds of devices: monitors, which are dormant processing requests passively waiting for expected constituents, and proposals, which are elementary hypotheses that will be actively evaluated against the input. When a monitor is triggered or a proposed hypothesis is confirmed, an event is created calling for the evaluation of a new hypothesis that, if acceptable, will become a new theory. In general, a number of events are competing for service by the processor at any moment. In human perception, there may be full parallel processing of such events, but in a serial machine, these events must be processed one at a time. In our computational framework, events are maintained on a queue in order of priority, the top event being processed at each step. The processing of an event can result in new proposals being made, new monitors being set, and existing monitors being triggered to produce new events. Since so much hinges on the order in which events are chosen for processing, a major control strategy issue is that of assigning priorities to events in order to find the most likely interpretation of the input without exhaustively exploring the full range of possible hypothetical interpretations.

14-2.5 Scoring Philosophy

A major concern in our speech understanding research has been the development of a uniform scoring philosophy for combining the evaluations of hypotheses from different knowledge sources. In the initial incremental simulations, we sought an understanding of this problem by allowing a human experimenter to see a vector of scores from the individual components and form a subjective evaluation of the overall goodness of a hypothesis. In SPEECHLIS, the different component scores were combined in an ad hoc way in an attempt to approximate these human judgments. The individual components of the score were constructed by the separate knowledge sources, each in its own way. It was clear that in order to avoid comparing apples with oranges, we needed a principle for deciding how many points of syntactic score were worth one point of lexical matching score, how many points of lexical matching score were worth one point of verification score, etc.

One might assume (as a methodological premise) that a good overall theory score would be some weighted sum of the scores assigned by the different knowledge sources (not necessarily for theoretical reasons but just because it seems reasonable, and linear combinations are a good place to start). However, the issue of concern would still be choosing the correct

319

weights. For example, CMU adopted such a weighted sum strategy in their Hearsay-II system, but chose weights essentially by trial and error.

In HWIM, we have adopted a uniform scoring philosophy in which the score of each different knowledge source is statistically calibrated to a uniform scoring dimension. Each score is appropriately weighted so that the theoretically correct total score of a theory is simply the sum of the scores assigned by the individual knowledge sources. The scoring dimension chosen is that of log likelihood ratios, and the interpretation of a theory's score is an estimate of the log probability of its being correct. The computation of this score involves a straightforward application of Bayes' theorem, deriving the probability of a theory T_i given evidence E_j by the formula:

$$Pr(T_i|E_j) = Pr(E_j|T_i)*Pr(T_i) / Pr(E_j).$$

That is, the probability of a theory given the evidence is equal to the probability of the evidence given the theory times the <u>a priori</u> probability of the theory, divided by the <u>a priori</u> probability of the evidence (i.e., the probability of this particular evidence occurring independent of T_i).

When there are several types of evidence, each from a different knowledge source, or several components of evidence within a single knowledge source, this equation can be factored into components:

$$Pr(T_i|E_{j1}\&E_{j2}\&...\&E_{jn}) = (Pr(E_{j1}|T_i)/Pr(E_{j1}))*(Pr(E_{j2}|T_i)/Pr(E_{j2}))$$

$$...(Pr(E_{jn}|T_i)/Pr(E_{jn}))*Pr(T_i)$$

under the assumption that the different pieces of evidence are independent. (A corresponding equation can be derived that accounts for any significant dependencies.) In HWIM, this equation is used in combining evidence both from different knowledge sources (e.g., acoustic-phonetic recognition, verification, and prosodic), and also within any given knowledge source (e.g., each phonetic segment in the segment lattice contributing evidence for a particular word hypothesis).

We assume then that the score assigned to a theory by a given knowledge source K is an estimate of the ratio $Pr(E_{jk}|T_i)/Pr(E_{jk})$, where E_{jk} is the evidence that K consulted in assigning its score. A ratio of 1 corresponds to essentially no information. That is, the evidence is as likely to occur by chance in any theory as it is for the particular theory T_i. A ratio of less than 1 indicates that it is more likely to occur for some arbitrary theory than it is for this particular T_i. Positive logs thus represent theories that in some sense "account for" the evidence, while negative logs correspond to theories that are to some extent contraindicated.

Using the above scoring philosophy, the score returned by a given knowledge source should be the log of an estimate of the probability ratio $Pr(E_{jk}|T_i)/Pr(E_{jk})$ where E_{jk} is the evidence it examined. Performance statistics of an individual knowledge source are used to calibrate its scores so that they are compatible with the scores of all other knowledge sources (Woods et al., 1976).

14-3. DESCRIPTION OF THE HWIM SPEECH UNDERSTANDING SYSTEM

This section will present an overview of the final version of the HWIM speech understanding system. We begin with its structure, followed by brief descriptions of its components, which are the implementations of the sources of knowledge. We conclude with an outline of the final control strategy for using these components to understand an utterance.

14-3.1 The Structure of HWIM

The structure of the HWIM speech understanding system is shown in Fig. 14-1. HWIM is implemented on TENEX, a virtual memory time-sharing operating system for the PDP-10 (Bobrow et al., 1972). HWIM is made up of a number of individual TENEX processes in a single multiple-process job structure. Each box shown in Fig. 14-1 is implemented as a separate TENEX process. The reasons for this multiprocess structure derive from:

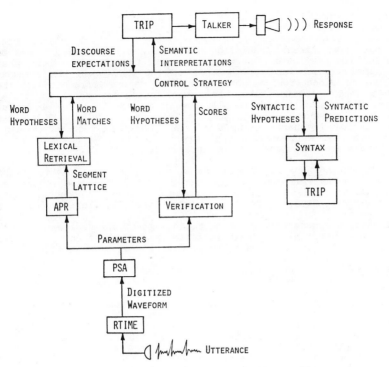

Fig. 14-1. Structure of the HWIM speech understanding system.

1. Differences in the implementation languages of the various components
   (TRIP, Control, and Syntax are written in INTERLISP, Lexical Retrieval
   and APR in BCPL, and Verifier, PSA, RTIME, and TALKER in combinations of
   BCPL, FORTRAN, and PDP-10 machine language.)

2. Storage demands (The program and data structure requirements of all the
   components far exceed the 262,144-word size of a single TENEX address
   space.)

3. Modularity (Knowledge source components were developed individually.
   Intercomponent communication is by means of common files, so components
   can be tested as individual stand-alone programs or in combination with
   other processes. In effect, the entire speech understanding system is
   assembled from these components at run time by means of instantiating
   the proper set of these processes.)

4. Convenience (The TRIP component contains in its semantic network factual
   information useful to the parsing of an utterance. Rather than
   re-implement this information and its accessing routines in the Syntax
   component, we merely created a second instantiation of TRIP below the
   Syntax component, so that Syntax can communicate with it. The reason
   for a second instantiation rather than the same one is so that the
   Speech Control system can be run without the top TRIP process.)

14-3.2 Knowledge Components
    This subsection describes each of the knowledge components shown in Fig.
14-1, with the exception of the Control Strategy, which is treated in Secs.
14-3.3 and 14-4.3. Also described here are the Dictionary Expansion process
and work on a Prosodics component.

14-3.2.1 RTIME and PSA - RTIME is a process used to acquire (digitize at
20,000 samples per second and store) the speech signal, and PSA is the signal

processing component, which converts the speech signal into a parametric representation used by the APR and Verification components.

The digitized waveform is pre-emphasized by first differencing. A 13-pole selective linear prediction analysis (Makhoul, 1975) is performed over the 0-5 kHz portion of the signal spectrum using a 20 ms Hamming window. (The original design was to make use of the full 0-10 kHz spectrum for classifying unvoiced sounds, but this was never implemented.) Formant frequencies are estimated from the lowest bandwidth poles of the linear prediction analysis. Fundamental frequency is estimated by a downsampled center-clipped autocorrelation algorithm (Gillmann, 1975). Other parameters are overall energy, energies in low-, mid-, and high-frequency bands, zero crossing rate, and a spectral shape measure (Woods et al., 1976, Vol. II). All parameters are computed at 10 ms intervals.

14-3.2.2 <u>Acoustic-Phonetic Recognizer</u> - The Acoustic-Phonetic Recognizer (APR) operates on the parametric representation of the utterance with acoustic-phonetic rules in order to produce bottom-up phonetic hypotheses (Schwartz and Zue, 1976; Woods et al., 1976, Vol. II). This process consists of three tasks:
1. Segmentation - determining the phonetic segment boundaries
2. Labeling - determining a rough phonetic characterization for each segment
3. Scoring - determining a quantitative description of each segment

The segmentation and labeling are performed together, but iteratively, by an ordered set of some 35 acoustic-phonetic "rules". These rules are not expressed in any rule formalism but are simply pieces of a program that operate on the parameters and the results of the application of the previous rules. The first rules to be applied perform very gross segmentation and labeling (e.g., sonorant, obstruent), and later rules operate on the results of the earlier ones, modifying the earlier segment boundaries, creating new ones, and changing or refining the earlier segment labels.

The APR program attempts to determine both manner and place of articulation for all phonemes. In addition, the program detects affricates, flapped dentals, and intervocalic glottal stop. It also detects and labels prevocalic and postvocalic glides, sentence initial /h/ and glottal stops, and unreleased plosives at the end of a sentence. Formant transitions are used in labeling consonants, and duration is used extensively as a cue in all phases of both segmentation and labeling. The program also detects unreleased plosive-plosive pairs, medial pauses, syllabic nasals, and vowel-schwa pairs (as in "give me a list").

The result of the segmentation and labeling phase is a data structure called the <u>segment lattice</u>, which is illustrated in Fig. 14-2. The segment

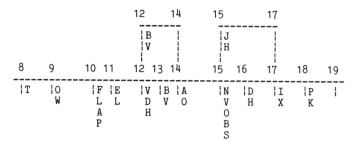

Fig. 14-2. Segment lattice fragment for the words "total budget". Time runs horizontally from left to right. The numbers denote segment boundaries, and the characters denote segment labels.

lattice allows for the representation of alternate segmentation paths where the acoustic evidence is not sufficiently unambiguous to permit unique segmentation decisions at this level. Each segment label, although shown as a single mnemonic label for the convenience of the experimenter, is in fact a vector of likelihood ratios L_j, one for each dictionary <u>phoneme</u>, giving an estimate of the likelihood of each phoneme P_j in light of the acoustic evidence. That is,

$$L_j = \frac{Pr(\text{acoustic evidence} \mid \text{phoneme}_j \text{ is correct})}{Pr(\text{acoustic evidence})}$$

These likelihood ratios are computed during the third, or scoring phase of acoustic-phonetic recognition. Initial approximations to them are obtained from phoneme/segment confusion statistics of the APR. Then, depending on the segment label, the scores of certain phonemes are refined, using several acoustic features measured from the segment. For instance, for unvoiced plosive segments, the scores on the unvoiced plosive phonemes are recomputed from measured values of formant frequencies before the silence, burst frequency, burst energy, and voice onset time. The probability density functions for these score modifications have been derived from a data base of utterances by five male speakers by use of an Acoustic-Phonetic Experiment Facility (Schwartz, 1976).

14-3.2.3 <u>Lexical Retrieval</u> - The Lexical Retrieval component, which embodies the lexical and phonological knowledge sources, is used to match dictionary word pronunciations against the segment lattice (Klovstad, 1976; Woods et al., 1976, Vol. III). This component makes use of a distributed key representation of the dictionary that merges common parts of different words, as illustrated in Fig. 14-3a. This makes an effective search of the entire dictionary computationally feasible without having to consider each word separately.

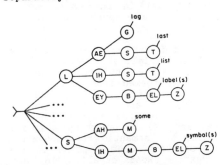

(a) Tree-structured dictionary

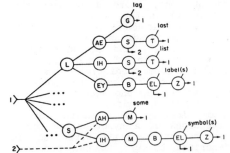

(b) Dictionary with across-word rules

Fig. 14-3.

Any lexical matching component for use with continuous speech must take account of the fact that the pronunciation of a word can be modified by the presence of neighboring words. For instance, "list" may be pronounced [L IH S] in the phrase "list some", but not in "list all". The general phonological rules that describe these effects are captured in the distributed key dictionary structure by extra paths that link some terminal nodes back to certain initial nodes in the network, as illustrated in Fig. 14-3b. In this example, "list" may be pronounced [L IH S], but the only words that are allowed to follow such a word match are those beginning with [S] (node 2). On the other hand, following a match for [L IH S T], any word may follow (node 1). (An analogous left-branching dictionary structure is used for matching words in the right-to-left direction.)

The Lexical Retrieval component can search for all words in the dictionary or for only those in a specified subset, and it can do so either in isolation or "anchored" to a previously found word match or set of word matches, in order that the across-word phonological effects be properly accounted for. The log likelihood score for a word match is computed from the segment/phoneme scores in the segment lattice using Bayes' Rule. The Lexical Retrieval component also considers the possibility of missing and extra segments in the lattice, scoring those possibilities using statistics derived from APR performance data.

14-3.2.4 <u>Verification</u> - The results of the Klatt-Stevens spectrogram reading experiment (Klatt and Stevens, 1973) suggest that an ability to verify word hypotheses against acoustic evidence would be a powerful aid to continuous speech recognition. The generative nature of phonological and coarticulation processes obscures the underlying phonetic structure of speech and makes bottom-up phonetic analysis particularly difficult. A top-down acoustic-phonetic verification process (Klatt, 1975), in which contextual information is known and can be taken into account, should provide a recognition ability that is largely independent of, and therefore complementary to, the bottom-up analysis provided by the APR.

HWIM's parametric word verification component is an implementation of this concept (Cook, 1976; Woods et al., 1976, Vol. II). Given a word hypothesized at a given position in the utterance, plus hypothesized context (if any), it looks up the pronunciations in a dictionary, generates an idealized time-varying spectral representation using a speech synthesis-by-rule program, and compares that against a region of the parametric representation of the utterance. This comparison makes use of a spectral distance metric and a dynamic programming time-warping algorithm given by Itakura (1975), with the addition of variable end points to allow for uncertainty in the hypothesized position of the word. The resulting spectral distances are converted to log likelihood scores.

14-3.2.5 _Syntax_ - The Syntax component embodies syntactic, semantic, and pragmatic knowledge sources, and by invoking a second instantiation of the TRIP component, accesses the factual knowledge source as well. Its parser is built around a "pragmatic" augmented transition network (ATN) grammar, which accepts only those utterances that are grammatical in the usual sense, meaningful in the travel budget management domain, and appropriate to the pragmatic circumstance of a single speaker talking to a computer data management system and given the previous conversation. In this grammar, the usual NP, VP, and PP constituents are replaced by structures such as "meetings", "trips", and "budget items". This specialization considerably increases the predictive power of the grammar, since it does not permit phrases like "her next workshop", which, although formed from words in the HWIM vocabulary and acceptable in normal English grammar, is not appropriate to this task domain. The functions of the Parser are (1) to judge the grammaticality of a given word sequence, (2) to predict the possible extensions of a hypothesized word sequence, and (3) to build up a formal representation of the utterance, in this case, the semantic representation described below. It can parse utterances starting at any point in the utterance and working in both directions thereafter (Woods et al., 1976, Vol. IV).

14-3.2.6 _TRIP_ - The TRIP component serves as the overall system controller, the data base manager and retriever, and the embodiment of HWIM's factual and discourse level knowledge sources (Woods et al., 1976, Vol. V). TRIP uses a semantic network to represent the travelers, destinations, meetings, trips, budgets, etc. that it must model. If it is presented with a typed request, it calls Syntax directly to parse and semantically interpret the request. If the request is spoken, then TRIP invokes the _Control Strategy_ component, passing to it discourse level expectations and receiving from it the semantic interpretation of the utterance. This interpretation, which is in a language akin to predicate calculus, is then manipulated by TRIP in its information retrieval role to carry out the user's request. During the processing of a spoken request, TRIP's data base is also used to check semantic and pragmatic constraints specified by the grammar.

The following are some examples of semantic interpretations:

```
Utterance:        Give me a list of the untaken trips.
Interpretation:   (FOR: ALL A0001/ (FINDQ: DB/TRIP (TIME (AFTER NOW)))
                  : T ; (OUTPUT: A0001))
(English paraphrase: "For every member of the class of trips that
                     start later than now, print it out.")
```

```
Utterance:              How much is in the Speech Understanding budget?
Interpretation:         (FOR: THE A0046 / (FINDQ: DB/BUDGET
                            (PROJECT (SPEECH UNDERSTANDING))) : T ;
                            (OUTPUT: (GET: A0046 MONEY/REMAINING)))
(English paraphrase: "Find the single entity that is the budget
                      for the speech understanding project, and
                      print out its amount of remaining money.")
```

TRIP's response to the user can be either typed or spoken, as appropriate. For the latter, TALKER, a speech synthesis program, is invoked (Woods et al., 1976, Vol. II).

14-3.2.7 Phonological Rules and Dictionary Expansion - The dictionary data structures used by the different components of the system are produced at system loadup time by a Dictionary Expansion component using a dictionary of baseform pronunciations and several sets of phonological rules. Although this program is not a part of the running system, it is an important source of knowledge for speech understanding. It is well known that words can be produced in continuous speech in a number of different ways (depending on the speaker as well as the acoustic environment), resulting in acoustic signals that are sometimes quite different. It is also well known that the acoustic realization of a word will vary with its phonological environment, such as the underlying vowels and consonants involved or the stress patterns, and that many of the systematic relationships can be captured in general phonological rules. The purpose of the dictionary expansion process is to produce automatically the full set of word pronunciations that are expected to be encountered in continuously spoken utterances.

In the current system, a baseform dictionary of 1138 words is expanded to 1363 words by means of rules for producing regular inflections. (Only 1097 of these words are known to the grammar, so that is the effective size of the vocabulary.) Some of these 1363 words have more than one baseform pronunciation (1789 in all). These are expanded into 3371 pronunciations by the application of within-word phonological rules, and then into a total of 8642 pronunciations by the across-word rules (Woods et al., 1976, Vol. III).

14-3.2.8 Prosodics - A Prosodics component (not shown in Fig. 14-1) was also developed in collaboration with Sperry Univac (Lea, 1978). Its function was to score the likelihood of major syntactic boundaries by reference to features of the fundamental frequency contour of the utterance (Woods et al., 1976, Vol. IV). This component was not sufficiently tested to be included in the final version of the HWIM system.

14-3.3 Control Strategy
The basic notion of a control strategy, and in particular, that of a central Control component that explicitly directs the process of hypothesis formation and extension, is derived from our early experiences with incremental simulation, as described in Sec. 14-2.2. In HWIM, this Control component uses the other components much like subroutines, making all decisions concerning resource allocation to alternative hypotheses. The control component is organized along the lines of the computational framework for perception presented in Sec. 14-2.4. Within this framework, we have developed a number of different control strategies, each one consisting of particular choices of ways for enumerating seed events, methods for refining partial hypotheses, and priority functions for determining what event to consider next. Because we have viewed the exploration of different control strategies as a central task, the Control component contains approximately 25 flag variables that control strategy options. The number of permissible combinations of these flags is in the thousands, although only a few dozen of the most promising have been explored.

The basic form of all of HWIM's present control strategies may be stated concisely as follows:

1. Having acquired and parameterized the utterance, and having formed a segment lattice, use Lexical Retrieval to scan a portion (or all) of the lattice for words that match well, independent of context. Place these seed matches, ordered by score, on an event queue.

2. Select the top-scoring event from the queue and present it as a _theory_ (i.e., hypothesis) to the Parser.

   a) If the theory is a complete sentence and spans the utterance, the Parser returns its semantic interpretation. This is accepted as the best model of the utterance (but in principle, the process could continue to find the second best interpretation, etc.).

   b) If the theory is grammatically unacceptable, it is rejected and step 2 is repeated.

   c) Otherwise, the Parser makes _proposals_ for all words and semantic categories of words that are possible at each end of the theory.

3. Give the proposals to Lexical Retrieval for _anchored scans_ from each end of the theory, taking into account any across-word phonological effects required by the words at each end. For each such word found, form a new _word event_, which is a one-word extension of the previous theory. Score each new event and place it in the proper position on the event queue.

4. Possibly rescore, remove, or add events on the queue, due to the detection of certain monitoring conditions. In particular,

   a) If the word being added to a theory in a new event has also been noticed by a theory on its other side, then a _collision event_, made up of the union of the word matches of the two "colliding" events, is formed and added to the queue (assuming a flag is set that enables this feature)

   b) If the theory evaluated has just reached a possible end of the utterance (and has not already been hypothesized to end there), an _end event_ is formed which hypothesizes that there are no more words at that end (with a possible score adjustment reflecting the likelihood according to the APR that the hypothesized point is actually the end of the utterance).

5. If a resource limitation on the number of theory evaluations allowed has been reached, then stop and report "no interpretation". Otherwise return to Step 2.

This cycle of syntactic proposals, scans for the words proposed in the context of the words already found, and formation of new events continues until an event is processed that spans the utterance, is acceptable to the grammar, and is consistent with the observed speech signal. Obviously, the number of such cycles (or new theories) required must be at least the number of words in the sentence plus 2 (for the end events), but such an optimum is rarely achieved. In some cases, the number of cycles required is on the order of 2 times the number of words; in others the number is much larger.

Among the variations possible on such a strategy are constraints on the region of the utterance in which seeds are formed and constraints on the directions in which theories are allowed to grow. Other strategy variations include several methods of computing priority scores, and whether and how to use word verification.

14-3.3.1 _Theory Formation_ - If the initial lexical scan for seed words is performed over the entire utterance and theories are permitted to grow in either direction, then a general "middle-out" interpretation strategy results. If the initial scan is restricted to possible left boundaries and theories are only permitted to grow to the right, then a strictly left-to-right strategy results. If the initial scan is performed on a small region of the utterance near the beginning of the utterance and theories are forced to grow only to the left until their left end is hypothesized (after which they grow only to the right), the result is what we refer to as a "hybrid strategy".

In general, a middle-out strategy will explore more theories before finding a spanning theory than will a strictly left-to-right strategy, due to competition for resources among events in different regions of the utterance.

A strictly left-to-right strategy, on the other hand, may have difficulty getting across the first word of an utterance if the acoustic score of that first word is not good. The hybrid strategies form a compromise that gains most of the efficiency of a left-to-right scan, but can anchor on a stressed content word near the beginning of the utterance and then back up to pick up unstressed and poorly articulated function words.

14-3.3.2 Priority Scoring - In developing control strategies that attempt to find the most likely interpretation of an utterance, it is necessary to distinguish two kinds of score that can be associated with a partial hypothesis: (1) A measure of quality, which expresses how likely a partial hypothesis is to be correct, and (2) a measure of priority, which is used to determine the order in which partial hypotheses are to be processed. The quality score can be used as a priority score (and one of the strategy options of HWIM is to do so), but this does not generally lead to the best overall interpretation of the utterance.

In HWIM, as we described earlier, the quality-score of a hypothesis is an estimate of the probability of the particular word sequence being correct, given the observed speech signal covered by that word sequence. The probabilities of different hypotheses are thus not directly comparable, since those different probabilities are based on different evidence. Intuitively, what is needed for a priority score is some estimate of the eventual score to be achieved by continuing to expand a hypothesis or some way to normalize the scores of different hypotheses to compensate for the fact that they may have different numbers of words and cover different portions of the utterance. Various such priority scores have been explored in the HWIM system, but the one that we have found the most effective is a measure called shortfall density. Briefly, it consists of scoring word matches and word match sequences, not by their lexical-matching (quality) scores, but by the extent to which their quality scores fall below a summed per-segment upper bound scoring function, which bounds the possible score contribution of each portion of the utterance to any theory covering it. This score difference, called the shortfall, is then divided by the duration of the region covered, to give a shortfall density. The items on the event queue are ordered by increasing shortfall density, rather than by decreasing quality score.

When used with a general middle-out control strategy including the island collision feature described above, the shortfall density scoring function provides an admissible search strategy (i.e., guarantees the discovery of the best possible interpretation). Moreover, there are several other control strategy options that increase efficiency while preserving this admissibility. Detailed discussions of these issues are contained in (Woods, 1977, in press). The shortfall density scoring measure has proven to be effective not only for these admissible strategies, but for various approximate strategies as well.

14-3.3.3 Verification - As mentioned above, one of the strategy options in HWIM is whether and how to use the word verification component in assigning scores. The Verification component yields a word match score that is largely independent of that given by Lexical Retrieval. Although conceptually, one should verify each new word match found by Lexical Retrieval, in order to bring as much knowledge as possible to bear on the ordering of the event queue, the computational cost of such a strategy is high. One way to avoid this cost is a strategy that we call "Verify-at-Pick", which selects for verification (at the beginning of Step 2 above) only those events from the top of the event queue that are necessary to ensure that the top of the queue is properly ordered. It does this by assigning to unverified events a default score that exceeds whatever verification score they may eventually receive, and then ordering them in the queue using this default. If such events fall sufficiently far down the queue, they are never actually verified. If they reach the top of the queue, however, they are verified at that time and reinserted into the queue at the appropriate point using their actual verification score. Thus, any event whose verification score could possibly be used to bring it to the top of the queue will be brought to the top by its default score, after which its actual verification score will be computed and used. To the extent that verification scores can be given an upper bound, this method provides all of the advantages of the full verification of every word match, but at a fraction of the cost.

14-4. SYSTEM PERFORMANCE

14-4.1 Knowledge Component Performance

HWIM's front-end knowledge sources are pattern recognizers in their own right, and it is of interest to report aspects of their performance. In this subsection, we briefly describe the performance of (1) the APR, (2) the APR and Lexical Retrieval, and (3) the Word Verification components. In assessing their performance, it should be kept in mind that these components were designed as components of a total system. As such, their task is not to make decisions as to rightness or wrongness. Rather it is to make hypotheses about the utterance and to evaluate the support for those hypotheses by means of log likelihood ratio scores.

14-4.1.1 Acoustic-Phonetic Recognition (APR) - The output of the APR is a lattice structure of phonetic segments, as described in Sec. 14-3.2.2 above. We may describe the APR performance in terms of its accuracy in segmenting the utterance into units of the appropriate size and in labeling those segments. The performance figures cited here were derived from the same set of 124 utterances by three male speakers that were used for the final system performance test (see Sec. 14-4.2 below).

Table 14-1 below describes the <u>segmentation</u> performance of the APR. Because the segment lattice produces multiple segmentation paths for some portions of the utterance, we describe the degree of ambiguity in segmentation in terms of the Branching Ratio, Segment Expansion Ratio, and Average Lattice Depth. The figures for missing and extra boundaries were

Total phonemes in ideal segmentation		2850
Total boundaries in lattices		3940
Total segments in lattices		5127
Branching Ratio (segments/boundaries)		1.35
Segment Expansion Ratio (segments/phonemes)		1.79
Average Lattice Depth		1.85
Total missing boundaries	48	1.7%
Total extra boundaries	67	2.3%

Table 14-1. APR segmentation performance.

measured over the best path through the segment lattice.

The APR's <u>labeling</u> performance is somewhat more difficult to characterize, since each segment bears a log likelihood score for each of the 71 possible dictionary phonemes; there is no notion of correct or incorrect, only the segment/phoneme scores. One measure of labeling performance is the proportion of segments in which the correct phoneme is within the N highest-scoring phonemes (again, over the best path through the lattice). This is illustrated in Fig. 14-4 below. However, this measure does not adequately describe the phoneme selectivity of the APR, since it is not the rank of the correct phoneme that matters, but the relative scores of the correct and most similar incorrect phonemes. Such performance measures and phonetic subclass labeling performance results are described in (Woods, et al., 1976, Vol. II; Cook and Schwartz, 1977).

14-4.1.2 APR and Lexical Retrieval - The Lexical Retrieval component uses as its input the segment lattice produced by the APR, so performance at the word-matching level reflects the operation of both of these components (as well as the adequacy of the dictionary). In the two tests to be described below, all 1363 entries in the full dictionary (more than the 1097 words known to HWIM's grammar) were candidates for matching against the segment lattice. No grammatical restrictions were invoked. The testing was done on the 124 new utterances used for HWIM's final performance test.

In the <u>sliding scan</u> test, the entire segment lattice was scanned for all dictionary words, and the 15 highest scoring word matches for the entire utterance were reported. A word match was counted as correct if it was a word in the sentence and was found in its proper position. Figure 14-5a shows a histogram of the rank of the highest scoring correct word.

328

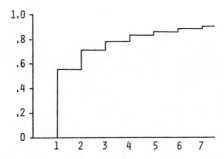

Fig. 14-4. APR labeling performance: proportion of correct phonemes within the top N (out of 71).

The <u>anchored scan</u> test is probably a more meaningful performance test. The first word is found at the beginning of the utterance, then an anchored scan (taking into account word-boundary effects) is made to its right, and so on until every word in the utterance has been found. Figure 14-5b shows a histogram of the rank of the correct word (out of a possible 1363) and also the cumulative distribution of these ranks.

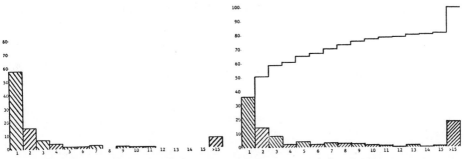

Fig. 14-5. APR/Lexical Retrieval histograms. (a) Sliding scans: rank of highest scoring correct word. (b) Anchored scans: rank of the correct word.

14-4.1.3 <u>Word Verification</u> - Figure 14-6 shows spectral score distributions obtained from the Verification component based on about 1200 words. These were words that had been actually matched by Lexical Retrieval and therefore proposed to Verification during the course of HWIM's normal operation, so they form a biased set of words that are acoustically somewhat similar to the correct words. All words are longer than 100 ms (shorter words are not given to Verification) and most of them were verified without contextual information. The extent to which the two distributions do not overlap illustrates the discriminability of the correct words from the entire set.

Another way of interpreting these two distributions is to consider partitioning them at the point where the log likelihood ratio score is zero (where the PDF for correct words equals the PDF for all words). Such a threshold partitions them in the ratios shown below.

	LLR$\geq$0	LLR<0
Correct	0.84	0.16
Incorrect	0.34	0.66

There will certainly always be some overlap, because words that differ only minimally (such as the names Bill and Bell) will never have vastly different scores. The threshold of 0 is an arbitrary one and does not imply acceptance/rejection. Verification scores, like those from other components,

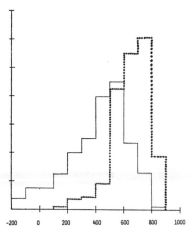

Fig. 14-6. PDF's of spectral distance scores for all words and correct words. The correct word distribution is outlined in dots.

are not thresholded but are used by Control in forming scores for entire multiword hypotheses about the utterance.

14-4.2 <u>Sentence Understanding Performance</u>
The final task in BBN's speech understanding research project was to make a meaningful test of its performance on understanding sentence length utterances. For this purpose, we recorded a new set of 124 utterances spoken by the three male speakers from whom previous utterances had been solicited. These utterances were processed by both a 409-word and a 1097-word version of HWIM using the LHSDVP strategy (Left-Hybrid strategy, using Shortfall Density scoring and the Verification component in Verify-at-Pick mode) (see Sec. 14-3.3). The system performance is summarized in Table 14-2.

	BIGDICT (1097 words)	MIDDICT (409 words)
Correctly understood	54 = 44%	65 = 52%
All words correct	51 = 41%	59 = 48%
Semantically correct	3 = 2%	6 = 4%
Incorrect	45 = 36%	40 = 32%
Close to correct	29 = 23%	25 = 20%
Less correct	13 = 10%	10 = 8%
Very wrong	3 = 2%	5 = 4%
No response	25 = 20%	19 = 15%
Gave up (150 theories)	24 = 19%	18 = 14%
System broke	1 = 1%	1 = 1%
Estimated average branching (words)	196	67
Speed (times real time)	1350	1050

Table 14-2. Summary of final performance results.

14-4.2.1 <u>Sentence Understanding Accuracy</u> - In Table 14-2, the term "Semantically correct" refers to utterances whose word list was not entirely correct, but whose semantic interpretation, as generated by the Parser, was identical to that of the correct sentence. This is regarded as "correctly understood" in the sense of Newell et al. (1973). For example:

```
Utterance:  How much is left?
Understood: What is left?
Semantic interpretation:
    (FOR: ALL A0007 / (FINDQ: DB/BUDGET)
    : T ; (OUTPUT: (GET: A0007 MONEY/REMAINING)))
    (That is, "for each budget, output the amount of money currently
    remaining there.")
```

Of the incorrectly understood utterances, most were quite close to the
correct sentence. For example:

```
Utterance:    Show me Bill's trip to Washington.
Understood:   Show only Bell's trip to Washington.
              (i.e., Alan Bell, rather than Bill Woods.)

Utterance:    The registration fee is twenty dollars.
Understood:   Their registration fee is twenty dollars.
```

Others were farther away from the correct sentence. For example:

```
Utterance:    Give me a list of the untaken trips.
Understood:   Give Bill's fifty untaken trips.
```

For some utterances, the system gave no response, as it was set to stop
searching if it had processed as many as 150 theories without finding a
theory that spanned the utterance. In all but a few such cases, at that
point there was little likelihood that HWIM would have correctly understood
the utterance had the search been continued. In two cases, the system was
unable to proceed because of a bug in some component.

The results comparing the smaller, 409-word task domain with the
1097-word task domain show a decrease in the correctly understood utterances
and a corresponding increase in the incorrect and "no response" cases for the
larger vocabulary, but the degradation is far from dramatic. This suggests
that the factor of 2.7 in vocabulary size (or the corresponding factor of 3
in average word branching) represents a much smaller change in the
"difficulty" of these tasks for HWIM than one might have expected.

14-4.2.2 Measures of Task Difficulty - It is very difficult to obtain an
objective measure of the inherent difficulty imposed by a task domain. It is
especially difficult to obtain such a measure that is uniformly applicable to
tasks with general context-free and context-sensitive grammars as well as
those with finite-state grammars. Goodman (1976) has made a start at
developing such a measure for tasks with finite-state grammars, but he does
not adequately model complex context-free and context-sensitive grammars.
Conceptually, the difficulty of a task language can be broken down into three
components: (1) the branching ratio, a measure of the number of alternative
words possible at a given point in a sentence, (2) a measure of the
confusability or similarity of the alternative words at such a choice point,
and (3) a measure of the similarity of the word sequences that could follow
two different word choices at a given point (i.e., a measure of how likely a
wrong choice will lead to subsequent mismatches that will drive the search
process back to the correct path). Goodman's method attempts to measure the
combined effects of (1) and (2), but doesn't deal with (3). Moreover, the
measures that he uses for (2) are not applicable for comparing systems with
fundamentally different methods of acoustic phonetic recognition and
different phonetic systems for recording lexical pronunciations. We are
left, then, with (1), the measure of branching ratio, which at best accounts
for only a gross level of difficulty and is not completely well defined for a
context-free or context-sensitive grammar (e.g., two different grammars
accepting the same language could have different branching ratios, depending
on how they were structured).

Subject to all of the above qualifications in the significance of the
number and its utility for comparison, we have computed a measure of average
branching ratio as a measure of task difficulty on HWIM's two grammars and
vocabularies. Wherever at the grammar's request the Lexical Retrieval
component is called to scan the segment lattice for a set of proposed words

                                331

and classes, the number of words possible at that point is noted. This number ranges from over 900, at the left end of the sentence, to 1, in cases where the context allows only a single word to follow. The "estimated average branching (words)" in Table 14-2 is the arithmetic mean of these branching factors. (Note that this number does not measure the average branching along only the correct path through the grammar; it includes all paths followed by the system in understanding the utterance.)

14-4.2.3 Speed - The speed of the system is shown in Table 1 in terms of "number of times real time", i.e., the PDP-10 CPU time for the run divided by the duration of the sentence, for those utterances that were correctly or incorrectly understood. The time required to understand an utterance is divided among the various components of the system in the following rough proportions:

RTIME/PSA	5%
APR	0
Lexical Retrieval	40
Verification	15
Syntax	20
Control	20

More details of the final performance testing may be found in (Woods et al., 1976, Vol. III).

14-4.3 Discussion of Control Strategies
Several of the control strategies implemented in HWIM can be shown to formally guarantee that the first complete theory found will be the best possible interpretation of the utterance, without having to exhaustively search the space of possibilities (Woods, 1977, in press). We will refer to such strategies as admissible, following a standard terminology for heuristic search algorithms. Other strategies, in particular the strategy of always working on the most likely current hypothesis, do not guarantee discovery of the best interpretation. We will refer to such strategies as approximate. Clearly an admissible strategy would be preferred, all other things being equal. However, it is frequently the case in heuristic search applications that the cost of obtaining an admissible solution is too great and that approximate methods are more cost effective.
There have been claims within the ARPA speech understanding community that an admissible search strategy is not appropriate for speech understanding, since such strategies are much more combinatoric than approximate strategies, and since a good approximate strategy may actually get the best interpretation most of the time (albeit without the assurance that it is the best). The evidence for such a claim is not completely clear. The BBN effort seems to have been the only project to seek admissible strategies explicitly and to try to make them efficient. The CMU Harpy and Hearsay II systems, on the other hand, have sought to develop fast approximate methods, on the premise that admissible methods are inherently inefficient. Our experience confirms that admissible strategies do evaluate more hypotheses in reaching an interpretation than do some of our approximate ones, but we have discovered one admissible search technique (the shortfall density method (Woods, 1977, in press)) that is vastly superior to other known admissible techniques in this domain and is not unreasonable to consider as a competitor for the approximate techniques. It has the characteristic that the amount of time required depends on the quality of the particular utterance and the number of false competing hypotheses that score well. For sufficiently good acoustic-phonetic performance, the number of theories considered is not at all unmanageable.
For reasons of time and resource limitations, our final test run of the HWIM system was made using one of the approximate strategies. Subsequently, a much smaller experiment was run to compare various control strategies on a set of ten utterances chosen at random from the larger set. Although this sample is much too small to be relied on, the results are nevertheless suggestive. For two comparable experiments using our best approximate method (Left-Hybrid Shortfall Density) and our best admissible method (Shortfall Density with "Ghosts", island Collisions, and Direction preference), both with a resource limitation of 100 theories and without using Verification, the results were as follows:

	LHSDNV	SD+GCD
Correct interpretation	6	5
Incorrect interpretation	2	0
No interpretation	2	5
Average number of theories evaluated	51	76

That is, the approximate strategy found the best (and in these cases the correct) interpretation in 6 of the 10 cases, while the admissible strategy found only 5 (not a significant difference for this size sample). On the other hand, the approximate method misinterpreted 2 additional utterances with no indication to distinguish them from the other 6. If this strategy were used in an actual application, the system would claim to understand about 80% of its utterances, but would actually misunderstand about 25% of those. The admissible strategy, on the other hand, would only claim to understand about 50% of the utterances, but would misunderstand a negligible fraction.

The admissible algorithm in the above experiments expanded only 50% more theories (and incidentally used only 30% more CPU time) than did the approximate strategy. The success rates of the two methods are not much different, except that the admissible method is less likely to make an incorrect interpretation. Moreover, the numbers of theories considered and the computation times are not vastly different. If one considers proposals to improve the performance of approximate strategies by having them continue to search for additional interpretations after the first one is found (and thus take the best of several), then the time difference shown above could easily be reversed and there would still be no guarantee that the best interpretation found would be the best possible.

14-4.4 Comparison with Other Speech Understanding Strategies

14-4.4.1 DRAGON - The DRAGON system (Baker, 1975) is the only other speech understanding system from the ARPA project that provides an admissible strategy. It does this by using a dynamic programming algorithm that depends on the grammar being a Markov process (essentially a finite-state grammar). It operates by incrementally constructing, for each position in the input and each state in the grammar, the best path from the beginning of the utterance ending in that state at that position. The computation of the best paths at position i+1 from those at position i is a relatively straightforward local computation, although for a grammar with n states, the number of operations for each step is n times the branching ratio. DRAGON performs such a step for each 10 millisecond portion of the utterance, using a state transition that "consumes" an individual segment of a phoneme.

The optimality of the solution found by this algorithm depends on a property of finite state grammars, namely that one sequence of words (or phonemic segments) leading to a given state is equivalent to any other such sequence as far as compatibility with future predictions is concerned (regardless of the particular words used). It is this property that permits the algorithm to ignore all but the best path leading to each state (even if competing paths score quite well!), and therefore permits it to find the best solution by progressively extending a bounded number of paths across the utterance from left to right. (This is a very attractive property, although in this case it requires one such path for each state in the grammar.) For more general grammars, where there may be extensive context-sensitive checking between two different parts of the utterance, the best path leading to a given state at a given position may not be compatible with the best path following it. In this case, second best (and worse) paths leading to a given state may have to be considered in order to find any complete paths at all, much less an optimum.

Although DRAGON's scores are estimates of probabilities of interpretations, its guarantee of optimality does not depend on that, but only on the fact that its grammar is finite-state and that therefore it suffices to carry a record of the best path leading to each state.

14-4.4.2 Harpy - The CMU Harpy system (Lowerre, 1976) is a development on the DRAGON theme that gives up the theoretical guarantee of optimality in exchange for computation speed. Like DRAGON, it takes advantage of the unique characteristic of finite-state grammars cited above, so that only the best path leading to a given state need be considered. However, it uses an adaptation of the dynamic programming algorithm in which not all of the paths ending at a given position are constructed. Specifically, at each step of the computation, those paths scoring less than a variable threshold are pruned from further consideration. This gives an algorithm that carries a number of paths in parallel (the number varying depending on the number of competitors above the threshold at any given point) but is not exhaustive. If the threshold is chosen appropriately, the performance can closely approximate that of the optimal algorithm, although there is a tradeoff between the speed gained and the chances of finding a less than optimal path.

The Harpy system has the best demonstrated performance statistics of any continuous speech understanding system to date. However, it derives this performance in large part from the use of a highly constraining (and advantageously structured) finite-state grammar. This grammar has an average branching ratio of approximately 10^* and characterizes a non-habitable, finite set of sentences, with virtually no "near miss" sentence pairs included. For example, "What are their affiliations" is in the grammar, but no other sentences starting with "What are their" are possible. The only two sentences starting with "What are the" are "What are the titles of the recent ARPA surnotes," and "What are the key phrases." These three sentences will almost certainly find some robust difference beyond the initial three words that will reliably tell them apart. Similarly, the grammar permits sentences of the form "We wish to get the latest forty articles on <topic>," but one cannot say a similar sentence with "I" for "we", "want" for "wish", "see" for "get", "a" for "the", "thirty" for "forty", or any similar deviation from exactly the word sequence given above.) Most of Harpy's grammar patterns (such as the last one) consist of a particular sentence with one single open category for either an author's name or a topic. A large number of them are particular sentences with no open categories (like the first three above). Such simple grammar patterns significantly reduce the number of possible "distractor" hypotheses that can compete with the correct interpretation of a test sentence, even when they are not used as test sentences themselves.

The Harpy algorithm makes no guarantee that the correct path will not be pruned from consideration if it starts out poorly, but at least for the structure of Harpy's current grammar (most of whose sentences start with stressed imperative verbs or interrogative pronouns), the correct interpretation is usually found.

The Harpy technique seems to be the algorithm of preference at present for applications involving carefully structured artificial languages with finite-state grammars and small branching ratios. However, it does not conveniently extend to larger and more habitable grammars. This is due to a number of factors, the most important of which is the combinatorics of expanding a large habitable grammar into a finite-state network (the branching ratio 10 grammar on which its performance is reported is about the largest Harpy can currently hold in its memory without paging). For example, the incorporation of a single context sensitive feature (such as number agreement between subjects and verbs) into a finite-state grammar requires the doubling of the number of states in a large sub-net of the grammar, the incorporation of two such features requires a quadrupling of states, and so on. In the worst case, implementing the constraint of a context free grammar that the number of "pushes" for self-embedding constituents must match the number of "pops" cannot be represented with any finite number of states, necessitating finite-state approximations that either accept sentences that

$*$ - - - - - - - - - - - - - -

$*$ Later references to this grammar refer to a "dynamic" branching ratio of 30. This ratio is computed by averaging the branching ratio along the paths of the correct interpretations of utterances, whereas the branching ratio of 10 results from averaging uniformly over the grammar as a whole. As a measure of the difficulty of a grammar for speech understanding, the average over the entire grammar is more appropriate, since it measures the potential for the grammar to permit viable "distractor" hypotheses that might be confused with a correct interpretation. In the actual searching of the hypothesis space for a correct interpretation, most of the hypotheses considered will in fact be such distractor hypotheses and not partial hypotheses along the correct path.

the original grammar doesn't or fail to accept some that it does. Such
finite-state grammars also have difficulty dealing with dynamically changing
situations such as constraints on utterances that depend on previous
utterances.

Neither the DRAGON nor the Harpy system uses density normalization or
any method to attempt to estimate the potential score that is achievable on
the as yet unanalyzed portion of the utterance. Such normalization is not
necessary, since they follow paths in parallel, all of which start and end at
the same point in the utterance, and therefore they never have to compare
paths of different lengths or in different parts of the utterance. Again, it
is worth emphasizing that the ability of these algorithms to keep manageable
the number of paths that need to be considered depends on the unique
characteristic of finite-state languages that requires only the best path to
each state be considered.

14-4.4.3 __IBM__ - A group at IBM (Bahl et al., 1976) has a speech
understanding system based on Markov models of language, which has
implemented two control strategies: a Viterbi algorithm (essentially the same
dynamic programming algorithm used by DRAGON) and a "stack decoder", a
left-to-right algorithm with a priority scoring function that attempts to
estimate the probability that a given partial hypothesis will lead to the
correct overall hypothesis. The latter apparently does not guarantee the
optimal interpretation, but is reported as getting more sentences correct
than the former (a circumstance that can happen if there are
acoustic-phonetic scoring errors such that the best scoring interpretation is
not correct, or if the transition probabilities of the Markov model do not
agree with the test set).

14-4.4.4 __Hearsay II__ - The Hearsay II system (Lesser et al, ., 1975)
permits the kind of generalized middle-out parsing described in this paper,
and does so for context free grammars (although apparently not for
context-sensitive or more powerful grammars). Moreover, it has a capability
for a kind of island collisions. However, its design philosophy specifically
rejects the use of an "explicit control strategy" as "inappropriate" (because
it "destroys the data-directed nature and modularity of knowledge source
activity") (Hayes-Roth and Lesser, 1976). Its scoring function for
hypotheses, which its authors refer to as the "desirability" of a KS
(knowledge source), is an __ad hoc__ combination of functions reflecting
intuitive notions of "value", "reliability", "validity", "credibility",
"significance", "utility", etc. Specifically, they state: "the desirability
of a KS invocation is defined to be an increasing function of the following
variables: the estimated value of its RF [response frame] (an increasing
function of the reliability of the KS and the estimated level, duration, and
validity credibility of the hypothesis to be created or supported); the ratio
of the estimated RF value to the minimum current state in the time region of
the RF; and the probability that the KS invocation will directly satisfy or
indirectly contribute to the satisfaction of a goal as well as the utility of
the potentially satisfied goal." (Hayes-Roth & Lesser, 1976). They go on to
say that even the above is not "complex enough" to "provide precise control
in all of the situations that arise" and proceed to describe various further
elaborations.

Although it is not easy to tell from the available published
descriptions exactly what Hearsay II does, the fact that the "desirability"
of a KS invocation is an increasing function of its duration definitely rules
out any interpretation of it as implementing the density method. The above
allusion to the "current state in the time region of the RF" refers to a
parameter that, for each point t in the utterance, specifies the maximum of
the "values" of all hypotheses "which represent interpretations containing
the point t." This "state" function at first glance seems similar to the
upper bound scoring function used in the shortfall algorithm, but in
actuality it is quite different (Woods, in press). Hearsay II's use of the
"state" parameter is reminiscent of SRI's "focus by inhibition" technique,
which was found to have generally undesirable effects, although it did offset
some of the costs of an island driving strategy (Paxton, 1976).

A superficial comparison of the Hearsay II system performance with that
of the BBN HWIM system might lead one to believe that the Hearsay II control
strategy is somehow more effective. However, it is more likely that the

difference in performance is due to the differences in difficulty of the two grammars or to differences in their acoustic "front end." The best reported performance results of the Hearsay II system are based on the same highly constrained, branching ratio 10 grammar used by Harpy.

14-5. CONCLUSIONS

14-5.1 The Current State

As mentioned in the preceding section, the performance of the current HWIM system is not a true indicator of its potential. The final performance tests described above mark the expiration of the original five-year program; they do not in any sense represent closure or completeness in the system. During the last five months of active development, performance increased at a rate of approximately 10% per month from a baseline of near zero as the individual components of the system began to come together, bugs and inconsistencies were ironed out, and new variations of control strategies and scoring algorithms were developed. There is no reason to expect that this trend of increasing performance had reached its apex when the project ended. On the contrary, there is every reason to believe that considerable improvements remained to be made.

For example, during the final weeks of the project, the 1097 word vocabulary was run for the first time, containing over 600 words that had never been seen before by the system. The final test run was made on this vocabulary with no alteration of the individual word pronunciations from the form in which they were copied from a standard pronunciation reference. These words introduced new acoustic-phonetic environments into the system, with the result that the APR component was functioning using an incomplete set of rules for the phenomena that it was being called on to label and a non-representative set of statistics. The fact that the system could perform at all with its vocabulary more than doubled without any feedback is evidence for the robustness of the techniques being used. The fact that our performance decreased only slightly with the increased vocabulary is interesting and contradicts the model that one might expect for the dependence of success rate on branching ratio. We believe that this is largely due to an APR that is generally very good, but whose acoustic phonetic knowledge still has gaps, causing it to make occasional serious mistakes with a frequency that is independent of branching ratio.

There are many other places in the system where individual components are functioning far below their potential capabilities. The major thrust of our research program has been towards developing effective techniques for handling the speech understanding problem for multiple speakers without individual training of the system to a speaker. This pursuit has been a major evolutionary effort, and modification and improvement of individual components has been sufficiently continuous that none of the components has been tuned to its full potential. For example, pronunciation likelihoods used in the dictionary base forms and in the phonological rules are intuitive human guesses, not statistically measured estimates. Moreover, while a method of checking the compatibility between syntactic hypotheses and prosodic information in the speech waveform has been implemented (Woods et al., 1976, Vol. IV), it has not yet been tested, much less tuned. A third source of untapped potential comes from the pronunciation features associated with individual word pronunciations. These are intended to be checked by the grammar to verify that the pronunciation of a word is consistent with a hypothesis about its use, but few places in the grammar have actually been annotated to make such checks, and the mechanism by which this information is made available to the parser has not yet been fully tested. In general, the reported performance can only be taken as an intermediate benchmark in a system that was still in a state of rapid development at that time.

The most significant conclusion that can be drawn from HWIM's performance is that a system with a vocabulary of over 1000 words and a grammar with a branching ratio of 196, with no tuning of the system to individual speakers and no discourse information being used, can function at approximately 50% sentence understanding level. Detailed analysis of HWIM's performance (Woods et al, 1976, Vol. III) shows that the speech confusions that are made are generally reasonable ones, many of which can be corrected by techniques already under development at that time. Some of them could be legislated away by artificial grammars designed to eliminate speech confusions. HWIM's grammar makes no such attempts, and in fact permits such minimal difference pairs as "What is the registration fee" and "What is their registration fee" (where, it should be noted, one of the pronunciations of "their" is [DH EH !O R], and an across-word gemination rule will merge the [R] with that of "registration"). It should also be pointed out that the system has been set up to use discourse context to resolve such pairs by using information such as whether there is a potential antecedent for the pronoun "their". However, due to the difficulty of setting up a test for sentence understanding in context and limited available time, the final demonstration test was performed on isolated sentences with the discourse model modified to return positive answers to any such questions. Thus, the expected performance of the system in context, even with no improvements in the system, would exceed that of the test conditions.

14-5.2 What has been Learned

In the course of our research, we believe that we have made significant advances in the technology required for continuous speech understanding. From an initial state of trial and error approximations and incremental simulations of human spectrogram readers, we have developed a number of theoretically interesting and demonstrably effective techniques. These include a general uniform scoring method for combining the scores of different knowledge sources, an efficient technique for incorporating generative phonological rules into a dictionary both within and across word boundaries, the use of pragmatic ATN grammars for combining syntactic, semantic, pragmatic, and prosodic information, an efficient bidirectional parsing algorithm for ATN grammars that permits them to be used in middle-out parsing without sacrificing predictive capability, a synthesis-by-rule Verification component that improves both performance and cost effectiveness by comparing word hypotheses with the input signal at the parametric level, and several overall control strategies, some of which can be guaranteed to find the best possible interpretation of an utterance without systematically enumerating all possibilities.

We have found that the vocabulary size problem does not seem to be as significant, at least for HWIM, as one would expect. On the other hand, although we have made significant progress, we have not yet gained closure on the set of acoustic-phonetic and phonological effects that are necessary to handle new vocabulary items and new speakers without specific training. Consequently, we do not know what the eventual performance of the system would be if that were achieved.

14-5.3 Promise for the Future

The results of the HWIM system provide an encouraging prospect for the future and complement those of the CMU Harpy system. Although the latter clearly has a much higher performance rate, sufficient to make it a viable candidate for near term applications, its restriction to finite-state grammars and limited branching ratio constrains these applications to ones for which a suitable artificial language can be designed. The system has already been tuned to near perfection, and there is no obvious place to turn for the improvements that would be necessary to get comparable levels of performance for more habitable grammars. HWIM, on the other hand, while its performance is much lower, has much more potential for growth. Even in its current state as a roughly implemented and untuned system, without all of the bugs fully worked out, it is making a creditable attack on grammars with branching ratios an order of magnitude larger and containing minimally different sentence pairs. Moreover, it seems that, unlike Harpy, HWIM's performance rate is relatively insensitive to branching ratio.

It is difficult to estimate what another year of development of the HWIM system might have achieved. The system performance increased rapidly in the last months of active development as bugs in components were being worked out and additional knowledge sources were being taken into account. This process had not been completed when the time arrived to run the final performance test. At that time, the system still contained untapped facilities for sophisticated discourse constraints, for checking compatibility between grammatical constructions, and particular word pronunciations and for making use of prosodic constraints. There was (and still is) a long list of particular acoustic phonetic phenomena to be studied and incorporated into

337

the APR, and there were still bugs in the system that were being uncovered. In short, there were a great many things that remained to be done to bring the system to its full level of capability. Consequently, the performance level that can be achieved by the techniques and approaches of the HWIM system is still very much an open question. We hope that it will be possible to find the answer to this question at some point in the future.

ACKNOWLEDGEMENTS

This research was supported by the Advanced Research Projects Agency of the Department of Defense and was monitored by ONR under Contract No. N00014-75-C-0053.

The research described in this chapter was the product of many present and former BBNers, who deserve as much credit as the authors. They are: Madeleine Bates, Geoffrey Brown, Bertram C. Bruce, Craig C. Cook, Laura Gould, Gregory Harris, Dennis H. Klatt, John W. Klovstad, John I. Makhoul, Bonnie L. Nash-Webber, Richard M. Schwartz, and Victor W. Zue.

REFERENCES

Bahl, L. R., J. K. Baker, P. S. Cohen, N. R. Dixon, F. Jelinek, R. L. Mercer, and H. F. Silverman, "Preliminary Results on the Performance of a System for the Automatic Recognition of Continuous Speech," Conference Record, 1976 IEEE Int. Conf. on Acoustics, Speech, and Signal Processing, April 12-14, 1976, Philadelphia, Pa., 425-429.

Baker, J. K., "The DRAGON System -- An Overview," IEEE Trans. Acoustics, Speech, and Signal Processing, ASSP-23, no. 1 (Feb. 1975), 24-29.

Bates, M., "The Use of Syntax in a Speech Understanding System," IEEE Trans. Acoustics, Speech, and Signal Processing, ASSP-23, no. 1 (Feb. 1975), 112-117.

Bobrow, D. G., J. D. Burchfiel, D. L. Murphy, and R. S. Tomlinson, "TENEX, a Paged Time Sharing System for the PDP-10," Comm. ACM, 15, no. 3 (March 1972), 135-143.

Cook, C., "Word Verification in a Speech Understanding System," Conference Record, 1976 IEEE International Conference on Acoustics, Speech, and Signal Processing, April 12-14, 1976, Philadelphia, Pa., 553-556.

Cook, C. C., and R. M. Schwartz, "Advanced Acoustic Techniques in Automatic Speech Understanding," Conference Record, 1977 IEEE International Conference on Acoustics, Speech, and Signal Processing, May 9-11, 1977, Hartford, Conn., 663-666.

Gillmann, R. A., "A Fast Frequency Domain Pitch Algorithm," J. Acoust. Soc. Am., 58, Supplement 1, (1975), S62.

Goodman, R. G., "Analysis of Languages for Man-Machine Communication," Ph.D. Thesis, Computer Science Dept., Stanford University, May 1972.

Hayes-Roth, F., and V. R. Lesser, "Focus of Attention in a Distributed-Logic Speech Understanding System," Conference Record, 1976 IEEE International Conference on Acoustics, Speech, and Signal Processing, April 12-14, 1976, Philadelphia, Pa., April, 1976, 416-420.

Itakura, F., "Minimum Prediction Residual Principle Applied to Speech Recognition," IEEE Trans. on Acoustics, Speech, and Signal Processing, ASSP-23, no. 1 (Feb. 1975), 67-72.

Klatt, D. H. "Word Verification in a Speech Understanding System," in Speech Recognition: Invited Papers Presented at the 1974 IEEE Symposium, ed. D. R. Reddy. New York: Academic Press, 1975.

Klatt, D. H., "Overview of the ARPA SPeech Understanding Project," Chapter 11 in this volume (1978).

Klatt, D. H., and K. N. Stevens, "On the Automatic Recognition of Continuous Speech: Implications from a Spectrogram-Reading Experiment," IEEE Trans. Audio Electroacoust., AU-21, no. 3 (June 1973), 210-217.

Klovstad, J. W., "Probabilistic Lexical Retrieval with Embedded Phonological Word Boundary Rules," in "Speech Understanding Systems, Quarterly Technical Progress Report No. 6," Report No. 3303, Bolt Beranek and Newman Inc., Cambridge, Mass., May, 1976 (DDC A026475).

Lea, W. A., "Prosodic Aids to Speech Recognition," Chapter 8 in this volume (1978).

Lesser, V. R., R. D. Fennell, L. D. Erman, and D. R. Reddy, "Organization of the Hearsay II Speech Understanding System," IEEE Trans. Acoustics, Speech, and Signal Processing, ASSP-23, no. 1 (Feb. 1975), 11-24.

Lowerre, B. T., "The Harpy Speech Recognition System," Ph.D. Thesis,
   Department of Computer Science, Carnegie-Mellon Univ., April 1976.
Makhoul, J. I., "Linear Prediction: A Tutorial Review," Proc. IEEE, 63, no. 4
   (April 1975), 283-296.
Nash-Webber, B., "Semantic Support in a Speech Understanding System," IEEE
   Trans. Acoustics, Speech, and Signal Processing, ASSP-23, no. 1 (Feb.
   1975a), 124-129.
Nash-Webber, B. L., "The Role of Semantics in Automatic Speech
   Understanding," in Representation and Understanding: Studies in Cognitive
   Science, ed. D. Bobrow and A. Collins. New York: Academic Press, 1975b.
Newell, A., J. Barnett, J. Forgie, C. Green, D. Klatt, J. C. R. Licklider, J.
   Munson, R. Reddy, and W. Woods, Speech Understanding Systems: Final Report
   of a Study Group. Amsterdam: North-Holland/American Elsevier, 1973.
Paxton, W. H., "A Framework for Speech Understanding," Technical Note 142,
   Stanford Research Institute Artificial Intelligence Center, Menlo Park,
   Calif., June 1977.
Rovner, P. D., J. I. Makhoul, J. J. Wolf, and J. J. Colarusso, "Where the
   Words are: Lexical Retrieval in a Speech Understanding System," Proc. IEEE
   Symposium on Speech Recognition, 15-19 April 1974, Pittsburgh, Pa.,
   160-164.
Rovner, P. D., B. Nash-Webber, and W. A. Woods, "Control Concepts in a Speech
   Understanding System," IEEE Trans. Acoustics, Speech, and Signal
   Processing, ASSP-23, no. 1 (Feb. 1975), 136-140.
Schwartz, R. M., "Acoustic-Phonetic Experiment Facility for the Study of
   Continuous Speech," Conference Record, 1976 IEEE International Conference
   on Acoustics, Speech, and Signal Processing, April 12-14, 1976,
   Philadelphia, Pa., 1-4.
Schwartz, R., and J. Makhoul, "Where the Phonemes Are: Dealing with
   Ambiguity in Acoustic-Phonetic Recognition," IEEE Trans. Acoustics,
   Speech, and Signal Processing, ASSP-23, no. 1 (Feb. 1975), 50-53.
Schwartz, R. M., and V. W. Zue, "Acoustic-Phonetic Recognition in BBN
   SPEECHLIS," Conference Record, 1976 IEEE International Conference on
   Acoustics, Speech, and Signal Processing, April 12-14, 1976, Philadelphia,
   Pa., 21-24.
Vicens, P., "Aspects of Speech Recognition by Computer," Ph.D. Thesis,
   Computer Science Dept., Stanford University, 1969.
Woods, W. A., "Motivation and Overview of SPEECHLIS: An Experimental
   Prototype for Speech Understanding Research," IEEE Trans. Acoustics,
   Speech, and Signal Processing, ASSP-23, no. 1 (Feb. 1975), 2-10.
Woods, W. A., "Shortfall and Density Scoring Strategies for Speech
   Understanding Control," Proc. 5th Int. Joint Conf. on Artificial
   Intelligence - 1977, Cambridge, Mass., Aug. 22-25, 1977, 18-26.
Woods, W. A., "Optimal Search Strategies for Speech Understanding Control,"
   submitted for publication in Artificial Intelligence.
Woods, W. A., M. Bates, G. Brown, B. Bruce, C. Cook, J. Klovstad, J. Makhoul,
   B. Nash-Webber, R. Schwartz, J. Wolf, and V. Zue, "Speech Understanding
   Systems - Final Technical Progress Report," Report No. 3438, Vols. I-V,
   Bolt Beranek and Newman Inc., Cambridge, Ma., 1976 (DDC ADA035165,
   ADA035166, ADA035167, ADA035277, ADA035278).
Woods, W. A., R. M. Kaplan, and B. L. Nash-Webber, "The Lunar Sciences
   Natural Language Information System: Final Report," Report No. 2378, Bolt
   Beranek and Newman Inc., Cambridge, Mass., 1972 (NTIS N72-28984).
Woods, W. A., and J. Makhoul, "Mechanical Inference Problems in Continuous
   Speech Understanding," Proc. Third Int. Joint Conf. on Artificial
   Intelligence, Palo Alto, Calif. 200-207, 1973 (also Artificial
   Intelligence, 5, no. 1 (Spring 1974), 73-91).

THE HARPY SPEECH UNDERSTANDING SYSTEM

Bruce Lowerre
Raj Reddy
Carnegie-Mellon University
Pittsburgh, PA 15213

15-1. ABSTRACT

Harpy is one of the first systems to demonstrate that high performance, large vocabulary connected speech recognition systems can in fact be realized economically for task-oriented (restricted) languages. In this chapter we present, using simple examples, the principles of organization of the Harpy system. We will illustrate how knowledge sources (KSs) are specified, how the knowledge compiler integrates the KSs into a unified directional graph representation, and how this knowledge is utilized. In conclusion, we will discuss many of the limitations of the present system and how these can be eliminated or reduced in future systems.

15-2. INTRODUCTION

Harpy is one of the systems developed as part of the five year ARPA speech understanding research effort. A study group headed by Allen Newell proposed a set of specific performance goals in 1971 to be achieved within a five year period (Newell, et al., 1971). Figure 15-1 presents the original stated goals and the performance of the Harpy system. It is interesting to note that Harpy not only met all the specifications but exceeded several of the stated object- ives. In particular, the system ran an order of magnitude faster with only about half the error rate, in a noisy environment using a poor frequency- response close speaking microphone.

A comprehensive review of the recent speech recognition research including the ARPA speech program is given in Reddy (1976), Klatt (1977), and Lea (this volume). Here, we will briefly mention some of the prior research which directly contributed to the success of the Harpy System.

The parametric representation and the distance metric used in the Harpy system are based on LPC coefficients (Atal, 1971; Itakura, 1968; and Markel, 1972) using minimum distance residual metric (Itakura, 1975). The segmenta- tion and labeling are extensions of techniques used in Hearsay II (Erman, this volume), Hearsay I (Reddy, et al., 1973), and earlier work of our group (Reddy, 1967). Other significant early work in this area is by Tappert et al. (1970) using the transeme approach. The juncture rules were all empirically derived but were influenced by the work of Oshika, et al., (1975) and Cohen & Mercer, (1975). The integrated network representation of knowledge is based on the Dragon system developed by Jim Baker at Carnegie-Mellon University. The best-few beam search technique is an extension of the best-first technique used in the Hearsay I system. Of all these, the single most important intellectual legacy upon which Harpy is based is the representation and delayed-decision techniques first used effectively in the Dragon system (Baker, 1975). It is also important to note the intellectual ferment created

Targets (from 1971)	HARPY Performance (1976)
Accept connected speech	Yes
from many	5 (3 male, 2 female)
cooperative speakers of the General American Dialect	Yes
in a quiet room	Computer terminal room
using a good quality microphone	Ordinary microphone
with slight tuning/speaker	Substantial tuning (20-30 utterances/speaker)
requiring only natural adaptation by the user	No adaptation required
permitting a slightly selected vocabulary of 1000 words	1011 words, no post-selection
with a highly artificial syntax and highly constrained task	Combined syntactic and semantic constraints → Avg. branching factor of 10
providing graceful interaction	modest interaction capabilities
tolerating < 10% semantic error	9% sentence error -- 5% semantic
in a few times real-time* [on a 100 MIPS machine]	80 times real-time on a* .35 MIPS PDP-KA10 Using 256K of 36-bit words With a simple program organization Costing about $5 per sentence
and be demonstrable in 1976 with a moderate chance of success.	Operational 13 August 1976

* A few times real-time on 100 MIPS processor is anywhere from 200 to 500 MIPSS (Millions of Instructions executed Per Second of Speech). The actual performance of Harpy was about 28 MIPSS, i.e., 80 times real-time on a .35 MIPS processor.

Figure 15-1.
Performance of the Harpy system.

341

by the large ARPA effort and continued interactions with several other groups actively pursuing similar research objectives.

15-3. KNOWLEDGE SOURCES

An important tenet that distinguishes speech understanding systems from recognition systems is the assumption that the speech signal does not have all the necessary information to uniquely decode the message and that one must use linguistic and context dependent knowledge sources to infer (or deduce) the intent of the message. However, this distinction appears to be getting fuzzy as time progresses and systems use not all the available sources of knowledge, but only a few of the knowledge sources, e.g., phonological, prosodic, lexical, and syntactic knowledge. Harpy belongs to this class of systems. Although we have implemented two tasks (chess and abstract retrieval) for which we have included task and context specific knowledge, most tasks implemented on Harpy do not include this knowledge. However, the structure and implementation of the Harpy system do not preclude the use of such knowledge.

In this section we will illustrate, by means of a simple example, typical knowledge sources used in a task and their specification and modification by the user. Figure 15-2 contains all the knowledge sources for a Mini-Query-Language (MQL). This is the usual form in which a user specifies various knowledge sources. Figure 15-3 illustrates some of these knowledge sources as directed graph representations. If an interactive graphics display terminal is available, knowledge sources can be specified directly in this network form by the user. This is the more natural form of specification as the knowledge compiler (Sec. 15-4) operates on the directed graph representation.

15-3.1 Syntactic Knowledge.

The syntax of the language is given in Fig. 15-2a as a set of four syntax equations. This is a special form for representing a class of phrase structure languages and is often called in computer science literature Backus Normal Form (BNF). Sentences "Please help me." or "Please show us everything." are legal in this language. The first equation states that a sentence in this language consists of a begin symbol ([) followed by phrase <SS> (in the second equation) followed by an ending symbol (]). The second equation states that the symbol <SS> may be defined in terms of two alternative phrase structures: please followed by help followed by any phrase defined by symbol <M> or please followed by show followed by <M> followed by phrase <Q>. Equation 3 states the phrase <Q> can be either everything or something. Equation 4 states that the phrase <M> can be either me or us. Figure 15-3a shows how these equations would be specified in directed graph representation.

Specifying the grammar for a new task is the role of a language design expert. He needs to have a deep understanding of the implications of each of the design decisions. The language must permit as much flexibility and graceful interaction as possible without sacrificing the recognizability and accuracy. Controlling the branching factor and the vocabulary ambiguity are two basic techniques available to the language designer. Goodman (1976) provides a formal model combining both of these aspects. Some of the language design tools developed by Goodman were instrumental in the development of a family of languages for the Harpy system which led to the successful demonstration in 1976. Although time pressures made it difficult to fine-tune these languages, it is clear that constrained and yet habitable languages can

```
<SENT> ::=      [ <SS> ]

<SS> ::=        please help <M>
                please show <M> <Q>

<Q> ::=         everything
                something

<M> ::=         me
                us
```

Figure 15-2(a). Grammar of MQL.


```
everything    (-,0) (EH,EH2) V R IY2 TH IH3 NX
help          (-,0) HH AA3 EL3 (← (-,0), -) P
me            (-,0) M IY
please        (← (-,0), -) (P (L,L2), PL (L,0)) IY (Z{4}, (Z,0) S)
show          (-,0) SH AA5 (OW,0)
something     (-,0) S AA M TH IH3 NX
us            (-,0) IH6 S (HH,0)
[             -
]             -
```

Figure 15-2(b). Pronunciation dictionary for MQL.


```
#,-↑-{,100}

-,#↑.-{,100}

-,-↑-{1,40}

0,-↑.< -{1,40}

Z,HH}

[Z,S],SH{

P,M{

OW,IH6↑(.< (>,0), >)

IY,[EH,EH2]↑(.< (>,0), >)

0,<{
```

-	1	5	HH	3	6	AA	4	10
←	1	8	M	3	6	AA3	6	12
P	3	8	NX	5	12	AA5	3	8
PL	4	10	R	2	5	OW	2	20
V	3	6	L	2	4	IH3	3	7
Z	2	10	L2	2	5	IH6	2	6
TH	3	8	EL3	8	14	IY	4	20
S	4	12	EH	6	14	IY2	4	8
SH	4	12	EH2	2	7			

Figure 15-2(c). Word   Figure 15-2(d). Phone templates for MQL.
   juncture rules for MQL.

Figure 15-2. Knowledge source for a
           Mini-Query-Language (MQL).

343
```
```

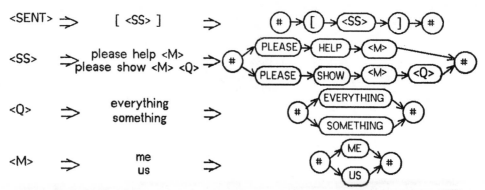

Figure 15-3(a). Representation of the grammar in Fig. 15-2(a).

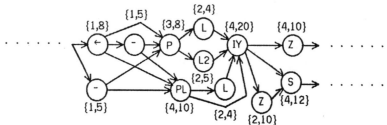

Figure 15-3(b). Representation of the word "please".

Change the maximum permissible duration of sentence initial (final) silence to 100

Change Z,SH juncture to allow either or both

Optional P at P/M juncture

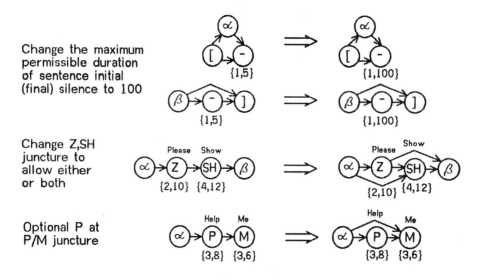

Figure 15-3(c). Representation of some of the juncture rules.

Figure 15-3. Directed graph representation of some of the knowledge given in Fig. 15-2.

be designed for use in specific task domains.

15-3.2 Lexical Knowledge.

Figure 15-2b gives the pronunciation dictionary for the MQL. Alternative pronunciations of each word are represented in a special notation (Lowerre, 1976, pg. 41). This is a string representation of the pronunciation graph. Figure 15-3b gives the graph representation for the word please. In the string notation, parentheses are used to indicate alternative choices and commas separate the alternatives. "0" is used to indicate null choice. Curly brackets are used to specify duration in centi-seconds, if the expected duration differs from the normal range of durations given as part of phone specification.

Note that the pronunciation graph in Fig. 15-3b is significantly more complex than what would normally appear as a baseform in a pronunciation dictionary. This is because the Harpy dictionary attempts to capture all the intra-word phonological phenomena as part of pronunciation. In the example given in Fig. 15-3b we see several such phenomena: /l/ in please may be partly or wholly devoiced and /z/ may be voiced, devoiced, or mixed. For each of these alternative phones, spectral patterns expected may be different for different allophones and require distinct symbolic notation.

Making up pronunciation dictionaries for a new vocabulary is perhaps the most time consuming task at present. Our initial attempts to derive all the intra-word phenomena from a set of pre-defined phonological rules operating on a baseform proved to be a failure. It appears that numerous subtle and complex processes have to be modeled very carefully before we can derive the pronunciation graph at the level of detail required by the Harpy system. Our present plan is to develop automatic and/or interactive knowledge acquisition techniques for learning the word structure directly from examples without the use of any predefined model.

15-3.3 Juncture Rules.

Another aspect of speech knowledge that is important for the successful operation of Harpy relates to the phenomena that occur at word boundaries. Unlike written text, where word boundaries are clearly defined, in spoken language word boundaries tend to overlap making it difficult to detect the end of one word and the beginning of the next. Knowledge about such phenomena is represented in Harpy in the form of Juncture Rules.

Figure 15-2c gives a set of word juncture rules for MQL. In general juncture rules contain examples of insertion, deletion, and change of phones occuring at word junctures. For this simple task, only a few juncture rules are required. Lowerre (1976, pg. 42) gives the notation used for specifying juncture rules. The exact details are unimportant here. What is interesting to observe is that many of these rules can be rewritten in the form of graph-rewriting rules (as illustrated in Fig. 15-3c) and many of the known phonological phenomena can be represented in this form. Figure 15-3c contains an example of duration change at sentence initial and final positions, an example of feature assimilation, and an example of phone deletion at word boundaries.

The approach taken in the design of Harpy is to manually tailor the juncture rules to the task at hand. This is a time consuming process. In the long run a complete set of rules capturing a wide variety of juncture phenoma has to be collected, revised, and refined. Phonological rules available in the literature do not provide the necessary level of detail to be used directly in Harpy-like systems. This is a case where automatic knowledge acquisition from examples is likely to be very helpful.

15-3.4 Phonemic Knowledge.

Figure 15-2d shows the list of phones used in MQL and the range of durations permissible for each phone, in centi-seconds. The durations are determined empirically. Missing in the figure are the phone templates which are represented as a transformation of linear prediction coefficients.

In general, the phone list for a given task consists of all the allophones (with distinct spectral characteristics) necessary to uniquely represent the expected spectral sequences in the word list. Each distinct allophone of a given phoneme is identified by adding a digit at the end of the phoneme symbol.

The generation of the spectral templates for various allophones is one of the significant innovations within the Harpy system. Lowerre (1977) describes this process in detail. There are three sources of variability that affect the phone template characteristics: environmental noise, transducer char- acteristics, and speaker characteristics.

In the Harpy system a single composite template is generated automatically for each allophone, capturing all three sources of variability. A speaker is asked to repeat 20 or so predefined sentences in the environment using the microphone. The Harpy system analyzes these sentences using a speaker independent set of templates to identify the location of each word and each phone within the word (more on the recognition process in Sec. 15-5). All instances of a given allophone in the 20 or so training sentences are averaged to generate a speaker specific, microphone specific, and environment specific template. Note that the template generation process is entirely automatic. Since any number of instances of an allophone can be averaged to generate the template, the same technique can be used to generate speaker independent or microphone independent templates by averaging over an appropriate set.

15-4.   KNOWLEDGE COMPILER

An interesting aspect that distinguishes the speech problem from many other knowledge intensive systems in AI is the diversity of the knowledge sources (KSs). Each deals with a different aspect of the problem, and each "speaks a different language." Yet the KSs must cooperate somehow in decoding an unknown utterance. The Hearsay II System (Erman, in this volume) provides one interesting solution to the problem. The so-called "blackboard" model is used to effect communication and cooperation. The Harpy system attempts to structure all knowledge into a unified directed graph representation. Some KSs syntax are easily represented as a graph. But many other aspects: juncture rules, pronunciation variability, and duration effects, are not as easily represented as a graph and often require considerable ingenuity. Much of the Harpy's success is the result of solving the difficult technical problems associated with forcing all the diverse KSs into a unified framework.

As we saw in Sec. 15-3, the KSs are specified by the user as independent units, each with its own notation (Fig. 15-2). Translating KSs represented in different notations into a single unified graph requires using a knowledge compiler. This process is not unlike translating programs specified in a higher level language into machine code using a language compiler. Figure 15-4 gives a flowchart of knowledge compiling process in the Harpy system. This is by far the most computer-intensive process of the Harpy system. It took over 13 hours of DEC System/10 (KL) time to compile the 1011 word vocabulary document retrieval task into a 15,000 state network.

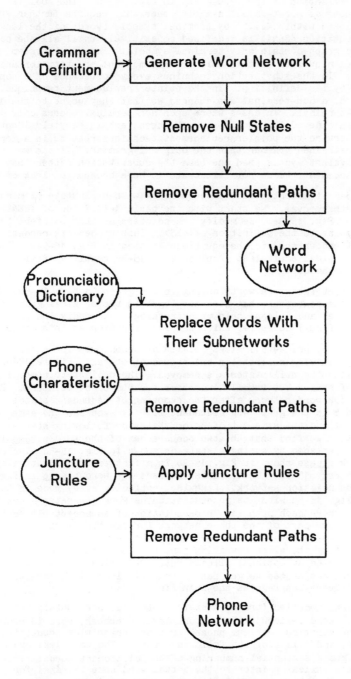

Figure 15-4. Flowchart of the knowledge compiler.

The first step in the compiling process is to generate a word network from the BNF specification of the type given in Fig. 15-2a. The goal is to replace all occurrences of non-terminal symbols (ones that require further specification; enclosed within <...>) by terminal symbols (words of the language). In the top equation <SENT> is redefined repetitively until all the paths in the directed graph contain only terminal symbols. The Harpy system uses two different techniques to achieve this transformation: substitution and pointer replacement. In the substitution technique every occurrence of a non-terminal is replaced by its definition. In the pointer replacement technique all occurrences of a non-terminal are changed so that they point to the definition of that non-terminal. In cases where each non-terminal occurs only once on the righthand side of the equation, both these techniques yield identical graphs. Otherwise the pointer replacement technique results in a more compact but less constrained grammar than the original grammar. If one wants an exactly equivalent syntax then one uses the substitution rather than the pointer replacement. We do not illustrate it here because of lack of space.

Figure 15-5 illustrates this process along with null state elimination and redundant path removal. We start with the basic definition of <SENT> as shown at the top of Fig. 15-3a. We modify the pointers so that pointers to <SS> are altered to point to the definition of <SS>. This process is repeated for each non-terminal encountered in the equations as seen in Fig. 15-5a. Figure 15-5b shows a topological equivalent graph to Fig. 15-5a resulting from pointer replacement technique.

Two important facts are worth noting in the graph in Fig. 15-5b. Note that it permits some sentences that were not legal in the original grammar, e.g., "please show me" and "please help me everything". Secondly the graph has a large number of null nodes (#) which serve no function at this stage.

Lowerre (1976, pp. 44-51) gives details of techniques for state space reduction by removing null states and redundant states. Figure 15-5c shows the graph after the null states are removed. The null state removal reduces the number of states but usually increases the number of pointers. Figure 15-5d shows the word network after the removing of redundant states. Two states A and B in the graph are redundant if: 1) each has the same terminal lexical symbol and the same set of prior states or following states. Using this definition we find that the two occurrences of the word please in Fig. 15-5c can be replaced by a single state as shown in Fig. 15-5d. The pronunciation network please shown in Fig. 15-3b is a further specification of please appearing in Fig. 15-5d. Thus, we can replace the word please in Fig.15-5d with its pronunciation network. Likewise, replacing every node in the word network in Fig. 15-5d with its pronunciation network generates a new finite state graph, where each path is a pronunciation of an acceptable sentence. Figure 15-6 shows part of the phone network for our MQL example. We remove redundant states in the phone network using the same techniques as in the word network. Applying the graph rewriting juncture rules,the examples given in Fig. 15-3c, adding an optional silence before the final state and again removing redundant states we get part of the final compiled knowledge network for our Mini-Query-Language as shown in Fig. 15-7.

In its final compiled form each state in the network contains the following information: word lexicon number, phone lexicon number, word id number, minimum phone duration, maximum phone duration, transition count, intersection state marker, and a list of its following states. The word lexicon number is calculated from a sequential numbering of the dictionary words. This serves as an internal lexical pointer to the actual word name (string) for recognition. The phone number is likewise calculated from a sequential numbering of the phones and serves as a pointer to the phone name.

The word id is used to uniquely identify every occurrence of a terminal

348

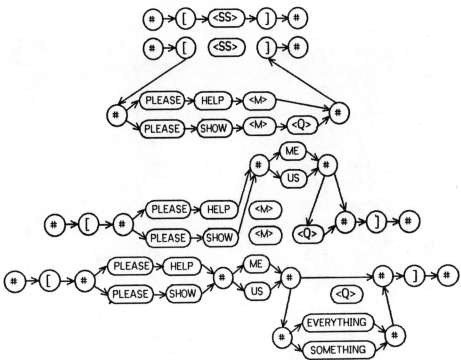

Figure 15-5(a).

Generation of the word network from the grammar specifications.

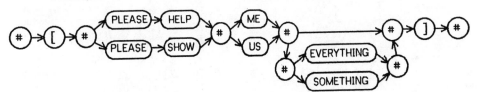

Figure 15-5(b). Word network after expansion.

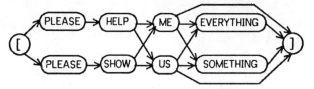

Figure 15-5(c). Removal of null states.

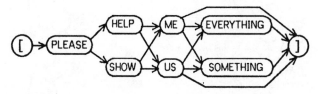

Figure 15-5(d). Removal of redundant states.

Figure 15-5. Generation of word network.

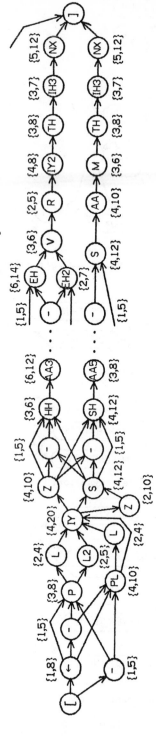

$\{m,n\}$ = {min duration,max duration}

Figure 15-6. Network after replacing all words with phone subnetworks (part of network not shown).

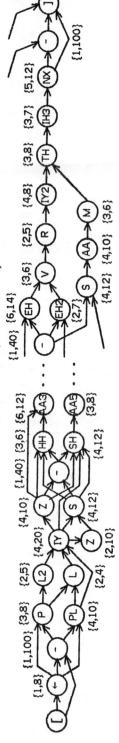

$\{m,n\}$ = {min duration,max duration}

Figure 15-7. Network after removal of redundant paths, application of juncture rules and addition of optional silence before final state (part of network not shown).

350

symbol (word) in the BNF grammar. Some words may occur more than once in the grammar. However, each will be given a unique id number. This is necessary for the recognition process to recognize that a transition has been made from one word to the next. This problem is especially prevalent in cases where the same word can occur two or more times in a row, such as in a series of digits. In this case, the BNF grammar must be constructed so that there are two lists of digits where the first list is linked to the second and the second is linked back to the first. This will generate connected network states with the same word lexical number but with different word id numbers.

The minimum duration is the minimum expected phone duration in centi-seconds. This is used by the recognition process in calculating transition probabilities. An inter-state transition which does not allow minimum duration in the exited state will be penalized. Similarly an intra-state transition which causes the maximum duration to be exceeded will be penalized.

The transition count is the minimum number of inter-state transitions needed to reach the final state. This is used by the recognition process to prune "dead-end" paths. For example, if state J has a transition count of N, and at a point in the recognition the number of segments left to go is less than N, then state J is pruned from consideration since its path cannot reach the final state before the end of the utterance. A side effect of this pruning is that on the last segment, the only state being considered is the final state (with transition count of 0).

Discussion. There are several other technical aspects of the knowledge compiler such as subsumption, intersection states, determination of transition count, and other details that are omitted for lack of space. Many of these tend to be efficiency issues in space and time. We have omitted discussion on how semantic, pragmatic, and prosodic knowledge would be incorporated into the network. We have been able to formulate solutions to these problems in several cases and do not anticipate any major difficulties in using these classes of knowledge within the Harpy framework.

15-5. THE RECOGNITION PROCESS

In this section we will describe how knowledge is used in the recognition of an unknown utterance. Figure 15-8 gives the complete graphical trace of an utterance recognition. The unknown sentence is digitized, segmented, matched with phone templates, and compared with the sentences in the language using the knowledge network. The utterance with the best score is chosen as the sentence and displayed at the bottom of the waveform. In the rest of this section we will briefly described each of these steps in the recognition process using the example in Fig. 15-8.

15-5.1 Digitization

All the experiments using the Harpy system were conducted in a computer terminal room environment (approx. 65 dbA) using an Electrovoice head-mounted close speaking microphone (model no. RE51). The signal was low pass filtered at 4.5 KHz using a Kronhite (model no. 3750R) and sampled at 10 KHz sampling rate. The time sharing operating system was modified to accept high data rate signal without any data loss. Utterance begining and end detection was done using amplitude and zero-crossing measurements of the signal (Gill, et al. 1978). The digitized waveform is displayed as in Fig. 15-8. Note that the second line of the waveform is a continuation of the first and the third is a continuation of the second.

351

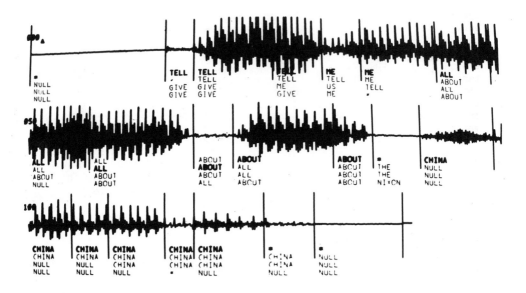

I heard "TELL ME ALL ABOUT CHINA"

Figure 15-8. A graphical trace of the recognition process.

15-5.2 Segmentation

The continuous speech signal is segmented into discrete components using ZAPDASH (zerocrossings and peaks in smoothed and differenced waveforms) parameters. The segmentation process is described in detail by Gill et al., (1978). A recursive top down segmentation procedure is used to identify segments based on features such as silence, voicing, frication, peak detection and dip detection. Figure 15-8 shows a typical segmentation achieved by the system. Note that segmentation boundaries are marked by vertical bars. Note that vowels are usually divided into two or more segments. There is one missing segment boundary at the juncture of the words all and about. The l-schwa boundary is missing. But given the constraints of the language the system recovers from this error.

15-5.3 Phone Template Matching

Spectral characteristics of each segment are determined by using LPC analysis at the midpoint of the segment. The average segment length is about 5 centi-seconds, resulting in a factor 5 improvement in signal analysis over systems which perform LPC analysis each centi-second. For each segment the LPC coefficients of the segments are matched with speaker dependent templates generated using the procedure described in Sec. 15-4.4. The LPC minimum distance residual metric is based on Itakura (1975). In certain versions of the Harpy system only templates which are permissable in that context are computed. Note that implicit within this discussion is the assumption that given enough allophone templates it is reasonable to attempt labeling of segments using pattern matching techniques. This was by no means an accepted approach to phone labeling until recently.

15-5.4 Recognition and Match

We will illustrate the steps in matching and search process using Fig. 15-9. Figure 15-9a is part of a knowledge network in which the sentence "Tell me all about China." is legal. Only the first few states of the knowledge network are shown. Note that given this network, only four phone labels are permissible in the sentence initial position, namely IH2, G, -, and T. Given this information, the phone template matching procedure only performs these matches. The values of the acoustic match distance are given on the right side of the boxes in Fig. 15-9b. Note that the silence phone /-/ has the smallest distance of 0.23 for the first segment, /T/ has distance of 1.46, /g/ a distance of 1.57, and /IH2/ has a distance of 2.26. Since these are the only legal phones for this position, none of the other phone distances are evaluated.

As the acoustic matches are generated, Harpy begins the recognition process. The goal of the recognition task is to find an optimal sequence of phones satisfying two criteria. The sequence must represent a legal path through the knowledge network and should consist of phones with high acoustic match probabilities (the actual calculation produces "- log probability").

The beam search technique used by the Harpy system is a heuristic search technique which locates a near-optimal sequence of phones that is consistent with the network. Beam search is a technique in which a group of near-miss alternatives around the best path are examined. By searching many alternatives simultaneously, this method avoids the need for backtracking. The search is executed by creating and examining a tree structure of phones whose connections are consistent with transitions in the knowledge net. Each ply (or column) in the recognition tree, given in Fig. 15-9b, represents the matching associated with one segment of the digitized utterance.

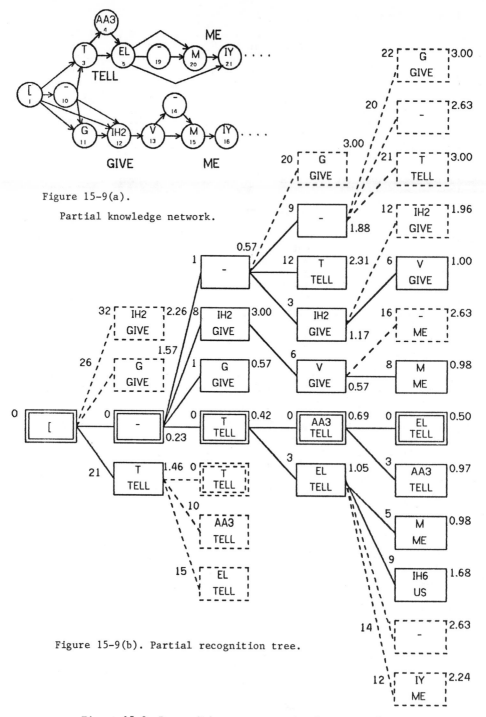

Figure 15-9(a).

Partial knowledge network.

Figure 15-9(b). Partial recognition tree.

Figure 15-9. Recognition process using beam search.

The root node of the tree is the sentence beginning state "[" of the network in Fig. 15-9a. Harpy begins the search by taking all the legal phones that can follow from the sentence initial state and entering them in the recognition tree. Refering to Fig. 15-9b, each box in the second ply (column) gives phone and the word associated with candidate state. Next, a path probability is calculated for each candidate. This is a cumulative value based on the path probability of the previous node and the acoustic match probability of the current node. The path probability value is indicated on the left side of each box. The path with the best probability (boxes with double lines in Fig. 15-9b) is determined. In this case the "-" state has the best value. All the remaining candidates are then compared with it. Those candidates that fall below a threshold of acceptability are pruned from further searching. In Fig. 15-9b the pruned states are indicated by dotted boxes. The successors of each surviving candidate are expanded, based on the information in the knowledge network.

As can be seen from Fig. 15-9a, there are four successors to the /-/ state and three successors to the /t/ state. Note that, although not shown in Fig. 15-9a as a specific pointer, each state can transition to itself. This permits two or more segments to be matched to the same state. Thus, the segmentation can introduce extra segment markers without significant penalty while a missing segment causes problems. Therefore, potential missing states must be created as optional states during the network creation time.

When the successor states are copied onto the recognition tree as candidates for match with the next segment in the segment list, two or more states may generate the same successor. Instead of retaining two independent paths through the same node, we can collapse them into a common path, avoiding redundant computation. In Fig. 15-9b both the /-/ and the /t/ states generate /t/ as a successor. Only the path with the highest prior value is relevant at this point. The deleted path is indicated by a double broken-line box. Thus, lesser-valued paths can be discarded because their path probabilities can never exceed the one with the highest value. The path probabilities are calculated as before, the best path is established and unpromising alternatives are pruned.

The forward search continues, expanding the recognition tree and saving those connections that satisfy the threshold, until we reach the end of the utterance. It was not possible to show the entire tree. Figure 15-9b shows only a portion of the recognition tree, i.e., up to the fourth segment of the waveform shown in Fig. 15-8. Returning to Figure 15-8, we see under each segment the words associated with the best four states in the candidate list for that segment.

So far we have explained the beam search technique informally by means of an example. The following algorithmic description of the search process provides a more formal and precise definition of the search and matching process.

```
Start:
Put the initial state in the list of previous states:
Repeat the following for each segment:
  For each state A in the list of previous states:
      Take A out of the list
      For each successor B of state A:
          Compute the cumulative loglikelihood P of
              transitioning from A to B as:
          P(A →B) = P associated with A + acoustic match between the
              phoneme associated with B and the current segment
          If the list of candidate paths contains a path X→ B
              If P(A→B) is greater than P(X→ B)
                  replace X→ B and P(X→ B) with A→ B
                  and P(A→B) in the list of candidate paths
          Else store A →B and P(A→B) in the list of
                  candidate paths
          If P(A →B) is better than any other loglikelihood computed
              so far for this segment:
                  P(A →B) becomes the best loglikelihood P(best)

  Compute the beamwidth E as function of segment duration
  For each path in the list of candidate paths:
    If the distance between the loglikelihood associated with
      the path and P(best) is less than E:
        put the "to" state of the path (B) in the list of previous states.
```

Of all the paths that survive at the end of the utterance, the one with the best path probability is the solution we are seeking. This is the only path that satisfies the two criteria of the recognition process. It provides the best interpretation of the acoustic matches, while satisfying the constraint of the knowledge network.

A backtrace through the recognition tree reveals the desired solution indicating the phone and word assignments associated with the best path. Since the pointers for each surviving path in the beam of the recognition tree are retained till the end, this turns out to be a straight forward look-up operation and does not involve any search. Note that what appears to be the best choice for each segment in the forward search may not, in fact, be part of the globally best sequence discovered by delaying the decision till the end. Thus, local errors introduced by segmentation and acoustic matches are recovered by delaying commitment to a particular path until the forward search is completed. Therefore the forward search may be errorful without affecting the final solution. Refering to Fig. 15-8 again, the final word choice selected by the backtrace is indicated brighter than the rest of the candidate choices. Note that on line two of the waveform the assignment of all and about involves the second best choices.

Occasionally, the heuristics associated with the beam search miss the optimal path, but because the acoustic matches are less than perfect, attempting to find the optimal path at great cost and effort leads to little or no improvement in the overall performance.

356

15-6. PERFORMANCE

In this section we will present a summary of the Harpy system performance for several tasks. A more detailed description of these results is given in Reddy et al., (1976). Table 15-1 summarizes some of the interesting results from these experiments. The first four tasks essentially have no syntactic or other higher level knowledge. The rest of the tasks use some form of syntactic and other task-dependent information.

Table 15-1 contains several relevant dimensions for each task. Each task was tested with several speakers, as shown in column 2. The pair of numbers in parentheses indicates the number of male and female speakers in each group. Column 3, 4, and 5 are indicative of the measure of complexity of each task. Size of the vocabulary is usually quoted as a measure of complexity. This is usually acceptable for languages which do not use syntactic or other task dependent constraints. The average branching factor is a measure of lexical fanout (Reddy, et al., 1977 pg. 41) allowed by the grammar. The branching factor based on entropy (2 $\uparrow$ entropy) of the language has been used by Cohen and Mercer (1975) and Goodman (1976). The IBM group uses the term "perplexity" to refer to this measure. The last two columns give performance of the Harpy system on these tasks: word error rate and millions of instructions executed per second of speech.

Effect of telephone: We conducted an experiment to evaluate the effect of telephone input on Harpy performance. We note from Table 15-1 (task 2) that using telephone speech increases the word error rate by a factor of 3 to 4.

Effect of speaker: Task 3 in Table 15-1 shows the effect of using speaker independent phone templates. Again, we see that there is a significant increase in error rate. Rabiner and Sambur (Rabiner, 1976) state that they get about 4% word error using a speaker independent recognition system. The IBM group (Bahl, 1978) reports less than 1% word error rate using speaker dependent training in a quiet environment.

Effect of vocabulary: The principal effect of the vocabulary size appears to be to increase the space required. It appears to have very little effect on the accuracy or speed of the system.

Effect of branching factor: Clearly, increase in branching factor increases the error rate and processing required. Different groups seem to prefer different measures. The IBM group (Bahl, 1978) claims that the performance of their system correlates highly with the entropy based perplexity measure. The Harpy system does not exhibit any such clear correlation. Both the digits task (perplexity 10) and the 1011 word abstract retrieval task (perplexity 5) both have the same error rate. Further, the retrieval task with a perplexity of 5, is 8 times slower than the digits task with higher "perplexity". Further, Harpy has a better error rate of only 12% with the spelling task (perplexity 26) while the IBM group reports an error rate of 30% using a task with a perplexity of 20. Independent of what measure is best to use, Harpy clearly demonstrates that it is possible to have high performance connected speech input for task-oriented constrained languages.

357

	No of Speakers	Vocab. Size	Average Branching Factor	Entropy based B.F., "Perplexity"	Word* Error rate (%)	MIPS* required to process a second of speech
Connected digits -Speaker dependent	10 (7+3)	10	10	10	2	3.5
Connected digits -Telephone	4 (3+1)	10	10	10	7	3.5
Connected digits -Speaker independent templates	20 (14+6)	10	10	10	7	3.5
Alphabet -Spelling task	2 (2+0)	26	26	26	12	5.2
Abstract retrieval	5 (3+2)	1001	33	5	2	28

Table 15-1

*Results as of September 1976

15-7. DISCUSSION

There are several important factors that contributed to the success the Harpy system. Foremost among them are the representation of knowledge and the beam search technique. Several speech related decisions that led to improved performance were: use of large number of allophone templates, dynamic adaptation of template characteristics for a new speaker, the decision to encode intra-word phonological phonememe into the pronunciation dictionary, lpc analysis, Itakura metric, and so on. Several questions arise about the generality and extendability of Harpy-like systems. We will raise some of these and present our current views on these topics.

1. Doesn't finite state grammar restriction make Harpy useless for use with natural language? From a computational point of view the answer appears to be "No". If one is willing to place a restriction on the length of sentence then the language can be modeled using finite state graph (FSG) representation. A simple FSG where any word can follow any other word, would accept all legal sentences but would permit many more illegal sentences as well. However, one need not take such a drastic step. As we observed in Sec. 15-5, if one is willing to accept some loss of constraints, the language can be represented by a suitable FSG which covers the language.

2. Doesn't FSG representation require a large amount of memory for complex tasks? The answer is "Yes" but given the advances in computer technology it doesn't matter. A graph structure that attempts to capture every possible variation requires a great deal of memory. Our current estimate is that a complex language may require a few million states (the 1011 word task has about 15,000) and that semiconductor memories capable of holding such state

358

information would be available for a few hundred dollars. We have also been studying issues of paging knowledge networks from secondary memory and the possibility of using multi-level networks rather than a single integrated network. Multi-level networks require a greater degree of dynamic interpretation during execution. Both of these appear technically feasible. It will be purely a question of space-time-cost trade-off in system organization.

3. How can Harpy handle sentences that are not part of its grammar? In general it cannot, but neither can any other system or human. To be able to handle new words and new sentence constructs that are not part of one's vocabulary and language one needs a knowledge acquisition facility. We have been developing concepts that would permit Harpy-like systems to acquire new words and new constructs. This requires an ability for the system to recognize that the unknown utterance is inconsistent with its internal knowledge and activate partial matching and word spotting type networks which are substantially less constrained. If all the words are known but they are ungrammtical (as in "sleep roses dangerously young colorless"), the sentence construct, if desired, can be assimilated into the word network. If one or more words are unknown then one needs a "speak and spell" program to learn the new words or variations of existing words.

In conclusion, we see that there are many possible avenues for evolving Harpy-like systems. It appears that many of the present limitations of the system can be removed without losing the high performance aspects of the system. However, these changes are likely to take many years to come given the limited research activity in the area.

15-8. ACKNOWLEDGEMENTS

The research reported here was supported by the Defense Advanced Research Projects Agency and monitored by the Airforce Office of Scientific Research under contract number F44620-73-C-0074.

We would like to thank Gary Goodman and Ron Cole for their helpful comments on this manuscript and John Zsarnay for his help in generating the illustrations.

15-9. REFERENCES

Atal, B.S., & S.L. Hanauer, "Speech analysis & synthesis by linear prediction of the speech wave", J. Acoust. Soc. Amer. vol 50, no 2, 1971.

Bahl, et al., "Automatic recognition of continuously spoken sentences from a finite state grammar", in Proc. IEEE-ICASSP Conf. 1978, Tulsa, Okla.

Baker, J.K., "The DRAGON system - An overview", IEEE Trans. ASSP, vol 23, 1975.

Baker, J.K., "Stochastic modeling for automatic speech understanding", in Speech Recognition: Invited Papers of the IEEE Symp., D.R. Reddy (ed.), 1975.

Cohen, P.S., & R.L. Mercer, "The Phonological component of an automatic speech recognition system", in Speech Recognition: Invited Papers of the IEEE Symp., D.R. Reddy(ed.), 1975.

Erman, L.D. & V.R. Lesser, "A multi-level organization for problem solving using many, diverse cooperating sources of knowledge", in Proc. 4th IJCAI, 1975, Tbilisi, USSR.

Erman, L.D., "The Hearsay-II speech understanding system", ch.16 this volume.

Gill, G.S. et al., "A recursive segmentation procedure for continuous speech", tech. rep., Computer Science Dept., Carnegie-Mellon U., 1978.

Goodman, G., "Analysis of Languages for man-machine voice communication", tech. rep., Computer Science Dept., Carnegie-Mellon U., 1976.

Itakura F., & S. Saito, "Analysis synthesis telephony based on the maximum likelihood method", Proc. 6th Int. Congr. Acoustics, 1968.

Itakura, F., "Minimum prediction residual principle applied to speech recognition", IEEE Trans. ASSP, vol 23, 1975.

Klatt, D.H., "Review of the ARPA Speech Understanding Project", .J. Acoust. Soc. Amer. vol 62, no 6, 1977.

Lea, W.A., "Speech Recognition: Past, Present, Future", ch. 4 this volume.

Lowerre, B., "The Harpy speech recognition systems", Ph.D. dissertation, Computer Science Dept., Carnegie-Mellon U., 1977.

Markel, J.D., "Digital inverse filtering - A new tool for formant trajectory estimation", IEEE Trans. Audio Electroacoust., vol AU-20, 1972.

Newell, A. et al., Speech Understanding Systems: Final Report of a Study Group, 1971. (Reprinted by North-Holland/American Elsevier, Amsterdam, Netherlands, 1973).

Oshika, B.T. et al., "The role of phonological rules in speech understanding research", IEEE Trans. ASSP, vol 23, 1975.

Rabiner, L.R., "Preliminary results in recognition of connected digits", IEEE Trans. Acoust., Speech, Signal Processing, April 1976.

Reddy, D.R., "Computer recognition of connected speech", J. Acoust. Soc. Amer. vol 42, 1967.

Reddy. D.R., et al., "The Hearsay speech understanding system: an example of the recognition process", Proc. IJCAI-73, 1973, Stanford, CA.

Reddy, D.R., "Speech recognition by machine: A review", Proc. of the IEEE (Apr. 1976).

Reddy, D.R., et al., "Speech Understanding Systems: summary of results of the five-year research effort at CMU", Computer Science Dept., Carnegie-Mellon U., 1977.

Tappert, C.C., et al., "The use of dynamic segments in the automatic recognition of continuous speech", tech. rep., RADC-TR-70-22, IBM, Systems Development Div. Research, Triangle Park, N.C., 1970.

16.

THE HEARSAY-II SPEECH UNDERSTANDING SYSTEM:
A TUTORIAL[1]

Lee D. Erman
Carnegie-Mellon University

Victor R. Lesser
The University of Massachusetts

16-1. INTRODUCTION

In 1971-72, the Hearsay-I speech understanding system was developed at
Carnegie-Mellon University -- the first of a series of such systems.
Hearsay-I [Reddy Erman & Neely 73, Reddy Erman Fennell & Neely 73] was a
successful attempt to solve the problem of machine understanding of speech in
specialized task domains. In this early system, the size of the vocabulary
(fewer than 100 words) and complexity of the grammar were very limited.
Experiences with Hearsay-I led to the more generalized Hearsay-II
architecture [Lesser Fennell Erman & Reddy 75, Erman & Lesser 75, Lesser &
Erman 77] in order to handle more difficult problems (e.g., larger
vocabularies and less-constrained grammars).

The active development of Hearsay-II extended over three years. During
this period, a number of different knowledge-source configurations were
constructed within the Hearsay-II framework. The most important of these are
called configurations C0 (January, 1975), C1 (January, 1976), and C2
(September, 1976). This last configuration was very successful: it came
close to the original ARPA performance goals set out in 1971 to be met by the
end of 1976 [Newell et al, 73]. Its performance in September, 1976, was 90%
correct semantic interpretation of sentences over a 1011-word vocabulary and
constrained syntax [CMU 77].

This presentation is divided into three major sections. First, the
Hearsay-II system architecture is presented (Sec. 16-2). The next section
(Sec. 16-3) discusses in detail the C2 configuration -- the particular types
of knowledge that are contained in this configuration, and how this knowledge
interacts in order to recognize spoken utterances. Section 16-4 contains a
detailed example of C2 recognizing an utterance.

16-2. THE HEARSAY-II ARCHITECTURE

The Hearsay-II architecture is based on the view that the inherently
errorful nature of processing connected speech can be handled only through
the effective and efficient cooperation of multiple, diverse sources of
knowledge. Additionally, the experimental approach needed for system

---
1 This work was supported at Carnegie-Mellon University by the Defense
  Advanced Research Projects Agency (F44620-73-C-0074) and is monitored by
  the Air Force Office of Scientific Research.

development requires the ability to add and replace sources of knowledge and to explore different control strategies. Thus, such changes must be relatively easy to accomplish; there must also be ways to evaluate the performance of the system in general and the roles of the various sources of knowledge and control strategies in particular. This ability to experiment conveniently with the system is especially crucial because the amount of knowledge is large and many people are needed to introduce and validate it.

A major focus of the design of the Hearsay-II system was the development of a framework for experimenting with the representation of and cooperation among these diverse sources of knowledge. Based on our experiences with Hearsay-I, we expected to need types of knowledge and interaction patterns whose details could not be anticipated at the outset of the project. Therefore, instead of designing a specific speech understanding system, we considered Hearsay-II as a model for a class of systems and a framework within which specific configurations of that general model could be constructed and studied. One can think of Hearsay-II as a high-level system for programming speech understanding systems of a certain type -- i.e., those that conform to the Hearsay-II model.

In the Hearsay-II architecture, each of the diverse types of knowledge needed to solve the speech problem is encapsulated in a <u>knowledge source</u> (KS). For speech understanding, typical KSs incorporate information about syntax, semantics, acoustic-phonetics, prosodics, syllabification, coarticulation, etc. The C2 configuration has about ten KS modules. KSs are kept separate, anonymous, and as independent as possible, in order to make the creation, modification, and testing of KS modules as easy as possible.

As one knowledge source makes errors and creates ambiguities, other KSs must be brought to bear to correct and clarify those actions. This KS cooperation should occur as soon as possible after the introduction of an error or ambiguity in order to limit its ramifications. The mechanism used for providing this high degree of cooperation is the <u>hypothesize-and-test</u> paradigm. In this paradigm, solution-finding is viewed as an iterative process. Two kinds of KS actions occur: 1) the creation of an <u>hypothesis</u>, an "educated guess" about some aspect of the problem (e.g., that a particular word was spoken during a specified portion of the utterance), and 2) tests of the plausibility of some hypothesis or sets of hypotheses. For both of these steps, the KS uses <u>a priori</u> knowledge about the problem, as well as the previously generated hypotheses. This "iterative guess-building" terminates when some subset of the hypotheses generated describes the spoken utterance "well-enough" to satisfy some halting criteria.

16-2.1 The Blackboard

The requirement that knowledge sources be independent implies that the functioning (and very existence) of each must not be necessary or crucial to the others. On the other hand, the KSs are required to cooperate in the iterative guess-building, using and correcting one another's guesses; this implies that there must be interaction among the KSs. These two opposing requirements have led to a design in which each KS interfaces to the others externally in a uniform way that is identical across KSs and in which no knowledge source knows which or how many other KSs exist. The interface is implemented as a dynamic global data structure, called the <u>blackboard</u>.

The blackboard is partitioned into distinct information levels (e.g., "phrase", "word", "syllable", and "phone"); each level holds a different representation of the problem space. The current state of problem solution is represented in terms of <u>hypotheses</u> on the blackboard. An hypothesis is an interpretation of a portion of the spoken utterance at a particular level (e.g., an hypothesis might be that the word 'today' occurred from millisecond 100 to millisecond 600 in the utterance). All hypotheses, no matter what their level, have a uniform attribute-value structure. For example, each hypothesis has attributes containing its level, begin- and end-time within the utterance (which can include notions of fuzziness), and plausibility ratings. The level and time attributes place a two-dimensional structure on hypotheses which partitions the blackboard and can be used for addressing hypotheses. Note that two or more hypotheses at the same level with significantly overlapping times are <u>competitors</u>; i.e., they represent competing interpretations of a portion of the utterance.

Hypotheses at different levels are connected through an and/or directed graph structure. Through these connections, hypotheses at each level can be described approximately as abstractions of hypotheses at the next lower level. A partial solution (i.e., a group of hypotheses) at one level can be used to constrain the search at an adjacent level. For example, consider a KS which can predict and rate words based on acoustic information and another KS which knows about the grammar of the language. The first KS can generate a set of candidate word-hypotheses. The second KS can use these hypotheses to generate phrase hypotheses which can be used, in turn, to predict words likely to precede or follow. These predictions can now constrain the search for the first KS.

16-2.2 <u>Knowledge-Source Activation</u>

Each knowledge source is activated in a data-directed manner, based on the occurrence on the blackboard of patterns of hypotheses specific to its interests. For example, a KS which knows how to make hypotheses about words given hypotheses about syllables is activated whenever any KS creates new syllable hypotheses. Once activated, a KS may examine the blackboard, typically in the vicinity of the hypotheses that activated it. Based on its knowledge, the KS may then modify those hypotheses or other hypotheses, or create new hypotheses. Such actions establish new patterns on the blackboard; these patterns may cause other KSs to be activated. This mechanism for KS activation implements a data-directed form of the hypothesize-and-test paradigm.

Each KS has two major components: a <u>precondition</u> and an <u>action</u>. The purpose of the precondition is to find a subset of hypotheses that is appropriate for action by the KS and to invoke the KS on that subset; the subset is called the <u>stimulus frame</u> of the KS instantiation. For example, the precondition of the KS that generates word hypotheses based on syllables looks for new syllable hypotheses. To keep from having to fire continuously to search the blackboard, each precondition declares the primitive kinds of blackboard changes in which it is interested. Each precondition is triggered only when such primitive changes occur (and is then given pointers to all of them). Whenever a precondition is executed, it checks all blackboard events in which it is interested that have occurred since the last time it was executed. For example, a "new hypothesis" to an executing precondition is any hypothesis which was created since the last time the precondition was executed.

The action part of a KS is a program for applying the knowledge to the stimulus frame and making appropriate changes to the blackboard. A stylized description of the likely action that the KS instantiation will perform (if and when it is allowed to execute) is called the <u>response frame</u>. For example, a response frame for the syllable-based word hypothesizer indicates that the action will be to generate hypotheses at the word level and in a time area that includes at least that of the stimulus frame. The stimulus and response frames, which are generated by the precondition component of the KS, provide information for comparing the desirability of execution of a KS instantiation to that of other KS instantiations; this information is used for the scheduling of KS instantiations.

16-2.3 Scheduling of Knowledge-Sources

At any point, there are, in general, a number of pending tasks to execute
-- both invoked knowledge sources and triggered preconditions. (In practice,
the number of pending tasks often exceeds 200.) If very, very large amounts
of processing power (and memory) were available, one could consider actually
activating all KSs in all their possible contexts. This would expand the
blackboard with many (competing) hypotheses. Assuming this would eventually
terminate (i.e., at some point no new contexts are created), a decision
process could then try to pick from all the competing hypotheses that subset
which best describes the data -- this would be the system's "solution" to the
problem. Because of this combinatoric explosion of possibilities (caused
mostly by the problems of variability and incompleteness in the signal and
errorfulness of the KSs), this complete expansion is not feasible.
Therefore, the control strategy can pick only a small subset of the
applicable KS activations; this can be thought of as exploring a limited
portion of the (potential) fully-expanded blackboard.

This selection process is implemented by a scheduler which calculates a
priority for each waiting task and selects for execution the task with the
highest priority. The priority calculation attempts, based on the specific
stimulus and response frames of the actions, to estimate the usefulness of
the action in fulfilling the overall system goal of recognizing the
utterance. A more detailed explanation of the scheduler is contained in the
next section and in [Hayes-Roth & Lesser 77].

16-2.4 The Hearsay-II Implementation

Based on the architecture just described, a high-level programming system
was constructed to provide an environment for programming knowledge sources,
configuring groups of them into systems, and executing them. Because KS
interactions occur via the blackboard (triggering on patterns, accessing
hypotheses, and making modifications) and the blackboard has a uniform
structure, KS interactions are also uniform. Thus, one set of facilities can
serve all KSs. Facilities are provided for

o defining the levels on the blackboard,
o configuring groups of KSs into runnable systems,
o accessing and modifying hypotheses on the blackboard,
o activating and scheduling KSs.

These facilities, along with other utilities for debugging and user
(researcher) interaction, are called the Hearsay-II 'kernel'. The kernel is
the high-level environment for creating and testing KSs and configurations of
them [Erman & Lesser 78].

Hearsay-II is implemented in the SAIL programming system [Reiser 76], an
Algol-60 dialect which has a sophisticated compile-time macro facility as
well as a large number of data structures (including lists and sets) and
control modes which are implemented fairly efficiently. The Hearsay-II
kernel provides a high-level environment for KSs at compile-time by extending
SAIL's data types and syntax through declarations of procedure calls, global
variables, and complex macros. This extended SAIL provides an explicit
structure for the specification of a KS and its interaction with other KSs
(through the blackboard). The high-level environment also provides
mechanisms that enable KSs to specify to the kernel (usually in non-
procedural ways) a variety of information which the kernel uses when
configuring a system, scheduling KS activity, and controlling user
interaction.

The knowledge in a KS is represented using SAIL data structures and code,
in whatever form the KS developer finds appropriate. The kernel environment
provides the facilities for structuring the interface between this knowledge
and other KSs, via the blackboard. For example, the syntax KS contains a
grammar for the specialized task language that is to be recognized; this

grammar is in a compact, network form. The KS also contains procedures for
searching this network, for example, to parse a sequence of words. The
kernel provides facilities (1) for triggering this KS whenever new word
hypotheses appear on the blackboard, (2) for the KS to read those word
hypotheses (in order to find the sequence of words to be parsed), and (3) for
the KS to create new hypotheses on the blackboard, indicating the structure
of the parse.

16-3. THE KNOWLEDGE-SOURCES OF SEPTEMBER, 1976

In this section, a description of the September, 1976, version of the
Hearsay-II system -- configuration C2 -- is given in terms of the functions
and interactions of its knowledge sources. Included is an example run of the
system.
    The task for the system is to answer questions about and retrieve
documents from a collection of computer science abstracts (in the area of
artificial intelligence). Example sentences are
    "Which abstracts refer to theory of computation?"
    "List those articles."
    "What has McCarthy written since nineteen seventy-four?"
The vocabulary contains 1011 words (in which each extended form of a root,
e.g., the plural of a noun, is counted separately, if it appears). The
grammar which defines the legal sentences is context free and includes
recursion. The style of the grammar is such that there are many more non-
terminals than in conventional syntactic grammars; the information contained
in the greater number of nodes provides semantic and pragmatic constraint
within the grammatical structure. For example, in place of 'Noun' in a
conventional grammar, this grammar includes such non-terminals as 'Topic',
'Author', 'Year', 'Publisher', etc.
    The grammar allows each word to be followed, on the average, by seventeen
other words of the vocabulary.[2] The standard deviation of this measure is
very high (about 51), since some words can be followed by many others (up to
300 in several cases). For the sentences used for performance testing, the
average length is seven words and the average number of words that can follow
any initial portion of the sentence is thirty-four.
    Figure 16-1 gives a schematic of configuration C2 as it was operational in
September, 1976. The levels are indicated by solid horizontal lines and are
labeled at the left. KSs are indicated by vertical arcs with the circled end
indicating the level where its stimulus frame is and the pointed end
indicating the level of its response frame. The name of a KS is connected to
its arc by a dashed horizontal line.

16-3.1 Signal Acquisition, Parameter Extraction, Segmentation, Labeling (SEG)
    An input utterance is spoken into a medium-quality Electro-Voice RE-51
close-speaking headset microphone in a fairly noisy environment (>65 db).
The audio signal is low-passed filtered and 9-bit sampled at 10 KHz. All
subsequent processing, as well as controlling the A/D converter, is digital
and is done on a time-shared PDP-10 computer. Four parameters (called
"ZAPDASH") are derived by simple algorithms operating directly on the sampled
signal [Goldberg Reddy & Gill 77]. These parameters are extracted in real-
time and are used initially to detect the beginning and end of the utterance.
    The ZAPDASH parameters are next used by the SEG knowledge-source as the
basis for an acoustic segmentation and classification of the utterance. This

---

2 Actually, a family of grammars was generated, varying in the number of
  words (terminals) and in the number and complexity of sentences allowed.
  The grammar described here and used in most of the testing is called "X05".

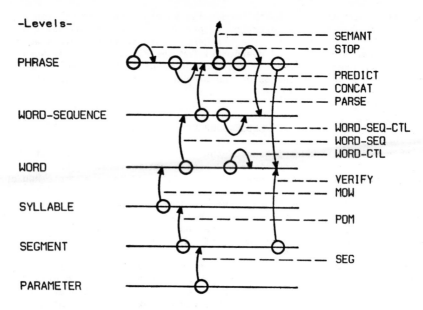

-Levels-

PHRASE ———————————————————— SEMANT
———————————————————— STOP

———————————————————— PREDICT
———————————————————— CONCAT
———————————————————— PARSE

WORD-SEQUENCE ———————————————————— WORD-SEQ-CTL
———————————————————— WORD-SEQ
———————————————————— WORD-CTL

WORD ———————————————————— VERIFY
———————————————————— MOW

SYLLABLE ———————————————————— POM

SEGMENT ———————————————————— SEG

PARAMETER

Figure 16-1.   The levels and knowledge sources of configuration C2.

segmentation is accomplished by an iterative refinement technique: First, silence is separated from non-silence; then, the non-silence is broken down into the sonorant and non-sonorant regions, etc. Eventually, five classes of segments are produced: silence, sonorant peak, sonorant non-peak, fricative, and flap. Associated with each classified segment is its duration, absolute amplitude, and amplitude relative to its neighboring segments (i.e., local peak, local value, or plateau). The segments are contiguous and non-overlapping, with one class designation for each.

Finally, the SEG KS does a finer labeling of each segment. The labels are allophonic-like; there are currently 98 of them. Each of the 98 labels is defined by a vector of auto-correlation coefficients [Itakura 75]. These templates are generated from speaker-dependent training data that have been hand-labeled. The result of the labeling process, which matches the central portion of each segment against each of the templates using the Itakura metric, is a vector of 98 numbers; the i'th number is an estimate of the (negative log) probability that the segment represents an occurrence of the i'th allophone in the label set.

16-3.2 Word Spotting (POM, MOW, WORD-CTL)
The initial generation of words, bottom-up, is accomplished by a three-step process.

First, using the labeled segments as input, the POM knowledge source [Smith 76] generates hypotheses for likely syllable classes. This is done by first identifying syllable nuclei and then "parsing" outward from each nucleus. The syllable-class parsing is driven by a probabilistic "grammar" of "syllable-class -> segment" productions; the rules and their probabilities are learned by an off-line program which is trained on hand-labeled utterances. (The current training, which is speaker-dependent, uses 60 utterances containing about 360 word tokens.) For each nucleus position, several competing syllable-class hypotheses are generated -- typically three to eight.

The syllable classes are used to hypothesize words. Each of the 1011

366

words in the vocabulary is specified by a pronunciation description. For word hypothesization purposes, an inverted form of the dictionary is kept, in which there is associated with each syllable-class all the words which have some pronunciation containing that syllable-class. The MOW KS [Smith 76] looks up each hypothesized syllable class and generates word candidates from among those words containing that syllable-class. For each word that is multi-syllabic, all of the syllables in one of the pronunciations must match above a threshold. Typically, about 50 words of the 1011-word vocabulary are generated at each syllable nucleus position.[3]

Finally, the generated word candidates are rated and their begin- and end-times adjusted by the WIZARD procedure [McKeown 77]. For each word in the vocabulary, WIZARD has a network which describes the possible pronunciations. This rating is calculated by finding the path through the network which best matches the labeled segments, using the distances associated with each label for each segment; the rating is then based on the difference between this best path and the segment labels.[4]

The result of the processing to this point is a set of words. Each word includes a begin-time, an end-time, and a confidence rating. MOW selects a subset of these words, based on their times and ratings, to be hypothesized; it is these selected word hypotheses that form the base for the "top-end" processing. Typically, these hypotheses include about 75% of the words actually spoken (i.e., "correct" word hypotheses). Each correct hypothesis has a rating which ranks it on the average about three, as compared to the five to twenty-five or so incorrect hypotheses which compete with it (i.e., which significantly overlap it in time). The non-selected words are retained internally by MOW for possible later hypothesization.

The amount of hypothesization that MOW does is controlled by the WORD-CTL ('Word Control') KS. WORD-CTL creates "goal" hypotheses at the word level; these are interpreted by MOW as indicating how many word hypotheses to attempt to create in each time area. One can think of MOW as a generator of word hypotheses (from the candidates it creates internally) and WORD-CTL as embodying the policy of how many to hypothesize. This clear separation of policy from mechanism has facilitated experimentation with various control schemes. For example, a trivial change to WORD-CTL, such that goal hypotheses are generated only at the start of the utterance ("left-hand end"), results in MOW creating word hypotheses only at the start, thus forcing all top-end processing to be left-to-right.

WORD-CTL fires at the start of processing of an utterance in order to create goal hypotheses. Subsequently, it may re-trigger if the over-all search process stagnates; this condition is recognized as there being no waiting KS instantiations above a certain priority (as described in Sec. 16-3.3.8) or as the global measures of current state of the problem solution not having increased in the last several KS executions.

16-3.3 Top-End Processing

16-3.3.1 Word-Island Generation (WORD-SEQ, WORD-SEQ-CTL) - The WORD-SEQ knowledge source [Lesser Hayes-Roth Birnbaum & Cronk 77] has the job of

---

3 Since the September, 1976, version, the POM and MOW KSs have been replaced by Noah [Smith 77, Smith & Sambur 78 (section 7-3.2.2.3)]. This KS outperforms POM-MOW on the 1011-word vocabulary (in both speed and accuracy) and is able to handle much larger vocabularies -- it has a performance degradation which is only logarithmic in vocabulary size in the range of 500 to 19,000 words.

4 WIZARD is, in effect, a miniature version of the HARPY speech recognition system [Lowerre 76, Lowerre & Reddy 78], except that it has one network for each word, rather than one network with all words and all sentences.

generating, from the word hypotheses generated bottom-up, a small set (about three to ten) of word sequence hypotheses. Each of these sequences, or islands, can be used as the basis for expansion into larger islands, hopefully culminating in an hypothesis that spans the entire utterance. Multi-word islands are used rather than single-word islands because of the relatively poor reliability of ratings of single words as well as the limited syntactic constraint supplied by single words.

WORD-SEQ uses two kinds of knowledge to generate multi-word islands:

o A table derived from the grammar indicates for every ordered pair of words in the vocabulary (1011 x 1011) whether that pair can occur in that order in some sentence of the defined language. This binary table (which contains about 1.7% "1"'s) thus defines "language-adjacency".

o Acoustic-phonetic knowledge, embodied in the JUNCT ('juncture') procedure, is applied to pairs of word hypotheses and is used to decide if that pair might be considered to be time-adjacent in the utterance. JUNCT uses the dictionary pronunciations and examines the segments at their juncture (gap or overlap) in making its decision.

WORD-SEQ takes the highest-rated single words and generates multi-word sequences by expanding them with other hypothesized words that are both time- and language-adjacent. This expansion is controlled by heuristics based on the number and ratings of competing word hypotheses. The best of these words sequences (which occasionally includes single words) are hypothesized.

The WORD-SEQ-CTL ('Word-Sequence-Control') KS controls the amount of hypothesization that WORD-SEQ does by creating "goal" hypotheses which are interpreted by WORD-SEQ as indicating how many hypotheses to create. This provides the same kind of separation of policy and mechanism achieved in the MOW/WORD-CTL pair of KSs. WORD-SEQ-CTL fires at the start of processing of an utterance in order to create the goal hypotheses. Subsequently, WORD-SEQ-CTL triggers if stagnation is recognized; it then modifies the word-sequence goal hypotheses, thus stimulating WORD-SEQ to generate new word-sequence islands from which the search may be be more fruitful. WORD-SEQ will generate the additional hypotheses by decomposing word-sequence islands already on the blackboard or by re-generating islands which were initially discarded because their ratings were too low.

16-3.3.2 Word-Sequence Parsing (PARSE) - Because the syntactic constraint used in the generation of the word sequences is only pair-wise, a sequence longer than two words might not be syntactically acceptable. The PARSE knowledge source of the SASS module [Hayes-Roth Erman Fox & Mostow 77, Hayes-Roth Mostow & Fox 78] can parse a word sequence of arbitrary length, using the full constraints given by the language. This parsing does not require that the word sequence form a complete non-terminal in the grammar nor that the sequence be sentence-initial or sentence-final -- the words need only occur contiguously somewhere in some sentence of the language. If a sequence hypothesis does not parse, the hypothesis is marked as "rejected". Otherwise, a phrase hypothesis is created. Associated with the phrase hypothesis is the word sequence of which it is composed, as well as information about the way (or ways) the words parsed.

16-3.3.3 Word Predictions from Phrases (PREDICT) - The PREDICT knowledge source of the SASS module can, for any phrase hypothesis, generate predictions of all words which can immediately precede and all which can immediately follow that phrase in the language. In doing the computation to generate these predictions, this KS uses the parsing information attached to the phrase hypothesis by the parsing component.

16-3.3.4 Word Verification (VERIFY) - An attempt is made to verify the existence of or reject each such predicted word, in the context of its predicting phrase. This verification is handled by the <u>VERIFY</u> knowledge source. If verified, a confidence rating for the word must also be generated. First, if the word has been hypothesized previously and passes the test for time-adjacency (by the JUNCT procedure), it is marked as verified and the word hypothesis is associated with the prediction. (Note that a single word hypothesis may thus become associated with several different phrases.) Second, a search is made of the internal store created by MOW to see if the candidate can be matched by a previously-generated candidate which had not been hypothesized. Again, JUNCT makes a judgment about time-adjacency. Finally, WIZARD compares its word-pronunciation network to the segments in an attempt to verify the prediction.

For each of these different kinds of verification, the approximate begin-time (end-time) of the word being predicted to the right (left) of the phrase is taken to be the end-time (begin-time) of the phrase. The end-time (begin-time) of the predicted word is not known and, in fact, one requirement of the verification step is to generate an approximate end-time (begin-time) for the verified word. In general, several different "versions" of the word may be generated which differ primarily in their end-times; since no context to the right (left) of the predicted word is given, several different estimates of the end (beginning) of the word may be plausible based solely on the segmental information.

16-3.3.5 <u>Word-Phrase Concatenation (CONCAT)</u> - For each verified word and its predicting phrase, a new and longer phrase may be generated. This process, accomplished by the CONCAT knowledge source of SASS, which is similar to the PARSE knowledge source, involves parsing the words of the original phrase augmented by the newly verified word. The extended phrase is then hypothesized and includes a rating based on the ratings of the words that compose it.

If a verified word is already associated with some other phrase hypothesis, CONCAT tries to parse that phrase with the predicting phrase. If successful, a new, larger phrase hypothesis is created which represents the merging of the two phrases.

16-3.3.6 <u>Complete Sentences and Halting Criteria (STOP)</u> - Two unique "word" hypotheses are generated before the first and after the last segment of the utterance to denote begin and end of utterance, respectively. These same "words" are included in the syntactic specification of the language and appear as the first and last terminals of every complete sentence. Thus, any verified phrase that includes these as its extreme constituents is a complete sentence and spans the entire utterance. Such a sentence becomes a candidate for selection as the system's recognition result.

In general, the control and rating strategies do not guarantee that the first such complete spanning hypothesis found will have the highest rating of all possible spanning sentence hypotheses that might be found if the search were allowed to continue, so the system does not just stop with the first one generated. However, the characteristics of such an hypothesis are used by the <u>STOP</u> knowledge source to prune from further consideration other partial hypotheses which, because of their low ratings, are unlikely to be extendible into spanning hypotheses with ratings higher than the best already-discovered spanning sentence. This heuristic pruning procedure is based on the form of the ratings function (i.e., how the rating of the phrase is derived from its constituent words). The pruning procedure considers each partial phrase and uses the ratings of other word hypotheses in the time areas not covered by the phrase to determine if the phrase might be extendible to a phrase rated higher than the spanning hypothesis; if not, the partial phrase is pruned. This pruning process and the rating and halting policies are discussed in [Mostow 77].

The recognition processing finally halts in one of two ways: First, there may be no more partial hypotheses left to consider for predicting and extending. Because of the combinatorics of the grammar and the likelihood of finding some prediction that is rated at least above the absolute rejection threshold, this form of termination happens when the pruning procedure has been effective and has eliminated all competitors. Second, the expenditure of a predefined amount of computing resources (time or space) also halts the recognition process; the actual thresholds used are set according to the past performance of the system on similar sentences (i.e., of the given length and over the same vocabulary and grammar).

Once the recognition process is halted, a selection of one or more phrase hypotheses is made to represent the result. If at least one spanning sentence hypothesis was found, the highest-rated such hypothesis is chosen; otherwise, a selection of several of the highest-rated of the partial phrase hypotheses is made, biasing the selection to the longest ones which tend to overlap (in time) the least.

16-3.3.7 <u>Hypothesis Ratings (RPOL)</u> - The <u>RPOL</u> KS runs in high priority immediately after any KS action that creates a new hypothesis or that modifies an existing hypothesis. RPOL uses rating information on the hypothesis, as well as rating information on hypotheses to which the stimulus hypothesis is connected, to calculate the over-all rating of the stimulus hypothesis.

16-3.3.8 <u>Attention Focussing</u> - The top-end processing operations include (a) word-island generation, (b) word sequence parsing, (c) word prediction from phrases, (d) word verification, and (e) word-phrase concatenation. Of these, (c), (d), and (e) are the most frequently performed. Typically, there are a number of these actions waiting to be performed at various places in the utterance. The selection at each point in the processing of which of these actions to perform is a problem of combinatoric control, since the execution of each action usually generates other actions to be done.

To handle this problem, the Hearsay-II system has a statistically-based scheduler [Hayes-Roth & Lesser 77] which calculates a priority for each action and selects, at each time, the waiting action with the highest priority. The priority calculation attempts to estimate the usefulness of the action in fulfilling the over-all system goal of recognizing the utterance. The calculation is based on the stimulus and response frames specified when the action is triggered. For example, the word verifier is triggered whenever words are predicted from a phrase hypothesis; the information passed to the scheduler in order to help calculate the priority of this instantiation of the verifier includes such things as the time and rating of the predicting phrase (in the stimulus frame) and the number of words predicted (as given in the response frame). In addition to the action-specific information, the scheduler keeps track of the overall state of the system in terms of the kinds and quality of hypotheses in each time area.

16-3.4 <u>Interpretation and Response (SEMANT, DISCO)</u>

The <u>SEMANT</u> knowledge-source [Fox & Mostow 77] accepts the word sequence(s) result of the recognition process and generates an interpretation in an unambiguous format for interaction with the data base that the speaker is querying. The interpretation is constructed by actions associated with "semantically interesting" non-terminals (which have been pre-specified for the grammar) in the parse tree(s) of the recognized sequence(s). If recognition results in two or more partial sequences, SEMANT constructs a consistent interpretation based on all of the partial sentences, taking into account for each partial sentence its rating, temporal position, and semantic consistency, as compared to the other partial sentences.

370

The <u>DISCO</u> ('discourse') knowledge-source [Hayes-Roth Gill & Mostow 77] accepts the formatted interpretation of SEMANT and produces a response to the speaker. This response is often the display of a selected portion of the queried data base. In order to retain a coherent interpretation across sentences, DISCO has a finite-state model of the discourse which is updated with each interaction.

16-4. AN EXAMPLE OF RECOGNITION

Following is a description of the recognition of the utterance "ARE ANY BY FEIGENBAUM AND FELDMAN?" by configuration C2 of Hearsay-II.[5] Each major <u>step</u> of the processing is shown; a step usually corresponds to the action of a knowledge source. Execution of the preconditions is not shown explicitly, nor is indication given of knowledge-source instantiations which are never scheduled. Also, executions of RPOL are not shown.

The name of the KS activated at each step follows the step number. If the KS name is followed by an asterisk, this indicates that the hypotheses in the stimulus frame of this KS instantiation are all correct. Single numbers in parentheses after hypotheses are their ratings (on a scale of 0-100). All times given are in centi-second units; thus the duration of the whole utterance, which was 2.25 seconds, is 225. When begin- and end-times of hypotheses are given, they appear as two numbers separated by a colon (e.g., 52:82). Hypotheses which are correct are marked with an asterisk.

The waveform of the spoken utterance is shown in Fig. 16-2.a. The "correct" word boundaries (determined by human inspection) is shown in Fig. 16-2.b for reference. The remaining sections of Fig. 16-2 contain all the hypotheses created by the KSs on the blackboard (except that the goal hypotheses created by WORD-CTL and WORD-SEQ-CTL are not shown). Each hypothesis is indicated by a box; the hypotheses are grouped by level -- segment, syllable, word, word-sequence, and phrase. Within each hypothesis box, the number preceding the colon indicates the step number in which the hypothesis was created. The symbol following the colon names the hypothesis. At the word level and above, a "*" following the symbol indicates that the hypothesis is correct. The trailing number within the hypothesis box is the rating, on a scale of 0 (lowest) to 100.

None of the <u>links</u> between hypotheses are shown in Fig. 16-2. In general, each hypothesis is connected via multiple binary links to hypotheses above and below it. For example, a word hypothesis has downward links connecting it to each of the syllables which compose it and upward links connecting it to each phrase and/or word-sequence in which it takes part.

1. KS: WORD-CTL
   Stimulus: Start of processing.
   Action: Create goal hypotheses at the word level. These will control the amount of hypothesization that MOW will do.

2. KS: WORD-SEQ-CTL
   Stimulus: Start of processing.
   Action: Create goal hypotheses at the word-sequence level. These will control the amount of hypothesization that WORD-SEQ will do.

3. KS: SEG
   Stimulus: Creation of ZAPDASH parameters for the utterance.
   Action: Create segment hypotheses with vector of estimated allophone

---

5 For reasons of clarity, the description differs from the actual run in a few details.

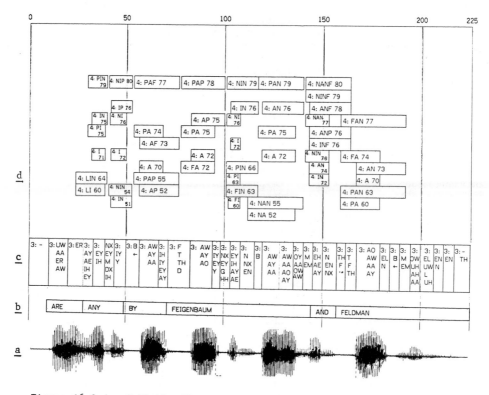

Figure 16-2.d. Syllable-Classes.
Figure 16-2.c. Segments.
Figure 16-2.b. The correct words (for reference).
Figure 16-2.a. The waveform of "Are any by Feigenbaum and Feldman?".

Fig. 16-2. The example utterance.

probabilities. (The several highest-rated labels of each segment are shown in Fig. 16-2.c.)

4. KS: POM
    Stimulus: New segment hypotheses.
    Action: Create syllable-class hypotheses.

Figure 16-2.d shows the syllable-class hypotheses created. Each class name is made up of single-letter codes representing classes of phones, as follows:

Code	Phone-class	Phones in class
A	A-like	AE,AA,AH,AO,AX
I	I-like	IY,IH,EY,EH,IX,AY
U	U-like	OW,UH,U,UW,ER,AW,OY,EL,EM,EN
L	liquid	Y,W,R,L
N	nasal	M,N,NX
P	stop	P,T,K,B,D,G,DX
F	fricative	HH,F,TH,S,SH,V,DH,Z,ZH,CH,JH,WH

372

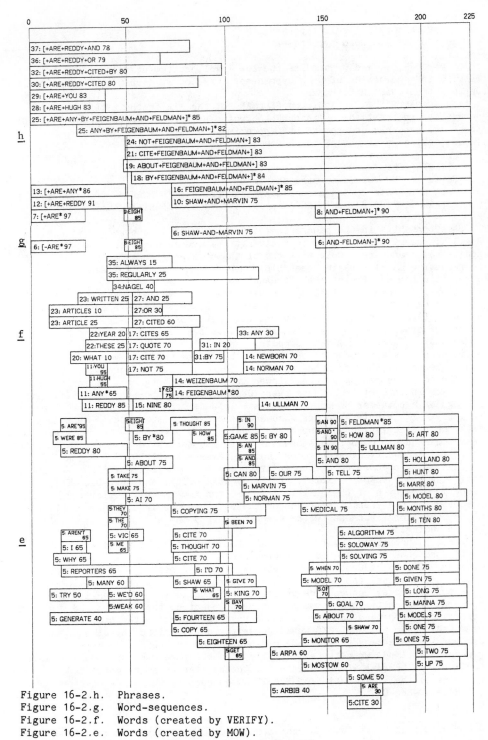

Figure 16-2.h. Phrases.
Figure 16-2.g. Word-sequences.
Figure 16-2.f. Words (created by VERIFY).
Figure 16-2.e. Words (created by MOW).

Fig. 16-2 (continued).

5. KS: MOW
   Stimulus: New syllable hypotheses.[6]
   Action: Create word hypotheses.

Steps 1, 3, 4, and 5 comprise the low level, bottom-up processing; this results in a selection of word hypotheses (created in step 5). Figure 16-2.e depicts these word hypotheses.

Four words (ARE, BY, AND, and FELDMAN) of the six in the utterance were correctly hypothesized; 86 incorrect hypotheses were generated. The 90 words that were hypothesized represents approximately 1.5% of the 1011-word vocabulary for each one of the 6 words in the utterance.

6. KS: WORD-SEQ
   Stimulus: New words created bottom-up.
   Action: Create 4 word-sequence hypotheses: AND-FELDMAN-]*(90,145:225), [-ARE*(97,0:28), SHAW-AND-MARVIN(75,72:157), EIGHT(85,48:57).

Step 6 results in the generation of 4 multi-word sequences. (See Fig. 16-2.g.) These will be used as initial, alternative anchor points for additional searching. Note that two of these islands are correct, each representing an alternative search path that potentially can lead to a correct interpretation of the utterance.

In earlier versions of KS configuration of the system (e.g., C1), low-level processing was not done in the serial, lock-step manner as in steps 3, 4, and 5 (i.e., level-to-level, where each level is completely processed before processing on the next higher level is begun). Rather, processing was done in an asynchronous, data-directed manner (i.e., as interesting hypotheses were generated at one level, they were immediately propagated to and processed by KSs operating at higher levels). It was found that the asynchronous processing at these lower levels (e.g., segment, syllable, and word) was inappropriate because there was not enough accuracy in credibility ratings of hypotheses to form hypothesis islands that could direct the search reliably. It is only with the word-sequence hypotheses produced in step 6 that the reliability of the hypothesis ratings is high enough that selective search can be employed. This conclusion is substantiated by experiments with several island-driving strategies [Lesser Hayes-Roth Birnbaum & Cronk 77].

High level processing on the multi-word sequences is accomplished by the following KSs: PARSE, PREDICT, VERIFY, CONCAT, STOP, and WORD-SEQ-CTL. Since an execution of the VERIFY KS will often immediately follow the execution of the PREDICT KS (each on the same hypothesis), we have combined the descriptions of these two KS executions into one step for ease of understanding.

Steps 7 through 10 involve the PARSE KS. The PARSE KS verifies whether a multi-word sequence (created in step 6) is a legal language fragment of the grammar. If the sequence is grammatical, a phrase hypothesis is constructed from it; otherwise, the sequence is marked rejected. In this example, all four multi-word sequences were verified to be valid language fragments. However, if a multi-word sequence had been rejected, the WORD-SEQ KS might be reinvoked to generate additional multi-word sequences in the time area of the rejected sequence. WORD-SEQ would generate the additional hypotheses by decomposing word-sequence islands already on the blackboard or by re-generating islands which were initially discarded because their ratings were too low. Additional word-sequence hypotheses might also be generated in response to the modification of "goal" hypotheses at the word-sequence level by the WORD-SEQ-CTL.

---

6 MOW will also be re-invoked upon a modification to the word goal hypotheses by WORD-CTL.

The scheduling strategy is so parameterized that processing at the phrase level is delayed until an adequate number of highly-rated phrase hypothesis islands are generated. This strategy is not built directly into the scheduler, but rather is accomplished (1) by appropriately setting external scheduling parameters (i.e., the high setting of the priorities of WORD-SEQ and PARSE KS actions in contrast to those of PREDICT, VERIFY, and CONCAT),[7] and (2) by taking into account the current state of hypotheses on the phrase level of the blackboard in evaluating the usefulness of potential KS actions as described by their response frames.

7. KS: PARSE*
   Stimulus: [-ARE* (word sequence)
   Action: Create phrase: [+ARE* (97,0:28)

8. KS: PARSE*
   Stimulus: AND-FELDMAN-]* (word sequence)
   Action: Create phrase: AND+FELDMAN+]* (90,145:225)

9. KS: PARSE
   Stimulus: EIGHT (word sequence)
   Action: Create phrase: EIGHT (85,48:57)

10. KS: PARSE
    Stimulus: SHAW-AND-MARVIN (word sequence)
    Action: Create phrase: SHAW+AND+MARVIN (75,72:157)

Each of the four executions of the PARSE KS (steps 7-10) results in the creation of a phrase hypothesis; each phrase is shown in Fig. 16-2.h. Each of these hypotheses causes an invocation of the PREDICT KS. The PREDICT KS attempts to extend a phrase hypothesis through the predictions of words that can, according to the grammar, follow or precede the hypothesis. Its action is to attach a "word-predictor" attribute to the hypothesis which specifies the predicted words. Not all of these PREDICT KS instantiations are necessarily executed (and thus indicated as a step in the execution history). For instance, further processing on the phrases [+ARE and AND+FELDMAN+] is sufficiently positive that the scheduler never executes the instantiation of PREDICT for the phrase SHAW+AND+MARVIN (created in step 10). In turn, VERIFY is invoked by the placing of a word-predictor attribute on a phrase hypothesis. For each word on the attribute list that VERIFY verifies (against the segmental data), it creates a word hypothesis (if one does not already exist) and the word is placed on a "word-verification" attribute of the phrase hypothesis. (Such newly-created word hypotheses are shown in Fig. 16-2.f.) CONCAT is then invoked on phrase hypotheses which have word-verification attributes attached. For each verified word, the phrase and new word are parsed together and a new, extended phrase hypothesis is created (and shown in Fig. 16-2.h). If all word predictions to the right or left of the phrase had been rejected, the phrase hypothesis is marked as "rejected", as is the underlying word-sequence hypothesis if all the phrase hypotheses it supports are rejected. (Note that this last action will re-trigger WORD-SEQ to generate more word sequences.)

11. KS: PREDICT & VERIFY*
    Stimulus: [+ARE* (phrase)
    Action: Predict (from the grammar) 292 words to right. Reject (using the
      acoustic information) 277 of them. The four highest-rated of the

---

7 These settings are determined empirically by observing a number of training runs. They are not adjusted during test runs of the system.

fifteen verified words are REDDY(85,26:52), ANY*(65,24:49), HUGH
(55,30:39), and YOU(55,28:39).

12. KS: CONCAT
    Stimulus: [+ARE* (phrase), REDDY (word)
    Action: Create phrase: [+ARE+REDDY (91,0:52)

13. KS: CONCAT*
    Stimulus: [+ARE* (phrase), ANY* (word)
    Action: Create phrase: [+ARE+ANY* (86,0:49)

In steps 11 through 13, the highly-rated phrase [+ARE is extended and
results in the generation of the additional phrases [+ARE+REDDY and
[+ARE+ANY. These phrases, however, are not immediately extended because the
predicted words REDDY and ANY are not rated sufficiently high. Instead, the
scheduler, pursuing a strategy more conservative than strict best-first,
investigates phrases that look almost as good as the best one. This
scheduling strategy results in the execution of the PREDICT and VERIFY KSs on
two of the other initial phrase islands: AND+FELDMAN+] and EIGHT.

14. KS: PREDICT & VERIFY*
    Stimulus: AND+FELDMAN+]* (phrase)
    Action: Predict 100 words to left. Reject 76 of them. The best of the
    verified 24 (in descending rating order) are FEIGENBAUM*(80,72:150),
    WEIZENBAUM(70,72:150), ULLMAN(70,116:150), NORMAN(70,108:150), and
    NEWBORN(70,108:150)

15. KS: PREDICT & VERIFY
    Stimulus: EIGHT (phrase)
    Action: Predict the word NINE to right and verify it (80,52:82). Predict
    SEVEN to left, reject prediction.

The attempted extension of the phrase EIGHT at step 15 is not successful
-- none of the grammatically predicted words is acoustically verified, even
using a lenient threshold. Thus, this phrase is marked rejected and is
dropped from further consideration.

16. KS: CONCAT*
    Stimulus: FEIGENBAUM* (word), AND+FELDMAN+]* (phrase)
    Action: Create phrase: FEIGENBAUM+AND+FELDMAN+]* (85,72:225)

Beginning with step 16, the highly-rated left word extension FEIGENBAUM to
the phrase AND+FELDMAN+] looks sufficiently promising that processing now
continues in a more depth-first manner along the path FEIGENBAUM+AND+
FELDMAN+] through step 25.[8] Processing on the path [+ARE+REDDY does not
resume until step 26.

17. KS: PREDICT & VERIFY*
    Stimulus: FEIGENBAUM+AND+FELDMAN+]* (phrase)
    Action: Predict eight words to left. Reject one (DISCUSS). Find two
    already on blackboard: BY*(80,52:72) and ABOUT(75,48:72). Verify five
    others: NOT(75,49:82), ED(75,67:72), CITE(70,49:82), QUOTE(70,49:82),
    CITES(65:49:82).

---

8 The rating on an hypothesis is only one parameter used by the scheduler to
  assign priorities to waiting KS instantiations. In particular, the length
  of an hypothesis is also important. Thus, FEIGENBAUM with a rating of 80
  looks better than REDDY with a rating of 85 because it is much longer.

In steps 18 through 24, alternative word extensions of FEIGENBAUM+AND+
FELDMAN+] are explored. As a result of this exploration, the phrase
BY+FEIGENBAUM+AND+FELDMAN+] is considered the most credible.

18. KS: CONCAT
    Stimulus: BY* (word), FEIGENBAUM+AND+FELDMAN+]* (phrase)
    Action: Create phrase: BY+FEIGENBAUM+AND+FELDMAN+]* (84,52:225)

19. KS: CONCAT
    Stimulus: ABOUT (word), FEIGENBAUM+AND+FELDMAN+]* (phrase)
    Action: Create phrase: ABOUT+FEIGENBAUM+AND+FELDMAN+] (83,48:225)

20. KS: PREDICT & VERIFY
    Stimulus: ABOUT+FEIGENBAUM+AND+FELDMAN+] (phrase)
    Action: Predict one word to left: WHAT. Verify it (10,20:49).

21. KS: CONCAT
    Stimulus: CITE (word), FEIGENBAUM+AND+FELDMAN+] (phrase)
    Action: Create phrase: CITE+FEIGENBAUM+AND+FELDMAN+] (83,49:225)

22. KS: PREDICT & VERIFY
    Stimulus: CITE+FEIGENBAUM+AND+FELDMAN+] (phrase)
    Action: Predict four words to left. Reject two of them: BOOKS, PAPERS.
      Verify THESE(25,28:49), YEAR(20,30:49).

23. KS: PREDICT & VERIFY*
    Stimulus: BY+FEIGENBAUM+AND+FELDMAN+]* (phrase)
    Action: Predict ten words to left. Reject five: ABSTRACTS, ARE, BOOKS,
      PAPERS, REFERENCED. Find two already on blackboard: ANY*(65,24:49),
      THESE(25,28:49). Verify three more: ARTICLE(25,9:52), WRITTEN
      (25,24:52), ARTICLES(10,9:52).

24. KS: CONCAT
    Stimulus: NOT (word), FEIGENBAUM+AND+FELDMAN+]*
    Action: Create phrase: NOT+FEIGENBAUM+AND+FELDMAN+] (83,49:225)

25. KS: CONCAT*
    Stimulus: ANY* (word), BY+FEIGENBAUM+AND+FELDMAN+]* (phrase)
    Action: Create phrase: ANY+BY+FEIGENBAUM+AND+FELDMAN+]* (82,24:225)
      [+ARE+ANY+BY+FEIGENBAUM+AND+FELDMAN+]* (85,0:225) is also created, from
      [+ARE+ANY and BY+FEIGENBAUM+AND+FELDMAN+].

In step 25, the word ANY is concatenated onto the phrase BY+FEIGENBAUM+
AND+FELDMAN+]. However, instead of only creating this new combined phrase,
the CONCAT KS also notices that the word ANY is the last word of the phrase
[+AND+ANY; this leads the CONCAT KS to merge the two adjacent phrases
[+ARE+ANY and BY+FEIGENBAUM+AND+FELDMAN+] into a single enlarged phrase,
after first ascertaining that the resulting phrase is grammatically allowed.
This merging bypasses the several single-word PREDICT, VERIFY, and CONCAT
actions that would be necessary to generate the enlarged hypothesis from
either of the two original hypotheses in an incremental fashion. Thus, the
recognition process is sped up, not only because the several single-word
actions are eliminated, but also because KS actions on competing non-correct
hypotheses are avoided since these actions do not appear to the scheduler as
attractive as actions on the new, enlarged hypothesis. Such mergings occur
in approximately half of the runs on the 1011-word grammar with the small
branching factor ("X05"); in grammars with higher branching factors, the
merging of phrase hypotheses occurs with even higher frequency.

It has been our experience that, just as a multi-word island is more credible than the individual words that compose it, so a merged phrase hypothesis is more credible than its two constituent phrases. For example, about 80% of the mergings in X05 runs produce correct hypotheses. In more complex grammars, this statistic drops to about 35%, but there are correspondingly more phrase mergings that occur.

The newly-created merged phrase also happens to be a complete sentence; i.e., it has begin- and end-of-utterance markers at as its extreme constituents. Thus, it is a candidate for the interpretation of the utterance.

26. KS: STOP
    Stimulus: [+ARE+ANY+BY+FEIGENBAUM+AND+FELDMAN+]* (complete phrase)
    Action: Deactivation of several score hypotheses.

STOP responds to the creation of a complete phrase. STOP tests each phrase hypothesis on the blackboard to see whether there is any possibility of extending it to produce a complete phrase that is rated higher than the one just created. It performs this heuristic test by trying to combine the phrase, just based on simple time adjacency constraints, in the best possible way with words already hypothesized. Each phrase that cannot be extended by this process into a word sequence that spans the entire utterance and is better than the newly created complete phrase is discarded. Subsequently, the RPOL KS (whose executions are not shown here) will discard hypotheses as they are created if they also cannot pass the same test.

Of the hypotheses not discarded, extensions to the phrase [+ARE now appear as the most likely candidates to produce new and better complete phrases. This search for better complete phrases results, in steps 27 through 36, in the examination of numerous alternative extensions, each of which is promising.

27. KS: PREDICT & VERIFY
    Stimulus: [+ARE+REDDY
    Action: Predict three words to right. Verify CITED(60,52:86), OR (30,52:67), AND(25,52:82).

28. KS: CONCAT
    Stimulus: [+ARE (phrase), HUGH (word)
    Action: Create phrase: [+ARE+HUGH (83,0:39)

29. KS: CONCAT
    Stimulus: [+ARE (phrase), YOU (word)
    Action: Create phrase: [+ARE+YOU (83,0:39)

30. KS: CONCAT
    Stimulus: [+ARE+REDDY (phrase), CITED (word)
    Action: Create phrase: [+ARE+REDDY+CITED (80,0:86)

31. KS: PREDICT & VERIFY
    Stimulus: [+ARE+REDDY+CITED (phrase)
    Action: Predict two words to right. Verify BY(75,83:98), IN(20,86:114).

32. KS: CONCAT
    Stimulus: [+ARE+REDDY+CITED (phrase), BY (word)
    Action: Create phrase: [+ARE+REDDY+CITED+BY (80,0:98)

33. KS: PREDICT & VERIFY
    Stimulus: [+ARE+REDDY+CITED+BY (phrase)
    Action: Predict one word to right. Verify ANY(30,105:126).

34. KS: PREDICT & VERIFY
    Stimulus: [+ARE+HUGH (phrase)
    Action: Predict one word to right. Verify NAGEL(40,42:63).

35. KS: PREDICT & VERIFY
    Stimulus: [+ARE+YOU (phrase)
    Action: Predict three words to right. Reject USUALLY. Verify REGULARLY
       (25,39:116), ALWAYS(15,39:72).

36. KS: CONCAT
    Stimulus: [+ARE+REDDY (phrase), OR (word)
    Action: Create phrase: [+ARE+REDDY+OR (79,0:67)

37. KS: CONCAT
    Stimulus: [+ARE+REDDY (phrase), AND (word)
    Action: Create phrase: [+ARE+REDDY+AND (78,0:82)

38. KS: STOP
    Stimulus: Stagnation
    Action: Stop search and accept [+ARE+ANY+BY+FEIGENBAUM+AND+FELDMAN+]*.

    KS STOP is again executed; this execution is caused by the lack of any KS
instantiations that are rated sufficiently high. STOP here makes a decision
to terminate the search process and accept the phrase [+ARE+ANY+BY+
FEIGENBAUM+AND+FELDMAN+] as the correct interpretation.

39. KS: SEMANT*
    Stimulus: Recognized utterance: [+ARE+ANY+BY+FEIGENBAUM+AND+FELDMAN+]
    Action: SEMANT parses the utterance, using the same grammar, but with
       semantic routines on some of the non-terminal nodes. The execution of
       these routines incrementally produces the following structure:
    F:[U:([ARE ANY BY FEIGENBAUM AND FELDMAN])
        N:($PRUNE!LIST
            S:($PRUNE!LIST!AUTHOR K:(A:((FEIGENBAUM * FELDMAN)))))
       ]
    "F" denotes the total message. "U" contains the utterance itself. "N"
    indicates the main type of the utterance (e.g., REQUEST, HELP, etc.),
    "S" the sub-type. "K" denotes the different attributes associated with
    the utterance (e.g., "A" is the author and "T" is the topic).
    This structure is passed on to the discourse component, which queries
    the data base and responds to the speaker.

                        16-5. CONCLUSIONS

    The Hearsay-II system has been successful. It came very close to meeting
the ARPA performance goals: In September, 1976, the C2 configuration
achieved correct semantic interpretation of 90% of a test set of utterances
(with 73% of the utterances being recognized word-for-word correctly). This
performance was with the highly constrained "X05" grammar over the 1011-word
vocabulary. The test set contained twenty-two utterances, averaging seven
words each. These utterances were totally new to the system and were run
"blind". The processing time averaged 85 mipss (million instructions per
second of speech) on a PDP-10 computer. (Subsequently, some trivial
implementation modifications reduced the processing costs to about 60 mipss.)
    In addition to its successful performance, the structure of the system is
interesting. An attempt was made from the start to develop a clean model for
the kinds of complex interactions that would be required of the various

                                379

sources of knowledge. Although the system was modified substantially as
experience was gained, it retained its fidelity to that model, indicating its
validity. A detailed discussion of the evolution of the architecture with
respect to the model can be found in [Lesser & Erman 77]. Several other
problem areas have been attacked with organizations strongly influenced by
the Hearsay-II structure: image understanding [Prager et al 77], reading
comprehension [Rumumelhart 76], protein-crystallographic analysis [Engelmore
& Nii 77], signal understanding [Nii & Feigenbaum 78], and complex learning
[Soloway 77].

16-6. ACKNOWLEDGMENTS

Raj Reddy has provided much of the vision and energy for this work, most
of the central ideas in the Hearsay model, and much technical expertise in
many of the knowledge sources in the Hearsay-II system. Richard Fennell and
Rick Hayes-Roth have been particularly instrumental in formulating and
testing the Hearsay-II architecture. All members of the CMU "speech group"
have contributed to this work; their substantial efforts are gratefully
acknowledged. Lucy Erman and Mark Fox have made helpful suggestions for this
paper.

16-7. REFERENCES

Abbreviations: ASSP -- Acoustics, Speech, and Signal Processing
                CMU -- Computer Science Dept., Carnegie-Mellon Univ.,
                       Pittsburgh, Pa.
                IJCAI -- International Joint Conference on Artificial
                       Intelligence

CMU Computer Science Speech Group (1977). Summary of the CMU Five-year ARPA
    effort in speech understanding research. Technical Report, CMU.
Engelmore,R.S. & H.P.Nii (1977). A knowledge-based system for the
    interpretation of protein x-ray crystallographic data. Technical Report
    Stan-CS-77-589, Stanford Univ., CA.
Erman,L.D. & V.R.Lesser (1975). A multi-level organization for problem
    solving using many diverse cooperating sources of knowledge.
    Proc. 4IJCAI, Tbilisi, USSR, 483-490.
Erman,L.D. & V.R.Lesser (1978). System engineering techniques for artificial
    intelligence systems. In A.Hanson and E.Riseman (Eds.), Computer Vision
    Systems, Academic Press, 1978.
Fox,M.S. & D.J.Mostow (1977). Maximal consistent interpretations of errorful
    data in hierarchically modelled domains. Proc. 5IJCAI, Cambridge, Mass.,
    165-171.
Goldberg,H., R.Reddy, & G.Gill (1977). The ZAPDASH parameters, feature
    extraction, segmentation, and labeling for speech understanding systems.
    In [CMU 77], 10-11.
Itakura,F. (1975). Minimum prediction residual principle applied to speech
    recognition. IEEE Trans. ASSP, 23, 67-72.
Hayes-Roth,F., L.D.Erman, M.Fox, & D.J.Mostow (1977). Syntactic processing
    in Hearsay-II. In [CMU 77], 16-18.
Hayes-Roth,F., G.Gill, and D.J.Mostow (1977). Discourse analysis and task
    performance in the Hearsay-II speech understanding system. In [CMU 77],
    24-28.
Hayes-Roth,F. & V.R.Lesser (1977). Focus of attention in the Hearsay-II
    system. Proc. 5IJCAI, Cambridge, Mass., 27-35.
Hayes-Roth,F., D.J.Mostow, & M.Fox (1978, in press). Understanding speech in
    the Hearsay-II system. In Natural Language Communication with Computers.
    L.Bloc (Ed.) Springer-Verlag, Berlin.

Lesser,V.R., R.D.Fennell, L.D.Erman, & D.R.Reddy (1975). Organization of the Hearsay-II speech understanding system. IEEE Trans. ASSP, 23, 11-23.

Lesser,V.R. & L.D.Erman (1977). A retrospective view of the Hearsay-II architecture. Proc. 5IJCAI, Cambridge, Mass., 790-800.

Lesser,V.R., F.Hayes-Roth, M.Birnbaum, & R.Cronk (1977). Selection of word islands in the Hearsay-II speech understanding system. Proc. IEEE Inter. Conf. ASSP, Hartford, Conn., 791-794.

Lowerre,B.T. (1976). The Harpy speech recognition system. Technical Report, CMU (Ph.D. Dissertation).

Lowerre,B.T. & R.Reddy (1978). The Harpy speech understanding system. In Trends in Speech Recognition, W.A.Lea (Ed.), Prentice-Hall (this book), Chap. 15.

McKeown,D.M. (1977). Word verification in the Hearsay-II speech understanding system. Proc. 1977 IEEE Inter. Conf. ASSP., Hartford, Conn., 795-798.

Mostow,D.J. (1977). A halting condition and related pruning heuristic for combinatorial search. In [CMU 77], 158-166.

Newell,A., J.Barnett, J.Forgie, C.Green, D.Klatt, J.C.R.Licklider, J.Munson, R.Reddy, & W.Woods (1973). Speech Understanding Systems: Final Report of a Study Group. North-Holland. (Originally appeared in 1971.)

Nii,H.P. & E.A.Feigenbaum (1978). Rule-based understanding of signals. In D.A.Waterman & F.Hayes-Roth (Eds.) Pattern-Directed Inference Systems, Academic Press.

Prager,J., P.Nagin, R.Kohler, A.Hanson, & E.Riseman (1977). Segmentation processes in the VISIONS system. Proc. 5IJCAI, Cambridge, Mass., 642-643.

Reddy,D.R., L.D.Erman, & R.B.Neely (1973). A model and a system for machine recognition of speech. IEEE Trans. Audio and Electroacoustics, AU-21, 229-238.

Reddy,D.R., L.D.Erman, R.D.Fennell, & R.B.Neely (1973). The Hearsay speech understanding system: An example of the recognition process. Proc. 3IJCAI, Stanford, Cal., 185-193.

Reiser,J.F. (1976). SAIL. Stanford Artificial Intelligence Lab., Memo AIM-289.

Rumelhart, D. E. (1976). Toward an interactive model of reading. Technical Report 56, Center for Human Information Processing, Univ. of Cal. at San Diego.

Smith,A.R. (1976). Word hypothesization in the Hearsay-II speech system. Proc. IEEE Int. Conf. ASSP, Philadelphia, Pa., 549-552.

Smith,A.R. (1977). Word hypothesization for large-vocabulary speech understanding systems. Technical Report, CMU (Ph.D. Dissertation).

Smith,A.R. & M.R.Sambur (1978). Hypothesizing and verifying words for speech recognition. In Trends in Speech Recognition, W.A.Lea (Ed.), Prentice-Hall (this book), Chap. 7.

Soloway,E.M. & E.M.Riseman (1977). Levels of pattern description in learning. Proc. 5IJCAI, Cambridge, Mass., 801-811.

17.

SPECIFIC CONTRIBUTIONS OF THE ARPA SUR PROJECT

Wayne A. Lea
June E. Shoup
Speech Communications Research Laboratory

17-1.   INTRODUCTION

We focus here on the specific contributions of the largest project ever undertaken in speech recognition; namely, the 5 year, $15 million Speech Understanding Research project sponsored by the Advanced Research Projects Agency of the United States Department of Defense (the "ARPA SUR project"). The detailed designs·and performances of the four final recognition systems are presented in previous literature and in Chaps. 12 to 16, and an overview of the project appears in Chap. 11. What we add here is a detailed assessment that provides the reader with lists of ideas, techniques, results, and comparisons which can be relevant in future work. We begin with generalities, then go into details, and end with general conclusions. Thus, Sec. 17-2 gives a brief overview of the limited capabilities in recognition that formed the context in which the project began, and a summary of how the major goals defined for the project were met or exceeded. Then we list some detailed contributions in system design (Sec. 17-3), and detailed contributions to various components or aspects of recognition (Sec. 17-4). Readers interested only in general contributions might well skip or skim over sections 17-3 and 17-4. Rising again from details to more general evaluations we venture (in Sec. 17-5) our list of the primary contributions of the ARPA SUR project. The expected impact on future work is summarized in Sec. 17-6. Many reports and publications were studied in preparing this chapter, and are listed in Sec. 17-7 or in Chaps. 11 to 16.

17-2.   BEFORE AND AFTER ARPA SUR

During two decades of research prior to the ARPA SUR project, there had been repeated calls for overcoming the major hurdle separating moderately successful isolated-word-recognition systems from the unattained ideal of more natural uninterrupted voice communication with computers. Review articles had repeatedly called for the full use of language structures such as acoustic phonetics, coarticulation regularities, phonological rules, prosodic structures, and especially syntax and semantics (Lindgren, 1965; Hill, 1971; Lea, 1972). The ARPA SUR project was the first large-scale effort to use artificial intelligence ideas and higher-level linguistic information to provide a technology for understanding spoken sentences. In this section, we take a look back at the context in which the project began, and assess how the initial goals were met.

Figure 17-1 summarizes some important aspects of the state of speech recognition technology when the ARPA SUR project began in 1971. No one had shown that continuous speech could be recognized. Existing examples at that time (e.g., Vicens and Reddy, 1969) were too limited to be extendable. <u>Isolated</u> word recognition had become quite accurate (over 95% correct) in a few prototype systems using high-quality speech, but their techniques had not been employed to reliably recognize words in sentence contexts. Nothing like a 1000-word vocabulary had ever been attacked, and it seemed that such large vocabularies could lead to combinatoric problems of major magnitude. No complete systems had been built using <u>multiple forms of incomplete knowledge</u> like acoustics, phonetics, lexical processing (word matching), prosodics, syntax, semantics, and pragmatics, plus appropriate control structures. Only the acoustic phonetics and word matching procedures were actually functional in available recognizers.

- PROTOTYPE ISOLATED WORD
  RECOGNIZERS

  - SMALL VOCABULARIES
    (10-200 Words)
  - ACCURACY = 95%
  - NO COMMERCIAL
    PRODUCTS
  - HIGH-QUALITY
    SPEECH ONLY

- LITTLE DATA ON ACOUSTIC
  CHARACTERISTICS OF SENTENCES

- SCATTERED SOURCES FOR
  PHONOLOGICAL RULES

- INCOMPLETE MEASURES OF
  PERFORMANCE

- NO CONTINUOUS SPEECH RECOGNIZERS

- NO MULTIPLE-KNOWLEDGE-SOURCE SYSTEMS

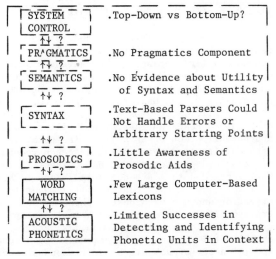

Fig. 17-1. The state of ASR at the beginning of the ARPA-SUR Project (1971)

Not only were there no adequate <u>systems</u> in 1971; even the necessary knowledge, ideas, and experimental data were limited and spotty. Very little data was available on the acoustic characteristics of phonetic segments or prosodics in spoken sentences. Scattered throughout the linguistics literature and various acoustic phonetic studies were phonological rules that had not been compiled in one place or used in speech analysis or recognition. There was also considerable uncertainty about how to use phonetic and prosodic data and phonological rules along with higher-level linguistic constraints. The only syntactic parsers were text-based, and they couldn't deal with errorful input strings or parsing from arbitrary starting points in the sentence. "Top-down" control strategies (whereby syntax first hypothesizes words that are then verified from acoustic data) were being suggested as a promising alternative to traditional bottom-up strategies (which did phonetic analysis first, hypothesized words, and finally would weed out wrong word sequences with linguistic constraints). Other system strategies were possible, but untried.

While researchers expected final accuracy of semantic understanding to be different from accuracy of phonetic segmentation and word matching, they didn't know just how much improvement syntax and semantics would make, or how low phonetic classification accuracy could be and still allow adequate accuracy of semantic understanding. They had little more than the vocabulary size and number of words in a sentence that could help gauge the complexity of a recognition task, so they didn't know whether 70% accuracy on a hard task was better or worse than 90% accuracy on an easier task. Most recognition techniques were not real-time processes, and the speed of complex speech understanding systems could only be guessed at.

The ARPA SUR project brought some answers in each of these problem areas, and others as well. This is _not_ to say that other projects haven't also made major contributions since 1971, or that there weren't others also aware of the problems addressed by the ARPA SUR project. Indeed there were, but general review of other work is not our concern here. (See Chap. 4 for a review of other relevant work.)

17-2.2 Meeting the Original Goals

In the spring of 1970, an adhoc study group was formed in response to a request by Dr. Larry Roberts, then Director of the Information Processing Technology (IPT) branch of the Advanced Research Projects Agency. The study group consisted of experts taken from the then-current ARPA contractors working on artificial intelligence, and consisted of Allen Newell and Raj Reddy of Carnegie Mellon University, James Forgie, Dennis Klatt, and J.C.R. Licklider of MIT, Jeffrey Barnett of System Development Corporation, John Munson of Stanford Research Institute, William Woods of Bolt Beranek and Newman, and Cordell Green of ARPA IPT. The committee was charged with exploring the "feasibility of demonstrating a speech recognition system with useful capabilities and greater power than current isolated word recognition systems". They concluded that a reasonable chance to achieve such a system would take at least five years, requiring: (1) major technical advances in the systematization and use of acoustic-phonetic and phonological structures; (2) cooperative efforts by several technical disciplines (including acoustics, phonetics, phonology, syntax, semantics, and task constraints); (3) intermediate experimental systems to be demonstrated around the mid-term of the project; and (4) a set of ambitious but reasonable specifications for evaluating the performance of the final systems. The study group, and the project itself as first initiated, did not require that the project provide a careful investigation of the potential uses of speech understanding in practical DOD applications, but the study group did expect that the demonstration of technical feasibility would represent a significant step toward a capability suitable for practical applications (Newell, et. al., 1973, p. 3).

Given the fledgling state of continuous speech recognition in 1971, and the defensive posture the field had following Pierce's (1969) pessimistic evaluation of speech recognition work, the goals defined by the ARPA study group were very ambitious. Yet, the study group recognized that some practical constraints had to be placed on the overall task of understanding continuous speech if useful systems were to emerge in the near future. They thus defined the goals shown in Fig. 17-2, and called for their fulfillment in a five year intensive program.

GOAL : ACCEPT CONTINUOUS SPEECH FROM MANY COOPERATIVE SPEAKERS,

HARPY : Primary test with 184 ⎫
HEARSAY II: Tested with   22 ⎬ sentences from
HWIM : Tested with   124 ⎪
SDC : Tested with   54 ⎭

⎧ 3 Male, 2 Female ⎫
⎪ 1 Male   ⎪
⎨ 3 Male   ⎬ speakers,
⎩ 1 Male   ⎭

GOAL : IN A QUIET ROOM, WITH A GOOD MIKE, AND SLIGHT TUNING/SPEAKER,

HARPY :   ⎫
HEARSAY II: ⎬ in a computer terminal room,
HWIM :   ⎪   with a close talking mike, and
SDC : in a quiet room, with a good mike, and

⎧ 20 ⎫
⎨ 60 ⎬ training sentences
⎩ NO ⎪   per speaker,
     NO ⎭

GOAL : ACCEPTING 1000 WORDS, USING AN ARTIFICIAL SYNTAX & CONSTRAINING TASK,

HARPY :   ⎫ 1011 words, finite state language, ⎧ BF=33   ⎫ for document
HEARSAY II: ⎬   ⎨ BF=33,46 ⎬   retrieval,
HWIM : 1097 words, restricted ATN grammar, BF=196, for travel management,
SDC : 1000 words, context-free grammar,   BF=105, for data retrieval,

GOAL : YIELDING < 10% SEMANTIC ERROR, IN A FEW TIMES REAL TIME (≈300 MIPS)

HARPY :   ⎫   ⎧ 5%   ⎫
HEARSAY II: ⎬ yielding ⎨ 9%,26% ⎬ semantic error, with
HWIM :   ⎪   ⎪ 56%   ⎪
SDC :   ⎭   ⎩ 76%   ⎭

⎧ 28 MIPS ⎫
⎨ 85 MIPS ⎬
⎪ 500 MIPS (1350 R.T. on .35 ⎪
⎩ 92 MIPS   MIPS) ⎭

Fig. 17-2. Goals and performance characteristics for final (1976)
            ARPA SUR Systems.

Occasionally we have heard the ARPA SUR project criticized in terms of how
it missed a target defined post facto by those who wished the project had
attacked problems it did not set out to deal with. We think it is first
appropriate to consider how the project results related to the initial goals,
and how the difficulties encountered compared with the initial projections of
the study group. The study group outlined 19 technical problems (or "dimensions of difficulty") involved in recognition, some of which are shown in
Fig. 17-2, along with results for the final four systems.

17-2.2.1 Continuous Speech - One of the primary "breakthroughs" sought was
to show the feasibility of understanding continuous speech, and each of the
final systems was demonstrated (with varying degrees of accuracy) by handling
a modest number of spoken sentences. There is little or no doubt that
restricted forms of continuous speech recognition are now possible. (The
restrictions will be clarified as we discuss the other problems or dimensions
listed in Fig. 17-2.) Indeed, Harpy's success with continuous speech has
encouraged the development of a Harpy-like integrated network for recognizing
connected speech in computer-assisted training of air traffic controllers at
the Naval Training Equipment Center and Logicon. The Harpy continuous speech
task was later used as a benchmark task for evaluating the IBM continuous
speech recognizer (Bahl, et al., 1978). All of the ARPA SUR systems, even
including the intermediate systems like the Lincoln system, the SRI system,
SPEECHLIS, HEARSAY I, and the SDC vocal data management system, did directly
attack the continuous speech problem, and none shirked from that responsi-

385

bility. <u>How well they did</u> is another issue.

17-2.2.2 <u>Multiple Speakers, Single Dialect</u> - A second problem area addressed by designers of ARPA SUR was the multiple-speaker problem. The ARPA SUR systems were targeted to work with "many" speakers. Harpy was tested with 5 speakers, on its document retrieval task, and with 20 speakers on a 3-digit-string recognition task. HWIM dealt with 3 speakers in its final test, and incorporated a procedure for estimating the talker's vocal tract length for automatic talker normalization. While one to five speakers may not be "many", the problem of handling multiple speakers was directly addressed, with considerable success at least for Harpy. In contrast, after 15 years of various projects, IBM and other long-term contributors to the field were still handling the speech of only one male speaker in 1978 (Bahl, et al.). Speaker dialect and sex comprised another (third) problem listed by the study group, and you may note from Fig. 17-2 that the Harpy system used both male and female talkers of a similar dialect, as originally called for in the project design. The limited populations of speakers shown in Fig. 17-2 are more an indication of the limited testing of the systems than they are an indication of inability or unwillingness to handle multiple speakers.

Many applications, such as military systems and even many factory installations, permit or require only a few talkers to speak to the machine, so that systems (like the 1976 ARPA SUR systems or the 1978 IBM system) which can handle only one or a few talkers are quite acceptable. Indeed, most commercial recognizers are speaker-dependent, and some researchers (e.g. Neuberg, 1975) suggest that the multiple-speaker problem shouldn't be given high priority, especially if a system can be readily tuned to a new talker.

17-2.2.3 <u>Tuneability</u> - A related design problem concerns how much training of the machine to the individual characteristics of the speaker is needed. H.   and HEARSAY II need only about 20 to 60 sentences of training data before they can accurately recognize a new talker of similar dialect. HWIM and the SDC system actually tried to get along without any training to the individual talker. All these results were directly in accord with the original ARPA SUR goal of only "slight tuning to the speaker", and may be contrasted to systems like IBM's that require over <u>one hour</u> of training utterances to determine a priori probabilities and other required statistics for each speaker.

17-2.2.4 <u>Input Environment</u> - Environmental noise was another problem listed in the ARPA SUR plan, and on this aspect the final systems exceeded the initial goals, by dealing with somewhat noisy (65dBA) speech recorded in computer terminal rooms, rather than in antiseptic conditions of acoustically-insulated <u>quiet rooms</u>. Most laboratory models of recognizers (e.g., IBM's recent system; Bahl, et al., 1978) have been tested only with high quality speech.

While the original goals also called for easing the recognition difficulty by use of high quality microphones, Harpy, HEARSAY II and HWIM were tested with inexpensive close-talking, noise-cancelling microphones. H   was also tested with telephone speech. The <u>telephone</u> and <u>microphone</u> conditions are thus among those goals in the initial study that were dealt with by the best-performing of the ARPA SUR systems. Yet, further studies are needed to determine how system performances degrade with various amounts of input distortion such as noise, bandwidth, and frequency distortions.

17-2.2.5 <u>Vocabulary and Language Constraints</u> - The project produced significant advances on other dimensions of the recognition problem, also. The systems were supposed to handle a large <u>vocabulary of 1000 words</u>, and they each did so. The 1000-word vocabulary was a major advance from the 16-word vocabulary used in previous continuous speech recognition (Vicens, 1969), or the small vocabularies (ranging only in a few cases above 100 words) used in speaker-dependent isolated word recognition. Perhaps equally important were the studies of how vocabulary size and other complexities of the task affect recognition performance, as will be discussed in Sec. 17-3.3.

The original project plan also focused on how to use syntactic, semantic, and pragmatic information to support recognition. Systems were expected to use an artificial syntax which highly restricts what can be said. Harpy and HEARSAY II used the most constrained grammars, with a finite state language, or Markov model. HWIM used a powerful grammar called an augmented transition network or ATN grammar, and the SDC system used a moderately difficult "context free" grammar. One way to measure the complexity of the recognition problem is the so-called branching factor, or "BF" shown in Fig. 17-2, which is the average number of words that could appear next in an allowable sentence of the language. Thus, the larger the BF, the more difficult the task, though this one metric is hardly adequate as a full measure of complexity of a recognition task. Still, one reason for the success of the Harpy system, in particular, was its effective use of syntax to constrain the possible wordings that might reasonably be hypothesized and distinguished. In evaluating the limited successes of the HWIM and SDC systems, the complexities of their tasks must be considered. We will consider these questions of task and language complexity, and effective use of constraints, in Sec. 17-3.3.

Semantic support, and the use of <u>user models</u> and modelling of the total <u>discourse</u> of interaction, had been called for in the initial study report, but they had less evident effects on the performance of the final ARPA SUR systems than did syntactic constraints. HEARSAY I, developed early in the project, had very strong constraints built in by the semantic and pragmatic information and the user model, and those constraints really helped recognition. SRI developed sophisticated semantics and discourse models that unfortunately were not incorporated into the final SDC system (Walker, 1976; also, Chap. 13 of this book).

17-2.2.6 <u>Accuracy and Other System Performance Measures</u> - Harpy exceeded the primary accuracy goal of the ARPA SUR project, by successfully understanding 95% of the sentences spoken to it, or, as is shown in Fig. 17-2, making a semantic error 5% of the time. The HEARSAY II system also matched the accuracy goal for that limited task, but when tried on another more challenging task with a branching factor of 46, its error rate tripled, to 26%. The HWIM system, with its challenging task represented by the large branching factor of 196, was wrong in its interpretation of a sentence in slightly over half the sentences it was tested with. System Development Corporation lost its major computer system only months before the final demonstration, so they had to drop their plans to use higher-level linguistic components designed at Stanford Research Institute, and develop a substitute system that only attained 24% correct understanding.

<u>Accuracy</u> is the one system parameter that has dominated the evaluative discussion of ARPA SUR systems, and stimulated the extensive interest in Harpy. However, it is important to place accuracy results in the full context of task complexity, extendibility of the system to new tasks, and other goals such as speed and cost of system design and operation. The reader should refer to Chap. 14 (Sec. 14-4.4) and Chap. 15 for some qualifications on Harpy's success.

While the goal was that the systems would give results in a few times real time on very large machines handling 100 million instructions per second (MIPS), it took minutes for responses to a few-second sentence in the fastest systems (working on moderate-size computers of less than 1MIPS),and an hour or more for the extremely slow HWIM system. However, even the 1350 times real time required for HWIM, using an 0.35 MIPS PDP-10 computer would correspond to only 5 times real time on the target 100 MIPS machines. Even though the computer technology had not advanced to providing the projected 100 MIPS, the systems were able to function under effective use of linguistic constraints. The expected demand for large memory and computer power due to combinatorial explosions of hypothesized words did not materialize to the degree feared. For Harpy, the speed goal was <u>exceeded by an order of magnitude</u> (cf. Lowerre and Reddy, Chap. 1). Harpy has subsequently been speeded up, so it now operates in near real time on a minicomputer with paged memory. Near-real-time analysis has been found to not only be useful for demonstrating the feasibility of practical systems, but also for speeding up research and permitting the processing of extensive data so that systems can be carefully tuned.

Not too many long-term projects succeed in matching or exceeding so many of their original goals, such as the ARPA SUR project did. Still, one could have hoped for a more thorough final performance evaluation than the hundred or so sentences with which even the most complete system tests were made. Such scientifically adequate evaluations were proposed but not funded.

17-3. DETAILED CONTRIBUTIONS: SYSTEM DESIGNS

While it is quite appropriate to evaluate the contributions of the ARPA SUR project in the light of its initial goals, it is also useful to ask in what ways the project has contributed to the total context of speech recognition work and other research and development work in speech science, computer science, and artificial intelligence. The detailed contributions in specific aspects of recognition techniques will be summarized in Sec. 17-4. Here we consider the <u>system</u> contributions, including the Harpy system structure (Sec. 17-3.1), the experimental testing of alternative structures and control strategies (Sec. 17-3.2), and the methods and results in performance evaluation (Sec. 17-3.3).

17-3.1 The Harpy System

Harpy has received considerable attention because it is one of the first systems to attain high performance in large vocabulary continuous speech recognition, and its contributions include its public demonstration of the credibility of task-constrained continuous speech input to computers. Ultimate practicality is suggested by the facts that this was accomplished at an order of magnitude faster than initially called for, with half the allowable error rate, under practical conditions of somewhat noisy speech tranduced by an inexpensive close talking microphone. As one developer of a competing system said to us, no one can now reasonably develop speech understanding systems without understanding Harpy, and using it as a "benchmark" system for comparisons with new recognizers.

To achieve success, Harpy used two primary system design contributions: the <u>integrated network representation of knowledge</u> and the <u>beam search technique</u>. The integrated network structure collapses knowledge at various <u>levels</u> (phonetic, phonological, lexical, and syntactic) into one generative model of acceptable pronunciations for recognizable sentences. As described in detail in Chap. 15, Harpy begins with a word network of acceptable word sequences, in which the nodes are words and any path through the network gives an acceptable sentence. Then each word node gets replaced by a pronunciation network, representing expected pronunciations of the word. Word boundary rules, initially entered by hand, operate on the network to handle phone string variations due to influences of each word on its neighbors. During the automatic compiling of a single composite network, optimization heuristics are used to yield an efficient network of correct pronunciations. The network for the "document retrieval" demonstration task had almost 15,000 nodes, and required 13 <u>hours</u> of PDP-10 computer time to develop. The nodes in this fully-expanded pronunciation network are "phones" or allophonic segments taken from a vocabulary of 98 alternative spectral templates.

Harpy finds the best match between each of the incoming acoustically-derived segments and the 98 phonetic templates, using Itakura's (1975) distance metric for scoring matches. At each segment in the left-to-right search, the best match and some near misses are retained for further testing. The number of near misses (or "beam width") retained at each point is dynamically adjusted as the search progresses through the network.

The finite state "network" representation (or "Markov model") is not new, and, in 1957, Chomsky argued that if one accepts no fixed upper limit on the complexity of English sentences, then English (and certain major subsets of English) could not be represented by such a finite state graph (cf. Lea, 1966). Indeed, unless the language initially designed for Harpy is in the restricted class of such "finite state languages", the network that does include all the acceptable pronunciations will necessarily also allow pronunciations that were <u>not</u> in the intended language. This is part of the reason why Wolf and Woods (Chap. 14) question the extendability of Harpy to other useful tasks. Harpy acts like an overgrown "word verifier", in matching expected pronunciations of the <u>total</u> utterance to the total incoming sequence of short time segments. It is a natural "next step" from previous isolated-word recognizers. In fact, it is basically a heuristic form of dynemic programming, which has become very popular in isolated word recognizers (White, 1978).

Dragon and IBM recognition systems have also used Markov models or finite state networks. What Harpy's developers did was to successfully combine the best features of previous systems such as Dragon's network representation and HEARSAY I's phonetic segmentation procedures. The beam search avoided the expensive, time consuming processes of an "admissable" recognition strategy (which Dragon used and HWIM was intended to use, to <u>guarantee</u> finding the optimal solution in the search for the best match with the input data). The network and beam search also achieved most of the delayed-decision advantages of HEARSAY I's "best-first" strategy, by pursuing how an apparently promising phonetic-sequence hypothesis fits at lexical and syntactic levels before pursuing less promising alternatives. (SRI also found that it is good to use information from several knowledge sources to avoid erroneous interpretations and reinforce choices of each knowledge source.) Backtracking (after a high-scoring hypothesis fails) was effectively avoided by Harpy's beam search. Occasionally the correct interpretation will <u>not</u> be among the high-scoring alternatives in the beam, so that a failure to recognize may occur, but obviously that did not occur frequently enough to reduce accuracy extensively.

Some problems with Harpy are noted in Chaps. 14 and 15. Making a pronunciation dictionary for a new vocabulary is very time consuming, and it would be useful to have automatic methods for learning new word structures (and new syntactic constructions) directly from example pronunciations. Network compiling is very expensive in computer time. Juncture rules, pronunciation variabilities, and duration effects are not easily represented as a graph. The juncture rules had to be manually tailored to the task. Here again, automatic knowledge acquisition would be valuable. Harpy is very sensitive to _missing_ states in the incoming phonetic sequence, unless extensive effort is devoted to creating optional states during the network creation time. In general, the collapsing of all types of information into a single network makes it difficult to revise minor parts of the incorporated knowledge, such as adding new words or new pronunciations to old words, incorporating newly learned word-juncture or phonological rules, adding new structures, introducing prosodic rules, etc.

An important contribution of Harpy was its demonstration of the value of _using_ syntactic (and other linguistic) constraints to _constrain_ the recognition problem, rather than just having the linguistic knowledge adequately model a large subset of English sentences. This was one of the original premises (or "dogmas"; Newell, 1975) of speech understanding that was vividly verified by Harpy's success.

17-3.2 Testing Alternative Structures and Control Strategies

17-3.2.1 _Several System Structures_ - There is a real danger that Harpy's success may overshadow other equally important contributions of the ARPA SUR project. Another major contribution was the variety of system structures and control strategies that were developed and applied for the first time to the recognition of continuous speech. HEARSAY II came very close to meeting the system specifications, using a generalized structure that is in some senses at the other extreme from Harpy; that is, HEARSAY II had clearly separated, cooperating knowledge sources that could be selectively modified, independently tested, and augmented by new knowledge sources without disrupting the total system. HEARSAY II's _blackboard_ permitted an anonymity and independence of system modules such that the function and the very existence of each knowledge source was not necessary or crucial to the others, yet they could use and correct each others hypotheses through the common blackboard. HWIM _complemented_ HEARSAY II's fixed structure but readily variable components by having more-fixed components, and flexible control strategies. It was no small task to implement such multiple knowledge source systems that could handle the variabilities in continuous speech.

Woods (in Walker, et al., 1977, p. 972) has aptly noted that several of the ARPA SUR systems used a "factored knowledge structure", in which common parts of different knowledge sources are _merged_ in such a way that retrieval processes can access them incrementally to progressively create more and more specific hypotheses about the utterance. Thus, Harpy merged grammar, lexical forms, rules, and pronunciations, while HWIM merged phonetic, phonological and lexical information in the phonetic lattice and lexical decoding network, and syntactic and semantic information in the ATN grammar. This trend seems to be a promising contribution.

For completeness, we should also note the performances of some intermediate systems developed in the course of the project, as shown in Fig. 17-3. The earlier systems worked with more limited vocabularies and tasks, achieving various low-to-moderate levels of sentence understanding accuracy. The HEARSAY I system used heavy _semantic_ constraints about the status of a chess board and the allowable and plausible moves to do 79% correct understanding of spoken chess moves. However, it did much poorer on other less-constrained tasks. CMU researchers believed HEARSAY I could have achieved the ARPA SUR goals, given the acoustic-phonetic capabilities of the final (1976) systems (Reddy, et al., 1976, p. 4). One of the attractive features of the HEARSAY I system was its use of <u>independent</u> cooperating knowledge sources or modules, which could be removed one at a time to establish the performance with versus without that module. Such "ablation studies" (Newell, 1975) help determine the contribution of each system component, and permit detecting "weak links" in the system operation.

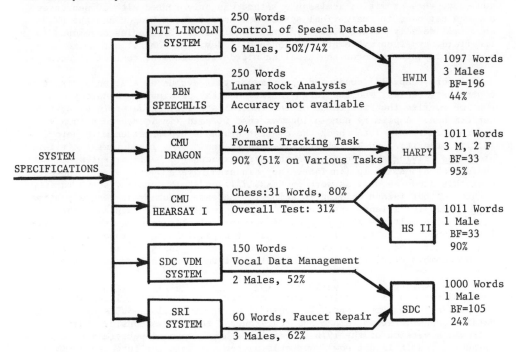

Fig. 17-3. Performance Results for Systems Developed Throughout the ARPA SUR Project. (Each task is briefly described, and accuracy percentages are given for correct <u>semantic</u> understanding.)

Lincoln Laboratory's system was one of the best performing intermediate systems, using a 250-word vocabulary and some of the best acoustic phonetic processing techniques available. Some of the "front-end" processing ideas of the Lincoln system were incorporated into the HWIM system and other systems (e.g., the Sperry Univac systems; Medress, et al., 1977). Dragon, the predecessor to HARPY, used a Markov model, no phonetic segmentation, and a highly constrained task to achieve fairly good performance. Also, SRI's system working with a small vocabulary of 60 words obtained 62% recognition at the midpoint of the ARPA SUR project. SDC achieved 52% on a 150 word vocabulary.

17-3.2.2 - <u>Experimenting with Alternative Control Strategies</u> - Besides building total systems with interesting structures, the ARPA SUR project also contributed extensive evidence about the advantages and disadvantages of various structures. BBN explored a number of different control strategies, including "left-to-right" versus "middle-out" analyses, and a "hybrid" strategy whereby analysis was initially anchored in the first stressed word in the utterance, then any extensions to the left (to the beginning of the utterance) were attempted before extensions to the right were attempted. They sought efficient "admissable" control strategies which guarantee the best possible interpretation, and found one superior admissable method based on their "shortfall density" concept for scoring alternative hypotheses (see Chap. 14). However, for efficiency they also developed (and finally used) "approximate" methods. They showed that their best admissable strategy took only slightly (30%) longer than the best approximate method and was almost as accurate, with fewer misleading acceptances of wrong interpretations. Unfortunately, this promising admissable method was only tested with 10 sentences, and was not used in their final system demonstrations. Dragon and the HWIM shortfall density method were the first "admissable" strategies developed in the field, and such systematic approaches to devising control strategies are a marked improvement over the usual ad hoc developments of control structures.

SRI (cf. Chap. 13) conducted experiments that evaluated sixteen alternative control strategies, and the large variations they obtained in accuracy and runtime confirm the importance of the control strategy in determining system performance. A primary conclusion was that it paid (in increased accuracy and reduced runtime) to check the context around a hypothesized word before setting priorities on all alternative hypotheses. They found that their forms of island driving and focusing on what are expected to be important areas of the speech did not help (in fact, they hindered) system performance. However, what this study as well as work on HEARSAY II and HWIM actually seems to indicate is that island driving is going to increase accuracy or reduce runtime only if (1) the islands are true "islands of reliability", such as might be assured with multiple-word islands or perhaps reliably-encoded stressed syllables; and (2) the expansion of islands by hypothesizing surrounding contexts can be controlled (such as by one-way expansions or BBN's hybrid strategy), so that combinatiorial explosions of alternative extensions do not arise.

17-3.2.3 Comparative Evaluations of the ARPA SUR Systems - Comparison of the ARPA SUR systems is a difficult but necessary part of the total assessment of the project's contributions. To begin with, we can exclude SDC's system from detailed consideration, since SDC researchers themselves consider that even a flawless version of the 1976 system would have improved performance only slightly, and it is not now a workable system suitable for further development without drastic changes. (They include in their list important changes needed in: the acoustic phonetic processor, the scoring algorithms, the phonological rules, the mapper, and the higher-level components such as semantics and discourse; cf. Chap. 12. Little of the system would stay the same.)

Harpy's accuracy makes it appear to be the leading system contribution, but the counter-arguments given by HWIM and HEARSAY II developers in Chap. 14 and 16 deserve attention, as do some frank admissions in Chap. 15 of the difficulties of building Harpy-like systems for new tasks. Harpy's developers note that Harpy involved some very time consuming tasks, including making pronunciation dictionaries, manually tailoring the juncture rules, and compiling the pronunciation network. They note that some knowledge such as juncture rules, pronunciation variability, and duration effects are not easily represented in a graph and require considerable ingenuity. However, their ingenuity and successful developments have already solved most of these problems, and they are working on automatic procedures for obtaining pronunciation dictionaries and juncture rules, plus ways of incrementally compiling minor changes in the network.

Harpy and Dragon, and to some extent HEARSAY II, achieved accuracy primarily by heavily constraining the task handled. (Earlier systems developed at CMU, SDC, Lincoln Laboratory, and SRI also highly constrained the task to achieve more accuracy.) In fact, Wolf and Woods (Chap. 14) argue that Harpy only dealt with an actual branching factor of 10, compared to HWIM's 196. They point out that Harpy's grammar allows mostly sentences that ease the recognition task by starting with stressed words, and the grammar allows very few sentence pairs that are similar in wording (and thus few that are readily confusable). They claim Harpy's language is non-habitable, so it could not be effectively used in most practical human-computer interactions. They assert that the performance of the 1976 HWIM system is not a true indicator of its potential, since (a) no vocabulary above 500 words was run on the system until the final weeks before demonstration; (b) the acoustic phonetic recognition component was incomplete; (c) many individual components were functioning far below potential and none had been tuned to its full potential; and (d) the prosodic component was not even tested, much less tuned. Using and debugging the system components "had not been completed when the time arrived to run the final performance test" (Wolf and Woods, Sec. 14-5.3). It is interesting that when we surveyed expert opinions about whether the ARPA SUR systems would have met the original specification if given one more year, more agreed that HWIM might have made it than any other system. All this may be rationalization or speculation, and to date there still is no proof that HWIM could achieve high accuracy on the complex task they undertook (or even on a more restricted task like Harpy's). All the ARPA SUR systems except Harpy have been "dormant" since the completion of the project.

Like HWIM, the HEARSAY II system was intended as a general purpose architecture with several separable knowledge sources. Its developers argue that changes in individual components or system structure are relatively easy to accomplish, with the system and its various sources of knowledge readily evaluated. HEARSAY II was successful (90% accurate) on the document retrieval task that Harpy used, and is expected to be applicable to larger tasks such as HWIM attempted. Yet, it is difficult to comparatively evaluate HEARSAY II and HWIM. HEARSAY II was much closer to being fine tuned than HWIM when it was demonstrated, but not as well tested and adjusted as Harpy. Its success makes it a safer bet than HWIM, but it could profit considerably by several ideas and techniques that were developed for HWIM, including: the uniform scoring procedure; the lexical decoding network; the versatile ATN grammar; and the shortfall density strategy (or some other admissable strategy).

There is no indisputable evidence that Harpy's language is unhabitable, or that either that language or some similarly small language with minimal complexity cannot be effectively used by talkers performing limited practical tasks. Alphonse Chapanis and his colleagues have found that humans do quite well in cooperative problem solving when restricted to vocabularies of a few hundred words, and can accomplish tasks almost as well if restricted to short (presumable simple) sentences (Chapanis, et al., 1977; cf. also Chap. 1 of this book). We still await any experimental evidence as to the "habitability" of any very small language, or the degree of degradation in human performance resulting from various complex constraints on what can be said. For many immediate practical applications, a Harpy-like language may prove adequate. It also should be noted that while Harpy did use a vocabulary with few similar words that could occur in similar structures, that careful selection of vocabulary and potential structural confusions would seem to be a reasonable and desirable feature to incorporate in a working system which must assure high accuracy.

We conclude that Harpy is the best choice for a recognition system that must accurately and quickly handle one small well-designed task. For systems that might be used for multiple small tasks or one or more large task, the choice is between HWIM and HEARSAY II. HWIM seems to be particularly suitable for cases where the developer wants relatively fixed, traditional components and wishes to explore alternative control strategies (especially efficient admissable strategies). HEARSAY II is suitable where a relatively fixed

system structure (knowledge sources and blackboard) is desired, along with an
excellent ability to evaluate individual knowledge sources that can be readily
changed. HEARSAY II does have some flexibility in control strategy via its
knowledge-source activation and scheduling procedures and its separation of
policy from mechanism (cf. Chap. 16). Since there are many control strategies
yet to be explored, and also many components or knowledge sources that are
still in definite need of improvement (or in some cases, that have not been
tested at all), both general approaches seem of current interest. However,
most experts we have surveyed are more concerned now about improved or new
components or <u>knowledge sources</u> (especially at the "front end" of the system)
than alternative strategies, so the HEARSAY II system would seem particularly
appropriate for further studies. If such an effort were attempted, the best
of the appropriate HWIM ideas should be incorporated (cf. Klatt, 1977).
Clearly, the ARPA SUR project contributed <u>several</u> excellent system structures
and alternative approaches for efficiently integrating diverse sources of
incomplete knowledge.

17-3.3 <u>Performance Evaluation</u>

   The original study report which formed the blueprint for the ARPA SUR project emphasized correct <u>understanding</u>, so that the performance of a system
would be measured by its capability to interpret an utterance and respond
appropriately, as opposed to its ability to exactly recognize subunits of the
utterance, such as phonemes, words, etc. Despite common impressions to the
contrary, this ultimate importance of machine response was not a new idea
originating with the study group, but was evident in various earlier writings
(e.g., Denes, 1953; Peterson, 1961; Lea, 1969, 1970) and is a natural extension of the communication theoretic notion that the ultimate purpose of a
communication is to induce a desired response in the hearer (cf. Shannon and
Weaver, 1949; Dean, 1953). However, the study group properly focused attention not on unimportant errors in phonetic strings or wording, but on ultimate interpretations and responses.

   An important contribution of the ARPA SUR work was the experimental verification of the value of syntactic and semantic constraints. For example, Fig.
17-4 shows, for various tasks handled by the HEARSAY I system, how the accuracy of recognition was substantially increased when syntactic constraints
were added to the acoustic information, and then increased further by the
addition of semantics (cf. Reddy, 1973). These tests were readily accomplished in HEARSAY I because of its ability to operate with or without knowledge sources like syntax and semantics.

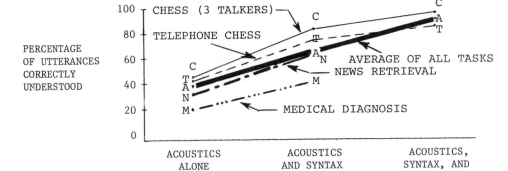

Fig. 17-4. Contributions of Syntax and Semantics to Accuracy of
           Recognition in the HEARSAY I System (Reddy, 1973)

Such systematic tests of the contributions of various system components and task constraints are generally valuable. As Paxton noted (in Walker, et al., 1977, p. 973), "if it is worth building a system ..., it is certainly worth making an effort to understand how the system actually works, and experimentation is an important technique for doing this". We have already noted SRI's and BBN's experiments with alternative control strategies (Sec. 17-3. 2.2).

Figure 17-5 shows some experimental results concerning how accuracy of understanding is affected by vocabulary size and utterance length, for various ARPA SUR systems. In general, it is clear, for systems tested with varied vocabularies, that vocabulary size has only a slight influence on the accuracy of recognition, while, at least for one system, utterance length significantly affects the likelihood of the utterance being correctly understood.

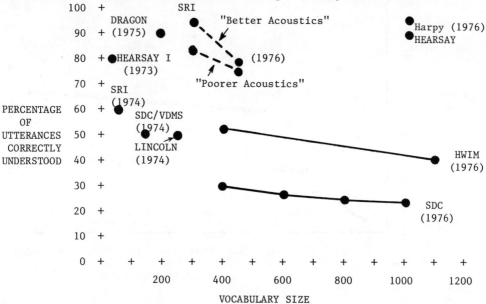

(a) Effects of vocabulary size on recognition accuracy

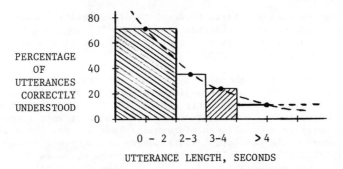

(b) Effects of utterance length on recognition accuracy, for 1976 SDC system (cf. Chap. 13)

Fig. 17-5. Effects of vocabulary size and utterance length on speech understanding accuracy, for various ARPA SUR systems.

Perhaps more important is the evidence regarding how accuracy relates to the complexity of the language, as illustrated in Fig. 17-6 by the error rate versus the static branching factor. Harpy and HEARSAY II seem to be highly sensitive to the static branching factor, while HWIM is not. An extension of the Harpy and HEARSAY II results to large branching factors like HWIM's 196 probably (but not with certainty) would have produced high error rates like those for HWIM. A valuable contribution of the ARPA SUR project was the development of the branching factor (and an old but largely unused measure of entropy; Goodman, 1976) as a measure of the complexity of a recognition task.

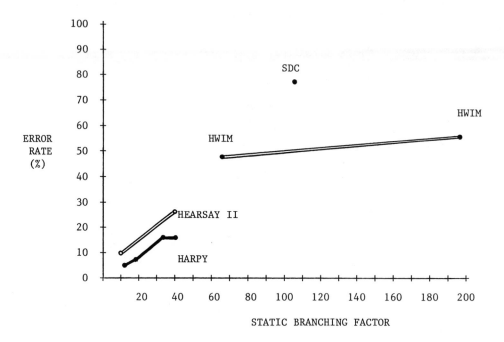

Fig. 17-6. Effects of static branching factor on recognition error rate.

There are very few data points in these plots of recognition accuracy (or error rate) versus vocabulary, utterance length, and language complexity, and we would hope that further studies will provide more extensive evidence about what influences recognition accuracy.

In general, the utility of phonology, syntax, semantics, and pragmatic information is evident in the final recognition accuracy scores given for the ARPA SUR systems. While HARPY correctly labeled (by top choice) only about 42% of the allophones in sentences, it attained 97% correct word recognition by its network constraints on allowable pronunciations. Also, while .97 taken to the seventh power would have predicted a seven-word sentence recognition accuracy of only 81%, the use of linguistic constraints produced 91% having no errors in any of their recognized words. Finally, the distinction between having all the words right and having correct understanding of the utterance was evident in that not just 91% but rather 95% of the sentences were correctly understood, so that the correct computer response would be possible, even if minor words were misidentified.

Similarly the SDC mapper was able to recover from the fact that only 1 in
167 syntactically predicted words was correct by using a combination of phonetic, lexical, and syntactic constraints to reject 97% of all word predictions
that were wrong. The long-sought-after goal of using linguistic constraints
to aid acoustic information has finally become a reality.

17-4.   DETAILED CONTRIBUTIONS: COMPONENTS AND IDEAS

Besides the total systems for speech understanding, the ARPA SUR project
produced several new or improved system components or "knowledge sources,"
and procedures or facilities for extensive analysis of connected speech.
These include improved acoustic analysis tools (Sec. 17-4.1), phonetic segmentation and labeling procedures (Sec. 17-4.2), phonological rules and lexical
processors (Sec. 17-4.3), prosodic aids (Sec. 17-4.4), syntactic analyzers and
parsers (Sec. 17-4.5), semantic and pragmatic analyses (Sec. 17-4.6), and
speech data bases and advanced knowledge of the speech signal (Sec. 17-4.7).

Every new idea or analysis technique benefits from having a _user_ that really
puts it to the test, and the ARPA SUR work actually contributed many intangible
results by using and testing earlier work from a variety of disciplines. Besides work by the five groups involved in system building, special research
contributions were made by the four "specialist contractors": Haskins Laboratories (phonetics and syllable studies); Speech Communications Research Laboratory (phonology and dictionaries); Sperry Univac (prosodic structures) and
University of California at Berkeley (prosodics and phonology).

17-4.1   _Acoustic Signal Processing_

Although, as Neuburg (1975 p.84) noted, the ARPA SUR project did not add
any promising new acoustic parameters[1], still it did provide some improved
techniques for extracting traditional ones. All the ARPA SUR contractors
cooperated in a 1973 workshop on acoustic parameterization, and exchanged
ideas and results of their various acoustic analyses of a common database of
thirteen sentences which were pertinent to the various systems. From that
workshop and later related interactions came decisions: to software pre-em-
phasize the speech to avoid erroneous low first formants in the LPC spectra;
to use the Sperry Univac version of Sondhi's (1968) autocorrelation method of
fundamental frequency tracking; to track formants by simple peak picking on
LPC spectra, and incorporate smoothing and correcting procedures developed at
Lincoln Laboratories (McCandless, 1974); to adopt BBN's "off-axis" LPC analysis and pole tracking to help resolve close formants to detect voicing from
band limited energies such as developed at Lincoln Laboratories; etc. SDC
used and modified Haskin's "convex hull" procedure for locating syllabic
nuclei (Mermelstein, 1975) and Sperry Univac's pitch tracker (Skinner, 1973;
Gillman, 1975) and phrase boundary detection ideas (Lea, 1973; Bernstein, et
al., 1976). Haskin's advocacy of the syllable as a useful recognition unit
impacted the design of the SDC and HEARSAY II systems. CMU's earliest simple
acoustic analyses with zero crossings were augmented by LPC and other parameters   used by Lincoln, BBN, and other systems.

BBN (Makhoul, 1974) developed a selective method of LPC analysis, whereby
fricative spectra were readily represented by a few poles, while sonorant
sounds were analyzed with the usual many (12 to 15) poles. Klatt (1976) proposed a perceptually-based filter bank as a reasonable alternative to LPC

[1]Janet Baker's (1975) instantaneous frequency measure based on local zero
crossing times might be considered a new acoustic parameter, but it apparently
has had negligible impact on subsequent systems.

analysis. CMU developed the simple ZAPDASH parameters and parameter-independent phonetic classifiers, and showed by comparative evaluations that several alternative sets of acoustic parameters gave nearly equivalent success in phonetic classification procedures (Goldberg, 1976). They also showed that PARCOR coefficients of LPC analysis were particularly attractive in speaker-independent recognition because, unlike most acoustic parameters, they could simply be additively averaged to obtain composite templates. Studies with semi-noisy computer rooms and telephone speech were acoustic advances that had rarely been attempted before.

General "dip detectors" (Weinstein, et al., 1975; Schwartz and Zue, 1976) were developed that can be used to detect potential boundaries between phonetic segments, at major changes in any acoustic parameter such as energy, formant frequency, spectral distance, etc.

17-4.2 Phonetic Segmentation and Labeling

Another basic parametric segmentation (preliminary to phonetic analysis) was involved in the detecting of syllabic nuclei from energy contours in systems at SDC, CMU, BBN, and Sperry Univac. Mermelstein (1975) of Haskins Laboratories provided a "convex hull" algorithm for locating about 93% of the syllabic nuclei, and his algorithm was incorporated into the SDC system. Sperry Univac's algorithm for locating syllabic nuclei (Lea, 1974; 1976) was tested on several speech data bases including a set of 255 sentences composed of only sonorant sounds (which represents a "worst-case" test of syllable detection capabilities), and the algorithm successfully located 91% of the syllabic nuclei, despite the lack of large energy dips in intervocalic sonorant consonants.

The syllable was a recognition unit in systems at CMU and SDC. The number of syllables in a word seems to be one reasonable metric of length, for normalizing word matching scores for words of different lengths. The number of syllables remaining in an utterance was also used by SDC and CMU as a length measure in rejecting hypotheses that could not properly account for the remaining data. Studies at SDC and SCRL suggested that syllable boundaries are too difficult to reliably locate to be used in recognition schemes, and in many phonological rules the syllable boundaries could be removed without altering the effects of the rule (Hanson, et al. , 1976). We still await any hard evidence that phonetic constraints are less across syllable boundaries than within syllables, even though such evidence, if available, would help justify syllables as units in speech analysis.

New and advanced phonetic segmentation and labeling strategies were developed. Harpy incorporated the concept of "allophones" in its 98 subphonemic templates, and made a firm decision on the best (or closest) of these for each acoustic segment. Lowerre (1976) showed that Harpy was more efficient than Dragon in part because Harpy had phonetic segmentation. Harpy's pronunciation networks and 98 phonetic templates seem to have been successful enough to prompt Klatt (1977; also, Chap. 25 of this book) to propose that no strict phonetic segmentation of speech be done, and that sequences of spectral templates be used to represent words. The "folding" of word juncture rules directly into Harpy's pronunciation networks was also noteworthy. The full implications of Harpy's phonetic methods are not yet known, but they seem to have been instrumental in creating a trend towards allophonic template representations and de-emphasis of more traditional phonetic segmentation and labeling methods (cf. Klatt, 1977; Bahl, et al., 1978; Newell, 1978).

The high interest in Harpy's phonetic analysis procedures is not necessarily because of high accuracy in phonetic labeling. Harpy (and Hearsay II) only had the correct phonetic label as the top choice on 42% of its segments, or within the top three choices 65% of the time. (HWIM correctly identified the phonetic segment by the correct top choice 52% of the time, or within the top three choices 80% of the time, while SDC had the correct top choice about 50% of the time.) An interesting conclusion is that, with the proper linguistic constraints, Harpy was able to succeed in 95% correct sentence understanding despite only 42% correct phonetic labeling. One would hope that substantial improvements in phonetic labeling would still be possible; the IBM phonetic analysis obtains about 65% correct labeling (cf. Klatt, Chap. 25). Also, experiments at CMU (Shockey and Reddy, 1974) with phoneticians and linguists transcribing the phones in a language they did not understand suggest that about 60-70% of the phones should be machine transcribable, and more recent experiments showed reliable human transcriptions of 90% of the phones in people's names (wherein syntax, etc. doesn't help disambiguate but the phonology of English is adhered to).

The phonetic lattice developed at BBN was an interesting contribution. It permits alternative conjectures as to what phonetic (or, quasi-phonemic) segments appear at various portions of the speech, and thus does not restrict word hypothesizing to only those words with the most likely ("nearest neighbor") phonetic segments in each region. However, that flexibility of alternative phonetic strings being preserved for higher levels can on occasion cause combinatoric explosions and confusions among alternative word sequences. Ambiguity arises not only from alternative segmentations (calling a region either one or two segments) but also from the assignment of a score for all possible segment categories at each position in the lattice. It has not been shown whether the ambiguity of the lattice helps or hurts phonetic recognition, and it is currently difficult to assess whether the lattice or Harpy's larger set of phonetic segments is better.

Despite the modest performance of the phonetic analyzers in the ARPA SUR systems, a number of definite improvements were made in detailed algorithms for detecting and identifying various speech sounds. Vowel identification procedures were improved, using speaker-dependent target frequencies for formants (at SDC, BBN, Sperry Univac, and Lincoln Laboratories). Formant trajectories were used for detecting, segmenting, and identifying glides, nasals, and dipthongs (at Lincoln and BBN). Haskins Laboratories also developed a nasal detector (Mermelstein, 1975). New or improved algorithms were provided for detecting retroflexives, laterals, flapped dentals, intervocalic glottal stops, initial glottal fricatives, plosives, fricatives, and affricates, and for determining place of articulation. A common feature in all the systems was an initial segmentation into broad ("manner-of-articulation") classes followed by refined categorization.

The ARPA SUR project also produced a number of phonetic research tools that should be of interest in future work. The ARPABET developed during the project is a useful agreed-upon quasi-phonemic labeling scheme that is computer-compatible and yet phonemically reasonable. BBN developed an acoustic phonetic analysis facility that provides an interactive environment for rapidly performing a wide variety of acoustic phonetic and phonological experiments on a large data base of continuous speech. One can specify phonetic contexts and find all their occurrences in the data base, run algorithms like acoustic parameterization or segmentation and labeling procedures, perform computer-assisted hand labeling of continuous speech, display parametric results or scatter diagrams like $F_1 - F_2$ plots, and have the computer tabulate statistical results (Schwartz, 1976).

In general, while it is beyond the scope of this chapter to comparatively evaluate all the ARPA SUR techniques in acoustics, phonetics, lexical analysis, syntax, etc. it would be a valuable contribution to the field if someone provided such objective evaluations (cf. Part II of this book for some evaluations). An extensive effort was devoted, in particular, to phonetic identification procedures, and all that was learned should not have to be tediously relearned by new investigators in future projects.

17-4.3 Phonological Rules and Lexical Analysis

One of the primary efforts of the ARPA SUR project was the compilation of over 200 phonological rules, and the selection of those that are most appropriate for use in systems. The rules selected were both analytic and generative in nature. They handled acoustic-phonetic, coarticulatory, junctural, and prosodic phenomena; but they did not handle derivational or morphophonemic information, since this knowledge was incorporated into the formation of the lexicons. The individual entries in the lexicons usually required more than one base form on which the rules would operate. The base forms were most useful if they were realizable, rather than abstract forms. The systems that were most successful were those that applied the rules before an entry was looked up. Indeed, in Harpy all the rules were precompiled into the network. The majority of rules were optional, rather than obligatory. Most of the rules included information regarding word boundaries, morpheme boundaries, and/or syllable boundaries, though studies were done to see which rules could be rewritten without boundary considerations.

The ARPA SUR project is the primary source of phonological rules used in speech recognition (along with the IBM system), so the reader is referred to Chap. 6 for further details and example rules. A companion contribution was the development and refinement of phonological rule compilers and testers, at SDC, BBN, and SCRL.

A primary trend from the project was the combining of phonological variability with lexical representations. Harpy had a different path through its network for each alternative pronunciation of a word, and it also had junctural (word-boundary) phenomena incorporated as allowable transitions in the network. SDC had spelling graphs for words, which were similar to Harpy's full expansions of alternative pronunciations for words (though SDC included syllable boundaries as segments in its pronunciations). HEARSAY II used a Harpy-like pronunciation network in its WIZARD word verifier. A major contribution in phonological and lexical analysis was HWIM's lexical decoding network, which merged common parts of pronunciations of different words and incorporated "wrap around" procedures for tying the ending of one word together with the beginning of the next word, allowing deletions and substitutions of elements based on coarticulatory regularities. Thus, as Klatt illustrates in Chap. 11, optional deletions like "list some" sounding like "lissum" can be efficiently represented.

Lexical analysis procedures seem to have become quite accurate, though rather expensive in computer processing time. The SDC mapper in isolation missed only 7% of the correct words and gave 7% false alarms (with more misses on polysyllables and more false alarms on monosyllables, as might be expected). When operating within their system, it yielded 8% misses and 3% false alarms. Figure 12-10 and Table 12-5 in Chap. 12 suggests that while there is no combinatorial explosion of mapping time for longer words, the mapper consumes a large portion of the processing time of the SDC system. In the 1976 HEARSAY II system about 50 words of the 1011-word vocabulary were generated at each syllabic nucleus position, and about 75% of the words actually spoken were correctly hypothesized. The word verifier in HEARSAY II accepted 94% of the correct words, but falsely accepted 49% of the incorrect words; cf. Chap. 11, Table 11-4. The lexical retrieval process in HWIM found a correct word as the highest scoring word about 57% of the time and then used word verification to accept about 84% of the correct words, but also falsely accepted 34% of the incorrect words. Lexical retrieval in HWIM consumed 40% of its processing time, and word verification required another 15%.

Experiments showed that the system performances were not drastically degraded with increases in the size of the vocabulary (cf. Fig. 17-4). The NOAH word hypothesizer introduced into HEARSAY II in 1977 performed with a degradation that was only logarithmic with vocabulary size in the full range of 500 to 19,000 words (cf. Chap. 7, Sec. 7-3.2.2.3).

Word verification came of age during the ARPA SUR project, and the parametric word verifier developed at BBN is considered one of the significant contributions (Klatt, 1977; also, Chap. 11). The verifier and synthesis procedures in HWIM apparently constitute the first attempt at actually using analysis-by-synthesis in a speech recognizer (Halle and Stevens, 1962).

Another significant BBN contribution related to lexical analysis is the uniform scoring procedure. Since all components of a system, especially the "front end", make hypotheses and offer priority "scores" about the content of an utterance, some means is needed for systematically combining the assessments of all components. This has usually been accomplished in an ad hoc manner, such as adding (or averaging) the scores on phonemes to get the score on a word, then adjusting scores based on prosodics, likely word sequences, etc. Each of the systems settled on a log likelihood method of scoring, and BBN carried that philosophy to a systematic combining of probabilities and the development of an admissable strategy for finding the best interpretation. Other system builders have since said they would like to incorporate a similar idea into their systems.

17-4.4 Prosodic Structures

Prosodic analysis facilities were among the new tools developed for speech recognition procedures by the ARPA SUR project. Besides the syllabification procedures mentioned previously, prosodic analysis algorithms included an improvement of Lea's earlier algorithm for detecting major phrase boundaries from fall-rise valleys in fundamental frequency contours (Lea, 1972; 1973 a,b; 1976). The location of the F_0 valley was shown to be just before the first stressed syllable of the following phrase. Another important algorithm that can be of use in various speech recognition systems is one that locates 89% of the perceived stressed syllables, from rising F_0 contours, and long-duration high-energy syllabic nuclei (Lea, 1973a; Lea and Kloker, 1975). Less reliable but simpler algorithms for phrase boundary detection and stressed syllable location (and determination of rate of speech) were developed and tested at SDC (Bernstein, et al., 1976), but no data is available on their utility in the SDC (or any other) system. Harpy used minimum and maximum phonetic durations as conditions on the likelihood of a phonetic segment being present, but the significence of such prosodic information in improving performance was not studied.

In general, while the acoustic data and parameter extractions were available for determining important prosodic features within each of the systems, prosodic features played only a minimal role in the final systems. Despite the development of a procedure for using intonational phrase boundaries in the BBN parser, no system actually used prosodic features to determine large-unit linguistic structures and to aid syntactic parsing. However, the facilities

are available for future use in studies of prosodic aids to speech understanding.

We reserve for Sec. 17-4.7 discussions of _experimental_ research conducted
on prosodic regularities. For further discussion of prosodic aids to speech
recognition, refer to Chap. 8.

17-4.5 Syntax, Semantics, and Pragmatics

Also of interest were the distinct _syntactic_ methods in the project, including the augmented transition network (ATN) grammar at BBN that combined
syntax and semantics into "pragmatic" grammars, and the SRI "total language
description" that focused on the grammar of speech as it is actually spoken,
not as it is described in a textbook model. While the incorporating of semantic information into the category symbols of the pragmatic ATN grammar significantly improved the efficiency of the syntactic aspects of the HWIM system (Woods et al., 1976, vol. IV), the resulting grammar was restricted to
highly task-specific constructions. Thus, even though the ATN structure may
handle versatile subsets of English (beyond finite-state or context-free
grammars), the pragmatic grammars actually implemented are highly task-constrained. This is in line with the ARPA SUR goals of a constraining task.
However, it then is a major job to develop a grammar that can handle a new
task, unless it fortuitously uses constructions like the travel-management
categories of "trips", "meetings", "fares", "sponsors", etc. Like Harpy, HWIM
thus requires extensive effort to efficiently handle new tasks. However, new
words and a few new constructions can be readily incorporated without re-
compiling the whole network, such as Harpy requires.

One of the major syntactic advances from the project was the ability to
parse _errorful_ strings, starting at _arbitrary points in the utterance_, so that
parsing was not restricted to the standard left-to-right text processing
methods. Word sequences could be parsed that did not form single non-terminal
"constituents" in the grammar, and could be saved for use with later hypotheses. Hypothesized constructions ("islands") were then extended by predicting adjacent words either to the right or to the left, and appropriate
words were filled in at short gaps between two non-contiguous portions of
hypothesized structure (e.g., cf. Woods, et al., 1976; Reddy, et al., 1976).
Not surprisingly, unconstrained right and left extensions of islands created
combinatorial explosions of hypothesized word sequences, and strategies were
(and are still) needed to constrain such island driving proceduring, such as
only using highly reliable (especiallymultiple-word) islands, and controlling
directions of extension (see Sec. 17-3.2). Parsing in the presence of error
requires abilities to handle and set priorities on alternative interpretations, and Harpy's beam search technique seems to be one of the best methods
to come out of the ARPA SUR project. Harpy's pre-compiled integrated network
was also particularly effective for constraining the possible word sequences
to be tested. HEARSAY II used constraints on word pairs that can be time-
adjacent to constrain sequences before higher-level syntactic analysis was
done.

Semantic networks, discourse constraints, and task constraints were also
included in the systems. For examples, HEARSAY I used chess board configurations plus legal and plausible moves, to help determine what was said in a
voice chess game. Allowable "next steps" in the assembly of apparatus were
to be used in the SRI/SDC system, and plausible things to say about trips,
meetings, budgets, etc., were incorporated into HWIM's "TRIP" component. SRI
conducted protocol analyses and used partitioned semantic networks and discourse information (such as antecedents for pronouns) in the development of

their "top end" components for a speech understanding system. However, semantic and pragmatic constraints had little impact on the performance of the final ARPA SUR systems. Response generation was also included in the system designs, but had no significant impact on final performance and was not even demonstrated in most final system tests. It might be said that, besides handling the error and island driving involved with speech, the ARPA SUR efforts in higher-level linguistics primarily served as users of previous ideas rather than as creators of new concepts.

Of major importance for future work was the development of methods for measuring phonetic and lexical ambiguity and language and task complexity. The syntactic branching factor (Goodman, 1976), while not a totally adequate measure of language complexity, is a major improvement over earlier measures like vocabulary size and the number of syntactic productions or non-terminals in a grammar. Goodman's concept of measuring complexity by information-loss in a recognition "channel" is also intrinsic in later measures, like "entropy" (Levinson, 1977) and "perplexity" (Bahl, et al., 1978).

17-4.6 Experimental Research

Not all of the research results in the ARPA SUR project could be directly incorporated into computer programs during the rush to complete the final demonstration systems. Also, while it was not a primary objective of the project to extend the basic knowledge of the speech signal, several significant contributions came from experimental research conducted by the system-builders and the specialist contractors.

We already noted in Sec. 17-3 several experiments with system structures, contributions of various knowledge sources, and associations between complexity and recognition accuracy. BBN introduced an interesting concept of "incremental simulations" whereby humans simulate the functions of system components until their actions are understood sufficiently to be implemented (Woods, 1975). Simulation studies may continue to be useful in guiding future system designs.

BBN researchers also explored how humans use phonetic information in spectrograms to hypothesize words in sentences, when the spectrographic display is "windowed" within 300 ms segments to prevent syntactic and semantic context from aiding recognition (Klatt and Stevens, 1972). One third of all phonetic segments were transcribed without error, while another 40% were partially identified error-free. As might be expected, they found that stressed cardinal vowels /ɑ, i, u /, single prestressed voiceless consonants, and single nasals had particularly low error rates. This agrees with Sperry Univac's experiments showing that single sonorant consonants and phonetic segments in stressed syllables were more reliably categorized by five different automatic (machine) transcriptions than were unstressed or reduced vowels or obstruents (Lea, 1973c; Chap. 8, Fig. 8-1). Only 3% of the vowels were undetected in the spectrograms, which is confirmed by usual high accuracies in machine detection of syllabic nuclei and vowels. Front-back distinctions were difficult to reliably make, and this too has been evident in automatic vowel labeling programs, including in the final ARPA SUR systems.

The transcribers were then asked to identify the words in the spectrograms. Klatt and Stevens estimated that for words containing 4 or 5 phonemes, the probability of correctly identifying the word was only about 0.25 (or less). However, word identification was greatly assisted by having a computer offer a list of words whose sound structures were similar to the transcribed sequence, and the transcriber could then select the best word. (A similar procedure was later used in the SDC lexical subsetter.) Indeed, in every case where the computer hypothesized the correct word, it was recognized and accepted by the experimenter. These experiments supported the idea of introducing word verification into HWIM and other systems.

Haskins Laboratories also conducted experiments on human detection of words from spectrograms. Their method was to match portions of the spectrogram of a sentence with reference spectrograms for alternative words. They found that even when most words were incorrectly matched, the number of syllables in the hypothesized word sequence generally agreed with the actual sentence. Thus, syllabic units were reliably detected. Feedback of a reference spectrogram (that is, acoustic "verification") for each hypothesized word did <u>not</u> help identify words unless most hypothesized words were already correct. As is now well-established, they found that <u>manner</u> and voicing of consonants were considerably more reliably detected than place of articulation. Haskin's researchers also explored perceptual guidelines for defining better <u>distance measures</u> for phonetic analysis (Mermelstein, 1976), and the dominant resonance in the front cavity of the talker's vocal tract was the best formant cue to <u>place</u> of articulation.

The ARPA SUR project required human transcriptions or judgments about the speech, as standards for evaluating machine results, so extensive work was done (primarily at SCRL and Sperry Univac) on repeatable and reliable techniques for providing orthographic, phonemic, phonetic, and prosodic transcriptions. The development of the ARPABET (cf. Chap. 6) as an agreed upon set of quasi-phonemic units was useful. SCRL transcribed 34 discourses orthographically and phonemically (using the ARPABET), and transcribed portions of 10 discourses in detailed phonetic form. SCRL also developed programs for generating subdictionaries, searching large databases or lexicons for various phonetic sequences or phonemes, or computing frequency of occurrence information within discourses. SCRL also selected final test sentences for the CMU and BBN systems.

A valuable part of the legacy from the project is the set of <u>speech data bases</u> compiled for various system tests and other purposes. CMU collected over 1,000 sentences, plus strings of digits. BBN and SDC each collected and processed several hundred sentences, and SDC and SRI collected 30 protocols of interactions. Other sentences were recorded and processed by intermediate systems like the Lincoln System, HEARSAY I, SPEECHLIS, and the SRI system. This listing is undoubtedly incomplete. Since designing and recording of speech data bases are   time consuming and expensive processes in testing aspects of recognition, we would recommend to speech researchers that they consider using the extensive data bases compiled during ARPA SUR. Each system builder, of course, has to develop a data base to test his system, so that many sentences are usually recorded, transcribed, digitized, and processed. Some particular data bases that would be appropriate for "benchmark" tasks for testing future systems would be those used to test the successful HARPY system. To compare alternative systems, they need to be tested with equivalent tasks and the same speech data, since we currently don't know how to decide whether system A that yields 50% correct understanding on a difficult task is better or worse than system B that yields 90% correct understanding on an easy task.

Speech data bases were also developed to test specific <u>components</u> of systems, such as acoustic phonetic and prosodic tests made with 84 sentences (21 by each of four talkers) that phonetician Peter Ladefoged carefully transcribed (giving phonetic segments, stress levels, and time boundaries) for SDC. A large data base of 1100 sentences, each recorded by three talkers, was developed at Sperry Univac to study prosodic patterns and a few phonetic phenomena in various English sentence structures. SCRL compiled a large database of over 10,000 seconds of discourses, interviews, and separate sentences, and provided transcriptions for 30 protocols. It still remains an important task for the speech community to catalog all such speech data bases and make them available to other researchers.

One major area in which knowledge of the sound structure of spoken sentences was advanced was in prosodics. Besides developing computer programs for prosodic analysis (including algorithms for F_0 tracking, syllabification, intonational phrase boundary detection, and stressed syllable location), Sperry Univac (cf. Lea, 1976) also conducted experiments that demonstrated the following useful regularities:

- Automatic phonetic labeling schemes work more accurately in stressed syllables. Stressed syllables are islands of phonetic and phonemic reliability.

- Listeners can consistently determine which syllables in connected speech are stressed, and machine detection of stress could be expected to be (at best) 95% correct.

- Certain word categories (nouns, verbs, etc.; cf. Chap. 8) are consistently stressed, except that subordination (and coordination with repetition of parts of the structure) will decrease the perceived stress levels. Stress levels may help determine sentence structures.

- Cues to phrase boundaries are found in intonation "valleys" (fall-rise contours), unusually long intervals between stressed syllables, and phrase-final lengthening of vowels and sonorants. Distinct durations of pause, and large F_0 variations, occur at clause and sentence boundaries.

- Time intervals between stresses are a good measure of speech rate, and correlate well with frequency of occurrence of errors in phonetic labeling (i.e., indicate where phonological distortions occur).

- Intonational phrase boundaries could help select structural hypotheses in a syntactic parser, and showed promise of more quickly finding the correct parse in the HWIM system.

- A prosodically-guided speech understanding strategy was defined (Lea, Medress, and Skinner, 1975).

These prosodics studies substantially improved the evidence that prosodic information can be used to aid speech recognition, and defined explicit ways for using prosodics in aiding phonetic and phonological analysis, word selections, and parsing. Yet, we still await any substantial use of prosodic information in speech understanding systems, and extensive basic research about prosodic correlates of linguistic structure still must be undertaken (Lea, 1976; also, Chap. 8 of this book).

Further details about the technical contributions of the ARPA SUR project are to be found in the final reports of the various contractors (Bernstein, et al., 1976; Reddy, et al., 1976; Walker, et al., 1976; Woods, et al., 1976;

Cooper, 1976; Lea, 1976; Hanson, 1976) and in publications and references
listed therein. BBN produced (in the years 1974 to 1976 alone) 39 presentations and publications, six quarterly technical reports, and a five volume
final report. Thirty five reports and publications were listed in the SDC
final report. SRI listed 22 publications and reports, and CMU's list included
57 reports, 11 journal articles, 10 chapters in books, three conference proceedings and books, and 53 papers presented at conferences and workshops.
The project also produced over 200 informal technical notes ("SUR notes").

17-5. PRIMARY CONTRIBUTIONS

In this section, we assess the various contributions of the ARPA SUR project that have already been detailed in Sec. 17-3 and 17-4. We consider some
expert opinions about the ARPA SUR contributions (Sec. 17-5.1), our assessment of the relative significance of the various contributions (Sec. 17-5.2),
and a summary of the resulting advances in the state of the art (Sec. 17-5.3).

17-5.1 Expert Opinions About ARPA SUR Work

To guide us in our assessment of primary ARPA SUR contributions, we visit-
ed all ARPA SUR contractors and almost all of the active speech recognition
groups in the United States, and conferred with other colleagues, including
workers from Japan, France, Germany, Canada, Poland, and Australia. We interviewed over 100 workers in speech recognition, and distributed a 30-page
questionaire to over 160 such workers (with only 34 formal replies), soliciting
opinions about the ARPA SUR project, the best current techniques in recognition, and the future needs and trends. Survey results are detailed in an
unpublished contract report (Lea and Shoup, 1978c, Appendix). Some of the
issues about which there was most agreement were that the ARPA SUR project
was ambitious and needed, and that it resulted in a significant advancement
bordering on a breakthrough.

When given a list of topics to rank order, the 34 respondents to the
questionaire gave average rankings which indicated that primary contributions
of the project (in decreasing order of significance) were in:

1. Control strategy and the integration of various knowledge
   sources;
2. Segmentation and labeling of phonetic units;
3. Word matching (and verification) procedures;
4. Phonological rules;
5. Prosodic analysis;
6. Acoustic phonetic analysis; and
7. Scoring procedures.

When the respondents were given the opportunity to write their own lists of
primary contributions, the most frequently mentioned contributions could be
grouped into the following categories (with numbers of explicit mentions as
indicated): system structure and control (21 mentions); phonological rules
(8); acoustic phonetics (7); parsing and higher-level linguistics (5) and
prosodics (4).

The significance of the ARPA SUR project is partly reflected in the fact
that HARPY, HEARSAY II, and HWIM were considered to be among the best current
speech understanding systems, along with the independently-developed IBM
system. A large majority agreed that the independent supporting research
efforts conducted by specialist contractors constituted a good aspect of the

project.

Other details of those expert opinions are beyond the scope of this chapter, and there is also some doubt about the representativeness of the 34 completed questionnaires, almost half of which came from former ARPA SUR workers. (However, it is noteworthy that the respondents had an _average_ experience of 10 years work in speech recognition, so they do represent an elite group of experts in the field.) We instead present next _our own_ overall assessments for which we take sole responsibility, but which we believe generally reflect the opinions and evaluations of most of the 100 or more experts with whom we have conferred.

17-5.2 Relative Significances of Various Contributions

Figure 17-7 illustrates our attempt at assessing the relative significances of various contributions from the project. Contributions with scores of "1" are considered the most significant, then come those whose bars reach level "2", then "3", and so on. Notice that major categories of significance include: meeting the system specifications (Sec. 17-5.2.1), providing several system control structures for speech understanding (Sec. 17-5.2.2), studying system control and search techniques (Sec. 17-5.2.3), studying linguistic constraints and system performances (Sec. 17-5.2.4), developing needed components or knowledge sources (Sec. 17-5.2.5), and conducting experimental research about speech analysis techniques (Sec. 17-5.2.6). Our listing here of primary contributions is unavoidably redundant for those who have carefully studied the contributions listed in Sec. 17-3 and 17-4, but the assignment of significances should be helpful.

17-5.2.1 _Meeting the System Goals_ - It is certainly significant that the project met the challenging system goals for understanding continuously-spoken sentences. While the attained _accuracy_ was a significant success, the handling of _large vocabularies_ and dealing with all the peculiar coarticulations and ambiguities of _continuous speech_ were also important. Researchers and system developers would be ill-advised to forget that this was accomplished by effective use of linguistic _constraints_. Of lesser, but still fairly high, significance were the _moderate speed_, _practical input environment_, and _multiple speakers_ involved in the final system performances.

17-5.2.2 _System Structures_ - Ultimately more significant than the accuracy of the final systems was the major stride in developing _alternative system structures for speech understanding_. The project focused attention on the large combinatorial space of alternative system designs, and showed advantages and disadvantages of many experimental system structures.

Harpy's success makes it an outstanding contribution, yet long after it's 1976 accuracy scores are out of date, its value will linger in its methods of _integrating knowledge into a composite pronunciation network_ and efficiently searching the network for acceptable pronunciations with the "_beam search technique_". It is the best available system for small recognizers of spoken sentences, and it will remain a _benchmark system_ for assessing future systems.

Harpy has its drawbacks, including the complex (costly and time-consuming) processes of determining allophonic templates, determining all dictionary pronunciations, handling word-juncture phenomena, compiling the network, and training for each talker. It does not lend itself to easy incremental modification or improvement (such as adding new words or structures). Its extendability to more complex tasks is uncertain, and the "habitability" (or ease of learning) of its finite state language is in question.

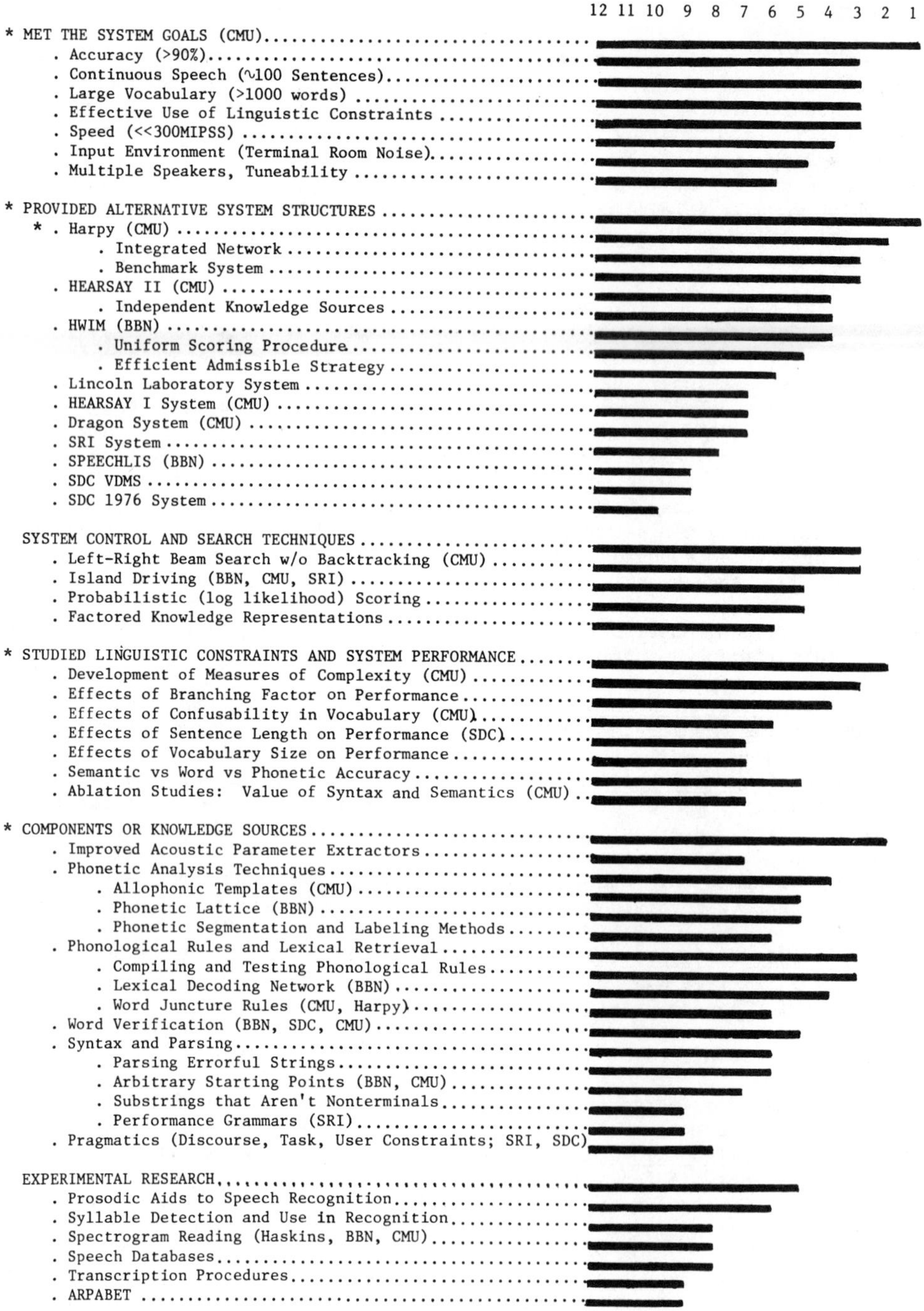

```
* MET THE SYSTEM GOALS (CMU).....................................
    . Accuracy (>90%)............................................
    . Continuous Speech (~100 Sentences)........................
    . Large Vocabulary (>1000 words) ...........................
    . Effective Use of Linguistic Constraints ..................
    . Speed (<<300MIPSS) ........................................
    . Input Environment (Terminal Room Noise)...................
    . Multiple Speakers, Tuneability ...........................

* PROVIDED ALTERNATIVE SYSTEM STRUCTURES .......................
    * . Harpy (CMU) .............................................
        . Integrated Network ...................................
        . Benchmark System .....................................
    . HEARSAY II (CMU) ..........................................
        . Independent Knowledge Sources ........................
    . HWIM (BBN) ................................................
        . Uniform Scoring Procedure.............................
        . Efficient Admissible Strategy ........................
    . Lincoln Laboratory System .................................
    . HEARSAY I System (CMU) ....................................
    . Dragon System (CMU) .......................................
    . SRI System ................................................
    . SPEECHLIS (BBN) ...........................................
    . SDC VDMS ..................................................
    . SDC 1976 System ...........................................

SYSTEM CONTROL AND SEARCH TECHNIQUES ...........................
    . Left-Right Beam Search w/o Backtracking (CMU) ............
    . Island Driving (BBN, CMU, SRI) ...........................
    . Probabilistic (log likelihood) Scoring...................
    . Factored Knowledge Representations .......................

* STUDIED LINGUISTIC CONSTRAINTS AND SYSTEM PERFORMANCE.........
    . Development of Measures of Complexity (CMU) ..............
    . Effects of Branching Factor on Performance...............
    . Effects of Confusability in Vocabulary (CMU).............
    . Effects of Sentence Length on Performance (SDC)..........
    . Effects of Vocabulary Size on Performance................
    . Semantic vs Word vs Phonetic Accuracy....................
    . Ablation Studies: Value of Syntax and Semantics (CMU)....

* COMPONENTS OR KNOWLEDGE SOURCES ...............................
    . Improved Acoustic Parameter Extractors...................
    . Phonetic Analysis Techniques .............................
        . Allophonic Templates (CMU) ...........................
        . Phonetic Lattice (BBN) ...............................
        . Phonetic Segmentation and Labeling Methods...........
    . Phonological Rules and Lexical Retrieval .................
        . Compiling and Testing Phonological Rules.............
        . Lexical Decoding Network (BBN).......................
        . Word Juncture Rules (CMU, Harpy).....................
    . Word Verification (BBN, SDC, CMU)........................
    . Syntax and Parsing........................................
        . Parsing Errorful Strings..............................
        . Arbitrary Starting Points (BBN, CMU)................
        . Substrings that Aren't Nonterminals..................
        . Performance Grammars (SRI)...........................
    . Pragmatics (Discourse, Task, User Constraints; SRI, SDC).

EXPERIMENTAL RESEARCH...........................................
    . Prosodic Aids to Speech Recognition......................
    . Syllable Detection and Use in Recognition................
    . Spectrogram Reading (Haskins, BBN, CMU)..................
    . Speech Databases..........................................
    . Transcription Procedures..................................
    . ARPABET ..................................................
```

Fig. 17-7. Primary ARPA SUR contributions and their relative significances.
(1= most; 12= least significant of the notable contributions;
*= highly significant contributions of score 3, 2, or 1)

Among all the other system structures investigated in the project, HEAR-SAY II and HWIM offer two notable ARPA SUR contributions. HEARSAY II offers a promising contrast to Harpy, in its structure of independently operating knowledge sources which can be separately tested and evaluated, and modified. It is probably the easiest structure to use for testing out new ideas within old components, or adding new knowledge sources, such as prosodics or user models. HWIM, on the other hand, offers some excellent traditionally important knowledge sources that are relatively fixed in form (and somewhat more difficult to alter), but which may be used in a variety of control strategies, including "admissable" strategies that are guaranteed to find the best possible interpretation of the detected phonetic string. As noted later in Fig. 17-7, among HWIM's notable contributions in <u>components</u> and recognition <u>knowledge sources</u> are its lexical decoding network, its phonetic lattice, its parametric word verifier, and its uniform (log likelihood or probabilistic) procedures for scoring hypotheses at all levels in the analysis.

It should be noted that HWIM, and to some degree, HEARSAY II also, were not carefully adjusted, tested with extensive data, or adequately analyzed to determine their weak or strong components. As HWIM developers have noted (Chap. 14), HWIM was just barely operational at the time of the final demonstrations, with half the vocabulary totally new to the system, some components totally untested and others not sufficiently adjusted, and the promising "shortfall density" strategy not operating during the main tests. While Harpy's success illustrates the value of freezing components and strategies early enough to permit extensive testing and "fine-tuning" of the system and its components, the final performance results for HEARSAY II and HWIM cannot be taken as accurate indicators of their ultimate potentials. Extensive performance evaluation studies were proposed, and still might be appropriate to undertake. If so, it would be useful to comparatively evaluate the HEARSAY II and HWIM systems and their individual components, perhaps by testing on a common task. Documentation of such complete performance evaluation could prove useful to developers of future speech understanding systems.

Earlier systems developed during the project became "throw-away systems" that guided the design of the final systems, but did not generally represent the best candidates for use in future speech understanding work. HEARSAY I (like HEARSAY II) still seems to be valuable for its ability to readily permit insertions of new components, or deletion of components to establish the specific contribution of each component. The Lincoln Laboratory intermediate system was impressively successful, and influenced HWIM substantially. Dragon was the predecessor of Harpy, but also influenced the later designs of the IBM systems (Bahl, et al., 1978).

17-5.2.3 <u>System Control and Search Techniques</u> - Significant contributions were made in experimenting with various system control and search strategies. Harpy's strict left-to-right search without backtracking helped limit the combinatorial expansion of alternative word sequences to hypothesize, while HEARSAY II and HWIM's island driving from arbitrary starting points in the utterance tended to create combinatorial explosions in alternative extensions of previously hypothesized word sequences. It appears that island driving, or middle-out analysis of an utterance, can be effective only if the islands are highly reliable, such as with multiple-word islands.

The systems converged on the idea of probabilistic (or log likelihood) scoring of hypotheses, and BBN developed a valuable uniform scoring procedure for relating assessments of hypotheses at all levels in a system's analysis. However, there was general agreement that <u>a priori</u> probabilities, whereby alternative hypotheses are selected on the basis of their frequency of occur-

409

rence in the language (or in previous data collections), should not be used, since they can cause the system to fatally reject correct but unexpected utterances or words. Unless one collects hours of statistical training data, such as the IBM system does (Bahl, et al., 1978), a priori probabilities can be in error due to fortuitous absence of acceptable utterances in the training data.

Another prominent trend from the project was the growing use of "factored knowledge representations" (cf. Chap. 14), whereby high-scoring knowledge from early hypotheses is used (at the same or other levels) in efficiently testing later hypotheses that also suggest similar local interpretations. (See Sec. 17-3.2.)

17-5.2.4 Studies of How Linguistic Constraints Influence Performance - A primary contribution of the ARPA SUR project was its simplifying of the recognition task by constraining it markedly via syntactic, semantic, and task constraints. This is comparable to lexical constraints in a small-vocabulary isolated-word recognizer. Because continuous speech recognition is a multiple-dimension problem, it can be constrained in many ways, and one question addressed by ARPA SUR work concerned which constraints were most effective in improving performance. System performances were found to be more closely associated with the branching factor of the language than with any other system variable. Harpy thus can not be unequivocably appraised "winner over HWIM, since its task was (on one measure) almost an order of magnitude easier. Interesting studies also showed that the confusions among similar words in the vocabulary influence system performance more than the numerical size of the vocabulary (Goodman, 1976). Length of utterance is also more likely to influence recognition than vocabulary size (Bernstein, et al., 1976; also Chap. 12). Focus of attention is now properly on language complexity (measured by branching factor, or perhaps by "entropy" or "perplexity"), word similarities, and utterance length, not vocabulary size.

Since final semantic accuracy (as high as 95%) was much higher than might be predicted from the low phonetic identification accuracy (40-50%) and multiplicative errors in word identification, it is evident that linguistic constraints substantially aided recognition. This was also graphically illustrated from ablation studies (comparisons of results with versus without syntactic and semantic components). These studies support the basic principles underlining the ARPA SUR effort, that acoustic information alone is not enough, that multiple sources of knowledge are needed, and that accurate "understanding" is different from accurate phonetic or word sequence "recognition" (Newell, 1975).

It will be important in the future to extend these valuable contributions from complexity metrics, ablation studies, and various system performance metrics, to provide quantitative ways of assessing performance of alternative systems even when they work on different tasks and with different knowledge sources and control strategies.

17-5.2.5 Components or Knowledge Sources - Major improvements were made in many previous recognition procedures, including acoustic parameter extractors, detailed procedures for detecting and identifying various vowels and consonants, and improved methods for word matching, but Fig. 17-7 lists only the most noteworthy new contributions. Formant tracking from LPC spectra, improved autocorrelation methods for pitch tracking, and accurate procedures for detecting syllabic nuclei were among the improved acoustic analysis tools. In phonetic segmentation and labeling, Harpy's 98 allophonic templates for classifying short sub-phonemic segments are considered a significant contribution, as is HWIM's phonetic lattice. However, we still don't know which of these (or other) phonetic analysis techniques is best for future work. Experts we have surveyed overwhelmingly agree that better acoustic phonetic analyses (or "front end" components) are high priority aspects in developing future speech understanding systems.

BBN's lexical decoding network is considered a substantial contribution to efficient phonological analysis and word hypothesizing, and is particularly noteworthy for its handling of influences of words on sound structures of neighboring words. Harpy's juncture rules perform a similar function, but are not well documented or readily learned by the developer or user of the system. The cooperative compilation and testing of a large set of phonological rules was a major contribution. Word verification (especially HWIM's parametric word verifier) is another interesting contribution.

In syntax and semantics, the most noteworthy advances were the ability to parse errorful strings, work both directions from arbitrary starting points in the structure, and parse word sequences (substrings) that do not constitute single nonterminals in the grammar. Prosodic aids to parsing are promising but largely untested additions. While interesting experiments and a few implemented procedures regarding pragmatics were introduced, much more seems possible in the areas of using discourse constraints, task constraints, and user models. The ARPA SUR project served more as a _user_ of higher-level linguistic components than as developer of new linguistic ideas and techniques.

17-5.2.6 _Experimental Research_ - Experiments at BBN, Haskins Laboratories, nd CMU showed that humans can transcribe speech from reading spectrograms, without knowledge of the linguistic context, and will be accurate about categorizing 70% of the phonemes in the utterances, and can be aided in identifying words in the spectrograms by computer-assisted survey of words of similar sound structure. Klatt and Stevens (1972) found that stressed cardinal vowels (/i, a, u/), prestressed consonants, and nasals that aren't in consonantal clusters were most reliably identified. Sperry Univac also showed that vowels and obstruents in stressed syllables were most reliably categorized by several available _machine_ transcriptions of speech. Vowels and syllabic nuclei were shown by such studies to be very reliably detected. Other experiments (principally at Sperry Univac) showed the importance of stressed syllables, intonational phrase boundaries, and rate of speech in recognition. Methods were developed for locating stressed syllables automatically, and extensive experiments showed that listeners could consistently decide which syllables were stressed. Valuable regularities were found in stress assignment for various word categories and phrase structures, and procedures were outlined for using such prosodic cues in speech recognition.

An agreed-upon ARPABET for transcribing and mechanically classifying speech sounds into phoneme-like units was developed, and procedures for orthographic, phonemic, and phonetic transcription were defined. Many large speech databases recorded and used during the project should be suitable for future research and system developments. Unfortunately, these databases, and the many computer algorithms for various aspects of recognition, have not been cataloged or made readily available to other researchers, and may be particularly difficult to obtain and use now that most (our survey shows 65%) of the ARPA SUR workers are dispersed and _not_ working on speech understanding or allied projects. The only contractors that still have most of their key ARPA SUR personnel are BBN and SRI.

17-5.3 Advances in the State of the Art

Figure 17-8 summarizes some important aspects of the <u>advances in the state of speech recognition technology</u> which the ARPA SUR project produced (cf. Fig. 17-1). Our discussion here closely parallels the description in Sec. 17-2.1 of the 1971 state of the art, so that the reader can readily make comparisons.

◉ COMMERCIAL ISOLATED WORD
    RECOGNIZERS

> ◉ SMALL VOCABULARIES
>   (10-200 Words)
> ◉ ACCURACY = 99%
> ◉ 6 COMMERCIAL SOURCES,
>   REDUCED COSTS
> ◉ HIGH-QUALITY SPEECH
>   OR TELEPHONE

• MORE DATA ON ACOUSTIC
  CHARACTERISTICS OF SENTENCES

• COMPILATIONS, TESTS, AND USAGE
  OF PHONOLOGICAL RULES

• USEFUL MEASURES OF
  COMPLEXITY AND PERFORMANCE

• ADVANCED SCORING PROCEDURES
  AND ADMISSABLE STRATEGIES

◉ PROTOTYPE RECOGNIZERS OF WORD
  SEQUENCES AND SENTENCES
  (Bell Laboratories, IBM, NEC,
  Sperry Univac)

    KEY: • ARPA SUR CONTRIBUTIONS
          ◉ Non-ARPA CONTRIBUTIONS

• HARPY CONTINUOUS SPEECH RECOGNIZER
  1,000 words, BF=33, Accuracy=95%

• SEVERAL MULTIPLE-KNOWLEDGE-SOURCE
  SYSTEMS

> • HEARSAY I, II; HWIM; others
>
>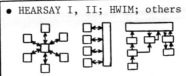
>
> • Systems With Acoustic Phonetics,
>   Phonology, Word Matching, Syntax,
>   Semantics, Pragmatics, and Some
>   Prosodics
>
> • Clear Evidence About Utility of
>   Syntax and Semantics
>
> • Speech Parsers Handle Errors and
>   Arbitrary Starting Points
>
> • Guidelines for Prosodic Aids to
>   Recognition
>
> • Large Lexicons That Handle Pro-
>   nunciation Variablities and Word
>   Boundary Effects
>
> • Improved Phonetic Unit Detectors;
>   Allophonic Templates and Phonetic
>   Lattice

Fig. 17-8. The state of ASR after the ARPA SUR Project (1976)

A primary contribution of the ARPA SUR project was in showing the feasibility of continuous speech recognition, so that now <u>restricted forms of sentence understanding</u> have attained a high (95%) level of accuracy comparable to that in the prototype word recognizers of 1971. Vocabularies of 1000 words <u>have</u> been attacked, and, what's more, experiments showed that large vocabularies did <u>not</u> lead to the expected combinatoric problems of major magnitude. System performance is only slightly degraded in expanding vocabularies from 200 to 1000 words. Several systems now <u>have</u> been built that use multiple forms of incomplete knowledge and any of several interesting control structures, to handle spoken sentences. In addition to previously available and <u>improved</u> acoustic phonetic and word matching procedures, ARPA SUR systems incorporated phonological rules, some prosodic features, word verifiers, speech parsers that could handle errorful hypothesized word sequences and arbitrary starting points for analysis, and semantic and pragmatic analyzers.

Not only is there now at least one adequate system (Harpy) and a few other partially-successful and promising speech understanding systems (particularly HEARSAY II and HWIM); even more important is the advanced knowledge attained about alternative system designs and improved components or knowledge sources. Promising ideas and techniques were developed in each aspect of system operation, and some experimental evidence is available about the effectiveness of alternative analysis techniques. A few experiments also advanced our corporate knowledge about the acoustic characteristics of phonetic segments and prosodics in spoken sentences. Phonological rules have been gathered from the literature and from new studies, and implemented and tested for their effectiveness in aiding speech understanding. Several effective methods have been devised and tested for using phonetic and prosodic data and phonological rules along with higher-level linguistic constraints. Syntactic parsers now <u>can</u> deal effectively with errorful input strings, and "island driving" ("middle-out" parsing from arbitrary starting points) is possible, though experiments showed that such island-driving is likely to yield combinatorial explosions of alternative word sequences unless the islands are very reliably identified and are extended in well-controlled ways. In addition to traditional bottom-up and top-down control strategies, we now have several effective new strategies, including the Harpy integrated network with beam search, the HEARSAY II "blackboard" model of an "hypothesize and test" strategy, the various BBN strategies, and many others experimented with at BBN, CMU, SRI, Lincoln Laboratory, and SDC.

As researchers had expected, final accuracy of semantic understanding (e.g., 95% in Harpy) was clearly shown to be different from accuracy of phonetic segmentation (42%) and word matching (97%). Thus, phonetic classification accuracy could be as low as 42% and still allow adequate accuracy of semantic understanding. Studies with HEARSAY I showed that adding <u>syntax</u> to acoustic phonetic recognition procedures increased the semantic accuracy by 25% (from 40% to 65%), and the further addition of a <u>semantic</u> component added another 25% improvement. Evidence is now in that heavy syntactic and semantic constraints substantially aid recognition. The ARPA SUR work added several new measures of task complexity other than vocabulary size or number of words in a sentence; the branching factor was shown to be a good (but not totally adequate) measure of language complexity, and word confusability and entropy were also introduced to help evaluate systems. Finally, speeds of complex speech understanding system are now known, and are expected to soon approach desirable real-time operation, even on moderate-sized computers.

While other systems have since been purported to meet or exceed the 1976 ARPA SUR capabilities, it is good to recall that the growth of other speech recognition projects after the beginning of ARPA SUR is not totally coincidental. That, too, is a fulfillment of an initial ARPA SUR goal, which was to <u>stimulate other projects</u> in continuous speech recognition (Newell, et al., 1971; p. 3). Recognition of continuous speech no longer is an unattained hope; it is an available reality in the form of HARPY-like systems, as well as in other restricted systems like those that recognize connected word sequences at Nippon Electric Company, IBM, Bell Laboratories, and Sperry Univac.

17-6. IMPACT ON FUTURE WORK

Immediately after successfully providing an initial technology base for restricted forms of continuous speech recognition, the ARPA SUR project ended in 1976. Extensive further work is still needed before practical commercial and military uses of speech understanding systems will become widespread. The limited final system tests did not provide a total scientific evaluation, and the HWIM system in particular needed extensive further testing and adjustments. Many "gaps" remain in speech understanding technology. For example, in our survey of expert opinions (Lea and Shoup, 1978a), we found that the following were considered the top-priority aspects of recognition that need attention (listed in descending order of priority, as determined from average rankings for 34 expert respondents):

- Acoustic phonetic analysis;
- Prosodic cues to linguistic structures;
- Performance evaluation;
- Using linguistics to constrain ambiguities;
- System tuning on extensive data;
- Fast or near-real-time processing;
- Scoring procedures; and
- Phonological rules

Figure 17-9 provides a more detailed list of prominent gaps in speech recognition, with our estimate of relative significances of the gaps, in parallel fashion to the list of the ARPA SUR contributions in Fig. 17-7. These areas in need of further work do not imply shortcomings or inadequacies in the ARPA SUR project, but indicate a composite grading of: (a) the importance of specific problems to overall system utility; (b) the degree to which needed performance must still be advanced, despite any previous advances coming from ARPA SUR work or other previous work; and (c) logical needs to answer some questions before others are pursued.

We can only briefly discuss these problem areas and their priorities here. In advancing system goals, studies with practical usage of isolated word recognizers indicate that 97% accuracy is usually needed, and at least that accuracy would probably be needed for the longer spoken sentences. Extensive testing and performance evaluating of total systems and their components is clearly needed for _all_ systems, whether they be isolated word recognizers or speech understanding systems. Work with better use of linguistic constraints and habitable languages seems important, while speed, input channels, and multiple speakers don't appear to be limiting the utility of recognizers. There is no evidence that significantly larger vocabularies are needed.

A four-pronged effort seems to be called for, in which: (1) Harpy-like systems are developed and applied; (2) research systems with independent knowledge sources are developed and used as test beds for various new ideas; (3) experimental research is conducted on topics relevant to speech recognition; and (4) practical applications are addressed. Harpy can be applied to various restricted tasks such as voice entry of cartographic data (Goodman, et al., 1977), training of air traffic controllers (Breaux, 1978; Grady, 1978), and various digit string recognition tasks. Extensions to Harpy that should really pay off include incremental compilation, automatic knowledge acquisition, and introduction of additional knowledge sources (such as pro-sodics). _Research systems_ which permit the introduction and testing of new or improved components are also vitally needed, and should be permitted to test system features like uniform scoring, admissable strategies and reliable island driving. Within those research systems, work is needed on phonetic, phonological, prosodic, and other types of components, with the specific tasks and priorities roughly as indicated in Fig. 17-9. Coupled with recognition studies should be necessary experimental research on prosodic structures, human factors issues (especially concerning what makes a language habitable), comparative evaluation of systems with common tasks, and general character-istics of spoken sentences.

Finally, practical applications should be examined carefully. The initial ARPA SUR goals did not call for explicit applications to military (or

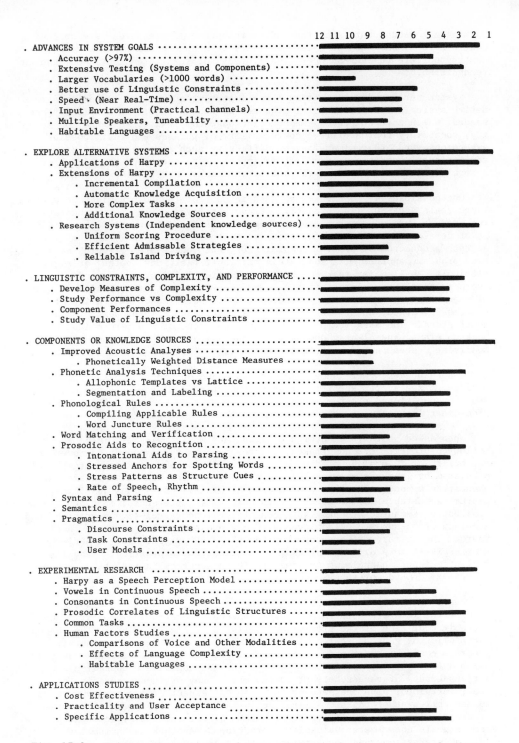

```
                                              12 11 10 9  8  7  6  5  4  3  2  1
. ADVANCES IN SYSTEM GOALS ·······················
  . Accuracy (>97%) ······························
  . Extensive Testing (Systems and Components) ·······
  . Larger Vocabularies (>1000 words) ················
  . Better use of Linguistic Constraints ············
  . Speed⸱ (Near Real-Time) ························
  . Input Environment (Practical channels) ··········
  . Multiple Speakers, Tuneability ·················
  . Habitable Languages ··························

. EXPLORE ALTERNATIVE SYSTEMS ·····················
  . Applications of Harpy ·······················
  . Extensions of Harpy ························
     . Incremental Compilation ··················
     . Automatic Knowledge Acquisition ··············
     . More Complex Tasks ·····················
     . Additional Knowledge Sources ··············
  . Research Systems (Independent knowledge sources) ···
     . Uniform Scoring Procedure ·················
     . Efficient Admissable Strategies ·············
     . Reliable Island Driving ··················

. LINGUISTIC CONSTRAINTS, COMPLEXITY, AND PERFORMANCE ····
  . Develop Measures of Complexity ················
  . Study Performance vs Complexity ···············
  . Component Performances ·····················
  . Study Value of Linguistic Constraints ···········

. COMPONENTS OR KNOWLEDGE SOURCES ·················
  . Improved Acoustic Analyses ··················
     . Phonetically Weighted Distance Measures ·······
  . Phonetic Analysis Techniques ·················
     . Allophonic Templates vs Lattice ·············
     . Segmentation and Labeling ················
  . Phonological Rules ························
     . Compiling Applicable Rules ···············
     . Word Juncture Rules ···················
  . Word Matching and Verification ················
  . Prosodic Aids to Recognition ·················
     . Intonational Aids to Parsing ··············
     . Stressed Anchors for Spotting Words ·········
     . Stress Patterns as Structure Cues ···········
     . Rate of Speech, Rhythm ·················
  . Syntax and Parsing ·······················
  . Semantics ····························
  . Pragmatics ···························
     . Discourse Constraints ··················
     . Task Constraints ·····················
     . User Models ·······················

. EXPERIMENTAL RESEARCH ·······················
  . Harpy as a Speech Perception Model ··············
  . Vowels in Continuous Speech ··················
  . Consonants in Continuous Speech ···············
  . Prosodic Correlates of Linguistic Structures ······
  . Common Tasks ··························
  . Human Factors Studies ·····················
     . Comparisons of Voice and Other Modalities ····
     . Effects of Language Complexity ··············
     . Habitable Languages ··················

. APPLICATIONS STUDIES ·······················
  . Cost Effectiveness ·······················
  . Practicality and User Acceptance ···············
  . Specific Applications ·····················
```

Fig. 17-9. Primary areas in speech recognition technology needing further work.

commercial) needs, but, near the end of the project, pressures were on the contractors to show the near-term military relevance of their work. It is now appropriate to address operational needs for restricted continuous speech recognition.

System performance evaluation is an important adjunct to exploring alternative system structures. Total measures of recognition task complexity are needed, which more completely measure language complexity, sentence complexity, vocabulary confusability, confusability of phrases and their possible extensions, and other dimensions of difficulty such as speaker population, environmental conditions, etc. It is important to determine the _causes_ of recognition errors, and the weak and strong links in system operation.

One possible way to bridge the gaps in current technology might be another large scale ARPA-SUR-like project. If another large scale speech understanding project were undertaken, our respondents (Lea and Shoup, 1978c) would favor development of several alternative systems, particularly if the systems address a spectrum of problem complexities, with one system directed at an easy problem, another at a moderately difficult task, and another at a quite difficult, challenging task. Other organizational features endorsed were the use of supporting research efforts conducted by specialist contractors, plus mid-term evaluations of the systems, extensive performance evaluation of the systems developed, and close interactions and frequent interchanges among contractors. The ARPA SUR project taught the value of mid-term milestones, back-up plans, and clearly demonstrated successes, rather than working on or modifying system features right up to the last minute.

The respondents were uncertain, or had mixed opinions, about completely defining fixed system specifications that must be achieved by fixed dates, and they questioned program management by committee. As one colleague said, "You can't legislate or schedule scientific breakthroughs."

When asked what system design choices they would make if a large scale follow-on project were undertaken, the respondents recommended: a moderate vocabulary of several hundred words or more; 10 to 100 speakers; three levels of system or language complexity; practical input through close talking microphones, telephones, or other communication channels of various qualities; systems adjustable to the speaker with only a few utterances; more substantial use of semantic and pragmatic constraints; near-real-time operation; and accuracy of 95-99%, to be achieved within a project period of three to five years. The primary differences from the ARPA SUR project are: a series of progressively more difficult tasks; more attention to practical needs like realistic input channels, many speakers, high accuracy in real time; and no programmed demand for success on a fixed deadline.

While such opinions may be of general interest, we do not necessarily endorse the idea of another large-scale speech understanding project. Admittedly, for each of the problem areas listed in Fig. 17-9 or in the respondents' list of gaps presented at the beginning of this section, separate programs could be undertaken. Yet, _coordinated_ programs should obviously be defined that permit, and indeed _promote_, interactions and cooperation among various groups of researchers or developers. Many of these specific topics are intertwined, with the methods taken in one aspect affecting the best way to accomplish other tasks. A large scale (ARPA-SUR-like) research program of cooperative and competitive developments of alternative systems with common goals does foster valuable interactions. Another mechanism for stimulating interactions and cooperation is the recently-established voice interactions Technical Advisory Group (or "TAG") set up among United States

Governmental funders of speech recognition work.

We recommend the establishment of two or three "speech science centers" with speech and linguistic expertise, powerful computer facilities, and mechanisms for visiting researchers to use such facilities to advance their work on various aspects of recognition, and to incorporate their advancements into the resident recognition systems. Such speech science centers could act as clearinghouses for useful speech databases, reports, research results, phonological rules, scoring procedures, recognition algorithms, and system structures, and could always offer working recognizers as research tools and testbeds for further advances. The centers could offer seminars and workshops for acoustic phonetic analysis, prosodics, phonological rules, interspeaker differences, etc. If affiliated with universities, they could provide the training and on-the-job experience appropriate for excellent new scholars in the field. Other speech research and development programs could be undertaken at the centers, such as in speech synthesis, speech transmission systems, clinical speech studies, and linguistic analysis. With stable funding from a variety of sources, and visiting scholars on sabbaticals or brief collaborative interactions, plus excellent facilities, such speech science centers could provide the concentrations of excellence needed to bridge the many gaps in current speech recognition technology.

Given the lead time needed to complete research projects and transfer the research into systems research should begin as soon as possible on improved acoustic phonetic analyses, phonological rules, prosodic analysis methods, and performance metrics and evaluation procedures. A coordinated program in the development of recognizers of several distinct capabilities could then be progressively undertaken.

17-7. REFERENCES

Bahl, L.R., J.K. Baker, P.S. Cohen, A.G. Cole, F. Jelinek, B.L. Lewis, and R.L. Mercer (1978), "Automatic Recognition of Continuously Spoken Sentences from a Finite State Grammar," Proceeding of the 1978 IEEE International Conference on Acoustics, Speech, and Signal Processing, Tulsa, OK., 418-421.

Baker, J.M. (1975) A New Time-Domain Analysis of Human Speech and Other Complex Waveforms, Technical Report CMUCSD, Ph.D. Dissertation, Carnegie-Mellon University, Pittsburgh, PA.

Bernstein, M., et al. (1976), Interactive Systems Research: Final Report to the Director, Advanced Research Projects Agency, for the Period 16 September 1975 to 15 September 1976, Report TM-5243/006/00, Systems Development Corporation, Santa Monica, CA.

Chapanis, A., R.N. Parrish, R.B. Ochsman, and C.D. Weeks (1977), Studies in Interactive Communication: II. The Effects of Four Communication Modes on the Linguistic Performance of Teams during Cooperative Problem Solving, Human Factors, 19, No. 2, 101-126.

Chomsky, N. (1957) Syntactic Structures. The Hague; Mouton.

Cooper, F.S. (1976) Acoustic Cues in Natural Speech: Their Nature and Potential Uses in Speech Recognition, Final Report on ONR Contracts N00014-67-A-0129-002 and N00014-76-C-0591, Haskins Laboratories, New Haven, CT.

Dean, H.H. (1953) Effective Communication. New York: Prentice-Hall.

Fry, D.B. and Denes, P. (1958), The Solution of Some Fundamental Problems in Mechanical Speech Recognition, Language and Speech, 1: 35-38.

Gillman, R.A. (1975), A Fast Frequency Domain Pitch Algorithm, J. Acoust. Soc. Amer., vol. 58, Suppl., Fall, 1975, S62 (A).

Goldberg, H.G. (1975) Segmentation and Labeling of Speech: A Comparative Performance Evaluation, Technical Report CMUCSD, Ph.D. Dissertation, Carnegie-Mellon University, Pittsburgh, PA.

Goodman, G. (1976) Analysis of Languages for Man-Machine Voice Communication, Technical Report CMUCSD, Ph.D. Dissertation (through Stanford University), Computer Science Department, Carnegie-Mellon University, Pittsburgh, PA.

Halle, M. and K.N. Stevens (1962), Speech Recognition: A Model and a Program for Research, IRE Transactions on Information Theory, IT-8: 155-159.

Hanson, B., et al. (1976) Techniques for Natural Speech Processing, ARPA SUR Note 209, Final Report on Contract   , Speech Communications Research Laboratory, Santa Barbara, CA.

Hill, D.R. (1971), Man-Machine Interaction Using Speech, in Advances in Computers (F.L. Alt, M. Rubinoff, and M.C. Yovits, Eds.). New York: Academic Press, 11: 165-230.

Itakura, F. (1975), Minimum Prediction Residual Principle Applied to Speech Recognition, IEEE Transactions on Acoustics Speech, and Signal Processing, Vol. ASSP-23, 67-72.

Klatt, D.H. (1976), A Digital Filter Bank for Spectral Matching, Proc. 1976 IEEE International Conference on Acoustics Speech and Signal Processing, Philadelphia, PA. (IEEE Catalog No. 76CH1067-8 ASSP), 537-540.

Klatt, D.H. (1977), "Review of the ARPA Speech Understanding Project," Journal of the Acoustical Society of America, 62: 1345-1366.

Klatt, D.H. and K.N. Stevens (1972), Sentence Recognition from Visual Examination of Spectrograms and Machine-aided Lexical Searching, Proceedings 1972 Conference on Speech Communication and Processing, IEEE and AFCRL: Bedford, MA., 315-318.

Lea, W.A. (1965), The 'Spectrum' of Weak Generative Powers of Grammars, Mechanical Translation, 9: 10-14.

Lea, W.A. (1969) The Impact of Speech Communication with Computers, Proceedings of the Sixth Space Congress, Vol. 1, Coco Beach, FL; Brevard Printers, March, 1969, pp. 15-19 to 15-31.

Lea, W.A. (1970a) Towards Versatile Speech Communication with Computers, International Journal of Man-Machine Studies, 2: 107-155.

Lea, W.A. (1970b) Evaluating Speech Recognition Work, Journal of the Acoustical Society of America, 47: 1612-1614.

Lea, W.A. (1972), Intonational Cues to the Constituent Structure and Phonemics of Spoken English, Ph.D. Dissertation, School of Electrical Engineering, Purdue University.

Lea, W.A. (1973a), An Approach to Syntactic Recognition Without Phonemics, IEEE Transactions on Audio and Electroacoustics, AU-21: 249-358.

Lea, W.A. (1973b), An Algorithm for Locating Stressed Syllables in Continuous Speech, Journal of the Acoustical Society of America, 55: 411(A).

Lea, W.A. (1973c), Evidence that Stressed Syllables Are the Most Readily Decoded Portions of Continuous Speech, Journal of the Acoustical Society of America, 55: 410(A).

Lea, W.A. (1974), Prosodic Aids to Speech Recognition: IV. A General Strategy for Prosodically-Guided Speech Understanding, Univac Report No. PX;0791. Sperry Univac, DSD, St. Paul, MN.

Lea, W.A. (1976e), Prosodic Aids to Speech Recognition: IX. Acoustic-prosodic Patterns in Selected English Phrase Structrues, Univac Report No. PX11963, Sperry Univac DSD, St. Paul, MN.

Lea, W.A. and D.R. Kloker (1975), Prosodic Aids to Speech Recognition: VI. Timing Cues to Linguistic Structures, Univac Report No. PX11534, Sperry Univac DSD, St. Paul, MN.

Lea, W.A., M.F. Medress, and T.E. Skinner (1975), A Prosodically-guided Speech Understanding Strategy, IEEE Transactions in Acoustics, Speech, and Signal Processing, ASSP-23, 30-38.

Lea, W.A., and J.E. Shoup (1978a), Gaps in the Technology of Speech Understanding, Proc. 1978 IEEE International Conference on Acoustics, Speech, and Signal Processing, Tulsa, OK, (IEEE Catalog No. 78CH1285-6 ASSP), 405-408.

Lea, W.A., and J.E. Shoup (1978b), Recommendations for Advancing Speech Recognition, Journal of the Acoustical Society of America, 63: Supplement 1, S78(A).

Lea, W.A., and J.E. Shoup (1978c), Review of the ARPA SUR Project and Survey of the Speech Understanding Field, Final Report on ONR Contract No. N00014-77-C-0570, Speech Communications Research Laboratory, Santa Barbara, CA.

Lindgren, N. (1965), Machine Recognition of Human Language, IEEE Spectrum Vol. 2, March, April, May issues.

Lowerre, B.T. (1976), The Harpy Speech Recognition System, Technical Report CMUCSD, Ph.D. Dissertation, Carnegie-Mellon University, Pittsburgh, PA.

Makhoul, J., and C.C. Cook (1974), Optimial Number of Poles in a Linear Prediction Model, Journal of the Acoustical Society of America, 56: S14(A).

McCandless, S.S. (1974), Use of Formant Motion in Speech Recognition, Proc. IEEE Symposium on Speech Recognition (IEEE Catalog No. 74H0878-9AE), Carnegie-Mellon University, Pittsburgh, PA., 211.

Medress, M.F., T.E. Skinner, D.R. Kloker, T.C. Diller, and W.A. Lea (1977), "A System for the Recognition of Spoken Connected Word Sequences," Proceedings of the 1977 IEEE International Conference on Acoustics, Speech, and Signal Processing, Hartford, CT, IEEE Catalog No. 77CH1197-3ASSP, 468-473.

Mermelstein, P. (1975), Automatic Segmentation of Speech into Syllabic Units, The Journal of the Acoustical Society of America, 58: 880-883.

Mermelstein, P. (1976), Distance Measures for Speech Recognition: Psychological and Instrumental, in Pattern Recognition and Artificial Intelligence. New York: Acedemic Press, 374-387.

Neuburg, E.P. (1975), Philosophies of Speech Recognition, in Speech Recognition: Invited Papers of the 1974 Symposium. New York: Academic Press, 83-95, (D. R. Reddy, Editor).

Newell, A. (1975), A Tutorial on Speech Understanding Systems. In Speech Recognition: Invited Papers Presented at the 1974 IEEE Symposium (D.R. Reddy, Editor), New York: Academic Press, pp. 3-54.

Newell, A. (1978), Harpy, Production Systems, and Human Cognition, unpublished report, Department of Computer Science, Carnegie-Mellon University, Pittsburgh, PA.

Newell, A., J. Barnett, J. Forgie, C. Green, D.H. Klatt, J.C.R. Licklider, J. Munson, D.R. Reddy, and W.A. Woods (1971), Speech Understanding Systems; Final Report of a Study Group, Carnegie-Mellon University, Pittsburgh, PA. (Reprinted by American Elsevier, Amsterdam, North-Holland, 1973).

Peterson, G.E. (1961), Automatic Speech Recognition Procedures, Language and Speech, 4: 200-219.

Pierce, J.R. (1969), Whither Speech Recognition?, Journal of the Acoustical Society of America, 46: 1049-1051.

Reddy, D.R. (1973), The CMU Speech Understanding Project-Progress Report, October 15, 1973, Department of Computer Science, Carnegie-Mellon University, Pittsburgh, PA.

Reddy, D.R., et al. (1976), Speech Understanding Systems: Summary of Results of the Five Year Research Effort at Carnegie-Mellon University (2nd version), Department of Computer Science, Carnegie-Mellon University, Pittsburgh, PA.

Schwartz, R.H. (1976), Acoustic-Phonetic Experiment Facility for the Study of Continuous Speech, Proc. 1976 Intern. Conf. on Acoustics, Speech, and Signal Processing, Philadelphia, PA., 1-4.

Schwartz, R.H. and V.W. Zue (1976), Acoustic-Phonetic Recognition in BBN SPEECHLIS, Proc. 1976 Intern. Conf. on Acoustics, Speech, and Signal Processing, Philadelphia, PA., 21-24.

Shannon, C.E. and W. Weaver (1949), The Mathematical Theory of Communication. Reprinted 1962, University of Illinois Press, Urbana.

Shockey, L. and D.R. Reddy (1974) Quantitative Analysis of Speech Perception: Results from Transcription of Connected Speech from Unfamiliar Languages, Speech Communication Seminar, Stockholm, Sweden.

Skinner, T. E.(1973), Speech Parameter Extraction: Fundamental Frequency, Spectral, and Formant Frequency Processing, Univac Report No. PX10376, Sperry Univac Defense Systems Division, Univac Park, St. Paul, MN.

Sondhi, M.M. (1968), New Methods of Pitch Extraction, IEEE Transactions on Audio and Electroacoustics, AU-16: 262-266.

Sondhi, M.M. and S.E. Levinson (1977), Relative Difficulty and Robustness of Speech Recognition Tasks that Use Grammatical Constraints, Journal of the Acoustical Society of America, 63: Supplement 1, S64(A).

Vicens, P.J. (1969), Aspects of Speech Recognition by Computer. Technical Report, Stanford University, AI Memo 85, Stanford, CA., (Ph.D. Dissertation).

Walker, D.E., et al. (1976), Speech Understanding Research, Final Technical Report, 15 October 1975 to 14 October 1976, Stanford Research Institute, Menlo Park, CA.

Walker, D.E., et al. (1977), Speech Understanding and AI; AI and Speech Understanding, panel discussion, Proceedings of the Fifth International Joint Conference on Artificial Intelligence, MIT, Cambridge, MA, August 22-25, 1977, Vol. Two, 970-974.

Weinstein, C.J., S.S. McCandless, L.F. Mondshein, and V.W. Zue (1975), "A System for Acoustic-Phonetic Analysis of Continuous Speech," IEEE Transactions on Acoustics, Speech, and Signal Processing, ASSP-23: 54-67.

White, G.M. (1978), Continuous Speech Recognition, Dynamic Programming, Knowledge Nets, and Harpy, Proceedings of Wescon, Los Angeles, CA, September 12-14, 1978, 28/2.

Woods, W.A. (1975), "Motivation and Overview of SPEECHLIS: An Experimental Prototype for Speech Understanding Research," IEEE Transactions on Acoustics, Speech, and Signal Processing, ASSP-23: 2-10.

Woods, W.A., et al. (1976), Speech Understanding Systems, BBN Report Number 3438 (5 volumes), Final Report on ONR Contract No. N00014-75-C-0533, Bolt Beranek and Newman, Cambridge, MA.

PART IV

RECENT DEVELOPMENTS IN SPEECH RECOGNITION

18.

Techniques for Expanding the Capabilities of Practical Speech Recognizers

J. L. Flanagan

S. E. Levinson

L. R. Rabiner

A. E. Rosenberg

Acoustics Research Department
Bell Laboratories
Murray, Hill, New Jersey 07974

ABSTRACT

The purpose of this paper is to give our assessment of the current opportunities and realities of automatic speech recognition. We differentiate between applications which the accumulated understanding and technology can support immediately, and those which require additional research for success. We describe our research experience and give performance data for several word-recognition systems, both talker-dependent and talker-independent. Our experience with programmed syntax analysis for increasing the recognition accuracy of sentence-length word strings is also described. We put forward the view that progress toward the ambitious goal of connected speech recognition might well be achieved through increments of effort directed toward sharply-defined and well-constrained subsets of the recognition problem.

18-1. A View of the Issues

Electronic recognition of speech emerged in its first forms some 25 years ago. The early developments were stimulated by two factors. Vacuum-tube electronics was advancing to a well-honed art (partly through intensive research and development during World War II), and a new understanding of the "information-bearing elements" of speech was evolving (largely as a result of the interest in analysis and synthesis of speech). On the first count, electronic circuits for signal analysis, logical decisions and switching functions were becoming available. On the second count, vocoder methods for bandwidth conservation, and signal analysis techniques for visual portrayal of speech information, clearly revealed the information-importance of the short-time amplitude spectrum. Not unnaturally, these factors combined to aid first efforts in automatic speech recognition (ASR).

Invariably, the early efforts aimed at recognition of individual words, and they relied upon the fundamental principle of matching a measured short-time spectrum (or related features) to a stored template. Distance measures for recognition decisions (or goodness of fit) were typically obtained by integration over the utterance. Remarkably good results were achieved on telephone quality speech, even with crude signal analysis. In one system (Davis et al., 1952), the formant frequencies were estimated from the axis-crossing rates of filtered waveforms. The stored templates took the form of matrices of resistors, the integrations were performed simply by large capacitors, and the recognition decisions were effected by circuits that selected the maximum voltage from among a modest set. Automatic recognition of spoken digits, by a designated talker (whose reference patterns were stored in the machine), were typically 97 to 99% correct.

Even at the outset, the difficulties of reliable recognition of connected speech by all talkers were well appreciated. The implied issues of coarticulation and automatic segmentation were well understood. Similarly, it became immediately clear that design trades could be made among circuit complexity, recognition accuracy, vocabulary size and talker population - the same interplays that exist today.

Given these early successes, why were they not exploited? They were not economically attractive. One of the most successful digit recognizers (AUDREY) occupied a six-foot high relay rack, was expensive, consumed substantial power and exhibited the myriad maintenance problems associated with complex vacuum-tube circuitry. More important, its reliable operation was limited to accurate recognition of digits spoken by designated talkers. It could therefore be used for voice dialing by, say, toll operators, or by especially affluent telephone customers, but this accomplishment was poorly competitive with manual dialing of numbers. In most cases, digit recognition is faster and cheaper by push-button dialing, rather than by speaking the successive digits.

While all of the early efforts recognized the difficulty of connected speech recognition, and hence concentrated on individual word utterances, it was generally appreciated that analysis in terms of linguistic elements smaller than a word, (i.e., phonemes, phonetic elements or syllables) was desirable, and that grammatical, linguistic and semantic constraints should be built into the recognizer if its capabilities were to be increased toward that of a human listener (Dudley, 1958; Dudley and Balashek, 1958; Fry and Denes, 1958). Early on the existing circuit technology placed severe limitations on the possibilities here, even if the understanding of how to quantify these factors existed, which it didn't. The technology likewise imposed limitations on extending and expanding the capabilities of successful word recognizers such as AUDREY. The obvious need was for reliable circuitry that could make accurate and sophisticated acoustic ("front-end") analysis, for enough memory and decision logic to permit the machine to have a respectably large vocabulary for a sizeable population of talkers, and for a better understanding of linguistic constraints. The late 1950's and early 1960's therefore represented something of a technology-imposed hiatus for speech recognition, until digital computers could be sufficiently advanced in development. The digital computer, with its capability for storage and fast arithmetic and logic, substantially changed the outlook.

Early applications of digital computers to spoken word recognition (in the 1960's) produced immediate and notable increases in vocabulary size and speaker population (Hughes, 1961; Martin et al., 1964; Reddy, 1967). But the cost of equipment and computation was relatively high, and the speed was uncomfortably low. Not surprisingly, the first computer implementations more or less duplicated and utilized the older concepts of spectrum analysis and template matching. But the potential of computers also stimulated a renewed interest in the broader problem - connected speech recognition by all talkers.

This broader interest was fostered by a five-year research program with government support (Klatt, 1977). The objective of this major project was a speech understanding system that could accurately comprehend unconstrained connected speech from at least one talker. The inclusion of grammatical, linguistic and semantic information was a primary interest. About the same time at least two industrial efforts commenced with somewhat more focussed objectives. One was the recognition of connected speech by a designated talker on restricted subject matter. The other represented a strong practical interest in recognition of individual words of a sizeable vocabulary and by a designated talker. Coming in at a later stage was additional modest effort in the communications sector. In terms of total effort, these commitments, as implemented during the 1970's, perhaps represent close to 200 man-years of research - a figure probably well in excess of all accumulated preceding effort in ASR.

With this recent and substantial experience, several things seem clear. The more ambitious of the broader objectives - unconstrained recognition of connected discourse - is still too ambitious. (There is the possibility that it may forever be.) The old trades among reliability, complexity, vocabulary size, talker population still exist, but the numbers pertaining to the economics have shifted. On the positive side, disciplined use of ASR is clearly practical and attractively reliable. By disciplined use we mean cooperative discourse using suitably constrained subsets of English speech. The subsets may range over single words, simple phrases or complete sentences that are acceptable in a prescribed grammar, either by designated talkers for more elaborate vocabularies, or talker-independent for more delimited vocabularies. These facts, if accepted and taken together with rapidly evolving device capabilities, make the present seem a singularly propitious time for ASR. For the first time, now, we can do clearly nontrivial automatic recognition, with high speed and low cost. We are in an increasingly good position to recover some of the past investment, and make ASR pay its own way, while the research frontiers are being inched forward. At this juncture, then, let us assess issues and chart some directions, be they admittedly parochial.

We have two simple purposes in our work. To harness and apply our accumulated ASR understanding, and to expand this understanding in an orderly way -- so that our reach never exceeds our grasp. Given this bias, how do these desired objectives take specific form? The examples we give represent our current commitments. All have a common point of departure - telephone quality speech, from conventional subscriber equipment, accessed over the switched network. Robustness is therefore a factor throughout.

Of those applications which the understanding and technology will immediately support, and which are worth doing, we cling to the older notion of highly reliable recognition of sizeable vocabularies by designated talkers and of smaller vocabularies that are talker-independent. Specific projects we wish to describe subsequently include a voice-actuated airline travel information system, a voice-actuated telephone directory assistance system, a speaker-independent system for connected digit recognition, and a highly-reliable recognizer for simple yes/no utterances. The objectives and rationales for these systems will unfold in the subsequent discussion. All these are essentially word recognizers. They utilize dynamic time-warping of spectral attributes of the input utterance onto one or more stored reference templates.

Of those needs and opportunities that presently require further research and understanding, we concern ourselves with two that are low-risk, high probability of pay-off undertakings, and one ambitious issue that has higher risk and lower probability of pay-off. In the former category, we are devising artificial languages that are "comfortable" and natural subsets of English, but by whose construction the recognizer gains powerful advantages. Our first efforts here centered on isolated-word sentence-length utterances made from vocabularies of 100-200 words, and on finite-state grammars that can achieve significant error-correcting abilities. Still in the former category, we press a strong interest in expanding the talker-independent capabilities of recognizers for all purposes. We therefore study multiple template storage, and clustering techniques for extracting representative templates for large talker populations.

On the higher-risk, more ambitious side, we are concerned with recognition of connected speech, but not in an unlimited context. There are two factors that make connected speech recognition of a limited-but-useful variety seem not completely hopeless. The recent successes in key-word spotting in running speech suggest that stressed content words, and especially polysyllabic words, can be reliably recognized in context (given enough compute power). This result depends upon a combination of good spectral description (either short-time amplitude spectrum computation or linear prediction computation) and dynamic time warping of stored templates along the connected speech stream. At the same time, understanding in the synthesis of connected speech directly from printed English text has progressed through the stage of practical syntax analyzers and stored pronouncing dictionaries (Allen, 1973; Coker, 1976; Lee, 1969). These factors, taken with the constraint that the input speech is from a prescribed subset of English and is spoken by a designated talker, make connected speech recognition appear a bit more tractable, and not much less interesting.*

We propose, therefore, to summarize our present standing in these research areas.

18-2. General Description of the Automatic Word Recognizer

Many of the speech recognition projects discussed in the remainder of the text are based on the speaker dependent, moderate size vocabulary (50-200 words), isolated word recognizer originally proposed by Itakura (Itakura, 1975).

A block diagram of the system is shown in Fig. 18-1. The input speech is first sent to an endpoint detector which locates the beginning and end of an unknown utterance. The utterance may then be preprocessed in one of several ways. For example, a simple high frequency preemphasis network is often used (Makhoul and Wolf, 1973). Other forms of preprocessing include simple bandpass filtering to remove noise, hum, etc. (Atal and Rabiner, 1976), or adaptive inverse filtering to remove the effects of the transmission system (Itakura, 1975).

Following preprocessing a p-pole autocorrelation analysis is performed. Values of p ranging from 6 to 10 have been used with analysis frame rates varying from 67 to 100 per second, depending on the specific application. Each frame of autocorrelation coefficients is converted to linear predictor

---

*It seems notable that, so far, all efforts in connected speech recognition have scrupulously avoided a marriage with the synthesis of connected speech from printed text. Maybe there is a good reason - maybe not.

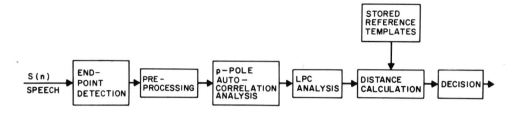

Fig. 18.1   Block diagram of the automatic word recognizer.

coefficients (LPC) for subsequent processing and/or storage as reference patterns. The autocorrelation method of LPC analysis is generally used (Markel and Gray, 1974).

Recognition consists of a matching process in which an unknown sample pattern of autocorrelation coefficients is compared with an ensemble of stored reference patterns previously established by the designated speaker. In the comparison a frame-by-frame scan of the sample pattern is carried out against each reference pattern. A distance score (or measure of dissimilarity) is calculated and accumulated using a dynamic programming technique (Sakoe and Chiba, 1971, 1976) as the scan proceeds. The vocabulary item corresponding to the reference pattern with the lowest accumulated distance is designated as the recognized word.

Especially significant in the matching process is the use of a dynamic programming algorithm. By means of a simple recursion formula a sequence of frames through each reference pattern is generated associated with a minimum accumulation of distance from beginning to end. This path is equivalent to a nonlinear time alignment and has been shown to be a significant factor in the performance of the recognizer especially for polysyllabic words (Itakura, 1975).

To speed up the distance calculation, and to eliminate unlikely reference patterns, an accumulated distance rejection threshold is often imposed. If at any frame during the scan against any reference pattern the accumulated distance exceeds the threshold the scan is aborted and the vocabulary item corresponding to the reference pattern is rejected as a candidate for recognition. If every reference pattern is aborted the outcome of the trial is said to be a rejection.

Although the result of a recognition trial is usually a single vocabulary item, it may also be taken to be a *set* of candidate items ordered by their distance scores. Such a result is useful when the recognition output is itself subject to further processing.

It should be noted that the only feature that determines whether the recognition system of Fig. 18-1 is trained to a speaker or is speaker independent is the reference template store. Thus by generating and storing speaker independent templates, the speaker specific constraint is eliminated. In this way the recognition system of Fig. 18-1 can be used in a wide variety of systems.

An evaluation of the system of Fig. 18-1 as a speaker dependent recognition system was carried out in which 13 participants dialed in to the system from their own phones daily over a 5-month period and provided test utterances. The tests words were an 84-item flight information vocabulary shown in Table 18-1, for which each speaker initially established two reference patterns per item. The median rate of recognition was 91.6%. In this on-line experiment if a given test word was not recognized on the first attempt, a second and, if needed, a third attempt was allowed. The complete results using this procedure are diagrammed in Fig. 18-2. After three attempts the rate of recognition is 98.5%. Note that the greatest improvement in performance takes place from the first to the second attempt. It is seen that the option for more than one attempt is highly desirable. Under the real-world conditions of dialed-up telephone lines and office environments initial attempts at recognition may fail for some reason such as noise interference or an abnormal utterance.

18-3. Digit Recognition Studies

As discussed in the introduction, when one is interested in recognition systems which are speaker independent, in order to maintain any degree of accuracy, the vocabulary size must be sharply limited. Thus, a great deal of research has been conducted in the area of digit recognition - both because of the small vocabulary size (10 digits from 0 to 9) and because of the utility of this vocabulary for data entry, telephone dialing, code identification, etc.

NO.	ITEM	PARTITION	NO.	ITEM	PARTITION
1	YES		42	CHICAGO	
2	NO	YES, NO	43	CINCINNATI	
3	MONDAY		44	CLEVELAND	
4	TUESDAY		45	COLUMBUS	
5	WEDNESDAY	DAYS OF	46	DALLAS	
6	THURSDAY	WEEK	47	DAYTON	
7	FRIDAY		48	DENVER	CITIES
8	SATURDAY		49	DETROIT	
9	SUNDAY		50	HARTFORD	
10	ONE		51	HOUSTON	
11	TWO		52	INDIANAPOLIS	
12	THREE		53	JACKSONVILLE	
13	FOUR		54	KANSAS CITY	
14	FIVE	HOURS OF	55	LAS VEGAS	
15	SIX	DAY	56	LOS ANGELES	
16	SEVEN		57	LOUISVILLE	
17	EIGHT		58	MEMPHIS	
18	NINE		59	MIAMI	
19	TEN		60	MILWAUKEE	
20	ELEVEN		61	MINNEAPOLIS	
21	TWELVE		62	MONTREAL	
22	AM		63	NASHVILLE	
23	PM	AM,PM	64	NEW ORLEANS	
24	NOON		65	NORFOLK	
25	MIDNIGHT		66	OKLAHOMA CITY	
26	ANY		67	OMAHA	
27	EITHER		68	PHILADELPHIA	
28	SEABASE		69	PHOENIX	
29	INTERNATIONAL		70	PITTSBURGH	
30	KENNEDY		71	PORTLAND	
31	LAGUARDIA	AIRPORTS	72	ROCHESTER	CITIES
32	NEWARK		73	SAINT LOUIS	
33	NATIONAL		74	SALT LAKE CITY	
34	DULLES		75	SAN ANTONIO	
35	SAN JOSE		76	SAN DIEGO	
36	OAKLAND		77	SAN FRANCISCO	
37	ATLANTA		78	SEATTLE	
38	BALTIMORE		79	SYRACUSE	
39	BOSTON		80	TAMPA	
40	BUFFALO		81	TORONTO	
41	CHARLOTTE		82	VANCOUVER	
42	CHICAGO		83	WASHINGTON	
			84	WINNIPEG	

Table 18-1

84-Word Flight Information System Vocabulary

In this section we describe two systems for recognizing digits in a speaker independent manner. The first system recognizes isolated digits using a heuristic, tree-search type algorithm based on a measured set of parameters, and a set of features which are estimated from the speech parameters. The second system is significantly more sophisticated in that it recognizes connected strings of a specified number of digits (3 in the case to be described) as would be appropriate for entering telephone numbers etc. This system uses a statistical pattern recognition approach to make the final recognition

MEDIAN CUMULATIVE ERROR RATES OVER 13 SPEAKERS

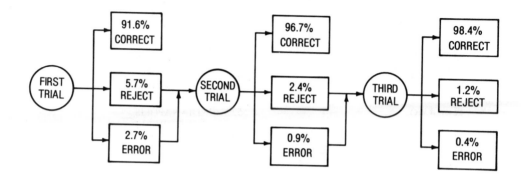

NO. OF FIRST TRIALS: TOTAL-9552

MEDIAN-732

Fig. 18.2   Evaluation results of automatic word recognizer using 84 word flight information vocabulary allowing three attempts at recognition.

decision. In addition, fairly advanced speech processing techniques are required to segment the digit string into the individual digits for subsequent recognition.

18-3.1 Isolated Digit Recognition System

Figure 18-3 shows a block diagram of the overall digit recognition system. The first block is an endpoint alignment algorithm (Rabiner and Sambur, 1975) whose function is to precisely determine the beginning and end of the utterance (the unknown digit). The speech is then analyzed every 10 msec (100 times per second) to obtain the following parameters:

1. *Zero crossing rate,* which is defined as the number of zero crossings in the 10 msec frame.
2. *Energy,* which is the sum of the squared values of the speech waveform in the 10 msec frame.
3. *Residual LPC error,* obtained from a 2-pole LPC analysis of the 10 msec frame a (Markel and Gray, 1974).
4. *Pole frequency (or frequencies),* obtained from the 2-pole LPC analysis of the 10 msec frame (Makhoul and Wolf, 1973).

The above parameters have been shown to form a highly robust set which can be used to reliably determine the presence or absence of key features of speech -e.g. nasality, frication, vowel type etc.

In parallel with the parameter measurements, the speech interval is segmented into three well-defined regions - i.e. beginning transient, middle region (vowel), and final transient. Each region is then characterized by the presence or absence of key speech features. All the speech information is fed in parallel into a preliminary decision-making algorithm that chooses one of several possible digit classes for the unknown digit - e.g. one class contains the digits 1 and 9. A final decision is then made based on the presence or absence of certain key features in the input speech (Sambur and Rabiner, 1975).

Table 18-2 gives a list of the sequence of features (sound classes) which are normally associated with the digits 0 through 9. For example the digit 4 is characterized by the sequence:

unvoiced consonant (f) - front vowel (o) - middle vowel (r)

Thus the heuristic classification looks for the above sequence to identify the digit as a 4. In order to

430

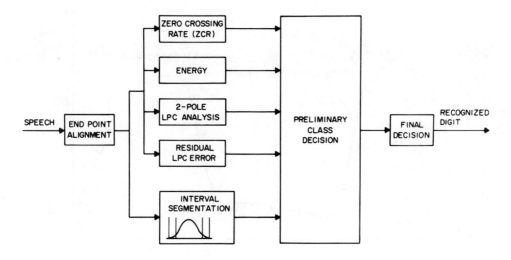

Fig. 18.3   Block diagram of isolated digit recognition system.

Digit	Sequence of Sound Classes
0	VNLC → FV → VLC → BV
1	VLC → MV → VLC
2	UVNLC → FV → BV
3	UVNLC → VLC → FV
4	UNVLC → BV → MV
5	UVNLC → MV → FV → VNLC
6	UVNLC → FV → UVNLC
7	UVNLC → FV → VNLC → FV → VLC
8	FV → UVNLC
9	VLC → MV → FV → VLC

VNLC = Voiced, noise-like consonant
UVNLC = Unvoiced, noise-like consonant
VLC   = Vowel-like consonant
FV   = Front vowel
MV   = Middle vowel
BV   = Back vowel

Table 18-2

Sound classes characteristic of the digits.

determine whether or not a feature of Table 18-2 is present in each of the 3 intervals, a description of the feature is used. By way of example a fricative is characterized by relatively high zero crossings, relatively low energy, relatively high residual error, and relatively high pole frequency. Figure 18-4 shows an example of the measurements for the digit six. The strong fricative regions at both the beginning and end of six are clearly seen in this figure.

431

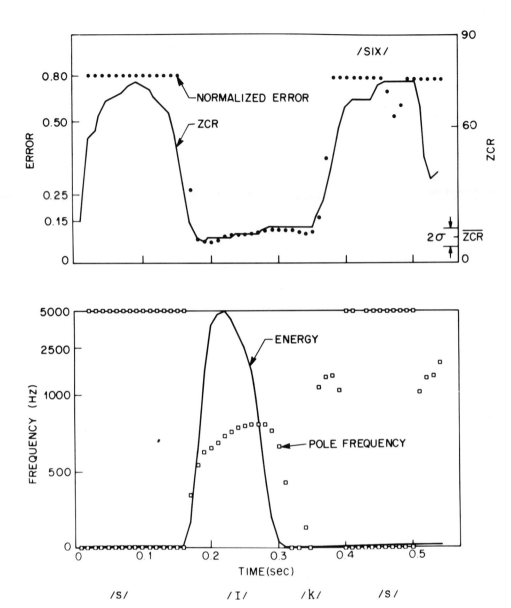

Fig. 18.4   Speech recognition measurements for the isolated digit "six".

A detailed discussion of the decision algorithm is beyond the scope of this paper; however it should be noted that a tree-like structure was used in which the most reliable decisions were used to guide the search and for which only the most unlikely digits were eliminated in the early stages (Sambur and Rabiner, 1975). In this manner digits with key features missing still had a good chance of being correctly recognized.

An experimental evaluation of the above system showed an error rate of about 2.7% in a test with 10 speakers (5 male, 5 female) each speaking the 10 digits, 10 times. The matrix of confusions indicated no major bias towards any specific confusion. In a second, more demanding, experiment, an error rate of 5.6% was obtained using 55 speakers (30 female, 25 male) with no prior experience in using a recognition system, and with recordings made "on-line" in a noisy computer room, and with a fairly low quality microphone.

The above set of experiments indicated that speaker independent, isolated digit recognition was well within the range of practical utility, at least for a class of cooperative talkers who have had some experience with man-machine communication systems.

18-3.2 Connected Digit Recognition Systems

The results in the preceding section provided strong impetus for experimentation with systems for recognition of connected digits. The motivation for considering connected digits is related to the applicability of such systems to the problems of voice dialing of telephone numbers, data entry, voice entry of identification codes etc. For such applications it is a considerably more natural communication mode to use connected digits, rather than a sequence of isolated digits. However, the tradeoff here is a considerable increase in system complexity, as well as a significant increase in the difficulty of the problem.

The major problem that is associated with recognition of connected digits is the segmentation of the digit string into the individual digits. The problem here is, in some cases, unsolvable in that a high degree of word coarticulation can occur such that no adequate boundary really exists. For example, for the digit string /199/ no clear boundaries exist anywhere since the final /n/ in "one" is coarticulated with the initial /n/ in "nine". A similar situation occurs at the end of the second digit. Thus segmentation is, at best, an extremely difficult problem.

A block diagram of the system which was ultimately used to recognize connected digits is given in Figure 18-5. There are three major (signal processing) parts of the system. These are:

1. Endpoint location - this is similar to the problem discussed in the preceding section. However, precise location of endpoints is not critical here since a more sophisticated "silence" detection is performed in subsequent parts of the system.

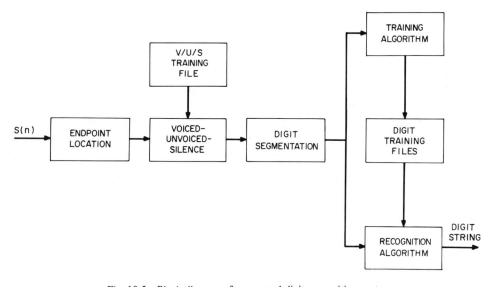

Fig. 18.5   Block diagram of connected digit recognition system.

2. Segmentation - the speech is analyzed every 10 msec, and each frame is classified as either voiced, unvoiced, or silence using a statistical decision approach based on 5 speech parameters (Rabiner and Sambur, 1976). A set of digit boundaries is then determined from the voiced-unvoiced-silence data, in conjunction with information about the energy, zero crossing rate, and relative durations of each region of the speech. The output of the segmentation algorithm is a set of markers which delineate the individual digits in the string.

3. Recognition - each digit in the string is dynamically time warped to each of a set of stored reference templates, and an average distance (similarity measure) is computed based on one of two distance computations. The first distance is the LPC log likelihood ratio of Itakura (Itakura, 1975) which measures average spectral similarity between the test and reference digits. If the

digit with minimum distance using the first measure does not satisfy a set of consistency checks (e.g. it should have a contour which is consistent with the measured voiced-unvoiced-silence contour), the distance computation is repeated using a covariance weighted measure which minimizes the effects of spectral differences during regions of the digit which are highly coarticulated, and maximizes the spectral matches during regions of low coarticulation. Figure 18-6 illustrates the frame-by-frame distances for the test digit 8 using both the log likelihood measure (D_1) and the covariance weighted measure (D_2). It is seen that a significant reduction in distance is obtained for the early frames of the word "eight" since these are highly influenced by the preceding digit, whereas none of the other choices has nearly as much variation in this region.

In order to use the recognition system, training sets of data are required to provide statistics for the voiced-unvoiced-silence files, and to create the reference templates for the digits. Techniques for creating such training data are well established (Sambur and Rabiner, 1976).

The connected digit recognition system was tested in two ways. First a set of digit templates were created for each of 6 individual speakers. Thus the system was first tested as a speaker trained system rather than a speaker independent one. For these six speakers (4 male, 2 female) the average recognition accuracy was 98.8% on strings of 3 digits. Thus it was clear that the system could handle coarticulation effects for a designated speaker.

A second test was run on 10 new speakers (all male) who had no training on this system. For these speakers the average recognition accuracy was 95.3% on a string of 3 digits, and the accuracy for all speakers was 90% or higher. The most common confusions in this experiment were between the digits 1 and 9.

The results of these experiments were again highly encouraging in that they demonstrated that connected digit strings could be reliably recognized in a carefully controlled environment.

18-4. Yes-No Recognition Systems

An interesting application of ASR that occurs within the telephone plant is reverse billing of long distance calls. For this application the requirements on the recognition system are extremely modest-namely, a 2 word vocabulary, yes and no. However, such a system must be extremely robust with an error rate well below 1% because of the high cost of making and correcting errors.

To understand this application we should review the current situation for making collect long distance calls. First an operator is required on the sending end to collect information about the calling party, to place the call, and to determine whether the called party will accept charges. In many circumstances an additional operator is required on the receiving end to assist in making connections, verifying the called party response etc. Thus the entire transaction is expensive and time consuming for all parties concerned.

With ASR the situation could become much less expensive. In such a case the calling party, upon dialing a code that indicates he is making a collect call, would receive a pre-recorded message (using a computer voice response system) asking him to clearly state his name at the beep. The caller's name would then be recorded, the caller would be put on hold, and the automatic system would place the call. When completed, the called party would be informed (again via a precorded message) that he has a collect call from the calling party (whose voice he would hear from the earlier recording). He then would be asked whether he accepted the charges by clearly speaking either yes or no at the beep. At this point the recognition system would decide which response was spoken and take appropriate action. The above transaction is simple, fast, inexpensive, and essentially requires no human intervention.

Of course there are potentially many human level problems with such a system that would have to be resolved - e.g. no name being recorded, or a response other than yes or no. However, such problems are human factors problems which involve careful system design and a certain amount of acclimation of the user to such systems.

The recognition system for this 2 word vocabulary is given in Figure 18-7. A simple statistical pattern recognition system is more than adequate for reliable recognition for such a small and distinct vocabulary. The features used are the LPC parameters, and the recognition algorithm is the minimum distance of the dynamically warped utterance to each template. The log likelihood distance is used in this system.

We have only made informal evaluations of this system, where we have found that no errors occurred when tested with "yeses" and "nos" of over 50 talkers. However, the true test of such a sys-

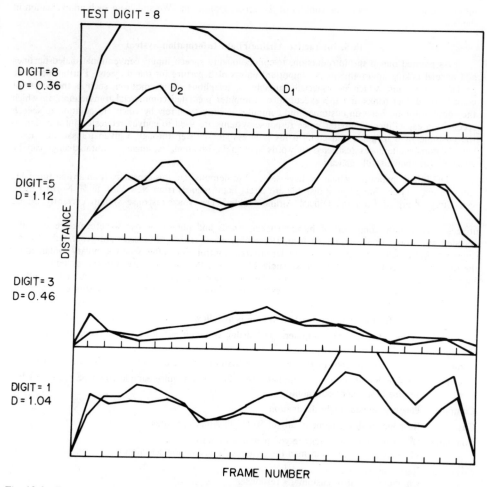

Fig. 18.6   Frame-by-frame distances for the test digit "eight" using two distance measures (D_1 and D_2).

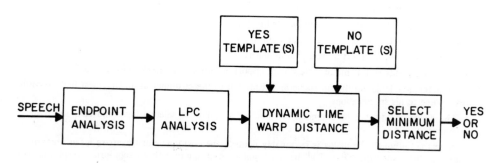

Fig. 18.7   Block diagram of "Yes-No" recognition system.

tem is "on-line" recordings in the context of the actual application. We anticipate such an evaluation in the future.

18-5. Interactive Airline Flight Information System

As pointed out in the introduction, telephone-quality speech input, conventional dialed-up lines and normal talking environments are important points of departure for our projects. Furthermore, we envision applications which are especially suitable for telephone communication, such as the access of computerized data banks and the execution of computer mediated commercial transactions, in which the communication between customer and computer is almost entirely by voice. In addition to speech recognition capabilities, computer voice response systems are used to convey requested information to the customer and to guide and confirm his progress step-by-step through a given transaction. Even with customer utterances restricted to words spoken in isolation, reasonably natural dialogs can be designed for many useful applications.

The initial application which we have selected to demonstrate this capability is an airline timetable information service. Stored on a disk file are direct flight records from New York to 50 North American cities excerpted from the Official Airline Guide.* The voice response system currently in use utilizes a vocabulary composed of human-spoken words and phrases whose waveforms are digitally encoded and stored in a compressed form (Rosenthal et al., 1974). Messages are generated by concatenating individual words and phrases under program control. Since the basic vocabulary contained in the time-table is relatively small (approximately 200 items), this type of voice response system is quite appropriate for this kind of application. In addition, since a given portion of the time-table can be specified by a relatively small number of descriptors, a limited vocabulary word recognition system is also quite appropriate.

The scenario for the flight information system is as follows:

The customer dials up the computer. The dialog commences with an identifying message from the computer.

Computer: This is the Bell Labs Flight Information System. Please dial your identification number.

Customer: Keys in his identification number. (At this point a voice sample could be requested for automatic speaker verification).

Computer: Please state your flight destination.

Customer: Responds with the name of any of 50 North American cities.

Computer: On what day of the week are you planning to depart to (city)?
(The computer has confirmed the customer's destination selection.)

Customer: Responds with day of the week.
Computer confirms customer's response.

Computer: At what hour of the day do you plan to depart?

Customer: Specifies hour, computer confirms.

Computer: AM or PM (or Noon or Midnight)?

Customer: Responds, computer confirms.

Computer: Do you wish complete flight descriptions?

Customer: Responds "yes" or "no", computer confirms.

Computer: From which airport do you plan to depart?

Customer: Responds with name of a New York airport or "any", computer confirms.

The computer now looks up the timetable and reads out to the customer up to four best flight records corresponding to his specifications.

The dialog could easily be extended to allow the customer to select a flight and date and request reservations.

Note that although the dialog is reasonably natural, the customer must exercise a fair amount of discipline in his responses. First of all he must answer each query with an appropriate response. An

---

*Kindly provided by the publisher, Reuben H. Donnelly Corporation, Oak Brook, Illinois.

inappropriate response will elicit either a rejection from the computer or the confirmation of an incorrect response. In the case of a rejection the question is repeated automatically to elicit another attempt at recognition from the customer. In the case of an error, repeating the question requires the intervention of the customer who must dial the appropriate repeat signal to the computer. Other precautions the speaker must take include exercising care to respond during the appropriate intervals, and avoiding extraneous noises and unusual pronunciations. However with a small amount of practice and orientation the process becomes quite routine and reliable.

It is important to note that a rudimentary syntax is imposed on this dialog by the proper response to each query. Advantage is taken of this by partitioning the reference patterns for each response, scanning only those corresponding to appropriate responses. Partitioning the vocabulary in this way reduces both the response time and the error rate. In the evaluation of the 84-word flight information vocabulary it was found that partitioning increased the *first* attempt recognition rate from 92% to 98%! The partitioning of the vocabulary appropriate to the dialog above is indicated in Table 18-1.

18-6. Airline Flight Information System with Sentence Input

Although the question-answer dialog is reasonably effective, it would be significantly more effective and efficient to specify a request for information in the form of a complete sentence. For example, the entire dialog described above might be replaced by a single sentence such as, "I would like to go from New York to Washington on Tuesday evening." Sentence input eliminates the need to thread through a sometimes tedious tree-like series of questions to specify a request. If there are many different types of requests, the tree structure may become unacceptably complex. Moreover, syntax for sentence input can exercise a far more significant influence on overall recognition capability than the rudimentary syntax associated with the question-answer dialog. Although the means are not available to us to accept sentences in the form of continuous discourse, it is relatively simple to adapt our

present isolated word recognizer to accept sentences in the form of strings of words spoken at once but with distinct pauses between them. To this end we have designed and implemented a speech recognition system comprising a modified speaker-dependent word recognizer and a programmed finite-state syntax analyzer which accepts reasonably natural English sentences in the task domain of requesting flight information and reservations (Levinson, 1977). The vocabulary consists of 127 words including many auxiliary and function type words permitting the construction of naturally formed sentences. The vocabulary is shown in Table 18-3 together with some sample sentence requests.

The system is optimal in the sense of maximum posterior probability. For each sentence input, w, the acoustic analyzer provides the syntax analyzer with an acoustic transcription, $\tilde{w}$, and a matrix of distance scores $\{d_{ij}\}$, $i = 1, 2, ..., N$, $j = 1, 2, ..., M$, where i represents the ith word in a sentence string of N words and j represents the jth item in the vocabulary of $M = 127$ words. The distance scores are obtained by scanning each calculated sample pattern in the sentence string against the entire set of reference patterns. Rejected reference patterns are assigned arbitrarily large distance scores. The syntax analyzer uses a dynamic programming algorithm similar to that of Viterbi (Viterbi, 1967) to find a sentence, $\hat{w}$, from the language whose overall distance $D = \min_{1 \leq j_i \leq M} \left\{ \sum_{i=1}^{N} d_{ij_i} \right\}$ is a minimum. The system is diagrammed in Fig. 18-8, ignoring the dashed lines.

Two important points need to be made about the procedure. First, it is algorithmic and optimal. It always finds the minimum distance sentence. Second, the execution time and storage requirements of the algorithm are linear in the length of the input sentence. Thus large languages having nearly 10^{10} sentences can be comfortably processed on only a moderately fast mini-computer.

An evaluation of the system (Levinson et al., 1976) was carried out using 7 speakers talking over dialed-up telephone lines. The median rate of correct word recognition at the output of the acoustic analyzer was 88%. The poorer performance with this vocabulary compared with the 84-word vocabulary is (besides the difference in vocabulary sizes) most likely attributable to the greater frequency of common, more easily confused words. The powerful correcting influence of the syntactic constraints imposed by the grammar is evidenced by the dramatic increase in word recognition at the output of the syntax analyzer (99.6%). The corresponding sentence recognition rate is 96%. (Since a single word error generates a complete sentence error, sentence recognition is generally worse than word recognition).

Although the beneficial effect of the use of grammatical constraints is obvious, one must not ignore the fact that the acoustic recognizer is well suited to this type of system. Over 98% of the time the correct word was among the first five choices. The point is that if one wishes practically low error

437

1	Evening	33	To	65	Reservation	97	Card
2	Nine	34	Charge	66	A	98	Saturday
3	October	35	Make	67	Fare	99	Pay
4	Douglas	36	Home	68	Bac	100	By
5	DC	37	Five	69	Departure	101	Ten
6	Arrival	38	Does	70	Of	102	March
7	Seattle	39	Go	71	Meal	103	Cash
8	Eleven	40	Seat	72	Flights	104	Miami
9	Los Angeles	41	From	73	What	105	Thursday
10	Friday	42	Time	74	I	106	American
11	January	43	On	75	When	107	Plane
12	AM	44	December	76	Sunday	108	Eight
13	April	45	June	77	Boston	109	Club
14	May	46	Would	78	Arrive	110	Master
15	Morning	47	Some	79	Twelve	111	Office
16	Detroit	48	Many	80	Leave	112	My
17	DO	49	In	81	August	113	Class
18	New York	50	Please	82	For	114	Six
19	At	51	Will	83	November	115	Three
20	Tuesday	52	Lockheed	84	Philadelphia	116	Washington
21	Oh	53	Want	85	February	117	night
22	Wednesday	54	Flight	86	Are	118	Phone
23	Need	55	Four	87	There	119	Area
24	Chicago	56	Depart	88	Return	120	Two
25	September	57	Repeat	89	Coach	121	Code
26	Is	58	Take	90	O'Clock	122	Nonstop
27	PM	59	Number	91	How	123	Seats
28	Boeing	60	Denver	92	Much	124	Seven
29	Information	61	Diners	93	Served	125	Times
30	Afternoon	62	Prefer	94	Credit	126	Stops
31	Express	63	July	95	The	127	First
32	Like	64	Monday	96	One		

SAMPLE TEST SENTENCES:

I would like some information please.

I would like one first class seat on flight number four four to Los Angeles on Saturday the oh one January.

Table 18-3

127-Word Flight Information System Vocabulary for Sentence Input

rates, a good "front end" is necessary.

More recently the system has been reconfigured into a syntax directed architecture (Levinson and Rosenberg, 1978), shown in Fig. 18-8 with the dashed lines, which is faster but no less accurate. Superficially this architecture resembles the classical hypothesize-and-test paradigm, with the syntax analyzer generating word hypotheses and the acoustic recognizer evaluating them. The important difference between our syntax-directed system and the well-known hypothesize-and-test methods of problem solving is that the algorithmic nature of the system is not compromised. Therefore, for any input, exactly the set of valid hypotheses is generated. Specifically, the syntax analyzer specifies to the acoustic analyzer which entries of $\{d_{ij}\}$ or, correspondingly, which reference patterns are required for each word position in the string.

Two such systems have been implemented — one which restricts the number of reference comparisons based on word position alone, and a second which makes use of the total number of words in

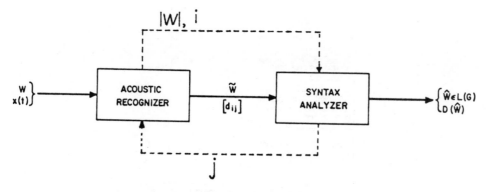

Fig. 18.8   Block diagram of sentence recognizer.

the sentence string in addition. As an example of the efficiencies attained, in the original implementation - when all 127 distances were computed for each word position - an average of 16.5 seconds per word was required for classification. With the first modification noted above this figure was reduced to 8.3 seconds and with the second a further reduction to 5 secs. was attained.

18-7. Spoken Spelled Input for Automatic Directory Assistance

We have investigated still another speech recognition system which derives benefit from the constraints among the elements of an input string. In this instance the vocabulary is spoken spelled letters of the alphabet and the strings are spoken spelled names (Rosenberg and Schmidt, 1977). The application is the retrieval of telephone directory information by spoken spelled inquiries. The same acoustical recognizer, modified for string input, is used. In effect, the acoustical recognizer provides an ordered set of alternative spellings of a name to be searched in a directory from ordered lists of candidate letters for each position in the spelled name string. The constraint on the string is the correct spelling of the name as listed in the directory. The point of departure for this system is an automatic directory information system which accepts Touch-Tone® spelled inquiries which has been demonstrated at Bell Laboratories (Lesk and McGonegal, 1976). The process is outlined in the simplified flow chart shown in Fig. 18-9.

The initial candidate string submitted for search in the directory is composed of the best candidate letters (associated with the smallest distance scores) for each letter position in the string. Each directory string within a specified search range is compared with the candidate string. The comparison consists of a scan from left to right to the first position of mismatch. If a complete match is found, the corresponding directory information is stored for output to the customer. If no match is found at the end of the search range a new candidate string is generated by replacing the candidate letter in the rightmost first mismatch position obtained in the last search range by the next best candidate letter in that position. When there are no more candidate letters available in a selected position that position is reset with its best candidate letter and the next preceding position is selected for modification.

Since a rejection threshold is imposed, it is possible for no candidate letters at all to be available in one or more positions. These positions are simply ignored in the matching process. In addition, if the search fails after all candidate letters provided by the acoustical recognizer have been exhausted, the search is restarted with an "ignore" or "wild card" condition imposed on selected positions one at a time.

We have carried out a small-scale evaluation with ten speakers providing speech input over dialed-up telephone lines. After establishing reference patterns for the vocabulary of spoken spelled letters, each speaker spelled out 50 names randomly selected from the 18000 entry Bell Labs directory. It is not surprising that the median word recognition rate (80%) for this vocabulary, which has many minimal distinctions between words, is worse than the other vocabularies discussed. Nevertheless the median rate for obtaining the correct name string from the directory is 96%! This result brings out once more the beneficial effects of coupling a speech recognition system to a task domain which imposes strong contextual constraints.

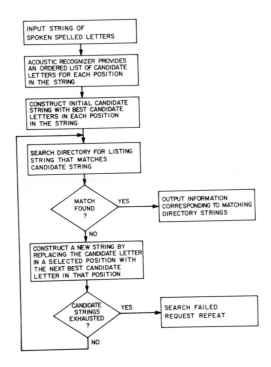

Fig. 18.9   Flow chart for spoken spelled input for automatic directory assistance.

18-8. Grammatical Constraints in ASR

As was stated in the introductory section of this paper, the very early researchers were well aware of the importance of linguistic, syntactic and semantic information to speech recognition. They simply lacked the mathematical and electronic tools to treat this problem in a reasonable way.

All of this changed rapidly with the development of electronic computing machinery and the concomitant growth of the theory of computation. This branch of mathematics, in conjunction with its physical embodiment - the modern digital computer - has enabled us to see computation not merely as fast numerical calculation, but as general manipulation of abstract symbols. Thus a powerful body of knowledge has been assembled providing a partial solution to the dilemma of the early researchers.

This section of the paper gives an overview of our understanding of syntactic information in ASR research. We have, as yet, not chosen to challenge the still mystifying areas of semantic and cognitive phenomena.

Using the notion of finite state grammar which we applied to the recognition system described in Sec. 18-6, we have derived mathematical formulae which permit a quantitative understanding of grammatical constraints and their effects on word recognition accuracy.

We have restricted ourselves to well defined and mathematically tractable problems. Thus, we have treated only finite languages in which sentences may be assumed to be equiprobable or to have probabilities which maximize the entropy of the language.

18-8.1 Measuring Grammatical Constraint

It is intuitively and empirically clear that judicial use of grammatical constraints will enhance speech recognition accuracy. An obvious question to ask is, given a speech recognition task language, how much "constraint" is built into it. In principle Shannon (Shannon, 1948, 1951) answered the question by defining the redundancy of a language and noting that in a very natural way this quantity measures grammatical constraint.

440

LANGUAGE	TASK	REF	PROPERTIES			RESULTS FOR EQUI-PROBABLE SENTENCES			RESULTS FOR SENTENCE PROBABILITIES THAT MAXIMIZE ENTROPY		
			$\|V\|$ (WORDS)	l_{max} (WORDS)	$\|\mathscr{L}(G)\|$ (SENTENCES)	$E\{\|w\|\}$ (WORDS)	$H(\mathscr{L}(G))$ BITS/WORD	$R(\mathscr{L}(G))$	$E\{\|w\|\}$ (WORDS)	$H(\mathscr{L}(G))$ BITS/WORD	$R(\mathscr{L}(G))$
FIRL	FLIGHT INFORMATION AND RESERVATIONS	[18]	127	22	6×10^9	17.6	1.85	.735	9.7	2.2	.685
IBM NEW RALEIGH	RANDOM ENGLISH SENTENCES	[9] C.8	250	9	1.6×10^8	8.4	2.83	.643	8.1	2.94	.630
LIZ	DESK CALCULATOR	[9] C.6	17	9	6.1×10^9	8.9	3.28	.197	3.9	3.79	.074
VP	VOICE COMPUTER PROGRAMMING	[9] C.7	37	18	4.7×10^{18}	17.9	3.47	.334	8.2	3.82	.266
HEARSAY I	CHESS MOVES	[9] C.5	30	15	10^7	12.2	1.91	.610	3.8	2.75	.438
LINCOLN LABS BASIC LANGUAGE	SPEECH ANALYSIS BY COMPUTER	[9] C.9	238	16	3.6×10^6	10.8	2.01	.745	4.4	2.75	.652
APEX	DATA RETRIEVAL	[9] 4-1	9	4	6	3.33	.775	.755	1.51	1.044	.670
VOCAL	VOICE COMPUTER PROGRAMMING	[16]	43	42	1.9×10^{28}	39.2	2.31	.574	15.3	2.60	.520

TABLE 18-4 REDUNDANCIES OF ASR TASK LANGUAGES

Using the mathematical notion of finite state grammar Sondhi and Levinson (Sondhi and Levinson 1977, 1978) have developed procedures for computing the relative redundancy of any finite language. Furthermore, these results are easily extended so that the relative redundancy of infinite languages may be approximated to any desired accuracy.

Before outlining these results, an important point must be made. Shannon's notion of redundancy is statistical in nature while the concept of finite state grammar is deterministic. In order to merge the two in a useful way one must make an underlying assumption about the probability distribution of sentences in the language. Two natural choices are: (a) equiprobable sentences, and (b) sentence probablities which maximize entropy.

The sequence of computations is as follows. First, one produces a formal specification of the task language, usually Backus Normal Form (BNF). Second the BNF is used to produce a finite state specification; for large languages this is best done mechanically. Finally, one applies some graph theoretic principles in order to efficiently count word and state occurences, state sequences and sentences of a given length.

Given this information one applies some information theoretic principles to derive formulas for relative redundancy based upon either of the two underlying assumptions.

When one actually makes these computations for existing speech recognition task languages one finds that the values of redundancy for subsets of English and "English-like" languages are very tightly clustered around 0.6. In addition, naive indicators of grammatical constraint such as vocabulary size, language size and sentence length are inconsistent among themselves. For example the HEARSAY I and VOCAL languages are of vastly different sizes but have nearly the same redundancies. The IBM NEW RALEIGH and LIZ languages have identical maximum sentence lengths but widely different redundancies. Also, the LINCOLN LABORATORIES BASIC and APEX languages have very different vocabulary sizes but nearly identical redundancies. A complete summary of our results is given in Table 18-4.

There is one aspect of this analysis which presently eludes us and that is the relationship between recognition robustness and redundancy. It is at least intuitively appealing that, for a given acoustic/syntactic classification system increasing redundancy should lower the error rate. At the

441

moment, however, our attempts to relate error probability to redundancy have resulted in intractable combinatorial problems and we have had to rely on empirical results (Levinson, 1976) and (Levinson et al., 1976) as verification of our intuition.

It is our hope that investigations such as these will afford further understanding of the speech recognition process so that new and more ambitious systems can be constructed on firm mathematical foundations.

18-9. Conclusion

We have given, in the preceding discussion, our current assessment of the opportunities and realities of automatic speech recognition (ASR). We started by outlining our view of techniques that can be implemented immediately, or in the near future with modest additional research, as contrasted with more ambitious and problematic achievements. Our overriding criterion in striving for new advances is to take prudent steps from established understanding and technology - so that reach never exceeds grasp, and so that significant research investment has realistic chance for practical reward.

At the outset we suggested that a number of the interacting factors which characterize present work are the same as those identified in the very beginning days of ASR. Trades can be made among vocabulary size, recognition accuracy, talker dependence, system complexity, cost, and speech connectivity. However, new understanding and technology have significantly shifted the weights among these factors. The advent of high-speed digital computation, in particular, has substantially impacted the issues of feasibility and economy.

On the side of those techniques which the understanding and technology immediately support, we believe that reliable and practically-attractive recognition of individual spoken words, and a few connected words and short phrases, can be satisfactorily accomplished over conventional telephone channels. Template matching and dynamic time registration by high-speed processors provide reasonably robust performance. Sizable vocabularies (more than a hundred words) can be realistically utilized with talker-dependent templates. Smaller vocabularies (on the order of one or two dozen words) can be reliably utilized in talker-independent systems.

On the side of those techniques that require continued fundamental research, we try to differentiate between short-time, low-risk, high-probability-of-payoff efforts *versus* more speculative, longer-range undertakings. In the first instance, our current research on talker classification, clustering analysis of templates to characterize intra and inter-talker effects, and multiple template stores for vocabulary items (as distinct from template averaging), strongly suggest that vocabulary sizes for both talker-dependent and talker-independent systems can be substantially expanded. Also, the recent successes with programmed parsers, and with well-defined languages that are finite subsets of English and are reasonably comfortable and natural, demonstrate the great leverage that syntax can provide to acoustic recognition. New and quantitative measures of language redundancy promise to aid the design of these recognition languages.

In the instances where we have consummate experience, we have tried to describe our efforts. In the areas where our work is ongoing and incomplete, we have tried to indicate our directions and expectations. In the former instance, a simple table of recognition percentages, shown as Table 5, permits some comparison and perspective on the systems outlined in the preceding pages.

Much more ambitious and problematic is the recognition of connected discourse. An important aspect here is to delimit a piece of the problem that has reasonable hope of useful solution. In our view, an appropriate way to circumscribe the problem is to limit it to talker-dependent recognition of connected speech for a finite subset of English, and perhaps confined to a specific topic. In this framework, connected speech recognition may be within grasp. In the unconstrained context, it may never be. Toward these objectives, too, it seems worthwhile to consider the insights gained from recent advances in the synthesis of speech by rule from printed English text (Coker, 1976). Likewise, new insights from recent research on keyword spotting in connected speech might provide helpful points of support (Christiansen and Rushforth, 1977). The trick in all these cases is to recognize where solid increments of accomplishment can be won, and to minimize large, speculative commitments. The next few years will tell us whether this view is justified.

System	% words correct	% strings correct
84-word Flight Information	91.6	-
84-word Flight Information (3 attempts allowed)	98.5	-
127-word Flight Information [20]	88	96
27-word Spelled Letters for Directory Assistance [29]	79.5	96
Isolated Digits [34] (speaker independent)	94.4	-
Connected Digits [33] (speaker dependent)	98.8	-
Connected Digits [33] (speaker independent)	95.3	-

Table 18-5

Summary of Performance for Several Recognition Systems

REFERENCES

Allen, J. B., "Speech Synthesis from Unrestricted Text," *Speech Synthesis,* ed. J. L. Flanagan and L. R. Rabiner. Stroudsburg, PA., Dowden, Hutchinson and Ross, 1973.

Atal, B. S. and Rabiner, L. R., "A Pattern Recognition Approach to Voiced-Unvoiced-Silence Classification with Applications to Speech Recognition," *IEEE Transactions on Acoustics, Speech and Signal Processing,* ASSP-24, no. 3 (June 1976), 201-12.

Coker, C. H., "A Model of Articulatory Dynamics and Control," *Proceedings of the IEEE,* 64, no. 4 (April 1976), 452-60.

Christiansen, R. W. and Rushforth, C. K., "Detecting and Locating Key Words in Continuous Speech Using Linear Predictive Coding," *IEEE Transactions on Acoustics, Speech and Signal Processing,* ASSP-25, no. 5 (October 1977), 361-67.

Davis, K. H., Biddulph, R., and Balashek, S., "Automatic Recognition of Spoken Digits," *Journal of the Acoustical Society of America,* 24, no. 6 (November 1952), 637-42.

Dudley, H., "Phonetic Pattern Recognition Vocoder for Narrow-band Speech Transmission," *Journal of the Acoustical Society of America,* 30, no. 8 (August 1958), 733-39.

Dudley, H., Balashek, S., "Automatic Recognition of Phonetic Patterns in Speech," *Journal of the Acoustical Society of America,* 30, no. 8 (August 1958), 721-39.

Fry, D. B. and Denes, P., "The Solution of Some Fundamental Problems in Mechanical Speech Recognition," *Language and Speech,* 1, no. 1 (January 1958), 35-38.

Goodman, R. G., *Analysis of Languages for Man-Machine Voice Communication.* Pittsburgh, PA: Department of Computer Science Technical Report, Carnegie Mellon University, 1976.

Hughes, G. W., *The Recognition of Speech by Machine.* Cambridge, MA: Research Laboratory of Electronics Technical Report, 1961.

Itakura, F., "Minimum Prediction Residual Principle Applied to Speech Recognition," *IEEE Transactions on Acoustics Speech and Signal Processing,* ASSP-23, no 1 (February 1975), 67-72.

Jelinek, F., "Continuous Speech Recognition by Statistical Methods," *Proceedings of the IEEE,* 64, no. 4 (April 1976), 532-56.

Klatt, D., "Review of the ARPA Speech Understanding Project," *Journal of the Acoustical Society of America,* 62, no. 6 (December 1977), 1345-66.

Lee, F. F., "Reading Machine: From Text to Speech," *IEEE Transactions on Audio and Electroacoustics,* AU-17, no. 4 (December 1969), 275-82.

Lesk, M. E. and McGonegal, C. A. *User Operated Directory Assistance,* Murray Hill, NJ.: Bell Laboratories Technical Memorandum, 1976.

Levinson, S. E., "The Vocal Speech Understanding System," *Proceedings of the 4th IJCAI,* Tbilisi, USSR, 1975.

Levinson, S. E., "Cybernetics and Automatic Speech Understanding," *Proceedings of the ICISS,* Patras, Greece, 1976.

Levinson, S. E., "Improving Word Recognition Accuracy by Means of Syntax," *Proceedings of the IEEE ICASSP-77,* Hartford, CT., 1977.

Levinson, S. E., Lipton, R. J. and Synder, L., "Some Results on Maximum a Posteriori Probability Parsing Algorithms," *Proceedings of the 1976 CISS,* Baltimore, MD., 1976.

Levinson, S. E., Rosenberg, A. E. and Flanagan, J. L., "Evaluation of a Word Recognition System Using Syntax Analysis," *Proceedings of the IEEE ICASSP-77,* Hartford, CT., 1977.

Levinson, S. E. and Rosenberg, A. E., "Some Experiments With a Syntax Directed Speech Recognition System," *Proceedings of the IEEE ICASSP-78,* Tulsa, OK., 1978.

Makhoul, J. and Wolf, J., *The Use of a Two-pole Linear Prediction Model in Speech Recognition.* Cambridge MA.: Bolt, Beranek and Newman, Inc. Report 2537, 1973.

Markel, J. D. and Gray, A. H., Jr., "A Linear Prediction Vocoder Simulation Based Upon the Autocorrelation Method," *IEEE Transactions on Acoustic, Speech and Signal Processing,* ASSP-22, no. 2 (April 1974), 124-34.

Martin, T. B., Nelson, A. L., Zadell, A. J., *Speech Recognition by Feature Abstraction* Techniques.

Dayton, Ohio: Wright-Paterson AFB Avionics Laboratories Report, 1964.

Olson, H. F., Belar, H., "Phonetic Typewriter, III," *Journal of the Acoustical Society of America,* 33, no. 11 (November 1961), 1610-15.

Rabiner, L. R. and Sambur, M. R., "Some Preliminary Results on the Recognition of Connected Digits," *IEEE Transactions on Acoustics, Speech, and Signal Processing,* ASSP-24, no. 2, (April 1976), 170-82.

Rabiner, L. R. and Sambur, M. R., "An Algorithm for Determining the Endpoints of Isolated Utterances," *Bell System Technical Journal,* 54, no. 2 (February 1975), 297-315.

Reddy, D. R., "Computer Recognition of Connected Speech," *Journal of the Acoustical Society of America,* 42, no. 2 (August 1967), 329-47.

Rosenberg, A. E. and Schmidt, C. E., "Recognition of Spoken Spelled Names Applied to Directory Assistance," *Journal of the Acoustical Society of America,* 62 Suppl. no. 1 (Fall 1977), S63.

Rosenthal, L. H., Rabiner, L. R., Schafer, R. W., Cummiskey, P. and Flanagan, J. L., "A Multiline Computer Voice Response System Using ADPCM Coded Speech," *IEEE Transactions on Acoustics, Speech, and Signal Processing,* ASSP-22, no. 5 (October 1974), 339-52.

Sakoe, H. and Chiba, S., "Comparative Study of DP-Pattern Matching Techniques for Speech Recognition," *Acoustical Society of Japan,* Report S73-22, 1973.

Sakoe, H. and Chiba, S., "A Dynamic Programming Approach to Continuous Speech Recognition," *Proceedings of the International Congress on Acoustics,* Budapest, Hungary, 1971.

Sambur, M. R. and Rabiner, L. R., "A Statistical Decision Approach to the Recognition of Connected Digits," *IEEE Transactions on Acoustics, Speech, and Signal Processing,* ASSP-24, no. 6 (December 1976), 550-58.

Sambur, M. R. and Rabiner, L. R., "A Speaker Independent Digit-Recognition System," *Bell System Technical Journal,* 54, no. 1 (January 1975), 81-102.

Schmidt, C. E. and Rosenberg, A. E., *"Bell Labs Flight Information System - an Application of the Voice Response System on the NOVA 800,"* Bell Laboratories Technical Memorandum, 1975.

Shannon, C. E., "Prediction and Entropy of Printed English," *Bell System Technical Journal,* 30, no. 1 (January 1951), 50-64.

Shannon, C. E., "A Mathematical Theory of Communication," *Bell System Technical Journal,* 27, no. 3 (July 1948), 379-423.

Sondhi, M. M. and Levinson, S. E., "Computing Relative Redundancy to Measure Grammatical Constraint in Speech Recognition Tasks," *Proceedings of the IEEE ICASSP-78,* Tulsa, OK., 1978.

Sondhi, M. M. and Levinson, S. E., "Relative Difficulty and Robustness of Speech Recognition Tasks that Use Grammatical Constraints," *Journal of the Acoustical Society of America,* 62, supp. no. 1 (Fall 1977), S64.

Viterbi, A. J., "Error Bounds for Convolutional Codes and an Asymptotically Optimal Algorrthm," *IEEE Transactions on Information Theory,* IT-13, no. 2 (April, 1967), 260-69.

19.

THE SPERRY UNIVAC SYSTEM

FOR

CONTINUOUS SPEECH RECOGNITION

Mark F. Medress
Sperry Univac

19-1. INTRODUCTION

As computers assume an ever-expanding role in so many of our activities, the need increases for a more natural and convenient means of communicating with them. Since the spoken word is our most natural means of communicating many kinds of information, the Defense Systems Division at Sperry Univac is meeting this need by developing technology and systems for effective verbal communication with computers.

A primary goal of our speech research program has been the development of a linguistically oriented computer system for recognizing naturally spoken phrases and sentences. In contrast to currently available isolated word recognizers, our system does not require users to either pause artificially between words, or to repeat every vocabulary word several times for system training. It is also able to recognize speech from a number of similar talkers without adjustments for individual voice characteristics. With suitable vocabulary and syntactic restrictions, the recognition of a wide variety of connected word sequences for practical speech input applications should be possible in the near future. Since a linguistic framework is used for recognition, the system can gracefully evolve to understand more complex sentences with the enhancement of syntactic and semantic analysis capabilities.

Other dimensions of the speech recognition problem are addressed by a related and complementary project. In this effort directed at word spotting, we are developing a system for locating specific words that occur in natural conversations over standard communication channels. And in the area of computer generation of speech, we have developed a number of voice response systems that produce very intelligible and natural sounding sentences for speech output. While the speech recognition and voice response systems can be applied to independent tasks, their combined use enables a speech recognition system to effectively interact with a user via spoken questions, requests, and other verbal messages.

In this chapter, we will describe Sperry Univac's continuous speech recognition system (Sec. 19-2), and discuss its current performance and planned improvements (Sec. 19-3). We will also review our related speech technology developments for word spotting and voice response (Sec. 19-4). The chapter concludes with a summary and discussion of future directions (Sec. 19-5).

19-2. THE RECOGNITION SYSTEM

The principal components of the system we are developing for continuous speech recognition are shown in Figure 19-1 (Medress, et. al., 1977). In the first step of the recognition process, an acoustic analysis produces a time-varying description of the incoming speech signal, including estimates of voice fundamental frequency, bandlimited energies, and vocal tract resonances, or formants. Next, a prosodic analysis component provides information about the syllabic structure of the utterance, including the preliminary locations of syllabic nuclei, as well as estimates of which syllables are stressed. A phonetic analysis component then hypothesizes the sound segments, or phonetic sequences, throughout the unknown utterance, including the locations and subclassifications of stops, sibilants, nasals, vowels, liquids, glides, and fricatives. This phonetic feature information is represented in a two-dimensional lattice of sound identifications versus time. In preparation for vocabulary matching, a segmental structuring component next transforms the lattice of phonetic information into a non-overlapping sequence of analysis segments, making various phonological and segmental adjustments during the transformation.

To complete the recognition process, a word sequence hypothesizer determines which sequence of vocabulary words best matches the analysis segments of the unknown utterance. It uses syntactic constraints to direct a word matching component, which aligns and scores segments from each potential word in the dictionary, or lexicon, with the appropriate analysis segments. The lexicon itself is produced with the aid of a generative phonological rules component, which automatically transforms standard dictionary pronunciations into likely alternative sequences of analysis segments. Using vowels as anchor points, and allowing both missed and extra segments with appropriate penalties, the word matcher aligns and scores the analysis and lexical segments. A key element in this process is a scoring matrix, which is generated by a statistical analysis processor that operates on a correlation of analysis segments with time-locked phonetic transcriptions for a data base of development utterances. Working from left to right, the word sequence hypothesizer then strings together good single word matches. The best scoring sequence of words that spans all the analysis segments and satisfies the syntactic constraints, is chosen as the recognized utterance.

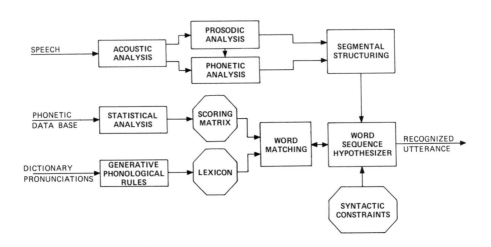

Figure 19-1. The Sperry Univac Continuous Speech Recognition System.

19-2.1 Acoustic Analysis

To produce an acoustic analysis of the unknown utterance, the analog speech waveform is low-pass filtered at 5 kHz and sampled at 10 kHz with a 12-bit A/D converter. An estimate of the rate of vocal cord vibration, or fundamental frequency, is determined from a 51.2 millisecond (ms), center-clipped and auto-correlated window of time waveform samples, which is advanced at 10 ms increments. Spectral analysis is performed with a 25.6 ms Hanning window of software-preemphasized time samples, which is also advanced at 10 ms increments. A 256-point Fast Fourier Transform (FFT) of each window produces spectra used to compute time functions of spectral change, spectral prominence, and bandlimited energies.

Smoothed spectra are also computed for each window, and are used in determining the first three formant frequencies. The smoothed spectra are produced by a 14-coefficient linear prediction analysis, and a 256-point FFT of the prediction coefficients. To enhance the spectral formant peaks, the linear prediction coefficients are biased off the jw-axis before the FFT computation, with the amount of bias being inversely related to fundamental frequency. The formant frequencies are then estimated by choosing the first three peaks, or relative maxima, in each linear prediction spectrum, with some adjustments to the resultant formant frequency contours so that they satisfy time continuity constraints. Table 19-1 contains a summary of the information provided by the acoustic analysis component for use in subsequent prosodic and phonetic processing.

Table 19-1. Speech Waveform Representation from the Acoustic Analysis
(Values Derived at 10 Millisecond Intervals).

Functional Representation	Frequency Range
From the Time Waveform Autocorrelation:	
1. Fundamental Frequency	60 — 400 Hz
From the Fourier Transform Spectra:	0 — 5000 Hz
2. Total Energy	60 — 5000 Hz
3. Sonorant Energy	60 — 3000 Hz
4. High Frequency Sonorant Energy	650 — 3000 Hz
5. Very Low Frequency Energy	60 — 400 Hz
6. Ratio of Low/High Frequency Energy	(60—900 Hz)/(3000 — 5000 Hz)
7. Frequency of Maximum Spectral Amplitude	60 — 5000 Hz
8. Spectral Derivative	60 — 5000 Hz
From the Linear Prediction Spectral Analysis:	0 — 5000 Hz
9. Linear Prediction Coefficients	
10. First Formant Frequency	
11. Second Formant Frequency	
12. Third Formant Frequency	

447

19-2.2 Prosodic Analysis

As the next step in the recognition system, the prosodic analysis component provides information about the syllabic structure of the utterance. Syllabic nuclei are located in regions of high sonorant energy bounded by significant dips. Other procedures determine which syllables are stressed, based on first detecting fall-rise valleys in fundamental frequency (Fo) contours to segment the speech into intonational phrases, and then associating stresses with high-energy syllabic nuclei near the initial Fo rise in a phrase, and near to substantial Fo inflections at later points in each phrase (Lea, 1976).

As part of the subsequent phonetic analysis, vowels are associated with, and identified at, the centers of the syllabic nuclei, after stripping away those portions of the nuclei that are automatically categorized as non-vowel sonorants. Long syllabic nuclei are candidates for diphthong identification, and syllable stress is used in assigning a reliability to each vowel.

19-2.3 Phonetic Analysis

The phonetic analysis process uses the acoustic functions representing the speech waveform, as well as the preliminary vowel nuclei found by the prosodic analysis, to hypothesize the locations and identities of phonetic segments throughout the utterance (Skinner, 1977a). Phonetic regions are first located and classified according to the different manners of articulation. These regions include vowels, liquids, glides, nasals, stops, sibilants, and fricatives, as shown in Table 19-2. Additional classification with regard to place of articulation is performed within each manner class. Stops, sibilants, and fricatives are then further distinguished with respect to their voicing feature. By using the manner, place, and voicing features, an attempt is made to uniquely identify each sound in the utterance with one of the 38 phonetic elements given in Table 19-2. In addition, three classifications not presented in the table — "voiced unknown," "unvoiced unknown," and "silence" — are used to identify utterance regions of significant duration for which no manner identification was previously given.

For vocalic sounds, the manner of articulation decisions are primarily based on formant characteristics. Retroflexive liquids (R) are required to have a low third formant frequency, with the second formant being close in frequency to the third. Lateral liquids (L) are characterized by low first and second formant frequencies, a high third formant frequency, and a discontinuity of the first formant at the junctures to adjoining sounds. Labial liquids (W) are identified by initially low first and second formant frequencies, with a significantly rising second formant frequency during the remainder of the segment and into the following vowel. A palatal glide (Y) must begin with a low first formant frequency and very high second and third formant frequencies, with subsequent transitions to more central values. The location of nasals (M, N, NX) is based on a low frequency concentration of energy (indicated by a high value of the ratio of low/high frequency energy), and a low frequency, narrow bandwidth first formant.

Table 19-2. Phonetic Analysis Categories.

Phonetic Category	Category Elements
Vowel:	
Monophthong	IY, IH, EY, EH, AE, AA, AO, AH, OW, UH, UW, ER
Diphthong	AY, OY, AW
Liquid	R, L
Glide	W, Y
Nasal	M, N, NX
Stop	P, B, T, D, K, G
Sibilant	S, Z, SH, ZH
Fricative	F, V, TH, DH, H, HV

Non-vocalic sounds are cued by abrupt changes in energy and/or characteristic energy distributions throughout the frequency range. A stop (P, B, T, D, K, G) must have a sudden increase in total energy and a large spectral derivative at the release. Sibilants (S, Z, SH, ZH) are indicated by their characteristic concentrations of energy at high frequencies (shown by a correspondingly low value of the ratio of low/high frequency energy). Fricatives (F, V, TH, DH, H, HV (non-phonemic voiced H)) are both sufficiently above the background noise and also below a specified energy level. Each remaining unidentified region of significant duration is then classified either as a "silence" if the total energy is at the background level, or as a "voiced unknown" or "unvoiced unknown." Every phonetic segment must have a minimum duration of 40 ms, and all sonorants must be at least partially voiced.

The further place-of-articulation decisions are based on the frequency of maximum spectral amplitude for stops and sibilants, and the second formant frequency for nasals. Monophthong vowels are identified as their nearest neighbor in the space of the first three formant frequencies, and diphthong vowels are identified by their initial vowel characteristics and the dynamics of their formant motion. Finally, the voicing decision for stops is based on the extent of the post-release delay in voicing onset, and the voicing decision for sibilants and fricatives is a function of the amount of concurrent voicing.

The results of the phonetic analysis process are organized in a two-dimensional lattice of phonetic classes versus time. As an example, the phonetic analysis lattice for the phrase "six seven nine" is shown in Figure 19-2. Across the top of the lattice is a time-synchronous, manually-specified orthographic and phonetic transcription. The remainder of the figure is analytically derived. Voicing was found during the vowel of "six" and continuously throughout "seven nine," beginning with the first vowel in "seven." Four vowel nuclei were appropriately located, and the identities of the second and fourth vowels exactly coincide with the transcription. A false /R/ was located at the /IH/-/K/ juncture in "six". As expected, no /L/'s, /W/'s, or /Y/'s were determined to be present during the utterance. Two nasals were found, the second of which was incorrectly identified as /M/. The voiced fricative /V/ was not found in the word "seven." Two sibilants were correctly located and subclassified as /S/'s during the analysis. The stop in "six" was

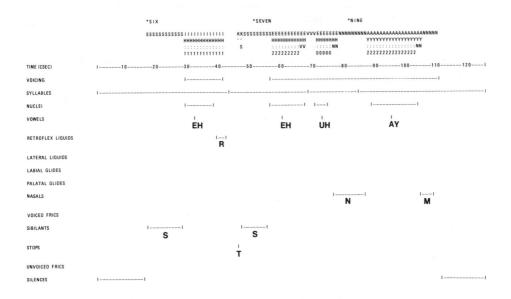

Figure 19-2. A Phonetic Analysis Lattice for the Phrase "Six Seven Nine."

449

also correctly located and subclassified with regard to voicing, but was incorrectly subclassified with respect to place of articulation, and thus was partially misidentified as a /T/. No unvoiced fricatives were found, and segments of silence were located preceding and following the utterance.

This example will be traced through the rest of the recognition process, because it illustrates a number of key features in a fairly compact format. It should be noted, however, that the same procedures are followed in recognizing longer phrases and complete sentences.

19-2.4 Segmental Structuring

In the next step of the recognition procedure, the lattice of phonetic information is organized into a non-overlapping sequence of segments to prepare for lexical matching. The midpoint of each sound type on the lattice is used to define the order of segments. During this transformation, various phonological or segmental adjustments are made: some previously undetected vowels are recovered by relabeling certain isolated "voiced unknown" regions; all /R-ER/ sequences are reordered to be /ER-R/ for consistency; all short silences occurring before stops are deleted; and whenever two consecutive segments have the same manner of articulation, the least reliable is deleted. Once the segment string has been produced, each vowel identity is then re-evaluated by using fundamental frequency and duration information, as well as frequency-of-occurrence probabilities (both context dependent and context independent), in combination with the formant frequencies.

Figure 19-3 presents the results of performing segmental structuring on the phonetic analysis lattice for "six seven nine" (see Figure 19-2). The analysis segments resulting at this stage are shown across the top of the figure. Vowel stress and consonant confidence measures are used to mark the analysis segments as highly reliable (HRS), optional (OPT), or intermediate in reliability (unmarked). The remainder of Figure 19-3 is described in the next section.

19-2.5 Word Sequence Hypothesization

To complete the recognition process, a word sequence hypothesizer directs a word matching component in building, from left to right, partial word sequences of appropriate lexical entries that match throughout the string of analysis segments (Kloker, 1976). As indicated in Figure 19-1, the word sequence hypothesizer uses syntactic constraints to limit the lexical items that must be considered at each step, and the word matcher accesses both a lexicon of segmental entries and a scoring matrix to accomplish the alignment and scoring. The lexicon contains expected phonetic

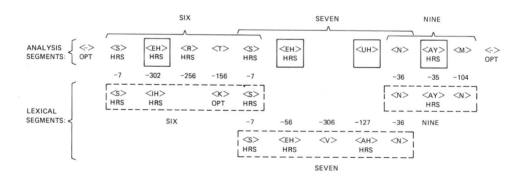

Figure 19-3. Analysis Segments and Lexical Matches for "Six Seven Nine."

descriptions of the vocabulary words, and the scoring matrix provides the log conditional probabilities for each lexical segment being spoken, given every possible analysis segment as being found. Log conditional probabilities for segmental misses and false alarms are also specified.

The strategy for building word sequences centers upon finding all good single word matches anchored around appropriate analysis vowels. Figure 19-3 presents the best scoring sequence of single word matches for this example. The process begins by aligning the first vowel of each syntactically allowed lexical entry with the first analysis vowel /EH/. Proceeding to the right of the initial vowel pair, all possible consonant alignments (including hits, misses, and false alarms) are considered, up to the next vowel pair or word or phrase boundary encountered. The consonants to the left of the initial vowel pair are treated similarly, and the best scoring alignment of consonants around this vowel pair is the one chosen. When new vowel pairs are found, they are automatically aligned and scored, and the process is repeated. In generating a potential alignment, the strategy ignores those alignments that would result in calling a segment marked "optional," a false alarm or a miss. The score used to compare partial alignments is the running average per-segment-score accumulated for the match up to that point. An attempted alignment will fail if the total number of misses plus false alarms exceeds a threshold dependent on the length of the word.

As Figure 19-3 illustrates, the best scoring alignment of the lexical entry for "six" around the first analysis vowel treats the analysis /R/ as an extra segment (i.e., a false alarm), and correctly associates the lexical /K/ with the analysis /T/. The numbers between the aligned segments are the log probability segment pair scores from the scoring matrix. The scores are all negative, since they are logarithms of numbers between zero and one. The score for "six" is -145, the average of the segment scores -7, -302, -256, -156, and -7.

After all syntactically allowed first words are aligned and scored, each good match is extended by anchoring possible second words at the next analysis vowel. In the example of Figure 19-3, the next analysis vowel after "six" is the second /EH/. The result of aligning and scoring the lexical entry for "seven" around this vowel shows that the word matcher can handle missed segments (the /V/ in "seven"). The alignment also indicates how the hypothesizer specifically deals with word boundary effects in continuous speech, by allowing consecutive words that end and begin with similar consonants to share consonantal analysis segments. Thus, the analysis /S/ that is aligned with the last /S/ in "six," is also used to begin the word "seven."

The word sequence hypothesizer continues to build high scoring word strings that satisfy the syntactic constraints until all the analysis segments have been accounted for. In the example of Figure 19-3, the extension of "six seven" is accomplished by anchoring lexical entries that can occur in third position, around the fourth analysis vowel /AY/. The alignment for "nine" again shows how one analysis segment (the /N/) can be used to both end one word and begin the next. At this point in the recognition procedure, all of the analysis segments have been utilized to create the word sequence hypothesis "six seven nine," which is then compared to other possible sequences to yield the recognized utterance.

Figure 19-4 shows the partial word sequences that are hypothesized in each step of this example. As in Figure 19-3, the analysis segments are given at the top of the figure, and the alignment of partial phrases is given below. To evaluate competing sequences, the hypothesizer uses the averages of the segment scores for each partial phrase, just as it does to compute the individual word scores, and these are listed on the right of the figure. As Figure 19-4 indicates, four words were considered worthy candidates to begin the utterance. By extending each of these words and retaining only the best scoring two-word sequences, the two lowest scoring first words are eliminated, and four partial phrases remain. In the last step of the recognition process, several three-word sequences are produced that span all the analysis segments. Since "six seven nine" scores best, it is correctly announced as the recognized utterance.

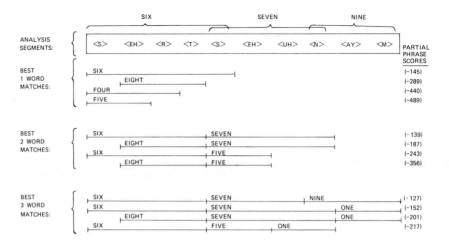

Figure 19-4. Partial Word Sequences in the Recognition of "Six Seven Nine."

19-2.6 Generation of the Lexicon and Scoring Matrix

As the preceding section illustrates, the lexicon and scoring matrix are important data structures in our continuous speech recognition system. The preparation of these data structures is substantially aided by automated procedures and a data base used for system development (refer back to Figure 19-1).

An initial version of a desired lexicon is produced by transforming standard dictionary pronunciations with a set of generative phonological rules, thus yielding lexical variants incorporating both phonological generalizations and systematic characteristics of our analysis system (Diller, 1977). Over 100 rules are currently in use; they are context sensitive, obligatory, and conjunctively ordered. The rules modify the dictionary pronunciations by inserting, deleting, and replacing segments to produce lexical entries that contain segment labels, segment reliabilities, and stress information. Approximately four lexical variants are generated for each dictionary pronunciation, and these variants reflect coarticulation effects both within and between words. A final set of variants is then produced by hand-tailoring the initial set to better capture the features of actual analysis tokens which are idiosyncratic to a given lexical item.

The scoring matrix is also generated automatically by performing a statistical analysis of a phonetic data base, as indicated in Figure 19-1. For each utterance in the data base, an orthographic and phonetic transcription is manually prepared to specify the locations and perceptions of every phonetic segment. The top of Figure 19-2 shows such a transcription for the utterance we have been using as a recognition example. Programs then automatically correlate the transcription segments with the segments produced during the analysis phase of our recognition system. One result is a segment confusion matrix containing the number of occurrences of each transcription-analysis phone pair, as well as the number of times each analysis phone was falsely hypothesized and the number of times every transcription phone was missed. These confusion statistics are then converted to log conditional probabilities to form the scoring matrix. The statistical analysis programs are also valuable for collecting phonetic parameter values from the data base to adjust algorithm thresholds, establish expected parameter value ranges, and automatically evaluate the performance of individual recognition components.

19-3. RECOGNITION PERFORMANCE

Our continuous speech recognition system has been developed and tested on a speech data base of phrases and sentences. The data base has been used to formulate algorithms and adjust threshold values and parameters, to generate such data structures as the scoring matrix and lexicon, and to evaluate system performance on phonetic, lexical, and utterance levels.

19-3.1 The Recognition Data Base

The data base we have used in our recognition development represents two application areas. The first of the task domains consists of two, three, and four word sequences of digits and "phonetic alphabet" words, a vocabulary and syntax characteristic of many data entry tasks. The 36-word vocabulary is divided into four subsets of eight to ten words, and nine varieties of sequences are defined. Examples of these alphanumeric sequences are listed in Table 19-3. The average branching factor (average number of word alternatives to the right of each word of the phrase) for this task is 9.4. The syntax defines 25,842 potential sequences.

The second task addresses the recognition of utterances typical of data management or information retrieval languages, and is based upon a potential speech input application in air traffic control. The seven command types listed in Table 19-3 define the permissable syntactic structures. The items in parentheses are fixed one-word subsets for that utterance type, while the underlined words are variable subsets consisting of the numbers 1–9, 10–19, or 20–90 by tens; the positions "up," "down," "left," or "right," the objects "field," "line," or "page"; ten airline names; and ten city names. The total vocabulary size is 64, and the average branching factor is 6.3. The syntax defines a potential of 919 different utterances.

For each task domain, 110 utterances were randomly selected for initial recording and processing. Three male talkers each recorded about one-third of the utterances, and these recordings were used for developing the recognition programs. No adjustments of the recognition system were made for individual talker characteristics.

About one year later, an additional set of 24 alphanumeric sequences and 23 data management commands were randomly selected from the two data bases to provide test material for the recognition system. Each of the three male talkers used for development recorded about one-third of the test utterances, which were reserved for processing after system development had been completed.

Table 19-3. Sample Phrases and Sentences for Speech Recognition Development and Testing.

ALPHANUMERIC SEQUENCES

— Vocabulary size = 36

— Average branching factor = 9.4

e.g. Hotel niner
Sierra Alfa Zulu
Quebec Papa four three

DATA MANAGEMENT COMMANDS

— Vocabulary size = 64

— Average branching factor = 6.3

1. (Shift line) twelve (to) (position number) ten

2. (Transmit line) eighteen (to) (station) two

3. (Cursor) down seven

4. (Erase) field

5. (Flight index for) American forty nine

6. (Weather forecast for) Minneapolis

7. (Current weather for) Boston

19-3.2 Phonetic Analysis Performance

The performance of the phonetic analysis procedures on the development portion of our data base is summarized in Table 19-4. The information in the table indicates the correspondence between a listener's transcription of phonetic segments and the automatically produced analysis segments, for the development data base of 220 alphanumeric sequences and data management commands. For each phonetic category, the listener decisions are indicated as number of segments transcribed. The system's performance is summarized in the dimensions of: number of segments detected, percentage of transcribed segments for which correct manner decisions were made, percentage of correct place and voicing decisions for those sounds having correct manner decisions (where appropriate), and percentage of false manner decisions. For example, the table shows that 670 released stops were transcribed by a listener, and 491 stops were hypothesized during the phonetic analysis process. Of the 670 transcribed stops, 63% (or 422) were actually found as stops during the analysis. Of these 422 stops, 72% received correct place of articulation classifications, and 87% were correctly identified with regard to voicing. Of the 491 stops detected during phonetic analysis, 14% did not correspond with stops in the utterance transcriptions, and were therefore counted as false alarms. From an examination of Table 19-4, it can be seen that best phonetic analysis performance occurred for vowels, retroflexives, and sibilants. Lateral liquids, labial glides, nasals, released stops, and unvoiced fricatives were classified with moderate success. Lowest phonetic analysis performance was obtained for palatal glides and voiced fricatives.

Table 19-4.   Phonetic Analysis Performance for 220 Development Utterances.

Phonetic Category (Manner)	Number Transcribed	Number Detected	Percent Correct			% False Alarms
			Manner	Place	Voicing	
Vowel						
Monophthong	1335	1247	94%	60%		2%
Diphthong	128	154		100%		
Retroflexive Liquid (R)	359	325	85%			6%
Lateral Liquid (L)	164	101	50%			19%
Labial Glide (W)	90	65	56%			23%
Palatal Glide (Y)	37	21	30%			48%
Nasal	426	313	63%	85%		15%
Released Stop	670	491	63%	72%	87%	14%
Sibilant	380	362	92%	94%	95%	3%
Unvoiced Fricative	278	254	77%			15%
Voiced Fricative	112	105	24%			74%

The consistency of the phonetic analysis results for the development utterances is reflected in several parts of the recognition system, and this accounts for some of the system's ability to correctly recognize utterances that have phonetic analysis errors. For example, the scoring matrix contains statistics from the development data base for missed, extra, and incorrectly identified segments. This matrix is used by the word matcher to align and score lexical entries with the analysis segments. In addition, the lexical entries themselves are modified to better represent the actual segments found for each vocabulary word in the development utterances.

19-3.3 Word and Phrase Recognition Results

After adjusting all components of the recognition system for the development portion of our data base, the system was stabilized. Then the remaining utterances, recorded by the same three male talkers a full year after the development recordings, were processed by the recognition system to obtain test results. Table 19-5 shows both the word and the phrase recognition results for the development and test portions of the alphanumeric sequences and the data management commands. The number of words or phrases in each category is given in parentheses beside the percentage correct results. For the alphanumeric sequences, 96% of the 110 development phrases and 79% of the 24 test phrases were recognized with no errors at all. Of the 329 individual words contained in the development phrases, 98% were correctly recognized. Similarly, 92% of the 72 words in the test phrases were also recognized correctly. For the data management commands, 97% of the development utterances and 87% of the test utterances were correctly recognized. Word recognition accuracies for the development and test utterances were 99% and 96%, respectively.

Table 19-5. Word and Phrase Recognition Performance for the
Development and Test Utterances.

Speech Data	ALPHANUMERIC SEQUENCES		DATA MANAGEMENT COMMANDS	
	% Correct Individual Word Recognition	% Correct Phrase Recognition	% Correct Individual Word Recognition	% Correct Phrase Recognition
Development	98% (329)	96% (110)	99% (380)	97% (110)
Test	92% (72)	79% (24)	96% (76)	87% (23)
Average	97% (401)	93% (134)	98% (456)	95% (133)

By combining the development and test utterances, we obtained average phrase recognition accuracies of about 94%, and average word recognition accuracies of about 98%. As expected, the individual word recognition accuracies were higher than those for complete utterances, since the presence of a single word error in a phrase results in that entire phrase being counted as incorrect. Analysis of the errors indicates that 14 of the 18 words found incorrectly had syllabication or phonetic errors that were not adequately represented in the scoring matrix or lexicon. The remaining four incorrect words resulted from problems in the word matching strategy, such as an incorrect word identification due to the sharing of consonants from adjacent words.

19-3.4 Future Recognition Development

Within the next few years, we expect to enhance our speech recognition system so that it can meet the performance requirements of a variety of practical applications for continuous speech input. Our current recognition system operates in about 80 times real time on our laboratory minicomputer, with approximately 75 percent of that time devoted to acoustic analysis. The system should operate in real time with the planned addition of a fast array processor, and with more efficient use of our minicomputer's hardware and software capabilities. Recognition accuracy should also increase as the result of incorporating both phonetic analysis improvements based on context information, and a word verification component being developed under our related word spotting project. Studies already under way of noisy, bandlimited speech should eventually lead to successful recognition over telephones and other communication channels. All of these planned improvements are designed to provide an effective and practical sentence recognition system for natural speech input to computers.

19-4. RELATED TECHNOLOGY DEVELOPMENT

The development of our continuous speech recognition system is complemented by two other closely related activities: word spotting and voice response. Each provides additional speech processing capability that can enhance the overall effectiveness of our recognition system.

19-4.1 Word Spotting

Our word spotting project is a major research activity that is using many of the same components and technologies from our continuous speech recognition system to develop procedures for spotting key information-carry words in natural conversations over normal communication channels (Medress, et. al., 1978). While the simple location of selected words is a more limited task than that of recognizing all of the words in a phrase or sentence, several new attributes introduce additional complexities to the problem. These include the limited bandwidth and added noise imposed by the telephone system; the variety of dialects and speech characteristics inherent in a large talker population; and the large fluctuations in amplitude, speaking rate, and articulatory preciseness that characterize conversational style speech.

A block diagram of our word spotting system is shown in Figure 19-5. The similarity between this system and the one we are developing for continuous speech recognition should be apparent from a comparison of Figures 19-5 and 19-1. The acoustic analysis, prosodic analysis, phonetic analysis and segmental structuring components produce a linear sequence of analysis segments representing the conversational speech material. While these components are basically the same as the corresponding ones in our speech recognition system, they are being suitably modified to better handle the limited signal bandwidth and wide variety of talkers (Skinner, 1977b). The word hypothesizer is also similar to that of our other system. Again using vowels as anchor points, it aligns and scores keyword representations from a segmental lexicon with the analysis segments, to determine where in the incoming speech are likely occurrences of keywords.

Each hypothesized keyword occurrence is then further evaluated by a new component developed for our word spotting system. Using dynamic programming for time registration, this word verifier provides an independent assessment of the acoustic similarity of a stored spectral pattern for the hypothesized word, with the spectral characteristics of the input speech at the region hypothesized. A novel feature of our verifier is its use of vowel nuclei for anchoring the alignment process. Finally, a keyword selector operates on the word scores provided by both the hypothesizer and verifier to produce a list of accepted keywords and their locations.

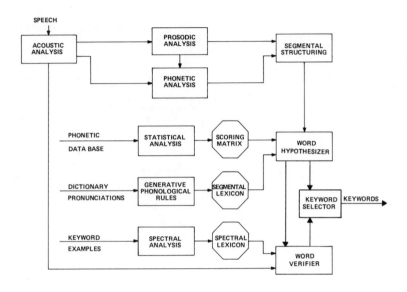

Figure 19-5. The Sperry Univac Word Spotting System.

An initial version of our word spotting system has been developed on 13 minutes of informal telephone conversations by eight talkers, and tested on 11 additional minutes of speech by two of the same talkers and eight new ones. Results of this test are encouraging, and development is continuing with a focus on improving acoustic and phonetic processing and word verification. The current test materials will be folded in as new development data, and the system will be retested using speech from 16 additional talkers. Studies are also under way to extend the system so it can perform acceptably with noisier speech.

19-4.2   Voice Response

The projects described so far have centered on the computer analysis of speech, with a major application being verbal input to computers.   Sperry Univac's voice response developments address the opposite problem: the computer generation of high quality, natural sounding sentences for speech output. Instead of creating speech by synthesis methods, our prerecorded voice response units use words and phrases that are first spoken by a trained announcer and then digitized and stored in a digital memory, as shown in Figure 19-6. To produce speech output, a host computer first specifies the sequence of words and phrases that form the desired output message. The voice response controller next retrieves the digitized speech from the vocabulary storage memory and strings the specified words and phrases together without undesirable intervening pauses. The audio decoder and data set interface portion then converts the digitized speech back into an analog signal, and the resulting voice output message is sent to a speaker, radio transmitter, or telephone circuit. The voice response unit is also able to accept touch-tone input characters for internal use or for transmission back to the host computer.

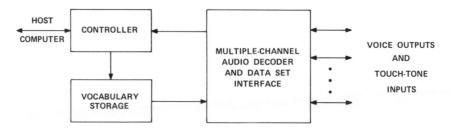

Figure 19-6. The Sperry Univac Voice Response Unit.

Our latest voice response unit, the VRU-400, is completely solid state and has several attractive features. The controller is implemented with a programmable microprocessor, providing a great deal of flexibility and internal processing capability. The vocabulary is stored in a solid state memory made of Charge Coupled Device (CCD) memory chips, resulting in increased reliability, faster access, and better modularity than a disk-based unit. By using Adaptive Differential Pulse Code Modulation (ADPCM), we are able to obtain high quality digitization of telephone bandwidth speech using only 24 kilobits per second of vocabulary, about half the bit rate needed with ordinary PCM encoding. The speech output quality is further enhanced by using variable-length vocabulary storage, and by composing messages from complete phrases whenever possible. We also record two versions of some vocabulary items, one version with flat inflection for use in the middle of a phrase, and the other with falling inflection for phrase-final position. The basic VRU-400 can handle up to 16 simultaneous and independent audio-output/touch-tone-input channels, and a vocabulary of up to 200 seconds of recorded speech. Additional vocabulary can be accommodated with extra vocabulary storage memory.

A number of practical applications have been successfully addressed by Sperry Univac's voice response units. They have been used by the Federal Aviation Administration to automatically generate voice messages in their air traffic control systems (Beck and Anderson, 1975). Typical examples include traffic advisories, metering and spacing messages, and minimum safe altitude warnings. The National Weather Service and the Department of Transportation have also used our voice response units to provide pilots with information about current and predicted weather conditions. Finally, we have recently installed a VRU-400 in a telephone ordering system for a large catalogue retailer in the Federal Republic of Germany. The voice response unit allows customers to place their orders over ordinary telephones, using touch-tone signals for input, and voice response messages (in German) for output. The voice response unit, which is on-line to the main order processing computer, provides real time confirmation of the item ordered, its availability, and its current price. Merchandise delivery time has also been significantly reduced, since the VRU-400 eliminates mail delays in placing orders.

19-5. SUMMARY

Sperry Univac is developing a continuous speech recognition system for understanding naturally spoken phrases and sentences by a number of talkers, without requiring extensive adjustments for individual voice characteristics. This linguistically oriented system first hypothesizes phonetic segments representing the incoming speech. Recognition is then completed by determining which sequence of vocabulary words best matches the hypothesized segments, and also satisfies applicable syntactic constraints. Current recognition performance is very encouraging, and within a few years we expect a practical version of this system to be available for a variety of speech input applications.

The utility of our continuous speech recognition system should be further enhanced by the technology we are developing for locating key information-carrying words in natural conversations. For this application, we are modifying and enhancing our recognition procedures to operate successfully with a large and diverse talker population communicating over standard telephone lines. In addition, we have already developed voice response systems that string together prerecorded words and phrases to produce high quality sentences for speech output. This voice response capability will allow our speech recognition system to interact naturally and conveniently with its users via spoken messages.

All of the development activities described in this chapter have a common goal: to make computer systems easier and more natural to use by enabling effective verbal communication between people and computers. Sperry Univac's current voice response systems already produce excellent speech output. We believe that our continuous speech recognition and word spotting systems now under development will provide the desired and complementary speech input capability for important practical applications.

ACKNOWLEDGEMENT

Sperry Univac's speech processing technology is a result of the combined efforts of all members of the Speech Communications Research Department at the Defense Systems Division. They include David P. Andersen, Donald E. Anderson, Timothy C. Diller, Dean R. Kloker, Larry L. Lutton, Henry N. Oredson, John F. Siebenand, and Toby E. Skinner. Tim, Dean, and Toby also provided much appreciated assistance in preparing material for this chapter.

REFERENCES

BECK, A.F., and D.E. ANDERSON (1975), "Computer-Generated Voice in Air Traffic Control Applications," Proceedings of the IEEE 1975 National Aerospace and Electronics Conference NAECON '75, IEEE Cat. No. 75 CHO956-3 NAECON 75, pp. 547–551.

DILLER, T.C. (1977), "Automatic Lexical Generation for Speech Recognition," Conference Record of the 1977 IEEE International Conference on Acoustics, Speech, and Signal Processing, IEEE Cat. No. 77 CH1197-3 ASSP, pp. 803–806.

KLOKER, D.R. (1976), "A Connected Word Sequence Matching Strategy for Speech Recognition," Sperry Univac Report No. PX 11649.

LEA, W.A. (1976), "Prosodic Aids to Speech Recognition: IX. Acoustic-Prosodic Patterns in Selected English Phrase Structures," Sperry Univac Report No. PX 11963.

MEDRESS, M.F., T.E. SKINNER, D.R. KLOKER, T.C. DILLER, and W.A. LEA (1977), "A System for the Recognition of Spoken Connected Word Sequences," Conference Record of the 1977 IEEE International Conference on Acoustics, Speech, and Signal Processing, IEEE Cat. No. 77 CH1197-3 ASSP, pp. 468–473.

MEDRESS, M.F., T.C. DILLER, D.R. KLOKER, L.L. LUTTON, H.N. OREDSON, and T.E. SKINNER (1978), "An Automatic Word Spotting System for Conversational Speech," Conference Record of the 1978 IEEE International Conference on Acoustics, Speech, and Signal Processing, IEEE Cat. No. 78 CH1285-6 ASSP, pp. 712-717.

SKINNER, T.E. (1977a), "Toward Automatic Determination of the Sounds Comprising Spoken Words and Sentences," Sperry Univac Report No. PX 12124.

SKINNER, T.E. (1977b), "Speaker Invariant Characterizations of Vowels, Liquids, and Glides Using Relative Formant Frequencies," Journal of the Acoustical Society of America, 62, S1 (A), p. S5.

20.

THE EXPANDING MARKET FOR COMMERCIAL SPEECH RECOGNIZERS

J. Michael Nye
Marketing Consultants International, Inc.

20-1. INTRODUCTION

One of the most misunderstood concepts about speech recognition is how
this technology would benefit mankind. Throughout the industrial revolution
"man" has been conditioned with a basic truth - in order to communicate and
control machines he must adapt the human method of communication to machine
language in order to tell the machine (or computer for that matter) what he
would like it to do.

Fundamentally, this decoding process on the part of the human many times
can lead to unconsious transposition errors, entry mistakes and most importantly unaccountability on the part of the human for machine input accuracy.
A reasonable example of this idea is in computer data entry. To input
computer data the human must exercise extreme caution in not violating any
protocol rules during communications which are normally taken for granted
in human to human verbal communications. The computer, as well as other
machines, is intolerant and unforgiving for simple transposition errors and
coding violation rules that easily develop because of the mental and physical
conversion functions necessary on the part of the human to accurately enter
information.

Automatic speech recognition offers the promise of solving this man/machine
control problem. The human can capture information at the source in "human
form" and transmit it to the computer or other machines without the intermediate decoding required to convert this information into machine readable
format.

Therefore a speech recognition device serves as an intermediate "interpreter" between the man and machine. Consequently, if the human desires
to record information like "right, door handle, missing - door stuck" a
device would recognize and verify to the human the information he wished
to enter. At this point the recognition device then decodes this information
into data strings acceptable to the machine (machine language) and then
transmits the data automatically.

Besides the obvious improvement in efficiency and user acceptance, this
technique provides for a method of accuracy accountability at the point of
data capture. Furthermore, no longer is it necessary for manufacturers to
devise clever man/machine dialog between the human and the recording device.
The speech recognition intermediary, if you will, automatically adapts to
the language idiosyncrasies of the human and converts them to machine language
without inconveniencing the human. This is a fundamental point about speech
recognition technology that is often lost in identifying new applications.

This chapter will describe a few representative examples of applications
in various segments of speech processing technology to "real world" problems.
New applications are successfully penetrated almost on a daily basis. In the

last few years industry has recognized the benefit and need for Distributed
Data Processing (DDP) systems to improve productivity in a plant environment.
With many major corporations "pioneering" the concept of Distributed Data
Processing/Source Data Entry the need for and applicability of speech processing technology has and will become more important. As costs of voice
input technology approach those of competing intelligent terminals or the
front-ends to the DDP systems, speech recognition offers the best operational
alternative from the end-user's point of view. Because of this obvious
industry trend no fewer than 50 companies are actively engaged in the development of various versions of automatic speech processing technology. Table
20-1 is an attempt to identify some of those organizations

TABLE 20-1

CURRENT & POTENTIAL SPEECH MANUFACTURERS
(May 1978)

COMPANY	COMMERCIAL PRODUCT	UNITS SOLD	RESEARCH	DISCRETE	CONTINUOUS
Threshold Technology,Inc.	Several	+200	Yes	Yes	FPA
Interstate Electronics,Inc.	Single	+ 10	Yes	Yes	FPA
Dialog Systems, Inc.	Single	+ 5	Yes	-	Yes
Perception Technology,Inc.	Single	+ 2	Yes	Yes	FPA
Texas Instruments,Inc.	No	+ 3	Yes	Yes	FPA
IBM Corporation	No	?	Yes	Yes	Yes
NEC America, Inc.	Single	+ 3	Yes	No	Yes
ITT - Defense Comm. Div.	No	?	Yes	Yes	FPA
System Development Corp.	No	-	Yes		FPA
Autonetics, Inc.	No	-	IR		FPA
Sperry Univac Corp.	No	-	Yes		FPA
Bell Labs	No	-	Yes	FPA	FPA
Boeing Computer	No	-	IR		FPA
Culler/Harrison	Single	+ 1	IR	No	Yes
Rockwell Systems Corp.	No	-	IR		FPA
E-Systems	No	-	IR		FPA
IGE Telefunken	No	-	IR		FPA
TRW	No	-	Yes		FPA
Motorola	No	-	IR		FPA
Honeywell	No	-	IR		FPA
Logicon, Inc.	Single	?	Yes	No	FPA
Heuristics, Inc.	Single-Hobby	+500	IR	Yes	No
Centigram, Inc.	Single	?	Yes	Yes	FPA
Phonics, Inc.	Single-Hobby	+ 25	Yes	Yes	No

IR - Industry Rumor
FPA - Future Product Assumed
? - Unknown Installations but Assumed

   This Table represents the author's knowledge about what may be happening
in the industry, particularly regarding the future. The inclusion or exclusion
of a specific company from this listing does not represent any recommendation
or endorsement by the author. It is provided as an information source to
demonstrate the growing interest in speech recognition. Any statistics
or information provided are the author's "best guess" based on published
information.

20-2. TECHNOLOGY REQUIREMENTS

Speech recognition devices can be segmented into several basic categories. Fundamentally, there are two primary operating technologies: 1) discrete word/isolated recognition systems, and 2) continuous word/connected recognition systems. In each category the technology segment would include adaptive and non-adaptive system performance. With an adaptive system a user must first orient (train) the system to the speaker's use of the vocabulary. However, with non-adaptive - speaker independent systems the requirement for advanced training is eliminated. Obviously, the technical difficulty is far greater with a speaker independent system as opposed to a speaker dependent system.

A general application discussion is provided which should be considered fairly typical of most of the existing uses of automatic speech recognition in "real" applications; that is, applications where the system is routinely used in conjunction with other systems to provide benefit to the customer in increased efficiency. It has been this author's experience that the need for non-adaptive technology has not been demonstrated. This is particularly true with most existing applications. Although non-adaptive systems will offer certain user convenience, it is useless if accuracy must be sacrificed for the sake of user convenience. Much has been stated about the need for larger vocabulary systems. As shown in Table 20-2, I estimate, from my six years of experience with various practical applications, that the bulk of application potential in discrete speech is with 75 words or less. With continuous speech 96% of the projected market needs a word list of 13 up to 200 words.

TABLE 20-2

TECHNOLOGY REQUIREMENTS

CAPABILITY	WORD SIZE	%
Discrete Speech	12	8%
	75	88%
	76+	4%
Continuous Speech	12	3%
	75	30%
	200	66%
	201+	1%

Proven applications of speech recognition have been identified in the areas of material handling/sorting, quality control/data entry, machine tool/ parts programming, source data collection/computer data entry, medical/ paraplegic machine control, and military tactical machine control problems. For the most part, these applications enjoy strong return on investments, even though they require adaptation to the individual speaker.

20-2.1 Material Handling

In the material handling applications segment, the primary application or system use has been identified as encoding operations for sortation equipment. With voice encoding systems the speech recognition device is interfaced to an existing material handling system which could be a conveyor sorter, tray sorter, or various other sortation equipment configurations. Basically, the system is used for encoding, that is, to tell the memory device of the sorter where to send an item that is being sorted. This type of application is fairly typical of warehouse operations in order assembly, shipping, receiving, and distribution systems.

A Baltimore area distribution center installed several voice encoders (from Threshold Technology, 1974) onto their existing conveyor sortation equipment. Originally, the facility maintained a facer and keyer encoding operation, Figure 20-1. To this system was added a voice encoding terminal which eliminated the need for the keying operation. Figure 20-2 illustrates how the facer operator can induct each package and encode the system simultaneously. Substantial productivity increases are achieved with the system, and the Baltimore facility currently uses approximately 15 encoding terminals.

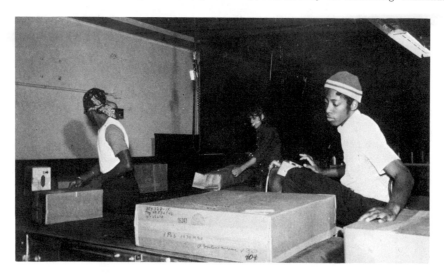

Figure 20-1. Package sorting by separate facing and keyboard encoding operations.

Figure 20-2. Packing sorting with simultaneous hands-free encoding.

20-2.2 Quality Control

In the area of quality control systems successful installations include Owens Illinois/TV tube inspection, Continental Can/pull ring beer can inspection, and Olin-Winchester/rifle serial number inspection and validation. Assembly plants for General Motors, Chrysler, and Ford Motor routinely use voice input for inspection operations.

Automotive assembly is a classic example for the need of Distributed Data Processing systems. In this application an inspector records vehicle build-up inspection defects on a vehicle travel ticket. This ticket is handled by various assemblers and inspectors throughout the assembly operation and eventually becomes the permanent, stored record on a particular vehicle. Because of the manual nature of the inspection reporting system it is difficult for quality control personnel to recognize trends in the manufacturing process or to isolate defective products going out the door.

Voice input eliminates the need for the travel ticket altogether and provides for real time feedback of what is happening in each assembly department as the vehicle proceeds down the assembly line. All open defects are instantaneously recorded and feedback information is provided for assembly errors to offending department. Benefits include system accuracy improvements, reduced defects, reduced inspection personnel, and a built-in discipline that requires assembly personnel to do the job they are being paid to do.

This problem appears to be universal throughout many routine assembly operations, not just automotive. The speech problem is simple because the average vocabulary size at each inspection station is under 40 words, and the data rate is less than 20 utterances per minute.

Manufacturers of finished goods products perform in-process visual inspection of products manufactured, in order to reduce the amount of rejects of completed products and to reduce warranty claims. Some of these tasks require the inspector to memorize numeric codes for an inspected item as well as the numeric code for the defect. Codes are important so the downstream, off-line, data entry functions would be simplified. Often this data is captured for historical purposes only because of its untimeliness.

These requirements add additional burden on the inspector and thereby contribute to system errors. The use of speech recognition in these types of applications eliminates the requirement for the operator to learn numeric code representations. It provides manufacturing personnel with more timely, meaningful data relative to what's really occuring in the manufacturing process.

Several years ago the General Motors Assembly Division tested voice data entry for a single station at the Southgate Assembly Facility in Los Angeles. Among other things the purpose of this test was to measure user acceptability, training requirements, system reliability, and in general the feasibility of capturing real time manufacturing information at the source. The results of the test were an unqualified success, although systems were not purchased for universal plantwide applications because the average cost, at that time, was approximately $35,000+ per voice input terminal. Since that time costs have been reduced significantly and, therefore many manufacturing/assembly plants are actively pursuing the installation of voice data collection systems.

As shown in Figure 20-3, an operator can ride with a vehicle as it proceeds down the assembly line, enter defeat information like "steering" wheel inoperative". The visual display is strategically located in the line of sight of the inspector who may verify what was entered and then continue. At the conclusion of the inspection process the user simply says a control word to indicate the inspection task is complete for this vehicle. A defect label printer produces a label that is affixed to the current travel ticket and follows the vehicle through the remaining assembly process. The defect label notifies repairmen which items need repair.

465

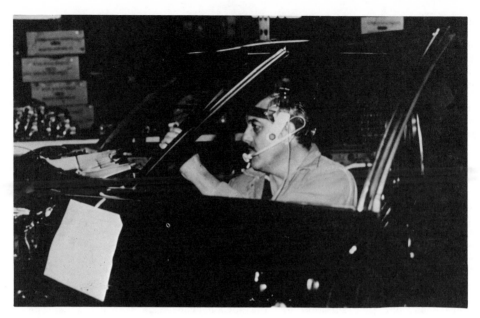

Figure 20-3. Voice entry of defects while inspecting a vehicle.

20-2.3 Medical

The medical market represents a rather unique opportunity for speech processing technology. Specifically the idea of using a small (low cost) voice recognition device to control the environment around incapacitated patients, paralyzed individuals, and people confined to wheelchairs has significant operational benefits. Unfortunately, until now and for some time to come costs of such technology prohibit widespread use in this market area.

20-3. MARKET FORECAST

The Distributed Data Processing market is projected by others to approach $4.6 billion by 1982. Of this total it is estimated that by 1979 the intelligent terminal market will exceed $800 million. According to International Data Corporation, it is expected that 250,000 general purpose terminals worth $1.5 billion will be shipped in 1978 alone from more than 70 suppliers in the industry.

It is generally conceded throughout industry that the intelligent terminal market will grow faster than any other segment of the computer industry. The consensus is that the annual growth rate for intelligent terminals will exceed 30% per year. Evidence of the spectacular growth rate in this industry can be demonstrated by the phenomenal successes of companies catering to this industry by offering custom terminals and total turnkey system services. Such notables as Four Phase Systems, Data Point, Sycor, and Incoterm Corporation collectively do in excess of $200 million annually (see Business Week, October 25, 1976, "Glowing Prospects for Brainy Computer Terminals").

With the total projection for intelligent terminals to reach $800 million by 1979 a significant portion of this market will probably still deal with the clerical/accounting activities of business and a lessor percentage concerned with actual data capture and manipulation at the factory level. User acceptance of this technology at the work station level in real world applications has been conservative with the acceptance of hardware on an application by application basis. This cautious acceptance trend implies a certain amount of "customization" for each customer, thereby, making it difficult to develop a standard intelligent terminal to meet general industry's needs economically. Because of this, excellent opportunity exists in the area of customized data entry systems.

It is reasonable to assume that speech recognition technology offers the universal customization needed by the end-user while at the same time providing for standardized hardware from the manufacturer's point of view. For years mainframe suppliers have met dismal defeat in the implementation of their standard intelligent terminal hardware in production oriented applications because the end-user was required to adapt their operation to the constraints of the standardized hardware configuration. Obviously speech recognition allows the user to customize the system operation to fit his specific requirements at a particular operation location, thereby, reducing training and increasing user acceptance of the invasion of the "computer" in the factory. This customization is usually under software control which can be implemented easily (economically).

Despite the "bullish" predictions for DDP, an available market forecast for speech recognition must be based on known, specific applications. Consequently, the assumptions made in Table 20-3 represent only known applications providing meaningful cost/benefit to the end-user.

TABLE 20-3

AVAILABLE MARKET FORECAST 1978-1988[*]

CAPABILITY	TERMINALS	% DOD/COMM. MIX	$VALUE(000)	% DOD/COMM. MIX
Discrete Speech	323,000	20/80	500,000	20/80
Continuous Speech	27,000	80/20	1,000,000	90/10
	350,000	25%/75%	$1,500,000	67%/33%

[*]Excludes Point of Sale, Financial (Cashless Society), Office of the Future, and Consumer Applications. (DOD = Department of Defense applications; COMM = Commercial applications)

The mix of Discrete versus Continuous is based on the assumption that continuous speech products will cost about 50% more than discrete terminals. However, if costs are greater than 50% the percentage mix will change drastically in those applications where discrete will marginally solve the problem. Their are applications, however, where only continuous speech will solve the problem (i.e., high speed multi-digit sorting), therefore, market growth will be slowed.

Of the data supplied in Table 20-3 it may be of interest to understand where the significant applications fall. For the commercial market, major application segment values are described in Table 20-4. Note that Manufacturing/SDC represents 60% of the total commercial market, as I forecast it.

Perhaps it is difficult to understand how a market of this size can be justified based on the performance of previous suppliers. Speech recognition is still in the pioneering stage of market development. The speech and success

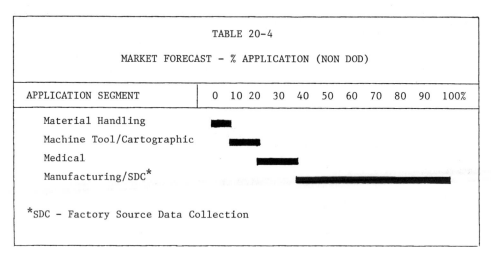

APPLICATION SEGMENT	0	10	20	30	40	50	60	70	80	90	100%

TABLE 20-4

MARKET FORECAST - % APPLICATION (NON DOD)

Material Handling

Machine Tool/Cartographic

Medical

Manufacturing/SDC*

*SDC - Factory Source Data Collection

rate of this pionerring effort is in direct relationship to the financial resources and strategy of the so-called "pioneers".

Another way to explain this pioneering effort is to refer to Figure 20-4.

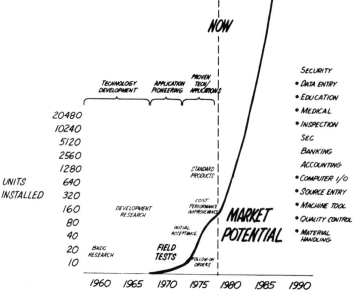

Figure 20-4. The "Technology Development Life Cycle" as applied to predicting the market potential in speech recognition.

This graph attempts to demonstrate the key events in the Technology Development Life Cycle. Only recently has speech recognition technology reached a point where cost and performance of initial products have achieved success with standard products developed with initial customer follow-on orders. Major applications for speech recogniiton have been penetrated successfully in areas as shown with dots on the right, and the other applications listed should provide further market potential.

The need is clear and the future bright for "humanized" man/machine communications.

SPEECH RECOGNITION RESEARCH

AT ITT DEFENSE COMMUNICATIONS DIVISION

George M. White
Marvin R. Sambur

21-1. INTRODUCTION

ITT Defense Communications Division (ITTDCD) believes that major markets for automatic speech recognition ASR equipment will develop gradually during the next ten years. This development is being guided and paced by Government spending which provides the major source of support for research in this field. The Government is presently interested in word-spotting, talker identification, language identification, "command and control," and secure (encrypted) speech transmission. ITTDCD is working on these Government applications. As cost drops and commercial usage rises, research sponsorship and applications will shift. There are, however, general problems that must be solved regardless of the sponsor or of the application. Some of these general problems are speaker independent speech recognition, telephone band limited speech recognition, noisy speech recogntion, and low cost implementation of signal processing algorithms. ITTDCD is now working on these problems. Our initial goals and approaches to these problems are the subject of this chapter.

The purpose of this chapter is not to present accomplishments of ITTDCD, but rather to indicate goals and ideas. Our emphasis is on tackling problems that have immediate application and which are also applicable to future systems in continuous speech recognition.

The organization of this chapter is as follows: In Sec. 21-1, ITTDCD computational facilities and staff are briefly discussed. This section reveals a significant committment on the part of ITTDCD to the field of automatic speech recognition. In Sec. 21-2, the application areas of ASR currently being investigated are described. These areas include "isolated word recognition", "slow speech dictation machines", "word-spotting" and "talker identification". In Sec. 21-3, basic research interests and goals are detailed. These interests include "dynamic programming", "feature selection", "recognition of noise degraded speech", and "optimization of dissimilarity measures" for speech recognition. Section 21-4 contains our ideas for low cost implementation of ASR systems. (ITTDCD believes that the eventual widespread use of ASR systems is based upon low cost. The lower the cost, the more the demand for the system.) Finally, a summary and discussion of the entire chapter is given in Sec. 21-5.

21-1 Computational Facilities, Staff and the ITT Voice Processor

ITTDCD is committed to the long term effort that is needed to effectively tackle the problems of automatic speech recognition. The staff presently consists of eight scientists who have done extensive R&D in the ASR field. This staff is expanding.

Research is carried out on two PDP-11 computers (one in San Diego, California, and one in Nutley, New Jersey), as well as on special purpose voice processing computers built internally by ITTDCD.

The ITT voice processing computers represent the state-of-the-art in LPC vocoding computers. Although the algorithms for speech compression will probably change and the computing machinery for exacting the algorithm will certainly change, a snapshot of today's processor is presented.

The ITT processor executes and LPC-10 analysis for the encoding operation, the characteristics of which are described below.

LPC-10 Characteristics

Predictor Order:	10
Sampling Rate:	8 kHz
Bit Rate:	2400 bps
Frame:	22.5 msec (54 bits per frame)
Analyzer:	Semi-Pitch Synchronous
Low Pass Filter:	4th Order Butterworth
Pitch:	AMDF function with Dynamic Programming (DYPTRACK) smoothing (50 Hz to 500 Hz,) 60 autocorrelation values).
Voicing:	2 decisions per frame based on Low Band Energy, zero crossing count and reflection coefficients RD1 and RC2.
Preemphasis:	$Z(n) - 15/16\ Z(n-1)$
Matrix Load:	Covariance (Modified ATAL)
Matrix Invert:	Modified Cholesky Decomposition
Coding of RCs:	Log Area Ratio for RC1 and RC2 and linear for others.
(The Synthesizer:	Uses Interpolation and is Pitch Synchronous)

The unit has one processor and two memories (a data memory and a program memory). The LPC-10 analysis code uses only 1238 words of program memory and 2900 words for data memory. It is very fast: 10 LPC (reflection) coefficients are generated in 2 msec, and pitch tracking and voicing analysis are performed in 4 msec for each 22.5 msec window. The total algorithm, including modem function, consumes about 13 msec. The processor itself weighs 50 pounds, consumes 60 watts of power, and uses about 180 TTL chips.

ITTDCD has (or soon will have) operational systems for "isolated word recognition", "talker identification" and "slow speech dictation recognition". These systems are described below.

21-2.1 Isolated Word Recognition

ITTDCD's isolated word recognition system is a versatile, extendable kernel for research in a variety of areas. It's basic function is to "spot" words in an input audio stream. It is used as an isolated word recognizer only to force the user to speak very distinctly to minimize coarticulation problems. The specifications for this system are listed in Table 1. The goal is to implement the system on ITT's fast processor. Dynamic programming will be used in the classifier stage. A key aspect of dynamic programming is that it is used to avoid beginning and ending of utterance detection, as well as segmentation and labeling. This produces an exceptionally simple program/machine architecture. The result is that the entire system could potentially be implemented on a dozen chips, if use is made of new signal processing chips such as devices being developed at Intel, Texas Instruments, or Reticon. For instance, these new chips could make it possible to realize an entire 20 channel filter bank or a 256 point Fourier transform on less than 6 chips. Even though the technology is in place to create these low-cost signal processing devices, their actual appearance on the marketplace remains to be seen. In the meantime, ITTDCD is developing low-cost classification algorithms and machine archetectures to take advantage of low-cost signal processors when they do become available.

Our future plans call for improving the kernel recognition system by making the word recognition system insensitive to variations in talkers, background noise, talking rate and channel characteristics. Specifically, the word recognition system should be capable of recognizing up to 50 words with better than 97% accuracy even when the system is tested on different speakers than the speakers whose speech was used to train the system. The system should also maintain a 95% accuracy for recognition over dialed up telephone lines. The specifications for this system are listed in Table 2. Our ideas for achieving these goals are detailed in Sec. 21-3.

21-2.2 Word Spotting

ITTDCD is developing algorithms to "spot words" in a stream of continuous speech for carefully pronounced speech with a good signal-to-noise ratio. Problems of temporal and spectral variation are the focal point of this research. The inherent temporal variability will be treated with new forms of dynamic programming. The inherent spectral variability found in continuous speech utterances will be studied with principal components analysis. Details of dynamic programming and principal components analysis are treated in a later section.

PERFORMANCE SPECIFICATIONS FOR KERNEL WORD RECOGNITION SYSTEM

(1)	Type of Speech	Isolate Utterances, Cooperative Speaker
(2)	Vocabulary Size	Up to 50 Polysyllabic Words
(3)	Accuracy	Better Than 99.0%
(4)	Type of Speaker	System Adaptation Required: i.e. a Training Period is Required – No Restriction on Users Language or Dialect
(5)	Recognition Speed (Using Existing Ram Processor)	10 Seconds Maximum 1 Second Design Goal
(6)	Speech Input Device	A Telephone Handset (But Not Over Dial Up Phone Line)

Table 1

PERFORMANCE SPECIFICATIONS FOR IMPROVED WORD RECOGNITION SYSTEM

(1)	Type of Speech	Isolated Utterances, Cooperative Speaker
(2)	Vocabulary Size	Up to 50 Words
(3)	Accuracy	Better than 97%
(4)	Type of Speaker	No System Adaption Required No Restriction on Users Language or Dialect
(5)	Recognition Speed (Using Existing Ram Processor)	Real Time
(6)	Speech Input Device	Dialed Up Phone Line

Table 2

21-2.3 Talker Identification

ITTDCD is investigating methods for "speaker identification," i.e. recognizing the identity of a speaker even if the text of the analyzed utterance is unknown. ITTDCD is also improving "speaker verification" (Is John Doe the speaker?) by making such systems more accurate and less expensive (see Sec. 21-4).

Two potentially powerful techniques for text independent speaker recognition which will be investigated are:

Orthogonal LPC approach

Long term average statistic approach

The idea to use orthogonal LPC for talker identification was inspired by an experimental study using eigenvector analysis to reduce data needed to achieve a high-quality synthesis [Sambur, 1975;1976].

It was observed that only a small subset of the parameters demonstrate any significant variation across the analyzed utterance. The remaining orthogonal parameters were essentially constant and, for purposes of synthesis, were completely specified by their measured mean values across the utterance. In a later experimental study it was shown that these remaining orthogonal LPC parameters were associated with the talker's identity. However, the experimental verification of this scheme leaves many unanswered questions. These questions include the following:

How much speech data is necessary to identify a person?

How does one generate the training data?

What is the optimum signal processing space for performing eigenvector analysis?

How many speakers can be accurately discriminated?

Can pitch information or long term average spectral data be used to supplement the orthogonal parameters?

These questions will be considered and the orthogonal method will be more extensively evaluated in a set of experiments that encompass a wide range of conditions and a great number of speakers.

Experiments have shown that long term statistics of speech (which include spectral and pitch distribution) can be determined by about 30 seconds of voiced speech, [Markel, et al., 1977]. This technique of talker identification has, under laboratory conditions, a fairly low error rate for up to 40 speakers. However, under real world condition (channel noise and distortion), the error rate is fairly high. The long term average statistic approach will be studied to learn whether other features might be more suitable for averaging.

These "other" features might include the 2 pole LPC derived pseudo-formant and vocal tract area function. In addition, the long-term average approach will be tested and evaluated in more depth than previously reported.

21-2.4 Slow Speech Dictation Machines

Automatic recognition of carefully pronounced words in continuous speech is becoming a reality in the laboratory although it will be several more years before true continuous speech automatic dictation machines emerge. However, a large vocabulary isolated word recognizer could be useful for automatic dictation and the technology for making it is available now. Moreover, there is evidence that a person can learn to speak to a recognition device with sufficient clarity to avoid the need for semantic support. Thus a continuous speech recognition system could be based on word spotting techniques combined with large vocabulary recognition techniques. This is the approach being followed at ITTDCD. The problem of stringing words or word fragments together into sentences is being treated with dynamic programming. The problem of short words embedded in longer words, and false word candidates being proposed for unknown utterance segments is also handled with dynamic programming. The problem of large vocabulary recognition is being treated with a dynamic search strategy which uses a "layered dictionary" approach to "hypothesize and verify" words. Layered dictionaries are dictionaries that contain the same utterances described at different levels of parametric compression. ITTDCD is building simple systems based on these techniques with the ultimate goals of developing a limited vocabulary automatic dictation machine for slow speech input.

21-3 RESEARCH AREAS

ITTDCD is tackling several fundamental problems common to both isolated word recognition and to continuous speech recognition. One such problem is that of time alignment. It is clear that dynamic programming will be a key component in most future ASR systems for solving the time alignment problem. Thus a portion of our research is devoted to enhancing the effectiveness of dynamic programming (Sec. 21-3). In addition, practical recognition systems must be able to effectively function in real word environments. Our research is directed at the fundamental problems of recognizing speech in noisy environments and/or over telephone lines (Sec. 21-3.2). The possibility of selecting acoustic features that are immune to degradation over phone lines or from background noise is of considerable interest. Our research is aimed at determining acoustic features that are relatively insensitive to noise and also to the identity of the speaker (Sec. 21-3.3). Finally, ITTDCD is investigating various methods for measuring acoustic dissimilarity (Sec. 21-3.4).

21-3.1 Dynamic Programming

ITTDCD's dynamic programming research has several different aspects. One aspect concerns constraints on the amount of nonlinear time warping that can be performed by dynamic proramming. The goal of our research is to restrict the degree of time warping to be commensurate with experimentally observed time axis deformations.

It is known that different pronunciations of the same word result in different segmental durations. Thus nonlinear time alignment strategies must be used to match polysyllabic utterances against standardized templates. However, the degree of temporal variability that should be permitted is not known. For example, some phonemes are characterized by their time rate of change while others are not; e.g. stop consonants are, most vowels are not. It would seem that a time alignment strategy that reflects this fact ought to be better than one that does not. Our hypothesis is that it is possible to improve on a strategy that would treat an entire utterance with constant constraints on non-linearity regardless of the types of phonemes found in the utterance. Perhaps piece-wise linear matching would be adequate. On the other hand, perhaps piece-wise linearity is inadequate even for segments as small as phonemes. The answers are not known at this time. We have partitioned our research into this problem as follows:

1. SPEECH DATA BASE ANALYSIS - to measure the extent to which subword segments exhibit differing degrees of temporal deformation;

2. ALGORITHM DEVELOPMENT AND TESTING - to discover computationally efficient means of encoding and utilizing information about the amount of temporal deformation for different speech segments during the classification process;

3. AUTOMATIC TEMPLATE GENERATOR DEVELOPMENT - to create a procedure which automatically generates templates that incorporate segment controlled deformation parameters, as well as the usual spectral information;

4. PERFORM RECOGNITION EXPERIMENTS - to quantify the improvement in recognition acuracy gained from using segment controlled deformation parameters.

1) The purpose of the "data base analysis" is to study the best match paths through dynamic programming matrices. Dynamic proramming matrices are defined to be matrices that contain speech sound similarity scores between short segments of two utternces. The row numbers and column numbers of the matrix represent the time indices in the two utterances. It is generally observed in dynamic programming matrices that there are broad rectangular regions of good similarity scores connected by narrow paths of good scores.

The goal of the study is to quantify the deviation from linearity for narrow paths and broad rectangular regions.

As a result of this study we hope to be able to tell how flexible different types of segments can be. We may discover that utterances can be represented by a mixture of flexible and inflexible segments. The inflexible segments would be those that are adequately modeled as straight lines of slope 1. If this is the case, it might not only allow more accurate recognition results, it might permit more compact storage of utterance templates.

2) "Algorithm development and testing" involves the development of algorithms for representing and employing variable template flexibility in dynamic programming pattern matching. In particular, the effects of varying A and B values in the dynamic programming equation will be studied:

$$D(i,j)=S(i,j) + MIN [A*D(i-1,j),B*D(i,j-1),D(i-1,j-1)]$$

$S(i,j)$ is the speech sound "dissimilarity" score (a low value means a good match). $D(i,j)$ is an entry in the dynamic programming matrix at location (i,j). Note that when A and B are larger than 1, this forces selection of $D(i-1,j-1)$ which means movement along a path of slope 1. The proper values of A and B would be determined experimentally and carried along in templates with each time frame to tell the dynamic programming classifier which values of A and B it should use. (See [White, 1978] for further information.)

3) "Automatic template generation" refers to the generation of templates that contain two types of information (spectral and temporal): (a) average signal parameters (spectral) and (b) constraints on path linearity (temporal). The "average signal parameters" are obtained by averaging parameters of several exemplars which are time-aligned with dynamic programming. The second step is to discover and encode a deformation parameter expressing the allowable temporal variation for each segment.

4) Finally, "recognition performance" will be studied using the above templates and A's and B's in the ITTDCD ASR kernel system.

21-3.2 Recognition of speech Degraded by Noise

The objective of this research is to determine an optimum method for reducing the effects of noise on the accuracy of automatic word recognition systems. Three approaches will be studied.

The first approach is a comparative evaluation of different features sets (basis vectors) to determine which feature set provides the highest recognition accuracy under noisy conditions. The feature sets to be examined are:

\# Linear predictive coefficients (LPC)

\# Vocal tract area functions

\# Autocorrelation coefficients

\# Cepstral coefficients

\# LPC derived pseudo formants

The first four feature sets are defined in the recent book by Markel and Gray [1977]. The LPC derived pseudo formants are obtained from the LPC coefficients by setting the magnitude of the last coefficient to unity and solving for the pole frequencies of the resulting LPC transfer function.

These feature sets will be studied in three environments:

1) a wideband quiet environment, 2) a telephone bandwidth quiet environment, and 3) a noisy telephone bandwidth environment. The overall optimum feature set will then be selected.

The second approach involves the use of a linear mean square (LMS) adaptive filtering approach for the removal of additive noise from the speech signal. The method can best be understood by considering the classical method of adaptive noise cancelling. Figure 1 illustrates the classical technique. The technique uses two sensors: One is located in the noise field far away from the speech and is used to establish the characteristics of the noise; the other sensor is near the speech source. However, the second sensor samples a signal, $x(n)$, that is composed of both speech and noise. The signal $wl(n)$ is adaptively filtered to produce the output $\hat{w}(n)$ that is an estimate of the additive noise $x(n)$. This output is then subtracted from the noisy signal $x(n)$ to produce the system output $\hat{s}(n)$. This output is used to control the adaptive filter and it is also transmitted as an estimate of $\hat{s}(n)$.

It can be shown that if the following conditions are satisfied, then $\hat{s}(n)$ is a best least squares fit to the clean speech $s(n)$. These conditions are:

1) $s(n)$ and $w(n)$ are uncorrelated;

2) $s(n)$ and $w1(n)$ are uncorrelated;

3) $w1(n)$ and $\hat{w}(n)$ are correlated;

4) The adaptive filter is adjusted such that the energy in $\hat{s}(n)$ is minimized.

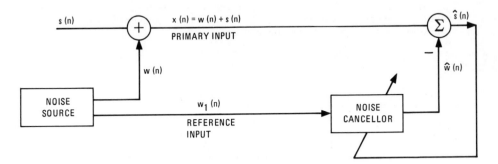

Figure 21-1. Classical Noise Cancelling Model

The use of a second sensor can be avoided by noting that speech is quasi periodic. Thus a section of speech delayed by 1 or 2 pitch periods will be highly correlated with the speech signal $s(n)$ and will be uncorrelated with the additive noise (provided $w(n)$ is sufficiently broadband).

Figure 2 illustrates how we can take advantage of the quasi-periodic nature of speech for effective noise removal. In this system, we take advantage of the fact that $s(n)$ and $s(n-T)$ are highly correlated and $w(n)$ and $w(n-10)$ are not correlated. Using the arguments of the previous paragraph, it can be seen that minimizing the energy in the system output $w(n)$ will result in a signal $\hat{s}(n)$ that is a best least squares fit to $s(n)$.

The adaptive filtering approach has been shown to help in perceptually removing the noise component from speech. We shall investigate how effectively it enhances the recognition of the noisy speech.

The third approach involves the investigation of a noise-reduced LPC parameter set recently proposed by Sambur. This parameter set is determined by subtracting a term proportional to the residual signal power from the diagonal of the autocorrelation matrix used to determine the standard LPC set.

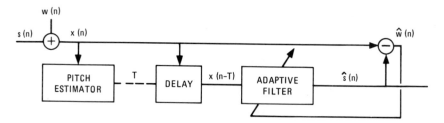

Figure 21-2. Adaptive Filtering Approach for Removing Noise from Speech

The new parameters have been shown to provide a more accurate representation of the speech spectrum in a noisy environment. These parameters may provide a superior feature set for recognition purposes as well.

2.3.3 Feature Selection

A speech utterance contains more information than the orthographic transcription of the spoken words. The speech conveys information about the identity of the speaker, his educational background, his emotional state, his sex, and even his physical makeup. Our goal is to develop a word recognition algorithm that will be insensitive to all these characteristics of individual speakers. Our strategy is to use parameters that carry relatively little information about the speaker. Three such parameter sets are LPC-derived pseudo formants, orthogonal LPC parameters, and vocal tract area functions.

LPC-derived pseudo formants are obtained from the LPC coefficients by setting the magnitude of the last coefficient to unity and solving for the pole frequencies of the reslting LPC transfer function. Assuming that the LPC derived transfer function is:

$$H_n(z) = \frac{1}{1 - a_1 z^{-1} - a_2 z^{-2} \cdots a_n z^{-n}}$$

with pole positions illustrated in Fig. 4, then the pseudo formants are obtained by setting $a(n) = 1$ and finding the corresponding poles. As noted in Fig. 3, the poles are now on the unit circle and have zero bandwidth. This result is a natural consequence of the fact that the last predictive coefficient is a product of all pole modulii of the vocal tract filter. By making the product unity, the individual pole modulus becomes unity, signifying that all poles are located on the unit circle.

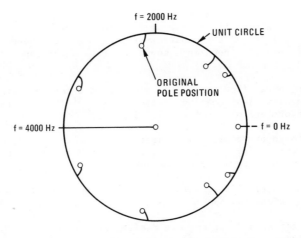

Figure 21-3. Root-Locus of Vocal Tract Filter as Last Filter Coefficient Approaches Unity

The pseudo formants are closely related to the actual formants, but unlike the formants, the pseudo formants vary smoothly across an analyzed utterance and can easily be labeled (see Fig. 4). In addition, due to the normalization of the speaker sensitive bandwidth information, pseudo formants should be even more effective than formants in providing a speaker independent representation of a speech word. The ability of pseudo formants to provide speaker independent recognition will be thoroughly examined and compared to other recognition features in ITTDCD's internal recognition system.

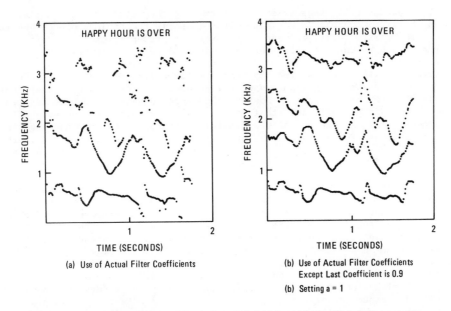

(a) Use of Actual Filter Coefficients

(b) Use of Actual Filter Coefficients Except Last Coefficient is 0.9

(b) Setting a = 1

Figure 21-4. Comparison of Pseudo Formant Trajectories and Formant Trajectories

As noted in Sec. 21-2.3, a set of orthogonal LPC parameters can be formed that convey a significant amount of information about the identity of the speaker. The utility of these parameters for use as speech recognition parameters will be examined and compared with other popular recognition features.

Vocal tract area functions are another attractive set of speaker independent recogniton features and will be examined. The advantages of vocal tract area functions arise from the following:

   a) The dynamics of vocal tract area functions are constrained by a physicological system imposing rules of continuity in movement and limits of velocity and acceleration.

   b) The normalization of physiological difference in vocal tract length is straightforward.

   c) Vocal tract area functions are easily calculated from LPC reflection coefficients.

The study of the vocal tract area functions will include:

   a) Transformations of area functions from one speaker to another to attempt to remove speaker differences.

   b) Vocal tract shapes useful for determining speech sound similarity for recognition.

21-3.4 Dissimilarity Measure

Two fundamental issues exist in determining the total match similarity scores between two utterances. The first issue is the obvious one of how to measure the dissimilarity between the acoustic representation of a reference utterance and an unknown utterance in a given frame of interest. The second issue is how to scale and combine the frame-by-frame scores. The first issue has traditionally been solved by using mathematical distance functions or filtering operations, e.g. convolving the autocorrelation functions of the two signals to be compared. Most matching procedures assume that adjacent frames are independent and that the total dissimilarity between two utterances is simply the sum of the dissimilarity for each corresponding time normalized frame. For instance, the principle of stochastic matching (Viterbi Algorithm) as used, for example, in the HARPY system, is based upon the independence of measurements in each analysis frame.

This independence is obviously not true. If the correlation could somehow be accounted for, a superior utterance matching algorithm would result. One approach for developing such an algorithm is proposed by Robert Wohlford. He suggests assigning a sound similarity score to speech segments rather than assigning sound similarity scores to individual frames of analysis. The hope is to produce an effective algorithm which computes segment sound similarity scores as a function of the frame by frame similarity score. If this can be done, we might avoid some of the problems associated with simply summing up individual analysis frames of constant duration. The success of this approach requires segmentation. It is proposed that segments be determined by comparing adjacent frames (using an appropriate similarity measure) to determine if they are sufficiently dissimilar to begin a new segment. A segment can be characterized by the average spectral parameters for each frame in the segment. ITTDCD shall experiment with these ideas to determine their utility for speech recognition.

20-4. LOW COST IMPLEMENTATION

A major barrier to commercial success of automatic speech recognition/ verification/synthesis devices has been the high cost of the signal processing components of the systems. Advances in microelectronics promise to dramatically reduce these costs. An order of magnitude improvement in the performance/cost ratio is technologically possible within five years due to advances in microelectronics, i.e. the commercial devices that today sell for $10,000 to $20,000 could be marketed for an order of magnitude less for many vocoding, speech recogniton, and speaker verification systems. This lower cost is expected to open up new markets for speech recognition/ verification/synthesis devices.

Considering speech recognition devices, for the task of recognizing a small vocabulary of isolated utterances, spoken by a small number of known cooperative speakers, in a relatively noise-free environment, over a high-quality microphone, several adequate solutions are well understood. There are many algorithms that achieve accuracies in excess of 99.0%. However, the relatively high cost of practical devices (typically more than $5,000) is prohibitive for most applications. The cost of such devices could soon be lowered dramatically by technological advances in LSI and charge transfer devices. ITT has considerable interest in new LSI device technology. Using newly-emerging analog and digital technologies, it is felt that isolated word recognition systems could be built for less than $500 per unit that would achieve better than 99% correct recognition scores for 50 word vocabularies of polysyllabic utterances that differ in more than one syllable. Of course, the actual costs will be strongly dependent on pro-duction volume and the $500 estimate is based on relatively high volume. The critical aspect is not the exact price estimate but the fact that the price is an order of magnitude below what a similar performing device would cost today.

Recogniton algorithms are evolving and it is difficult to predict what direction low-cost implementations will take. However, it is becoming clear that dynamic programming will be a key component in most systems regardless of their complexity. One reason for this is that dynamic programming is simple to implement on special purpose hardware and/or microcode. It would be straight forward to design a custom LSI chip that would be a totally self-contained recognition system using dynamic programming for 4 or 5 utterances if off-chip support included template memory, a signal processor, and a distance function evaluator. Such chips could be key components in large-vocabulary and continuous speech recognition systems, as well as small vocabulary isolated utterance devices.

21.5 DISCUSSION AND SUMMARY

Consequently, ITTDCD has only recently entered the automatic speech recognition field. This chapter focuses on future research rather than past results. The ITTDCD strategy is to build upon its well established capability in the speech compression (vocoding) area. The analyzer part of a vocoder is an ideal front end for a speech recognizer. A brief description of an ITTDCD voice processor was presented. ITTDCD's continuing research and development in low cost vocoding is expected to contribute to its ASR capability.

ITTDCD is developing operational systems for isolated word recogntion, word spotting, talker identification, and isolated word (slow speech) dictation. The areas of emphasis in each of these projects are "low cost technologies" (for use in isolated word recognition), dynamic programming (for use in word spotting), optimal signal parameters (for use in talker identification), and the multi-dictionary approach to large vocabulary recognition (for use in dictation machines). These ideas were discussed in some detail along with the fundamental problems common to all applications: noise immunity, speech sound similarity measures, time alignment, and signal parametric representations.

REFERENCES

Markel, J., Oshika, B. T., and Gray, Jr., A. H., "Long Term Feature Averaging For Speaker Recogniton," IEEE Transactions on Acoustics, Speech, and Signal Processing, ASSP-25, no.4, 1977, 330-337.

Markel, J. and Gray,Jr., A. H., Linear Prediction of Speech, New York: Springer Verlag, 1977.

Sambur, M. R., "An Efficient Linear Predictive Vocoder," Bell System Technical Journal, 34, 1975, 693-723

Sambur, M. R.,"Speaker Recognition Orthogonal Linear Prediction," IEEE Transactions on Acoustics, Speech, and Signal Processing, ASSP-24, no. 4, 1977, 283-289.

White, G. M., "Dynamic Programming, The Viterbi Algorithm and Low Cost Speech Recogniton," Proceedings of the IEEE ICASSP, Tulsa, Oklohoma, April, 1978, to appear.

22.

RECENT WORK ON SPEECH RECOGNITION IN JAPAN

Hisashi Wakita
Speech Communications Research Laboratory, Inc.

Shozo Makino
Tohoku University, Sendai, Japan

22-1. INTRODUCTION

The study of speech recognition became active in Japan during the 1950's and several experimental systems for speech recognition were built in the early 1960's. Noteworthy among the various efforts are (1) a system for the recognition of Japanese conversational speech (Sakai and Doshita, 1963); (2) phonemic classification experiments on Japanese mono-syllables (Suzuki and Nakata 1963); (3) recognition experiments on Japanese vowels (Suzuki and Oizumi, 1963), and (4) a study of spoken digit recognition (Kato, Chiba, and Nagata 1964) The recognition system in (1) was developed at Kyoto University and utilized "tri phonemes" as reference patterns. The "spectrum moment method" for extracting formant frequencies was used in (2). In study (3), at Tohoku University, learning processes were introduced to build a vowel recognition system. The recognition of spoken digits in (4), conducted at Nippon Electric Company (NEC), attained 98% correct recognition for 20 male speakers and 93% for 10 female speakers. Although these studies were exceedingly good, they also revealed the real difficulty of automatic speech recognition.

From the mid 1960's, various studies of coarticulation, phonetic perception, and new analysis techniques were undertaken. These studies led to the important development of the "maximum likelihood method" (Itakura and Saito, 1966) and the "PARCOR" analysis method (Itakura and Saito, 1968). These techniques are now well known as the linear predictive coding method, and made a considerable contribution not only to the area of speech recognition but also to other areas of speech research. Other important techniques developed in the late 1960's and early 1970's include the use of a word dictionary for the correction of acoustically recognized phonetic strings (Itahashi Suzuki, and Kido, 1971) and the introduction of the dynamic programming technique to attain nonlinear time axis warping (Sakoe and Chiba, 1971) in speech recognition. Particularly, the use of dynamic programming has influenced much of the subsequent recognition research in the United States, and the technique has been playing an important role in various recognition systems.

In the early 1970's, a software word recognizer using a word dictionary and phonological rules was attempted (Itahashi, Makino, and Kido 1973). They attained 92.3% correct recognition for 52 words spoken by a male speaker and an average score of 70% for 10 words spoken by each of 9 other male speakers. In addition to the use of linguistic information such as phonological rules, their system also used the distinctive features of speech and rules for sound duration.

A software recognition system for spoken digits was also attempted on the basis of the maximum likelihood method applied to phonemes and learning processes (Kohda, Hashimoto, and Saito, 1972). They obtained 99 8% correct recognition for 2637 spoken digits produced by 30 male speakers and 98.6% for 2601 spoken digits produced by 30 female speakers.

Sakoe and Chiba developed a method for efficient pattern matching on entire-word pattern units by introducing dynamic programming for nonlinear time axis warping. They obtained a recognition rate of 99.8% for 2400 single-digit samples spoken by 4 male speakers. They also did recognition experiments on double digits by using single digits as units, resulting in a recognition rate of 99.6% correct double-digit recognition. These techniques are currently being improved and the pursuit of new techniques is of great concern in Japan. We next consider the state of the art of automatic speech recognition and the available recognition systems in Japan. Major systems to be described below are tabulated in Tables 22-1 through 22-3 at the end of this chapter.

22-2. BASIC RESEARCH IN ATUOMATIC SPEECH RECOGNITION.

22-2.1 Speech Analysis Techniques and Feature Extraction

Since the maximum likelihood method developed by Itakura and Saito was quite efficient and effective for the estimation of spectral envelopes, extensions of the method have been attempted by various researchers. Various attempts were made to approximate speech spectral envelopes by a rational function having both poles and zeros in order to more accurately estimate the peaks and dips in the spectra. One such attempt was to compute the impulse response of an inverse filter for speech waveforms and estimate the poles and zeros of the spectrum from the impulse response and the transfer function of the filter on the basis of least mean square error (Fukabayashi and Suzuki, 1975). Another attempt was to estimate spectral zeros from the residual signal obtained by inverse filtering of the speech wave (Ishizaki, 1977) The parameters of the inverse filter were obtained on the basis of an autoregression model. In this method, the power spectrum is first obtained by applying a fast Fourier transform (FFT) to the residual signal, then the autocovariance is obtained by applying the inverse FFT to the inverse of the power spectrum. The parameters, which are obtained in the process of autoregression, correspond to those for a moving average process. Another pole zero estimation algorithm was developed by use of the "state-space method" (Morikawa, Fujisaki, and Hashimoto, 1977). Their algorithm assumed an "autoregression moving average" (ARMA) model for speech production and expressed the process in terms of "state and observation equations". From the speech signal, a state transition matrix and state variables are computed. The eigenvalues for the state transition matrix correspond to the poles of the spectrum, and the zeros are obtained from the state transition matrix and the autocorrelation function of the speech signal. This algorithm can also optimally determine the order of the model simultaneously. We can cite another method for estimating spectral poles and zeros by use of the maximum likelihood criterion (Sagayama, Furui, and Saito, 1976). Despite these studies for estimating spectral zeros, the techniques have not yet reached the point where they can actually be applied to speech recognition. Estimation of the order of poles and zeros, and the separation of spectral zeros associated with the vocal tract from those associated with the glottal source, remain unresolved.

Another improvement on the maximum likelihood method involves the estimation of formant frequencies. It was reported (Itakura, 1975) that a procedure for estimating formant frequencies could be greatly simplified by moving all the poles that are within the unit circle in the z plane onto the unit circle by assuming a complete reflection at the glottis end of the vocal tract. It was also reported (Itahashi and Yokoyama 1973) that the estimation of formant frequencies based on the linear prediction method is somewhat easier on a logarithmic frequency scale than on a linear frequency scale.

Another application of the linear prediction method is estimation of vocal-tract area functions from acoustic speech waveforms. An adaptive preemphasis filter to eliminate the source and radiation characteristics was introduced before applying the LPC analysis to the speech signal (Nakajima et al., 1973). The adaptive preemphasis circuits consisted of a second-order critical-damping digital filter and a third-order critical damping digital filter. They reported that reasonable looking area functions could be obtained for various speakers, and they further proceeded to an articulatory modeling to extract some articulatory parameters from estimated area functions (Nakajima and Ishizaki, 1974). However, the problem of adaptively eliminating the individual source characteristics still needs further investigation together with the other inherent problems involved in this technique.

Regarding the estimation of articulatory parameters, reasonable results for the Japanese vowels were obtained by extracting some articulatory parameters from the formant frequencies by applying a nonlinear regression analysis (Shirai and Honda, 1976).

22-2.2 Phoneme Recognition and Segmentation

In the basic research on segmentation and phoneme recognition, the identification of fricative consonants, voiceless plosives, and semivowels have been attempted. There have also been attempts to develop recognition algorithms which perform segmentation and phoneme recognition simultaneously. Some of the major works and results are summarized below.

1) A coarticulation model was proposed by approximating the temporal variation of formant frequencies as a response from a critically damped system, and an algorithm for the segmentation and identification of connected vowel utterances was investigated (Fujisaki, et al., 1973; Itahashi and Yokoyama, 1973).

It is also reported that the above model can be applied to the identification of semi-vowels and voiced plosives (Fujisaki, et al., 1975). Further experiments indicated that there is a reasonably good similarity in temporal structure between the coarticulatory model and human perception.

2) Spectral zeros are important for the discrimination of voiceless fricatives /s/ and /ʃ/ (Fujisaki and Kunisaki, 1975).

3) For discrimination of nasals from vowels, the deviation from the spectrum of the neutral vowel becomes one of the cues (Takeuchi, Kasuya and Kido, 1975).

4) Nasal spectra in natural utterances can be estimated on the basis of a nasal production model (Shirai Gomi, and Honda, 1977).

5) The place of articulation of a nasal sound can be estimated by use of the transition between the nasal and the following vowel (Ishizaki, 1977).

6) Discrimination of voiceless and voiced stop consonants was attempted on the basis of the linear prediction reflection coefficients (Sekiguchi and Shigenaga, 1975).

7) Spectral moment is useful for identification of voiceless stop consonants. Particularly, the spectral moments at the explosion and 10 msec after the explosion are useful (Kunisaki and Fujisaki, 1977)

8) A multistage dynamic processing is effective for the extraction of voiceless plosive information (Tanaka, 1977) A recognition rate of 90% was obtained for 90 samples taken from three male and three female speakers.

9) An articulatory model was proposed on the basis of a principal compenent analysis of vocal-tract area functions which were obtained by use

of the linear prediction method (Ohta and Iwamatsu, 1976). Articulatory movements of vowel and semi-vowel transitions were investigated by use of this method.

22-2.3 The Use of Linguistics Information.

Some of the major works on the application of linguistic information to speech recognition are summarized below.

1) An algorithm for correcting incorrectly identified phonemes, and for the deletion and insertion of phonemes was developed, which uses transitional information between phonemes, the confusion matrix of phonemes, and the dynamic programming technique (Makino, Suzuki, and Kido, 1974; Kido, Suzuki, Makino, and Matsuoka, 1974). By use of this algorithm, it is possible to automatically generate phonological rules.

2) In the study of automatic word and connected speech recognition, the following have been investigated.

a) Automatic construction of phoneme sequences to be stored in the dictionary, from the phoneme sequences obtained from training speakers (Shikano and Kohda 1973)

b) Conversion of phoneme sequences into word sequences (Sakimura, et al. 1973).

c) Effective word look-up in the dictionary based on phoneme sequence rules (Makino, Suzuki, and Kido, 1974).

d) Nine dimensional representation of a phonetic segment as applied to word recognition (Matsuoka and Kido, 1976).

e) Word recognition using Chinese characters as units (Matsuoka and Kido, 1976).

f) Properties of phoneme pairs which tend to cause recognition errors (Makino and Kido, 1976).

g) Comparison of various tree-search methods in identifying word sequences in continuous speech recognition (Niimi and Kobayashi, 1976).

h) Effectiveness of using syntactic information in continuous speech recognition (Takeya and Kawaguchi, 1973).

22-2.4 Individual Talker Characteristics

1) The effects of time differences between the recording of the training samples and the test samples on the recognition rate were studied (Kohda and Saito, 1973; Furui, 1977). It was found that the error rate went up by about 0.8% for a 20 day time difference between the two sets of samples. It was also reported in a five-year project that when the time difference between the two sets of samples exceeds six months, the error rate approaches a constant.

2) Talker normalization has been investigated in several studies. One of the approaches used expansion and compression of an interpolated autocorrelation function after an adaptive preemphasis was applied to the speech waves to eliminate the individual glottal characteristics (Furui, 1975). It is reported that the number of errors that occurred without normalization reduces to about half when this approach was used.

An approach to estimating the vocal tract length was proposed, on the basis of a certain information criterion applied to the linear prediction parameters (Ishizaki and Nakajima, 1975). This approach was used to extract some articulatory parameters from the vocal-tract area functions estimated from the speech waveforms. Talker normalization based on the formant frequencies was also investigated for the recognition of sustained vowels (Fujisaki, Katagiri, and Sato, 1977).

486

There have been quite active studies on isolated word recognition with limited vocabularies. We categorize the word recognition systems into the ones based on phoneme sequences and the others based on the word as an undivided unit. The summaries of those systems studied are given here.

22-3.1 Word Recognition Systems Based on Phonemes

A word recognition system to recognize the names of major cities in Japan was investigated at Tohoku University (Matsuoka and Kido, 1976; Kido, Matsuoka, Miwa, and Makino, 1976). This system employs the overall energy level and the local peaks of input spectra as major parameters. In this system, three major local peaks are extracted from the output of the bandpass filter bank every 10 msec. A set of phoneme candidates are assigned to each frame based on the local peaks thus computed. The temporal characteristics of the local peaks are used to identify phonemes such as /j/ and /w/, and the speech energy level in addition to the local peaks of spectra is used for identifying /r/ and /h/. The phoneme sequences obtained in this way are matched with the word dictionary by use of a similarity measure. In the experiments on identifying 20 city names, a recognition rate of 96% was obtained for the five speakers whose utterances were used to generate reference patterns. The recognition rate was 86% for three test speakers. For 166 city names which were spoken by three of the five reference speakers, the recognition rate was 82%. The above system was modified into an on-line recognition system (Miwa, Makino, Matsuoka, and Kido, 1976). In a recognition experiment conducted on this system, subjects were allowed to repeat up to three times. The result was 94% for 51 city names spoken by 25 speakers.

Another system at Tohoku University utilizes the parameters representing the gross spectrum of the input speech signal (Miwa, Makino, and Kido, 1977; Niitsu Miwa, Makino, and Kido, 1977). The input signal is passed through a 29 channel filter bank (1/6 octave bandpass filter (with Q = 6) from 250 Hz to 6300 Hz), and the output is digitized every 10 msec. After the slope of the spectrum is adaptively compensated, frame by frame, the system computes the local peaks (roughly corresponding to formants), plus linearly transformed parameters representing the spectral shape and the energy level. Determination of consonantal segments is made on the basis of the change in a spectral shape parameter and the energy level, especially taking into consideration their extrema. The consonantal segments thus determined are categorized into nasals, voiced plosives, voiced fricatives, liquids, laryngeal fricatives, voiceless fricatives, and voiceless plosives by use of the local peaks of the spectrum and the total energy. Besides these consonants, semi-vowels are also detected by using the spectral shape parameters, and nasals are detected on the basis of local peaks. If several phonemes are detected for the same segment, one phoneme is singled out for that segment based on certain phonological rules. The segments which are left out as non-consonantal segments are regarded as vowels, and the identification of vowels is also made using local peaks of the spectrum. For a recognized phoneme sequence, devocalized vowels and long vowels are detected by using phoneme concatenation rules. The phoneme sequence thus obtained is referenced to each item of the word dictionary by taking the probability of segmentation errors into consideration. The word which gives the largest similarity to lexical entries is output as the recognized word. For 20 city names spoken by 15 speakers, a recognition rate of 97.3% was obtained. For 51 city names, the rate was 95.3% and for 166 city names, the rate was 85.7%.

In another experiment (Makino, Suzuki, and Kido, 1971), the time sequence of distinctive features obtained from an input signal was matched via dynamic programming with reference sequences of distinctive features generated by use of a word dictionary and a phoneme duration dictionary. A recognition rate of 93.5% was obtained for 53 city names spoken by a single speaker who trained the system, a 90% recognition rate for 10 city names was obtained for 9 new speakers who did not train the system. At Waseda University, spoken digit recognition was attempted based on a transition diagram of phoneme sequences (Shirai and Fujisawa, 1974). A recognition rate of 94.3% was obtained for 2,500 digit samples produced by 5 speakers.

At Kyoto University, spoken digit recognition was also attempted (Sakai and Nakagawa, 1976), by a method in which only the reference patterns of vowels were generated by a learning process and the reference patterns for voiced consonants were estimated from neighboring vowels. For 1,500 samples provided by 20 speakers, a 97% recognition rate was reported.

A similar word recognition system is being studied at Tokyo University (Sato and Fujisaki, 1975). The system is to recognize 10 digits and three arithmetic symbols. Vowels in a word are identified separtely from consonants. The consonantal segments are represented as a time sequence of parameters and each sequence is matched with the reference patterns. For 975 samples produced by three male speakers, a recognition rate of 96.1% was obtained. The system was further improved, and for 560 samples of 28 words produced by two male speakers, the result was 99.6% accuracy (Nakai, Sato, and Fujisaki, 1976).

22-3.2 Word Recognition Systems Without Phoneme Identification

The most noteworthy work in the area of word recognition is a system developed at Nippon Electric Company (NEC). The system does not assume the phoneme as a recognition unit, but uses instead the undivided word itself as a unit. To solve the problem of speaking rate variation, they introduced the technique of dynamic programming (DP). This technique was also adopted into the system at NTT developed by Kohda et al. and also Itakura's system at Bell Laboratories. The use of dynamic programming greatly influenced the development of word recognition systems in the United States also.

Below is a brief description of the two-level dynamic programming method used in the latest NEC system (Sakoe, 1975).

Let the reference pattern for the nth word ($n=1, 2, \ldots, N$) be represented as:

$$B^n = b_1^n, b_2^n, \ldots, b_j^n, \ldots, b_{JN}^n \tag{1}$$

and let the input speech pattern of concatenative words be represented by:

$$c = c_1, c_2, \ldots, c_i, \ldots, c_I \tag{2}$$

The concatenation of two reference patterns, B^n and B^m is defined as:

$$B^n \oplus B^m = b_1^n, b_2^n, \ldots, b_{Jn}^n, b_1^m, \ldots, b_{Jm}^m$$

The pattern of k concatenated words ($n(1)$, $n(2)$, $\ldots, n(k)$) is approximated by concatenation of the reference pattern of each word as:

$$B = B^{n(1)} \oplus B^{n(2)} \oplus \ldots \oplus B^{n(k)} \tag{3}$$

B is regarded as the reference pattern for the concatenated word utterance and DP matching is applied to the input pattern C. In this case, $k = \hat{k}$ and $n(x) = \hat{n}(x)$ ($x = 1, 2, \ldots k$) are determined so as to make the similarity measure maximum, and thus the input pattern is determined as the concatenation of the $\hat{k}$ words $\hat{n}(1)$, $\hat{n}(2)$, $\ldots, \hat{n}(k)$. The algorithm can be described as below. First, the following calculation is made:

$$T = \max_{k, n(x)} [S(c, B^{n(1)} \ B^{n(2)} \ \ldots \ B^{n(k)})] \tag{4}$$

where S(A,B) is a similarity measure between A and B. The optimum $\hat{k}$ and $\hat{n}(1)$, $\hat{n}(2)$, $\ldots$,$\hat{n}(k)$ are determined from the above computation. This procedure is similar to the analysis-by-synthesis technique in that the reference pattern B is constructed so that the input pattern can best be approximated by B. If a partial pattern $C(\ell,m)$ of an input pattern is defined as a pattern starting at $i = \ell + 1$ and ending at $i = m$, the maximization of (4) is rewritten as:

$$T = \max_{k,\ell(x)} \left[\sum_{x=1}^{k} \max_{n(x)} \{ S(c(\ell(x-1), \ell(x)), B^{n(x)}) \} \right] \qquad (5)$$

The following is the basic algorithm for the two-stage dynamic programming.

(1) _Partial_ _Matching_: For a partial pattern $C(\ell,m)$ $(\ell \triangleleft m)$, the DP matching is made for all the references $B^n (n=1,\cdots,N)$ and a partial similarity $\hat{S}(\ell,m)$ and the number of partial reference patterns $\hat{N}(\ell,m)$ are computed and stored.

(2) _Total_ _Matching_: Based on the table of partial matchings, the optimum estimation of $k=\hat{k}$ and $\ell(x)=\hat{\ell}(x)$ are made so as to maximize T in (5). This maximization is attained by a dynamic programming method.

(3) _Decision_ _Process_: Based on the table of the results of partial matching, the following equation gives the recognition result:

$$\hat{n}(x) = \hat{N}(\hat{\ell}(x-1), \hat{\ell}(x)) \qquad (6)$$

In this way, the amount of computation is considerably reduced as compared with the amount of computation in (4). Letting N be the number of reference patterns, k the number of words in an input, J the average length of reference pattern, I the length of an input pattern, and R the matched window size, the number of computations based on the two-stage DP method is RJIN, whereas the number of computations based on (4) becomes RIN^k. The method was tested on 1-to-4-digit numbers produced by five male speakers (50 samples for each n-digit number, totaling 1000 samples) with an average recognition rate of 99.7%. In this experiment, the reference patterns were made from two utterances of each number for each speaker. The system, built in hardware with a micoprocessor, allows multi-channel input (4 channels), and will soon be available as a commercial device.

Another successful word recognition system is also one developed at NEC company (Chiba, Watari, and Watanabe, 1977). The system is intended to be speaker independent.

In this system, 10 autocorrelation function values are computed every 10 msec, after the input signal is preprocessed. Each reference category includes ten specific time points to be sampled in the input signal. Thus, each word is represented by a 100-order vector. Recognition is made by applying 100 dimensional piecewise nonlinear discriminant functions, which are constructed from the training samples spoken by many speakers, using the linear programing method. The training samples used in the experiment were one hundred words in Fortran commands, produced twice by 55 male and female speakers. A total of 3,500 words were spoken by 35 speakers from the training group; 1500 samples were also spoken three times by 5 non-training speakers. The results were 99.0% recognition for the 35 training speakers, and 99.3% for the 5 non-training speakers, resulting in an average recognition rate of 99.1%.

22-4. SPEECH UNDERSTANDING SYSTEM.

The study of speech understanding systems is rather active in Japan. Most of them are being developed for performing particular tasks. Two well known systems are described in this section.

22-4.1 Train Seat Reservation System

In 1976, a second revised on-line system for reserving train seats was completed for experimental use (Kohda, Nakatsu, and Shikano, 1976). In this system, recognition of input speech is performed with roughly two stages: an acoustic processor and a language processor. The acoustic processing and speech synthesis are done on an NEAC 3200/70 computer, and the language processing is done on a PANAFACOM U-400 computer. At the acoustic processing stage, a real-time correlator and a high-speed speech processor are used.

For phoneme recognition, a data base is prepared in the form of a phoneme lattice. This data base consists of (1) the location where the speech power becomes locally minimum, (2) a time series of a 10th order autocorrelation function, (3) a series of vowels extracted on the basis of maximum likelihood (including the first two choices of vowel categories giving the largest likelihood) and (4) an initial segment category for making a phoneme lattice. The input speech is categorized into vowel intervals, transition intervals, and pause intervals, based on (1) and (3) above, and, for a vowel interval, the vowel giving the largest likelihood is taken.

Based on the above data base, a final phoneme lattice is determined by use of the acoustic information described below.

The acoustic information includes phoneme concatenation rules, a phoneme process function, and reference VCV acoustic parameters. The phoneme concatenation rules give possible strings of segment features and phonemic symbols. If a portion of a phoneme lattice matches one of the reference segments and phoneme concatenations, that portion is processed by use of the phoneme process functions; that is, addition or deletion of segments and insertion and deletion of phonemes are done at this stage. By use of the phoneme process functions, the reference VCV acoustic parameters are used to identify the consonant in a VCV string. Based on the phoneme lattice thus obtained, plus information on phoneme duration, linguistic information is then applied to make a final decision on the recognition of the input sentence. The linguistic information includes (1) pragmatics (2) a syntactic representation, (3) a word dictionary, and (4) phonological rules. The pragmatics provide a procedure for syntactic analysis, depending upon the type of conversation, deep structure, and the length of the input speech. The syntactic representation is based on "phrase matching" and includes seven phrases regarding necessary reservation items, plus two others related to verbs and particles. The word dictionary contains 98 basic words, totaling 110 words including phonological variations. Each word is stored in terms of its corresponding phonemic string. The phonological rules provide some variational rules on phonemes in connected speech. All this information is used in a top-down fashion.

First, a sentence type is determined for an input utterance by use of pragmatics, and the words in the sentence are estimated by syntactic analysis. Then, phoneme sequences of estimated words are matched to the phoneme lattice by use of phonological rules. The above process utilizes a depth-first method of tree search.

In semantic analysis, some key words in the input sentence are stored for deep structure, the inference to reservation items and the possibility of reservations are checked in reference to the train time table, and the final decision about the details of the reservation is made.

Recognition experiments were conducted for seat reservation inquiries spoken phrase by phrase by 8 males in a 69 dB(A) room. The rates of phoneme recognition, and phrase recognition were 58.5% and 86.0% respectively. The final success rate of making reservations was 99.1%. The system operates in five times real time.

22-4.2 Computer Network Commands and Status Request

A system for understanding computer network commands and status requests has been developed at Kyoto University (Sakai and Nakagawa, 1977). Input speech is passed through a bank of 1/4 octave filters (20 channels) and sampled every 10 msec. By use of a total energy level, and a high-low freuency component ratio, pause, voiceless non-fricatives voiceless non-plosives, and voiced sounds are categorized. For voiceless sounds, identification is made by use of duration, existence of preceeding pause, and change in frequency spectrum. Voiced sounds are categorized into stationary and transitional intervals on the basis of spectral change. The stationary and quasi-stationary intervals are regarded as vowels. Long transitional intervals, and low-energy intervals are categorized as voiced consonants. A Baysean decision rule is applied to categorize the vowels and voiced consonants. As the results of acoustic analysis, the first phoneme candidate, plus its reliability, and the second phoneme candidate, and the phoneme durations are all sent to the linguistic processor. Once a phonemic sequence is obtained for an input utterance, some key words are searched for in the sequence. Then, from the end of the phoneme sequence, the predicate of the input sentence is searched for. From the beginning of the sequence, the neighboring words are determined. The word identifier in the system recognizes words on the basis of phoneme similarity, the word dictionary and a successive-word-matching method. The word predictor selects the possible words to follow next in the utterance by the aid of syntactic and semantic information and pragmatics. The input sentence is determined from selected word sequences, taking the likelihood of word sequences into account. Experiments were conducted for 200 sentence utterances (1983 words) spoken by 10 speakers. An average sentence recognition rate of 64% and an average word recognition rate of 93% were obtained.

Besides the speech understanding systems described above, recognition of the FORTRAN language (Sekiguchi, et. al., 1977) and of the Basic-1 language (Niimi and Asami, 1975; Niimi, Kobayashi, Asami and Miki, 1977) are being studied.

There are two conspicuous trends in research on automatic speech recognition in Japan. One is the estimation of articulatory parameters and their application to speech recognition. The articulatory parameters are investigated on the basis of vocal tract area functions obtained either by linear prediction analysis or from speech spectra. Although those parameters may eventually be utilized for sound segmentation and phoneme identification, various problems have to be resolved before those techniques become applicable for practical purposes: for instance, the problem of coarticulation; the use of linguistic information combined with articulatory information; the identification of consonants based on the articulatory parameters; etc.. Several interesting models of coarticulation are being investigated (e.g. Fujisaki et al.,1973; Itahashi and Yokoyama,1973), but many problems still remain unresolved. It is anticipated, however, that automatic recognition systems for continuous speech based on some sort of articulatory model will be developed in the near future.

The other trend is the development of word recognition systems and speech understanding systems based on linguistic information. The use of linguistic information for speech recognition system is far behind that in the United States, due mainly to the fact that relatively few linguists are involved in the development of recognition systems. The problems involved in the use of linguistic information include the establishment of a design method, the introduction of associative memories, and the structure and sorting of linguistic information.

Table 22-1

Word Recognizer Based on Phonemes

Reference	Vocabulary	Subjects	Results	Remarks
Makino et al. (1971)	53 city names 10 city names	1 male 9 test males	93.5% 90%	
Shirai & Fujisawa (1974)	10 digits	5 males	94.3%	2500 test utterances
Sato & Fujisaki (1975)	10 digits & 3 arithmetic symbols	3 males		975 test utterances
Matsuoka & Kido (1976)	20 city names	5 training males	96.0%	
Kido et al. (1976)		3 test males	86.0%	
Kido et al. (1976)	166 city names	3 training males	82.0%	
Miwa et al. (1976)	51 city names	25 males	94.0%	3 repetitions allowed on-line system
Miwa et al. (1977)	20 city names 51 city names 166 city names	15 males 15 males 15 males	97.3% 95.3% 85.7%	
Sakai & Nakagawa (1976)	10 digits	20 males	97.0%	
Nakai et al. (1976)	28 words	2 males	99.6%	560 test utterances

Table 22-2

Word recognition systems without phonemic identification.

Reference	Vocabulary	Subject	Results	Remarks
Sakoe (1975)	strings of 1-4 digits	5 males	99.7%	1000 test utterances
Chiba et al. (1977)	100 words FORTRAN commands	35 training speakers (includes 3 females)	99.0%	3500 words
		5 test males	99.3%	1500 words

Table 22-3

Speech Understanding Systems

Reference	Vocabulary	Subject	Results	Remarks
Kohda et al. (1976)	train seats reservations	8 males	58.5% (phonemes) 86.0% (phrases) 99.1% (success)	69dB(A) room
Sakai & Nakagawa	computer network	10 males	93.0% (word) 64.0% (sentence)	200 sentence utterances (1983 words)

Chiba S., M. Watari,Watanabe (1977), A word recognition system for unlimited speakers, paper presented at the meeting of the Institute of Electronic and Communication Engineers of Japan, August.

Fujisaki, H., Y. Katagiri, Y. Sato (1977), "Feature Extraction and Automatic Recognition of Sustained Vowels Uttered by a Number of Unknown Speakers," Technical Report on Speech of the Acoustical Society of Japan, S 77-08.

Fujisaki, H., O. Kunisaki (1975), "Analysis and Recognition of Voiceless Fricative Consonant in Japanese," Journal of the Acoustical Society of Japan, 31, 12, 741-742.

Fujisaki, H., H. Morikawa, M. Sugito (1976), "Temporal Organization of Articulatory and Phonatory Controls in Realization of Word Accent," Report of Spring Meeting of the Acoustical Society of Japan, 229-230.

Fujisaki, H., Y. Sato, Y. Noguchi, T. Yamakawa (1975), "Automatic Recognition of Semivowels in Spoken Words," Journal of the Acoustical Society of Japan, 31, 11, 696-697.

Fujisaki, H., M. Yoshida, Y. Sato, Y. Tanabe (1973), "Automatic Recognition of Connected Vowels Using a Functional Model of the Articulatory Process," Journal of the Acoustical Society of Japan, 29, 10, 636-638.

Fukabayashi, T., H. Suzuki (1975), "Speech Analysis by Linear Pole-Zero Model," Journal of the Institute of Electrical and Communication Engineers of Japan, No. 5, 270-277.

Furui, S. (1975), "Learning and Normalization of the Talker Differences in the Recognition of Spoken Words," Technical Report on Speech of the Acoustical Society of Japan, S75-25.

Furui, S. (1977), "Comparison Between the Effects of the Temporal Variation of the Speech Spectrum on Speaker and Speech Recognition," Reports of Spring Meeteng of the Acoustical Society of Japan, April, pp.361-362.

Ishizaki, S. (1977), "Pole-zero Model Order Identification in Speech Analysis," Journal of the Institute of Electrical and Communication Engers of Japan, 60-A, 4, 423-424.

Ishizaki, S. (1977), "Nasal Feature Extraction Based on Linear Prediction Model," Technical Report on Speech of the Acoustical Society of Japan, S77-37.

Ishizaki, S., T. Nakajima (1975), "Estimation of Vocal Tract Length by Use of an Information Criterion," Report of Autumn Meeting of the Acoustical Society of Japan, 135-136.

Itahashi, S., S. Chiba (1976), "On the Relation Between Auditory Phonemic Segment and Second Order Model," Report of Autumn Meeting of the Acoustical Society of Japan, 333-334.

Itahashi, S., S. Makino, K. Kido (1973), "Discrete Word Recognition Utilizing a Word Dictionary and Phonological Rules," IEEE Transactions on Audio and Electroacoustics, AU-21, 239-249.

Itahashi, S., H. Suzuki, K. Kido (1971), "Discrimination of Some Consonant in Words with the Aid of Dictionary," Journal of the Institute of Electrical and Communication Engineers of Japan, 54-C, 1, 10-17.

Itahashi, S., S. Yokoyama (1973), "Automatic Formant Trajectory Tracking and Its Application by a Second-Order Linear System," Journal of the Institute of Electrical and Communication Engineers of Japan, 29,11, 690-691.

Itakura, F., S. Saito (1970), "A Statistical Method for Estimation of Speech Spectral Density and Formant Frequencies," Journal of the Institute of Electrical and Communication Engineers of Japan, 53-A, 1, 35-42.

Itakura, F. (1975), "Line Spectrum Representation of Linear Predictor Coefficients of Speech Signal," Technical Report on Speech of the Acoustical Society of Japan, S75-34.

Itahashi, S., S. Yokoyama (1973), "Automatic Formant Trajectory Tracking and its Approximation by Second Order Linear System," Journal of the Institute of Electrical and Communication Engineers of Japan, 29, 11, 690-691.

Kato, Y., S. Chiba, K. Nagata (1964), "Spoken Digit Recognizer," Journal of the Institute of Electrical and Communicative Engineers of Japan, 47, 9, 1319-1325.

Kido, K., T. Matsuoka, J. Miwa, S. Makino (1976), "Spoken Word Recognition System for Unlimitted Adult Male Speakers," Proceedings of the 1976 International Conference on Acoustics, Speech, and Signal Processing, ,Philadelphia, 214-217.

Kido, K., H. Suzuki, S. Makino, T. Matsuoka (1974), "Recognition of Spoken Words by Use of Spectral Peaks and Lexicon," Proceedings of the IEEE Symposium on Speech Recognition, Pittsburgh, 45-54.

Kohda, M., R. Nakatsu, K. Shikano (1976), "On-line Recognition System of Conversational Speech," Technical Report on Speech of the Acoustical Society of Japan, S78-28.

Kohda, M., S. Saito (1973), "Influence of Long-term Variations of Learning and Unkown Samples on Recognition Rate of Spoken Digits," Report of Autumn Meeting the Acoustical Society of Japan, 141-142.

Kohda, M., S. Hashimoto, S. Saito (1972), "Spoken Digit Mechanical Recognition System," Journal of the Institute of Electrical and Communication Engineers of Japan, 55-D, 3, 186-193.

Kunisaki, O., H. Fujisaki (1977), "Parameter Extraction of Voiceless Stop Consonants," Report of Spring Meeting of the Acoustical Society of Japan, 363-364.

Makino, S., K. Kido (1976), "On the Confusion of Words Caused by Phoneme Recognition Error," Technical Report on Speech of the Acoustical Society of Japan, S76-26.

495

Makino, S., H. Suzuki, K. Kido (1971), "Recognition of Spoken Word Utilizing Word Dictionary," <u>Report of Spring Meeting of the Acoustical Society of Japan</u>, 163-164.

Makino, S., S. Suzuki, K. Kido (1974), "A Method of Looking Up the Item of Word Dictionary on Spoken Word Recognition," <u>Technical Report of the Institute of Electrical and Communication Engineers of Japan</u>, EA 73-55.

Makino, S., H. Suzuki, K. Kido (1974), "Error Correction of Phoneme Strings Using Transition Probability," <u>Technical Report on Speech of the Acoustical Society of Japan</u>, S74-02.

Matsuoka, T., K. Kido (1976), "Investigation on Phonemic Information of Static Properties of Local Peaks in Speech Spectra," <u>Journal of the Acoustical Society of Japan</u>, 32, 1, 12-23.

Matsuoka, T., K. Kido (1976), "Automatic Recognition of Spoken Words by Use of Spectral Local Peaks," <u>Technical Report of the Institute of Electrical and Communication Engineers of Japan</u>, PRL 76-7.

Matsuoka, T., K. Kido (1976), "Representation of Phoneme Group by nine Dimensional Vectors and Its Application to Speech," <u>Journal of the Acoustical Society of Japan</u>, 32, 7, 443-445.

Matsuoka, T., K. Kido (1976), "A Consideration of the Use of Linguistic Information for the Spoken Words Recognition," <u>Technical Report of the Institute of Electrical and Communication Engineers of Japan</u>, PRL 76-38.

Matsuoka, T., K. Kido (1977), "Investigation on Dynamic Properties of Local Peaks in Speech Spectra and their Use for Spoken Word Recognition," <u>Journal of the Acoustical Society of Japan</u>, 33, 1, 12-22.

Miwa, J., S. Makino, K. Kido (1977), "Phoneme Recognition by Use of Least Squares Fit Line of Speech Spectrum," <u>Technical Report on Speech of the Acoustical Society of Japan</u>, S77-10.

Morikawa, H., H. Fujisaki, K. Hashimoto (1977), "A State-Space Approach to an Adaptive Speech Analysis System," <u>Journal of the Institute of Electrical and Communication Engineers of Japan</u>, 60-A, 6, 543-550.

Nakai, Y., Y. Sato, H. Fujisaki (1976), "Comparison of Methods for Word Registration in Automatic Recognition of Words in a Limited Vocabulary," <u>Technical Report on Speech of the Acoustical Society of Japan</u>, S76-02.

Nakatsu, P., M. Kohda (1975), "Improvement of the Recognition Method of VCV Syllables," <u>Report of Autumn Meeting of the Acoustical Society of Japan</u>, 351-352.

Nakatsu, R., K. Shikano, K. Itoh, M. Kohda (1977), "On-line Question-Answering System by Conversational Speech," <u>Technical Report on Speech of the Acoustical Society of Japan</u>, S77-14.

Nakajima, T., S. Ishizaki (1974), "Dynamic Feature Extraction on Articulatory Parameters," <u>Technical Report on Speech of the Acoustical Society of Japan</u>, S74-28.

Nakajima, T., H. Omura, K. Tanaka, S. Ishizaki (1973), "Estimation of Vocal Tract Area Function by Adaptive Inverse Filtering Method," <u>Technical</u>

Report on Speech of the Acoustical Society of Japan.

Niimi, Y., T. Asami (1975), "The Use and Effects of Linguistic Knowledges in a Speech Recognition System, Journal of the Institute of Electrical and Cmmunication Engineers of Japan 58-P, 12, 741-747.

Niitsu, Y., J. Miwa, S. Makino, K. Kido (1977), "A Method of the Use of Linguistic Information for the Spoken Word Recognition System," Technical Report on Speech of the Acoustical Society of Japan,.

Niimi, Y., Y. Kobayashi (1976), "Experiments in the Contribution of Various Knowledge Sources to the Speech Recognition System," Technical Report on Speech of the Acoustical Society of Japan, S76-29.

Niimi, Y., Y. Kobayashi, T. Asami, Y. Miki (1977), "The Speech Recognition System of Spoken Basic-1 , " Journal of the Information Processing Society of Japan, 18, 5, 453-459.

Ohta, K., A. Iwamatsu (1976), "A Linear Articulatory Model and an Observation of Articulatory Movement of Semi-Vowels Based on the Estimated Vocal Tract Crossectional Area Functions," Technical Report on Speech of the Acoustical Society of Japan.

Sagayama, S., S. Furui, S. Saito (1976), "Maximum Likelihood Estimation of Speech Spectrum by Pole-zero Modeling," Report of Spring Meeting of the Acoustical Society of Japan, 321-322.

Sakai, T., S. Doshita (1963), "Speech Recognition System of Conversational Sounds," Journal of the Institute of Electrical and Communication Engineers of Japan, 41, 11, 696-1702.

Sakai, T., S. Nakagawa (1976), "A Classification of Spoken Words in Continuous Speech for Many Speakers," Journal of the Information Processing Society of Japan, 17, 7, 650-658.

Sakai, T., S. Nakagawa (1977), "A Speech Understanding System of Simple Japanese Sentences in a Task Domain," Journal of the Institute of Electrical and Communication Engineers of Japan, 60E, 1, 13-20.

Sakimura, H., S. Nakayawa, K. Ohtani, T. Sakai (1973), "Phoneme-to- Word Translation in Continuous Speech Recognition," Report of Autumn Meeting of the Acoustical Society of Japan, 101-102.

Sakoe, H. (1975), "Recognition of Continuously Spoken Words Based on Two Level DP Matching," Technical Report on Speech of the Acoustical Society of Japan, S75-28.

Sakoe, H., S. Chiba (1971), "Recognition of Continuously Spoken Words based on Time-Normalization by Dynamic Programming," Journal of the Acoustical Society of Japan, 7, 9, 483-490.

Sato, Y., H. Fujisaki (1975), "A Method for Recognition of Words in a Limited Vocabulary," Technical Report on Speech of the Acoustical Society of Japan, S75-27.

Sekiguchi, Y., H. Oowa, K. Aoki, M. Shigenaga (1977), "Speech Recognition System for FORTRAN Program," Journal of the Information Processing Society of Japan, 445-452.

Sekiguchi, Y., M. Shigenaga (1975), "Recognition of Stop Consonants," Report of Autumn Meeting of the Acoustical Society of Japan, 347-348.

Shikano, K., M. Kohda (1973), "Learning of Phoneme Sequences and Speech Recognition," Report of Autumn Meeting of the Acoustical Society of Japan, 105-106.

Shirai, K., H. Fujisawa (1974), "Spoken Digit Recognition through Phoneme Recognition," Journal of the Institute of Electrical and Communication Engineers of Japan, 57-D, 3, 155-162.

Shirai, K., T. Gomi, M. Honda (1977), "Detection of Nasal Sounds Using Model of Production Process," Technical Report on Speech of the Acoustical Society of Japan, S77-38.

Shirai, K., M. Honda (1976), "An Articulatory Model and the Estimation of Articulatory Parameters by Nonlinear Regression Method," Journal of the Institute of Electrical and Communication Engineers of Japan, 59-A, 8, 668-674.

Suzuki, J., K. Nakata (1963), "Phonemic Classification and Recognition of Japanese Mono-Syllable," Journal of the Institute of Electrical and Communication Engineers of Japan, 46, 11, 1680-1687.

Suzuki, H., J. Oizumi (1963), "The Binary Coding and learning for Recognition of Japanese Vowels," Journal of the Institute of Electrical and Communication Engineers of Japan, 46, 3, 291-299.

Takeuchi, S., H. Kasuya, K. Kido (1975), "A Method for Extraction of the Spectral Cues of Nasal Consonants," Journal of the Acoustical Society of Japan, 31, 12, 739-740.

Takeya, S., E. Kawaguchi (1973), "A Simulation of a Recognition System for Connected Speech Sounds Using Linguistic Information," Journal of the Institute of Electrical and Communication Engineers of Japan, 56-A, 9, 513-520.

Tanaka, K. (1977), "The Multistage Dynamic Processing Approach to Phonemic Information Extraction (Part II), Technical Report on Speech of the Acoustical Society of Japan, S77-09.

Tsuruta, H., Sakoe, Chiba, and Nakata (1977), "A Multichannel Recognition System of Continuously Spoken Words with Microprocessors," Paper presented at the meeting of the Institute of Electronic and Communication Engineers of Japan, August.

23.

SPEECH RECOGNITION WORK IN POLAND

Wiktor Jassem
Pracownia Fonetyki Akustycznej
Instytut Podstawowych Problemów Techniki
Polska Adademia Nauk

23-1. INTRODUCTION

Research and engineering work in the area of ASR began in Poland around 1967. Four centres have been engaged: the Institute of Automation (IA), the Department of Cybernetic Acoustics (DCA) of the Institute of Fundamental Technological Research and the Acoustic Phonetics Research Unit (APRU) of the same Institute, all of the Polish Academy of Sciences, and the Institute of Telecommunications and Acoustics (ITA) of the Technical University in Wroclaw.

At IA an analogue device was constructed which, using a small internal memory, could recognize a variable vocabulary of some 30 words by classifying phonetic segments into four different classes and storing, in coded form, up to five segments. The project was discontinued after a few years of experimentation.

The ASR work at DCA is part of a larger project of two-way man-machine communication involving both recognition and synthesis. Recognition is based on the measurement of zero-crossing density. The vocabulary will consist of a fixed set of some 40 words. The implementation of the technique, using a mini-computer is under way but, using a bigger machine, the recognition of the ten digits has been successfully completed.

At APRU the work is aimed at using a variable vocabulary of some 200 words and a hybrid (analogue-digital) system with a mini-computer. Todate most of the work has concentrated on developing detailed mathematical models and algorithms which are tested in the course of semi-automatic recognition in which data are collected by traditional measurement methods. The data are processed by a small general-purpose computer preparing procedures that can be implemented in relatively cheap hybrid systems. The immediate target is to recognize isolated words through the identification of at least some of the phones. The construction of the analogue pre-processor is completed and implementation of the procedures found to be optimal is under way.

At ITA, ASR is part of a broad project involving also speaker identification and speech synthesis. All-digital methods using FFT analysis and LPC are being developed and tested.

23-2. IA (WARSAW)

An ASR project was embarked on single-handedly by Wlodarczyk 1969a who set out to classify the Polish phonemes into a small number of classes according to the distribution of energy in the spectrum. He first attacked stationary signals, i.e., the vowels and the fricatives pronounced in isolation and distinguished three classes of sounds: (1) with most energy concentrated below 2 kHz -- all oral vowels; (2) with a relatively flat

499

spread of energy -- the fricatives /x f z ʒ ɣ/ and (3) with energy concentrated above 2 kHz -- the fricatives / s ʃ ɕ / . He next decided to select a low-frequency band (approx. 200--900 Hz) and a high-frequency band (approx. 5--10 kHz) and, by applying the output of one channel to one pair of the plates of a CRT and that of the other to the other pair, produced a classification of all the Polish phonemes based on the shapes of the "spots" on the screen of the CRT. He again distinguished three classes: (1) with more energy in the low-frequency band: syllabic and non-syllabic vowels, / b d g/ and /ɣ/; (2) with more energy in the high-frequency band: /t s ʃ ɛ ts tʃ tɕ /; (3) with approximately equal energy level in both bands: the remaining phonemes. Wlodarczyk 1969b contains some remarks on the modifications in the classification - now into four classes -- and the characteristic frequency bands were revised (130--570 Hz and 7--15 kHz). More details are given in Wlodarczyk 1970. Using an additional spectral criterion based on the total shape of the spectrum, four classes were distinguished (with /a/ and /x/ forming a separate type). Some experiments with isolated phones pronounced by the author were here described. The results lead Wlodarczyk to the conclusion that such acoustic-phonetic parameters as the formant frequencies are not stable enough to be used for purposes of classification, being strongly affected by fundamental frequency variations. This paper also contains a block diagram of a device intended for automatic classification of the Polish phonemes. It includes a bank of band-pass filters, a comparator circuit for the high-and low-frequency inputs and a logical system assigning the signals into the four types.

In 1971a Wlodarczyk presented a method of segmenting short words into phoneme-length stretches. The parameters were again the relative energy levels in the extreme frequency ranges. Assuming threshold values found experimentally, a binary code could be used for the classification of the segments. An added criterion for classification was now the over-all level of the segments.

In 1971b this author justifies the principle of recognizing isolated words for many practical purposes of man-machine communication. A device called SELFON-1, whose principles were outlined in Wlodarczyk's earlier publications (quoted above) is now described as a completed, practicable instrument, which is able to segment a speech signal (a word) and classify each segment on the basis of the binary "distinctive features" related to the energy level in the characteristic frequency bands. The number of segments in a word is found to be usually greater than that of the successive phonemes. Therefore, "proper" segments and "spurious" segments are distinguished. The appearance of a spurious segment is due to the lack of complete synchrony in the changes of the classificatory features. Some regularities in the appearance of the spurious segments were observed and some phonotactic constraints were noted so that a partial system of error-correction could be developed. SELFON-1 included a memory able to store up to 5 successive segments in the form of binary codes. The results of many series of experiments lead to some minor modifications of the frequency bands.

With (a) a maximum of 5 segments stored in the memory, (b) the assignment of each segment to just one of the four classes, (c) partial predictability of the spurious segments and (d) some phonotactic constraints, the number of different words was calculated that could be unambiguously recognized by the device. Several lists of words were constructed such that each item on the list was represented by a different higher-order code (one symbol per segment). A list could contain up to 20 different words. Also a few lists were tested with ambiguously coded words. The individual phonemes were found to differ as to their rates of correct classification. Consequently, the words also differed as to their correct-classification scores. The suggestion was made that for the practical purposes of voice-control of technical systems a small but effective vocabulary could be selected in which the classification scores might approach 100%.

Wlodarczyk's research and the device he constructed had a number of interesting features: (1) The analogue techniques that were employed are very attractive from an economic point of view. (2) The signal is described in terms of simple parameters which are used both for segmentation and segment classification. (3) Phonemic and phonotactic redundancy is used to advantage. (4) The recognizer is relatively immune against variations in voice effort, tone hight and rate of speech.

A full evaluation of Wlodarczyk's work is difficult because (a) his device was extensively tested with one voice only (the author's) and (b) the tests were not controlled so as to yield results that could be analyzed statistically.

The project was discontinued in 1972.

23-3. DCA (WARSAW)

Work on ASR was initiated at the Department of Cybernetic Acoustics by Kacprowski who, in his 1967a paper discusses the general issues and reviews some of the results obtained outside Poland in the 50's and early 60's. He also points out the practical applications of man-machine communication and specifies the main phonetic and linguistic problems involved. Another general and updated discussion of ASR problems, with a review of acoustic-phonetic work done in Poland and relevant to ASR is contained in Kacprowski 1972. His 1967a article was immediately followed by another (Kacprowski 1967b), in which the first concrete steps taken by him and his co-workers towards automatic recognition of the Polish speech signal were presented. The objects to be identified were isolated, sustained vowels. An analogue device including an analysis block, consisting of 7 band-pass filters, and a logical network was constructed. Optimal threshold values were found which could be used to quantize the smoothed outputs of the filters into discriminating binary signals from each. Every vowel sound was represented as a logical product of binary signals such as $\bar{A} \cdot B \cdot C \cdot D \cdot \bar{E} \cdot F \cdot G$, where the letters referred to the individual filters and the negation sign indicated that the threshold value of the smoothed voltage was not exceeded. Tests with appropriate speech material (isolated sustained vowels) revealed that most of the 128 codes were non-occurrent, a few were ambiguous whilst over 50 were reliably related to the individual phonemes. The logical net was built of semiconductor diodes in accordance with the unambiguous codes. The paper does not give any statistical results of tests performed with the complete device. Details of the design of the filters used to "segment" the vowel spectrum are given in Gubrynowicz 1967. The device is also described in Kacprowski and Gubrynowicz 1970, where results are given of tests performed with "a wide range of voices," different from those for which the pattern matrices had been prepared. The scores are between 58% correct for /ɨ/ and 88% correct for /a/. The instrument was not developed any further so as to be used for the recognition of higher-order linguistic units.

Since 1971 Gubrynowicz has been concentrating on the technique of zero-crossing density measurements for the purposes of ASR. In his 1971, 1972 and 1976 papers he applied this method to the recognition of vowels. Together with Kacprowski and others he published a series of studies on the classification and recognition of voiceless fricatives: Kacprowski and Gubrynowicz 1972, Gubrynowicz 1973 and Gubrynowicz, Kacprowski, Mikiel and Skalski 1976. The philosophy and the results of the two series of studies may be summarized as follows: It is proved mathematically that the zero-crossing density may be estimated with an accuracy of 1% provided the mean signal level exceeds an arbitrary signal-clipping level α by about 20 dB. It is also shown that in order to obtain satisfactory accuracy for running speech, the level of the quietest sounds (such as /f/) would have to exceed α by 17 dB. This, however, would be correct only if the distribution of the instantaneous amplitude

values were normal, which is approximately true only for voiceless fricatives. The distribution being exponential for voiced sounds the measurement
should be made at a signal level exceeding the threshold level by about 43
dB. The zero-crossing technique is therefore very vulnerable to poor S/N
conditions. Gubrynowicz also investigates, using rigorous mathematical
methods, the optimal averaging interval Δt to be used in running speech
analysis. In 1972 and 1976 he presents a detailed discussion of the accuracy
of formant frequency estimation using two distinct models of the speech signal, a deterministic and a stochastic one. Within the deterministic model
he considers a one-formant approximation to vowel-like sounds and a two-formant approximation. It is shown how the error in formant frequency estimation by zero-crossing measurement decreases with the increase of the order
of the harmonic and the fundamental frequency. In the most unfavourable case
of the first harmonic in a low male voice the error is about 50% but falls
rapidly down to about 6% for the 8th harmonic. A more realistic, two-formant
deterministic model is also discussed and it is shown how the measurement
accuracy of the lower and the higher formant frequency depends on the relations in the levels and the frequencies of the harmonics that are dominant
in each formant region. For the stochastic model, the effects of the relations between the formant frequencies and their bandwidths on the accuracy
of $\bar{q}_0$ measurement is discussed in detail (Gubrynowicz 1976). In order to
estimate the formant frequencies it is necessary to apply filters for each
formant region and the partial overlap of these regions (around 1 kHz) presents a difficulty. Some of the main conclusions drawn by Gubrynowicz are:
"The minimal quantization interval over which zero-crossings are counted
must not be smaller than the larynx-tone period, but it is desirable that it
should be at least several times longer, especially in the case of formants
situated in the range of the first three harmonics. When longer stretches
of the speech signal...are analyzed, it becomes necessary to consider the
significant transitional states... and then the quantization interval should
not exceed 20 ms (Gubrynowicz 1976, p. 267).

Using the zero-crossing technique Gubrynowicz (1973, 1974a) performed, in
an on-line system including a small, 32-K Russian computer, the recognition
of the 10 Polish digits with 19 voices (male and female) used in collecting
the data for the training set (880 utterances) and 22 voices (also male and
female) for the test data, obtaining over 95% correct-classification scores
for both sets. His general assumption was that, when dealing with a small,
fixed vocabulary, it is not necessary to identify the successive phonemes
and that it is not even always necessary to perform a complete phonemic
segmentation of the signal. General information, such as the occurrence of
some voiceless fricative in initial, or medial, or final position, the position of (possibly ambiguous) vowel-like segments, etc. is all that is needed.
The parameters extracted from the signal were: (a) approximate F   value,
(b) approximate F   value, (c) binary decision about the energy level below
500 Hz relative to a fixed threshold level, (d) total number of zero-crossings
and (e) binary decision as to the zero-crossing density exceeding 2500 per
second. On the basis of the training set of data a "logical tree" was constructed with the aid of which each spoken digit was coded into specific
sequences of binary symbols. These symbols indicated the "distinctive" segments and the digits in the test set were recognized by reference to the
codes. The processing time needed for the recognition of each spoken digit
was of the order of 20 ms.

In his 1974b paper Gubrynowicz presents a set of 39 words which he intends
to use in the near future for the voice-control of a machine. His voice-
operated system will include a mini-computer of the MERA-300 series. The word
list includes the Polish versions of the ten digits and such items as "punch,"
"printer," "disc," "program," "start," etc. A small number of sentences can
be formed by sequences of the words in the vocabulary using very simple
grammar.

In order to recognize a list of 39 words like the one suggested in
Gubrynowicz 1974b, it is necessary to obtain some phonemic information.
With this in view, a classification of the Polish voiceless fricatives based
on zero-crossing density measurements was attempted in Kacprowski and
Gubrynowicz 1972 and in Gubrynowicz, Kacprowski, Mikiel and Skalski 1976.
The materials consisted of CVC and VCV syllables with all the 5 Polish voiceless fricatives /f s ʃ ɕ x / and all the 6 Polish vowels /i   e a o u /
spoken by 10 subjects. The values of $\bar{\vartheta}_0$ were measured by a special digital
device at 20 ms intervals and printed sequentially. Segmentation was performed visually on the printouts. For each fricative phoneme a histogram
of the $\bar{\vartheta}_0$ values was prepared. It was found that (a) a normal-distribution
approximation could only be used in one phoneme and (b) that the overlaps of
the distributions were so great that there was no chance of reliably classifying the data according to the individual phonemes. This chance was increased, however, when similar phonemes were grouped together so that three
classes only were distinguished, viz. (1) /x/, (2) / ʃ ɕ / and (3) f s /.
In this case, recognition scores between 73 and 94% could be obtained. When
$\bar{\vartheta}_0$ values were calculated separately for each phoneme in each position, it
could be noted that this parameter was strongly affected by the phonetic context, especially the neighbouring vowel.

At present, Gubrynowicz is engaged in solving the many specific technical
problems of signal pre-processing, feeding data into the mini-computer and
preparing software for the recognition of his set of words and sentences
(Gubrynowicz and Zarnecki 1977).

23-4. APRU POZNAŃ

23-4.1 General principles

The general principles which underlie the current work on ASR at APRU may
be formulated as follows (Jassem in press):
1. The speech signal is transmitted in units of word length.
2. The number of operationally different voices is about 10.
3. The operators speak non-regional Standard Polish.
4. Distortion of the original signal (reverberation, noise, poor transmission characteristics, cross-talk, etc.) is reduced to a rational
   minimum.
5. The system will be tuned to the operator's voice.
6. The pronunciation is distinct, but natural.
7. The vocabulary is variable and contains, for a given operation, or
   series of operations, between several dozen and several hundred
   items.
8. No grammar is introduced.
9. The recognition process takes place at several levels, the lower-
   order linguistic elements being allophones and phonemes or phonoids.
10. Pragmatic and semantic information is not introduced (apart from a
    priori considerations in the selection of the current vocabulary).
11. The admissible error rate at the lower levels should not signifi-
    cantly impair recognition at the word level.
12. The digital processing is performed by a cheap mini-computer.
13. Fast-access external memory units are available.
14. The delay involved in the total process of recognizing a single
    utterance should not be greater than a few seconds.
15. The complete system must be realistic economically.
16. The complete system is a hybrid including an analogue pre-processing
    block.

These principles are derived from (a) a priori assumptions, (b) the results
of approx. 10 years of experimentation and (c) the assessment of ASR work done
in other places.

The formulation of the principles is regarded as flexible and may be revised as new results come in, but it is likely to remain essentially valid for the next four or five years. The aims are admittedly modest, but they are at least realistic in view of the man-power, facilities and resources that are now available and are likely to be available in the foreseeable future.

23-4.2 Isolated vowels

The phonotactic structure of Polish is such that each of the six phones representing the principal allophones of the six vowel phonemes may naturally be pronounced in isolation. They may even be regarded as complete words since they are names of six vowel letters. This convenient situation was taken advantage of in the first set on experiments in computer-aided quasi-automatic speech-sound recognition, as described in Jassem, Krzyśko and Dyczkowski 1972a, 1972b, 1974.

A six-phone series /i ɨ e a o u / was spoken by 16 male voices 5 times and spectrograms showed that each vowel sound may be considered a stationary event. The frequencies of the four formants were measured from "sections" and thus each phone was characterized by a variable vector in a four-dimensional space assumed to have a normal distribution $N(\mu_i, \Sigma_i)$ in the population π_i (1 = 1,2,...,6) with a mean vector μ_i and a covariance matrix Σ_i. The statistical parameters were estimated for each phone from the 16 x 5 = 80 observations. The control (test) set consisted of 10 utterances of each phone by 2 of the 16 speakers. The statistical models used for the classification (identification) assumed no equality of the covariance matrices (Box test). The first statistical method used a non-randomized Bayes model which divides the multidimensional space into non-overlapping subspaces, one for each object (phone). A test vowel was assigned to a phone according to the subspace in which it was found, the subspaces being separated by hypersurfaces determined by quadratic discriminant functions of the type.

$$v_{ij}(\underline{x}) = \underline{x}'(\Sigma_j^{-1} - \Sigma_i^{-1})\underline{x} + 2(\mu_i'\Sigma_i^{-1} - \mu_j'\Sigma_j^{-1})\underline{x} + \mu_j'\Sigma_j^{-1}\mu_j -$$

$$- \mu_i'\Sigma_i^{-1}\mu_i + \ln\frac{|\Sigma_j|}{|\Sigma_i|} + 2\ln\frac{q_i}{q_j} , \qquad (23\text{-}1)$$

where q_i and q_j are a priori probabilities. This model was used with all the four features F_1, F_2, F_3 and F_4 and also in a bivariate analysis using only F_1 and F_2.

All 120 vowels in the control set were classified using the subspaces determined by the training set. There were 4 (3,3%) misclassifications with two variables (F_1 and F_2) and 2 misclassifications (less than 2%) with four variables F_1 , F_2 F_3 and F_4 . The same material was also subjected to classification by a minimax method using linear discriminant functions of the general type

$$\underline{b}'\underline{x} + c = 0, \qquad (23\text{-}2)$$

the dividing hyperplane being used so that

$$\underline{b}'\underline{x}_0 + c \leqslant 0 \Rightarrow \underline{x}_0 \in \pi_1,$$

$$\underline{b}'\underline{x}_0 + c > 0 \Rightarrow \underline{x}_0 \in \pi_2.$$

The values of $\underline{b}'$ and c are derived from the mean vectors and the covariance matrices. (For details of the mathematical foundations of the Bayes and minimax methods as modified and adapted to the purposes of these investigations see especially Jassem, Krzyśko and Dyczkowski 1976).

With the minimax method, the assignment of a vowel sound to a class representing one of the six phones now consists in a process of successive eliminations which begins with the statistically most distant pair (this turned out to be /i/ and /a/ and continues for the next distant pair until the vowel is assigned to the most probable phone. This method was applied to the following feature combinations: F_1F_2, $F_1F_2F_3$, $F_1F_2F_4$, $F_2F_3F_4$ and $F_1F_2F_3F_4$. The overall results may be summarized as follows:
With all four formants all the 120 vowels were correctly identified. With F_4 ignored only one mistake occurred. With F_3 and F_4 ignored also one mistake only was made. When only F_2 was ignored, the score was 81% and with F_1 ignored 82% of the classifications were correct. Thus, very nearly all the necessary linguistic information is contained in F_1 and F_2. This conclusion was double-checked by applying a sequential method to the vowels in the training set. Very broadly, this method (based on a mathematical model involving the likelihood ratio) consists in finding out how many formants are necessary in order to obtain correct classification with a given probability, the formants being taken sequentially in all possible orders. With four variables there are $4! = 24$ permutations. The best results were obtained with the orders $F_1F_2F_3F_4$ and $F_1F_2F_4F_3$ and the worst results with the orders $F_4F_3F_1F_2$ and $F_4F_3F_2F_1$. This confirmed the conclusion concerning the relative importance of the formants. For details see Jassem, Krzyśko and Dyczkowski 1974b and 1976.

23-4.3 Vowels in sentences

In the next series of experiments (Lobacz and Jassem 1973, Lobacz 1974 and 1976), the materials were vowels in 6 utterances, each forming a complete sentence, so constructed that each of the six vowel phonemes should be represented at least once in each utterance. Three specially selected speakers pronounced the sentences once at three speeds: fast, normal and slow. Formant charts with F_1 and F_2 as co-ordinates were prepared for each tempo. A vowel sound was represented by a sequence of points in the F_1F_2 plane, each point corresponding to the two values as found in measurements of conventional spectrograms made at intervals $\Delta t = 20$ ms, with an accuracy of 50 Hz. The F_1-F_2 planes were divided into 6 regions, one for each vowel phoneme, by curves representing quadratic discriminant functions derived from data pooled for the three speakers. The functions were determined by the mean vectors and covariance matrices calculated for each vowel phoneme from all the measurement data for that phoneme in all utterances at a given speed. There were, then, three different charts, one for each speed. Each vowel sound was represented as a time-and-frequency quantized trajectory on the appropriate chart. In many cases this trajectory was found to be contained within one identification region and the vowel sound was classified accordingly. In other cases the trajectory passed through 2 or 3 regions and special algorithms were then used to assign the sound to exactly one phoneme. These algorithms were based on (a) the amount of time that the trajectory "remained" in a region and (b) the order of regions passed by the trajectory.

For the three speech rates the overall scores, pooled for the three speakers, were: fast 92%, normal 95%, slow 97% correct. Lobacz 1974 and 1976 contain detailed discussions of the effect of speech tempo on the identification regions and the recognition scores.

The results of Lobacz' work were decisive for the establishment of a method of (semi-) automatic recognition of vowels in continuous speech. The problems to be attacked next were (a) whether it was permissible, for satisfactory results, to pool data from different (male) speakers if a larger number of voices were involved and the voices were not pre-selected, (b) to what extent the results could be improved if the assumed recognizing device was tuned to the individual voice and (c) how good the mathematical models and the algorithms were for statistically representative or arbitrarily chosen linguistic

505

The next series of experiments was based on the analysis of spoken sentences so constructed that they should be maximally representative. These sentences (6 in number) were constructed on the basis of phoneme-frequency counts in spoken colloquial texts consisting of a total of over 100,000 phones. Jassem and Lobacz 1971 and 1976 give the frequencies of single phonemes, diads, triads and tetrads. The typical sentences included the most frequent phoneme sequences and represented natural, colloquial style Polish equivalents of such phrases as "What's the time?", "Can you keep quiet?", etc.

The material consisting of the typical phrases spoken by 11 randomly chosen male voices is analyzed, and the vowels are identified, in Jassem 1974a and 1974b, Jassem, Szybista 1976 and Jassem, Szybista and Dyczkowski (in press). In the first experiment each of the 11 speakers uttered the 6 typical phrases once. There were eleven variants of this experiment. In each variant the data from one speaker formed the test set, while the data from the remaining 10 speakers were pooled for the training set. In each variant a different speaker was tested. Again, F_1F_2 identification charts were constructed, with quadratic and linear discriminant functions. The measurement methods, the preparation of the computer-constructed identification charts and the identification procedure based on the trajectories in the F_1F_2 plane were the same as in the previous series of experiments. Depending on the type of discriminant function, the overall scores for the individual variants varied between 60% and 87% correct. The means were 78% (quadratic functions) and 76% (linear functions) for the training set of data and, respectively, 75% and 76% for the test data. In the second part of the experiment, the identification charts were prepared separately for each speaker on the basis of data from four replications of the typical phrases. The vowels in the fifth replications produced data for the test sets. The identifications were performed for each speaker separately using his own identification chart. Ten speakers were involved. The results of the classification (identification) were not significantly affected by the type of discriminant function. Neither were the scores for the data in the training set significantly better than those for the data in the test sets. But there were significant differences between the speakers, the overall scores varying between 79% correct and 96% correct. On an average, the scores for recognitions simulating the tuning of the recognition device to the operator's voice were better by 13% than those for which the "patterns" (the identification charts) were constructed by averaging over 10 different voices.

23-4.4 Fricatives

In Jassem 1975, Jassem, Szybista, Krzyśko, Stolarski and Dyczkowski 1976 and Jassem (forthcoming), methods of recognizing fricatives were investigated, the assumption being that only features of the spectrum envelope were taken into account. Two distinct methods of parametrically describing the spectral envelopes between 1 kHz and 8 kHz were applied. In the first, after appropriate normalization, mean levels in several frequency bands were taken as the random variables. The total frequency band was divided into 2, 3, 4, 5, 6, 7 or 12 frequency ranges and the classification was performed separately for each condition. Several criteria were applied for the optimization of the divisions, and for three frequency ranges a large number of different divisions were examined. It turned out that as long as the division was not too unequal, it di not greatly matter what the dividing frequencies were. For upwards of 3 frequency ranges, therefore, the total range was divided into bands of equal width.

The materials consisted of CVCVC nonsense words with C = $\left\{ \text{/f s } \int \text{ ɕ x /} \right\}$ and V = $\left\{ \text{/i a u /} \right\}$. Three speakers uttered the "words" in sequences of the type /fifif fafaf fufuf... ...sasas susus / five times. There were, then, altogether 675 spectra and the relative level was measured at $\triangle f = 200$ Hz. The analysis was performed with the aid of the conventional Sona-Graph provided with a specially constructed integrating circuit which permitted the distributions of energy density to be averaged over any multiple of 40 ms. The complete set of data was classified i.e., there was no division into a training and a test set. The individual fricatives were identified in multidimensional spaces. The identification regions were determined using quadratic discriminant functions, separately for the 2,3,...,12 dimensions. The experiment was performed according to two distinct designs. In the first, 5 populations were assumed, one for each phoneme. In the other, 45 populations were assumed: 9 positional variants for each phoneme. In the latter case it was further assumed that the classification was correct if the sound was classified as any of the 9 variants of the phoneme in question. Each of the three voices was tested separately against its own patterns. The results of the classification varied with phoneme, speaker and the number of features. Detailed scores are given in the publications quoted above, but some overall scores, averaged over the three speakers, may be given here. In the Tables below the figures indicate percent correct classifications.

Table 23-1

Overall recognition scores for the Polish fricatives /f s ∫ ɕ x/

number of features	5 objects (phonemes)	45 objects (positional variants)
2	64	not tested
3	79	90
4	90	99
5	95	
6	97	
7	98	
12	99	

With 99% correct classification with the "variant-to-phoneme" method, a larger number of variables was not tested.

A different principle of identification was next applied to the same materials. This time, the random variable was the projection on the frequency axis of the centre of gravity--the "weighted frequency - (a) of the entire energy distribution between 1 kHz and 8 kHz, (b) of two parts of the spectrum of equal width, (c) of three parts of the spectrum of equal width. Both the 5-object variant and the 45-object variant was used. Averaging over the three speakers, the overall scores were as shown in Table 23-2.

Table 23-2

Recognition scores obtained in the "weighted frequency" method

number of features	5 objects (phonemes)	45 objects (positional variants)
1	not tested	58
2	80	86
3	80	93

The frequency band getting narrower with the increase of the number of features, the weighted-frequency method is naturally inapplicable with a large number of variables. For practical purposes of fully automatic recognition in a hybrid system, this method with 45 objects and 3 features or the

507

"average levels" method with 5 objects and 5 features seems advisable.

A pilot experiment described in Jassem, Szybista, Krzyśko, Stolarski and Dyczkowski 1976 indicates that voiced fricatives can be identified with the same methods as the voiceless ones at least equally satisfactorily.

All the calculations as well as the construction of the charts and the logical procedures involved in the identifications were performed on a small general-purpose computer ODRA 1204.

23-4.5 Implementation and work in progress

An engineering team at APRU, under H. Kubzdela, has completed the construction of a hybrid system including a multi-channel analogue analyzer, a commutator and a A/D converter. The data are finally processed by a mini-computer MERA 303. The implementation of the methods described above in this hybrid system is under way. Meanwhile, D. Szybista is successfully applying them to a semi-automatic recognition of the vowels, the fricatives and the affricates in a vocabulary consisting of the 200 most frequent Polish words. Methods of automatic segmentation of continuous speech into phone-length segments are also being developed. This work largely follows the theoretical suggestions contained in Jassem 1971.

Due to considerable phonotactic redundancy in Polish, it has been found that assuming correct segmentation, voiced-voiceless distinction and an identification of only the vocalic and fricative segments with about the same accuracy as that found in the work presented above, items in an arbitrary vocabulary of 200 words will be correctly recognized approx. 90% of the time. Recognition of other types of segments will soon be undertaken with the aim of raising the score.

23-5. ITA (WROCLAW)

In Tyburcy and Zalewski 1976 and 1977 the FFT technique was applied to investigate the formant movements during transitions between vowels. The time interval Δt was 12.8 ms and the frequency range was 78 Hz to 5 kHz. By averaging over 25 successive spectral sections, each transition could be represented as a vector in a multidimensional Euclidean space. The identification of each case of a transition was performed by determining the distance between it and each of the pattern vectors (one for each of 15 types of transitions). 24 male voices and 25 female voices were tested. For the male voices 720 transitions were classified the number for the female voices is not given. By using an effectiveness coefficient for each dimension the dimensionality could be reduced from 64 to 18 without adversely affecting the identification scores. These varied between 83% and 100% with averages of 92% (male voices) and 93% (female voices). The FFT analysis was also used by Tyburcy, Pawlak and Worobiec (1977) for the purposes of segmentation in 25 words containing CVC and VCV syllables by finding the maximum rate of change of the short-term spectrum. The results were found to be in good agreement with boundaries visually determined in oscillograms and spectrograms, but relations between them and those obtained in listening tests using time filters were found to be complex.

Applying the LPC technique the formant frequencies were investigated by Jurkiewicz, Zalewski and Myślecki (1977). The autocorrelation and the co-variance formulation of LPC were compared. Five formants were determined in each of the 6 isolated Polish vowels uttered by 50 male speakers. The error in the imaginary part of the pole frequency (the formant frequency) was estimated at 1% and that of the real part (bandwidth) at 20%. The autocorrelation formulation was found to give better accuracy, which was tested by synthesizing and re-analyzing the vowels.

In Zalewski, Jurkiewicz and Hollien 1977 an attempt is made to recognize vowels using Itakura's log ratio prediction residual. Detailed results are not given.

23-6. SUMMARY

Two ASR projects using analogue systems had to be abandoned. The present
state of the art has to be judged under consideration of the time delay,
very moderate man-power investment and extremely modest resources and facilities as compared with those in such countries as the USA, the USSR, Japan,
etc. The work now carried on in three places is complementary. One group
concentrates on words in a small, fixed vocabulary using zero-crossing
techniques with implementation in a mini-computer. The second has a strong
acoustic-phonetic front-end orientation aiming at a medium-size variable
vocabulary in a hybrid system. The third group develops digital pre-processing techniques for a two-way man-machine communication system.

REFERENCES

Note: (P) in Polish; AA Archiwum Akustyki; SAS Speech Analysis and Synthe-
sis, W. Jassem ed. PWN Polish Scientific Publishers, Warsaw; OSA Proceedings
Open Seminar on Acoustics, Polish Acoustical Society. All items not marked
(P) are written in English.

GUBRYNOWICZ, RYSZARD, "Frequency quantization of the speech signal for the
    purposes of automatic vowel recognition" (P) AA 2, 1967, pp. 255-266.
GUBRYNOWICZ, RYSZARD, Estimation of spectral parameters using the method of
    zero-crossings, (P) Prace IPPT PAN 49/1971, Warsaw.
GUBRYNOWICZ, RYSZARD, An analysis of the zero-crossings of the speech signal
    having a harmonic structure (P) Prace IPPT PAN 37/1972, Warsaw.
GUBRYNOWICZ, RYSZARD, An algorithm for recognizing the 10 digits with the
    aid of the computer BESM-3M (P) 20 OSA, 1973, pp. 57-60.
GUBRYNOWICZ, RYSZARD, The application of the zero-crossing method to the
    analysis of the speech signal and the automatic recognition of a limited
    set of words (P) Prace IPPT PAN 37/1974 1974a.
GUBRYNOWICZ, RYSZARD, Automatic speech recognition in man-machine communica-
    tion, PRACE IPPT PAN 71/1974, Warsaw (1974b).
GUBRYNOWICZ, RYSZARD, "Estimation of formant frequencies by zero-crossing
    measurement," SAS 4, 1976, pp. 253-268.
GUBRYNOWICZ, RYSZARD, W. MIKIEL, J. KACPROWSKI and W. SKALSKI, "A classifica-
    tion of Polish fricatives using the analysis of zero-crossings, SAS 4,
    1976, 147-160.
GUBRYNOWICZ, RYSZARD and P. ZARNECKI, "A mini-computer system for on-line
    processing of selected parameters of the speech signal, (P) 24 OSA, 1977,
    pp. 116-119.
JASSEM, WIKTOR, Acoustic-phonetic foundations of automatic phoneme recognition
    (P), Prace IPPT PAN 14/1970.
JASSEM, WIKTOR, "Phonological segmental units in the speech signal," Form and
    Substance, L. I. Hammerich et al. eds. Akad. Forlag, Odense, 1971, pp.
    181-192.
JASSEM, WIKTOR, "Recognition of Polish vowels in typical phrases," ARSO
    Automatic Recognition of Auditory Patterns VIII/2, Lvov 1974 (1974a), pp.
    28-30.
JASSEM, WIKTOR, "Computer-aided recognition of Polish vowels in continuous
    speech," Speech Communication Seminar vol. 3, 1974 1974b, Almquist,
    Stockholm, pp. 175-181.
JASSEM, WIKTOR, "Classification of Polish fricative consonants," 22 OSA, 1975,
    pp. 81-84.
JASSEM, WIKTOR, Foundations of a general model of speech recognition, (P)
    Prace IPPT PAN, in press.
JASSEM, WIKTOR, Recognition of fricatives using wighted mean frequencies,
    Prace IPPT PAN, forthcoming.

JASSEM, WIKTOR, A. DYCZKOWSKI, D. SZYBISTA, "Semi-automatic classification and identification of vowels in typical phrases," SAS 4, 1976, pp. 135-145.

JASSEM, WIKTOR, M. KRZYŚKO, A. DYCZKOWSKI, Classification and identification of Polish vowels by formant frequencies (P) Prace IPPT PAN 64/1972 1972a, Warsaw.

JASSEM, WIKTOR, M. KRZYŚKO, A. DYCZKOWSKI, "Recognition of the Polish vowels by formant frequencies," 19 OSA, 1972b, pp. 268-271.

JASSEM, WIKTOR, M. KRZYŚKO, A. DYCZKOWSKI, "Identification of isolated Polish vowels," AA 9, 1974a, p. 261-287.

JASSEM, WIKTOR, M. KRZYŚKO, A. DYCZKOWSKI, "Identification of isolated Polish vowels," SAS 4, 1976, pp. 107-133.

JASSEM, WIKTOR, and P. LOBACZ, A phonotactic analysis of Polish texts (P) Prace IPPT PAN 63/1971.

JASEM, WIKTOR and P. LOBACZ, "Frequency of phonemes and their sequences Polish texts," SAS 4, 1976, pp. 241-251.

JASSEM, WIKTOR, D. SZYBISTA and A. DYCZKOWSKI,"Recognition of Polish vowels in typical Polish phrases,"(P) Prace IPPT PAN 43/1975, Warsaw.

JASSEM, WIKTOR, D. SZYBISTA, and A. DYCZKOWSKI, "Recognition of Polish vowels in continuous speech" (P) AA, in press.

JASSEM, WIKTOR, M. KRZYŚKO, P. STOLARSKI, A. DYCZKOWSKI, "Recognition of Polish fricatives by spectral features," (P) Prace IPPT PAN 4/1976.

JURKIEWICZ, JERZY, J. ZALEWSKI, W. MYŚLECKI, "Analysis of formant movements in short Polish phrases using linear prediction," 24 OSA, pp. 92-95.

KACPROWSKI, JANUSZ, Theoretical bases of the process of automatic speech recognition, (P) AA 2, pp. 123-151, 1967a.

KACPROWSKI, JANUSZ, "Theoretical bases of the method of automatic vowel recognition" (P), AA 2, pp. 227-253, 1967b.

KACPROWSKI, JANUSZ, "Acoustical aspects of man-computer communication using natural language" (P) AA, 7, 1972, pp. 201-212.

KACPROWSKI, JANUSZ, "The effect of phonetic context on the zero-crossing frequency of fricative consonants," 20 OSA, 1973, pp. 101-104.

KACPROWSKI, JANUSZ, R. GUBRYNOWICZ, 'Automatic recognition of Polish vowels using a method of spectrum segmentation," SAS 4, 1970, pp. 51-70.

KACPROWSKI, JANUSZ, R. GUBRYNOSICZ, A study of the spectral parameters of voiceless fricatives using the method of zero-crossing, Prace IPPT PAN, Warsaw, (P) 71/1972.

MOTYLEWSKI, JERZY, J. KACPROWSKI, Automatic recognition of words using a method of segmenting the spectrum of the speech signal (P) Prace IPPT PAN 29/1969, Warsaw.

LOBACZ, PIOTRA, Effect of speech rate on the formant movements in Polish speech (P), Prace IPPT PAN 64/1974, Warsaw.

LOBACZ, PIOTRA, "Speech rate and vowel formants," SAS 4, 1976, pp. 187-218.

LOBACZ, PIOTRA and W. JASSEM, "Identification of Polish vowels in running speech," (P) 20 OSA, 1973, pp. 183-188.

TYBURCY, EDWARD, J. ZALEWSKI, "transitions as distinctive features of phoneme sequences," (P) Instytut Telekomunikacji i Akustyki, 1976, pp. 28-29.

TYBURCY, EDWARD, J. ZALEWSKI, "Distinctive features of vowel sequences described by a phonetic function of speech," (P) 24 OSA, 1977, pp. 96-99.

TYBURCY, EDWARD, A. PAWLAK, Z. WOROBIEX, "Application of the phonetic speech function to the segmentation of continuous speech," (P) 24 OSA, 1977, pp. 80-83.

WLODARCZYK, HIPOLIT, "Objective classification of phonemes based on extreme bands of the speech spectrum," (P) AA 4, 1969, 1969a, pp. 263-279.

WLODARCZYK, HIPOLIT, "An automatic selector of isolated phonemes and words," (P), AA 4, 1969 (1969b), pp. 353-355.

WLODARCZYK, HIPOLIT, "On classifying isolated speech sounds independently of the manner of articulation," (P) AA 5, 1970, pp. 84-96.

WLODARCZYK, HIPOLIT, "Methods of automatic segmentation of the speech
signal and of classification of segments in the electronic system
SELFON-1, (P) AA 6, 1971 (1971a), pp. 79-96.

WLODARCZYK, HIPOLIT, "Automatic recognition of limited sets of words and
classification of phonemes by segmenting two pass-band signals, (P),
AA 6, 1971 (1971b), pp. 171-197.

ZALEWSKI, JANUSZ, J. JURKIEWICZ and H. HOLLIEN, "Application of the Ikatura
metric to the similarity between patterns obtained by predictive coding,
Instytut Telekominikacji i Akustyki, also 24 OSA, 1977, (P), pp. 100-103.

24.

SPEECH RECOGNITION WORK

IN WESTERN EUROPE

Jean-Paul Haton

Centre de Recherche en Informatique de Nancy (CRIN)

University of Nancy 1, France

24-1.   INTRODUCTION

Research into speech recognition is currently experiencing an important development in Western Europe, particularly in France, Germany and Italy. Those laboratories working in this field belong both to universities and to private companies.

The motivations behind this research are close to those of other researchers in the world in that the work is situated in the general framework of the simplification and diversification of man-machine communication : the applications envisaged for the speech recognition systems concern, thus, machine-control, quality-control, information centers, communication with a computer, etc... It must be noted, however, that at present the industrial development of isolated word-recognition systems has not reached the level of the U.S.A.

Many common points exist between the research undertaken in the USA and that in Western Europe, if only in the form of regular contact between the two communities (visits, ICASSP congresses, etc.). Nevertheless, European research-work has some specific characteristics : for example, the development in France, from 1971-72 onwards, of methods of dynamic comparison for isolated word-recognition, following the original research carried out by the Russians and the Japanese ; another characteristic of this work is the pre-eminence of acoustic-phonetic decoding in relation to the other processing levels found in the majority of practical realisations.

Research into speech recognition developed quite early in Europe thanks to precursors such as, for example, DREYFUS-GRAF who, from 1944 onwards, began his studies into the recognition of French by "Phonétographe" (DREYFUS-GRAF, 1950) ; FRY and DENES, in Great Britain, in 1958 who constructed a phoneme-recognition system using linguistic constraints (in this case the frequency of phonetic digrams) to improve the performances (DENES, 1959). On the other hand, research-work in the 1960's remained fragmentary and isolated in Germany, France and Italy as well as in Great Britain. It was not until 1970 that a certain coordination in research work began to appear, in, for example, the creation of the groups "Speech Communication" ("Communication Parlée") within the G.A.L.F. (French Acoustical Society) and "Speech Recognition" ("Reconnaissance de la Parole") within the A.F.C.E.T. (French Computer Society).

There exists, in this field, at present, about ten teams in France, around six in West Germany, two in Italy, about three in

Great Britain, and one in Sweden. These teams are tackling
different aspects of the problem : acoustic analyses of speech,
isolated-word recognition, recognition and understanding of
continuous speech.

We shall now review the methods in operation and the results
obtained, limiting ourselves, generally,to the most recent
research work . Our description is classed by theme and not by
country, this being, in our opinion,the most propitious way
of presenting a synthesis of European research in this field.

This survey paper does not pretend to draw the whole picture
of research work into Speech Communication in Europe. In fact,
we will not mention important studies undertaken in speech
synthesis, speech transmission, speaker verification, aids for
the handicapped often by the same teams that are working on
speech recognition. In addition, there are a number of
Laboratories in Europe interested in fundamental aspects of
speech and in Speech Communication. Even if they are not
involved in speech recognition these laboratories often influence
research in this field.

24-2. SPEECH ANALYSIS AND FEATURE EXTRACTION METHODS

The acoustic-phonetic levels of processing are of capital
importance in the chain of Speech Communication.

This is a fact recognized from the very beginning by
European researchers, as has already been said, and it is also
one of the conclusions of the SUR ARPA project.

On the question of acoustic speech-processing and feature
extraction, the methods used are generally similar to those
used by American or other researchers, but for a few exceptions,
as we shall see.

24-2.1. Speech Analysis

Spectral analyzers, of the Vocoder type, were among the first
devices used for speech analysis and are still used at present.
Certain particular types of spectral analyzers have been
conceived :
- the selective amplitude compressors of DREYFUS-GRAF.
- the binary spectral analyser used by HATON, LAMOTTE and
  coll. (HATON, 1974) in which the slope of the amplitude-
  frequency curve is coded on a bit. This coding allows an
  important compression of information ; however, the loss of
  pertinent information does not permit an identification of
  the phonemes in continuous speech. This machine is no longer
  used at present.
- the "Loudness analyzer" used by RUSKE and coll.(W.Germany)
  which yields 22 loudness functions covering the frequency
  range 70-10,000 cps and approximates the frequency and
  time resolution of the human ear. The description of this
  analyzer may be found in (VOGEL, 1975).
Two approaches, used by French teams, may be compared with
this method. The first concerns the use of an "artificial
cochlea" which consists of 96 bandpass filters whose central
frequencies have been chosen from measurements made on the
cochlea and from psycho-acoustic studies (ALINAT, 1975).

The second uses a mathematical model of the ear for the
analysis of speech. This model, developed by CAELEN in Toulouse

(CAELEN, 1976) comprises three parts :
- external and medium ear
- cochlea
- filtering and nervous coding.

The use of two different sources of analysis (spatio-temporal at the level of the cochlear spectrum, and frequential at the level of the neurons) helps to give a precise perceptive image of the sound.

Several teams also use, alone or concurrently with other methods, linear prediction coding (L.P.C.).This is the case in France for the E.N.S.T. in Paris (GUEGEN, MICLET), for the E.N.S.E.R.G. in Grenoble (CARRE, TUFFELLI), and for the C.R.I-Nancy (HATON and coll.). A special hardware processor for L.P.C. computation is being developed by E.N.S.E.R.G. and a micro-programmed processor was developed by C.R.I.-Nancy. The use of Kalman filtering methods in speech analysis has also been studied by GUEGUEN.

Some groups also use temporal methods in speech analysis. These methods make it possible to detect the pitch and to track formants directly from the speech wave. Two French groups have developed original techniques in this field. DOURS and FACCA (C.E.R.F.I.A., University of Toulouse) track formants by direct estimation of the impulse response of the vocal tract (DOURS, FACCA AND PERENNOU, 1974).

BAUDRY and DUPEYRAT (C.E.A.-S.E.R.F., Saclay, France)code the signal while conserving only its extrema, after digitalisation of this signal. The use of this coding and of histograms of the lengths of curve-segments and of zero-crossings, permits the detection of pitch and of formant frequencies. The method has the advantage of being simple and quick (BAUDRY AND DUPEYRAT, 1976).

24-2.2. Feature extraction

The parameters used for recognition are in most cases either the data provided by the spectral analysers or the formants.

Several studies have been undertaken to achieve the compression of spectral data by the use of methods such as factor analysis, Karhunen-Loeve expansion. Let us mention here the work of POLS in the Netherlands (POLS, 1977), of PAU at the E.N.S.T. Paris (PAU, 1972) and of HATON in Nancy (HATON AND LAMOTTE, 1972). These methods have permitted the recognition of isolated words as we shall see below. LIENARD and MARIANI (L.I.M.S.I. Paris) use the "differential spectrum" notion calculated from the difference between two short-time spectra of the speech-wave. This parameter possesses normalisation properties and gives good results in phonemic recognition, as we shall see. Some researchers use specialized hardware for the extraction of specific parameters from the vocal signal. Thus, VAN DER GIET and GLAVE (Universität Bonn) extract 7 binary acoustic features for the segmentation and identification of words (FRIEDRICH et al., 1976). Similarly, BELLISSANT (L.I.M.A.G., Grenoble) uses the parameters defined by VICENS (VICENS, 1969), i.e. amplitudes and zero-crossings in three frequency bands, plus the number of relative extrema in each band, which considerably improves recognition.

24-3. ISOLATED WORD-RECOGNITION

In this context, "word" means a single word and also a short phrase which can be processed as a single unit.

The practicability of limited systems for word recognition has grown to the point where such systems are becoming commercially viable. The industrial development of these systems, in Europe, is not yet the same as in the U.S.A. (i.e. VIP 100 and VIP 500) but it will become so, no doubt, in the near future. As we have already said, the applications envisaged are the same. We point out, however, that no European firms has launched itself in the commercialisation of a model of a recognition system proposed by a research laboratory.

Word-recognition systems may be classed into two categories : the first corresponds to a global approach, it consists of treating the entire word as an acoustic pattern which is classified by a global comparison with stored reference patterns. In the second category, on the contrary, an attempt is made to segment the speech-wave into small units (phonemes, syllables, diphones, or others), to identify each unit individually and to finally recognize a word by some kind of lexical search.

Most of the systems belong to the first category, which we shall begin by studying, limiting ourselves to the systems dating after 1970.

POLS (T.N.O., Netherlands) developed in 1971 a recognition system of about 20 words using a compression of spectral data by factor analysis (POLS, 1971). An analogous system, with similar performances, was proposed in 1972 by PAU (E.N.S.T., Paris)(PAU, 1972). This approach, also studied by HATON for vowel recognition (HATON, 1974), does not permit the recognition of large vocabularies. On the other hand, it does present an interest for speech re-education of deaf people as has been shown by the work of LAGNEAU at the E.N.S.T. Paris (LAGNEAU, 1975) and of HATON in Nancy : SIRENE project (HATON AND HATON, 1976). Following this work, a system of global recognition for words using the Karhunen-Loeve expansion has been realized in Nancy by LEM (LEM, 1976).

Several digit-recognition systems have been realized. Thus at C.N.E.T.-Lannion (France), associated with a desk calculator (GRESSER, 1973) and using stochastic decision functions. HINRICHS and GONSCHOREK (T.U. Braunschweig, W. Germany) have realized a 10-number-recognition system for 100 speakers, with a self-adaptation to the speech rate and intensity (HINRICHS AND GONSCHOREK, 1971). BECKER (AEG Telefunken, Ulm, W. Germany) uses a channel vocoder and linear or quadratic discriminant functions for the same purpose (BECKER, 1974). A more general version of this AEG-Telefunken system permits the recognition of 40 isolated words and is self adaptive to the speaker.

ROCHE (E.C.A.,Paris) has proposed an original approach to the problem of word-(or phoneme-)recognition using information theory. The recognition program is generated automatically from a composition law and from elementary operators working on data provided by a channel-Vocoder (ROCHE, 1972). These principles have been put into operation in a few very reduced cases.

Within the framework of word-recognition, BERGER-VACHON (University of Lyon, France) has made a study on the statistical approaches of the problem : validity of adopted

515

hypotheses, elaboration methods of paradigms (reference patterns) from examples (BERGER-VACHON, 1975).

MLOUKA (L.I.M.S.I., Paris) has proposed a word-recognition system using a 32-channel spectral analyzer. The words are represented by a series of differential spectra corresponding to transition zones in the word (c.f. the analysis method of LIENARD and MARIANI in Sect. 24-2). For a 100-word vocabulary and one speaker, after training, the recognition pourcentage is about 90 % (MLOUKA, 1974).

Those European systems that are among the most efficient in global word-recognition use temporal normalisations of the acoustic patterns, generally employing the principles of dynamic programming. These methods were first studied and implemented in Japon (SAKOE AND CHIBA, 1971) and the U.S.S.R.

These techniques, requiring time-consuming computations, nevertheless permit the making of comparisons which break away from the invevitable variations in length of a given word. A system of this type has been realized at the Plessey Laboratories (Maidenhead, G.B.) for the recognition of 10 numbers (WARREN, 1972). Another system, founded on CHIBA's algorithm, has been implemented at the C.N.E.T.-Lannion (BARS et al., 1973) with the use of a channel Vocoder. The system permits the recognition in real-time of a vocabulary of from about 10 to 100 words for one speaker with a success rate of about 95 %. Some off-line experiments have also been carried out for larger vocabularies (up to 1000 words). An original dynamic-matching algorithm has been proposed by HATON. This algorithm locally, not globally, optimal, turns out to be sufficient for speech patterns and much less time consuming. Real-time experiments using the binary spectrum analyzer described in Section 24-2   have given 97 % accuracy for a fifty-word vocabulary and one speaker, after training (one template for each word in the dictionary). This system has permitted the undertaking of studies on the drift of performances in the course of time when using an on-line recognition system (HATON,1974).A pre-industrial prototype was developed by CGE(Laboratories de Marcoussis) using these principles.

We shall now examine the realisations of the second category which correspond to an analytical approach of the problem. Systems of this type exploit,instead of ignoring, the syllabic and/or phonemic structure of speech. The techniques used in these systems turn out to be less efficient (in computation time and/or recognition rates) than global methods as far as recognition of small vocabularies is concerned. But these techniques may be useful for large vocabularies and they often are generalizable to connected speech recognition (see Section 24-3).

The DAWID system developed by VAN DER GIET and coll. (IRP, Bonn,W-Germany) uses a hardware analyzer (see Sect. 24-2) and describes an incoming word as a string of phonetic symbols which correspond to classes of phonemes (9 classes are distinguished : voiced and unvoiced fricatives,voiced and unvoiced plosives, vowels, initial segments,etc.).The matching process is based on the identity of any reference string with the actual string representing an unknown word (GLAVE, 1977).This system has been tested in isolated word sentence recognition as we shall see later.

Another system developed by RUSKE and SCHOTOLA(T.U. München, W-Germany)uses the "loudness analyzer" described earlier. Each word is segmented into decision units(i.e. initial consonant

clusters preceding the syllable nucleus or final consonant
following the nucleus).The use of a loudness function (i.e. the
sum of the outputs ot the analyzer) makes it easier to segment
a word into syllables which are the decision units of the
recognition process. Total processing time (including
segmentation and lexicon matching)is about 15 to 25 sec using
a vocabulary consisting of 230 names of German cities (RUSKE AND
SCHOTOLA,1978).Experiments have yielded up to 97% detection of
syllable nuclei in isolated words.

The systems developed by French groups are a little different
in that they provide a more precise phonemic transcription
of speech.

ALINAT(Thomson-CSF,France)uses an "artificial cochlea"(see Sect.
24-2)in order to derive phonemic transcriptions of words.The system
is under development and present work concerns the discrimination
of unvoiced plosives/p,t,k/ (ALINAT,1978).

The system developed by BAUDRY and DUPEYRAT(CEA,France)uses
the original time-domain analysis described above in order to
achieve multi-speaker word recognition(BAUDRY AND DUPEYRAT,1978).
Syntactic methods are used to detect the beginning of a voicing
period and to segment speech into phonemes.The sequence of
phonemes corresponding to an incoming word is then compared to
the transcriptions of all words of the vocabulary using an
anchor-point matching procedure.The system is being implemented
on a minicomputer and is intended to process very large
vocabularies.RIVOIRA and TORASSO(Politechnico di Torino,Italy)
present also a syntactic approach for all levels of recognition:
segmentation,phonetic labelling and lexical recognition(RIVOIRA
AND TORASSO,1977).A 24-channel spectrum analyzer in the range
50-10000 cps yields a description of the word.This description
is used to segment the word into three classes(voiced,unvoiced,
no energy).Phonemic classification and lexical recognition use
then fuzzy automata.Another approach to analytical word
recognition has been used by CARTIER and his colleagues at CNET-
Lannion(COURBON et al,1977).The CHARLES system is self adaptive
to any male or female speaker ;it uses DREYFUS-GRAF's idea on
the so called "Phonocodes"and can recognize any word composed of
the French phonemes CHOKINA with an average recognition rate of
about 90%.

The system developed by BLOMBERG and his colleagues(KTH,
Stockholm)is also based on a phonemic segmentation of the words.
Formants are extracted from a filterbank spectrum.This system
gives good results with several speakers : with a 41 word
vocabulary the recognition rate is about 98% for 6 male speakers
in the training group,and about 90% for 3 female speakers(no
women in the training group).Another system was implemented by
the same group for single speaker situations.This second system
is based on a global,pattern-matching approach and extracts the
first two formants from zero-crossings measurements.

Present work in isolated word recognition is characterized by
the search for multi-speaker or self-adaptive systems.For
instance, STENZEL and coll.(T.U.Braunschweig)have developed a
real_time speaker-independent system which gives 95% accuracy on
a 56-word vocabulary(with high quality recording).This system
uses a maximum-likelihood classifier for which the training set consists
of the utterances of the vocabulary by 100 persons.The acoustic
analysis is performed through a 10-channel spectral analyzer.
Another system,already mentioned,is a self adaptive system
developed by AEG-Telefunken.

A second trend in word recognition is the design of small, microcomputer-based systems.Such systems are being developed by several groups in W-Germany,France and they will certainly be of great practical interest in the near future for machine-control and other related applications.

Isolated word-recognition systems are also being used for sentence recognition.Of course,sentences must be pronounced word by word with a pause of a fraction of second between words. Applications where simple languages with rigid syntax are used can be foreseen for such systems.HATON has presented an application for programming a numerically-controlled machine-tool where the user specifies the sequence of actions the machine is to take (HATON,1974).The syntax of the language is represented by a finite-state grammar.The use of the syntax allows the system to discard all candidate-words which cannot appear according to previously recognized words;it has then to make a choice among subvocabularies of about 10 words or less (the total vocabulary is about 40 words). This is a first step in the use of syntactic and semantic constraints to increase the performances of a speech recognition system. In the application described here the recognition rate for sentences is about 100% for one speaker.The recognition of words is performed by the dynamic matching algorithm described earlier. THON (T.U. Braunschweig) has reported a similar experiment with the programming language FOCAL and a 54 word vocabulary. Experiments have shown a reduction of the error rate by two thirds by use of the syntax (THON,1976).Another experiment using the same language FOCAL has been carried out by VAN DER GIET and coll. (GLAVE AND VAN DER GIET,1978).The word recognition system is the DAWID system previously described.The finite-state grammar controls the recognition process and makes it possible to obtain 90% recognition with a 150 word vocabulary.Another application of this system is concerned with an information querying system.

GROC and TUFFELLI(ENSERG,Grenoble,France) have defined a HARPY-like structure for sentence recognition.Their system uses a metalanguage for the definition of the grammar.The grammar is precompiled under the form of a data base called "recognition net".This recognition net is implemented for the recognition of isolated word sentences. The acoustic preprocessing determines the poles for each word by a LPC algorithm.Dynamic programming and modified Itakura's distance serve for word recognition (TUFFELLI AND GROC,1977).Present work concerns the adaptation of the system to continuous speech(GROC AND TUFFELLI,1978).

24-4. CONTINUOUS SPEECH RECOGNITION

Continuous Speech Recognition implies that the words are strung together.The goals of continous speech recognition systems are either the very low-bit rate transmission of speech or the specification of all the words spoken.Some early attempts at speech recognition in Europe were already concerned with aspect of the field.Nevertheless significant realizations date from about 1973.

The system developed by DE MORI and his colleagues (Politechnico,Turin,Italy)makes extensive use of syntactic control at various stages of the recognition process.A finite-state automaton operating on spectral features segments the speech wave into syllables.Spectral data are obtained by FFT or inverse filtering(e.g. energy above 2.5 kHz,ratio low energy/high energy). Preclassification of segments into elemental fragments and final classification are also made by using finite-state grammars which can be learned by grammatical inference. The description of the speech input given by this system can be used for speech synthesis or as input to a Speech Understanding System (DE MORI et al., 1976).

ROSSI and STRINGA (ELSAG, Genova, Italy) use the basic idea of a linguistic model of a system for mail address optical recognition. That is the decisions are taken only at the full message level. The input speech signal is analyzed through a bank of 8 bandpass filters, it is then segmented and the segments labeled. The system is implemented on a special network of minicomputers (ROSSI AND STRINGA, 1977).

The system developed by MERCIER and his colleagues (CNET-Lannion) is based on a spectral analysis of the speech signal by a channel Vocoder (15 filters covering the telephone band-width). A segmentation into syllables is achieved by using intensity computed as the sum of the outputs of the 15 filters sampled at 100 cps. A phoneme segmentation is then made together with a hierarchical classification of these phonemes into broad classes. This preclassification takes into acount spectral parameters such as intensity in predetermined frequency bands, etc. Finally a complete identification of phonemes yields a phoneme lattice with about 70% phoneme recognition rate (GRESSER AND MERCIER, 1975). On the basis of a prosodic model of French (using only the fundamental frequency), work is also in progress in order to segment connected speech into prosodic words (VAISSIERE, 1977).

GUEGUEN and MICLET (ENST, Paris) have built a system that includes an "Adapted Channel Vocoder". This Vocoder is made up of the set of inverse digital filters, each filter being tuned for the recognition of a particular phoneme. This device yields every 10 ms an ordered list of possible phonemes. To each phoneme is associated an automaton in order to properly define the phoneme boundaries (GRENIER AND GUEGUEN, 1976). Present work is concerned with word identification at lexical level and grammatical inference (MICLET AND GUERIN, 1978).

Research carried out by LIENARD and MARIANI (LIMSI, Paris)in connected speech recognition mainly uses transient information for phoneme identification (MARIANI AND LIENARD, 1977). Two lexicous were constructed by a learning method, one for steady-state spectra and another for transitions between phonemes, or diphones. Each diphone is characterized by a differential spectrum reflecting the spectral change between two instants. The segmentation into steady states and transitions is based on variational principles (LIENARD et al., 1974). The steady-state segments are first labeled and the diphones are then identified according to surrounding phonemes. Phonemes and diphones are finally concatenated by using some heuristics. Preliminary results gave 50% of phonemes exactly recognized in first position. The phoneme lattice is transmitted to the upper levels of processing.

Two systems have been developed in Nancy. The first one uses a spectral analyser in order to make a phonemic segmentation of the speech wave. The identification of the phonemes is then carried out in optimal subspaces obtained by Karhunen-Loeve expansion (LEM, 1976). The second system works directly on the sampled speech wave. A syllabic and then phonemic segmentation is made by using temporal and prosodic parameters (intensity, voicing, zero-crossings rate). Specific operators have been defined for the preclassification and identification of phonemes; these operators use spectral and temporal features such as formant frequencies and bandwidths (obtained by LPC), zero-crossings, noice analyzes,... The system is based on an artificial intelligence approach in the sense that it is able to derive the optimal tree structure for recognizing the phonemes with the above-mentioned operators (HATON, MESSENET AND SANCHEZ, 1978). Two other studies carried out by the same group concern the recognition of connected digit sequences for ZIP code identification and the use of prosodic information (voicing, intensity and pitch variations) in connected speech segmentation and syntactic analysis of sentences (HATON et al., 1977).

The ARIA system developed at the University of Toulouse uses a temporal analysis of the speech wave which consists mainly of a direct estimation of the three formants. The method is related to the PINSON's method (PINSON, 1963) with several improvements (pitch detection, separate detection of each formant). The basic idea is to directly identify the impulse response of the vocal tract during time intervals where the glottis is closed. Results already obtained show that the method yields parameters of better quality than the one given by a channel Vocoder (DOURS, FACCA, AND PERENNOU 1974). As was mentioned in Sect. 24-2., this group also uses another kind of analysis of the speech wave (CAELEN, 1976). In the framework of the ARIA project PERENNOU and his colleagues are also developing a lexical analysis algorithm. This algorithm uses the syllable as a fundamental unit ; it has been designed for taking into acount syntactic and semantic filters in order to detect all the words within a sentence (CAUSSE et al., 1976).

One of the goals of a continuous speech recognition system can be the recognition of particular words in the speech wave. This goal is referred to as word-spotting in the literature BRIDLES and SEDGWICK (J.S.R.U., Ruislip, G.B.) have developed a word-spotting algorithm which mainly uses a representation of words by a set of variable-duration segmented templates containing informations about duration and spectrum of the segments. The segmentation is carried out by an optimal, dynamic programming algorithm. This word representation has been applied to word spotting is continuous speech by computation of a likelihood ratio between a given word representation and an unknown portion of the speech input. This computation also uses a dynamic programming algorithm (BRIDLES AND SEDGWICK,1977).

24-5. SPEECH UNDERSTANDING

We refer to Speech Understanding Systems (SUS) as to speech recognition systems which make extensive use of higher level constraints (syntactic, semantic, pragmatic) within a particular well-defined domain in order to perform a particular task. The first work in Western Europe was done by TUBACH at the University of Grenoble, France (TUBACH, 1970). TUBACH's system was able to understand with very good accuracy small programs written in a subset of ALGOL and spoken by a single speaker. The system used a spectral analysis at the acoustic level.

More recently, five research groups have reported on SUS in France and Italy. All these systems use as a front-end the acoustic-phonetic processors which were described in the previous section.

520

DE MORI and his colleagues have presented a project for a
SUS with learning capability (DE MORI,RIVOIRA AND SERRA, 1975).
Particular care is devoted in this system to the emission and
verification of hypotheses at syllabic level.The emission of
hypotheses uses a stochastic grammar related to the phonemic
composition of syllables. An error-correcting algorithm has been
designed for verifying these hypotheses.The use of fuzzy set
theory has been investigated at lexical and semantic levels.
Lexical hypotheses are emitted on the basis of syllable
hypotheses and lexical redundancy (DE MORI AND TORASSO, 1976).
The semantic knowledge in this system is represented in a graph
on which fuzzy relations have been defined. Some preliminary
results show a good performance of the semantic procedure
(SAITTA, 1978).

At the present time SUS that have been designed by French
groups for the past 3 or 4 years are less ambitious than the
systems developed in the USA in the framework of SUR ARPA
project.

A first system, called MYRTILLE 1 was designed in Nancy by
HATON and his colleagues for artificial language understanding.
MYRTILLE 1 uses basically a top-down strategy ; a hypothesis-
and-test paradigm was implemented at the syntactic level in
order to make it possible for the parser to control the
recognition process (PIERREL, 1975). Hypotheses emitted by the
parser are then verified at the lexical level by using a
generalized graph-search algorithm. The system is able to process
sentences in which some words have been omitted as far as the
meaning of these sentences remains obvious. It was implemented
in a telephone exchange application. With a fourty word
vocabulary and a thirty rule grammar,95% of sentences uttered by
one speaker are understood,directly or after a dialog between the
speaker and the system.The average computation time excludind
acoustic processing is about 0.5 sec. on a CII-Iris 80 computer
(HATON AND PIERREL,1977). A schematic block-diagram of MYRTILLE 1
is given in Fig. 24-1.

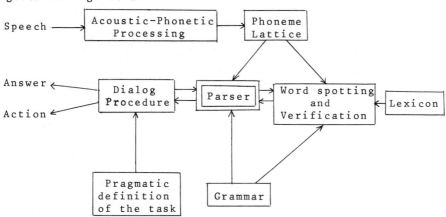

Fig. 24-1.

Organization of MYRTILLE 1 System

521

Another version of this system uses an island-driven,bottom-up parser which makes it possible to start processing a sentence from any reliable word of this sentence.Similar results have been obtained with the two versions (MOHR AND HATON,1976).

MYRTILLE 1 as well as the other SUS described below are not suited for natural language processing. A new system called MYRTILLE II is presently being developed for applications of some hundred word vocabulary and the syntax of basic spoken French. This system uses some kind of pseudo-parallel architecture for the cooperation of the various sources of knowledge : phonetic,prosodic,syntactic,semantic and pragmatic.

The KEAL System developed by MERCIER and his colleagues in Lannion is comparable to MYRTILLE 1 in its capabilities but it is basically a bottom-up system. An efficient lexical search algorithm determines a word lattice corresponding to an input sentence from the phoneme lattice produced by the acoustic processor. The parser then builds all possible syntactic structures according to the context-free grammar of the application. The structures with the best scores are examined first and the process is repeated until an acceptable structure for the whole sentence has been found (QUINTON, 1976). A dialog component defined as a finite state automaton is controlled by the pragmatic level within the framework of the application. Until now applications of computer aided design and information querying have been tested by using simple, artificial languages. With a sixty word vocabulary and a fifty production rule grammar sentence recognition of about 90% was obtained for one speaker in almost real-time on a CII-10070 computer (GAGNOULET et al.,1977).The organization of KEAL is illustrated in fig.24-2.

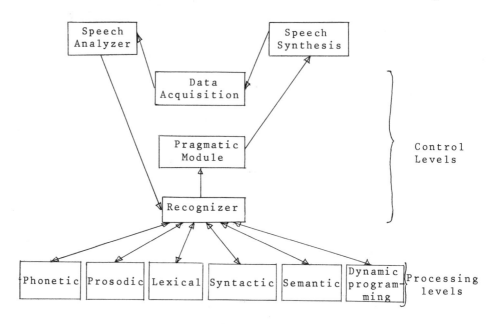

Fig. 24-2.

Organization of KEAL System

BATTANI and MELONI (University of Marseille-Luminy)have investigated the lexical, syntactic and semantic levels of a SUS by using PROLOG as a programming tool. The syntactic and phonological components work in a top-down manner with back tracking. A preliminary implementation was made by using a very simple language for teaching the IBM 360 system control language (BATTANI AND MELONI,1975).

More recently, MARIANI and LIENARD have proposed a top-down SUS based on the prediction-verification paradigm at all processing levels. This system assumes a high-quality acoustic-phonetic processing of the input sentence. The grammar is implemented under the form of a binary precedence matrix which allows an efficient parsing. The system is now under development; it has already been successfully tested on limited applications (MARIANI AND LIENARD,1978).

24-6. CONCLUSION

A lot of efforts have been made over the past twenty years in speech recognition in Western Europe. This work includes all aspects of the field from very simple isolated word recognition systems to natural language understanding systems. The former have already reached the point of practicality for some applications and work is in progress in order to bring the latter closer to this point.

ALINAT,P.,"Etude des phonèmes de la langue française au moyen d'une cochlée artificielle.Application à la reconnaissance de la parole". Revue Technique Thomson-CSF, 7, n°1,(1975),91-123.
ALINAT,P.,"Reconnaissance analytique de parole utilisant une cochlée artificielle", Congrès AFCET, "Reconnaissance des Formes", Paris, Fév. 1978.
BARS,J.F. et al.,"Application de la programmation dynamique à la reconnaissance des mots" 4èmes journées d'Etude sur la Parole, GALF, Bruxelles, 1973.
BATTANI,G. AND H. MELONI,"Compréhension automatique de la parole continue à l'aide de la phonologie,la syntaxe et la sémantique" 6èmes journées d'Etude sur la Parole, GALF, Toulouse, Mai 1975.
BAUDRY, M. AND B. DUPEYRAT, "Analyse du signal vocal.Utilisation des extrema du signal et de leurs amplitudes.Détection du fondamental et recherche des formants" 7èmes journées d'Etude sur la Parole GALF, Nancy, 19-21 Mai 1976.
BAUDRY, M. AND B. DUPEYRAT,"Utilisation de méthodes syntaxiques et de filtrage logique en reconnaissance de la parole" Congrès AFCET "Reconnaissance des Formes",Paris,Fév. 1978.
BECKER,D., "Weigleich eines linearen und eines nichlinearen Klassificators bei der Worterkennung" Wiss.Ber. AEG Telefunken, 47, n° 3-4, (1974), 77-84.
BELLISSANT, C. AND R. BOUTTAZ, "Un système d'entrée vocale sur ordinateur" Séminaire de programmation, Grenoble, 1975.
BERGER-VACHON,C., "Conception d'une entrée vocale automatique" Thèse d'Etat, Université de Lyon 1, 1975.
BRIDLE, J.S. AND N.C. SEDGWICK, "A Method for Segmenting Acoustic Patterns, With Applications to Automatic Speech Recognition" IEEE-ICASSP, Hartford, Conn.,May 1977.
CAELEN, J., "Un modèle mathématique de cochlée et son application à l'analyse du signal vocal "Thèse de Docteur-Ingénieur, Université de Toulouse, 1976.

CAUSSE, B. et al., "Evaluation d'une méthode ascendante d'analyse lexicale dans le discours continu", 7èmes journées d'Etude sur la Parole, GALF, Nancy, Mai 1976.

COURBON, L. et al., "Reconnaissance automatique de la parole CHARLES".Revue d'Acoustique, 43, n°4,(1977), 340-46.

DE MORI, R. AND P. TORASSO, "Lexical classification in a Speech Understanding System Using Fuzzy Relations" IEEE-ICASSP, Philadelphia, April 1976.

DE MORI, R., P. LAFACE AND E. PICCOLO, "Automatic Detection and Description of Syllabic Features in Continuous Speech" IEEE Trans. Acoustics, Speech and Signal Processing, 24, n° 5, (1976), 365-79.

DENES, P., "The Design and operation of the Mechanical Speech Recognition at University College London" J. Brit. IRE, 19, n°4, (1959), 219-29.

DOURS, D., R. FACCA AND G. PERENNOU, "Analyse temporelle du signal de parole comparée à l'analyse fréquentielle du point de vue de la reconnaissance "Journées d'Etude sur la Parole, GALF, Orsay, Mai 1974.

DREYFUS-GRAF, J., "Sonograph and Sound Mechanics" J.A.S.A.,22, (1950), 731-39.

FRIEDRICH, L. et al., "DAWID II, Beiträge zur automatischen Spracherkennung" Buske, Hamburg(IKP-Forschungsbericht Bd 39), 1976.

GAGNOULET, C. et al., "A Multi-Purpose Speech Understanding System" IEEE-ICASSP, Hartford, May 1977.

GLAVE, R.D., "Performance Evaluation of the DAWID Speech Recognition System" 9th Int. Cong. Acoustics, Madrid, July 1977.

GLAVE, R.D. AND G. VAN DER GIET, "The DAWID Speech Recognition System" IEEE-ICASSP, Tulsa, USA, Ap. 1978.

GRENIER, Y. AND C. GUEGUEN, "Un vocoder à canaux adaptés, son apprentissage : application à la parole continue" 7èmes journées d'Etude sur la Parole, GALF, Nancy, Mai 1976.

GRESSER, J.Y., "Reconnaissance automatique de la parole et dialogue homme-machine" Echo des Recherches, Oct.,(1973), 10-21.

GRESSER, J.Y. AND G. MERCIER, "Automatic Segmentation of Speech Into Syllabic and Phonemic Units, Application to French Words and Utterances" In "Auditory Analysis and Perception of Speech" G. FANT,M.A.R. TATHAM ed., Academic Press, 1975.

GROC, B. AND D. TUFFELLI, "Compilation d'un mét alangage de définition de structures relationnelles et son utilisation en reconnaissance de la parole" Congrès AFCET "Reconnaissance des Formes", Paris, Fév. 1978.

HATON, J.P. AND M. LAMOTTE, "Selection of Features by Information Compression in Speech Recognition" Machine Perception of Patterns and Pictures, Conf. Series no 13,Teddington, G.B., Ap. 1972.

HATON,J.P. "Contribution à l'analyse, la paramétrisation et la reconnaissance automatique de la parole"Thèse d'Etat, Université de Nancy 1, jan. 1974.

HATON, J.P., "A Practical Application of a Real-Time Isolated Word Recognition System Using Syntactic Constraints" IEEE Trans. Acoustics, Speech and Signal Processing, 22, n°6, (1974), 416-19.

HATON, J.P. AND J.M. PIERREL, "Organization and Operation of a
    Connected Speech Understanding System at Lexical,Syntactic
    and Semantic levels" IEEE-ICASSP, Philadelphia, Ap. 1976.
HATON, M.C. AND J.P. HATON, "Un système de rééducation vocale
    assistée par ordinateur des mal-entendants" 8th Int.Cong.
    Cybernetics, Namur, Sept. 1976.
HATON, J.P. G. MESSENET AND C. SANCHEZ, "Etude et utilisation
    des indices acoustiques et des traits pour la reconnaissance
    phonétique" 9èmes journées d'Etude sur la Parole, GALF,Aix,
    Mai 1978.
HINRICHS, O. AND J. GONSCHOREK, "Ein Spracherkennungsgerät mit
    selbstätiger Anpassung an Sprachgeschwindigkeit und
    Lantstärke" NTZ, 24, n°4,(1971), 177-82.
LAGNEAU, M., "Un système d'aide visuelle aux sourds profonds"
    6èmes journées d'Etude sur la Parole,GALF, Toulouse,Mai 1975.
LEM, H., "Compression de l'information, Application à la
    paramétrisation et à la reconnaissance automatique de la
    parole" Thèse de 3ème cycle, Université de Nancy 1,1976.
LIENARD, J.S. et al., "Real-time Segmentation of Speech"Speech
    Communication Seminar,KTH, Stockholm, Aug. 1974.
MARIANI, J.J. AND J.S. LIENARD, "Acoustic-Phonetic Recognition
    of Connected Speech Using Transient Information" IEEE-
    ICASSP, Hartford, Conn., May 1977.
MARIANI, J.J., "Contribution à la reconnaissance automatique
    de la parole utilisant la notion de spectre différentiel".
    Thèse de Docteur-Ingénieur, Université de Paris 6,1977.
MARIANI, J.J. AND J.S. LIENARD, "ESOPE O : un programme de
    compréhension automatique de la parole procédant par
    prédiction-vérification aux niveaux phonétique, lexical
    et syntaxique" Congrès AFCET "Reconnaissance des Formes"
    Paris, Fév. 1978.
MICLET, L. AND C. GUERIN, "Inférence multiple en grammaire
    régulière " Congrès AFCET "Reconnaissance des Formes",
    Paris, Fév. 1978.
MLOUKA, M., "Reconnaissance automatique de la parole : une
    expérience de reconnaissance par mots" Thèse de 3ème cycle,
    Université de Paris 6, 1974.
MOHR, R. AND J.P. HATON "A Parsing Algorithm For Imperfect
    Patterns And Its Applications" 3d I.J.C.P.R.,Coronado,
    Nov. 1976.
PAU, L.F., "Statistical Reduction and Recognition of Speech
    Patterns ; Normalization of some Phoneme Parameters"
    Machine Perception of Patterns and Pictures, Conf. Series
    n° 13, Teddington, G.B., Ap. 1972.
PAU, L.F., "Méthodes statistiques de réduction et de reconnais-
    sance des formes. Normalisation des paramètres phonémiques.
    Application à la reconnaissance" Thèse, Université de
    Paris, 1972.
PIERREL, J.P. "Contribution à la compréhension automatique du
    discours parlé" Thèse de 3ème cycle,Université de Nancy 1,
    1975.
PINSON, E.N. "Pitch-Synchronous Time-Domain Estimation of
    Formant Frequencies and Band Widths"J.A.S.A., 35,(1963),
    1265-73.
POLS, L.C.W., "Real-time Recognition of Spoken Words" IEEE
    Trans. Computers, 20, (1971), 972-78.

POLS, L.C.W., "Speech Analysis And Identification of Dutch Vowels in Monosyllabic Words" Institute for Perception, TNO, 1977.

QUINTON, P., "A Syntactic Analyzer Adapted to Speech Recognition" IEEE-ICASSP, Philadelphia, Ap. 1976.

ROCHE, C., "Information utile en reconnaissance des formes et en compression de données, application à la génération automatique de systèmes de reconnaissance optique et acoustique" Thèse d'Etat, Université de Paris 6, Déc. 1972.

ROSSI, C. AND L. STRINGA, "A Linguistic Approach to Speech Recognition Via a Minicomputer Set" IEEE-ICASSP, Hartford, Conn., May 1977.

RUSKE, G. AND T. SCHOTOLA, "An Approach to Speech Recognition Using Syllabic Decision Units" IEEE-ICASSP, Tulsa, Ap. 1978.

SAITTA, L. "Fuzzy Semantic Network for a Speech Understanding System-An Experimental Study" IEEE-ICASSP, Tulsa, April 1978.

SAKOE, H. AND S. CHIBA, "A dynamic Programming Approach to Continuous Speech Recognition" 7th Int. Cong. Acoustics, Budapest, Aug. 1971.

SLUSKER, G.S. "Nelinejnyp method analiza recevych signalov" Trudy N.I.I.R., n°2, (1968), 76-82.

THON, W., "Some Contributions of Information Theory to the Use of Context in Automatic Speech Recognition" NTZ, 29, n° 12, (1976), 906-11.

TUFFELLI, D. AND B. GROC, "Word Recognition and Encoding Using Poles" IEEE-ICASSP, Hartford, Conn., May 1977.

VAISSIERE, J., "Premiers essais d'utilisation de la durée pour la segmentation en mots dans un système de reconnaissance" 8èmes journées d'Etude sur la Parole, GALF, Aix-en-Provence, 1977.

VICENS, P., "Aspects of Speech Recognition by Computers" PhD Thesis, Stanford University, 1969.

VOGEL, A., "Ein Gemeinsames Funktionschema zur Beschreibung der Lautheit und der Rahigkeit" Biol. Cybernetics, 18, (1975), 31-40.

PART V

FUTURE NEEDS AND TRENDS

527

SCRIBER AND LAFS:
TWO NEW APPROACHES TO SPEECH ANALYSIS

Dennis H. Klatt

Massachusetts Institute of Technology

25-1 INTRODUCTION

This chapter will be concerned with new techniques for speech analysis given the objective of automatic sentence recognition by machine. We summarize here the advantages of several speech analysis techniques developed by other investigators, and then propose two new systems for speech analysis: the SCRIBER phonetic transcription system and the LAFS lexical hypothesis generator.

Figure 25-1a illustrates steps that appear to be necessary in going from a speech waveform to a string of lexical hypotheses for an unknown sentence. Parameters are extracted from the speech waveform, a phonetic representation of the input is derived, and lexical hypotheses are proposed. The chapter will be divided into sections concerning criteria for selecting relevant parametric representations, methods for extracting these parameters, techniques for phonetic classification, and techniques for taking into account sentence-level phonological recoding rules during the process of selecting candidate words from a large lexicon.

The SCRIBER phonetic transcription system shown in Fig. 25-1b will be proposed as an attractive alternative to the more traditional methods of phonetic analysis. Knowledge of auditory psychophysics is used to represent speech as a sequence of spectra. Phonetic decoding rules then take the form of a network of expected sequences of static spectra for each possible transition between phonetic segments.

Also considered is the problem of generating lexical hypotheses from speech input. The LAFS lexical-access-from-spectra system shown in Fig. 25-1c will be proposed as a method for generating lexical hypotheses directly from the acoustic representation of an unknown sentence. Acoustic-phonetic knowledge and word-boundary phonology is precompiled into a lexical decoding network structure.

Prosodic Analysis. We will not consider prosodic analysis in this chapter. Prosodic cues (fundamental frequency, segmental duration, and the intensity contour) suggest a stress pattern for the incoming syllable string, and thus could assist in lexical hypothesization. Prosodic cues also indicate clause boundaries, phrase boundaries, and, to a minor extent, word boundaries.

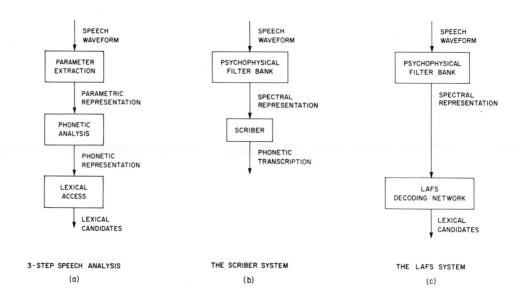

Fig. 25-1. The block diagram of part (a) describes an analysis procedure leading to the hypothesization of lexical items contained in an unknown sentence. Parts (b) and (c) outline the structure of two new methods of speech analysis to be described in Sect. 25-5 and 25-6 respectively.

While relatively little use has been made of prosodic information in most recognition systems described to date, some ideas for prosodic analysis have been proposed and tested (Lea, Medress, and Skinner, 1975).

25-2 PARAMETRIC REPRESENTATIONS OF THE SPEECH WAVEFORM

This section reviews two very different approaches to the selection of acoustic parameters appropriate for phonetic decoding. One parameter set is based on the acoustic theory of speech production. The other is based on aspects of auditory physiology and psychophysics. In the first approach, formant analysis or articulatory inference plays a central role, while in the second, all that matters is the distribution of energy in a set of broadly-tuned filters.

It is assumed that the input speech waveform has been recorded using a high-quality microphone in a relatively noise-free environment. Of course many of the techniques described here can be applied to telephone-quality speech or to recordings made under conditions of high ambient noise, but there will always be a loss of information in these applications that must be overcome by the appropriate use of lexical restrictions and higher-level syntactic and semantic constraints.

Noise-Reducing High-Pass Filter. No matter what the choice of parametric representation to be used for phonetic analysis, the first step in the processing of an input waveform should be high-pass filtering to remove very low frequency background noise. Typical environmental noises contain the greatest energy below about 100 Hz (Pearsons et al., 1976), whereas speech contains very little energy below 100 Hz -- and filtering out spectral components below about 200 Hz has a negligible effect on intelligibility (French and Steinberg, 1947). Ideally, a noise-reducing high-pass filter should have a relatively sharp cutoff frequency of about 100 Hz, a linear phase response and less than 0.5 dB ripple in the passband for minimal distortion to the remaining frequency components.

25-2.1 Analysis Techniques Based on a Model of Speech Production

According to an acoustic theory of speech production (Fant, 1960; Stevens and House, 1961), a speech sound can be represented as the result of a sound source exciting the vocal tract which acts as a resonating linear system. The sound output from the lips then radiates out into free space. The resulting pressure waveform measured at some distance from the lips has a spectrum that is the product of a source spectrum, a vocal tract transfer function, and a radiation characteristic. These considerations suggest that the set of acoustic parameters given in Table 25-1 are relevant for determining the identity of any speech sound.

Table 25-1. A parameter set for speech analysis based on the acoustic theory of speech production.

1. Whether the source spectrum is periodic (as in a sonorant), aperiodic (as in a voiceless fricative or aspirate), or periodic at low frequencies and aperiodic at high frequencies (as in a voiced fricative).

2. The fundamental frequency F0 (if periodic voicing is present).

3. The frequency locations of the lowest three or four resonant frequencies of the vocal tract (formants), if discernible as distinct spectral peaks, as e.g. in a non-nasalized sonorant.

4. The relative amplitudes of the lowest 3 or 4 formants in a non-nasalized sound.

5. The gross spectral shape up to about 6 kHz during voiceless consonants.

Another possible analysis parameter suggested from the acoustic theory of speech production is the presence and frequency of any transfer-function zeros. Atal and Schroeder (1978) have reported some success in developing a linear-prediction analysis procedure that extracts both poles and zeros. However, interpretation of spectral zeros is difficult because in some cases, they may be due to source irregularities.

Similarly, formant bandwidths may seem attractive candidates as parameters for distinguishing between some speech sounds. However, the differences in bandwidth between sonorants are small, and source irregularities make it extremely difficult to determine bandwidths accurately.

Automatic Parameter Extraction Procedures. A voicing decision (whether a spectrum is voiced, voiceless, contains both voicing and noise, or silence) is more difficult to determine automatically than one might think given the ability of the human eye to do so. Rabiner and Sambur (1977) have proposed a simple spectrally-based decision strategy which uses the idea that voiced sounds contain more low-frequency energy than voiceless sounds. An improved approach might be to include various spectral or temporal periodicity criteria (Rabiner et al., 1976) and to use different criteria for different gross types of spectra.

The problem of fundamental frequency extraction is complicated by the fact that voicebars and voiced fricatives may exhibit a nearly sinusoidal waveform, while in a sonorant, many of the higher harmonics are significantly more intense than the fundamental component. If a speech sound is voiced, the fundamental frequency of vocal fold vibrations can be estimated with acceptable accuracy (except at transitions between voiced and unvoiced portions of the waveform) using any of a number of techniques (Rabiner et al., 1976).

Formant frequency estimation can be accomplished by techniques that range from simple peak-picking on filter-bank spectra to complex analysis-by-synthesis strategies (Bell et al., 1961). More recently, techniques making use of linear prediction analysis (Makhoul, 1975) have been employed with good success. In these methods, speech is usually low-pass filtered to 5 kHz, digitized at 10,000 samples per second, and processed at 10 msec intervals by multiplying the waveform by a 25.6 ms Hamming window, taking the first difference of adjacent waveform samples to emphasize higher frequencies, and performing a 12 to 14-pole linear prediction analysis using the autocorrelation method. An example of a linear-prediction spectrum is shown in part (e) of Fig. 25-2. Formant frequencies are then estimated as the locations of peaks in the linear-prediction spectrum.

For some voices and some segment types, formants are missed or extra formant-like peaks appear in the spectrum. When two formant frequencies come close and result in a single peak in the linear-prediction spectrum, the locations of both formants may be resolved by evaluating the spectrum inside the unit circle (Makhoul and Wolf, 1972). Improved accuracy is also obtained if instead of peak-picking, the roots of the linear-prediction polynomial are found. In this case, only roots having bandwidths smaller than some criterion are accepted. One can also impose continuity constraints concerning permitted formant frequency changes from analysis frame to analysis frame (McCandless, 1974) or e.g. median smoothing (Rabiner et al., 1975) to correct occasional analysis frames containing gross errors in formant estimation.

Linear-prediction formant tracking algorithms work quite well in determining the frequency positions of the lowest two or three formants of most voices during the production of non-nasalized sonorants. However, if the fundamental frequency is very high, e.g. over 250 Hz, the linear predictor may track only the strongest harmonic, in which case errors of 100 Hz or more are possible. Since nasalized vowel spectra containing extra pole-zero pairs are also difficult to handle, it must be said that formant tracking techniques are still far from perfect. Formant tracking is a useful procedure most of the time, but gross errors in formant estimation are possible, and these can lead to serious errors in phonetic transcription. It would be better if the error behavior of the parameter set used in phonetic analysis were more graceful and always led to errors that were phonetically similar to the correct segment.

Assuming that the frequency locations of the lowest three formants have been found, it is easy to compute the amplitudes of the formant peaks in dB directly from the linear-prediction spectrum. Formant bandwidths could also be estimated from the linear-prediction analysis, but such estimates have proven to be unreliable due to source irregularities and other factors.

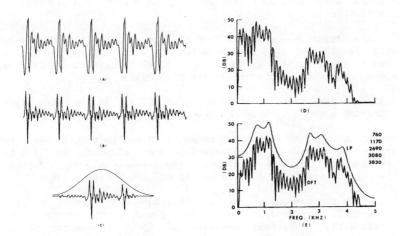

Fig. 25-2. The waveform segment shown in (a) is first differenced in (b), and multiplied by a 25.6 ms Kaiser window in (c). The magnitude of the discrete Fourier transform of the windowed waveform is computed and shown in (d). The magnitude spectrum of the first-differenced windowed waveform is approximated by a linear prediction spectrum in (e). Peaks in this smoothed spectrum can often be associated with formant frequencies.

Since formant amplitudes cannot be determined unless formant frequencies are known, it is desirable to have a parameter that reflects relative formant amplitudes and general spectral shape in fricatives and plosive bursts where frequencies of lower formants are not visible. The linear prediction spectrum itself is an excellent candidate because it is easily computed and there exist several measures for comparing spectra against stored templates for each segment type (e.g. Itakura, 1975).

Acoustic-to-Articulatory Transformations. The shape of the vocal tract can be estimated from formant frequency data (Mermelstein, 1967) or from the waveform of a voiced segment (Wakita, 1973), but the transformation is not unique -- there are usually many vocal tract shapes that result in the same frequency positions for the lowest three formants (Atal et al., 1978). Given this ambiguity, it appears necessary to impose further constraints such as requiring that the vocal tract shape be produced by a highly constrained and simplified vocal tract model (Atal, 1975; Hafer, 1974). Articulatory parameters derived in this way have not been used very much in speech recognition research, but they are clearly worthy of future investigation.

25-2.2 Analysis Techniques Based on a Model of Speech Perception

Examination of data on the behavior of the peripheral auditory system (Green, 1976) and on the psychophysics of simple acoustic stimuli (Licklider, 1951) suggest that the perceptually most important acoustic parameters to be extracted from the speech waveform consist of a spectral representation that takes into account critical bands (Sharf, 1970), masking

---

Table 25-2. Psychophysical considerations in the design of a spectral representation for speech processing.

1. Include frequency components from at least 270 to 5600 Hz since this is the minimum passband for which there is no measurable loss in intelligibility when compared with systems containing wider bandwidths (French and Steinberg, 1947).

2. Include a dynamic range of at least 50 dB so as to adequately represent spectra of both the intense and weak speech sounds.

3. Provide a temporal resolution of about 10 ms since this is the best current guess as to the shortest spectral window employed by the auditory system, and since otherwise certain rapid formant transitions and brief plosive bursts might be missed.

4. Take into account the observation that our ears cannot resolve individual harmonics of a voiced sound if the harmonics are spaced within a critical bandwidth of about a quarter of an octave (Sharf, 1970; Plomp and Mimpen, 1968).

5. Take account of the fact that the contribution to intelligibility from different portions of the spectrum is not uniform (French and Steinberg, 1947). The relative importance to speech intelligibility of different frequency components is in good agreement with a theory stating that each critical bandwidth contributes about equally to intelligibility, at least over the range from 270 to 5600 Hz.

6. Design the slopes of the critical band filters so as to account for the spread of masking, at least over intensities commonly observed during listening to conversational speech (i.e. low frequencies mask weak higher-frequency components better than vice-versa, so the filters have more gradual low-frequency skirts).

7. Express the output of each filter in dB (because decibels are an approximately equal-interval scale for loudness), and quantize filter outputs to about 1 dB (because the just-noticeable difference for changes to formant amplitudes change is 1 dB or more, depending on the circumstances (Flanagan, 1957)).

8. Process only the _magnitude_ of the spectrum because the phase spectrum is not too unpredictable to be used in phonetic decoding.

9. Use a number of overlapping critical-bandwidth filters sufficient to discriminate spectral changes caused by formant frequency changes of about 3 to 5 percent since this is the just-noticeable difference for a formant frequency shift (Flanagan, 1957).

10. Employ a preemphasis filter based on a pure tone threshold curve which indicates that there is an effective emphasis of frequencies in the 2 to 3 kHz range.

(Egan and Hake, 1950), and loudness concepts (Zwicker and Sharf, 1965). An appropriately designed spectrum analyzer can produce a spectral representation that is similar to the "neural spectrogram" memory buffer that is assumed to exist in the auditory system. The spectral representation should take into consideration the factors listed in Table 25-2.

Several attempts have been made to build a spectral analyzer satisfying most of these design criteria (Zwicker, 1970, Plomp, 1970; Klatt, 1976a). Examples of spectra produced by one such spectral analyzer are shown in Fig. 25-3. A linear-log frequency scale is employed to reflect the greater perceptual importance of lower frequencies. Formants do not always show up as distinct spectral peaks in this display, suggesting that formant extraction by spectral peak picking is probably not a perceptual strategy used by humans (on the other hand, analysis-by-synthesis procedures could be used to determine whether two formants are hiding under an observed peak, so no firm conclusions can be drawn concerning the use of formants from this kind of evidence). The perceptual considerations listed in Table 25-5 suggest a set of acoustic parameters for determining the identity of any speech sound that are listed in Table 25-3.

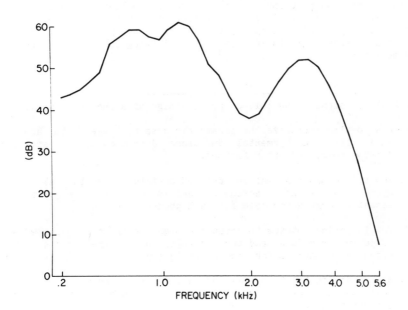

Fig. 25-3. The outputs in dB from a set of thirty critical bandwidth filters (whose design is based on psychophysical data) have been computed for the waveform segment shown in part (c) of Fig. 25-2. The perceptually-based filter-bank representation is plotted on a frequency scale in which equal intervals have roughly equal perceptual importance.

Automatic Parameter Extraction Procedures. The magnitude spectrum can be obtained by sharp low-pass filtering the input waveform at 6 kHz, digitizing the speech at 12,000 samples per second, using a digital

---
Table 25-3. A parameter set for speech analysis whose design is based on psychophysical considerations.

1. A sequence of magnitude spectra computed about every 10 ms, as produced by a spectral analyzer that takes into account the points listed in Table 25-2.

2. Voicing fundamental frequency.
---

preemphasis filter to account for the greater emphasis of frequencies around 2-3 kHz, multiplying by a 25.6 ms Kaiser window or Hamming window, computing the discrete Fourier Transform, and weighting and summing different Fourier components to produce effective filter bandwidths of the appropriate shape, and converting to decibels.

25-3 WHAT TO DO WITH THE PARAMETRIC DATA

Whether one chooses to work with the acoustically-motivated parameter set or the perceptually-motivated set, one still faces the same problems in developing techniques for comparing parameter changes over time against expected characteristics for different phonetic segments. A list of the five basic problems facing anyone wishing to design a system for speech analysis is presented in Table 25-4. The following subsections discuss each of these issues.

Table 25-4. Problems to be solved in the design of a phonetic analyzer.

1. How to time normalize the parametric data to take into account variability in segmental durations due to changes in speaking rate, stress, and other factors.

2. How to frequency normalize the parametric data to take into account differences across talkers in vocal tract length and in acoustic targets employed for each phonetic segment.

3. How to define metrics to compute distance between an observed set of parameter values (and their changes over time) against the expected properties for each phonetic segment.

4. How to divide the time axis into units corresponding to phonetic segments on the basis of parameter changes over time (the segmentation problem).

5. How to identify and characterize algorithmically the acoustically-reliable, perceptually-important aspects of phonetic contrasts in terms of the parameter set that has been adopted.

25-3.1 Time Normalization.

Segmental durations are influenced by many factors, including speaking rate, locations of syntactic boundaries, syllable stress, and features of adjacent segments (Klatt, 1976b). When a segment is shortened or lengthened, relatively stationary portions are shortened or lengthened more than transitional portions. In addition, segments shortened beyond some limit display acoustic manifestations of articulatory target undershoot.

The duration of an acoustic event can play a decisive role in a number of phonetic contrasts in English. Whether a plosive or affricate is voiced or voiceless depends on the duration of a delay in voicing onset relative to consonant release. Voiceless fricatives are longer in duration than voiced fricatives (and the duration of a previous sonorant is longer before a voiced fricative). The vowel /AE/ is longer than the phonetically similar vowel /EH/, and the contrasts between other vowels are also dependent on durational information.

Unfortunately, the durational dividing line for each of these phonetic contrasts depends on speaking rate, location of syntactic boundaries, syllable stress, and local phonetic environment. We are faced with a classical chicken/egg problem -- phonetic decision strategies depend in part on higher-level factors that cannot be resolved until the phonetic decisions have already been made. It appears that the only way out of this dilemma is to make higher-level and phonetic decisions simultaneously (see Sec. 25-6) or to proceed in an analysis-by-synthesis mode where tentative phonetic decisions are verified after lexical items have been identified (Klatt, 1975; Woods, et al., 1976).

How important are durational considerations to phonetic processing? Aside from the examples cited above, the answer is not known. It has been said that the rate of formant motions helps to distinguish plosive-vowel transitions from sonorant-vowel transitions (Liberman et al., 1956). However, the perceptually most relevant cue may be transition rate, transition duration, or simply the duration of the initial sonorant-like spectrum.

Linear time warpings (Dixon and Silverman, 1976) or dynamic programming techniques (Itakura, 1975) can be employed to align sequences of unknown spectra with sequences of reference spectra and various kinds of scoring penalties can be imposed for time warpings that are greater than some maximum distortion. The Harpy "beam-search" strategy (Chapter 15) is similar to dynamic programming except that some warpings are forbidden by temporal constraints, and the search is non-exhaustive so that it is possible to miss the best alignment.

25-3.2 Talker Normalization.

Talkers differ (1) in the size and length of their vocal tracts, (2) in the articulatory/acoustic targets corresponding to different phonetic segments, (3) in the amount of anticipatory and perseveratory coarticulation and target undershoot that is realized under different conditions of stress and speaking rate, (4) in the dialect they employ, (5) in the phonemic forms for certain lexical items such as [K AE T S AX P] vs. [K AE CH AX P], and (6) in the conditions under which the recording is made -- e.g. level and spectrum of the background noise and frequency response of the recording equipment. [It is convenient to group recording conditions with talker-specific factors since the solutions to both problems may be similar, see below.]

The average vocal tract length for an adult male is about 17 cm. The average vocal tract length for an adult female is about 15 percent shorter. This should result in a 15% increase in the frequency positions of all formants for a female voice, all else being equal. However, all else is not equal since the majority of the male-female difference in vocal tract length is restricted to the pharynx. It also appears that sex-specific dialectal differences can exist (Fant, 1966). Still, Nordstrom and Lindblom (1975) and Wakita and Kasuya (1977) report good results using an acoustically based estimate of the vocal tract length to normalize formant frequencies by a single talker-specific linear scale factor. Gerstman (1968) has also reported success using a related technique.

As a practical matter, it is desirable to find a talker-normalization procedure that not only normalizes for vocal tract length, but simultaneously takes into account as many of the six types of talker differences listed above as possible. The Harpy sentence recognition system (Lowerre, 1976; Lowerre and Reddy, Chapter 15) provides a dynamic learning mechanism for talker normalization that shows great promise. The Harpy phonetic decoding network contains only 98 different spectral template types, and a learning algorithm has been defined to modify these templates dynamically to reflect characteristics of a new talker. If the system can recognize a sentence using a set of talker-independent average templates (true about 90% of the time for a simple task grammar), then templates used in the correct path through the network are modified in accordance with the data observed from the sentence spoken by the new talker.

The advantages of talker-specific spectral templates are that they compensate for (1) vocal tract length differences, (2) speaker-specific differences in acoustic properties of phonetic targets, (3) recording conditions, and, to some extent, (4) differences in coarticulatory strategies. Differences in dialect and lexical representations can only be handled by placing the alternatives in the lexicon (Cohen and Mercer, 1975) or by restricting the analysis to talkers of a single uniform dialect.

Some form of self-normalization may also be necessary within this framework so that a new talker can function with an initial set of talker-independent average templates. for example, a first-order frequency scaling based on estimated vocal tract length, average fundamental frequency over an utterance (Schwartz and Zue, 1976), or formant extrema in vocalic portions of an input utterance might be employed.

If a high-performance phonetic recognition capability is desired, major changes would have to be made in the present Harpy strategy. The lexical decoding network would have to be replaced by a phonetic decoding network, the template inventory would have to be doubled or tripled in order to permit more refined phonetic classifications, and the linear-prediction spectrum and minimum-residual error metric would have to be replaced by an improved spectral representation of the kind discussed in Sec. 25-2.2. The SCRIBER system to be described in Sec. 25-5 incorporates these modifications.

25-3.3 Metrics.

We consider here (1) static metrics for comparing parametric data obtained at a single point in time, and (2) cumulative metrics for combining scores over time. A non-diphthongized non-nasalized sonorant can be represented statically by the frequencies of the lowest three formants F1, F2, and F3, as measured at the temporal midpoint of the segment. A metric that has been proposed for comparing sonorants x and y is the weighted Euclidean distance:

$$D_{xy} = A(F_{1x}-F_{1y})^2 + B(F_{2x}-F_{2y})^2 + C(F_{3x}-F_{3y})^2 \qquad (25-1)$$

where A > B > C. The metric seems intuitively reasonable and has yielded satisfactory results (Kameny, 1976). Another possibility is to use log(F1/F3) and log(F2/F3) as parameters in the Euclidean metric (Skinner, 1977) since dividing by the third formant tends to normalize for differences in vocal tract length among men, women, and children. However, Bernstein (1976) has shown that this entire class of metrics diverges from perceptual judgements of distance between sustained vowels whenever formant frequencies get fairly close because the amplitudes of these formants increase. Of course the metric also results in seriously misleading distance scores if a formant tracking error has been made.

Harpy and a number of other systems have employed the minimum prediction residual error measure (Itakura, 1975) to compare linear prediction spectra. This distance is simple to compute and is based on similarity in spectral shape, but the residual error does not take into account possible gross differences in signal level, and it weights high-frequency components as being just as important as low-frequency components.

Plomp (1970) has proposed a Euclidean metric for comparing spectra obtained from a perceptually based spectrum analyzer:

$$Dxy = \sum_n [DBx(n) - DBy(n)]^2 \qquad (25-2)$$

The distance Dxy is the sum over channel numbers n of the squares of differences in dB between unknown and reference spectra. Lindblom (1978) has shown that this metric agrees remarkably well with perceived distance among a set of Swedish vowels. However, the metric should probably be modified slightly to tease out overall intensity as a separate factor, and to be able to compensate for differences in conditions between recording sessions (Klatt, 1976a).

Assuming one used the distance metric of Equation 25-2 to compare spectra every 10 ms, how should one then combine distance scores over time to arrive at a phonetic matching score? Simply adding the scores from successive 10-ms frames may give too much weight to differences in long-duration stationary vowels and too little weight to e.g. differences during a brief plosive burst. Schroeder (1968) proposed a time-independent measure as a solution to this problem, but other alternatives are needed.

If distance scores always increase with duration, one also runs the risk of biasing the system to divide the input into more small phonetic chunks than are really there in order to minimize the distance per phone. Thus distance per unit time is a more appropriate measure than distance per phonetic segment. One way to avoid monotonic distance score increases with time is to convert each static distance score into an estimated log-likelihood probability that the unknown and reference spectra are the same (Klovstad and Mondshein, 1975). Then adding scores is the same as multiplying probability estimates for successive time frames.

25-3.4 Segmentation.

If the speech waveform could be segmented reliably into chunks corresponding to phonetic segments, the job of identifying each segment would be much simplified. A number of investigators have proposed strategies for performing a preliminary segmentation of the speech waveform on the basis of cues to broad manner-of-articulation classes such as silence, voiceless, voiced obstruent, and voiced sonorant (Weinstein et al., 1975; Mermelstein,

1975; Goldberg and Reddy, 1976; Dixon, 1977). The performance of these
algorithms is not good enough to be relied upon as a final segmentation, but
if error correction at a later stage is possible, the algorithms serve as a
useful first step in the phonetic identification process.

The problem is that accurate segmentation on the basis of simple
acoustic criteria is impossible. For some segmentation decisions, a detailed
knowledge of the relations between English phonology, articulation, and
acoustics is necessary. A few decisions are arbitrary (such as the
phonologically based convention that "each" contains two segments while "eats"
contains three, or that "Foyt" contains a single vowel nucleus while "saw
each" contains a two-vowel sequence) -- segment boundaries can be redefined in
these cases to suit the convenience of the investigator. Other cases, such as
distinguishing how many segments are in "bail" versus "braille", or in
locating the second vowel in "be a" are more difficult to deal with. The
formant motions corresponding to the schwa of "be a" are acoustically similar
to many vowel-consonant formant transitions and are also similar to the
schwa-like offglide of lax vowels in words such as "bid".

Splitting up fricative sequences such as occur in the word pair
"fi_sh _store" are just as difficult in that they depend on sophisticated tests
of spectral change that have to be tuned so as to reject spectral changes to
e.g. the [S] spectrum during plosive closure gestures as in "_spin". Two
plosives in row (as in "i_t _passed") cannot always be distinguished from a
single plosive because the first is rarely released, and the closure interval
is not significantly longer than a closure interval for a single prestressed
plosive. Finally, there are examples of spurious third formant dips
associated with changes in formant cavity affiliations during some
consonant-vowel transitions such as in the word "ya" that give the appearance
of an extra segment if one is relying on formant trajectory maxima and minima
to segment sonorant sequences (perhaps maxima and minima in F1 and F2 only
should be counted).

The BBN speech understanding system (Woods et al., 1976) uses a
segmentation and labeling strategy in which alternative segmentations of the
input waveform are arranged in a lattice. Difficult segmentation decisions
are avoided by placing both alternatives in the lattice for consideration by
lexical decoding strategies. Ambiguity is further represented by listing
matching scores for all possible phonetic segments at each position in the
lattice. The phonetic labeling performance of this system is perhaps the best
of all the systems developed under the ARPA project.

The issue of how to represent uncertainty during segmentation and
phonetic labeling is important to the success of any speech recognition
system. It has not been shown that the ambiguity of a lattice helps or hurts
relative to a best-guess segmentation strategy because alternative
segmentations may produce too many high-scoring false word matches. (The
lattice concept does not obviate the need for scoring algorithms that treat
missing and extra segments in correct words.) If a way could be found to do
automatic phonetic transcription without first attempting segmentation, one
could perhaps avoid these problems and avoid having to correct bad
segmentation guesses (see Sec. 25-5).

25-3.5 Representation of Acoustic-Phonetic Knowledge.

Specific strategies for phonetic recognition will be reviewed in the
next section. We only note here that there are a number of good reasons why
the performance of current phonetic recognition strategies is disappointing.
Our knowledge of acoustic phonetics is incomplete and is not represented

algorithmically. The focus of early systematic studies (see Lehiste, 1968 for a representative collection) has usually been to document average formant values and systematic changes to formant targets due to coarticulatory influences. Thus one advantage of formant-based recognition strategies is the availability of theory and data on expected formant motions for many consonant-vowel combinations.

But formants are not the whole story, of course. There are many potentially useful acoustic cues of a spectral nature such as onset spectra, general spectral tilt, etc. (Schwartz and Zue, 1976). What is needed is more basic acoustic-phonetic research directed toward the quantification of all potentially useful cues in a form useful for automatic recognition strategies. Not only are full descriptions of the expected acoustic properties of isolated consonant-vowel syllables largely unavailable, but data on the expected variability in sentence contexts are also scanty. Until more such data are made available, strategies based on e.g. a large inventory of diphone templates derived from data rather than theory (Dixon and Silverman, 1976) stand a better chance of succeeding than phoneme recognition strategies based on an acoustic theory or hypothesis as the identity of invariant cues.

25-4 PHONETIC RECOGNITION STRATEGIES

The purpose of phonetic recognition is to access the lexicon of a speech recognition system. This should be kept in mind since not all lexical access strategies need use an intermediate phonetic level of representation (see Sec. 25-6). Techniques for phonetic analysis to be examined in this section include (1) formant-based recognition strategies, (2) articulatory-to-phonetic transformations, (3) phonetic feature detector systems, (4) theories of phonetic/spectral invariance, and (5) diphone recognition strategies. For a discussion of additional techniques, see Chapter 5.

Formant-Based Recognition Strategies. Vowel identification strategies that have employed formant data include algorithms based on the use of stationary formant targets (Gerstman, 1968), formant motions for diphthongs (Weinstein et al., 1975), and coarticulatory influences with adjacent segments (Kameny, 1976). The sonorants /W, Y, R, L/ have also been identified on the basis of formant behavior.

Place of articulation for stops can be determined from formant motions into the adjacent vowel (Liberman et al., 1967), although the rules are complex. Place of articulation for all the plosives and nasals has been determined on the basis of formant motions in one system (Woods et al., 1976), and simple strategies such as spotting velar stops from the proximity of the second and third formants have worked well (Weinstein et al., 1975). However, formant-based decoding strategies require that parameter extraction, preliminary segmentation, and normalization procedures be performed successfully, and there are many cases where this is difficult.

Articulatory-to-Phonetic Decision Rules. Vocal tract shape estimation procedures (Wakita, 1973; Atal, 1975) have been used in attempts to automatically segment speech (Broad, 1975). However, there have not been any complete phonetic decoding systems based on these techniques as yet. The advantage of rule systems couched in articulatory terms is that one might be able to infer articulatory targets from observed articulator trajectories and thus deduce the phonetic intentions of the talker.

Phonetic Feature Detector Systems. One theory of speech perception postulates a stage in the processing of speech where a set of phonetic feature detectors indicate the presence or absence of selected attributes in the signal such as voicing, nasality, stop, labiality, etc. Machines have been programmed to detect selected acoustic attributes in the signal such as the presence of voicing energy, but it has been difficult to define detectors for higher-level phonetic features of the type described by Fant (1970) and others. If such detectors could be built, one would still have the problem of aligning feature changes along the time axis so as to determine which segments are present. It is an interesting theoretical issue whether this model is an accurate description of human sentence processing, but the model seems less attractive for machine processing of speech.

Theories of Phonetic/Spectral Invariance. Blumstein, Stevens, and Nigro (1977) have proposed that there are invariant cues to place of articulation for stops in the onset spectra seen at stop release. Alveolars have several prominent high-frequency spectral peaks, while velars have a single prominent energy concentration in the mid-frequency range, and labials have a generally falling spectrum. They argue that stops are not highly encoded in the sense of Liberman et al. (1967), and that phonetic decoding in general is much more direct than previously believed.

Many past speech recognition schemes have been designed on this premise, although perhaps not with the right acoustic cues as a basis. Molho (1976) used a low-order linear predictor to characterize the spectra of fricatives and plosive bursts and to compare them against linear prediction templates. He found that a single average template for each obstruent resulted in about 50% correct performance. The BBN system (Schwartz and Zue, 1976; Cook and Schwartz, 1977) distinguishes among fricatives and unvoiced plosives with about 70 to 75% accuracy using similar measures.

The Harpy speech understanding system (Chapter 15) used a single talker-specific 12-pole linear prediction spectral template to characterize each fricative and plosive burst, plus additional sequences of voiced templates to characterize consonant-vowel formant transitions. The Harpy system was quite successful in the task domain for which it was designed, but its phonetic discrimination capabilities are limited to less than 50% accuracy (Klatt, 1977).

Diphone Recognition Strategies. A diphone is defined as the interval from the middle of one phonetic segment to the middle of the next. There are about 1200 to 1500 different diphone types in English. The diphone is said to constitute a better recognition unit than the phone because diphones take into account coarticulation between adjacent segments, while coarticulatory rules are still difficult to characterize in terms of recognition algorithms for phones.

Dixon and Silverman (1976) describe a phonetic recognition strategy in which a set of diphone-like templates called transemes were developed to generate a phonetic transcription of the speech of a single talker. The input speech is first segmented into steady-state regions, and then the transitions between steady states are identified from a set of over 1000 transemes. Transemes were defined in terms of seven sequential DFT spectra, and a linear time expansion/contraction was used to stretch an unknown speech segment to fit each template. Results approach 61 to 69% phonetic accuracy and about 12% segmentation errors, but may not generalize easily to new talkers if the system has inadvertently made use of idiosyncratic cues.

Performance Evaluation. Recent spectrogram-reading experiments (Cole, et al., 1978) have shown that the acoustic signal is rich in phonetic information. An expert spectrogram reader can produce a broad phonetic transcription that agrees with a panel of listeners from 85 to 90 percent of the time. The performance of present systems for producing a phonetic transcription of a sentence range from about 49% for Harpy to 63% for a system described in Cook and Schwartz (1977) and 61 to 69% for a single-speaker system described in Dixon and Silverman (1976). Why haven't these systems been able to approach the performance of the human spectrogram reader? There seem to be two main reasons: the spectrogram reader cannot verbalize the visually based algorithm he uses in sufficient detail, and the systems constructed thus far are so complex as to be difficult to optimize.

25-5 THE "SCRIBER" PHONETIC RECOGNIZER

This section is concerned with the design of a new algorithm for generating a phonetic transcription of the acoustic waveform corresponding to an unknown English sentence. The system is called SCRIBER, and is presently under development in the Speech Communication Laboratory at M.I.T. This preliminary report is concerned only with the design philosophy for such a system since we have no results to report as yet. We are indebted to R. Schwartz and J. Klovstad of BBN for help in resolving computational issues associated with SCRIBER design.

Phonetic Inventory. A tentative set of 55 output phonetic categories for SCRIBER is presented in Table 25-5. The phonetic inventory is large enough to preserve distinctions useful in lexical decoding (e.g. postvocalic allophones of the liquids, unstressed and unreleased allophones of the plosives), but it is by no means intended to produce a narrow phonetic transcription.

Representation of Acoustic-Phonetic Knowledge. It is assumed that transitions between phonetic segments can be represented succinctly and accurately by sequences of a few static spectra. For example, Fig. 25-4 illustrates a sequence of four spectra used to characterize the transition between [TT] and [AA] in the phrase "the top of the hill". Such a transition from the middle of one phone to the midpoint of the next is called a diphone.

The spectral representation that has been chosen is based on the psychophysical considerations given in Section 25-2.2. A 25.6 ms chunk of waveform is multiplied by a Kaiser window and converted into a 30-point spectral representation (Klatt, 1976a). Several examples of these psychophysical spectra are shown in Fig. 25-4.

It is up to the experimenter to select by hand sufficient sample times to characterize each possible phonetic transition of English. There are 55 phonetic segment types in the inventory of SCRIBER, but many of the 55-by-55 possible acoustic transitions are not allowed. Only about 2000 diphones are phonologically legal. Many of these are unnecessary if one wishes to take advantage of accidental gaps observed in phonetic sequences from a particular corpus of words (Dixon and Silverman, 1976).

Transition Definitions. In many cases, the tedious task of identifying spectral sequences for each phonetic transition (diphone) is simplified if one can rely on previous acoustic-phonetic analyses of speech to define a framework for combining portions of diphones. For example, Figure 25-5 indicates expected spectral sequences for the prestressed aspirated consonant [TT] followed by any stressed vowel of English. The decoding

---

Table 25-5. Inventory of 55 phonetic categories produced by SCRIBER.

IY	beat,Betty,beer	FF	fit,if	PP	pet,hip
IH	bit	VV	vet,of	PX	spin,happy,lips
EY	bait,Monday	TH	thin,with	PU	apt,ebbtide
EH	bet	DH	this,lathe	BB	bet,web
AE	bat,combat	SS	sit,mass	TT	tin,it
AY	bite,reply	ZZ	zen,is	TX	stem,its
AA	pot,hilltop	SH	shed,wish	TU	hotbox,Edger
AW	bout,rebound	ZH	--,azure	DD	deal,said
AH	but	CH	chin,itch	DX	latter,ladder
AO	bought	JH	jet,edge	TQ	Latin
OW	boat,auto	WW	wet,--	QQ	we_eat
OY	boy	YY	yet,--	KK	cat,hook
UH	book	RR	red,--	KX	skim,acre,hooks
UW	boot	XR	--,beer	KU	act,tugboat
ER	bird,butter	LL	let,--	GG	get,egg
AX	about	XL	--,call	MM	met,am
IX	wishes	EL	bottle	EM	put'em
		HH	hit,--	NN	net,in
		HX	we have	EN	button
				NG	--,sing

---

structure summarizes the obvious fact that the closure (silence) spectrum for [TT] is the same before any vowel, and the observation that onset spectra for [TT] are virtually identical before all front vowels, identical before all back unrounded vowels, and identical before all rounded vowels (Klatt, in preparation). As indicated in the figure, spectral characteristics observed during aspiration are dependent on both [TT] and the vowel.

Temporal Features of Transition Definitions. The sequence-of-spectra concept is attractive for a number of reasons discussed below, but it has one major deficiency -- temporal cues to phonetic contrasts such as voice onset time or rate of spectral change are not represented in a sequence of spectral templates. In order to overcome this deficiency, we borrow an idea from the Harpy sentence recognition system (Chapter 15) and place constraints on the duration of the input that can be associated with each spectral template of a phonetic transition definition. Thus each state of the network of Figure 25-5 is assigned an explicit feedback path specifying the minimum, maximum, and expected number of input spectra that can be associated with the state during recognition. For example, the number of input spectra associated with the burst spectrum plus the number associated with the aspiration spectrum in Figure 25-5 must be greater than 4 (i.e. the voice onset time must exceed 40 ms) for a [TT] to be recognized. Then differences between expected and observed durations of the input assigned to a spectral template contribute to the distance score.

We do not represent rate of spectral change by this means because it appears that cases where rate seems important (e.g. in distinguishing between /ba/ and /wa/) depend more on the duration of the initial sonorant-like portion, and thus can be better represented by specifying the minimum (or maximum) duration of an initial steady state spectrum and specifying that a certain spectral sequence be traversed. This is an important claim since rate of formant transitions or rates of other spectral changes are difficult to represent in discrete networks of this sort. If rate turns out to be an

544

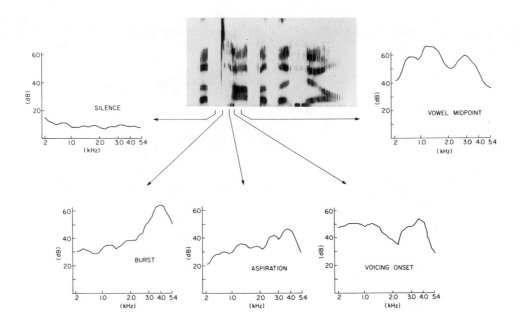

Figure 25-4. A broadband spectrogram is shown in of the phrase "the top of the hill" in order to indicate times at which spectra were computed in order to characterize the transition from the middle of closure for [TT] to the middle of the vowel [AA] in the SCRIBER phonetic decoding network.

important acoustic cue, we would have evidence against the entire approach outlined here.

     Recognition Strategy. The input waveform is processed by computing a spectrum every 10 ms (using overlapping 25.6 ms chunks of windowed waveform). The psychophysical spectral representation described in Sec. 25-2.2 is employed, and the Euclidean distance metric of Equation 25-2 is used to compute matching scores for each comparison of an input spectrum with a spectral template. A complete spectral sequence phonetic decoding network is compiled automatically from transition definitions of the type shown in Fig 25-4. This network is used during input recognition in a manner very similar to the strategy employed in the Harpy sentence recognition system (Chapter 15). The idea is to find the path through the network that best represents the observed input spectra. This path defines the optimal phonetic transcription.

     One can conceive of trying all possible paths in the search for the best-scoring path (Baker, 1975), but practical considerations limit the search to a reasonably large number of the most promising alternatives. The strategy that has been adopted is simple: input spectra are processed one at a time and used to try to extend only the best "phonetic theories", i.e. those theories that score within some range of the best-scoring theory. A theory consists of a state in the decoding network, how long one has been in that state, a

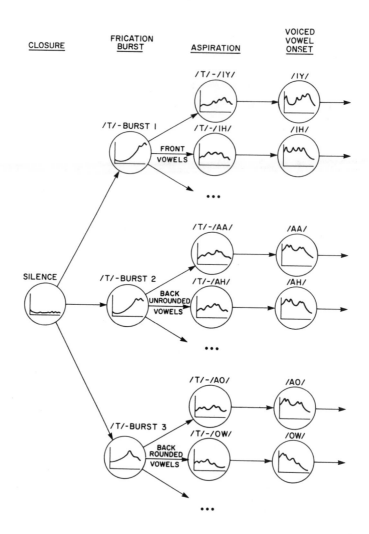

Fig. 25-5. A small portion of the SCRIBER spectral sequence phonetic decoding network is shown to illustrate the defining characteristics of prestressed prevocalic [TT]. Each state of the network (circle) is characterized by a spectral template (dB versus frequency, as shown inside the circle). Not shown are durational constraints in the form of a feedback path to each state indicating limits on the number of input 10-ms spectra that can be associated with each state during recognition.

cumulative spectral matching score, and the last two phones of the implied phonetic transcription. The cumulative score of a theory is the sum of all the spectral matching scores used to get to that state in the network.

Talker Normalization. One criticism of previous spectral template models of speech recognition is that they cannot be modified very easily to handle different talkers. There is wide variation in the spectra characterizing phonetic segments spoken by various men, women, and children. However, Lowerre (1977) has proposed a way to dynamically modify spectral templates to be more representative of the current talker. He restricted the Harpy sentence recognition network to have only 98 different spectral templates, and all words had to be represented in terms of these 98 templates. If a sentence could be recognized using templates representative of an average talker (true with a sentence error rate about four times as great as when talker-specific templates are available), then the observed input spectra were used to modify those spectral templates that were matched during recognition. An added advantage of this approach is that it captures some idiosyncratic aspects of acoustic targets employed by each talker in realizing different phonetic segments.

In the SCRIBER system, many more than 98 spectral templates are required to make fine phonetic contrasts (about 300?), but the dynamic talker normalization procedure of Harpy can still be applied. In addition, we will also seek generalized methods of template selection such as starting with an average female template if the new talker seems female, or modifying all templates on the basis of average spectral properties of a new voice.

Time Normalization. Variations in segmental durations due to speaking rate, syntactic factors, stress, and phonetic environment make it very difficult to rely on absolute durational constraints to distinguish among phonetic segments. The SCRIBER system will incorporate an estimate of current speaking rate to adjust selected durational thresholds, but other higher-level variables that influence segmental durations present durational ambiguity that simply cannot be overcome unless those lexical and syntactic factors are taken into account. This is one reason why we feel that a minimum-use-of-duration strategy is wise in any attempt to build a phonetic recognizer.

The SCRIBER system includes a method nearly as powerful as dynamic programming to align input spectra with the spectral sequences defining phonetic transitions. Since the number of spectra in a transition definition is always less than the minimum duration of an input phonetic transition, the system should always find a reasonable best path. Explicit time normalization (see e.g. Dixon and Silverman, 1976) is thereby avoided.

Performance Optimization. There is a uniform method of representing acoustic-phonetic knowledge in the SCRIBER system. All acoustic-phonetic facts are represented in a network in terms of sequence of spectra and durational constraints. Knowledge appears in a simple transparent form that makes optimization relatively easy. The SCRIBER system is also tunable in a sense that is not true of many phonetic recognizers. If the cause of any observed transcription error is localized to a particular portion of the network, a local change in the network to fix an error does not have unpredictable global consequences.

We plan extensive tuning of the SCRIBER system, first with one talker, and then with many talkers, in order to establish the limits of its performance capabilities. A second motivation for constructing such a system is to attempt to characterize acoustic-phonetic knowledge in a concise useful form.

The keys to success of this approach are the selection of a good set of spectral templates and development of a diphone dictionary that captures the acoustic characteristics of English phone sequences. Stated in this way, the task ahead is still formidable, but it is an interesting and well-defined challenge. The missing pieces must come from speech science: the computer

547

sciences have done the job of providing a structure in which to embed speech knowledge for recognition purposes.

25-6 LAFS: LEXICAL ACCESS FROM SPECTRA

A lexical access module of a speech recognition system generates lexical hypotheses from the input speech waveform. Before describing how one might design a system that searches for lexical hypotheses without use of an intermediate phonetic level of representation, we examine two primary reasons why lexical access is difficult: (1) the phonetic transcription that serves as input to a lexical hypothesizer contains substitution errors, intrusions and omissions which will lower the matching scores for correct words and promote fortuitous matches with incorrect words (especially in a large lexicon), and (2) there are extensive rule-governed changes to the way that words are pronounced in different sentence contexts.

Table 25-6. Examples of word-boundary phonology.

"Did you hit it to Tom"

[d ɪ ǰ ə h´ɪ ɾ ɪ t̥ ə t´a m]

1. Palatalization of /d/ before /y/.
2. Reduction of unstressed /u/ to schwa in "you".
3. Flapping of intervocalic /t/ in "hit it".
4. Reduction to schwa and devoicing of /u/ in "to".
5. Reduction of geminate /t/ in "it to".

<u>Phonological Recoding at Word Boundaries</u>. The expected phonetic realization of a word depends on the sentence context in which it appears. Consider for example the phonetic string observed for the spoken utterance "Did you hit it to Tom?" that is shown in Table 25-6. No word boundaries are indicated in the phonetic transcription because acoustic cues to word boundary locations are rarely present.

Each of the simplifications listed in Table 25-6 can be described by general phonological rules. Such rules presuppose an underlying basic representation for each word or morpheme (called the phonemic representation). For example, the phonemic string that would be stored in the lexicon for "did" and for "you" might be / d ɪ d / and / y u /. An (optional) word-boundary phonological rule / d # y / --> [ǰ] transforms the word-final phoneme / d / and the word-initial / y / into the phonetic segment [ǰ].

In most systems for sentence recognition, such modifications must be viewed as a kind of "noise" that makes it more difficult to hypothesize lexical candidates given an input phonetic transcription. To see that this must be the case, we note that each phonological rule example of Table 25-6 results in irreversible ambiguity -- the phonological rule does not have a unique inverse that could be used to recover the underlying phonemic representation for a lexical item. For example, the [ǰ] observed in the sample phonetic transcription of Table 25-6 could be the first or last segment of a word like "judge", or it could be the surface manifestation of an underlying /d/-#-/y/. The schwa vowels of Table 25-6 could be the first vowel in a word like "about" or the surface realization of almost any English vowel appearing in a sufficiently destressed word. The tongue flap [ɾ] could have come from a /t/ or a /d/. The [t] of "it to" could be the single /t/ of "it is" or the surface form of two identical segments separated by a word boundary. The voiceless vowel in "to" could represent the release stage of a word-final /t/ or the devoicing of a short vowel between two voiceless consonants. Deletions of segments (e.g. the /t/ in "list some") complicate the picture even more, for now one must entertain the possibility that any moderately long-duration [s] seen in the input is really an underlying /s t/-#-/s/.

A Partial Solution: Precompiled Phonological Knowledge. The BBN system (Woods, et al., 1976; Klovstad, 1978) deals with ambiguity generated by phonological recoding rules by precompiling knowledge of the rules into a decoding network. The first step is to construct a tree of expected phonemic sequences for all words of the lexicon, as shown in Fig. 25-6a. Then the end of each word in the tree is attached to all word-beginning states and a set of phonological rules are applied to modify the connectivity pattern. The result is a phonetic-sequence lexical decoding network of the type shown in Fig. 25-6b. The effect of the [s t # s] --> [s] phonological rule in Fig. 25-6b is to create an extra path from near the end of words ending in [s t] to the second phonetic segment of words beginning with [s]. Phonology seems to have come of age over the past few years in that formal rules of considerable predictive power have been developed (Woods et al., Vol. 3, 57-72, 1976; Cohen and Mercer, 1975; Oshika et al. 1975).

Given the BBN decoding network in which words are represented in terms of phonetic segments (and phonological rule phenomena are represented in the connectivity pattern), one still needs a sophisticated matching strategy to select words corresponding to a phonetic string for an unknown utterance. If the input is processed from left-to-right, one needs a metric to determine penalties for mismatches and for segmental intrusions or deletions because the automatic phonetic analyzer will make many errors of these types. Experience with the BBN lexical network has shown that metrics to handle errors are very important because unexpected transcription errors may otherwise result in a fatal mismatch with the correct word. One possible reason for the limited success of the BBN system appears to be the large decrements to the score of the correct theory that occurred when novel transcription errors were encountered.

A Second-Generation Solution: LAFS. The ideal way to deal with transcription errors would be to go back to the acoustic data to see if the expected phonetic sequence scores reasonably well. A phonetic transcription intentionally throws away this information in order to make the lexical search problem computationally tractable. It is possible to avoid the problem of recovering from errorful intermediate phonetic decisions by combining the best elements of SCRIBER with a BBN-like lexical decoding network. The result is LAFS, a lexical-access-from-spectra decoding network that has no intermediate phonetic level of representation.

A LAFS lexical decoding network is constructed in three stages, as illustrated in Fig. 25-7. The first step is to create a tree of phonemic representations for all lexical items. Word terminations are then connected back on the tree root in step 2, and phonological rules are applied to create a network of alternative phonetic representations for all possible (grammatical and ungrammatical) word sequences of the lexicon. These two steps exactly parallel the lexical decoding network developed at BBN (Klovstad, 1978).

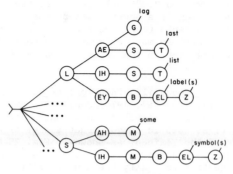

(A) INITIAL TREE STRUCTURE

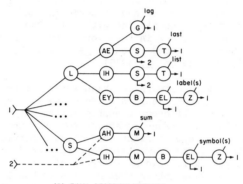

(B) FINAL DECODING NETWORK

Fig. 25-6. The partial lexical tree for the phonetic representation of several English words shown in part a is transformed into a lexical decoding network for the recognition of sequences of words by application of a set of word-boundary phonological rules (Klovstad, 1978).

The third step is to replace each phonetic transition by a sequence of spectral templates. Transition definitions are obtained from the SCRIBER diphone dictionary. A network very similar in structure to SCRIBER results, and the decoding strategy of SCRIBER, i.e. find the best path using a simple spectral metric, can be applied. An example of a portion of a LAFS network is shown at the bottom of Fig. 25-7.

The network is quite large, but only on the order of 3 to 5 times as large as a lexical decoding network made up of phonetic segments. We believe that lexical hypotheses can be generated rapidly and more accurately in a LAFS structure than in any two-step model (phonetic recognition followed by lexical access) containing the same acoustic-phonetic and phonological knowledge.

Morphemes versus Words. If the lexicon is broken down into morphemes (e.g. books=book+s, baseball=base+ball), there can be considerable savings in both storage and processing time. Allen (1973) has assembled a morpheme dictionary that can represent more than ten times as many English words as

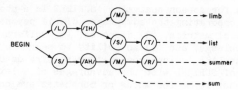

STEP I: LEXICAL TREE (PHONEMIC)

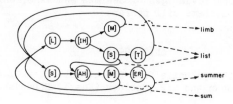

STEP 2: LEXICAL NETWORK (PHONETIC)

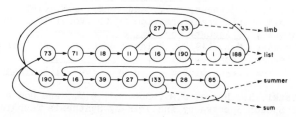

STEP 3: LEXICAL ACCESS FROM SPECTRA (SPECTRAL TEMPLATES)

Fig. 25-7. The LAFS lexical-access-from-spectra decoding network that is shown in part (c) is derived by first constructing a tree of phonetic representations for all words in the lexicon (a portion of which is shown in part (b), and then applying a set of phonological rules to the tree while connecting all word terminations to word beginnings in order to form a phonetic sequence lexical decoding network, as shown in part (b). The numbers inside the states in the spectral sequence decoding network of part (c) refer to spectral templates from an inventory of about 300.

there are morphemes. LAFS should probably be organized in terms of morphemes, but for phonetic recognition purposes, a lexical decoding network must keep separate representations for morphemes that change pronunciation when bound together (e.g. applicability=apply+able+ity).

A LAFS lexical decoding network could serve as a front-end component of a moderately large speech understanding system. A possible interface with an augmented transition network grammar (Woods, 1970) is described in Klatt (1977). A LAFS network could also be constructed in the form of a complete speech understanding system for a task involving a finite grammar, as was done in the Harpy application.

We have reviewed techniques for acoustic analysis, phonetic analysis, and lexical access in this chapter. On the basis of the review, we have proposed two new systems for speech analysis. SCRIBER is a phonetic transcription system incorporating the advantages of (1) psychophysical spectra, (2) psychophysical metrics, (3) diphones, (4) uniform representation of acoustic-phonetic knowledge, and (5) an ability to search a large network for an optimum path. The LAFS lexical-access-from-spectra decoding network combines the advantages of SCRIBER with the advantages of a lexical network structure in which abstract forms for words or morphemes are combined and restructured by a set of phonological rules that capture detailed phonetic properties of word strings as spoken in normal sentence frames. We have identified the theoretical advantages of SCRIBER and LAFS; only time will tell how well these proposed systems will perform.

References

Allen, J. (1973), "Speech Synthesis from Unrestricted Text", in Speech Synthesis, J.L. Flanagan and L.R. Rabiner (Eds.), Stroudsberg, PA: Dowden, Hutchinson and Ross.

Atal, B.S. (1975), "Towards Determining Articulator Positions from the Speech Signal", in G. Fant (Ed.), Speech Communication, Vol. 1, 1-9.

Atal, B.S., Chang, J.J., Mathews, M.V., and Tukey, J.W. (1978), "Inversion of Articulatory-to-Acoustic Transformation in the Vocal Tract by a Computer Sorting Technique", J. Acoust. Soc. Am. 63, in press.

Atal, B. and Schroeder, M.R. (1978), "Linear Prediction Analysis of Speech Based on a Pole-Zero Representation", J. Acoust. Soc. Am., in press.

Baker, J. (1975), "The Dragon System -- An Overview", IEEE Trans. ASSP-23, 24-29.

Bell, C.G., Fujisaki, H., Heinz, J.M., Stevens, K.N., and House, A.H. (1961), "Reduction of Speech Spectra by Analysis-by-Synthesis Techniques", J. Acoust. Soc. Am. 33, 1725-1736.

Bernstein, J.C. (1976), "Vocoid Psychophysics, Articulation, and Vowel Phonology", Ph.D. Thesis, Univ. Michigan, Ann Arbor, Mich.

Blumstein, S.E., Stevens, K.N., and Nigro, G.N. (1977), "Property Detectors for Bursts and Transitions in Speech Perception", J. Acoust. Soc. Am. 61, 1301-1313.

Broad, D. (1975), "Basic Directions in Automatic Speech Recognition Research", Int. J. Man-Machine Studies 4, 105-118.

Cohen, P.S. and R.L. Mercer (1975), "The Phonological Component of an Automatic Speech Recognition System", 275-320 in Reddy (1975).

Cole, R.A., Rudnicky, A., Reddy, R., and Zue, V. (1978), "Speech as Patterns on Paper", in Perception and Production of Fluent Speech, R. Cole (Ed.), Erlbaum.

Cook, C.C. and R.M. Schwartz (1977), "Advanced Acoustic Techniques in Automatic Speech Understanding", 663-666 in Silverman (1977).

Dixon, N.R. (1977), "An Application Hierarchy for Heuristic Rules in Automatic Phonetic Segmentation of Continuous Speech", IEEE Int. Conf. ASSP, 671-674, IEEE Catalog No. 77CH1197-3 ASSP.

Dixon, N.R. and Silverman, H.F. (1976), "The 1976 Modular Acoustic Processor (MAP)", IEEE Trans. ASSP-25, 367-378.

Egan, J.P. and Hake, H.W. (1950), "On the Masking Pattern of a Simple Auditory Stimulus" J. Acoust. Soc. Am. 22, 622-630.

Fant, G. (1966), "A Note on Vocal Tract Size Factors and Non-Uniform F-Pattern Scaling", Speech Transmission Labs. QPSR-4, 22-30.

Fant, G. (1970), "Analysis and Synthesis of Speech Processes" in Manual of Phonetics, B Malmberg (Ed.), Amsterdam: North-Holland, 173-277.

Fant, G., (Ed.) (1975), *Proc. Stockholm Speech Communications Seminar*, Almqvist and Wiksell (Stockholm) and Wiley (New York).

Flanagan, J.L. (1957), "Estimates of the Maximum Precision Necessary in Quantizing Certain Dimensions of Vowel Sounds", *J. Acoust. Soc. Am. 29*, 533-534.

French, N.R. and J.C. Steinberg (1947), "Factors Governing the Intelligibility of Speech Sounds" *J. Acoust. Soc. Am. 19*, 90-119.

Gerstman, L.J. (1968), "Classification of Self-Normalized Vowels" *IEEE Trans. AU-16*, 78-80.

Goldberg, H.G. and Reddy R. (1976), "Feature Extraction, Segmentation and Labeling in the Harpy and Hearsay-II Systems", *J. Acoust. Soc. Am. 60*, S11 (A).

Green, D.M. (1976), *An Introduction to Hearing*, New York: Wiley.

Hafer, E.H. (1974), "Speech Analysis by Articulatory Synthesis", S.M. Thesis, Dept. Computer Science, Northwestern Univ.

Itakura, F. (1975), "Minimum Prediction Residual Principle Applied to Speech Recognition", *IEEE Trans. Acoustics, Speech, and Signal Processing ASSP-23*, 67-72.

Jelinek, F. (1976), "Continuous Speech Recognition by Statistical Methods", *Proc. IEEE 64*, 532-556.

Kameny, I. (1976), "Automatic Acoustic-Phonetic Analysis of Vowels and Sonorants", 166-169 in Teacher (1976).

Klatt, D.H. (1975), "Word Verification in a Speech Understanding System", 321-341 in Reddy (1975).

Klatt, D.H. (1976a), "A Digital Filter Bank for Spectral Matching", 537-540 in Teacher (1976).

Klatt, D.H. (1976b), "Linguistic Uses of Segmental Duration in English: Acoustic and Perceptual Evidence", *J. Acoust. Soc. Am. 59*, 1208-1221.

Klatt, D.H. (1977), "Review of the ARPA Speech Understanding Project", *J. Acoust. Soc. Am. 62*, 1345-1366.

Klatt, D.H. (1978), "A New Look at the Problem of Lexical Access", in *Perception and Production of Fluent Speech*, R. Cole (Ed.), Erlbaum.

Klatt, D.H. and K.N. Stevens (1973), "On the Automatic Recognition of Continuous Speech: Implications of a Spectrogram-Reading Experiment", *IEEE Trans. Audio and Electroacoust. AU-21*, 210-217.

Klatt, D.H. (in preparation), *Analysis and Synthesis of Consonant-Vowel Syllables in English*.

Klovstad, J.W. (1977), "Computer-Automated Speech Perception System", Ph.D. thesis, MIT.

Klovstad, J. W. and L.F. Mondshein (1975), "The CASPERS Linguistic Analysis System", *IEEE Trans. Acoustics, Speech, and Signal Processing ASSP-23*, 18-123.

Lehiste, I. (1968), *Selected Readings in Acoustic Phonetics*, Cambridge: MIT Press.

Liberman, A.M., F.S. Cooper, D.S. Shankweiler, and M. Studdert-Kennedy (1967), "Perception of the Speech Code", *Psych. Review 74*, 431-461.

Liberman, A.M., Delattre, P., Gerstman, L., and Cooper, F. (1956), "Tempo of Frequency Change as a Cue for Distinguishing Classes of Speech Sounds", *J. Exp. Psychol. 52*, 127-137.

Licklider, J.R.C. (1951), "Basic Correlates of the Auditory Stimulus", in *Handbook of Experimental Psychology*, New York: Wiley.

Lindblom, B. (1978), "Phonetic Aspects of Linguistic Explanation", *Studia Linguistica 22*, in press.

Lowerre, B.T. (1976), *The Harpy Speech Recognition System*, Ph.D. Thesis, Dept. of Computer Science, Carnegie-Mellon Univ., Pittsburgh, PA 15213.

Lowerre, B.T. (1977), "Dynamic Speaker Adaptation in the Harpy Speech Recognition System", 788-790 in Silverman (1977).

Makhoul, J. (1975), "Linear Prediction: A Tutorial Review", *Proc. IEEE 63*, 561-580.

Makhoul, J.I. and Wolf, J.J. (1972), "Linear Prediction and the Spectral Analysis of Speech", Bolt Beranek and Newman Inc. Report No. 2304, Cambridge, MA.

McCandless, S.S. (1974), "An Algorithm for Automatic Formant Extraction Using Linear Prediction Spectra", IEEE Trans. ASSP-22, 135-141.

Mermelstein, P. (1967), "Determination of the Vocal Tract Shape from Measured Formant Frequencies", J. Acoust. Soc. Am. 41, 1283-1294.

Mermelstein, P. (1975), "Automatic Segmentation of Speech into Syllable Units", J. Acoust. Soc. Am. 58, 880-883.

Molho, L.M. (1976), "Automatic Acoustic-Phonetic Analysis of Fricatives and Plosives", 182-185 in Teacher (1976).

Nordstrom, P.E., and Lindblom, B. (1975) "A Normalization Procedure for Vowel Formant Data", Proc. 8th Int. Congress on Phonetic Sciences, Leeds, England.

Oshika, B., V.W. Zue, R.V. Weeks, H. Neu, and J. Aurbach (1975), "The Role of Phonological Rules in Speech Understanding Research", IEEE Trans. Acoustics, Speech, and Signal Processing ASSP-23, 104-112.

Pearsons, K.S., Bennett, R.L., and Fidell, S. (1976), "Speech Levels in Various Environments", Bolt Beranek and Newman Inc. Report No. 3281, Cambridge, MA.

Peterson, G.E. (1961), "Automatic Speech Recognition Procedures" Language and Speech 4, 200-219.

Plomp, R. (1970), "Timbre as a Multidimensional Attribute of Complex Tones", in Frequency Analysis and Periodicity Detection in Hearing, R. Plomp and G.F. Smoorenburg (Eds.) 397-414, Sijthoff, Leiden, the Netherlands.

Plomp, R. and Mimpen, A.M. (1968), "The Ear as a Frequency Analyzer II", J. Acoust. Soc. Am. 43, 764-768.

Rabiner, L.R. and M.R. Sambur (1975), "An Algorithm for Determining the Endpoints of Isolated Utterances", Bell Syst. Tech. J. 54 297-315.

Rabiner, L.R., and Sambur, M.R. (1977), "Application of an LPC Distance Measure to the Voiced-Unvoiced-Silence Detection Problem", IEEE Trans. ASSP-25, 338-343.

Rabiner, L.R., Sambur, M.R., and Schmidt, C.E. (1975), "Applications of a Nonlinear Smoothing Algorithm to Speech Processing", IEEE Trans. ASSP-23, 552-557.

Rabiner, L.R., Cheng, M.J., Rosenberg, A.E., and McGonegal, C.A. (1976), ""Comparative Performance Study of Several Pitch Detection Algorithms", IEEE Trans. ASSP-24, 399-417.

Reddy, D.R. (1975), Speech Recognition: Invited Papers Presented at the 1974 IEEE Symposium, Academic Press.

Reddy, D.R. (1976), "Speech Recognition by Machine: A Review", Proc. IEEE 64, 501-531.

Schroeder, M.R. (1968), "Similarity Measures for Automatic Speech and Speaker Recognition", J. Acoust. Soc. Am. 43, 375-377.

Schwartz, R.M. and Zue, V.W. (1976), "Acoustic-Phonetic Recognition in BBN SPEECHLIS", in Teacher (1976), 21-24.

Sharf, B. (1970), "Critical Bands", in Foundations of Modern Auditory Theory, Vol. 1, J.V. Tobias (Ed.), 157-202, New York: Academic Press.

Silverman, H.F. (Chairman) (1977), "Conference Record of the 1977 IEEE International Conference on Acoustics, Speech and Signal Processing", Hartford, May 9-11, 1977, IEEE Catalog No. 77CH1197-3 ASSP.

Silverman, H.F. and N.R. Dixon (1976), "The 1976 Modular Acoustic Processor (MAP): Diadic Segment Classification and Final Phoneme String Estimation", 15-20 in Teacher (1976).

Sivian, L.J. and White, S.D. (1933), "On Minimum Audible Sound Fields", J. Acoust. Soc. Am. 4, 288-321.

Skinner, T.E. (1977), "Speaker-Invariant Characteristics of Vowels, Liquids, and Glides Using Relative Formant Frequencies", J. Acoust. Soc. Am. 62, Supple. 1, 55 (A).

Smith, A.R. (1976), "Word Hypothesization in the Hearsay-II Speech Understanding System", 549-552 in Teacher.

Stevens, K.N. and House, A.S. (1961), "An Acoustical Theory of Vowel Production and Some of its Implications", _J. Speech and Hearing Research_ 4, 303-320.

Tappert, C.C. (1975), "Experiments with a Tree-Search Method for Converting Noisy Phonetic Representations into Standard Orthography", _IEEE Trans. Acoustics Speech and Signal Processing ASSP-23_, 129-135.

Tappert, C.C., N.R. Dixon, and A.S. Rabinowitz (1973), "Application of Sequential Decoding for Converting Phonetic to Graphic Representation in Automatic Speech Recognition of Continuous Speech (ARCS)", _IEEE Trans. Audio Electroacoust. AU-21_, 225-228.

Teacher, C., (Chairman) (1976), _Conference Record of the 1976 IEEE International Conference on Acoustics Speech and Signal Processing_, Philadelphia, PA., April 12-14, 1976, (IEEE Catalog No. 76CH1067-8 ASSP).

Wakita, H. (1973), "Direct Estimation of the Vocal Tract Shape by Inverse Filtering of Acoustic Speech Waveforms", _IEEE Trans. AU-21_, 417-427.

Wakita, H. and Kasuya, H. (1977), "A Study of Vowel Normalization and Identification in Connected Speech", in Silverman (1977), 648-651.

Weeks, R.V. (1974), "Predictive Syllable Mapping in a Continuous Speech Understanding System", 154-158 in Erman (1974).

Weinstein, C.J., S.S. McCandless, L.F. Mondshein, and V.W. Zue (1975), "A System for Acoustic-Phonetic Analysis of Continuous Speech", _IEEE Trans. Acoustics Speech and Signal Processing ASSP-23_, 54-67.

Woods, W.A. (1970), "Transition Network Grammars for Natural Language Analysis", _Commun. Ass. Comput. Mach. 13_, 591-602.

Woods, W.A., Bates, M., Brown, G., Bruce, B., Cook, C. Klovstad, J., Makhoul, J., Nash-Webber, B., Schwartz, R., Wolf, J., and Zue, V. (1976), "Speech Understanding Systems: Final Technical Progress Report", Bolt Beranek and Newman Inc. Report No. 3438, Cambridge, MA (in 5 volumes).

Woods, W.A. and V. Zue (1976), "Dictionary Expansion via Phonological Rules for a Speech Understanding System", 561-564 in Teacher (1976).

Zwicker, E. (1970), "Masking and Psychological Excitation as Consequences of the Ear's Frequency Analysis", in R. Plomp and G.F. Smoorenburg (Eds.), _Frequency Analysis and Periodicity Detection in Hearing_, Sijthoff, Leiden, the Netherlands, 376-393.

Zwicker, E. and Sharf, B. (1965), "A Model of Loudness Summation", _Psychol. Rev. 72_, 3-26.

26.

WHITHER SPEECH RECOGNITION?

George R. Doddington
Texas Instruments

26-1. INTRODUCTION

Technology forecasts in general tend to err on the conservative side. This is especially true in computer technology, where largely unanticipated technological breakthroughs have revolutionized the pervasiveness of electronics. In speech technology, however, forecast speech recognition capabilities have remained a tantalizing mirage. Except for an occassional grump here and there, knowledgable people have continued to forecast speech recognition capabilities which have either never materialized or have fallen far short of expectations.

The excessive optimism and expectation of progress in speech recognition are attributable in part to the ease of speech recognition by humans. More important, however, is the ease of achieving wonderful speech recognition performance in the laboratory. Such performance creates high expectation. But complex dependence of the speech signal on a virtually limitless number of parameters (such as vocabulary, dialect and discipline) makes the task of transforming laboratory performance into useful capability hard and unrewarding.

Nevertheless, this forecast dares to be another of those which would look optimistically into the future of automatic speech processing and speech recognition. This optimism stems from ongoing revolutions in the cost, power and speed of digital computers, being brought to us courtesy of progress in semiconductor technology. Progress in automatic speech recognition will ride this wave of computer technology. Breakthroughs in cost will spawn a myriad of applications for speech input, while faster, more powerful computers will facilitate advances in recognition technology.

26-2. RESEARCH ISSUES

26-2.1 Research Dimensions

The development of speech recognition technology is a multi-disciplinary endeavor requiring knowledge and research in machine intelligence, acoustic phonetics, signal processing, speech perception and human factors. Speech science, as reflected in current recognition capability, appears as a vast uncharted ocean of ignorance. Because of this general problem environment, there are two prerequisites for a successful and efficient program of speech recognition development. First, the program must be large; that is, it must involve the coordinated efforts of many people for many years. Specifically, the typical one-year, one-person research sortie is of limited value unless it is well coordinated with a larger overall program objective. Second, a well-defined application objective must be established, to serve the important function of focusing research effort on a few important issues and thus foster the building of a sound recognition technology.

A favorite myth among many speech recognition scientists is that speech must be truly understood before it can be adequately recognized. Although intimate knowledge of the language is certainly crucial to human recognition in adverse environments, such knowledge cannot hope to compensate for a devastating lack of perceptual adequacy at the acoustic/syllabic level. Emphasis on "understanding" what is being said needs to be deferred until the basic level of perceptual adequacy is substantially improved.

Support for this argument is provided by results of experiments conducted at Texas Instruments, to test the recognition ability of human listeners in a context devoid of semantic or syntactic information. In the first of two such experiments, 20 listeners listened to words spoken in isolation, selected from a 26,000 word vocabulary. The speaker for each word was chosen randomly from a set of 10 male and 10 female speakers. Results as a function of vocabulary size are shown in Table 26-1.

Table 26-1

Human Recognition Performance for
Speaker Independent Isolated Word Recognition

Vocabulary Size # words	Error Rate (%)	Substitution (%)	Rejection (%)
50	1.0		
120	0.8		
1500	1.2		
26000	2.3	1.8	0.5

Note that the error rate in this table appears relatively insensitive to vocabulary size. This is at least partially attributable to the vocabulary construction. (The vocabularies comprise the N most frequently used words and therefore the smaller vocabularies tend to have the shorter, more difficult to recognize words.) Another interesting note is that female speakers were recognized as well as male speakers, which deviates from the norm in machine recognition.

A second experiment attempted to measure the performance of humans in the recognition of connected spoken digits. Fifteen listeners listened to a total of 195 six-digit sequences, each spoken by a different speaker. Only 5 misrecognitions were committed (most appeared due to inattention), for a resultant error rate of .03%. If only our machines could do as well!

The first priority in speech recognition research should be to develop a basic recognition capability that agrees with perception as closely as possible. A research program is needed which combines recognition developments and perceptual experiments. Mutually beneficial interaction will thus result by direct assimilation and evaluation of perceptual theories.

26-2.3 Research computer
It is hardly necessary to mention the need for a computer system in carrying out a legitimate program in speech recognition development. This system, key to program success, must provide three capabilities: the development and execution of speech processing algorithms; an interactive

research interface including an A/D and D/A sampled data subsystem and a graphics capability that will support speech spectrogram generation; and a real-time operational interface to simulate complete systems and study the interaction between application and performance. Of special importance is the ability to store and manipulate large data bases involving many speakers. This need arises from the statistical variability among speakers and the need to comprehend this variability. Minimally adequate on-line data storage requirements for research purposes range from 100 to 1000 Mbytes and up.

26-3. FORECAST

This forecast is likely to be more provocative than sage. I begin by forecasting some applications of speech recognition, because it is through these applications that speech technology will be developed.

26-3.1 Applications Forecast

Fuzzy thinking tends to dominate the application of speech recognition. An amusing example of this is a news article I read recently in which the reporter claimed that speech input soon will "enable a pilot to fly his plane using his voice, thus freeing his hands for other functions". On a more serious note, speech input systems are often touted as highly efficient, cost effective means of data entry for sorting and inspection applications. Often phenomenal productivity improvements are measured. But what is the contribution to this productivity from speech input, as opposed to system automation and source data entry? The contribution from speech is usually marginal. In many such applications speech can be viewed as a marketing tool, used to help sell the computerized data management system.

So how does one determine a proper application for speech input? First, speech recognition must be viewed as an interface technology. As such it is part of a larger system. It also is in competition with other modes of input such as keyboard data entry and totally automated data entry. A speech input mode should obviously not be chosen if an alternate modality is a better choice. In making this choice one must consider many factors including cost, productivity, error performance and human factors.

During the next 3 to 10 years cost will continue to be the major factor limiting the growth in applications of speech recognition, despite the favorable rapid decline in the cost of computation. This cost problem mandates applications for which speech input provides a unique solution. Such applications include voice verification for use in physical access control and data security, and voice data input for use in telephone transaction systems. Automatic telephone transaction systems such as bank-by-phone and airline reservation systems are an especially attractive opportunity for speech input. Such systems, with their pre-existing voice communication network, have potential for strong productivity improvement by reducing the staff of human operators that currently provides the interface for user data entry into the system. Such systems may also be easily formalized to provide a well-defined speech recognition environment involving a relatively small vocabulary. Other desirable attributes of these telephone applications include a low potential cost of the speech recognition service (achieved through a centralized, multiplexed system) and a capability to perform voice verification and thus validate the transaction.

Further into the future, office automation products will benefit from the addition of speech interfaces. There is increasing pressure for productivity improvement in the office, because office productivity gains lag an order of magnitude behind factory gains. Therefore, increasing importance of office productivity will help to offset the initial high cost of speech interfaces to office automation equipment.

26-3.2 Technology Forecast

Just as applications tend to motivate development of speech technology, so technological advances in various speech processing problem areas will help guide the selection of viable applications. There are three major problem categories in automatic speech recognition. In increasing order of difficulty, they are vocabulary size, connected speech, and between-speaker differences. To date, successful practical speech recognition technology has required discrete speech, speaker dependent, small vocabulary constraints, and little progress has been made during the past 5 to 10 years in overcoming these limitations.

A major reason for this lack of progress has been misplaced emphasis on "higher level" information to aid the recognition progress, with a corresponding neglect of the development of an adequate acoustic/perceptual feature representation. During the coming years, acoustic phonetic processing will be elevated beyond its current status as a simple "phoneme server" to the intelligent recognition processor. Two speech technology trends, which have already begun to a limited degree, will enable this breakthrough in acoustic processing. First, intermediate descriptions of the speech signal at the syllabic level will become highly effective both in improving performance and in providing extensibility to larger and different vocabularies. Prosodic attributes of inflection and timing, important in human recognition, will be more easily utilized at the level of syllabic representation. Second, a well-defined structure must be developed for establishing and evaluating multiple acoustical/perceptual hypotheses regarding speech segments without mutual interference among competing hypotheses. The traditional approach of "first segmentation, then recognition" is doomed to failure because low-level errors in segmentation invariably create fatal complexities and limitations at the higher recognition levels.

Present applications of dynamic programming to time registration for both word recognition (NEC's word recognition product) and speaker verification (TI's voice verification technology) demonstrate successful practical use of the concept of establishing multiple parallel hypotheses. But much greater development and refinement of these concepts is needed to provide useful perceptual ranking of parallel syllabic hypotheses and of phonemic hypotheses within the syllable.

The application of dynamic programming will also find widespread use in speech processing for improving the measurement reliability of abstract features. As an example, fig. 26-1 demonstrates the construction of reliable pitch and formant contours with the aid of sequential optimization techniques. Also important in establishing an adequate perceptual representation of speech will be the use of relational measures involving, for example, average syllable duration, formant amplitude and pitch frequency.

26-3.3 Performance Forecast

With the prospect of truly comprehensive recognition technology, one might anticipate unlimited performance possibilities. Unfortunately, there will still be severe performance limitations in machine recognition of speech, and we need to understand these limitations in order to guide our applications and our research. First, I would not hope in the near future for a machine speech recognition capability which requires a true understanding of content beyond a highly formalized context. Let us look then at our anticipated performance capabilities and limitations.

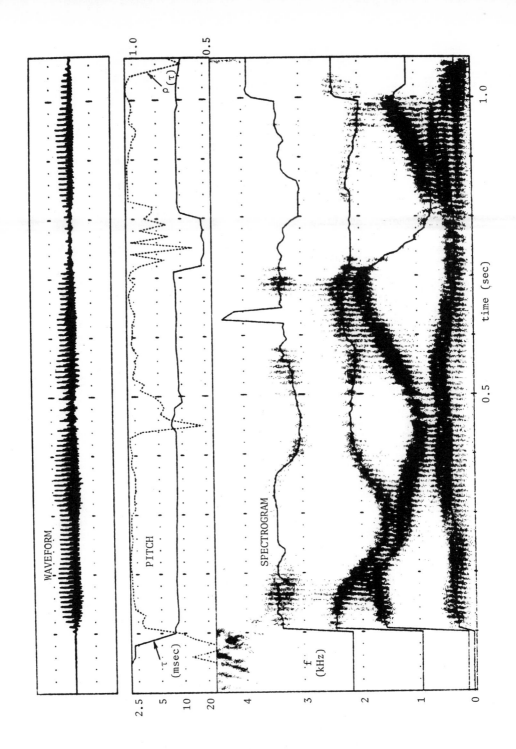

Figure 26-1. Example of sequentially optimized
pitch and formant trajectories.

Performance will continue to be inhomogeneous across various speaker subsets: The traditional, highly skewed distribution of performance among speakers will not be eliminated;* recognition performance will always be better for men than for women; performance degradation will be experienced for unexpected dialects (in speaker independent systems); and performance for experienced speakers will be better than for naive, inexperienced speakers. However, improved recognition capabilities should provide greater ability for the user to self-adapt to the system to improve his recognition performance.

Advances in recognition technology will provide substantial improvement in the capability to recognize connected speech independent of speaker within the next five years. These capabilities will at long last begin to support applications in a truly useful and unique way. With increased recognition competence, error rate will be found to be relatively insensitive to vocabulary size. As far as recognition error rates are concerned, I anticipate very low substitution rates (less than 1% on a word basis) with moderate reject rates of 2-5%. Such a reject level will be acceptable for interactive speech input.

In summary, the level of speech recognition performance in the past has been sub-marginal and has not provided unequivocally satisfactory system operation. During the next five years however, a threshold of competence will be reached in the laboratory which will have profound impact upon the acceptance and growth of speech input applications during the next decade.

---

* We at Texas Instruments symbolize the skewed distribution by categorizing speakers as either "sheep" or "goats". The sheep, for whom the system works well, comprise the bulk of the population, say 80-90%. But the goats, despite their minority, have greatest influence on the performance of the system, because most of the recognition errors are attributable to them.

27.

SPEECH RECOGNITION: WHAT IS NEEDED NOW?

Wayne A. Lea
Speech Communications Research Laboratory

27-1. INTRODUCTION

The future of speech recognition holds challenge and promise, but much is needed to make that future all we could hope it would be. Here we consider some aspects of what the future requires. In Sec. 27-2, I attempt to summarize the open discussion on "Speech Recognition: What is Needed Now?", which was the culmination of a session on that topic at the December 1977 International Congress on Phonetic Sciences ("IPS-77""), held in Miami, Florida. I then (Sec. 27-3) discuss various opinions expressed in an opinion poll of speech recognition experts, which June Shoup and I conducted in 1977-1978 regarding the current issues and future needs in speech recognition. I end (in Sec. 27-4) with my own suggestions of future needs and trends. A few references are listed in Sec. 27-5. The reader is also encouraged to read the "future" section of Chap. 4, and Sec. 17-6, for further details about specific projects, priorities of various issues, and mechanisms for meeting future needs. Most of the details of my ideas for future work have been incorated in those sections, to permit this chapter to focus on primary issues, goals, and plans.

27-2. SUMMARY OF THE IPS-77 OPEN DISCUSSION

To prevent misrepresenting the opinions and competencies of the individual discussants (both invited speakers and audience) at the IPS-77 open discussion (which I moderated and tape recorded for later study), and to maintain the generality of that discussion, the following summary provides only a brief overview of the issues and positions expressed during that session. Some of the invited papers presented at that session dealt with work performed during the ARPA SUR project, and of course the evaluation of that recently-completed project was one issue of concern to the audience. Those historical conditions somewhat influenced the discussion, but the issues raised should be of interest for years to come. We will number key issues as they are raised in this discussion, but the numbers here do not necessarily imply order of importance.

A lively discussion showed the following to be a popular and controversial issue:

      (1) What is the significance of the distinction between "understanding" versus "recognition" of speech? Which type of systems should be pursued now, or in the foreseeable future?

It was observed that Harpy, the most successful of the ARPA SUR systems, was more of a recognizer than an "understanding system", in that it used the acoustic data to select word sequences, admittedly within strict syntactic constraints, but with no (or almost no) semantics. Despite two decades of strong advocation of the use of higher-level linguistic information to constrain the recognition task, controversy still exists about whether you absolutely need syntax and semantics, or whether our knowledge of them is sufficiently advanced, to warrent their inclusion in recognizers of continuous speech. Some noted that syntax, semantics, and discourse increase recognition accuracy and are used by the successful human prototype system, and that speech has linguistic communication of intended meanings as its ultimate intent. Others argued that the basic pattern matching techniques, statistical analyses, and mathematical methods (without elaborate syntax, semantics, or pragmatics) have produced the best successes in actual recognizers. Advocates of the more mathematical view criticized available semantic and syntactic models as ad hoc. They noted the diversion that such higher-level modules have been, in detracting from needed work on the acoustic "front-ends" of recognizers. The question of which knowledge sources really warrent extensive effort and money being spent seems to be open for further discussion, though there seems to be strong agreement that a primary area was the "front-end", involving acoustic, phonetic, prosodic, and phonological analyses, or the equivalent in acoustic pattern matching processes.

A related issue raised in the discussion was:

> (2) Which levels of task complexity, and thus which types of systems (isolated word recognizers, digit string recognizers, Harpy-like sentence recognizers, HWIM or HEARSAY-II multiple-knowledge-source speech understanding systems, etc.) are needed and should be given attention?

While some viewed the ARPA SUR work as evidence of the futility of trying to do too much too soon, others were concerned that too short-sighted a view may seriously delay the introduction of important information and advanced system components. Some concluded that the best answer seems to be to pursue all levels of system complexity, including, but definitely not confined to, the use of sophisticated higher levels in complex systems.

Whenever one poses the question of what types of systems are needed, the following question can arise, as it did at the IPS-77 discussion:

> (3) What are the practical applications for speech recognizers, and the important well-established advantages of voice as a modality for communication with machines?

Among those who raised this question were several who have actively worked on building recognizers, but who have sensed the need to know needs before future system specifications are defined. One experienced developer of practical systems observed that the main advantage of speech is certainly not one of speed, but rather one or more of the following: the hands-and-eyes-busy situations, the reduced training that voice commanding involves, and/or the mobility that voice permits (especially with a wireless microphone). The "bottom-line" is reduced cost of operation, due to reduced personnel needs and more efficient data entry. For more discussion of these topics, see Chaps. 1 to 4 in this book, and various other articles by Martin, Chapanis, and Welch, as referenced in those chapters.

Another issue raised by the discussion of types of systems and their practical applications is this one:

> (4) Why recognize continuous speech? Is it really needed?

This remains an issue for further study, although some discussion of this question was presented in Chaps. 1 to 4, and at other points throughout this book. It can, of course, be asked in opposite manner: Why _not_ use connected speech, and why use isolated words?

Regarding the alternative approaches to accomplishing recognition, this question (which may or may not be subsumed in the answers to questions 1 and 2) was raised:

> (5) What is the role of the phonetician, linguist, or speech scientist in future work, versus that of the mathematician or acoustic-pattern-matching advocate?

Acoustic pattern matching schemes have dominated the successes in the field, yet some question their extendibility to large tasks in sentence recognition. A related question is:

> (6) What is the role in future work for _research_ (on various phonetic, prosodic, linguistic, artificial intelligence, or theoretical speech or computer science topics)?

A provocative question raised at the IPS-77 session was:

> (7) What should be done next for another $15 million? Is there any application, or set of related applications, that warrants that amount of effort? Can we predict them in advance, or do we need the "solution" before the "problem" that needs that solution is fully apparent (cf. Chap. 2)?

These questions are among the most intriguing ones that can be raised in this field, although I am sure many readers could offer several others of general concern. Companion questions also arise regarding the impact of speech recognition work on other fields of study, such as:

> (8) What does speech recognition tell us about how human communication operates? Can we take successful limited recognizers as potential models of human perception of speech?

> (9) What is the social impact of speech recognizing machines? Will voice input aspects of automation cause loss of good jobs, or free personnel for more satisfying responsibilities?

Other more technical and specialized issues raised during the IPS-77 discussion dealt with the current status and future needs in such specific topics as understanding coarticulation and phonological regularities, measuring syntactic complexities, determining the size of vocabularies needed in various tasks, etc. These have been addressed at various points thoughout the book.

27-3. OPINIONS ABOUT FUTURE NEEDS AND TRENDS

In Chaps. 4 and 17, and in a detailed report (Lea and Shoup, 1979), June Shoup and I have summarized the opinions expressed to us via replies to a 32-page questionnaire or in personal interviews with over 100 workers in this field. Here I will attempt to express the consensus of those opinions, using the questions of Sec. 27-2 as initiators of topics (though the questions asked in the survey were _not_ specifically those listed in Sec. 27-2).

(A1 = Answer to question 1): The consensus seems to be that multiple-knowledge-source systems for sentence "understanding" remain interesting for research and advanced development, but that the distinction between "recognition" and "understanding" is somewhat artificial; more-limited systems can best be developed rapidly with pattern matching techniques, but even they can benefit from severe constraints on the recognition task, by highly constrained syntax and small subvocabularies of alternative next words. (A2) Systems to be pursued in the next five years or so should include recognizers of:(1) connected word sequences and digit strings; (2) isolated word recognizers with syntax and low cost; (3) restricted speech understanding (Harpy-like, but extendable) systems; and (4) research systems for multiple-knowledge-source sentence understanding.

(A3) There are a variety of applications that warrant use of speech recognizers, as listed in priority order by Lea and Shoup (1979, p. 104); they primarily depend upon the naturalness, mobility, freedom of hands and eyes, multimodal communication, increased communication capacity, and compatibility with the telephone that speech offers.

(A4) The predominant role of continuous speech in the listed types of needed future systems suggests the general consensus that continuous speech is desired, though there is little evidence about its being <u>necessary</u> or unquestionably more useful for known applications. This is a topic that needs continued investigation, with special consideration given to its role in specific applications areas.

(A5) The important roles to be played by phoneticians, linguists, and other speech-oriented scientists are evident in the experts' advocation of acoustic phonetics, prosodics, coarticulatory and phonological rules, and assessment of language and task complexity as topics of high priority in future work. (A6) Progress on the "front-ends" of systems, and other high-priority topics such as effective use of linguistic constraints and development of measures and methods for performance evaluation will require extensive further research. We need to know the acoustic phonetic, prosodic, and linguistic characteristics of naturally spoken sentences. This research will pay off in the long-range advancement of the field, and cannot be scheduled to match short-term deadlines on practical system developments.

(A7) If another large-scale ($15 million) project were undertaken, it should address a variety of tasks of increasing complexity, and have the characteristics described in Sec. 4-5.1 (cf. also Lea and Shoup, 1979; 105-107). There is probably no one applications area that is known to unquestionably warrant that level of investment, though the potential market for recognizers seems quite large (cf. Chap. 20 and Lea and Shoup, 1979, 104-105). (A8 and A9) Not too much is yet known about the implications of speech recognition on human sciences, or about the social impact of recognizers.

27-4. SUGGESTIONS ABOUT FUTURE NEEDS AND TRENDS

In Chap. 17 (and in Lea and Shoup, 1979; cf. also Sec. 4-5.2), June Shoup and I have advocated four types of projects:

1. Applications studies with available commercial recognizers;

2. Comparative evaluations of alternative devices and specific improvements in current systems (without major redesigns);

3. Advanced development projects to substantially expand recognition capabilities; and

4. Research on necessary knowledge sources and basic concepts relevant to future successes in recognition.

You may notice that while we endorse the value of carefully limited projects to meet realistic short-term goals, such as are advocated separately by Neuburg and Doddington, in Chap. 2 and 26, respectively, we also include longer-range more linguistically-based approaches. This is a rapidly growing field, and we are going to require all the tools we can bring to bear on advancing towards more versatile systems that will meet an expanding spectrum of future needs.

I have confidence that in years to come some of the authors in this book will be properly pursuing some of the best acoustic pattern matching techniques and focusing on the best next steps in speech recognition. These are the types of people who have produced encouraging successes and given credibility to this field. Also, while I do not advocate the centisecond modeling methods that have been recently "rediscovered" in this field (remember that this was one of the primary ways of characterizing continuous speech throughout the 1960's), I expect that some capable groups will pursue those methods with considerable success (cf. Chap. 4, pp. 70-71). Many readers may choose to add to the advances made with such techniques.

Also, I expect that the spectral template approaches of Itakura and the Harpy system, and as so impressively extended by Klatt in Chap. 25, will hold interest for a long time to come. These also seem to be a part of the tools for making the best "next steps" in recognition.

Perhaps due to bias from long years of linguistic studies, I am more confident about linguistically-based speech recognition procedures being extendable to new and more-difficult tasks. The more versatile the interaction with the machine, the more important the linguistic information would seem to be. The ultimate decision of the recognizer is linguistic; that is, what was the intended message, as measured by the correct (intended) response being produced. I think some workers have misinterpreted Harpy's success. It was not simply an efficient dynamic programming algorithm, some great acoustic templates, or an efficient mathematical search that made Harpy succeed. It was not lacking in speech knowledge or linguistic prowess; indeed, the carefully developed templates and "hand-tailored" juncture rules reflected very much speech knowledge, and the basically simple, but effective, use of syntactic constraints in the network helped reduce the search space and avoid combinatoric explosions that would accompany any neglect of such linguistic constraints. Harpy was a good marriage of good acoustic analysis and pattern matching techniques with some of the more robust and dependable aspects of currently known linguistic and phonetic regularities. As with any marriage, the effectiveness of that union will require continued compromise, mutual respect, an effective complementation of roles, and a willingness to change and adjust as more is learned in subsequent activity.

Hence, in addition to the interesting projects advocated elsewhere in this (and I find none that is without considerable merit), I would advocate several specific projects:

- Extensions and major revisions of a Harpy-like system;

- A HEARSAY-II-like system of independent knowledge sources, interacting through a flexible "blackboard-like" data

structure, but incorporating some of the best components from
HWIM and other recent systems, plus easy insertion of new
knowledge sources;

- Development of procedures for performance evaluation, systematic
  comparisons of recognizers, and measurement of task complexities;

- Research on the acoustic phonetic, prosodic, and phonological
  characteristics of spoken English sentences; and

- Study of what makes "habitable" languages for effective
  interaction with computers.

All of these projects refer to reserch and advanced development work; more
practical and shorter-range projects have been itemized elsewhere (Chaps.
4 and 17; also Lea and Shoup, 1979, Sec. 5, and Lea, 1979).

I think Harpy is the current "benchmark" for comparatively evaluating
future systems that handle continuously spoken sentences. Yet, it needs
several minor extensions and major revisions to make it more useful for a
variety of tasks. The total network must be recompiled everytime any
change is made, such as adding a new word or new structure, or altering
the expected pronunciations of a word. This takes hours of compiling time
on a large computer. Current work is going on at Carnegie-Mellon University (CMU), and at the SpeechCommunications Research Laboratory to alleviate
this and other problems by incrmental compilation and multiple-level networks.
CMU has developed methods for running Harpy on a PDP-11 computer, with
paging of the memory to handle the large networks despite limited core. CMU
is preparing a user's manual for use of transportable versions of the Harpy
system, and the transported version of the Harpy system (actually the
Locust PDP-11-based system) is currently being implemented at the Speech
Communications Research Laboratory.

Harpy (or Locust) can be augmented with new knowledge, like prosodics
and new acoustic phonetic analysis procedures. Procedures are needed for
automatically acquiring aspects of the knowledge, such as word pronunciations
or new structures. CMU researchers are also considering methods for handling
more difficult problems with more powerful grammars. (Personal communications
with Raj Reddy, Gary Goodman, and Fil Alleva.)

A project for the on-going development and enhancement of a powerful
multiple-knowledge-source speech understanding system seems to be called
for by the successes and lessons learned from the ARPA SUR project. The
HEARSAY-II structure seems particularly flexible and suitable for such an
effort, but the phonetic lattice, lexical decoding network, scoring ideas,
and limited ATN grammars such as BBN used in HWIM should be considered as
powerful condidates for incorporation into such a research system. Primary
attention should be on the front-end (acoustics, segmentation and labeling,
prosodics, phonological rules, and lexical decoding) of the recogniton
process, where the critical gaps in current capabilities are known to exist.
This kind of project is also discussed in Chaps. 4 and 17.

There are a number of closely related issues involving performance
evaluation of systems, systematic comparisons of recognizers, and measurement of task complexities that warrant substantial investigation. We need
improved ways of measuring the overall performance of a system, including
the interactions among recognition accuracy, speed, computational requirements, all dimensions of recognition task difficulty (cf. Chap. 1), and
assessment of major contributors and "weak links" in the series of component

processes in the system. Current commercial recognizers, and future systems that will be developed, need to be carefully compared to assess their relative merits and their applicabilities for various tasks. The complexities of various tasks need to be measurable, so we can assess systems dealing with different tasks and so that performance on new tasks can be estimated in advance of actual recognition experiments. Dimensions in the assessment of task complexity include the branching factor, entropy, and other syntactic complexities of the interactive language, plus the assessment of the confusability of words in the vocabulary (Lea, 1979). These investigations could form one cohesive long-term research project, or be accomplished by a coordinated set of smaller studies.

Repeatedly throughout this book, I (and several other authors) have advocated work on the front-end of a recognizer. Yet, there is need for basic research projects to gather more necessary knowledge about characteristic features of continuous speech. This research will typically take years before it has direct impact on speech recognizers, so work should begin soon on these topics.

Finally, I would certainly like to see research be done on what makes a limited language "habitable" (easy to learn and to keep within the constraints of). Studies could be done on the effectiveness of communication with machines under various conditions on vocabulary, syntax, protocol structure, etc., to determine what makes interaction most effective and the language easy to successfully use (Lea, 1970). Such results should then be incorporated into the design of languages for human-machine interaction.

There are some additional general needs in future work. We need a cohesive _theory_ of speech recognition. Knowledge of _human perception_ should be considered more in future work. _Syntactic_ pattern recognition schemes should supplement current statistical techniques. I think it would be good if we could get away from the general tendency to make a large number of uncertain guesses about the wording or structural units in an utterance, and then weeding them out after expensive processing finds that they fail. Good project management would suggest that systems be designed so that public demonstrations of systems are usually possible and encouraged, that intermediate milestones and goals are defined and used to "freeze" systems early enough so they can be readied for demonstration, and that back-up plans be made, so that if an ideal goal is not reached, informative performance can be demonstrated on less demanding tasks. It is now time to work on practical environmental conditions like noise, telephone speech, large speaker populations, etc.

There is a diversity of needed projects, but a need for some sharing of databases, coordination of projects, and goal-directed planning. We need new methods for stimulating _research_ on fully systematic ideas, which may require funding alternatives to the usual today-oriented funding agencies. Hopefully, the many ideas presented throughout this book will spur new ideas, new projects, new advances, and a growing enthusiasm for the field.

The possibilities and practical benefits seem almost unbounded in using speech recognizers to aid busy computer users. It is encouraging that, after years of commercial and governmental use of limited isolated-word recognizers, the number of companies developing such ideas , and the general market, seem to be expanding. I believe that in the future we can expect increased commercial use of such systems. I also expect that the advantages of speech input will become even more apparent as capabilities are _expanded_ to handling

connected speech that is more natural and rapid. Voice input does promise
to be a fascinating and productive thrust in the future of computer
technology.

27-5. REFERENCES

Lea, W.A. (1970), Towards Versatile Speech Communication with Computers,
International Journal of Man-Machine Studies, 2, 107-155.

Lea, W.A. (1979), Critical Issues in Airborne Applications of Speech Recognition, Final Task Report, Naval Air Development Center (Code 6041)
Contract Number N 62269-78-M-3770, Warminster, PA.

Lea, W.A. and J.E. Shoup (1979), Review of the ARPA SUR Project and Survey
of Current Technology in Speech Understanding, Final Report on ONR
Contract Number Noool4-77-C-0570, SpeechCommunictions Research Laboratory report to Office of Naval Research, January, 1979.

INDEX

pragmatic, 54
of SDC system, 277
semantic template, 214, 222
slot and frame, 51, 52
transformational, 52
types of, 14
Grammatical constraints, 440-442

H

Habitability, of a language, 4
Hand occupation, voice data entry
  with, 26-27, 33-34
Handwriting, vs. vocal communication,
  6, 8, 9
Hardware, cost of, 26
Harpy system
  achievements of, 69-70, 388-390,
    398-399, 407, 566
  vs. BBN-HWIM, 333-334, 337
  described, 261-263, 340-342
  digit string recognition in, 72
  drawbacks of, 392-393, 407
  extensions to, 91
  grammar of, 264, 333-334
  knowledge compiler in, 346-351
  knowledge sources in, 342-346
  LOCUST version of, 16
  message recognition in, 56
  performance of, 357, 358
  recognition in, 351-356
  spectral templates in, 266
HCDE test, 34, 35
Hearsay-I system, 55, 361, 390-391,
  394
  restricted nature of, 12
Hearsay-II system
  achievements of, 379-380, 390, 392-
    394, 409
  architecture of, 361-365
  vs. BBN-HWIM, 335-336
  constraints in, 223-224
  described, 259-261
  focusing strategy in, 245
  knowledge sources in, 362, 363-371
  recognition in, 371-379
  sentence hypotheses in, 225-226,
    227
  word hypothesizer of, 154-155
Hear What I Mean system (see BBN-HWIM
  system)
High Complexity Data Entry test, 34,
  35
High Speed Data Entry test, 34, 35
HWIM (see BBN-HWIM system)
Hypotheses
  accepting sentence, 225-227
  choosing among, 55-57

in Hearsay-II, 362-363
word, 150-162

I

"IBM shoebox recognizer," 63
IBM system, 14, 335
Information transfer, rate of
  with continuous speech, 66
  human-machine, 6-7
Inspection, recognizers used for, 77,
  465
Intelligent terminals, market for,
  466-467
International Congress on Phonetic
  Sciences, 562
Interstress intervals
  as phrase boundary markers, 178-179
  spanning pauses, 182, 183
  as speech rate measure, 180-181
Intonation, as linguistic cue, 184-
  193
Invariance condition, 49-51
IPS-77, 562
Island driving
  in ARPA SUR projects, 392, 402, 409,
    413
  as search strategy, 243, 244
  in SRI system, 305-310, 312, 313
Island generation, in Hearsay-II,
  367-368
Islands of phonetic reliability, 170
Isolated digit recognition system,
  430-433
Isolated vowels, in Polish, 504-505
Isolated word recognition, 10, 21
  available technology for, 75, 76, 77
  vs. continuous, 24-25
  development of, 59-66
  at ITTDCD, 471, 472
Iterative matching, hypothesizing by,
  152, 153
ITTDCD, research at, 469-482

J

Japan, speech recognition work in,
  483-493
JUNCT procedure, 368, 369
Juncture rules, in Harpy, 345

K

KEAL system, 522
Kernel
  of Hearsay-II, 364, 365

DATE DUE

~~FEB 18~~	SEP 27 '93		
MAR 23 '87	OCT 1 '93		
MAY 11 '87	MAY 20 '94		
APR 19 '88	NOV 1 '95		
JUN 19 '88			
OCT 16 '88			
NOV 14 '88			
DEC 27 '88			
FEB 15 '89			
APR 16 '89			
MAY 13 '89			
OCT 4 '89			
NOV 16 '89			
DEC 19 '89			
FEB 7 '90			
MAY 17 '93			